Fodor's 07

CAPE COD, NANTUCKET & MARTHA'S VINEYARD

Where to Stay and Eat
for All Budgets

Must-See Sights
and Local Secrets

Ratings You Can Trust

Fodor's Travel Publications   New York, Toronto, London, Sydney, Auckland
www.fodors.com

CAPE COD, NANTUCKET & MARTHA'S VINEYARD 2007 917
Editor: Michael Nalepa

.4 FOD

Editorial Production: Bethany Cassin Beckerlegge
Editorial Contributors: Andrew Collins, Sandy MacDonald, Laura V. Scheel
Maps: David Lindroth, *cartographer;* Bob Blake and Rebecca Baer, *map editors*
Design: Fabrizio La Rocca, *creative director;* Guido Caroti, *art director;* Moon Sun Kim, *cover designer;* Melanie Marin, *senior picture editor*
Cover Photo (Brant Point Lighthouse, Nantucket): Atlantide Phototravel/Corbis
Production/Manufacturing: Colleen Ziemba

SPECIAL SALES

This book is available for special discounts for bulk purchases for sales promotions or premiums. Special editions, including personalized covers, excerpts of existing books, and corporate imprints, can be created in large quantities for special needs. For more information, write to Special Markets/ Premium Sales, 1745 Broadway, MD 6-2, New York, New York 10019, or e-mail specialmarkets@ randomhouse.com.

AN IMPORTANT TIP & AN INVITATION

Although all prices, opening times, and other details in this book are based on information supplied to us at press time, changes occur all the time in the travel world, and Fodor's cannot accept responsibility for facts that become outdated or for inadvertent errors or omissions. So **always confirm information when it matters,** especially if you're making a detour to visit a specific place. Your experiences—positive and negative—matter to us. If we have missed or misstated something, **please write to us.** We follow up on all suggestions. Contact the Cape Cod, Martha's Vineyard, and Nantucket editor at editors@fodors.com or c/o Fodor's at 1745 Broadway, New York, New York 10019.

PRINTED IN THE UNITED STATES OF AMERICA

10 9 8 7 6 5 4 3 2 1

Be a Fodor's Correspondent

Your opinion matters. It matters to us. It matters to your fellow Fodor's travelers, too. And we'd like to hear it. In fact, we *need* to hear it.

When you share your experiences and opinions, you become an active member of the Fodor's community. That means we'll not only use your feedback to make our books better, but we'll publish your names and comments whenever possible. Throughout our guides, look for "Word of Mouth," excerpts of your unvarnished feedback.

Here's how you can help improve Fodor's for all of us.

Tell us when we're right. We rely on local writers to give you an insider's perspective. But our writers and staff editors—who are the best in the business—depend on you. Your positive feedback is a vote to renew our recommendations for the next edition.

Tell us when we're wrong. We're proud that we update most of our guides every year. But we're not perfect. Things change. Hotels cut services. Museums change hours. Charming cafés lose charm. If our writer didn't quite capture the essence of a place, tell us how you'd do it differently. If any of our descriptions are inaccurate or inadequate, we'll incorporate your changes in the next edition and will correct factual errors at fodors.com *immediately*.

Tell us what to include. You probably have had fantastic travel experiences that aren't yet in Fodor's. Why not share them with a community of like-minded travelers? Maybe you chanced upon a beach or bistro or B&B that you don't want to keep to yourself. Tell us why we should include it. And share your discoveries and experiences with everyone directly at fodors.com. Your input may lead us to add a new listing or highlight a place we cover with a "Highly Recommended" star or with our highest rating, "Fodor's Choice."

Give us your opinion instantly at our feedback center at www.fodors.com/feedback. You may also e-mail editors@fodors.com with the subject line "Cape Cod Editor." Or send your nominations, comments, and complaints by mail to Cape Cod Editor, Fodor's, 1745 Broadway, New York, NY 10019.

You and travelers like you are the heart of the Fodor's community. Make our community richer by sharing your experiences. Be a Fodor's correspondent.

Happy Traveling!

Tim Jarrell, Publisher

CONTENTS

PLANNING YOUR TRIP

About This Book 6
What's Where 7
Quintessential Cape Cod 14
When to Go 16
If You Like 17
Great Itinerary 19
On the Calendar 21

CAPE COD

1 APPROACHING THE CAPE 25
Plymouth 28
Fall River 36
Westport 37
South Dartmouth 39
New Bedford 39
Marion 42

2 THE UPPER CAPE 46
Bourne 48
Sandwich .55
Falmouth .63
Mashpee .79

3 THE MID CAPE 85
Barnstable 88
Yarmouth .110
Dennis 121

4 THE LOWER CAPE 133
Brewster .136
Harwich 148
Chatham .153
Orleans 168
Eastham .177

5 THE OUTER CAPE 188
Wellfleet & South Wellfleet 193
Truro 210
Provincetown 217

6 MARTHA'S VINEYARD 247
Vineyard Haven (Tisbury) 252
Oak Bluffs 257
Edgartown 262
Chappaquiddick Island 268
West Tisbury 269
Chilmark .272
Menemsha 274
Aquinnah .276

7 NANTUCKET 280
Nantucket Town 282
Siasconset & Wauwinet 309

SMART TRAVEL TIPS A TO Z . . .319

INDEX 345

ABOUT OUR WRITERS 352

MAPS

Massachusetts 8–9
Cape Cod 10–11
Approaching Cape Cod 31
The Upper Cape 51
The Mid Cape 92
Hyannis 95
Where to Stay & Eat in Hyannis 101
The Lower Cape 139
Chatham 154
Where to Stay & Eat in Chatham 160
The Outer Cape 190
Provincetown 218
Where to Eat in Provincetown 225
Where to Stay in Provincetown 227
Martha's Vineyard 250–251
Where to Stay & Eat in
    Vineyard Haven 253
Where to Stay & Eat in Oak Bluffs . . .258
Where to Stay & Eat in Edgartown . .264
Where to Stay & Eat Up-Island 271
Nantucket .283
Nantucket Town 285
Where to Eat in Nantucket Town 290
Where to Stay in Nantucket Town . . .295
Siasconset, Polpis & Wauwinet 311
Where to Stay & Eat Outside
    Nantucket Town 313

CLOSEUPS

Portrait of a Pilgrim 33
Cuttyhunk Island 41
Time to Fly 55
Powwow, Wampanoag Style 80
The New Face of Hyannis 97
Riding the Rail Trail 130
The Cape Cod Baseball League 165
Rotary 101 .170
Year-Round on the Cape 184
Rainy Day Fun 196
Truro's Edward Hopper 211
Provincetown: America's Gay Summer
    Playground 237
Dune Shacks 241
Martha's Vineyard Trivia 274
Navigating the Rental Market 298
Nantucket Reds 309

ABOUT THIS BOOK

Our Ratings

Sometimes you find terrific travel experiences and sometimes they just find you. But usually the burden is on you to select the right combination of experiences. That's where our ratings come in.

As travelers we've all discovered a place so wonderful that its worthiness is obvious. And sometimes that place is so unique that superlatives don't do it justice: you just have to be there to know. These sights, properties, and experiences get our highest rating, **Fodor's Choice**, indicated by orange stars throughout this book.

Black stars highlight sights and properties we deem **Highly Recommended**, places that our writers, editors, and readers praise again and again for consistency and excellence.

By default, there's another category: any place we include in this book is by definition worth your time, unless we say otherwise. And we will.

Disagree with any of our choices? Care to nominate a place or suggest that we rate one more highly? Visit our feedback center at www. fodors.com/feedback.

Budget Well

Hotel and restaurant price categories from ¢ to $$$$ are defined in the opening pages of each chapter. For attractions, we always give standard adult admission fees; reductions are usually available for children, students, and senior citizens. Want to pay with plastic? **AE, D, DC, MC, V** after restaurant and hotel listings indicate whether American Express, Discover, Diners Club, MasterCard, and Visa are accepted.

Restaurants

Unless we state otherwise, restaurants are open for lunch and dinner daily. We mention dress only when there's a specific requirement and reservations only when they're essential or not accepted—it's always best to book ahead.

Hotels

Hotels have private bath, phone, TV, and air-conditioning and operate on the European Plan (aka EP, meaning without meals), unless we specify that they use the Continental Plan (CP, with a continental breakfast), Breakfast Plan (BP, with a full breakfast), or Modified American Plan (MAP, with breakfast and dinner) or are all-inclusive (including all meals and most activities). We always

list facilities but not whether you'll be charged an extra fee to use them, so when pricing accommodations, find out what's included.

Many Listings
- ★ Fodor's Choice
- ★ Highly recommended
- ⊠ Physical address
- ⊹ Directions
- ⊕ Mailing address
- ☎ Telephone
- 🖷 Fax
- ⊕ On the Web
- ✎ E-mail
- 💳 Admission fee
- ☉ Open/closed times
- ▶ Start of walk/itinerary
- Ⓜ Metro stations
- ▭ Credit cards

Hotels & Restaurants
- 🏨 Hotel
- ⤸ Number of rooms
- ⭢ Facilities
- ⭢|⭢| Meal plans
- ✕ Restaurant
- ⭢ Reservations
- 🏠 Dress code
- ⭢ Smoking
- ⭢⭢ BYOB
- ✕🏨 Hotel with restaurant that warrants a visit

Outdoors
- 🏌 Golf
- ⭢ Camping

Other
- ☾ Family-friendly
- 🔒 Contact information
- ⭢ See also
- ⊠ Branch address
- ☞ Take note

APPROACHING THE CAPE 	Heading for the Cape from either Boston or Providence, you pass southeastern Massachusetts towns that range from intriguing historic villages to former industrial cities to a handful of bucolic seaside communities with perhaps as much charm as—and far fewer crowds than—the Cape itself. Along Boston's South Shore, the city of Quincy celebrates the legacy of two hometown presidents, John Adams and John Quincy Adams. It's well-worth exploring the Adams National Historic Park, which comprises 11 historic buildings. A bit farther south, the region's must-see draw is Plimoth Plantation, a stellar living-history museum in the family-friendly town of Plymouth. If you're approaching from the south and west, Fall River's Battleship Cove provides a floating piece of WWII history, while New Bedford gives a powerful image of the country's whaling days and early industrial era. These cities are both a bit rough around the edges, but these key attractions merit a visit. If you have time to meander, venture off the interstate and pass through the pastoral seafront villages of Westport, South Dartmouth, and Marion, which hark back to the old-time New England pleasures of lobster boils, sugary beaches, and long summer days.
THE UPPER CAPE 	The region nearest the bridges is the most suburban and sprawling chunk of Cape Cod as well as the most historic—increasingly, it's also becoming more and more upscale in character, as affluent Boston and South Shore commuters continue to snap up homes in the area's two biggest towns, Falmouth and Sandwich. Many old B&Bs have been turned into private homes, but the infusion of money has also led to a better selection of fine restaurants and shops that remain open year-round. Proximity to the bridges also makes this a relatively more accessible area than the rest of the Cape, and it's handy for short getaways. Along the northern bay side lie the Cape's oldest towns—Sandwich was settled back in 1637. Nearby Mashpee, where more than 600 residents are descended from the original Wampanoags, is one of two Massachusetts towns with Native American–governed areas. The west coast from Bourne through North and West Falmouth mixes residential suburbs with hidden coves and beaches lining the bay, while Falmouth proper is an established year-round community with a particularly strong fine and performing arts scene. Nearby Woods Hole brims with maritime attractions and is where a ferry chugs year-round to Martha's Vineyard.

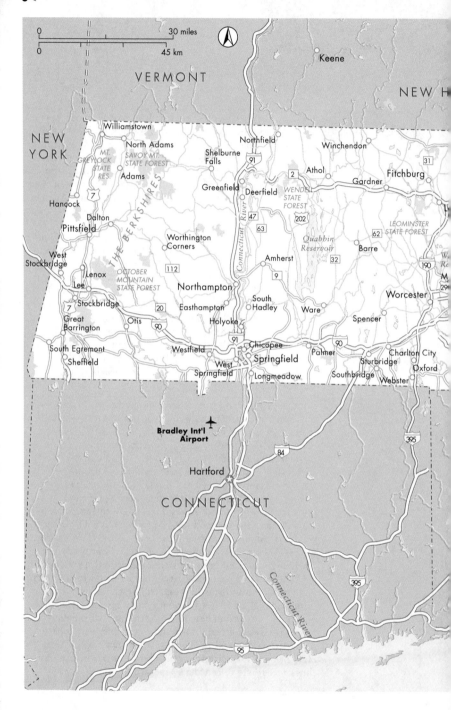

0   30 miles
0   45 km

VERMONT

Keene

NEW H

NEW
YORK

Williamstown
North Adams
Northfield
Winchenden
Shelburne
Falls
MT.
GREYLOCK
STATE
RES.
SAVOY MT.
STATE FOREST
Adams
Athol
Gardner
Fitchburg
Greenfield
Deerfield
WENDELL
STATE
FOREST
31
2
Hancock
THE BERKSHIRES
47
63
202
LEOMINSTER
STATE FOREST
Dalton
Pittsfield
7
Worthington
Corners
Quabbin
Reservoir
Barre
62
West
Stockbridge
Amherst
32
190
Lenox
OCTOBER
MOUNTAIN
STATE FOREST
112
9
Lee
Northampton
Worcester
Stockbridge
20
Easthampton
South
Hadley
Ware
Spencer
7
Great
Barrington
Otis
90
Holyoke
91
South Egremont
Westfield
Chicopee
Palmer
90
Charlton City
Sheffield
West
Springfield
Springfield
Longmeadow
Sturbridge
Southbridge
Webster
Oxford

CONNECTICUT

Bradley Int'l
Airport

84

395

Hartford

Connecticut River

395

Connecticut River

95

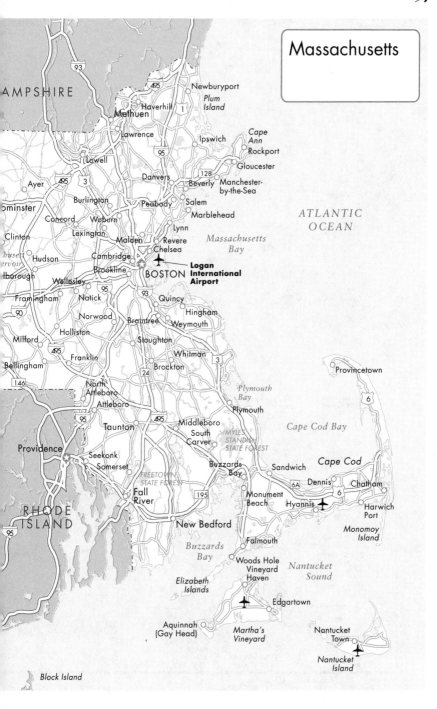

Massachusetts

NEW HAMPSHIRE

93

Ayer
Leominster
Clinton

495

Newburyport
Plum
Island

Haverhill
Methuen
Lawrence

Ipswich
*Cape
Ann*
Rockport
Gloucester

*ATLANTIC
OCEAN*

Lowell
3
Danvers
Beverly
Manchester-
by-the-Sea

Burlington
Peabody
Salem
Marblehead

Concord
Woburn
Lexington

*husetts
ervoir*
Hudson

Malden
Lynn
Revere
Chelsea

*Massachusetts
Bay*

Cambridge
Brookline
BOSTON

Wellesley
Framingham
Natick

90
95
93

Milford
Holliston
Franklin

Norwood
Braintree
Weymouth

Quincy
Hingham

**Logan
International
Airport**

Bellingham
146

495

North
Attleboro
Attleboro

Stoughton
Whitman
3

Brockton
24

*Plymouth
Bay*

Provincetown

6

Providence

Taunton
Middleboro
South
Carver

*MYLES
STANDISH
STATE FOREST*

Plymouth

Cape Cod Bay

Cape Cod

Seekonk
Somerset

*FREETOWN
STATE FOREST*

195

Buzzards
Bay

Sandwich

6A
Dennis
Chatham

RHODE
ISLAND

95

Fall
River

Monument
Beach

Hyannis
6

Harwich
Port

New Bedford

Falmouth

*Monomoy
Island*

*Buzzards
Bay*

Woods Hole
Vineyard
Haven

*Nantucket
Sound*

*Elizabeth
Islands*

Edgartown

Aquinnah
(Gay Head)

*Martha's
Vineyard*

Nantucket
Town

*Nantucket
Island*

Block Island

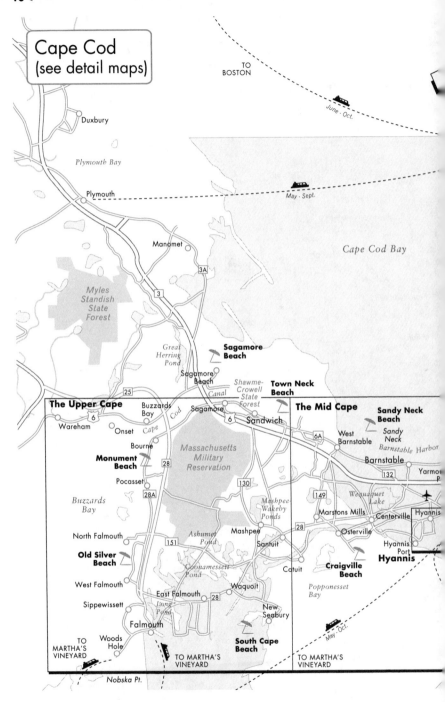

Cape Cod
(see detail maps)

TO
BOSTON

Duxbury

Plymouth Bay

June - Oct.

Plymouth

May - Sept.

Manomet

Cape Cod Bay

3A

3

*Myles
Standish
State
Forest*

*Great
Herring
Pond*

**Sagamore
Beach**

Sagamore
Beach

Canal

*Shawme-
Crowell
State
Forest*

**Town Neck
Beach**

25

The Upper Cape

Buzzards
Bay

Cod

Sagamore

6

Sandwich

The Mid Cape

**Sandy Neck
Beach**

6
Wareham

Onset

Cape

6A

West
Barnstable

*Sandy
Neck*

Barnstable Harbor

Bourne

*Massachusetts
Military
Reservation*

Barnstable

**Monument
Beach**

28

132

Yarmo
P

Pocasset

28A

130

149

*Wequaquet
Lake*

*Buzzards
Bay*

*Mashpee-
Wakeby
Ponds*

Marstons Mills

Centerville

Hyannis

North Falmouth

151

*Ashumet
Pond*

Mashpee

28

Osterville

Hyannis
Port

**Old Silver
Beach**

*Coonamessett
Pond*

Santuit

Catuit

Hyannis

West Falmouth

**Craigville
Beach**

*Popponesset
Bay*

Sippewissett

East Falmouth

28

Waquoit

*Long
Pond*

New
Seabury

May - Oct.

Falmouth

Woods
Hole

**South Cape
Beach**

TO
MARTHA'S
VINEYARD

TO MARTHA'S
VINEYARD

TO MARTHA'S
VINEYARD

Nobska Pt.

WHAT'S
WHERE

THE MID CAPE 	The Mid Cape has a bit of a Jekyll-and-Hyde complex. Along the northern fringes, narrow Route 6A snakes through the peaceful, all-American, colonial hamlets of Barnstable, Yarmouth Port, and Dennis. It's a sophisticated, adult-minded area filled with antiques shops, smart taverns, and romantic B&Bs with creaky floorboards and wavy-glass windows. At the southern end of the area, booming Hyannis acts as a transportation and social hub for a more family-oriented—in some places honky-tonk—patch of seaside fun. It's chock-full of both hip and casual restaurants and galleries and has dozens of motels as well as some charming country inns. Traffic-clogged and rather tacky, Route 28 cuts east from Hyannis into South Yarmouth and West Dennis, the Cape capitals of motor lodges and minigolf courses. In the other direction, though, Route 28 runs west through the more low-key, old-money enclaves of Centerville, Cotuit, and Osterville.
THE LOWER CAPE 	The Lower Cape is really a microcosm of everything that is Cape Cod. Brewster is a continuation of the subtle, historic charms of Route 6A, while Harwich Port and Orleans both see some of the same commercial exuberance—and excess—along Route 28 and other parts of Cape Cod's southern shore. Pristine and lightly developed Eastham is the gateway to Cape Cod National Seashore. And blue-blooded Chatham feels like a cross between the tony sections of Falmouth and Sandwich mixed with the restrained elegance of Nantucket—it's more expensive and conservative than just about any town on Cape Cod. In addition to the Cape, nature lovers can explore remote Monomoy National Wildlife Refuge as well as dozens of inviting ponds and beaches, plus one of the best stretches of the Cape Cod bike path. There's virtually nothing on Cape Cod—opulent inns and resorts, casual lobster shacks, funky galleries, historic lighthouses and windmills—that you won't find in considerable abundance in the Lower Cape.
THE OUTER CAPE 	The narrow "forearm" of the Cape—less than 2 mi wide between Cape Cod Bay and the Atlantic Ocean in some spots—includes two of the Cape's least-developed areas, Wellfleet and Truro. That being said, Wellfleet fosters one of the most sophisticated and intriguing gallery and boutique scenes in coastal Massachusetts; its discreetly developed downtown is rife with fine window-browsing opportunities. Truro is super laid-back, the quintessence of subdued yet stunningly beauti-

ful seclusion. U.S. 6 hooks around to the west from Truro and terminates in one of the world's great hubs of bohemian life, Provincetown, which ranks among the nation's leading gay vacation getaways. Increasingly high housing costs, however, have steadily turned Provincetown from quirky to snazzy—bring your credit cards if you plan to visit the town's bevy of high-end galleries, home-furnishing shops, and bistros. But in the end, this entire area represents the Cape of dunes and beach grasses, of crashing surf and scrubby pines—the Cape that most attracts creative minds and seekers of solitude.

MARTHA'S VINEYARD

This fabled island just off the southwest tip of Cape Cod, about 5 mi south of Falmouth by boat, makes for an easy daytrip from the mainland but merits several days' worth of exploration if you want a real sense of its allure. The three towns that compose Down-Island (the east end of Martha's Vineyard)—Vineyard Haven, Oak Bluffs, and Edgartown—are the most popular and the most populated. Here you'll find the ferry docks, the shops, and a concentration of things to do and see, including the centuries-old houses and churches that document the island's history. However, much of what makes the Vineyard special is found in its rural reaches, in the agricultural heart of the island and the largely undeveloped lands south and west of the Vineyard Haven–to–Edgartown line known as Up-Island. Country roads meander through woods and tranquil farmland, and dirt side roads lead past crystalline ponds, abandoned cranberry bogs, and conservation lands.

NANTUCKET

A bit smaller than Martha's Vineyard and quite a bit farther from mainland Cape Cod (about 25 mi south of Hyannis), Nantucket is divided into town and country. Town, where the ferries dock, is the center of island activity, with historical homes and inns and boutiques, galleries, and restaurants leading up from the harbor and waterfront. The rest of the island is largely residential (trophy houses abound), and nearly all roads from town terminate at one of the island's teeny (and seasonal) beach communities. Surfside, 3 mi to the south of Nantucket Town, is the island's premier beach (although Jetties also draws a crowd). The Village of Siasconset (known locally as Sconset) lies 8 mi to the east of town, past Windswept Cranberry Bog, and has spectacular rose-covered cottages worth a peek.

QUINTESSENTIAL CAPE COD

Two-Wheel-Drive

There's no better mode of transportation for touring the Cape than a bike. It's along one of several outstanding trails that you can see verdant forests, hear birds chirp, and smell the salt air.

The Cape's many well-developed bike trails satisfy avid and occasional cyclists alike. The definitive route, the Cape Cod Rail Trail, offers a particularly memorable ride along 25-mi of paved right-of-way of the old Penn Central Railroad. The Cape Cod National Seashore maintains three bicycle trails that wind through stunning wilderness, amid dunes, marshes, and ponds. And Falmouth's Shining Sea Trail offers an easy 3½-mi route along the coast, providing views of Vineyard Sound and dipping into oak and pine woods. In fact, there's good biking in just about every town on Cape Cod, plus a number of bike-rental shops.

Play Ball!

America's national pastime, baseball, takes on special meaning each summer on Cape Cod. It's here that you can watch the sport in its purest form, without having to deal with pricey tickets, prima donna ballplayers, and riotous crowds. The Cape Cod Baseball League comprises 10 teams and has been going strong since the 1950s, attracting top college ballplayers from around the country.

These guys are talented—on par with midrange minor-league professional players. In fact, dozens of today's big stars began playing on the Cape, from Nomar Garciaparra to Jeff Bagwell. The games are held at relatively simple yet classic ball fields, so grab a hot dog and catch a game of baseball the way it was meant to be played.

If you want to get a sense of Cape Cod culture, and indulge in some of its pleasures, start by familiarizing yourself with the rituals of daily life. These are a few **highlights**—things you can take part in with relative ease.

Lobster Lovin'

Scores of eateries and markets on the Cape serve lobster, usually the traditional way—boiled whole in the shell with drawn butter—but also in pies, bisques, quesadillas, and omelets. At the Yarmouth House Restaurant, you can order a delicious filet mignon topped with fresh-picked lobster meat. Or opt for the standard summer lunch treat, a lobster roll—light lobster salad with just a hint of mayo on a plain white frankfurter roll.

Wherever you try it, don't leave Cape Cod without sampling this revered culinary offering. And if you get a hankering for lobsters once you get home, just call Quality Fresh Seafood in Bourne—they can airmail you a full clambake, complete with a whole lobster ready for steaming.

Seeing the Light

In addition to traditional Cape-style houses, Cape Cod is known for another distinctive architectural type: lighthouses. You'll find them up and down the Cape, some still active, others decommissioned.

Each has its own personality and profile. There's Highland Light in Truro, the Cape's oldest. Eastham's oft-photographed Nauset Light ranks among the most beautiful, and both Chatham Light and Falmouth's Nobska Light afford some of the best views. In Martha's Vineyard, be sure to journey out to Aquinnah Lighthouse, which stands atop a bluff above the beach and crashing surf. It's definitely worth ascending any lighthouse open for tours (several are, albeit with limited hours) to enjoy a magical perspective of the Cape's spectacular landscape.

WHEN TO GO

Memorial Day through Labor Day (or, in some cases, Columbus Day) is high season on Cape Cod. This is summer with a capital *S,* a time for barbecues, beach bumming, swimming, and water sports. In summer everything is open for business on the Cape, but you can also expect high-season evils: high prices, crowds, and traffic.

The Cape, however, is increasingly a year-round destination. For more insight into Cape Cod's off-season, *see* Year-Round on the Cape on page 184.

Climate

The following are average daily maximum and minimum temperatures for Hyannis. For local Cape weather, coastal marine forecasts, and today's tide times, call the weather line of **WQRC** (☎ 508/771–5522) in Hyannis; average temperatures on the islands are similar.

🖪 Forecasts **Weather Channel** (⊕ www.weather.com).

IF YOU LIKE

Beachcombing

Cape Cod has more than 150 beaches, enough to keep inveterate beachcombers happy—and covered in sand—all year long. Remember, strolling the beach can be just as enjoyable on a winter morning, when crowds are sparse and the surf is intense, as on a sultry summer afternoon.

Bay-side beaches generally have more temperate waters and gentler waves. South-side beaches, on Nantucket Sound, have rolling surf and, though still a bit chilly, are moderated by the Gulf Stream. Inland, you'll find dozens of freshwater ponds, many with warm water and sandy beaches ideal for kids. The Cape Cod National Seashore offers the greatest "wow" factor: chilly water, serious surf, long and wide expanses of sand, magnificent dunes, and mesmerizing views. Here are some favorite spots to dip your toes into the sand.

- The **Massachusetts Audubon Wellfleet Bay Wildlife Sanctuary,** in South Wellfleet, with its numerous adult and children's programs and its beautiful salt-marsh surroundings, is a favorite migration stop for Cape vacationers year-round.

- **Nauset Light, Coast Guard, Marconi, and Race Point beaches** stretch majestically along the length of the Cape Cod National Seashore. Backed by dunes, they are *the* classic Cape beaches.

- Across from the scenic Bass River, the Mid Cape's **West Dennis Beach** is long and wide, with pristine marshland. It's great for windsurfing.

- One of the nicest beaches on the approach to the Cape, Westport's **Horseneck Beach State Reservation** stretches for 2 mi and offers access to great kayaking and boating on the Westport River.

Art & Antiques

The Cape's off-the-beaten-path locale and glorious setting helped turn it into a prominent art colony in the mid-19th century. Today, its concentration of art galleries is among the highest in the nation, with everything from modestly priced crafts and pen-and-ink drawings to priceless nautical paintings and contemporary bronzes. The Cape's prosperous history as a shipping and whaling center accounts for its plethora of fine antiques shops. If it's fine artwork and vintage furnishings you're after, this is the place. Here are a few areas worth scouring.

- Driving along **Route 6A from Sandwich to Brewster** you'll pass dozens of fine antiques shops and more than a few excellent galleries. Pay special attention as you drive through the village of Dennis. There are also two great antiques auction houses in this area, Robert C. Eldred Co. in East Dennis and Sandwich Auction House in Sandwich.

- Historic **Nantucket Town** is worth ferrying to for its abundance of very fine—and pricey—galleries and antiques emporia.

- Along laid-back **Wellfleet's Main and Commercial streets,** numerous galleries offer everything from stained glass to nautical watercolors to African carved-wood sculptures. South of downtown, the Wellfleet Flea Market—great for bargain hunting—is held four days a week in summer.

- **Commercial Street in Provincetown,** especially along the stretch in the East End, abounds with high-quality options. Just in the past few years, dozens of new and increasingly prestigious establishments have opened along here.

IF YOU LIKE

Ice-Cream Shops

However you spend the day on Cape Cod—whether beachcombing or biking, sailing or sidewalk shopping—break up the action with a sweet treat from one of the region's many distinctive ice-cream shops. Devotees debate the merits of soft-serve versus hard ice cream, and waffle versus sugar cones. And some loyalists frown upon the recent influx of newfangled gelato shops, not to mention restaurants serving such offbeat variations as deep-fried ice cream. Whatever you do, avoid ubiquitous franchise operations, and try to stick with parlors selling homemade ice cream—there are plenty to choose from. Consider the following local faves.

- Set in a rustic mid-19th-century barn decorated with a working nickelodeon, Dennisport's **Sundae School Ice Cream Parlor** serves great homemade ice cream, real whipped cream, and old-fashioned sarsaparilla and cream soda (there are additional locales in Harwich Port and East Orleans).

- In Chatham, **Buffy's** serves delicious, rich ice cream that you can savor outside beneath a prodigious apple tree. Don't overlook the fresh-squeezed lime rickies and tangy smoothies.

- Since 1889, **Hallet's**—a quaint country drugstore in Yarmouth Port—has served tasty and justly famous ice-cream concoctions from its all-marble soda fountain with swivel stools.

- **Jerry's Seafood and Dairy Freeze** in West Yarmouth ranks among the Cape's favorite purveyors of soft-serve ice cream.

Boating Adventures

Given that the Cape is completely surrounded by water, it's no wonder that one of the best ways to appreciate it is from a boat, whether a charter fishing yacht or a nimble kayak. Companies renting all types of boats and offering a wide range of tours and excursions exist all around the Cape, and whale-watching cruises rank among the most popular options. Even just riding one of the region's many ferryboats offers a great chance to enjoy the high seas and wonderful views of the land. Here are a few great ways to take to the water in and around Cape Cod.

- Take a boat trip out to **Monomoy National Wildlife Refuge,** a 2,500-acre preserve that comprises the Monomoy Islands, a fragile 9-mi-long barrier-beach area south of Chatham. Several companies offer excursions out this way.

- Cruise the Outer Cape on Provincetown's **Bay Lady II Excursion Schooner,** a beautiful 73-foot sailing vessel that heads out for two-hour cruises three times daily. You're welcome to bring your own spirits and snacks for this scenic and peaceful sail.

- Book an excursion with **Great Marsh Kayak Tours,** which has offices in West Yarmouth and Barnstable and offers a range of great trips, from fly-fishing runs to sunset jaunts—you can also customize your own itinerary.

- **Hy-Line,** in Hyannis, offers cruises on reproductions of old-time Maine coastal steamers. The one-hour tours of Hyannis Harbor and Lewis Bay include a view of the Kennedy compound and other points of interest.

GREAT ITINERARY

CAPE COD: CLASSIC BEACHES & BUSTLING VILLAGES

Day 1: Falmouth

Begin by crossing the Bourne Bridge and taking Route 28A south through some lovely little towns until you reach Falmouth, an excellent base for exploring the Upper Cape. Here you can stroll around the village green, look into some of the historic houses, and stop at the Waquoit Bay National Estuarine Research Reserve for a walk along the estuary and barrier beach. Take some time to check out the village of Woods Hole, the center for international marine research and the year-round ferry port for Martha's Vineyard. A small aquarium in town has regional sea-life exhibits, and there are several shops and museums. If you have any extra time, spend it north of here in the lovely old town of Sandwich, known for the Sandwich Glass Museum and the beautiful grounds and collection of antique cars at Heritage Museums and Gardens.

Days 2 & 3: Hyannis

The crowded Mid Cape is a center of activity, and its hub is Hyannis. Here you can take a cruise around the harbor or go on a deep-sea fishing trip. There are shops and restaurants along Main Street and plenty of kid-worthy amusements. Kennedy fans shouldn't miss the JFK Museum. End the day with a concert at the Cape Cod Melody Tent. Spend your second day exploring the northern reaches of the Mid Cape with a drive along scenic Route 6, which passes through the charming, slow-paced villages of Barnstable, Yarmouth Port, and Dennis. There are beaches and salt marshes, museums, antiques shops and galleries, and old graveyards along this route. Yarmouth

Port's Bass Hole Boardwalk makes for a particularly beautiful stroll. In Dennis there are historic houses to tour, and the Cape Museum of Fine Arts merits a stop. End the day by climbing 30-foot Scargo Tower to watch the sun set. At night you can catch a film at the Cape Cinema, on the grounds of the Cape Playhouse.

Days 4 & 5: Chatham

Chatham, with its handsome Main Street, is a perfect base for strolling, shopping, and dining. A trip to the nearby Monomoy Islands is a must for bird-watchers and nature lovers. Back in town, you can watch glassblowing at the Chatham Glass Company, visit the Old Atwood House and Railroad Museums, and drive over to take in the view from Chatham Light. Spend your second day detouring up to Brewster to check out the eclectic mix of antiques shops, museums, freshwater ponds for swimming and fishing, and miles of biking and hiking trails through Nickerson State Park. Don't miss the Cape Cod Museum of Natural History. On the way north from Chatham, take the less-commercial end of Route 28 to Orleans, driving past sailboat-speckled views of Pleasant Bay. On the way up toward Provincetown, stop in Eastham at the National Seashore's Salt Pond Visitor Center.

Days 6 & 7: Provincetown

Bustling Provincetown sits at the very tip of the Cape, and there's a lot to see and do here. Catch a whale-watch boat and take a trolley tour in town or bike through the National Seashore on its miles of trails. Climb the Pilgrim Monument for a spectacular view of the area—on an exceptionally clear day you can see the Boston skyline. Visit the museums and shops and art galleries, or spend the afternoon swimming and sunning on one of the beaches. To escape the crowds, spend a day driving south through sleepy but scenic Truro and then park your car in Wellfleet's historic downtown, where you'll find a bounty of intriguing shops and galleries. Continue a bit south to historic Marconi Station, which was the landing point for the transatlantic telegraph early in the 20th century. It's also worth walking the short but stunning White Cedar Swamp Trail.

Alternatives

On Day 2, hop the ferry for a day trip to either Martha's Vineyard or Nantucket. Both islands offer breathtaking scenery and village centers chock-full of great shops and restaurants. And if you're really keen on exploring either island, consider spending the night. Martha's Vineyard requires a shorter ferry ride and is your best choice if time is tight.

On either your first or final day—especially if you're a history buff or you're traveling with kids—pass through Plymouth, on the mainland just north of Sagamore Bridge, and make a visit to Plimoth Plantation, one of the most impressive living-history museums in the country.

TIPS

❶ Keep in mind that traffic leading onto the Cape is particularly horrendous on Friday, and traffic leading off the Cape is rough on Sunday. Try to time your visit to avoid these times, but if you must travel to or from the Cape on these days, cross as early in the day as possible.

❷ If you're traveling with kids, you might want to pass on some of the itinerary's more adult-oriented highlights described above—such as shopping in Wellfleet and driving along scenic Route 6A from Barnstable to Dennis—and instead set aside some time in the southern sections of Yarmouth and Dennis, where Route 28 passes by countless amusement centers, minigolf courses, and other kid-friendly amusements.

❸ A car is the best way to explore the Cape, but in the busier town centers—such as Falmouth, Hyannis, Chatham, and Provincetown—you can get around quite easily on foot. Plan to park your car at your accommodation and avoid using it except to explore less densely populated areas of the Cape.

ON THE
CALENDAR

The Massachusetts Office of Travel & Tourism offers events listings and a whale-watch guide for the entire state. Also see the events calendar in "CapeWeek," an arts-and-entertainment supplement published every Friday in the *Cape Cod Times*; it's available online at ⊕ www.capeweek.com.

WINTER Early December	Many Cape towns ring in the Christmas season in grand style. To take in the best-known celebration, plan an excursion to nearby Nantucket for the annual Christmas Stroll Weekend (☎ 508/228–1700), which takes place the first weekend of the month. Carolers and musicians entertain strollers as they walk the festive cobblestone streets and sample shops' wares and seasonal refreshments. Activities include theatrical performances, art exhibitions, crafts sales, and a tour of historic homes. To avoid the throngs, visit on one of the surrounding weekends (festivities begin the day after Thanksgiving and last through New Year's Eve).
	Various Cape towns also have holiday strolls; call the Cape Cod Chamber of Commerce (☎ 508/862–0700) for a free brochure.
	Falmouth's Holidays-by-the-Sea (☎ 508/548–8500 or 800/526–8532), held the first full weekend of December, includes lighting ceremonies at the Village Green, caroling at Nobska Light in Woods Hole, a house tour, church fairs, and a parade.
December	Chatham's Christmas by the Sea weekend (☎ 508/945–5199), generally the first weekend of the month, includes caroling, a Festival of Trees, and other special events. The events are part of a month-long celebration beginning just after Thanksgiving and ending with a lavish First Night celebration, with fireworks over Oyster Pond on New Year's Eve.
SPRING Late April	The weekend-long Brewster in Bloom (☎ 508/896–3500) greets the spring season with a daffodil fest each year during the last weekend in April. Geared to promote small-town life, the festival includes arts-and-crafts shows, a parade, tours of historic homes and inns, a golf tournament, and a giant antiques and collectibles market.
Mid-May	The Green Briar Nature Center and Jam Kitchen in Sandwich holds its annual Green Briar Herb Festival (☎ 508/888–6870), where you can pick up perennials, wildflowers, and dozens of herb varieties.
	During Cape Cod Maritime Days (☎ 508/362–3225 ⊕ www.capecodmaritimedays.com) lighthouse tours, guided shorefront walks, and special exhibits Cape-wide help celebrate the Cape's nautical heritage.

ON THE CALENDAR

SUMMER June–August	Summer theater, town-band concerts, and arts-and-crafts fairs enliven most every Cape town.
Early June	The Cape Cod Antique Dealers Association Spring Antiques Show (☎ 508/888–3300 ⊕ www.ccada.com) at Sandwich's Heritage Plantation is attended by 60 dealers of fine 18th- and 19th-century English and American furniture, folk art, Sandwich glass, jewelry, paintings, and quilts.
Mid- to late June	The Portuguese Festival (☎ 508/487–3424) honors Provincetown's Portuguese heritage with a lively weekend of ethnic foods and crafts, bands playing in the streets, a children's fishing derby, traditional dances, fireworks, and other events.
	The Blessing of the Fleet in Provincetown concludes the Portuguese Festival weekend. On Sunday, a parade ends at the wharf, where anglers and their families and friends pile onto boats and form a procession. The bishop stands on the dock and blesses the boats with holy water as they pass by.
Early July	Falmouth welcomes the Soundfest Chamber Music Festival (☎ 508/548–2290 ⊕ www.coloradoquartet.com), including the Colorado Quartet and guest artists. Daily events during the two-week festival include student performances, concerts, master classes, and lectures.
July 4 weekend	The Mashpee Powwow (☎ 508/477–0208) brings together Wampanoags from North and South America for three days of dance contests, drumming, a fireball game, and a clambake, plus the crowning of the Mashpee Wampanoag Indian princess on the final night.
	Fireworks displays are a part of July Fourth celebrations in several Cape towns; Falmouth has one of the most spectacular shows.
Mid-July	The Barnstable County Fair (☎ 508/563–3200 ⊕ www.barnstablecountyfair.org) in East Falmouth, begun in 1844, is Cape Cod's biggest event. The nine-day affair includes livestock and food judging; horse, pony, and oxen pulls and shows; arts-and-crafts demonstrations; carnival rides; lots of food; and appearances by formerly famous performing artists bent on comebacks.
Late July	The Cape Symphony Orchestra sets up at the Mashpee Commons for the first of two annual Sounds of Summer Pops Concerts (☎ 508/362–1111).

August	The **Cape & Islands Chamber Music Festival** (☎ 508/945–8060 or 800/818–0608 ⊕ www.capecodchambermusic.org), three weeks of top-caliber performances, including a jazz night, is held at various locations in August. The festival also sponsors an off-season concert series; call or check the Web site for the schedule.
Early August	The Boston Pops Esplanade Orchestra wows the crowds with its annual **Pops by the Sea concert** (☎ 508/362–0066 ⊕ www.artsfoundationcapecod.org), held at the Hyannis Village Green at 5 PM. Each year a guest conductor strikes up the band.
	New Bedford's **Feast of the Blessed Sacrament** (☎ 508/979–1745 or 800/508–5353 ⊕ www.portuguesefeast.com) is one of the largest celebrations of Portuguese culture in the country. Music, dance, a parade, carnival rides, and traditional foods—particularly the giant *carne de espeto* outdoor barbecue—are all part of the four-day event.
Mid-August	The 7-mi **SBLI Falmouth Road Race** (☎ 508/540–7000 ⊕ www.falmouthroadrace.com) is a world-class race covering the coast from Woods Hole to Falmouth Heights; to participate, apply by mail the fall or winter before the race.
Late August	The Cape Symphony Orchestra comes to Eldridge Field Park in Orleans for its **Sounds of Summer Pops Concert** (☎ 508/362–1111).
	The annual **New England Jazz Festival** (☎ 508/477–2580 ⊕ www.bochcenterarts.com), produced by the Boch Center for the Performing Arts, takes place at Mashpee Commons.
	The Osterville Historical Society holds its annual **antiques show** (☎ 508/428–5861) on the third or fourth Thursday in August.
FALL September	The **Annual Bourne Scallop Fest** (☎ 508/759–6000) attracts thousands of people to Buzzards Bay for three days of music, parades, carnival rides, and, of course, fried scallops.
	The **Harwich Cranberry Festival** (☎ 508/430–2811 ⊕ www.harwichcranberryfestival.org) includes an arts-and-crafts show, a carnival, fireworks, pancake breakfasts, an antique-car show, and much more.
Mid-October	During **Seafest** (☎ 508/945–5199), an annual tribute to the maritime industry, Chatham Light is open to the public.
Late October	**Fall foliage.** The leaf season usually peaks around the end of October. Colors might flame a few weeks earlier or later, however, depending on the weather during the preceding months.

| Thanksgiving Eve | The Lighting of the Monument festivities (☎ 508/487–1310) commemorate the Pilgrims' landing, with the lighting of 5,000 white and gold bulbs draped over the Pilgrim Monument in Provincetown. The lighting occurs each night until just after the New Year. A musical performance accompanies the lighting, and the monument museum holds an open house and tours. Other events include dramatic readings of the Mayflower Compact (which was signed in Provincetown Harbor), fireworks, and numerous Thanksgiving dinner celebrations. Various arts-and-crafts events kick off around the same time and continue through the holiday season. |

Approaching the Cape

PLYMOUTH, FALL RIVER, WESTPORT, SOUTH
DARTMOUTH, NEW BEDFORD & MARION

WORD OF MOUTH

"[In Plymouth] the 'rock' is not the draw, but the historical actors do a great job of bringing history alive. Tour the Mayflower as well as the Plantation. You'll find it absolutely amazing that all those people traveled all those days on that small 'flotation device' in the middle of the Atlantic. It's a great cloudy day activity, or when you've had just enough of the beach!"

—Dreamer2

www.fodors.com/forums

Updated by
Laura V. Scheel

YOUR PRIMARY GOAL may be to get to Cape Cod sooner rather than later, but that doesn't mean you shouldn't stop to see some of the eclectic towns you'll pass through as you approach the region—they're a mix of suburbanized colonial hamlets, low-key yachting enclaves, and riches-to-rags industrial communities enjoying varying degrees of resurgence. Though the approach to the Cape may not have the cachet of the Cape proper, there's plenty to interest travelers looking for something to do on a rainy day—or even those who just want to take a break from the road. In the communities that line the principal routes to Cape Cod, you'll find some of New England's seminal historic attractions (all of them well suited to kids), a handful of bewitching beaches, a few pretty-damn-quaint seaside villages, and a passable selection of pleasing restaurants and accommodations.

In Plymouth you can see that monument you've heard about since childhood, Plymouth Rock, and walk the decks of the *Mayflower II*. A few miles down the road, don't miss Plimoth Plantation, a re-created 17th-century Puritan village where trained staff members vividly dramatize the everyday lives of the first English settlers. Watch them make cheese, forge nails, and explain where and when they bathe (hint: not often). If you have the time, as you leave Boston and pass through Quincy, exit from Route 3 onto the South Shore's slower but infinitely more scenic highway, Route 3A. It runs for about 50 mi down through the South Shore along Massachusetts Bay, from Quincy through Scituate, Duxbury, and Plymouth and on to Cape Cod Canal. It takes an extra hour to go this way, but you'll avoid Route 3's occasionally vicious traffic jams, and this drive is great fun if you're a fan of road-tripping.

If you're coming by way of I–195, consider stopping in the seafaring city of New Bedford, a major whaling port in the 19th century. It now delights visitors with the nation's largest museum on the history of whaling. If you have the time, and especially if you're intrigued by the macabre legacy of the 19th century's most infamous trial, in which Lizzie Borden was accused, and acquitted, of dispatching her parents with "40 whacks" of an ax, stop in Fall River, where this riveting drama played out. Fall River has seen better days, but it's also home to the largest collection of historic naval ships and submarines all open for exploration—Battleship Cove. Not far from I–195 and the Fall River–New Bedford corridors, along the coves of Buzzards Bay, you'll find charming seaside towns and sandy beaches, the best known of which is Horseneck Beach in Westport. The pretty villages of South Dartmouth, Fairhaven, and Marion are also worth a stop.

Exploring the Approach to the Cape

If you're approaching the Cape by car, you have three key options. If you're coming from metro Boston and points due north, you'll likely approach the Cape via Route 3 (which is a major four-lane, limited-access highway, just like any interstate). If you're approaching from points south and west (i.e., Rhode Island, Connecticut, New York City), you'll likely take I–195, which cuts over from I–95 in Providence. And if you're approaching from central or western Massachusetts (i.e., Worcester or Springfield) or from Vermont, New Hampshire, or Maine, you'll probably take I–495, which cuts down in a southeasterly direction toward the Cape from the Mass Pike.

We've organized this chapter by covering first Plymouth, the region's must-see destination, which lies along Route 3, and then the engaging communities on or near I–195, from the cities of Fall River and New Bedford to the mellow but arresting villages of Westport, South Dartmouth, and Marion. There aren't many notable stops off I–495, but if you're coming that way and are keen on visiting some of the towns in this chapter, you can easily jog northeast to Route 3 or south to I–195. Again, Plymouth is the star of the region, and even if you approach Cape Cod from a different direction, it's worth making a day trip back out to America's so-called hometown—it's easy to reach Plymouth from the Upper Cape.

Numbers in the margin correspond to points of interest on the Approaching the Cape map.

About the Restaurants

Like other Massachusetts shorefront towns, the communities approaching the Cape have plenty of seafood restaurants, where you find everything from clam shacks to more upscale dining options. In New Bedford and Fall River, which have large Portuguese populations, you can sample traditional Portuguese dishes made with spicy *linguica* (sausage) or *bacalau* (salt cod), and pick up some soft, doughy Portuguese sweet bread to sustain you as you explore.

About the Hotels

Plymouth's numerous lodgings include quaint bed-and-breakfasts and chain properties. Choices on the coast are more limited, although the area does have several worthwhile small inns and B&Bs. If you're traveling with kids, be sure to ask whether they are welcome at smaller properties; some are not set up for youngsters.

WHAT IT COSTS					
	$$$$	$$$	$$	$	¢
RESTAURANTS	over $30	$22–$30	$16–$22	$10–$16	under $10
HOTELS	over $260	$200–$260	$140–$200	$90–$140	under $90

Restaurant prices are per person for a main course at dinner. Hotel prices are for a standard double room, excluding 6% sales tax (more in some counties) and 1%–4% tourist tax.

Timing

The fair-weather days of autumn make for a good time to visit Plymouth and the surrounding area. The Thanksgiving holiday is filled with special events at Plimouth Plantation, the site of the first permanent European settlement in southern New England in 1620. Heavy traffic is the norm on summer weekends and holidays on all major routes approaching the Sagamore and Bourne bridges. It's not uncommon for bridge backups to extend several miles, tacking on extra travel time.

Plymouth

❶ *40 mi southeast of Boston.*

On December 26, 1620, 102 weary British men, women, and children disembarked from the *Mayflower* to found the first permanent European settlement north of Virginia. (Virginia was their intended destination, but storms pushed the ship off course. Their first landing site, in Provincetown on the tip of Cape Cod, proved inhospitable; they set sail after spending nearly five weeks there, crossing Cape Cod Bay and ending their journey in Plymouth.) Of the settlers, now known as the Pilgrims, a third were members of a Puritan sect of religious reformers known as the Separatists, so called because they wanted to establish their own church separate from the national Church of England. This separation was considered treasonous, and the group had previously fled to the city of Leiden in the Netherlands seeking religious freedom. After more than 10 years there, they joined with other emigrants to start a new life in the New World.

While in Provincetown, the expedition's leaders drew up the Mayflower Compact, a historic agreement binding the group to the law of the majority. This compact became the basis for the colony's government. After a rough start (half the original settlers died during the first winter), the colony stabilized and grew under the leadership of Governor William Bradford. Two other founding fathers—military leader Myles Standish and John Alden—acquired mythical status via a poem by Henry Wadsworth Longfellow, *The Courtship of Miles Standish.*

Forty miles south of Boston, Plymouth today is characterized by narrow streets, clapboard mansions, shops, and antiques stores. Some commercial names would make the Pilgrims shudder: the John Alden Gift Shop and Mayflower Seafoods. But it's easy to overlook these and admire the picturesque waterfront. The town also holds a parade, historic-house tours, and other activities to mark Thanksgiving. It's simple to get around Plymouth on foot or via the **Plymouth Rock Trolley** (☎ 508/747–4161); $15 gets you unlimited rides for the day.

Plymouth is dotted with historical statues, including depictions of William Bradford on Water Street, a Pilgrim maiden in the verdant Brewster Gardens, and Massasoit (chief of the local Wampanoag tribe) on Carver Street. The largest freestanding granite statue in the country, the **National Monument to the Forefathers** stands high on a grassy hill. Designed by Hammet Billings of Boston in 1854 and dedicated in 1889, it depicts Faith surrounded by Liberty, Morality, Justice, Law, and Education, and includes scenes from the Pilgrims' early days in Plymouth. ✉ *Allerton St.*

PLEASURES & PASTIMES

BEACHES
With a coastline that meanders in and out of Buzzards Bay, southeastern Massachusetts has plenty of choice seaside areas. Westport's Horseneck Beach is a long stretch of sand that's hugely popular on weekends. Plymouth has several popular beaches, from Plymouth Beach near town to the long crescent of sand at White Horse Beach to the south. But there are also smaller beaches and coves where you can enjoy the shore in relative quiet—in Fairhaven, South Dartmouth, Mattapoisett, Marion, and other small towns that dot the area.

If you're more interested in being on the water than in it, try a cruise from Onset Harbor or take a whale-watching trip. Whale-watch excursions run from Plymouth daily between June and September and on a more limited basis in April, May, and October; they usually last three to four hours.

OUTDOOR ACTIVITIES
The approach to the Cape provides numerous opportunities to get close to nature. The 16,000-acre Myles Standish State Forest in Plymouth is great for hiking, as is the Freetown–Fall River State Forest. The numerous rivers and inlets on Buzzards Bay—for example, the Westport, Mattapoisett, Paskamanset, Agawam, and Weweantic rivers—are excellent for canoeing and kayaking.

THE ARTS
A great variety of musical and theatrical events are staged in a classic setting at the Zeiterion Theatre in New Bedford from September through May. You might catch a performance by blues maven Etta James, spend the evening with Garrison Keillor, or sit on the edge of your seat as you watch the vaudeville antics of the Flying Karamazov Brothers. On the second Thursday evening of every month, New Bedford holds AHA! Nights, which highlight the city's art, history, and architecture. Various performing arts events are also held regularly in Plymouth as well as at the excellent Marion Art Center, which presents everything from music to dance.

TOURING & SHOPPING
U.S. 6 from New Bedford to Buzzards Bay contains numerous specialty, antiques, and kitschy shops both inside and outside the villages. The same is true, perhaps to a lesser extent, of Route 3A from Plymouth to Sagamore. In any case, it's a pleasant drive to get off the main highway for a stretch.

MUSEUMS
For rainy- and sunny-day activities alike, the area approaching the Cape is rich in interesting, unique museums, including Plymouth's *Mayflower II* and Plimoth Plantation, Fall River's Battleship Cove, and New Bedford's Whaling Museum.

Several historic houses are open for visits, including the 1640 **Sparrow House,** Plymouth's oldest structure. You can peek into several rooms furnished in the spartan style of the Pilgrims' era. A contemporary crafts gallery also on the premises seems somewhat incongruous, but the works on view are of high quality. ⊠ *42 Summer St.* ☎ *508/747–1240* ⊕ *www.sparrowhouse.com* 🎫 *$2; gallery free* ⊙ *Apr.–late Nov., Thurs.–Tues. 10–5.*

Operated by the Plymouth Antiquarian Society, the 1749 **Spooner House** was home to the same family for 200 years; today you can take a guided tour through its restored interior and well-tended gardens. The **Hedge House Museum,** a massive Federal home from 1809, reveals the wealthier side of successful 19th-century living. As of this writing, the society was restoring a third historic property, the **Harlow Old Fort House,** a 1677 gambrel-roofed dwelling, which is slated to reopen for tours in 2007. ⊠ *27 North St.* ☎ *508/746–0012* 🎫 *$5* ⊙ *Early June–early Oct., Thurs.–Fri. 2–6, Sat. 10–1.*

Like Plimoth Plantation, the **Mayflower II,** a reproduction of the 1620 *Mayflower,* is manned by staff, some clad in period dress, and docents who regularly present demonstrations on board, from knot tying to cooking. The ship was built in England through research and a bit of guesswork, and then sailed across the Atlantic in 1957. In addition to touring the ship, you can peruse the several interesting exhibits on the pier next to it. ⊠ *State Pier* ☎ *508/746–1622* ⊕ *www.plimoth.org* 🎫 *$8; free with Plimoth Plantation combination ticket* ⊙ *Late Mar.–Nov., daily 9–5.*

A few dozen yards from the *Mayflower II* is **Plymouth Rock,** popularly believed to have been the Pilgrims' stepping-stone when they left the ship. Given the stone's unimpressive appearance—it's little more than a boulder—and dubious authenticity (as explained on a nearby plaque), the grand canopy overhead seems a trifle ostentatious.

SPOOKY WALKS

Whether you're into local lore or creepy tales of the paranormal, walking tours through Plymouth's historic areas are a great way to learn more about the town's past. The most popular offering from **Dead of Night Ghost Tours** (☎ 508/866–5111 or 508/277–2371 ⊕ www.deadofnightghosttours.com 🎫 $12; reservations required) is the Twilight Lantern Ghost Tour; there are also sunset cemetery tours and scavenger hunts for kids. The walks meet at Plymouth Rock; each lasts about 90 minutes. Choose from a 90-minute ghostly tour or a narrated history tour—you even get to carry your own lantern—with **Colonial Lantern Tours** (☎ 800/698–5636 or 508/747–4161 ⊕ www.lanterntours.com 🎫 $15). The Ghostly Haunts & Legends Tour departs nightly from the John Carver Inn at 25 Summer Street; the history tour meets at 86 Water Street.

Across the street from Plymouth Rock is **Cole's Hill,** where the company buried its dead—at night, so the local Native Americans could not count the dwindling numbers of survivors. Just past the hill, on what was once called 1st Street, is the site of the original settlement; in 1834

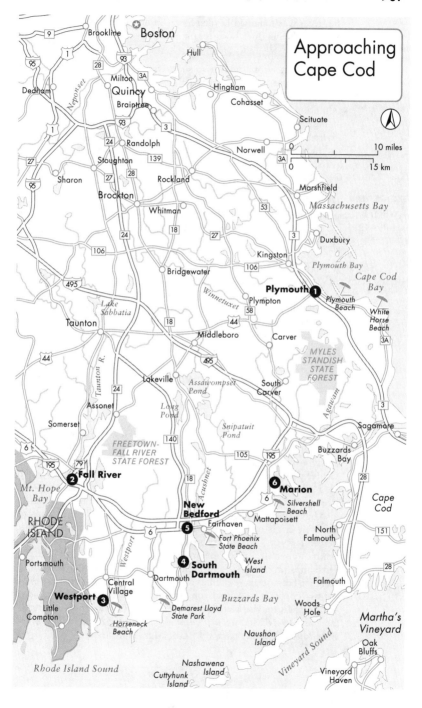

Approaching Cape Cod

10 miles

15 km

Boston
Brookline
Hull
Milton
Quincy
Hingham
Dedham
Braintree
Cohasset
Scituate
Randolph
Norwell
Stoughton
Sharon
Rockland
Marshfield
Brockton
Whitman
Massachusetts Bay
Bridgewater
Kingston
Duxbury
Plymouth Bay
Taunton
Plympton
Cape Cod Bay
Plymouth ❶
Plymouth Beach
White Horse Beach
Middleboro
Carver
MYLES STANDISH STATE FOREST
Lake Sabbatia
Lakeville
South Carver
Assawompset Pond
Assonet
Long Pond
Sagamore
Somerset
Snipatuit Pond
FREETOWN-FALL RIVER STATE FOREST
Buzzards Bay
❷ **Fall River**
Mt. Hope Bay
❻ **Marion**
Silvershell Beach
New Bedford
Cape Cod
RHODE ISLAND
Mattapoisett
❺
Fairhaven
North Falmouth
Fort Phoenix State Beach
West Island
Portsmouth
❹ **South Dartmouth**
Falmouth
Central Village
Dartmouth
Buzzards Bay
Westport ❸
Demarest Lloyd State Park
Woods Hole
Little Compton
Horseneck Beach
Naushon Island
Martha's Vineyard
Oak Bluffs
Rhode Island Sound
Nashawena Island
Cuttyhunk Island
Vineyard Sound
Vineyard Haven
Nemasket
Winnetuxet
Taunton R.
Acushnet
Westport
Agawam
Plympton

the street was renamed Leyden Street in honor of the Dutch city that sheltered the Pilgrims. Look for plaques designating the locations of the original lots.

From the waterfront sights it's a short walk to one of the country's oldest public museums. The **Pilgrim Hall Museum,** established in 1824, transports you back to the time just before the Pilgrims' landing with its exhibition of items carried by those weary travelers to the New World. Included are a carved chest, a remarkably well-preserved wicker cradle, Myles Standish's sword, John Alden's Bible, Native American artifacts, and the remains of the *Sparrow Hawk,* a sailing ship that was wrecked in 1626. ⊠ *75 Court St. (Rte. 3A)* ☎ *508/746–1620* ⊕ *www.pilgrimhall. org* 🖃 *$6* ☉ *Feb.–Dec., daily 9:30–4:30.*

■ NEED A
BREAK?
Sample fruit wines—the cranberry variety is particularly refreshing—at the **Plymouth Bay Winery** (⊠ 114 Water St. ☎ 508/746–2100), open March–December, Monday–Saturday 10:30–5, Sunday noon–5. It's a short walk from the *Mayflower II.*

(ↄ)
Fodor'sChoice
★
When you see the sign at the entrance of **Plimoth Plantation** welcoming you to the 17th century—take it seriously! Against the backdrop of the Atlantic Ocean, a Pilgrim village has been painstakingly re-created, from the thatch roofs, cramped quarters, and open fireplaces to the longhorn livestock. Throw away your preconceptions of white collars and funny hats; through ongoing research, the Plimoth staff has developed a portrait of the Pilgrims that's more complex than the dour folk pictured in elementary-school textbooks. Listen to the accents of the "residents," who never break character. You might see them plucking ducks, cooking rabbit stew, or tending garden. Feel free to engage them in conversation about their life, but expect only curious looks if you ask about anything that happened later than 1627.

Elsewhere on the plantation is **Hobbamock's Homestead,** where descendants of the Wampanoag Indians re-create the life of a Native American who chose to live near the newcomers. In the **Carriage House Crafts Center** you'll see earthenware, candles, clothing, and other items created using the techniques of 17th-century English craftsmanship—that is, reproductions of what the Pilgrims might have imported (you can also buy samples). There are always a few artisans on hand demonstrating early crafts-making techniques, too. At the **Nye Barn** you can see descendants of 17th-century goats, cows, pigs, and chickens, bred to resemble animals raised on the original plantation. The visitor center has gift shops, a cafeteria, and multimedia presentations. Dress for the weather, because many exhibits are outdoors. Admission tickets are good for two consecutive days; if you have time, you may want to spread out your plantation visit to take in all the sights. ⊠ *Warren Ave. (Rte. 3A)* ☎ *508/746–1622* ⊕ *www.plimoth.org* 🖃 *$21; $24 including entry to Mayflower II (2-day passes)* ☉ *Late Mar.–Nov., daily 9–5.*

CLOSE UP

Portrait of a Pilgrim

1

AT PLIMOTH PLANTATION, the living history interpreters you meet are not just quaintly costumed actors. Beyond the bonnets, sweeping skirts, breeches, and cloaks of these folks going about 17th-century everyday business are glimpses and representations of actual, documented Pilgrim residents.

Once an interpreter is assigned their character for the year, the studying begins—role players closely examine primary sources from the 1627 village, learning biographical backgrounds, regional dialects, typical skills, and customs. Associate Director of Colonial Interpretation John Kemp says that this type of training instills "a sense of responsibility to a real person in history. We want every person to really connect with the character they are portraying."

The staff, says Kemp, is a combination of "curious experts and passionate learners." There are those who have a great knowledge of Renaissance foodways, agriculture, and livestock; others have studied 17th-century woodworking, blacksmithing, or military history. It's definitely not your average seasonal job; after all, these "Pilgrims" spend their days creating a world that existed almost 400 years ago. Keep this in mind when you ask them where the bathrooms are—they won't have any idea what you're talking about.

—Laura V. Scheel

OFF THE BEATEN PATH

JOHN ALDEN HOUSE MUSEUM – The only standing structure in which original Pilgrims are known to have lived is about 10 mi north of Plymouth in the town of Duxbury, settled in 1628 by Pilgrim colonists Myles Standish and John Alden, among others. Alden, who served as assistant governor of Plymouth colony, occupied this house, which was built in 1653, along with his wife, Priscilla, and eight or nine of their children. One bedroom has a "seven-day dresser" with a drawer for each day of the week; the Sunday drawer, which held formal church wear, is the largest. ✉ *105 Alden St., Duxbury* ☎ *781/934–9092* ⊕ *www.alden.org* 🎫 *Guided tours $5* ☉ *Mid-May–mid-Oct., Mon.–Sat. noon–4.*

Where to Stay & Eat

$–$$$ ✕ **East Bay Grille.** A boisterous locals' favorite with subtle nautical decorations (oars, half-model ships), the East Bay looks natty enough for a special occasion but works as a casual family option, too. You'll find a menu here that suits many tastes and budgets, from mammoth lobster rolls and juicy burgers to more substantial fare, such as Chilean sea bass topped with tropical-fruit salsa, and charbroiled steak tips. Also note the several fine salads and the tasty steamed mussels appetizer. There's a popular Sunday brunch, and a pianist performs many evenings. ✉ *173 Water St., Town Wharf* ☎ *508/746–9751* ▭ *AE, D, MC, V.*

★ ¢–$$ ✕ **Lobster Hut.** This casual, cafeteria-style eatery at the waterfront offers seafood in the classic breaded-and-fried style, plus sandwiches and luncheon specials. The interior is Formica-basic, but the fish is tasty, and the water views are excellent. You can eat inside or outdoors on the patio under a tent. ⊠ *Town Wharf* ☎ *508/746–2270* ⊟ *MC, V* ✆ *Closed Jan.*

¢–$$ ✕ **Wood's Seafood.** Furnished with a simple counter for ordering fish and a handful of plastic tables and chairs, this harborside seafood shack looks authentically and endearingly shabby. If you're looking for reasonably priced seafood (fried clams, lobster rolls, crab cake sandwiches, and assorted fish plates) with a water view, it's a great choice. You can also buy live lobsters to take with you, or have them shipped to anywhere in the country. ⊠ *Town Wharf* ☎ *508/746–0261* ⊟ *AE, MC, V.*

¢ ✕ **The All-American Diner.** The look is nostalgia—red, white, and blue with movie posters. The specialties are beloved American foods—Monte Cristo–style egg sandwiches and banana Belgian waffles for breakfast (served all day) and cheeseburger club sandwiches, chicken-fried steak, and meat loaf for lunch. ⊠ *60 Court St.* ☎ *508/747–4763* ⊟ *AE, DC, MC, V* ✆ *No dinner.*

$$–$$$ ✕🖃 **John Carver Inn.** This three-story colonial-style redbrick building is steps from Plymouth's main attractions. The public rooms are lavish, with period furnishings and stylish drapes. The guest rooms are more matter-of-fact, but the six suites have hot tubs and working fireplaces; two-room suites have fireplaces and whirlpool baths. The indoor pool has a *Mayflower* ship theme and an 80-foot waterslide. At its Hearth 'n Kettle Restaurant, staff in colonial attire serve a huge selection of predictable American favorites, including seafood and hearty sandwiches. ⊠ *25 Summer St., 02360* ☎ *508/746–7100 or 800/274–1620* 🖷 *508/746–8299* ⊕ *www.johncarverinn.com* ⤲ *79 rooms, 6 suites* ⌂ *Restaurant, cable TV, Wi-Fi, pool, gym, bar, video game room, meeting rooms* ⊟ *AE, D, DC, MC, V.*

★ $$ 🖃 **Beach House Oceanfront B&B.** At the end of a long dirt road, this contemporary gray-shingle home overlooking the Atlantic makes a perfect hideaway. Although it's only about 10 minutes south of Plymouth center, the house feels like it's a world away. The deck, screened porch, and living room–dining room with floor-to-ceiling windows all face a wide expanse of ocean, and steps lead down the cliff to a small private beach. Inside, the theme is white—from the leather sofas in the living room to the lace curtains and quilts in the bedrooms. ⊠ *45 Black Pond La.* 🖅 *429 Center Hill Rd., 02360* ☎ *508/224–3517 or 888/262–2543* ⊕ *www.beachhouseplymouth.com* ⤲ *3 rooms, 1 suite* ⌂ *Beach; no smoking* ⊟ *MC, V* ⦿I *BP.*

$–$$ 🖃 **Best Western Cold Spring.** This neat-as-a-pin motel, about ½ mi from downtown Plymouth, is a good choice for families. Several buildings cluster around the parking areas and a lush green lawn, and inside, the rooms are nicely maintained, if nondescript, with floral bedspreads and sturdy wooden furnishings. Deluxe rooms are a tad more spacious than standard ones, and a few second-floor rooms look out toward the harbor. ✉ *188 Court St., 02360* ☎ *508/746–2222 or 800/678–8667* ☝ *508/746–2744* ⊕ *www.coldspringmotel.com* ⬐ *55 rooms, 3 suites, 2 cottages* ⛬ *Cable TV, Wi-Fi, pool, business services* ▭ *AE, D, MC, V* ⑂ *CP* ☽ *Closed Jan.–Mar.*

$–$$ ⌂ **Governor Bradford on the Harbour.** The waterfront location here (directly across from the *Mayflower II*) is a big plus. Rooms are motel-basic, each with two double beds, a small refrigerator, and free HBO. A Continental Plan is available from May to October. ✉ *98 Water St., 02360* ☎ *508/746–6200 or 800/332–1620* ☝ *508/747–3032* ⊕ *www.governorbradford.com* ⬐ *94 rooms* ⛬ *Refrigerators, cable TV, pool, no-smoking rooms* ▭ *AE, D, DC, MC, V.*

$–$$ ⌂ **Pilgrim Sands Motel.** This is the closest accommodation in town to Plimoth Plantation, and one of the few beachfront properties in the region. It's run by a friendly and helpful staff; and while the rooms themselves lack personality and feel a bit dated, they're clean and functional—you're paying more for the location. ✉ *150 Warren Ave., 02360* ☎ *508/747–7263 or 800/729–7263* ☝ *508/746–8066* ⊕ *www.pilgrimsands.com* ⬐ *62 rooms* ⛬ *Cable TV, Wi-Fi, 2 pools (1 indoor), hot tub, beach* ▭ *AE, D, MC, V* ⑂ *CP.*

Sports & the Outdoors

BEACHES **Plymouth Long Beach** (✉ Warren Ave. [Rte. 3A]), south of town, has restrooms, showers, and lifeguards (in season). Daily parking fees are $10 weekdays, $15 weekends.

White Horse Beach (✉ Taylor Ave.) is a popular long, sandy beach in a neighborhood of summer cottages, off Route 3A south of Plimoth Plantation. Parking is very limited.

BICYCLING Plymouth's gently sloping terrain and scenic streets make excellent terrain for bicycling. You can rent bikes at **Martha's Cyclery** (✉ 300 Court St. ☎ 508/746–2109).

GOLF Play a fine, challenging 18-hole game at **Atlantic Country Club** (✉ 450 Little Sandy Pond Rd. ☎ 508/759–6644).

Crosswinds Golf Club (✉ 424 Long Pond Rd. ☎ 508/830–1199) has great views, a driving range, and 18- and 9-hole course options.

Shoot 9- or 18 holes at **Waverly Oaks Golf Club** (✉ 444 Long Pond Rd. ☎ 508/224–6700), which also has plenty of practice space.

STATE PARKS **Myles Standish State Forest** (✉ Cranberry Rd., South Carver, Exit 5 off Rte. 3 ☎ 508/866–2526 ⊕ www.mass.gov/dcr) has more than 16,000 acres for hiking, biking, swimming, picnicking, and canoeing.

TOURS **Andy Lynn Boats** (☎ 508/746–7776), at Plymouth Town Wharf, runs whale-watch trips June–September; call for their schedule.

Capt. John Boats (☎ 508/746–2643 or 800/242–2469 ⊕ www.whalewatchingplymouth.com) offers several daily whale-watch cruises from Plymouth Town Wharf June–early September, and on a more limited schedule in April, May, and early September and October.

Fall River

2 *18 mi east of Providence, 54 mi southeast of Boston.*

This fading port and textile-milling center is today a prosaic, mostly industrial town that's en route to the Cape if you're coming from the south and west through Rhode Island. Fall River is home to the impressive nautical museum Battleship Cove and was the site of the infamous 19th century Borden murders. Otherwise, this once-thriving city—better known today as the hometown of celeb chef Emeril Lagasse—has little to attract visitors.

The best place to learn about the Borden case is the **Fall River Historical Society,** which is packed with Borden memorabilia, including courtroom evidence, photographs, and the handleless hatchet believed to be the murder weapon. The 1843 Greek Revival mansion also contains exhibits on the Fall River steamship line and the city's days as the world's largest cotton cloth manufacturer. One-hour tours begin on the hour. ☒ *451 Rock St.* ☏ *508/ 679–1071* ⊕ *www.lizzieborden.org* ▦ *Tours $5* ☽ *Apr., May, Oct., and Nov., Tues.–Fri. 9–4:30; June–Sept. and Dec., Tues.–Fri. 9–4:30, weekends 1–5.*

> ### LIZZIE BORDEN
>
> It's a famous rhyme of woe: "Lizzie Borden took an axe / And gave her mother forty whacks. / When she saw what she had done, / She gave her father forty-one." And yet Lizzie, the maiden daughter of Fall River's prominent banker, was found innocent of the 1892 bludgeoning deaths of her father and stepmother in the most sensational trial of its time.

If you're strong of heart and stomach, you may want to take in the **Lizzie Borden Bed & Breakfast Museum,** in the Bordens' former home, the site of the murders, which has been transformed into a B&B. Even if you don't spend the night here, you can stop in to see the display of Lizzie-related items. ☒ *92 2nd St.* ☏ *508/675–7333* ⊕ *www.lizzie-borden.com* ▦ *Tours $10* ☽ *Tours daily on the hr 11–3.*

A visit to Fall River can skirt Lizzie Borden's sad saga entirely. The town's industrial docks and enormous factories recall its past as a major textile center in the 19th and early 20th centuries. In the past, Fall River ⟳ served as a port; today the most interesting nautical site is **Battleship Cove,** a "floating" museum complex docked on the Taunton River. You can go aboard the 35,000-ton battleship USS *Massachusetts;* the destroyer USS *Joseph P. Kennedy, Jr.;* a World War II attack sub, the USS *Lionfish;* two PT boats from World War II; and a Cold War–era Russian-built warship. Also on the grounds is the wooden **Fall River Carousel,** which was built in the 1920s. Rides cost 50¢. ☒ *5 Water St., at Davol St., off Rte. 79* ☏ *508/678–1100 or 800/533–3194* ⊕ *www. battleshipcove.org* ▦ *$14* ☽ *Apr.–June, daily 9–5; July–early Sept., daily 9–5:30; early Sept.–Oct., daily 9–5; Nov.–Mar., daily 9–4:30.*

1

Where to Stay & Eat

$–$$ ✕ **Waterstreet Café.** This casually sophisticated café, with exposed brick and sponge-painted walls, serves hummus and tabbouleh wraps, falafel, and other Middle Eastern–inspired salads and sandwiches, along with creative American and Mediterranean specialties such as maple-chipotle char-grilled pork chops or Greek Island Shrimp sautéed with artichoke hearts and feta cheese. It's a short walk from Battleship Cove. There's brunch on Sunday and live music many nights. ⊠ *36 Water St.* ☎ *508/672–8748* ⊕ *www.waterstreetcafe.com* 🖃 *AE, D, MC, V* ☉ *Closed Mon. and Tues. No dinner Wed.*

¢–$ ✕ **T. A. Restaurant.** Fall River has a substantial Portuguese community, and this modest but excellent eatery serves some of the best examples of that culture's cuisine in the state. *Alentejana* (marinated pork with clams and potatoes), garlicky shrimp Mozambique, and baked cod with onions and tomatoes are among the specialties. A shop next door sells Portuguese foods and provisions. ⊠ *408 S. Main St.* ☎ *508/673–5890* 🖃 *AE, D, MC, V.*

$$–$$$ 🏨 **Lizzie Borden Bed & Breakfast Museum.** Could you stand to sleep in the same house where Lizzie Borden's father and stepmother met a bloody end? Choose from one of the original bedrooms, some of which can be combined into adjoining suites, or three rooms converted from attic space—all are lavishly appointed with fine Victorian pieces. A full breakfast and a house tour are included, as well as a map of the "Lizzie Trail" (related sites in the Fall River area). You can also watch videos about the Borden case. Owners Donald Woods and Lee Ann Wilbur have restored and rejuvenated the entire property, using fabrics, paints, and furnishings that more closely resemble how the Borden house would have looked at the time of its infamy. ⊠ *92 2nd St., 02721* ☎ *508/675–7333* ⊕ *www.lizzie-borden.com* 🛏 *6 rooms, 2 suites, 3 with shared bath* ♿ *Wi-Fi, shop; no room phones, no room TVs, no smoking* 🖃 *AE, D, MC, V* ⦿ *BP.*

Westport

❸ *12 mi southeast of Fall River.*

As you venture south and east of Fall River, the urban landscape gives way to farm country. You'll pass rows of corn, old stone walls, and pastures of cows and horses. About 12 mi from Fall River, Westport is comprised of farmland and summer homes in a small village and scattered throughout the countryside; it also has one of the area's nicest beaches.

The **Westport Rivers Vineyard and Winery** has earned considerable acclaim for their sparkling, white, and rosé vintages, which they've been producing since the early '90s using grapes they grow on an 80-acre vineyard—the sparkling wines are particularly well regarded. You can sample the wines, and there's a small art gallery above the store with changing exhibits. Free winery tours are offered on weekends, and the winery holds special food-and-wine events and festivals throughout the year. ⊠ *417 Hixbridge Rd., off Rte. 88* ☎ *508/636–3423* ⊕ *www.*

westportrivers.com ☼ *Tasting room, shop, and gallery May–Dec., daily 11–5; Jan.–Apr., weekends 11–5.*

NEED A BREAK?

Traditional baking techniques are still employed at **Butler's Colonial Donut House** (✉ 459 Sanford Rd. ☎ 508/672-4600). Specialties include cream puffs, Long Johns, and a variety of old-time favorites, all handmade with real cream. Rounding out the offerings are tasty pastries and pies.

Where to Stay & Eat

$$–$$$$ ✕ **The Back Eddy.** Fresh, creatively prepared seafood—such as applewood
Fodor'sChoice bacon–wrapped sea scallops with corn-and-tomato succotash, and rare
★ grilled yellowfin tuna with wasabi oil and house-made kimchee—is the specialty at this laid-back waterfront restaurant where some diners arrive by boat and many patrons greet each other by name. The casual, wood-floor dining room is boisterous, with a lively bar scene, and most of the large windows overlook the busy harbor, an ideal place to watch the sunset. Expect to wait for a table. ✉ *1 Bridge Rd.* ☎ *508/636–6500* ⊕ *www.thebackeddy.com* ▭ *AE, D, MC, V* ⌦ *Reservations not accepted* ☼ *Closed Jan.–Mar. No lunch weekdays.*

¢–$$ ✕ **Marguerite's.** The scene is pure country kitchen inside this gray-shingle house—from the wooden tables to the cheerful waitresses who circulate with ever-full coffeepots. Diner-style breakfasts and old-time New England specialties, from stuffed quahogs (clams) and chowder to broiled scrod, liver and onions, and chicken pie, make up most of the menu; the daily specials offer some jazzier flourishes, such as grilled swordfish with lemon-dill butter. It's all fresh and homemade, which has earned this little house a devoted local following. Note that dinner is served only until 8 PM weeknights and until 8:30 on Friday and Saturday. ✉ *778 Main Rd., Village Commons shopping center* ☎ *508/636–3040* ▭ *No credit cards* ☼ *Closed Sun.*

$$ ▭ **Paquachuck Inn.** Built in 1827 as a supply house for whaling ships, this wood-shingle building on Westport Point is now a modest, comfortable inn. The wood-floor rooms with exposed beams aren't large, but several have four-poster beds and all offer at least a glimpse of the water. Unfortunately, none has a private bath (the nine rooms share four baths), although one shared bath does have a whirlpool tub, and there's also an outdoor shower. The large, sunny breakfast room with comfy couches leads to a patio and yard—note the three whale vertebrae that are now a garden sculpture. ✉ *2056 Main Rd., 02791* ☎ *508/636–4398* ⊕ *www.paquachuck.com* ⇱ *9 rooms* ♿ *Coffee shop, dock; no a/c, no room phones, no room TVs, no smoking* ▭ *MC, V* ❙❁❙ *CP.*

Sports & the Outdoors

BEACHES One of the nicest beaches in southeastern Massachusetts, **Horseneck**
★ **Beach State Reservation** (✉ Rte. 88 ☎ 508/636–8816 ⊕ www.mass.gov/dcr) draws summer crowds to its 2 mi of sand, with access to kayaking and boating on the Westport River. There are restrooms with showers, and lifeguards in season. Parking is $7 a day from May through early September.

South Dartmouth

❹ *4 mi east of Westport.*

As in nearby Westport, the South Dartmouth countryside is dotted with farms and summer homes, but residents who work in nearby New Bedford also make their homes here year-round. One of the prettiest spots is Padanaram (pronounced pay-duh-*nair*-um) Village, where Gulf Road and Dartmouth Road meet. Built around the sailboat-filled harbor, its a little oasis of shops, galleries, and cafés. Nearby, the village of Russells Mills houses one of the region's oldest general stores and a pottery studio.

Where to Stay

$$ ⌂ **Residence Inn.** This comfortable extended-stay Marriott is near shopping and golf; Horseneck Beach is 12 mi away. The spacious suites have full kitchens, high-speed Internet access, and separate sleeping and living areas; some units have fireplaces. There's a complimentary full breakfast, and you can order in from local restaurants through a delivery service. ✉ *181 Faunce Corner Rd., North Dartmouth 02747* ☎ *508/ 954–5858 or 800/331–3131* 🖷 *508/747–3032* ⌕ *96 suites* △ *Kitchens, in-room data ports, Wi-Fi, indoor pool, gym, hot tub, laundry facilities, laundry service, concierge, some pets allowed (fee)* ▭ *AE, D, DC, MC, V* ⏍ *BP.*

Sports & the Outdoors

BEACHES   **Demarest Lloyd State Park** (✉ Barney's Joy Rd. ☎ 508/636–8816 ⊕ www. mass.gov/dcr) may be hard to find, but it's worth seeking out for its long beach of soft, white sand on a sheltered Buzzards Bay cove. Behind the beach is a wooded area with picnic tables and barbecue grills. The bathhouse has restrooms and showers. In season (late May–early September) there are lifeguards, and parking is $7 a day.

Shopping

Davoll's General Store (✉ 1228 Russells Mills Rd. ☎ 508/636–4530), established in 1793, sells antiques and collectibles, as well as clothing, deli sandwiches, and a small selection of groceries.

Salt Marsh Pottery (✉ 1167 Russells Mills Rd. ☎ 508/636–4813 or 800/ 859–5028 ⊕ www.saltmarsh.com) makes platters, bowls, and other unique ceramic pieces decorated with wildflowers.

New Bedford

❺ *15 mi east of Fall River, 50 mi south of Boston.*

In 1652, colonists from Plymouth settled the area that now includes New Bedford. The city has a long maritime tradition, which began when it was a shipbuilding center and small whaling port in the late 1700s. By the mid-1800s New Bedford had flourished into a center of North American whaling.

Today New Bedford still has the largest fishing fleet on the East Coast, and although much of the town is industrial, the restored historic district near the water is a pleasant stop. It was here that Herman Melville set some of the opening sections of his masterpiece, *Moby-Dick*. New Bedford's whaling tradition is commemorated in the **New Bedford Whaling National Historical Park,** encompassing 13 blocks of the waterfront historic district. The park visitor center, in an 1853 Greek Revival former bank, provides maps and information about whaling-related sites. Free walking tours of the park leave from the visitor center at 10 AM and noon in July and August. You can also view an orientation film about American whaling and the New Bedford historic sites; the film is free and is shown on the hour, daily 10–3, at the nearby New Bedford Whaling Museum. ⊠ *33 William St., Downtown* ☎ *508/996–4095* ⊕ *www. nps.gov/nebe* ⊘ *Daily 9–5.*

★ ☺ The **New Bedford Whaling Museum,** established in 1903, is the world's largest museum devoted to the history of whaling. A highlight is the skeleton of a 66-foot blue whale, one of only three on view anywhere in the world. An interactive exhibit lets you listen to the underwater sounds of whales, dolphins, and other sea life, plus the sounds of a thunderstorm and a whale-watching boat—all as a whale might hear them. You can also peruse the collection of scrimshaw, visit exhibits on regional history, and climb aboard an 89-foot half-scale model of the 1826 whaling ship *Lagoda*—the world's largest ship model. ⊠ *18 Johnny Cake Hill, Downtown* ☎ *508/997–0046* ⊕ *www.whalingmuseum.org* ☺ *$10* ⊘ *Daily 9–5; late May–early Sept. until 9 on Thurs.*

Seaman's Bethel, the small chapel described in *Moby-Dick,* is across the street from the whaling museum. ⊠ *15 Johnny Cake Hill, Downtown* ☎ *508/992–3295* ⊘ *Weekdays 10–5.*

The **New Bedford Art Museum,** a compact gallery space in the 1918 Vault Building (a former bank), showcases the work of area artists. Included are paintings by 19th- and early-20th-century New Bedford artists Albert Bierstadt, William Bradford, and Charles Henry Gifford. ⊠ *608 Pleasant St., Downtown* ☎ *508/961–3072* ⊕ *www.newbedfordartmuseum. org* ☺ *$3* ⊘ *Late May–early Sept., Mon.–Wed. and Fri.–Sun. 10–5, Thurs. 10–7; early Sept.–late May, Wed. and Fri.–Sun. noon–5, Thurs. noon–7.*

For a glimpse of upper-class life during New Bedford's whaling heyday, head ½ mi south of downtown to the **Rotch-Jones-Duff House and Garden Museum.** This 1834 Greek Revival mansion, set amid a full city block of gardens, housed three prominent families in the 1800s and is filled with elegant furnishings from the era, including a mahogany piano, a massive marble-top sideboard, and portraits of the house's occupants. A self-guided audio tour is available. ⊠ *396 County St.* ☎ *508/997– 1401* ⊕ *www.rjdmuseum.org* ☺ *$5* ⊘ *Mon.–Sat. 10–4, Sun. noon–4.*

Where to Stay & Eat

$–$$$ ✕ **Davy's Locker.** A huge seafood menu is the main draw at this spot overlooking Buzzards Bay. Choose from more than a dozen shrimp preparations or one of several Caribbean-inspired treats, such as swordfish with mango-salsa jambalaya. An almost daunting array of surf-and-turf combos, steaks, salmon grills, lobster platters, and fried seafood plates

CLOSE UP

Cuttyhunk Island

1

FOR A TASTE of old New England island magic without the development or crowds of Cape Cod, Martha's Vineyard, or Nantucket, visit bucolic Cuttyhunk Island, which is accessible only by boat or seaplane. Cuttyhunk, which is about 10 mi south of New Bedford, sits at the southwestern end of the Elizabeth Islands, an isolated 16-mi chain extending from Woods Hole and separating Vineyard Sound from Buzzards Bay. The rest of these lovely islands (Noamesset, Uncatena, Naushon, Nashawena, and Pasque) are privately owned and inaccessible to the public. Cuttyhunk was first explored by Bartholomew Gosnold in 1602 and was settled in 1641. In the days of sail, Cuttyhunk served as home to the pilots who guided the whaling ships safely into New Bedford harbor. Today's year-round population is fewer than 100, a living testament to the island's reputation for isolation. In summer, the population swells to several hundred. You'll see very few cars here—golf carts are the vehicle of choice for residents—but there's little need for one. At just 2½ mi long and less than 1 mi wide, Cuttyhunk is easily navigable on foot.

Upon arrival at the dock, you will be surrounded by many boats both large and small. You need not bother to bring much pocket money, as there's little to buy except perhaps some fresh oysters and an ice-cream cone. Outdoor public restrooms are available. A short uphill walk brings you to the center of the island, where you'll be treated to majestic views of Vineyard Sound. Here you will find a small general store, a one-room schoolhouse, a church, a library, a seasonal café, a small museum, and a B&B. An unpaved dirt road leads to the far end of the island, where you can find a pond among pastoral natural surroundings. This is a quiet place where you can truly relax amid peaceful, natural surroundings.

If you want to stay overnight, contact the **Cuttyhunk Fishing Club B&B** (☎ 508/992-5585 ⊕ www.cuttyhunkfishingclub.com), which rents rooms, apartments, and houses from mid-May to mid-October. **Pete's Place Rentals** (☎ 508/992-5131 ⊕ www.cuttyhunk.com/rental.html) has a small number of water-view properties available for weekly rentals from late May to mid-October.

The **M/V** *Alert II* **ferry** (☎ 508/992-1432 ⊕ www.cuttyhunk.com) makes the one-hour trip from New Bedford's Fisherman's Wharf (Pier 3) to Cuttyhunk daily mid-June to mid-September. The ferry departs New Bedford at 10 AM and returns from Cuttyhunk at 3 PM (with additional trips on Friday, Saturday, and Sunday); same-day round-trip fares are $24.

–By James W. Rohlf

round out the enormous menu. Ice-cream smoothie cocktails, such as the toasted almond (with amaretto, Kahlua, and vanilla ice cream), make for toothsome desserts. ⊠ 1480 E. Rodney French Blvd. ☎ 508/992-7359 ⊟ AE, D, MC, V.

¢-$$ ✕ **Antonio's.** If you'd like to sample the traditional fare of New Bedford's large Portuguese population, friendly, unadorned Antonio's serves hearty portions of pork and shellfish stew, bacalau (salt cod), and grilled sardines, often on plates piled high with crispy fried potatoes and rice. ✉ 267 *Coggeshall St., near intersection of I–195 and Rte. 18* ☎ *508/990–3636* ▱ *No credit cards.*

★ ¢–$$ ✗ **Freestone's City Grill.** Housed in an 1877 former bank in the historic district, Freestone's serves soups and chowders, sandwiches and salads, plus scrod casino (topped with seafood stuffing and bacon bits), Asian-veggie stir-fry, and broiled flat-iron steak with Jack Daniels sauce. Traditional details—mahogany paneling, marble floors, and brass rails—blend with contemporary art. ✉ *41 William St., Downtown* ☎ *508/993–7477* ⊕ *www.freestones.com* ▱ *AE, DC, MC, V.*

$ ▥ **Edgewater Bed & Breakfast.** One of New Bedford's most pleasant places to stay is just across the Acushnet River in Fairhaven, a residential suburb. The Edgewater's slogan is "So close to the water, you'll think you're on a boat," and it's true—this house, built in 1760 and expanded in the 1880s, has water views from three sides. All rooms are simply and traditionally furnished; the window-lined Captain's Suite, with a working fireplace and a king-size bed, has the best views. Owner Kathy Reed, who has run the B&B since the early 1980s, has plenty of ideas for things to see and do. ✉ *2 Oxford St., Fairhaven 02719* ☎ *508/ 997–5512* ᨇ *508/997–5784* ⊕ *www.rixsan.com/edgewater* ⬡ *3 rooms, 3 suites* ⬙ *Cable TV; no room phones, no kids under 5, no smoking* ▱ *AE, D, MC, V* ⦿⧵ *CP.*

Nightlife & the Arts

On the second Thursday of every month from 5 to 9 PM, New Bedford hosts **AHA! nights** (☎ 508/264–8859 ⊕ www.ahanewbedford.org), a downtown gallery night program that highlights the city's art, history, and architecture. Museums and galleries, including the Whaling Museum and the New Bedford Art Museum, have extended hours and offer free admission. Concerts, crafts demonstrations, and other special events are often on the program.

A variety of musical and artistic events are held at the **Zeiterion Theater** (☎ 508/994–2900 ⊕ www.zeiterion.org), a wonderful old building in New Bedford's historic district.

Sports & the Outdoors

BEACHES **Fort Phoenix State Beach Reservation** (✉ Green St., Fairhaven, Off U.S. 6 ☎ 508/992–4524 ⊕ www.mass.gov/dcr), the site of the Revolutionary War's first naval battle, has a small sandy beach. Parking is free, and there are restrooms with showers.

Marion

➏ *20 mi east of Fall River, 50 mi south of Boston.*

Small-town charm pervades the modest village center of Marion, a town that has worked hard to preserve its historic buildings and landmarks. Nineteenth-century and even some earlier homes, many with white picket fences and well-tended flower gardens, line the narrow streets. The present home of the **Sippican Historical Society,** an integral part of the Town of Marion, was built in 1834 by Dr. Walton Nathan Ellis. The **Marion**

Art Center was once the Universalist Church, built in 1833 by a group of people who wanted to start a "new religion" in Sippican Village. **Handy's Tavern,** built in 1812, was a popular place for the seafaring men to gather after their ships docked at the foot of Main Street. What is now the **Marion General Store** was a place of worship from 1799 to 1841.

During the early and mid-1800s, Marion was mainly a home for sea captains and sailors carrying cotton to Europe and cargoes to the Orient, and returning with products from the East. Many of them became wealthy, and some built magnificent homes in Marion, which was also a small shipbuilding community. Today, the year-round community of about 6,000 is tenacious about preserving its historic character and private to the point of not encouraging publicity and shunning tourism. The majority of out-of-towners come to visit children boarding at **Tabor Academy,** a private school for grades 9–12 whose campus stretches along a half mile of Sippican Harbor, or to attend a high-end antiques show every August. Still, Marion is worth a stop to view the spectacle of more than 700 boats moored in scenic **Sippican Harbor** and to soak up the historical beauty of this hidden treasure of a town.

NEED A BREAK? | **Maggie's Homemade Ice Cream** offers more than 25 flavors of homemade ice cream, Maggie's own hot fudge, homemade Danish waffle cones, custom-made ice cream cakes and pies, and freshly baked cookies. ⊠ *Spring St. at U.S. 6* ☎ *508/748-9711.*

Where to Eat

¢–$$ ✕ **Sippican Café.** Historically, Marion has been a one-restaurant town, and when Kathleen and Bob Bost bought and renovated a local breakfast joint, this became the place to go for dinner. Chef Loretta Imbriglio, alumna of the Meridien and the Chatham Bars Inn, delights locals with her light-handed, inventive twists on fresh seafood, beef, chicken, and pasta. Like the place itself, the menu is small but enticing, with three or four specials nightly and even a cheese course. Take note: it's BYOB. ⊠ *167 Spring St.* ☎ *508/748-0176* ▭ *AE, MC, V* ☉ *No dinner Sun.–Tues.*

¢ ✕ **Uncle John's Cafe & Cookies.** Marion's local java joint serves breakfast and lunch, doling out coffee, scones, muffins, bagels, sandwiches, soups, and salads, which you can enjoy at tables or at the counter. Despite its name, the cookie selection is small. ⊠ *356 Front St.* ☎ *508/748-0063* ▭ *No credit cards* ☉ *No dinner.*

Nightlife & the Arts

The **Marion Art Center** (⊠ 80 Pleasant St. ☎ 508/748-1266 ⊕ www.marionartcenter.org)—comprising two galleries; a small, intimate theater; and a studio—offers classes in art, music, dance, and theater arts year-round to both children and adults. Local artists have shows here, and four major theatrical productions are performed each year. In the late 19th century, during Marion's "Gilded Age," many famous writers and artists—including Henry James, Charles Dana Gibson, Sanford White, and the Barrymores—came to the area to share ideas and each other's company.

EN ROUTE

As you head east toward Cape Cod, a wet and wild adventure for the kids awaits at the **Water Wizz Water Park,** with a 50-foot-high waterslide complete with tunnels and dips, a wave pool, a river ride, three tube rides, two enclosed water-mat slides, a children's slide, a pool, miniature golf, and food. The enclosed Black Wizard waterslide descends 75 feet in darkness. ⊠ *U.S. 6 and Rte. 28, Wareham, 2 mi west of Bourne Bridge* ☎ *508/295–3255* ⊕ *www.waterwizz.com* ⊠ *$28* ☉ *Mid-June–mid-Aug., daily 10–6:30; mid-Aug.–early Sept., daily 10–6.*

Sports & the Outdoors

BEACHES   **Silvershell Beach,** at the south end of Front Street, is open to the public. Facilities include lifeguards and a playground.

Shopping

Marion Sports Shop (⊠ 290 Front St. ☎ 508/748–1318) is one of the oldest tennis specialty shops in New England, but the impressive selection of tennis gear at the back of the store is not all it has to offer. Owner Frank Fletcher, a former tennis instructor, also stocks hip clothing lines for both men and women by up-and-coming designers and unusual jewelry and accessories, items procured during his regular buying trips to Manhattan.

APPROACHING THE CAPE ESSENTIALS

To research prices, get advice from other travelers, and book travel arrangements, visit www.fodors.com.

BY BOAT & FERRY

From mid-spring through early autumn, ferries run from New Bedford to Cuttyhunk Island and to Oak Bluffs and Vineyard Haven on Martha's Vineyard, and from Plymouth to Provincetown.

For details, ⇨ Boat & Ferry Travel *in* Smart Travel Tips located in the back of the book.

BY BUS

Dattco offers service from Boston to New Bedford. Bonanza Bus Lines runs frequent direct service between Boston and Fall River, as well as service to both Fall River and New Bedford from Providence. From Fall River and New Bedford to the Cape, Bonanza provides service to Bourne, Falmouth, Woods Hole, and Hyannis. Plymouth & Brockton Street Railway buses stop in Plymouth en route to the Cape from Boston. From the Plymouth stop, you can take Plymouth Area Link buses to the town center or to Plimoth Plantation.

🚌 Bus Depots **Plymouth & Brockton Plymouth depot** ⊠ Visitor's Center Park/Ride lot, Rte. 3, Exit 5, Plymouth ☎ 508/746-0378. **Southeastern Regional Transit Authority Fall River Terminal** ⊠ 221 2nd St., Fall River ☎ 508/679-2335. **Southeastern Regional Transit Authority New Bedford Terminal** ⊠ 134 Elm St., New Bedford ☎ 508/999-5211.

🚌 Bus Lines **Bonanza Bus Lines** ☎ 888/751-8800 ⊕ www.bonanzabus.com. **Dattco** ☎ 508/993-5040 ⊕ www.dattco.com. **Plymouth & Brockton Street Railway** ☎ 508/746-0378 ⊕ www.p-b.com. **Plymouth Area Link** ☎ 508/746-0378 ⊕ www.gatra.org/pal.htm.

BY TAXI

🛈 Taxi Companies **Central Transportation** ⊠ Plymouth ☎ 508/746-0018. **Yellow Cab** ⊠ Fall River ☎ 508/674-4633. **Yellow Cab** ⊠ New Bedford ☎ 508/999-5213.

VISITOR INFORMATION

Plymouth Waterfront Visitor Information Center is generally open between April and November.

🛈 Tourist Information **Destination Plymouth** ⊠ 170 Water St., Suite 10C, Plymouth 02360 ☎ 508/747-7533 ⊕ www.visit-plymouth.com. **Plymouth County Convention & Visitors Center** ⊠ 32 Court St., 2nd fl., Plymouth 02360 ☎ 508/747-0100 or 800/231-1620 ⊕ www.seeplymouth.com. **Fall River Chamber of Commerce** ⊠ 200 Pocasset St., Fall River 02721 ☎ 508/676-8226 ⊕ www.fallriverchamber.com. **Bristol County Convention & Visitors Bureau** ⊠ 70 N. 2nd St., New Bedford 02741 ☎ 508/997-1250 or 800/288-6263 ⊕ www.southofboston.org. **New Bedford Office of Tourism** ⊠ Waterfront Visitors Center, Old City Pier 3, New Bedford 02740 ☎ 508/979-1745 or 800/508-5353 ⊕ www.destinationnewbedford.org.

The Upper Cape

WORD OF MOUTH

"Sandwich is one of the least commercialized towns on the Cape. Heck, we just got our first movie theater a few years back, and there still isn't a fast food restaurant in sight! If you like to shop, you could easily spend some of your days driving along 6A from Sandwich down into Barnstable and even Yarmouth, stopping along the way at dozens upon dozens of antiques stores and unique shops. There are also many nice restaurants along the way."

—klw25

Updated by
Laura V. Scheel

THE CLOSEST PART OF THE CAPE TO THE MAINLAND, the Upper Cape has none of the briny, otherworldly breeziness of the Outer Cape and little of the resort feel of Lower Cape towns like Chatham. Instead, its year-round population is substantial, its beaches are intimate, and more of its attractions—freshwater ponds, conservation areas, and small museums—are inland. You'll discover plenty of history here: Sandwich is the oldest town on the Cape, and Bourne was the Pilgrims' first Cape Cod settlement and an important trading area. The first Native American reservation in the United States was established in Mashpee, which still has a large Wampanoag population and a tribal-council governing body.

Being able to find peace and quiet so close to the mainland and the traffic-clogged bridges is an unexpected and much-appreciated characteristic of the Upper Cape. Sandwich, its village streets lined with historic houses and museums, is remarkably well preserved. Heading east, Route 6A meanders past antiques shops, bed-and-breakfasts, and salt marshes. Falmouth, to the south, is an active year-round community, more suburban than seaside, though its easy-to-reach beaches are popular with families. In the villages of North and West Falmouth, along Buzzards Bay, tree-lined country lanes lead to sandy coves, and in East Falmouth and Waquoit, narrow spits of land jut into marshy inlets; plenty of secluded sites for hiking and walking are yours for the taking. Woods Hole, a small but bustling village on the Cape's southwestern tip, is a center for international marine research; it's also the departure point for ferries to Martha's Vineyard.

Exploring the Upper Cape

On the north shore, Sandwich, gracious and lovely, is the Cape's oldest town. Centered inland, Mashpee is a long-standing Native American township in which Native American–owned land is governed by local Wampanoags. Falmouth, the Cape's second-most populous town, is still green and historic, if seemingly overrun with strip malls. Woods Hole, the major port for ferries to Martha's Vineyard, is world renowned for its biological research institutions. Along the west coast, in parts of Bourne and West and North Falmouth, you can find wooded areas ending in secluded coves; the south coast has long-established resort communities.

About the Restaurants

Much like the rest of Cape Cod, the Upper Cape's dining scene ranges from basic seafood shacks to contemporary restaurants that draw inspiration from the far corners of the globe—plus everything in between. Overall, the restaurant options tend toward the traditional, with fried clams, baked scrod, and boiled lobster gracing the most popular menus. Restaurants are more widely scattered in the Upper Cape towns—there are few "restaurant rows"—but if you like to wander and check out your dining options, try Main Street in Falmouth Center or Water Street in Woods Hole.

About the Hotels

Sandwich and other towns along the north-shore Route 6A Historic District have quiet, traditional villages with an old-Cape feel and charming B&Bs. Along Route 6A you can also find family-friendly motels, ranging from the modest to the better equipped. Historic B&Bs fill the center of Falmouth, and other small inns line the shore and the neighboring streets of Falmouth Heights. Lodging options are fewer in Bourne and West and North Falmouth, but a few B&Bs hidden away on country lanes provide glimpses of old New England. You can also rent modern town houses and condominiums with extensive resort amenities in Mashpee's New Seabury community.

WHAT IT COSTS				
$$$$	$$$	$$	$	¢
RESTAURANTS over $30	$22–$30	$16–$22	$10–$16	under $10
HOTELS over $260	$200–$260	$140–$200	$90–$140	under $90

Restaurant prices are per person for a main course at dinner. Hotel prices are for a standard double room, excluding 6% sales tax (more in some counties) and 1%–4% tourist tax.

Timing

Although summer on the Upper Cape is the quintessential New England vacation experience, the ideal time of the year to visit may be early autumn. You can enjoy the beaches and water activities on Cape Cod Bay, Buzzards Bay, and Nantucket Sound in tranquillity between mid-September and late October, when the summer crowds have left but the weather is still mild. The Bourne Scallop Festival takes place in mid-September for three days.

Bourne

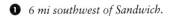 *6 mi southwest of Sandwich.*

The town of Bourne includes nine villages—Bourne Village, Bournedale, Buzzards Bay, Cataumet, Gray Gables, Monument Beach, Pocasset, Sagamore, and Sagamore Beach—along Buzzards Bay and both sides of the Cape Cod Canal. The villages range from souvenir shop-dominated commercial districts to bucolic waterfront suburbs. With a mix of year-round and summer residents, the area includes places for learning about the region's marine life and early commercial history, as well as several attractive recreation areas, established and maintained by the Army Corps of Engineers, for biking, hiking, and fishing along the canal.

The Pilgrims established their first Cape Cod settlement in Bourne in 1627, but back then it was still part of Sandwich; Bourne didn't become a separate town until 1884. By that time it had grown into a popular summer colony whose part-time residents included President Grover Cleveland and *Boston Globe* publisher Charles Taylor. Present-day Bourne's

PLEASURES & PASTIMES

2

BEACHES

Water surrounds the Upper Cape on three sides, giving beach lovers plenty of options. The south-side beaches, on Nantucket Sound, have rolling surf and are warmed by the Gulf Stream. Along Buzzards Bay, many small coves have sandy stretches (although most restrict parking to residents or permit holders in season). To the north, on Cape Cod Bay, the beaches generally have more temperate waters and gentle waves, but watch out for pebbles mixed in with the sand, particularly in the Sandwich area. Remember that you can also swim inland—the Upper Cape has many child-friendly freshwater ponds with sandy beaches and calm waters.

BICYCLING

Several short bike trails—including the Shining Sea Trail between Falmouth and Woods Hole and the Cape Cod Canal Trail, which follows both sides of the canal—make the Upper Cape a good place for easy day rides. Many of the less-traveled roads in Bourne, West and North Falmouth, and in the interior between Sandwich and Falmouth are also good biking areas. The beaches of Buzzards Bay, their parking restricted to those with resident stickers, make excellent destinations for bike rides.

NIGHTLIFE & THE ARTS

There's plenty of entertainment on the Upper Cape, especially in season; choices range from the summer concerts at Sandwich's Heritage Museums and Gardens to the staged readings at the Cape Cod Theatre Project (in Falmouth and Woods Hole) to the year-round concerts sponsored by Mashpee's

Boch Center for the Performing Arts. Bourne, Sandwich, and Falmouth all hold summer town-band concerts, and festivals with entertainment take place throughout the year. If you're looking for art galleries and crafts shows, explore the Falmouth downtown area, Route 6A in East Sandwich, and Mashpee Commons.

SPORTS & THE OUTDOORS

Hikers and walkers will find plenty of places to wander on the Upper Cape. Several recreation areas line the Cape Cod Canal, and trails crisscross the region's wildlife sanctuaries and nature reserves, including the Ashumet Holly sanctuary, Waquoit Bay National Estuarine Research Reserve, and the Mashpee River Woodlands. Canoeing and kayaking are great around the marshy inlets of both Cape Cod Bay and Buzzards Bay and on the Upper Cape's many freshwater ponds. Also, the ponds, as well as the banks of the canal, are popular fishing sites.

maritime orientation was created by the Cape Cod Canal, which opened in 1914. The 17½-mi canal cut the distance for shipping traffic between Boston and New York by 75 mi and eliminated the often-treacherous journey around the Cape. The Army Corps of Engineers took over the canal's operation in the late 1920s and embarked on a project to widen it; the current Bourne and Sagamore bridges were built in the 1930s as part of this project.

☾ The **National Marine Life Center,** on the mainland near the chamber of commerce office, has a small exhibit area devoted to whales, dolphins, seals, and other marine life. In summer there are marine-life educational programs for children and evening lectures about the ocean environment for adults. The center hopes to break ground on an expanded facility for rehabilitating stranded marine animals that will include a marine animal hospital and nursery, eight rehabilitation pools, and additional exhibit space as soon as the necessary funds can be raised. ✉ *120 Main St., Buzzards Bay* ☎ *508/743–9888* ⊕ *www.nmlc.org* ✉ *Free, donations accepted* ☉ *Late May–early Sept., Mon.–Sat. 10–5, Sun. noon–5.*

On the mainland side, the **Massachusetts Maritime Academy,** founded in 1891, is the oldest such academy in the country. Future members of the Merchant Marines receive their training at its 55-acre campus in Buzzards Bay. The library has nautical paintings and scale models of ships from the 18th century to the present and is open to the public at no charge (hours are extensive but vary widely depending on whether school is in session; call ahead). For a 30- to 60-minute tour of the academy (weekdays only; times vary), call 48 hours in advance. The tours are designed for prospective students and their families but are open to all. ✉ *Taylor's Point, Buzzards Bay* ☎ *508/830–5000* ⊕ *www.mma.mass.edu.*

A monument to the birth of commerce in the New World, the **Aptucxet Trading Post Museum** was erected on the foundation of the original post archaeologically excavated in the 1920s. Here, in 1627, Plimoth Plantation leaders established a way station between the Native American encampment at Great Herring Pond 3 mi to the northeast, Dutch colonists in New Amsterdam (New York) to the south, and English colonists on Cape Cod Bay. Before the canal was built, the Manomet River connected Herring Pond with Buzzards Bay (no, scavengers don't frequent it—it was misnamed for the migrating osprey that do), and a short portage connected the pond to Scusset River, which met Cape Cod Bay. The Native Americans traded furs; the Dutch traded linen cloth, metal tools, glass beads, sugar, and other staples; and the Pilgrims traded wool cloth, clay beads, sassafras, and tobacco (which they imported from Virginia). Wampum (beads made from polished shells) was the medium of exchange.

Inside the post, 17th-century cooking utensils hang from the original brick hearth; beaver and otter skins, furniture, and other artifacts such as arrowheads, tools, and tomahawks are displayed throughout. Also on the grounds are a gift shop in a Dutch-style windmill, a saltworks, herb and wildflower gardens, a picnic area overlooking the canal, and a small Victorian railroad station built for the sole use of President Grover Cleve-

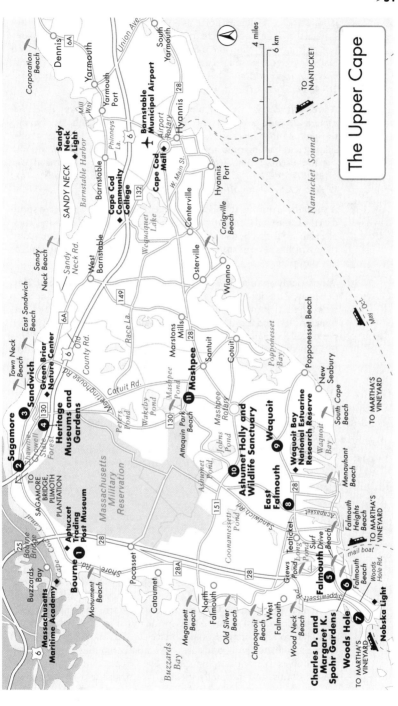

The Upper Cape

land, who had a summer home in Bourne. To get here, cross the Bourne Bridge; then take the first right from the Bourne Bridge rotary onto Trowbridge Road and follow the signs. Note that the site is also open on holiday Mondays in season. ⊠ *24 Aptucxet Rd.* ☎ *508/759–9487* ⊕ *www. bournehistoricalsoc.org* ⌦ *$4* ⊗ *May, June, and Sept.–mid-Oct., Tues.–Sat. 10–4, Sun. 2–5; July and Aug., Mon.–Sat. 10–4, Sun. 2–5.*

☾ A break for energetic children pent up in a car for too many miles, **Adventure Isle** has a go-kart track, bumper-boat lagoon, 18 holes of miniature golf, 25-foot Super Slide, batting cages, kiddie rides, laser tag, a roller skating and blading rink, and an arcade with snack bar. Check the Web site for discount coupons. ⊠ *Rte. 28, 2 mi south of Bourne Bridge* ☎ *508/759–2636 or 800/535–2787* ⊕ *www.adventureisle.com* ⊗ *Apr.–Oct., call for off-season hrs; July–early Sept., daily 10 AM–11 PM.*

❷ A short drive northeast of Bourne proper, the village of **Sagamore** straddles the Cape Cod Canal and is perhaps best known for the bridge, completed in 1935, that bears its name. Primarily a small suburban community, the town has several stores for those interested in bargain hunting or gift shopping.

Watch richly colored lead crystal being hand-blown at **Pairpoint Glass Company,** America's oldest glass factory (founded in 1837). The shop sells candlesticks, vases, stemware, sun catchers, cup plates, lamps, perfume bottles, and reproductions of original Boston and Sandwich glass pieces. ⊠ *851 Sandwich Rd. (Rte. 6A)* ☎ *508/888–2344 or 800/899–0953* ⊕ *www.pairpoint.com* ⌦ *Free* ⊗ *Showroom weekdays 9–6, Sat. 10–6, Sun. 11–6. Demonstrations May–Dec., weekdays 9–4; Jan.–Apr., call before visiting; demonstration hrs are limited.*

Where to Stay & Eat

BOURNE   ✗ **Chart Room.** Located harborside at the marina in a former cargo
$–$$ barge, this traditional watering hole has been serving up seafood classics since 1966. Clam chowder, lobster rolls, broiled scrod, seafood Newburg, baked stuffed shrimp—they're all here, as are sirloin steak, broiled lamb chops, and even grilled cheese-and-tomato sandwiches. ⊠ *1 Shipyard La., at Kingman Yacht Center, Cataumet* ☎ *508/563–5350* ⊟ *AE, DC, MC, V* ⊗ *Closed mid-Oct.–late May and weekdays late May–late June and early Sept.–mid-Oct.*

$ ✗ **Stir Crazy.** Fresh ingredients with lively Cambodian, Thai, and Viet-
FodorsChoice   namese flavors dominate every dish that graces the menu here (owner
★   Bopha Samms hails from Cambodia). Try the *nhem shross* (an appetizer of vegetables and shrimp) and the refreshing *bar bong* (chilled noodles topped with pork, egg rolls, and coconut-peanut sauce). ⊠ *570 MacArthur Blvd. (Rte. 28 S), Pocasset* ☎ *508/564–6464* ⌲ *Reservations not accepted* ⊟ *MC, V* ⊗ *Closed Mon. No lunch Sat.–Thurs.*

$ ▦ **Wood Duck Inn.** Behind this cozy B&B, a 17-acre working cranberry bog and acres of conservation land spread out as far as you can see. The small but comfy Cottage Room has lace curtains and a brass bed with a floral comforter, and both suites have a bedroom plus a sitting room that doubles as extra sleeping space. The Garden Suite is done in romantic florals, and the family-friendly Treetops Suite resembles a contemporary apartment in forest green and white; it has a tiny but fully equipped kitchen and sweeping views. The innkeepers deliver breakfast to your door. ✉ *1050 County Rd., Cataumet 02534* ☎☎ *508/564–6404* ⊕ *www.woodduckinnbb.com* ↘ *1 room, 2 suites* ⚫ *Some kitchens, microwaves, refrigerator, cable TV, in-room VCRs; no a/c in some rooms, no smoking* ⊟ *No credit cards* ⟊ *CP.*

SAGAMORE   ✕ **Sagamore Inn.** Old Cape Cod traditions with an Italian twist can be
$–$$ found at this local favorite, owned by the Pagliarani family since 1963. Pressed-tin walls and ceilings, fans, old wooden booths and tables, lace curtains, and white linen add up to a dining room so casual you almost overlook its elegance. The seafood platter is a knockout, and the chicken potpie and prime rib are substantial. Luncheon specials attract regulars from all over town, and the service is friendly. A cozy, handsome old bar is under the same roof. ✉ *1131 Rte. 6A* ☎ *508/888–9707* ⚫ *Reservations not accepted* ⊟ *AE, MC, V* ⊘ *Closed Tues.*

$ ⚠ **Scusset Beach State Reservation.** Encompassing 300 acres adjacent to the Cape Cod Canal (there's a fishing pier for anglers), the park has a beach on Cape Cod Bay and 98 RV sites plus 5 tent sites, some wooded. There are cold showers on the beach and hot showers in the campground. ⚫ *Beach, full hookups* ↘ *103 sites* ✉ *140 Scusset Beach Rd., off Rte. 3 at Sagamore Bridge rotary* ☎ *877/422–6762 campsite reservations, 508/888–0859 general information* ⊕ *www.reserveamerica.com* 🎫 *Tent sites $15; $20* ⊟ *MC, V.*

Nightlife & the Arts

The **Army Corps of Engineers** (☎ 508/759–4431), which maintains the Cape Cod Canal via a field office in Buzzards Bay, offers free daily programs in summer, including evening campfire programs on canal-related topics (with marshmallow roasting). Call for program details and locations.

In Bourne, Thursday evening **town-band concerts** (✉ Main St. ☎ 508/759–6000) in July and August start at 7 in Buzzards Bay Park.

Sports & the Outdoors

The **Army Corps of Engineers** (☎ 508/759–4431) sponsors guided walks, bike trips, and hikes, including canal and area natural-history walks.

BASEBALL   The **Bourne Braves** of the collegiate Cape Cod Baseball League play home games at **Coady School** (✉ Trowbridge Rd. ☎ 508/432–6909 ⊕ www.bournebraves.org) from mid-June to mid-August.

BEACHES   **Monument Beach,** off Shore Road, is a small but pretty crescent of sand adjacent to the town dock, facing Buzzards Bay just south of Bourne Bridge. The beach has a snack bar, restrooms, and a parking lot, which is restricted in season to those with resident permits. From Shore Road, turn right onto Emmons Road just past the old train depot.

Sagamore's **Scusset Beach State Reservation** is a pleasant place for a swim, walk, or bike ride near the mainland side of the Sagamore Bridge. The beach sweeps along Cape Cod Bay, and its pier and canal breakwater are popular for fishing and viewing boat traffic; other activities include hiking, picnicking, and camping. There's a parking fee from mid-April to mid-October. ✉ *140 Scusset Beach Rd., off Rte. 3 at Sagamore Bridge rotary* ☎ *508/888–0859* ⊕ *www.mass.gov/dcr* ✆ *Mid-Apr.–mid-Oct., parking $7* ☉ *Daily 8–8.*

BICYCLING   An easy, straight trail stretches on either side of the **Cape Cod Canal**, 6½ mi on the south side, 7 mi on the north, with views of the bridges and ship traffic on the canal. Contact the **Army Corps of Engineers** (☎ 508/759–4431) for information about canal trail access and parking. Directly across the street from the canal bike path on the mainland (near the Massachusetts Maritime Academy), **P&M Cycles** (✉ 29 Main St., Buzzards Bay ☎ 508/759–2830) rents mountain- and hybrid bikes at reasonable rates.

FISHING   The Cape Cod Canal is a great place to fish—from the service road on either side—for the big blues and striped bass making their way through the passage seasonally (April–November).

HIKING &   Run by the Army Corps of Engineers, the **Herring Run Visitor Center** (✉ U.S.
WALKING   6, Bournedale ☎ 508/759–4431, 508/759–5991 tides, weather, and special events), on a bank of the canal with an excellent view, has picnic tables (close to noisy U.S. 6), access to the canal bike path, a herring run through which the fish travel on their spawning run in May, and short self-guided walking trails through woodland. The visitor center is on the mainland side of the canal, between the bridges.

On the Cape side of the canal, the Army Corps of Engineers manages the **Tidal Flats Recreation Area** (✉ Shore Rd. ☎ 508/759–4431), a small but peaceful canal-side park near the Cape railroad bridge. It's a pleasant site for picnicking or fishing, with a great view of the canal's ship traffic. There's also access to the canal bike path. In the late afternoon, between 5 and 7, you can watch the bridge lower to allow a service train to cross the canal; these times are approximate and can vary widely because of traffic and bridge work. To reach the recreation area, cross the Bourne Bridge and follow Trowbridge Road to Shore Road.

ICE-SKATING   **John Gallo Ice Arena** (✉ 231 Sandwich Rd. ☎ 508/759–8904) is the place to go for ice-skating year-round (except May). Lessons are offered and skate rental is available; admission is $2.

Shopping

Cape Cod Factory Outlet Mall (✉ Factory Outlet Rd., Exit 1 off Rte. 6 ☎ 508/888–8417 ⊕ www.capecodoutletmall.com) has more than 20 outlet stores, including Corningware-Corelle-Revere, Carter's, Van Heusen, Izod, Bass, and Reebok.

Christmas Tree Shops (✉ Cranberry Hwy. [Rte. 6A], Exit 1 off Rte. 6 ☎ 508/888–7010 ⊕ www.christmastreeshops.com) sell dishware and a wide variety of other household goods at bargain prices. There are other locations in Falmouth, Hyannis, Yarmouthport, West Yarmouth, West Dennis, and Orleans.

CLOSE UP

Time to Fly

SO YOU'RE heading south on Route 3 toward the Cape, about 8 mi from the Sagamore Bridge. You're still speeding along, and you're beginning to feel relaxed, even a little smug. And why not? After all, you've carefully planned your schedule, cleverly outsmarting tens of thousands of other vacationers with a similar destination. But then, a sickening sense of dread poisons your mood as you catch a glimpse of a red sea of brake lights blurred by a haze of engine exhaust. Suddenly, you're not going anywhere.

The Sagamore Bridge, completed in 1935, was built to accommodate approximately 35,000 motorists heading to Cape Cod each day during peak season. Before crossing the bridge, travelers would safely navigate a rotary, branching off perhaps to fill their gas tanks or have lunch. At least that was the plan. Today the bridge handles nearly 90,000 cars, minivans, and SUVs, all overflowing with bicycles, kayaks, baggage, and impatience. The quaint rotary, with its pretty plantings and convenient pit stops, has become many a driver's personal hell.

The elimination of this much-despised rotary sits at the center of the massive Sagamore "flyover." Long awaited, hotly debated, and slated for completion just in time for the 2007 summer season, the project will be the state's most ambitious transportation undertaking since Boston's perpetual Big Dig. Costing an estimated $58 million, the work will directly connect Route 3 to the Sagamore Bridge, diverting local traffic through a series of underpasses. The goal is to benefit those who want an unhindered passage over the bridge as well as local residents who simply want to drive across town without getting mired in the rotary. Estimates predict savings of anywhere from 18 to 33 minutes, but you'll likely still experience slowdowns, outright traffic jams, and some level of aggravation. So you won't always be flying . . . but hopefully you'll be moving faster than before.

Sandwich

★ ❸ *3 mi east of Sagamore Bridge, 11 mi west of Barnstable.*

A well-preserved New England village, Sandwich wears its history proudly, despite having become increasingly suburban in character over the past few decades, its population soaring to more than 30,000. The oldest town on Cape Cod, Sandwich was established in 1637 by some of the Plymouth Pilgrims and incorporated on March 6, 1638. Driving through town past the white-column town hall, the gristmill on Shawme Pond, the First Church of Christ with its spindlelike spire, and the 18th- and 19th-century homes that line the streets is like driving back in time—you may feel as if you should be holding a horse's reins rather than the steering wheel of a car. When you reach Main Street, park the car and get out for a stroll. Look at old houses on Main

Street, stop at a museum or two, and work your way to the delightful Shawme Pond. Unlike other Cape towns, whose deepwater ports opened the doors to prosperity in the whaling days, Sandwich was an industrial town for much of the 19th century. The main industry was the production of vividly colored glass, called Sandwich glass, which is now sought by collectors. The Boston and Sandwich Glass Company's factory here produced the glass from 1825 until 1888, when competition with glassmakers in the Midwest—and finally a union strike—closed it. While you walk, look for etched Sandwich glass from the old factory on front doors. There probably aren't two identical glass panels in town.

The **Sandwich Glass Museum,** with its 9,000 square feet of exhibits, has information about the history of the company, including a diorama showing how the factory looked in its heyday, an "ingredient room" showcasing a wide spectrum of glass colors along with the minerals added to the sand to obtain them, and an outstanding collection of blown and pressed glass in many shapes and shimmering hues. Large glass lamps, vases, and pitchers are impressive, as are the hundreds of candlesticks and small saucers on display. Glassmaking demonstrations are held in summer. A few galleries contain relics of the town's early history (the museum is also the Sandwich Historical Society). The extensive, ornate gift shop sells some handsome reproductions, including some made by local and national artisans. The museum also sponsors several walking tours of the town in July and August. ⊠ *129 Main St., Sandwich Center* ☎ *508/888-0251* ⊕ *www. sandwichglassmuseum.org* ⊠ *$4.75* ⊘ *Apr.–Dec., daily 9:30–5; Feb. and Mar., Wed.–Sun. 9:30–4.*

A lovely place for a stroll or a picnic is the park around **Shawme Pond** (⊠ Water and Grove Sts., Sandwich Center), a favorite fishing site for children. The ducks and swans love to be fed, though posted signs warn you not to indulge them. Across the way—a perfect backdrop for this setting—stands the spired, white 1848 First Church of Christ, inspired by a design by British architect Christopher Wren.

Where Shawme Pond drains over its dam, a little wooden bridge leads over a watercourse to the waterwheel-powered **Dexter Gristmill,** built in 1654. In season the miller demonstrates the grinding process, talks about the mill's operation, and sells its ground corn. ⊠ *Water and Grove Sts., Sandwich Center* ☎ *508/888-4910, Sandwich Town Hall* ⊠ *$3; combination ticket with Hoxie House $4* ⊘ *Late May and early Sept.–late Sept., Sat. 10–4:45; June–early Sept., Mon.–Sat. 10–4:45.*

NEED A
BREAK?

The delightful **Dunbar Tea Shop** (⊠ 1 Water St. [Rte. 130], Sandwich Center ☎ 508/833-2485) is in a former billiards room–carriage house, now converted into a country cottage with paneled walls and assorted antiques and kitschy doodads. Lunch (from a smoked-fish platter with salad to quiche or a salmon tart), English cream tea, and tasty sweets are served from 11 to 5 daily, July through October (until 4:30 the rest of the year). A gift shop sells British tea, specialty foods, and home-decorating items.

The **Thornton W. Burgess Museum** is dedicated to the Sandwich native whose
tales of Peter Cottontail, Reddy Fox, and a host of other creatures of
the Old Briar Patch have been part of children's bedtimes for decades.
Thornton Burgess (1874–1965), an avid conservationist, made his characters behave true to their species to educate children as he entertained
them. Storytelling sessions, often including the live animal that the
Burgess story is about, take place regularly in July and August. In the
Discovery Room, kids can use their imaginations in the prop-filled
classroom. On display are some of Burgess's 170 books (although children are welcome here, the exhibits are of the don't-touch variety). The
small gift shop carries puppets, Burgess books, and Pairpoint Crystal
cup plates decorated with Burgess characters. ⊠ *4 Water St. (Rte. 130),
Sandwich Center* ☎ *508/888–4668* ⊕ *www.thorntonburgess.org* ✉ *Donations accepted* ☉ *May–Oct., Mon.–Sat. 10–4, Sun. 1–4.*

Overlooking Shawme Pond is the **Hoxie House,** a remarkable old saltbox virtually unaltered since it was built in 1675. Even though people
lived in it until the 1950s, the house was never modernized with electricity or plumbing. Furnishings reflect daily life in the colonial period,
with some pieces on loan from the Museum of Fine Arts in Boston. Highlights are diamond-shaped lead-glass windows and a collection of antique textile machines. ⊠ *18 Water St. (Rte. 130), Sandwich Center*
☎ *508/888–1173* ✉ *$3; combination ticket with Dexter Gristmill $4*
☉ *Late May–mid-June, Sat. 10–5, Sun. 1–5; mid-June–mid-Oct.,
Mon.–Sat. 10–5, Sun. 1–5.*

The **Old Town Cemetery** (⊠ Grove St., Sandwich Center), on the opposite side of Shawme Pond from Hoxie House, is a classic, undulating
New England graveyard. You can stop in for a peaceful moment and
trace the genealogy of old Sandwich. On Thursday in July and August,
you can hear tales during narrated walking tours about the cemetery's
more illustrious inhabitants; call the Sandwich Glass Museum for additional information.

❹ Heritage Museums and Gardens, 100 beautifully landscaped acres overlooking the upper end of Shawme Pond, includes gardens and a café as
well as an impressive complex of museum buildings with specialty collections ranging from cars to toys. In 1967 pharmaceuticals magnate
Josiah K. Lilly III purchased the estate and turned it into a nonprofit
museum. A highlight is the Shaker Round Barn, which showcases classic and historic cars—including a 1930 yellow-and-green Duesenberg
built for Gary Cooper, a 1919 Pierce-Arrow, a 1915 Milburn Light Electric, and a 1911 Stanley Steamer—as well as art exhibitions. The American History museum houses the Cape Cod Baseball League Hall of Fame
as well as antique firearms, a collection of 2,000 hand-painted miniature soldiers, military uniforms, and Native American arts. The art museum has an extensive Currier & Ives collection, Americana (including
a mechanical-bank collection), antique toys such as a 1920 Hubley
Royal Circus, and a working 1912 Coney Island–style carousel that both
adults and little ones can ride as often as they like. A shuttle bus—equipped
with a wheelchair lift and space to stow baby strollers—transports visitors every few minutes from the car museum to other exhibit sites.

Paths crisscross the grounds, which include gardens planted with daylilies, hostas, heather, herbs, and fruit trees. Rhododendron enthusiasts will recognize the name of onetime estate owner and hybridizer Charles O. Dexter; the rhododendrons are in full glory from mid-May through mid-June. Daylilies reach their peak from mid-July through early August. Families visiting with youngsters should ask at the ticket office for Family Funpacks with children's activities, or the Clue tours, scavenger-hunt games for exploring the grounds. In summer, concerts are held in the gardens, often on Wednesday or Saturday evening or Sunday afternoon. The center of the complex is about ¾ mi on foot from the in-town end of Shawme Pond. ⊠ *67 Grove St.* ☎ *508/888–3300* ⊕ *www. heritagemuseumsandgardens.org* ⊡ *$12* ☉ *Apr.–Nov., daily 10–5; Nov.–Mar., call for very limited hrs.*

At the **Cape Cod Canal Visitor Center,** run by the Army Corps of Engineers, exhibits and video presentations describe the canal's history, area wildflowers, and local "critters." Among the special ranger-led programs are beach and dune walks, as well as evening star watches. The visitor center is opposite the Coast Guard Station, near Joe's Fish Market. ⊠ *Ed Moffitt Dr.* ☎ *508/833–9678* ⊡ *Free* ☉ *Mid-May–mid-Oct., call for hrs.*

For a view of the bay, you can walk to Town Neck Beach on the **Sandwich Boardwalk,** built over a salt marsh, creek, and low dunes. In 1991 Hurricane Bob and an October nor'easter destroyed the previous boardwalk. Individuals and businesses donated planks to rebuild it, which volunteers then installed. The donors' names, jokes (GET OFF OUR BOARD), thoughts (SIMPLIFY/THOREAU), and memorials to lovers, grandparents, and boats are inscribed on the planks. The long sweep of Cape Cod Bay stretches out around the beach at the end of the walk, where a platform provides fine views, especially at sunset. Stone jetties, dunes, waving grasses, and the entrance to the canal are in the foreground, and you can look out toward Sandy Neck, Wellfleet, and Provincetown or toward the white cliffs beyond Sagamore. The sandy strip on this mostly rocky beach is near the rugosa rose–patch dunes; the flowers have a delicious fragrance, and it's a good place for birding. The creeks running through the salt marsh make for great canoeing. From the town center it's about a mile to the boardwalk; cross Route 6A on Jarves Street and at its end turn left, then right, and continue to the boardwalk parking lot.

☾ At the **Sandwich Fish Hatchery,** the oldest fish hatchery in the country, you can see more than 200,000 brook, brown, and rainbow trout at various stages of development; they are raised to stock the state's ponds. The mesh over the raceways keeps kingfishers and herons from snagging a free lunch. You can buy feed for 25¢ and watch the fish jump for it. ⊠ *164 Rte. 6A* ☎ *508/888–0008* ⊡ *Free* ☉ *Daily 9–3.*

OFF THE BEATEN PATH

GREEN BRIAR NATURE CENTER AND JAM KITCHEN – Is it the soothing pondside location or its simple earthiness—who's to say? Whatever the reason, this center, owned and operated by the Thornton Burgess Society, is a solid symbol of the old Cape. You pass a wildflower garden on your way in, and the Smiling Pool sparkles out back. Birds flit about the grounds, and great smells waft from vintage stoves in the Jam Kitchen, where you can watch as jams and pickles are made according to Ida Putnam's recipes, used here since 1903 (sun-cooked fruit preserves are especially superb). Come weekdays mid-April through mid-December to see jam being made in the Jam Kitchen; you can even take a jam-making class some evenings or Saturdays. The nature center has classes for adults and children, as well as walks, lectures, and a May herb festival, where herbs, wildflowers, and perennials are for sale. The Briar Patch Conservation Area behind the building has nature trails—take a walk and visit the real live animals that inspired Peter Cottontail, Grandfather Frog, and other beloved Thornton Burgess characters. ⊠ *6 Discovery Hill Rd., off Rte. 6A, East Sandwich* ☎ *508/888–6870* ⊕ *www.thorntonburgess.org* ▧ *$2 suggested donation* ☉ *Apr.–Dec., Mon.–Sat. 10–4, Sun. 1–4; Jan.–Mar., Tues.–Sat. 10–4.*

Where to Stay & Eat

★ **$–$$$**   ✕ **Aqua Grille.** At this smart-casual and reasonably priced bistro by the marina, offerings range from Cape basics (clam chowder, fried seafood, boiled lobsters) to more creative contemporary fare, such as nut-crusted halibut with an orange beurre blanc. The excellent lobster salad comprises a hearty serving of greens, tomatoes, avocados, baby green beans, and big, meaty lobster chunks. Sandwiches (salmon burgers, turkey wraps) are also available. ⊠ *14 Gallo Rd.* ☎ *508/888–8889* ⊕ *www.aquagrille.com* ▤ *AE, DC, MC, V* ☉ *Closed late Oct.–Mar.*

$–$$ ✕ **Bee-Hive Tavern.** This informal and friendly colonial-style tavern hasn't been here since Revolutionary times (it opened in the early '90s), but the cozy dark-wood booths and wide-board floors look the part. The kitchen turns out solid American fare, such as burgers and sandwiches, fried seafood, Yankee pot roast, ribs, and steaks. Dinner-size salads are also available. ⊠ *406 Rte. 6A, East Sandwich* ☎ *508/833–1184* ▤ *MC, V.*

$–$$ ✕ **Sushi by Night.** Located rather oddly in what is a standard American deli during the day, Sushi by Night morphs into a full-service Japanese and sushi restaurant in the evenings, serving delicious food and a nice selection of sakes and imported beers. Try the alligator roll (with tempura shrimp, tobiko, avocado, and eel), the yellowtail carpaccio with ponzu sauce, or the soft-shell crab appetizer. A number of sushi, tempura, and noodle combination platters and bowls are also offered. This is some of the best sushi on the Cape. ⊠ *Merchant's Square Shopping Center, 4 Merchant's Rd.* ☎ *508/833–5015* ▤ *AE, MC, V* ☉ *No lunch.*

¢–$ ✕ **Marshland Restaurant and Bakery.** Sandwich's version of down-home is this homey coffee shop tucked into a parking lot. For breakfast try an Italian omelet, a rich mix of Italian sausage, fresh vegetables, and cheese. The lunch specials—a grilled chicken club sandwich, the Cobb salad, a turkey Reuben, a daily quiche, and the like—are the best choices midday, and for dinner the prime rib does not disappoint. ⊠ *109 Rte. 6A* ☎ *508/888–9824* ▤ *No credit cards* ☉ *No dinner Mon.*

¢–$ ✕ **Seafood Sam's.** Fried seafood reigns supreme at Sam's, across from the Coast Guard station and a stone's throw from the Cape Cod Canal. Order from the counter, take a number, and sit in an airy dining room where the munch of fried clams accompanies the sound of lobsters cracking open. Sam's also has branches in Harwichport, Falmouth, and

South Yarmouth. ⊠ *6 Coast Guard Rd.* ☎ *508/888–4629* ⊕ *www. seafoodsams.com* ⊟ *D, MC, V* ⊘ *Closed early Nov.–early Mar.*

$$–$$$$
Fodor'sChoice
★

✕🖭 **Belfry Inne & Bistro.** This delightful one-of-a-kind inn comprises a 1902 former church, an ornate wood-frame Victorian, and an 1830 Federal-style house clustered on a main campus, plus a fourth building—a 1638 former meetinghouse, the oldest standing structure in Sandwich—just a short walk down the road. Room themes in each building nod to their respective histories—the Drew House's charmingly appointed rooms, for example, are named after former inhabitants. The luxurious rooms in the Abbey, named for the six days of creation, have whirlpool tubs and gas fireplaces, and are set along a corridor overlooking the restaurant below. (If it's available, splurge on the Tuesday room—the incredible stained glass "compass" window will take your breath away.) The meetinghouse contains some of the most over-the-top, sumptuous accommodations on the Cape. The Bistro ($$–$$$$) serves dazzling, globally inspired dishes such as black grouper roasted with tamarind-yogurt sauce in a striking setting—look up at the church's original arches and stained glass as you dine. Next door in the Victorian building, the Painted Lady restaurant ($–$$) serves innovative renditions of home-style American favorites, including a delicious baked mac-and-cheese. ⊠ *8 Jarves St., 02563* ☎ *508/888–8550 or 800/844–4542* 🖷 *508/ 888–3922* ⊕ *www.belfryinn.com* 🛏 *26 rooms* ♿ *2 restaurants, some in-room hot tubs, cable TV, massage, bar; no kids under 10, no smoking* ⊟ *AE, D, DC, MC, V* ❢◎❢ *BP.*

$$–$$$

✕🖭 **Dan'l Webster Inn and Spa.** Built on the site of a 17th-century inn, the Dan'l Webster is a contemporary hotel within the heart of Sandwich's historic downtown. Rooms are decked out in high-end colonial-inspired cherrywood and mahogany furnishings in traditional colors. You might find a Sheraton reproduction armoire in one room, a pencil-post four-poster bed in another; some units have fireplaces, and most have balconies overlooking the nicely manicured gardens. The restaurant ($$–$$$$) is a longtime favorite. Upscale, modern Continental dishes, such as roast rack of lamb stuffed with spinach and olives and served with a cabernet sauce, take their places beside veal Oscar, roast prime rib, and other classics. A casual tavern serves pizzas, burgers, and salads. The spa offers a full slate of massage, facial, and beauty treatments. ⊠ *149 Main St., 02563* ☎ *508/888–3622 or 800/444–3566* 🖷 *508/888– 5156* ⊕ *www.danlwebsterinn.com* 🛏 *45 rooms, 9 suites* ♿ *2 restaurants, room service, some in-room hot tubs, cable TV, Wi-Fi, pool, spa, meeting rooms* ⊟ *AE, D, DC, MC, V.*

★ $–$$

🖭 **Inn at Sandwich Center.** Across from the Sandwich Glass Museum, this 18th-century house with fine colonial and Victorian furnishings is listed on the National Register of Historic Places. In addition to such decorative flourishes as ornate nonworking fireplaces and Oriental rugs, rooms contain high-thread-count linens, robes, and Gilchrist & Soames bath amenities. A gazebo on a nearby hill houses a secluded spa where you can arrange to have a professional massage. A hearty breakfast is served in the keeping room, which contains a fireplace and an antique table (older than the inn) that seats 10. Gracious hosts Jan and Charlie Preus know a lot about the region and have created a warm and inviting inn

2

that's appealing whether you seek quiet seclusion or the opportunity to mingle with fellow guests. ⊠ *118 Tupper Rd., 02563* ☎ *508/888–6958 or 800/249–6949* 🖷 *508/888–2746* ⊕ *www.innatsandwich.com* ⤴ *5 rooms* ⚲ *Wi-Fi; no room phones, no room TVs, no kids under 10, no smoking* ▤ *MC, V* ⊘ *Closed Jan.–Mar.* ⫶⊙⫶ *BP.*

$–$$ 🏨 **Sandwich Lodge & Resort.** This glorified motel on 10 rolling acres has several different types of accommodations. Suites and efficiencies have kitchens with refrigerators and two-burner stoves or microwave ovens; some even have two-person whirlpool tubs. The modern indoor pool is a highlight, conveniently accessible from many of the rooms. The homey on-site restaurant serves lunch and dinner (ample portions, great prices). ⊠ *54 Rte. 6A Box 1038, 02563* ☎ *508/888–2275 or 800/282–5353* 🖷 *508/888–8102* ⊕ *www.sandwichlodge.com* ⤴ *24 rooms, 44 suites, 4 efficiencies* ⚲ *Some in-room hot tubs, some kitchens, microwaves, refrigerators, cable TV, Wi-Fi, 2 pools (1 indoor), hot tub, Ping-Pong, shuffleboard, bar, laundry facilities, some pets allowed (fee)* ▤ *AE, D, MC, V* ⫶⊙⫶ *CP.*

¢–$ 🏨 **Earl of Sandwich Motor Manor.** Single-story Tudor-style buildings form a "U" around a duck pond and wooded lawn set with lawn chairs. Rooms, attractively, if simply, furnished, are nicely sized with large windows and dark pine headboards and doors. Many rooms have canopy beds. A Continental plan is offered from late May to October. ⊠ *378 Rte. 6A, East Sandwich 02537* ☎ *508/888–1415 or 800/442–3275* 🖷 *508/833–1039* ⊕ *www.earlofsandwich.com* ⤴ *24 rooms* ⚲ *Refrigerators, cable TV, pool, some pets allowed; no smoking* ▤ *AE, D, DC, MC, V.*

¢ ⛰ **Shawme-Crowell State Forest.** Less than a mile from the Cape Cod Canal, this 742-acre state forest is a good base for local biking and hiking, and campers get free day use of Scusset Beach. Open-air campfires are allowed at the wooded tent and RV (no hookups) campsites. Heated bathroom and shower facilities are a blessing on chilly mornings. The campground is generally open year-round, but if you're planning a winter trip, call to confirm before visiting. ⤴ *285 sites* ⊠ *Rte. 130* ☎ *508/888–0351, 877/422–6762 reservations* ⊕ *www.reserveamerica.com* ▥ *Basic sites $12* ▤ *MC, V.*

Nightlife & the Arts

THE ARTS **Heritage Museums and Gardens** (⊠ 67 Grove St. ☎ 508/888–3300) sponsors jazz and other concerts in its gardens from June to mid-September; bring chairs or blankets. Most concerts are free with admission to the complex. **Town-band concerts** (⊠ Bandstand, Henry T. Wing Elementary School, Rte. 130 and Beale Ave., Sandwich Center ☎ 508/888–5144) are held Thursday evening from July through late August starting at 7:30.

NIGHTLIFE **Bobby Byrne's Pub** (⊠ 65 Rte. 6A ☎ 508/888–6088), with other locations in Hyannis and Mashpee, is a comfortable pub, with a jukebox, and good light and full menus.

British Beer Company (⊠ 46 Rte. 6A ☎ 508/833–9590 ⊕ www.britishbeer. com), with other locations in Cedarville, Falmouth, and Plymouth, has a traditional British "public house" atmosphere with a great menu that includes fish, ribs, and pizza.

Sports & the Outdoors

BEACHES   **East Sandwich Beach,** on North Shore Road, lies behind the grass-covered dunes beyond a row of gray-shingle beach cottages. It's a long stretch of sand, but nearby parking is very limited (and restricted to residents between 8 AM and 4 PM in season). From Route 6A follow Ploughed Neck Road to North Shore Road.

Town Neck Beach, off Town Neck Road, is a long, dune-backed bay beach with a mix of sand and pebbles. You need a resident parking sticker to leave your car in the large parking area between 8 AM and 4 PM in season. There are restrooms and a snack bar.

GOLF   **Sandwich Hollows Golf Club** (⊠ 1 Round Hill Rd., East Sandwich ☎ 508/888–3384 ⊕ www.sandwichhollows.com) has an 18-hole, par-71 course that's open to the public.

Shopping

★ The **Brown Jug** (⊠ 155 Main St., Sandwich ☎ 508/888–4669) is a tantalizing gourmet food shop in a cozy brown-shingle house in the center of Sandwich—the perfect place to pick up delicious picnic supplies. You'll find cheeses, chocolate, and all sorts of hard-to-find imported foods; you can also order tasty sandwiches to go.

Fodor'sChoice   The **Giving Tree** (⊠ 550 Rte. 6A, East Sandwich ☎ 508/888–5446 or ★   888/246–3551 ⊕ www.givingtreegallery.com), an art gallery and sculpture garden, sells contemporary crafts, jewelry, ceramics, and prints. It has walking paths through a peaceful bamboo grove, along the marsh, and over a narrow wooden suspension bridge. The shop is open Memorial Day through Christmas.

Joe's Lobster Mart (⊠ Cape Cod Canal ☎ 508/888–2971), opposite Seafood Sam's and the Coast Guard station, sells fresh-from-the-tank lobsters. Call ahead, and they'll boil your crustaceans to order—a great idea for an easy dinner at your cottage or hotel or for a picnic overlooking the canal. Joe's also sells many varieties of fresh fish.

Sandwich Auction House (⊠ 15 Tupper Rd. ☎ 508/888–1926 ⊕ www.sandwichauction.com), which auctions antiques, general merchandise, and Oriental rugs, is a great place to spend part of a Wednesday night (Saturday in the off-season); come after 2 PM to preview the items for sale. This local institution has weekly sales; in addition, specialty sales every six to eight weeks feature upscale antiques received during that period. Sales are also held for antique and modern rugs.

Titcomb's Bookshop (⊠ 432 Rte. 6A, East Sandwich ☎ 508/888–2331 ⊕ www.titcombsbookshop.com) stocks used, rare, and new books, including a large collection of Cape and nautical titles and Americana, as well as an extensive selection of children's books.

EN
ROUTE   **Route 6A** heads east from Sandwich, passing through the oldest settlements on the Cape. Part of the Old King's Highway historic district, the route is protected from development. Classic inns and enticing antiques shops alternate with traditional gray-shingle homes on this tree-lined road, and the woods periodically give way to broad vistas across the

marshes. In autumn the foliage along the way is bright; maples with their feet wet in ponds and marshes put on a good display. Along Route 6A just east of Sandwich Center, you can stop to watch cranberries being harvested in flooded bogs. If you're heading down-Cape and you're not in a hurry, this is a lovely route to take. And if you do wish to take the faster but less-interesting U.S. 6 as your primary route through the region, it's easy to hop off here and there and travel certain stretches of parallel Route 6A.

Falmouth

❺ *2 mi south of West Falmouth, 15 mi south of Bourne Bridge, 4 mi north of Woods Hole.*

Falmouth, the Cape's second-largest town, was settled in 1660 by Congregationalists from Barnstable who had been ostracized by their church and deprived of voting privileges and other civil rights for sympathizing with the Quakers (then the victims of severe repression). The town was incorporated in 1686 and named for Falmouth, England. The Falmouth area, sprawling over 44 square mi, includes eight villages: Falmouth, North Falmouth, West Falmouth, Hatchville, Teaticket, East Falmouth, Waquoit, and Woods Hole.

Much of Falmouth today is suburban, with a mix of old and new developments and a large year-round population. Many residents commute to other towns on the Cape, to southeastern Massachusetts, and

> **WORD OF MOUTH**
>
> "Try to bike the Shining Sea Bike Trail or drive along Surf Drive from Woods Hole to Falmouth."   –Gene

even to Boston. The town has a quaint village center, with a typically old New England village green and a shop-lined Main Street. South of town center, Falmouth faces Nantucket Sound and has several often-crowded beaches popular with families. To the east, the Falmouth Heights neighborhood mixes inns, B&Bs, and private homes, nestled close together on residential streets leading to the sea. Bustling Grand Avenue, the main drag in Falmouth Heights, hugs the shore and the beach. Parks and ponds dot the town; one of the nicest, Grews Pond in Goodwill Park, is north of the town center—it's a lovely site for a picnic on a summer afternoon.

Today attractive old homes, some built by sea captains, flank the **Village Green,** which is listed on the National Register of Historic Places. It served as a militia training field in the 18th century and a grazing ground for horses in the early 19th century. Also on the green is the 1856 **Congregational Church,** built on the timbers of its 1796 predecessor, with a bell made by Paul Revere. The bell's cheery inscription reads: THE LIVING TO THE CHURCH I CALL, AND TO THE GRAVE I SUMMON ALL.

The **Falmouth Museums on the Green** represent life in colonial Cape Cod. The 1790 **Julia Wood House** retains wonderful architectural details— a widow's walk, wide-board floors, lead-glass windows, and a colonial kitchen with wide hearth. Antique embroideries, baby shoes and clothes, toys and dolls, portraits, furniture, and the trappings of an authentically equipped doctor's office, all from the house's onetime owner, fill the premises. Out back, a re-creation of the Hallett Barn displays antique farm implements, a 19th-century horse-drawn sleigh, and other interesting items. Next door, the smaller **Conant House,** a 1794 half-Cape (an asymmetrical 1½-story building), holds military memorabilia, whaling items, scrimshaw, sailors' valentines, and a genealogical and historical research library. One collection includes books, portraits, and other items relating to Katharine Lee Bates, the native daughter who wrote "America the Beautiful." The Falmouth Historical Society also owns the 1812 white Cape house where Bates was born, off-site at 16 Main Street. The house is no longer open to the public, but a plaque out front commemorates Bates's birth in 1859.

Guides give tours of the museums, and a pretty formal garden with a gazebo and flagstone paths is adjacent. You can take a break with "Tea in Julia's Garden," which offers tea sandwiches, scones, and other refreshments on Thursday from 1 to 3 in July and August. There are also historical trolley tours in season; call for prices and times. Free walking tours of the town are available Tuesday at 4 in July and August. ⊠ *Village Green, 55 Palmer Ave., Falmouth Center* ☏ *508/548–4857* ⊕ *www. falmouthhistoricalsociety.org* ☒ *Museums $5; tea $12, including museum admission* ☉ *Late June–Sept., Tues.–Fri. 10–4, Sat. 10–1.*

❻ The privately owned **Charles D. and Margaret K. Spohr Gardens,** three planted acres on Oyster Pond, are a pretty, peaceful place. The springtime explosion of more than 700,000 daffodils gives way in turn to the tulips, azaleas, magnolias, flowering crab apples, rhododendrons, lilies, and climbing hydrangeas that inspire garden goers in summer. A collection of old millstones, bronze church bells, and ships' anchors decorates the landscape. ⊠ *45 Fells Rd., off Oyster Pond Rd.* ☏ *508/548– 0623* ⊕ *www.spohrgardens.org* ☒ *Free* ☉ *Daily sunrise–sunset.*

☾ Video-game rooms and candlepin bowling make the **Leary Family Amusement Center** a great place to take the kids on a rainy day. ⊠ *23 Town Hall Sq., off Rte. 28, Falmouth Center* ☏ *508/540–4877.*

❼ The village of **Woods Hole,** which dangles at the Cape's southwestern tip, has a unique personality shaped by its substantial intellectual community. As a major departure point for ferries to Martha's Vineyard, it draws crowds of through traffic in season. Well known as a center for international marine research, Woods Hole is home to several major scientific institutions. The National Marine Fisheries Service was here first, established in 1871 to study fish management and conservation. In 1888 the Marine Biological Laboratory (MBL), a center for research and education in marine biology, moved in across the street. Then in 1930 the Woods Hole Oceanographic Institution (WHOI) arrived, and the U.S. Geological Survey's Branch of Marine Geology followed in the 1960s.

Most of the year Woods Hole is a peaceful community of intellectuals quietly going about their work. In summer, however, the basically one-street village overflows with thousands of scientists and graduate students who come from around the globe either to participate in summer studies at MBL, WHOI, or the National Academy of Sciences conference center or to work on independent research projects. A handful of waterside cafés and shops along Water Street compete for the distinction of having the most bicycles stacked up at the door. Parking, limited to a relatively small number of metered spots on the street, can be nearly impossible. If you're coming from Falmouth to wander around Woods Hole, either ride your bicycle down the straight and flat Shining Sea Trail or take the Cape Cod Regional Transit Authority's WHOOSH trolley.

Scientific forces join together at the **Marine Biological Laboratory–Woods Hole Oceanographic Institution Library** (⊠ 7 Marine Biological Laboratory St., off Water St. ☎ 508/289–7423 ⊕ www.mbl.edu), one of the best collections of biological, ecological, and oceanographic literature in the world. The library has access to more than 200 computer databases and subscribes to more than 5,000 scientific journals in 40 languages, with complete collections of most. During World War II the librarian made arrangements with a German subscription agency to have German periodicals sent to neutral Switzerland and stored until the end of the war. Thus the library's German collections are uninterrupted, whereas even those of many German institutions are incomplete. All journals are always accessible, as they cannot be checked out, and because the library is open 24 hours a day. The Rare Books Room contains photographs, monographs, and prints, as well as journal collections that date from 1665.

> ## THINK TANK
>
> Wood's Hole's incredible concentration of scientific minds is due in part to the variety and abundance of marine life in the area's unpolluted waters and the village's natural deepwater port. Researchers here can easily exchange ideas and information and attend stimulating daily lectures and discussions (many open to the public) given by important scientists. The pooling of resources among the various institutions makes for economies of scale that benefit each while allowing all access to highly sophisticated equipment.

Unless you are a scientific researcher, the only way you can get to see the library is by taking the **Marine Biological Laboratory tour** (☎ 508/289–7623). The one-hour tours (mid-June–August, weekdays at 1 and 2), led by retired scientists, include an introductory slide show as well as stops at the library, the Marine Resources Center (where living sea creatures collected each day are kept), and one of the many working research labs. It's a good idea to call for reservations and meeting instructions at least a week in advance.

The **Woods Hole Oceanographic Institution** is the largest independent, private oceanographic laboratory in the world. Several buildings in the village of Woods Hole house its shore-based facilities; others are on a 200-acre campus nearby. During World War II its research focused on underwater explosives, submarine detection, and the development of antifouling paint. Today its $93 million annual budget helps to operate many laboratories with state-of-the-art equipment. A graduate program is offered jointly with MIT. WHOI's research vessels roam the world's waters; its staff led the successful U.S.–French search for the *Titanic* (found about 400 mi off Newfoundland) in 1985.

The Woods Hole Oceanographic Institution is open to the public only on guided tours, but you can learn about it at the small **WHOI Exhibit Center,** with videos and exhibits on the institution and its various projects, including its research vessels. **One-hour walking tours** (☎ 508/289–2252) of the institution and its piers are offered in July and August, weekdays at 10:30 and 1:30; tours begin at the WHOI Information Office at 93 Water Street and are free, but reservations are required. ⊠ *15 School St.* ☎ *508/289–2663* ⊕ *www.whoi.edu* 🎫 *$2 suggested donation* ☉ *Early May–late May and early Sept.–Oct., Tues.–Fri. 10–4:30; late May–early Sept., Mon.–Sat. 10–4:30. Closed Jan.–Mar.; call for off-season hrs.*

☾ The compact **National Marine Fisheries Service Aquarium** displays 16 FodorśChoice tanks of regional fish and shellfish in several rooms, cramped but ★ nonetheless crammed with stuff to see. Magnifying glasses, a dissecting scope, and mini-squeegees hanging from the frosty tanks (a favorite tool for kids passing through) help you examine marine life. Several hands-on pools hold banded lobsters, crabs, snails, starfish, and other creatures. The top attraction is two harbor seals, on view in the outdoor pool near the entrance in summer; you can watch their feedings weekdays at 11 and 4. ■ TIP→ The aquarium's status as a federal facility mandates a check of your driver's license or other valid ID at the door, so come prepared with credentials and expect to wait in line for a few minutes, particularly on rainy days. ⊠ *Albatross and Water Sts.* ☎ *508/495–2267, 508/495–2001 recorded information* ⊕ *www.nefsc.nmfs.gov/nefsc/aquarium* 🎫 *Free* ☉ *June–Aug., Tues.–Sat. 11–4; call for hrs off-season.*

NEED A BREAK? **Pie in the Sky** (⊠ 10 Water St. ☎ 508/540–5475), a small bakery with indoor and outdoor seating, sells cookies, pastries, and coffees, as well as sandwiches. The Oreo cookie bars are truly decadent. It's a short walk from the ferry terminal, and a good bet for breakfast.

The **Woods Hole Historical Museum** (formerly known as the Bradley House Museum) is a three-building complex that houses paintings, a restored Woods Hole Spritsail boat, boat models, and a model of the town as it looked in the 1890s. One room is filled with elegant ladies' clothing from the late 1800s. The archives hold old ships' logs, postcards, newspaper articles, maps, diaries, and photographs; more than 200 tapes of oral history provided by local residents; and a 100-volume library on maritime history. Free guided walking tours of the village depart from the museum, which is across from the Martha's Vineyard ferry parking lot, Tuesday at 4 in July and August. ⊠ *573 Woods Hole Rd.* ☎ *508/548–7270* ⊕ *www.woodsholemuseum.org* 🎫 *Free* ☉ *Museum mid-June–mid-Oct., Tues.–Sat. 10–4; archives yr-round, Tues. and Thurs. 10–2.*

The 1888 **Episcopal Church of the Messiah,** a stone church with a conical steeple and a small medicinal herb garden in the shape of a Celtic cross, is a good place for quiet reflection. The garden, enclosed by a holly hedge, has a bench for meditation. Inscriptions on either side of the carved gate read ENTER IN HOPE and DEPART IN PEACE. ✉ *22 Church St.* ☎ *508/ 548–2145* ☜ *Free* ☉ *Daily sunrise–sunset.*

Impressive **Nobska Light** (✉ Church St. ⊕ www.lighthouse.cc/nobska) has spectacular views from its base of the nearby Elizabeth Islands and of Martha's Vineyard, across Vineyard Sound. The 42-foot cast-iron tower, lined with brick, was built in 1876 with a stationary light. It shines red to indicate dangerous waters or white for safe passage. Since the light was automated in 1985, the adjacent keeper's quarters have been the headquarters of the Coast Guard group commander—a fitting passing of the torch from one safeguarder of ships to another. The lighthouse is open to the public only sporadically for tours; check with the Falmouth Chamber of Commerce for details.

The bucolic villages to the east (well, bucolic once you leave Route 28 ❽ and its strip malls) have much to offer nature lovers. **East Falmouth** and ❾ **Waquoit** sit on narrow fingers of land that poke out toward Nantucket Sound, so water is never far away here and comes in the form of quiet inlets and marshy bays rather than the crashing surf of the open ocean. Residential neighborhoods, with both seasonal and year-round homes, often end in dirt lanes that lead to the water. Menauhant Beach, the nicest beach in these towns, sits on a thin sliver of land with the sound on one side and a grass-lined cove on the other. Inland, the land is more rural, with a number of farms (and farm stands) still operating.

Overseen by the Massachusetts ❿ Audubon Society, **Ashumet Holly and Wildlife Sanctuary** is true to its name and its original plantsman, Wilfred Wheeler, with its 1,000-plus holly trees and shrubs composed of 65 American, Asian, and European varieties. Like Heritage Museums and

> ### ROAD NAME GAME
>
> As you head east from Falmouth Center on Route 28, the street signs change names as you travel through different areas. The road is Main Street until you pass Falmouth Heights Road, when Route 28 becomes Davis Straits. Farther east it becomes Teaticket Highway, then East Falmouth Highway, and then Waquoit Highway.

Gardens in Sandwich, this 45-acre tract of woodland, shady groves, meadows, and hiking trails was purchased and donated by Josiah K. Lilly III to preserve local land. Grassy Pond is home to numerous turtles and frogs, and in summer 35 nesting pairs of barn swallows live in the open rafters of the barn. Maps for self-guided tours cost $1. Tours to nearby Cuttyhunk Island (on a 50-foot sailing vessel) leave Woods Hole every Sunday from mid-July to early October; trips run from 9 to 5 and cost $50. ✉ *286 Ashumet Rd., East Falmouth* ☎ *508/362–1426* ⊕ *www. massaudubon.org* ☜ *$3* ☉ *Trails daily sunrise–sunset.*

♻ **Waquoit Bay National Estuarine Research Reserve** encompasses 2,500 acres of estuary and barrier beach around the bay, making it a good birding site. **South Cape Beach** is part of the reserve; you can lie out on the sand or join one of the interpretive walks. **Flat Pond Trail** runs through several different habitats, including fresh- and saltwater marshes. **Washburn Island** (☎ 877/422–6762 camping permit) is accessible by boat (your own) or by Saturday-morning tours (call to reserve); it offers 330 acres of pine barrens and trails, swimming, and 11 wilderness campsites (a permit is required). At the **reserve headquarters,** a 23-acre estate, an exhibit center includes displays about the bay's plants and animals, the Cape Cod watershed, and local Wampanoag culture. An interactive exhibit, outside on the lawn, allows you to trace the path of a raindrop; pick up a ball (the pseudo-raindrop) and follow its journey from cloud to land to river and on through the water cycle. In July and August the center has nature programs for children and families, as well as a Saturday-afternoon open house from 2 to 4 PM with family programs and a Tuesday-evening lecture-performance series (you can bring a picnic). ⊠ *149 Rte. 28, 3 mi west of Mashpee rotary, Waquoit* ☎ *508/457–0495* ⊕ *www.waquoitbayreserve.org* ⊗ *Exhibit center late June–early Sept., Mon.–Sat. 10–4; late May–late June, weekdays 10–4.*

Tony Andrews Farm and Produce Stand has pick-your-own strawberries (June), peas and beans (June and July), herbs (July and August), and tomatoes (August), as well as other produce on the stand. The farm schedules hayrides in fall, and a haunted house is set up in October. You can pick your own pumpkins in fall and choose your Christmas tree in December. ⊠ *394 Old Meeting House Rd., East Falmouth* ☎ *508/548–4717* ⊗ *June–Oct.; call for hrs and for information about special events.*

★ ☺ **Coonamessett Farm** operates a farm store where you can assemble your own gift baskets or purchase produce and specialty foods, as well as a small café serving soups, salads, baked goods, and beverages. Members of the farm's Pick-Your-Own club ($15-per-year membership; non-Cape residents can buy a one-day membership for $5) can pick strawberries, lettuces, herbs, rhubarb, and other fruits and vegetables. Members can also tour the greenhouses and fields, learn about hydroponic growing systems, and visit the animals (call ahead to arrange tours). The farm also rents canoes for use on the adjacent Coonamessett Pond. On Friday nights in summer, don't miss the wonderful organic vegetarian buffet dinners with live music. ⊠ *277 Hatchville Rd., East Falmouth* ☎ *508/563–2560* ⊕ *www.coonamessettfarm.com* ⊗ *Call for seasonal hrs.*

Rows and rows of grapevines—8,000 in all—line the fields of Kristina and Antonio Lazzari's **Cape Cod Winery.** It now produces seven wines; the Nobska red won a bronze medal at an International Eastern Wine Competition. ⊠ *681 Sandwich Rd., East Falmouth* ☎ *508/457–5592* ⊕ *www.capecodwinery.com* ⊗ *July and Aug., tastings Thurs.–Sun. noon–4; late May, June, and Sept.–late Dec., tastings weekends noon–4.*

Where to Stay & Eat

EAST FALMOUTH
& WAQUOIT
¢–$

✕ **McGann's of Falmouth Pub and Restaurant.** McGann's calls itself "a touch of Ireland on Cape Cod," and the McGann family should know—they also have a pub in the town of Doolin, County Galway, Ireland. The place has the slightly frayed grit of an Irish country tavern, and the filling if heavy bar food comes with an Irish twist: Irish-style fish-and-chips, or Gaelic chicken in an Irish whiskey-and-bacon sauce, for example.

Though Guinness reigns, the bar has 20 beers on draft. There's live music Friday, Saturday, and Sunday; Thursday is karaoke night. ✉ *734 Rte. 28, East Falmouth* ☎ *508/540–6656* ⌖ *Reservations not accepted* ⊟ *AE, D, MC, V.*

¢–$ ✕ **Moonakis Café.** Breakfast gets high marks at this humble roadside diner. You'll find all the standards and then some—eggs, pancakes, fruit salad—all nicely done. The chunky hash browns are fried with just the right amount of onions, and if the omelet with roasted tomatoes, olives, and goat cheese is on the menu, it's an excellent choice. Also recommended (if you're not on a diet) are the decadent Belgian waffles buried under strawberries, bananas, and whipped cream. Specials are always offered and change frequently. ✉ *460 Rte. 28, Waquoit* ☎ *508/457–9630* ⊟ *No credit cards* ☉ *No dinner.*

$$–$$$ 🛏 **Green Harbor Waterfront Lodging.** Although the modest rooms here are clean and adequate, it's the friendly summer camp–like feel that makes this attractive compound great for families. There are old-fashioned lawn swings, a swimming pool, umbrella-topped picnic tables, and barbecue grills, but the main attraction is the waterfront. It's not open ocean here but a peaceful tree-lined inlet, with rowboats and pedal boats for guests' use. Some of the no-frills rooms in the 1960s-vintage motel have microwaves and small refrigerators; others have kitchenettes. A spacious three-bedroom cottage has three full baths, an eat-in kitchen, and a living room with a fireplace and two sofa beds. It's down a quiet lane off Route 28. ✉ *134 Acapesket Rd., East Falmouth 02536* ☎ *508/548–4747 or 800/548–5556* 🖷 *508/540–1652* ⊕ *www.gogreenharbor.com* 🛏 *34 rooms, 1 cottage* ⌖ *Picnic area, some kitchenettes, some microwaves, some refrigerators, cable TV, pool, wading pool, boating, volleyball, laundry facilities, some pets allowed (fee); no smoking* ⊟ *AE, D, DC, MC, V* ☉ *Closed Nov.–Apr.*

$–$$$ 🛏 **Cape Wind.** If you're traveling with children who need space to run, this gray-shingle motel on 5 acres is a dependable though modest option. The rooms face a broad green lawn that slopes down to the bay; it's a great place to launch your canoe or kayak. The rooms are decidedly basic, with standard motel furnishings that are being continually updated and refreshed. All have refrigerators and coffeemakers, and some have microwaves; others have kitchenettes. The spacious one-bedroom apartment has a private terrace, but its half-basement location makes the interior rather dark. The motel is in a quiet residential neighborhood. ✉ *34 Maravista Ext., Teaticket, East Falmouth 02536* ☎ *508/548–3400 or 800/267–3401* 🖷 *508/495–0316* ⊕ *www.capewind.com* 🛏 *31 rooms, 1 apartment* ⌖ *Some kitchenettes, some microwaves, refrigerators, cable TV, Wi-Fi, pool; no smoking* ⊟ *D, MC, V.*

FALMOUTH ✕ **RoöBar City Bistro.** Sibling to the Chatham and Hyannis restaurants
★ $$–$$$ of the same name, the RoöBar brings a distinctly urban hipness to Falmouth. The bar is a popular watering hole, and the menu—scallop and smoked-bacon chowder, Asian duck confit pizza, Gorgonzola-crusted filet mignon—draws its inspiration from many cultures. There's also a terrific wine list. ✉ *285 Rte. 28, Falmouth Center* ☎ *508/548–8600* ⊕ *www.theroobar.com* ⊟ *AE, MC, V* ☉ *No lunch.*

$–$$$ ✕ **Firefly Woodfire Grill and Bar.** Both the menu and the interior change seasonally here, but you can watch your food being prepared in the open kitchen year-round. Much of the food is cooked with the heat of a wood-flamed fire, either in the beachstone oven or on the grill for which the restaurant is named; try one of the pizzas, or any grilled meat or seafood dish, such as cedar-plank maple-glazed salmon with sweet-potato hash and panfried mushrooms. There's also a full bar with an extensive wine list and beer selection, in addition to colorful cocktails. Pop and folk bands perform here regularly. ✉ *271 Rte. 28* ☎ *508/548–7953* ⊕ *www.fireflywoodfiregrill.com* ⊟ *AE, D, MC, V.*

$–$$ ✕ **La Cucina Sul Mare.** Northern Italian and Mediterranean cooking is the specialty at this classy, popular place. The staff is friendly and the setting is both intimate and festive, if a bit crowded. Calamari, warm green salad with goat cheese and cranberries, a classic lemon chicken sautéed with shallots and capers, and a variety of specials—including plenty of local fresh fish—adorn the menu. The *zuppa de pesce,* a medley of seafood sautéed in olive oil and garlic and finished in a white wine herb-and-tomato broth, is a specialty. Make sure to come hungry—the portions here are huge—and expect a long wait during prime hours in season. ✉ *237 Rte. 28* ☎ *508/548–5600* ⊟ *AE, D, MC, V.*

FodorsChoice
★

$–$$ ✕ **Quarterdeck Restaurant.** Part bar, part restaurant—but all Cape Cod—this spot is across the street from Falmouth's town hall, so the lunch talk tends to focus on local politics. The stained glass is not authentic, but the huge whaling harpoons certainly are. Low ceilings and rough-hewn beams seem a good match for the menu, which includes hearty sandwiches such as Reubens and grilled chorizo at lunch and specials at night. The swordfish kebab, skewered with mushrooms, onions, and green peppers and served over jasmine rice, is especially good. ✉ *164 Rte. 28 Falmouth Center* ☎ *508/548–9900* ⊟ *AE, D, DC, MC, V.*

¢–$ ✕ **Betsy's Diner.** A classic American treasure, Betsy's is a shiny, happy, busy place with a reassuring pink neon sign urging you to EAT HEAVY. The generous dining room, gleaming counter, and stools and booths by the big windows are done in pretty pastel mauve-and-cream tones. Memorabilia and neon grace the walls. Pancakes, waffles, and omelets are served all day, and typical dinner options include meat loaf and mashed potatoes, knockwurst and sauerkraut, and charbroiled pork chops. ✉ *457 Rte. 28, Falmouth Center* ☎ *508/540–0060* ⚏ *Reservations not accepted* ⊟ *AE, D, MC, V* ⊙ *No dinner Sun.*

¢–$ ✕ **The Clam Shack.** Fried clams top the menu at this basic seafood joint right on Falmouth Harbor. The clams are crisp and fresh; the meaty lobster roll and the fish-and-chips platter are good choices, too. Place your order at the counter and then take your tray to the picnic tables on the roof deck for the best views. More tables are on the dock in back, or you can squeeze into the tiny dining room. Just don't plan on a late night here—the Shack closes most evenings around 8. ✉ *227 Clinton Ave., Falmouth Harbor* ☎ *508/540–7758* ⊟ *No credit cards* ⊙ *Closed early Sept.–late May.*

¢ ✕ **Maryellen's Portuguese Bakery.** It's easy to drive right past this no-frills spot hidden behind a Dairy Queen. Take a seat at the counter or at one of the few tables, and then order up breakfast with a Portuguese twist.

Try the savory Portuguese omelet, filled with spicy *linguica* (sausage), parsley, onions, and cheese, or the French toast made with Portuguese bread. The lunch menu starts with BLTs and burgers but quickly moves on to kale soup and *cacoilha* (marinated pork). ⊠ *829 Rte. 28, near Falmouth Heights Rd.* ☎ *508/540–9696* ⊟ *No credit cards* ☾ *No dinner.*

$$–$$$$ ✕▥ **Holiday Inn.** This chain hotel is a dependable option for families. A tried-and-true comfort formula has been applied here: large rooms with contemporary furnishings, suites with king-size beds, and a large pool area surrounded by patio furniture and greenery. The Kansas City Steakhouse ($$–$$$$) restaurant serves breakfast and dinner year-round; you'll find Cape Cod specialties as well as huge quantities of beef—it's an unexpectedly good restaurant despite its setting inside a chain property. The hotel is adjacent to a pond and is close to Falmouth Center. ⊠ *291 Jones Rd., 02540* ☎ *508/540–2000 or 800/465–4329* 🖷 *508/548–2712* ⊕ *www.capecodhi.com* ⮌ *93 rooms, 5 suites* ⚒ *Restaurant, room service, cable TV, Wi-Fi, indoor pool, gym* ⊟ *AE, D, DC, MC, V.*

$$–$$$ ✕▥ **Coonamessett Inn.** At this delightful old-Cape-style inn-restaurant that's a famous setting for weddings and special occasions, five buildings of one- and two-bedroom suites ring a landscaped lawn that leads to a scenic wooded pond. Rooms are casually decorated, with bleached wood or pine paneling and New England antiques or reproductions. A large collection of Cape artist Ralph Cahoon's work appears throughout the inn. In the main dining room ($$–$$$$), a few contemporary flourishes enhance the traditional menu; you can still find rack of lamb and baked-stuffed lobster, but you might also see cumin-scented scallops with Israeli couscous. Lighter but still excellent food is served in the cozy Eli's Lounge ($), which has live music Friday and Saturday. ⊠ *311 Gifford St., at Jones Rd., 02540* ☎ *508/548–2300* 🖷 *508/540–9831* ⊕ *www.capecodrestaurants.org/coonamessett* ⮌ *28 suites, 1 cottage* ⚒ *Restaurant, cable TV, bar; no smoking* ⊟ *AE, D, MC, V* �🍴 *CP.*

★ $$$–$$$$ ▥ **Inn on the Sound.** At this understated but stylish inn, perched on a bluff overlooking Vineyard Sound, the living room and most of the guest rooms face the water. Most have queen-size beds, and all contain unfussy contemporary furnishings such as natural oak tables, unbleached cottons, ample shelf space, and ceiling fans; four have private decks. Common areas include an art-laden living room with a boulder fireplace, oversize windows, and modern white couches; a bistrolike breakfast room; and a porch with more stunning water views. ⊠ *313 Grand Ave., Falmouth Heights 02540* ☎ *508/457–9666 or 800/564–9668* 🖷 *508/457–9631* ⊕ *www.innonthesound.com* ⮌ *8 rooms, 1 apartment* ⚒ *Cable TV, Wi-Fi, beach; no a/c, no kids under 18, no smoking* ⊟ *AE, D, MC, V* �🍴 *CP.*

$$$ ▥ **The Inn at Siders Lane.** Housed in a contemporary Federalist reproduction building nearly indistinguishable from its authentic neighbors, this elegant B&B blends traditional New England hospitality and 19th-century style with modern amenities. Opened in 2005 just steps from downtown's bustle, the Inn feels private and intimate on its quiet corner by the Village Green. Upstairs, the two spacious guest rooms are tastefully appointed with graceful furnishings in pale neutral tones. Each has a queen bed, private bath, and cable TV; the house also has central air-conditioning. Hosts Jim and Maureen Trodden serve a superb hot breakfast, and you can join them again in the afternoon for tea and fresh-baked cookies. ⊠ *51 W. Main St., 02540* ☎ *508/495–4359* ⊕ *www.innatsiderslane.com* ⇗ *2 rooms* ♌ *Cable TV; no smoking* ⊟ *MC, V* ⦿| *BP.*

★ **$$$** 🖼 **Mostly Hall B&B.** With its deep, landscaped yard and wrought-iron fence, this elegant inn with a wraparound porch resembles a private estate. (The house got its name when a young guest is said to have exclaimed, "Look! It's mostly hall!") The imposing 1849 Italianate house has an upscale European style with painted wall murals in several bedrooms; the Tuscany Room's walls suggest an intimate Tuscan garden. Three of the rooms are more traditionally decorated, with colonial antiques; all have canopy beds. Breakfast is served in the formal parlor or outside on the veranda. Although the inn is steps from the town center, you can lounge in the gardens and feel a world away. ⊠ *27 Rte. 28, 02540* ☎ *508/548–3786* 🖶 *508/548–5778* ⊕ *www.mostlyhall.com* ⇗ *6 rooms* ♌ *Cable TV, in-room DVDs, Wi-Fi, bicycles, library; no kids under 16, no smoking* ⊟ *AE, D, MC, V* ☻ *Closed mid-Dec.–mid-Apr.* ⦿| *BP.*

$$–$$$ 🖼 **Palmer House Inn.** This turn-of-the-20th-century Queen Anne home stands on a tree-lined street, just a short stroll from Falmouth's Village Green. The Victorian interior of Falmouth's largest B&B is pretty if slightly over the top, with heavy period furniture, endless lace, and ornate stained-glass windows—many rooms have fireplaces. One good bet is the third-floor Tower Room, which has a view across the treetops. The large rooms in the 1910 carriage house are airier, with more tailored appointments, and four newer rooms, all with whirlpool baths, are less ornate. There's a two-bedroom suite in a separate cottage (where young children are permitted). A candlelight breakfast is served, and afternoon refreshments are available. ⊠ *81 Palmer Ave., 02540* ☎ *508/548–1230 or 800/472–2632* 🖶 *508/540–1878* ⊕ *www.palmerhouseinn.com* ⇗ *16 rooms, 1 cottage,* ♌ *Some in-room hot tubs, cable TV, bicycles; no smoking* ⊟ *AE, D, DC, MC, V* ⦿| *BP.*

$–$$$ 🖼 **Admiralty Inn.** This large roadside motel outside Falmouth Center has several types of rooms and suites, and its child-friendly facilities make it a good bet for families. Standard rooms have two queen-size beds or one queen-size- and one Murphy bed. King Jacuzzi rooms have king-size beds and whirlpool tubs in the bedroom. Town-house suites have cathedral ceilings with skylights, two baths (one with whirlpool), a loft with a king-size bed, a living room with a sofa bed, and a queen- or king-size bed. ⊠ *51 Rte. 28, East Falmouth 02536* ☎ *508/548–4240 or 800/341–5700* 🖶 *508/457–0535* ⊕ *www.theadmiraltyinn.com* ⇗ *70 rooms, 28 suites* ♌ *Restaurant, some in-room hot tubs, refrigerators, cable TV, some in-room VCRs, 2 pools, hot tub, bar* ⊟ *AE, D, DC, MC, V.*

$$ 🖼 **Capt. Tom Lawrence House.** A lawn shaded by old maple trees surrounds this pretty white house, which is steps from downtown yet set back from the street enough to feel secluded. Built in 1861 for a whaling captain, the intimate B&B has romantic rooms with antique and painted furniture, Laura Ashley or Ralph Lauren linens, French country wallpaper, and thick carpeting. An efficiency apartment is bright, spacious, and suitable for families, with a fully equipped eat-in kitchen. Breakfast and afternoon snacks are served near the fireplace in the common room. The owners are extremely friendly and helpful. ✉ *75 Locust St., 02540* ☎ *508/ 548–9178* 📠 *508/457–1790* ⊕ *www.captaintomlawrence.com* 🛏 *6 rooms, 1 efficiency* ⚷ *Refrigerators, cable TV, bicycles; no room phones, no children under 5 (except in efficiency), no smoking* ▭ *AE, MC, V* �’❘ *BP* ⊙ *Closed Jan.*

NORTH & WEST FALMOUTH

★ $–$$$

✕ **Chapoquoit Grill.** Comfortable and bustling, this unassuming local favorite has an Italian slant, starting with creative pastas and wood-fired pizzas. The long list of daily specials might include wood-grilled duck with orange-molasses glaze or sirloin with a tamarind-mango glaze. A fireplace and coral-color walls make the front room intimate, and the larger rear dining room seems vaguely tropical (with a palm tree in the middle). Expect daunting waits for a table on summer weekends; come early or late. ✉ *410 Rte. 28A, West Falmouth* ☎ *508/540–7794* ⚷ *Reservations not accepted* ▭ *MC, V* ⊙ *No lunch.*

$$$$

🏨 **Inn at West Falmouth.** This luxurious 1899 estate-house inn is in a secluded area of exclusive West Falmouth. A combination of contemporary and antique furnishings and polished hardwood floors set an elegant but relaxed mood. Guest rooms have king- or queen-size beds (some with canopies), Italian marble bathrooms with whirlpool tubs, phones, hair dryers, and wall safes; some have fireplaces and private decks or balconies. Beyond the French doors, off the pale pink-and-green breakfast room, a patio spilling over with potted plants and trees overlooks woods, gardens, and a tennis court and leads to the small pool and deck with distant views of the bay. It's a 15-minute walk from the beach. ✉ *66 Frazar Rd., Box 1208, West Falmouth 02574* ☎ *508/540– 7696 or 800/397–7696* 📠 *508/540–9977* ⊕ *www.innatwestfalmouth. com* 🛏 *6 rooms* ⚷ *In-room hot tubs, cable TV, tennis court, pool, billiards; no smoking* ▭ *MC, V* ❘❉ *CP.*

$$–$$$$

🏨 **Sea Crest Resort.** Location and amenities are strong draws at this modern conference center and resort, whose eight buildings sprawl along one end of beautiful Old Silver Beach—guests enjoy some 700 feet of frontage right along the sand. Rooms, done in dark blues and pastels, are crisp and clean; many have ocean views, and some have gas-log fireplaces. A number of lodging packages are available. The poolside deli, Oscars, is a good bet for a quick burger or sandwich if you don't want to stray far from the beach; it's easily accessible to nonguests. The resort gets high marks for its kids' day camp. ✉ *350 Quaker Rd., North Falmouth 02556* ☎ *508/540–9400 or 800/225–3110* 📠 *508/548–0556* ⊕ *www.seacrest-resort.com* 🛏 *258 rooms, 8 suites* ⚷ *Restaurant, room service, refrigerators, cable TV with movies and video games, WiFi, putting green, 2 tennis courts, 2 pools (1 indoor), health club, hot tub, sauna, shuffleboard, piano bar, children's programs (ages 3–12; summer only), meeting rooms* ▭ *AE, D, DC, MC, V.*

$$–$$$

🏨 **Beach Rose Inn.** In 2002, owners David and Donna McIlrath rehabbed this rambling 1863 farmhouse on a quiet lane to create a comfortable country-style B&B. The rooms—some in the main inn, some in the adjacent carriage house—are furnished with quilts and a mix of antiques and reproductions. The Falmouth suite has an airy, private sunporch; this room, and those in the adjacent carriage house, have whirlpool tubs. A three-bedroom apartment on the second floor of the carriage house (without a full kitchen, though it does have a refrigerator, microwave, coffeemaker, and toaster) and a separate, tiny two-bedroom cottage both rent by the week. One room is reserved for guests with pets. ✉ *17 Chase Rd., off Rte. 28A, West Falmouth 02574* ☎ *508/540–5706 or 800/498–5706* 🖶 *508/540–4880* 🌐 *www.thebeachroseinn.com* 🛏 *7 rooms, 1 suite, 1 apartment, 1 cottage* ♿ *Some in-room hot tubs, some kitchenettes, some microwaves, some refrigerators, Wi-Fi, some pets allowed (fee); no room phones, no room TVs, no kids under 10 (except in cottage), no smoking* 🟰 *MC, V* 🍴 *BP.*

$$–$$$ 🏠 **Chapoquoit Inn.** Four-poster beds, pastel quilts, and garden views fill the rooms at this cozy B&B in a 1739 former Quaker homestead surrounded by woodland and flower beds. Owners Kim and Tim McIntyre (she's a former marketing exec, he's a landscape designer) have furnished their inn with antiques and other family heirlooms. In the sunny breakfast room, which opens to the deck, you might find lemon pancakes or crème brûlée French toast. The sands of Chapoquoit Beach are a short 10-minute walk away. ✉ *495 Rte. 28A, West Falmouth 02574* ☎ *508/540–7232 or 800/842–8994* 🌐 *www.chapoquoit.com* 🛏 *8 rooms* ♿ *Cable TV, some in-room VCRs, Wi-Fi; no room phones, no TV in some rooms, no kids under 12, no smoking* 🟰 *MC, V* 🍴 *BP.*

$–$$ 🏠 **Ideal Spot Motel.** Neat as a pin, quiet, and a bit old-fashioned, this gray-shingle motel in the heart of quiet West Falmouth village has simple, good-size, family-friendly rooms. Efficiencies have a queen-size bed or two doubles, plus a kitchen and a sitting area with a sofa bed; the large motel rooms have refrigerators. There's no pool, but Chapoquoit Beach is a mile away. The lovely grounds are decked with well-manicured greenery. ✉ *641 Rte. 28A, at Old Dock Rd., Box 465, West Falmouth 02574* ☎ *508/548–2257 or 800/269–6910* 🌐 *www. idealspotmotel.com* 🛏 *12 efficiencies, 2 rooms* ♿ *Some kitchens, some refrigerators, cable TV; no smoking* 🟰 *D, MC, V* 🕐 *Closed Dec.–Mar.*

WOODS HOLE   ✕ **Landfall.** Request a window table overlooking the water at this clas-
$$–$$$$ sic Cape seafood spot, where lobster pots, buoys, and other nautical paraphernalia hang from the ceilings. Lobster, fried clams, and baked scrod lead off the menu of traditional seafood fare. Though the kids will need their restaurant manners, it's still family friendly, and the children's all-you-can-eat specials are a great value. ✉ *2 Luscombe Ave.* ☎ *508/548–1758* 🌐 *www.woodshole.com/landfall* 🟰 *AE, MC, V* 🕐 *Closed Dec.–Mar. and Mon.–Wed. Apr.–late May and early Sept.–Nov.*

$$–$$$ ✕ **Captain Kidd Restaurant & Bar.** The stately bar, festive atmosphere, and a small number of cozy tables that cluster around a woodstove and overlook Eel Pond make this a year-round favorite for locals. Baked halibut, pan-seared scallops, lemon-herb roasted chicken, lamb medallions, and fried calamari are a few of the favorites, served in a publike atmosphere. In the bar area, a lighter and less expensive menu is offered, including pizzas, pastas, fish-and-chips, and fried seafood platters. ✉ *77 Water St.* ☎ *508/548–8563* 🟰 *AE, MC, V.*

$–$$$ ✕ **Shuckers World Famous Raw Bar and Cafe.** Some of the harborside tables at this casual nautical-theme restaurant are so close to the dock that you almost feel as if you're sitting in the bobbing sailboats. The menu ranges from jerk chicken to pasta primavera to lobster ravioli, but it's best to stick with the grilled fish and other simple seafood dishes. The "world-famous" lobster boil—a boiled lobster, steamed clams and mussels, and an ear of corn—is justifiably popular. ⊠ *91A Water St.* ☎ *508/540–3850* ⊕ *www.woodshole.com/shuckers* ▤ *AE, D, MC, V* ⊗ *Closed Nov.–Apr., and Mon.–Thurs. mid-May–late May and early Sept.–mid-Oct.*

$$ 🏨 **Sands of Time Motor Inn and Harbor House.** Essentially two lodgings in one, this property on a hill above Woods Hole village houses both a motel and a Victorian-era inn. In the family-friendly motor inn, the furnishings are standard motel-style; the best views, looking out to the water, are from the second-floor rooms, some of which have private balconies. The Harbor House is more eclectic—a canopy bed here, a claw-foot tub there; some rooms have fireplaces or private patios. ⊠ *549 Woods Hole Rd., 02543* ☎ *508/548–6300 or 800/841–0114* 🖷 *508/457–0160* ⊕ *www.sandsoftime.com* 🛏 *35 rooms* ⚭ *Cable TV, pool; no smoking* ▤ *AE, D, DC, MC, V* ⊗ *Closed mid-Nov.–Apr.* �ⵔ *CP.*

$–$$ 🏨 **Capeside Cottage.** This classic Cape house, built in 1942, has country-style rooms with the same basic touches: double beds, lace curtains, and fluffy quilts. The seasonal Garden Room, next to the kidney-shape in-ground pool, has a king bed (or two twins) and a sleeper sofa, refrigerator, cable TV, and microwave; this room is also pet friendly. You can eat breakfast out by the pool or in the comfortable common room, which has a fireplace and lots of amenities, including a refrigerator and an assortment of teas, as well as a TV and VCR. ⊠ *320 Woods Hole Rd., 02543* ☎ *508/548–6218 or 800/320–2322* 🖷 *508/457–7519* ⊕ *www.capesidecottage.com* 🛏 *6 rooms* ⚭ *Pool; no room phones, no room TVs, no smoking* ▤ *AE, MC, V* ⵔ *BP.*

★ $–$$ 🏨 **Woods Hole Passage.** A century-old carriage house and barn have been converted into a romantic showcase. The large rose-hue common room radiates comfort with its lace curtains and overstuffed furniture. One guest room (the smallest) is in the main house; the others are in the restored barn, where the upstairs rooms have soaring ceilings. Gregarious and helpful owner Deb Pruitt sells Martha's Vineyard ferry tickets at cost so you can avoid lines at the dock. You can enjoy a delicious breakfast on the patio in the lovely yard; early risers can request "breakfast-in-a-bag" to take on the road. Kids are accepted, by prior arrangement. ⊠ *186 Woods Hole Rd., 02540* ☎ *508/548–9575 or 800/790–8976* 🖷 *508/540–4771* ⊕ *www.woodsholepassage.com* 🛏 *5 rooms* ⚭ *Wi-Fi, bicycles, croquet, horseshoes; no room phones, no room TVs, no smoking* ▤ *AE, D, MC, V* ⵔ *BP.*

Nightlife & the Arts

THE ARTS The **College Light Opera Company** (⊠ Highfield Theatre, off Depot Ave., Falmouth ☎ 508/548–0668 ⊕ www.collegelightopera.com) presents nine musicals or operettas for one week each, the results of a summer program involving music and theater majors from colleges around the country. The company includes more than 30 singers and an 18-piece orchestra. Be forewarned: the quality can vary from show to show.

The **Cape Cod Theatre Project** (☎ 508/457–4242 ⊕ www.capecodtheatreproject.org) helps develop new American plays through a series of staged readings. Each summer the project presents three or four readings, which are followed by audience discussion with the playwright. Productions have included works by Gloucester Stage Company director Israel Horovitz and by Pulitzer Prize winners Lanford Wilson and Paula Vogel. Performances take place at **Falmouth Academy** (✉ 7 Highfield Dr., off Depot Ave., Falmouth) and in the **Woods Hole Community Hall** (✉ Water St., Woods Hole).

Performing at the same venues as the College Light Opera Company, the **Falmouth Theatre Guild** (✉ Highfield Theatre, off Depot Ave. ☎ 508/548–0400 ⊕ www.falmouththeatreguild.org) is a first-rate community theater that presents four plays—a mix of musicals and dramas—from fall through spring.

Falmouth's summer **town-band concerts** (✉ Scranton Ave. ☎ 508/548–8500 or 800/526–8532) are held in Marina Park on Thursday evening starting at 8.

The **Woods Hole Folk Music Society** (✉ Community Hall, 68 Water St. ☎ 508/540–0320 ⊕ www.arts-cape.com/whfolkmusic) presents professional and local folk and blues in a smoke- and alcohol-free environment, with refreshments available during intermission. Concerts by nationally known performers take place the first and third Sunday of the month from October to April.

Woods Hole Theater Company (✉ Community Hall, 68 Water St. ☎ 508/540–6525 ⊕ www.woodsholetheater.org), the community's resident theater group since 1974, presents several productions each year, generally between late spring and early fall.

NIGHTLIFE **Coonamessett Inn** (✉ 311 Gifford St., Falmouth Center ☎ 508/548–2300) has dancing to soft piano, jazz trios, or other music in its lounge on weekends year-round.

Liam Maguire's (✉ 281 Rte. 28, Falmouth Center ☎ 508/548–0285) is a festive, authentic Irish pub with nightly Irish and other acoustic music and dependable pub fare.

Nimrod Inn (✉ 100 Dillingham Ave., Falmouth Center ☎ 508/540–4132) presents jazz and contemporary music at least six nights a week year-round. The Nimrod is also a great spot for late-night dining.

Sea Crest Resort (✉ 350 Quaker Rd., North Falmouth ☎ 508/540–9400) has a summer and holiday-weekend schedule of nightly entertainment on the outdoor terrace, including dancing to country, Top 40, reggae, and jazz bands and a big-band DJ.

Sports & the Outdoors

BASEBALL The **Falmouth Commodores** (✉ 790 Rte. 28, Falmouth ☎ 508/432–6909 ⊕ www.falcommodores.org) of the collegiate Cape Cod Baseball League play their home games at Guv Fuller Field from mid-June to mid-August.

BEACHES **Chapoquoit Beach** (⊠ Chapoquoit Rd., West Falmouth), a narrow stretch of white sand, lines a peninsula that juts dramatically into the bay. Resident parking stickers are required at the beach lot in season, but the surrounding roads are popular with bicyclists. The beach has lifeguards and portable toilets.

2

Falmouth Heights Beach on Grand Avenue is an often-crowded arc of sand on Nantucket Sound, backed by a row of inns and B&Bs. The beach has lifeguards (in summer) and portable toilets. There's a small strip of metered parking on Grand Avenue between Walden Avenue and Crescent Park Avenue.

Grews Pond in Goodwill Park, a pretty tree-lined freshwater pond with a sandy beach and lifeguarded swimming area, is popular with local families. You'll find several sites for picnicking, along with restrooms and a volleyball net; there's also a playground nearby. You can enter the park from Route 28 just north of Jones Road or from Gifford Street opposite St. Joseph's Cemetery. Parking is free.

Megansett Beach (⊠ County Rd., North Falmouth), hidden in a residential neighborhood, is a small, family-friendly location. Weathered gray-shingle homes line the cove, and boats moored at the adjacent yacht club bob in the bay. The beach has lifeguards and a portable toilet but no other services. Resident parking stickers are required at the beach lot in season.

Menauhant Beach, on Menauhant Road in East Falmouth, is a long, narrow stretch of sand with a pond in a quiet residential neighborhood. Its slightly more secluded location means it can be a bit less crowded than the beaches near Falmouth Center. The beach has lifeguards, restrooms, outdoor showers, and a small snack bar. Public parking is available; in season the fee is $10.

★ **Old Silver Beach** (⊠ Off Quaker Rd., North Falmouth) is a long, beautiful crescent of soft white sand bordered by the Sea Crest Resort at one end. It's especially good for small children because a sandbar keeps it shallow at the southern end and creates tidal pools full of crabs and minnows. The beach has lifeguards, restrooms, showers, and a snack bar. There's a $20 fee for parking in summer.

Surf Drive Beach, a family-friendly sandy cove on Surf Drive, faces Nantucket Sound with views out toward the Vineyard. The beach has restrooms and showers as well as lifeguards. Public parking is available; in summer the daily parking fee is $10.

Wood Neck Beach (⊠ Wood Neck Rd., West Falmouth), in the Sippewisset area, is a sandy bay-side beach backed by grass-covered dunes. At high tide the beach is very narrow, but sandbars and shallow tidal pools make this a good place for children when the tide is out. Resident parking stickers are required in season.

BICYCLING The **Shining Sea Trail** is an easy 3½-mi route between Locust Street, Falmouth, and the Woods Hole ferry parking lot. It follows the coast, providing views of Vineyard Sound and dipping into oak and pine woods;

a detour onto Church Street takes you to Nobska Light. A brochure is available at the trailheads. If you're going to Martha's Vineyard with your bike, you can park your car in one of Falmouth's Steamship Authority lots and ride the Shining Sea Trail to the ferry. (The free shuttle buses between the Falmouth lots and the Woods Hole ferry docks also have bike carriers.) There are plans to eventually extend the trail another 8 mi or so up through West Falmouth.

Corner Cycle (⊠ 115 Palmer Ave., Falmouth ☎ 508/540–4195) rents bikes (including tandems and children's bikes) by the hour, day, or week. It also rents Burley trailers for carrying small children and does on-site repairs. The shop is two blocks from the Shining Sea Trail. **Holiday Cycles** (⊠ 465 Grand Ave., Falmouth Heights ☎ 508/540–3549) has surrey, tandem, and other unusual bikes.

FISHING   Freshwater ponds are good for perch, pickerel, trout, and more; you can obtain the required license (along with rental gear) at tackle shops, such as **Eastman's Sport & Tackle** (⊠ 150 Rte. 28, Falmouth ☎ 508/548–6900 ⊕ www.eastmanstackle.com).

Patriot Party Boats (⊠ 227 Clinton Ave., Falmouth Harbor ☎ 508/548–2626 or 800/734–0088 ⊕ www.patriotpartyboats.com) has deep-sea fishing from party or charter boats. Advance bookings are recommended, particularly for weekend trips.

HORSEBACK   **Haland Stables** (⊠ 878 Rte. 28A, West Falmouth ☎ 508/540–2552) of-
RIDING   fers lessons and trail rides by reservation Monday through Saturday.

ICE-SKATING   Skaters take to the ice at the **Falmouth Ice Arena** (⊠ 9 Skating La., off Palmer Ave. ☎ 508/548–7080 ⊕ www.falmouthicearena.com) fall through spring. You can rent skates from the pro shop.

RUNNING   To run in the world-class **SBLI Falmouth Road Race** (⌂ Box 732, Falmouth 02541 ☎ 508/540–7000 ⊕ www.falmouthroadrace.com) in mid-August, send a self-addressed, stamped envelope to request an entry form. The race typically closes to entrants in early spring. A crowd of 75,000-plus spectators lines the streets of the 7-mi course, which covers a combination of winding and hilly terrain, flat stretches, and stunning ocean scenery. There are 10,000 registered runners (the spring application window is quite small, and if you cannot run a mile in less than 12 minutes, you are asked not to enter), as well as about 2,000 unofficial ones, making this an immense event for such a small town.

TENNIS &   The huge **Falmouth Sports Center** (⊠ 33 Highfield Dr. ☎ 508/548–7433)
RACQUETBALL   has three outdoor- and six indoor tennis courts and two racquetball-handball courts, as well as steam rooms and saunas, a full health club, and physical therapist services. Day and short-term rates are available.

Shopping

★ **Bean & Cod** (⊠ 140 Rte. 28, Falmouth Center ☎ 508/548–8840 or 800/558–8840 ⊕ www.beanandcod.com), a specialty food shop, sells cheeses, breads, and picnic fixings, along with pastas, coffees and teas, and unusual condiments. The store also packs and ships gift baskets.

Eight Cousins Children's Books (⊠ 189 Rte. 28, Falmouth Center ☎ 508/548–5548) is the place to find reading material for toddlers through young adults. In addition to comprehensive sections on oceans and marine life, Native American peoples, and other Cape topics, the well-stocked shop also carries audiotapes, CDs, and games.

Europa (⊠ 628 Rte. 28, West Falmouth ☎ 508/540–7814) is a small boutique in a charming old house with a great selection of jewelry, accessories, gift items, and fun clothing at fair prices. A second room is devoted to lamps and lamp repair.

Handworks (⊠ 68 Water St., Woods Hole ☎ 508/540–5291), tucked in the back of the Community Hall building next to the drawbridge, is a cooperative arts-and-crafts gallery showcasing the work of local artists.

Howlingbird (⊠ 91 Palmer Ave., Falmouth Center ☎ 508/540–3787) stocks detailed hand-silk-screened marine-theme T-shirts and sweatshirts, plus hand-painted cards and silk-screened hats and handbags.

Maxwell & Co. (⊠ 200 Rte. 28, Falmouth Center ☎ 508/540–8752) has traditional men's and women's clothing with flair from European and American designers, handmade French shoes and boots, and leather goods and accessories.

Rosie Cheeks (⊠ 233 Rte. 28, Falmouth Center ☎ 508/548–4572), whose name was inspired by the owner's daughter, specializes in creative women's clothing and jewelry, with a particularly nice selection of hand-knit sweaters.

Mashpee

 7 mi east of East Falmouth, 10 mi south of Sandwich.

Mashpee is one of two Massachusetts towns with both municipally governed– and Native American–governed areas (the other town is Aquinnah, formerly known as Gay Head, on Martha's Vineyard). In 1660 the Reverend Richard Bourne, a missionary, gave a 16-square-mi parcel of land to the Wampanoags (consider the irony—an outsider "giving" Native people their own land). Known as the Mashpee Plantation and governed by two local sachems, it was the first Native American reservation in the United States. In 1870 Mashpee was founded as a town. In 1974 the Mashpee Wampanoag Tribal Council was formed to continue its government with a chief, a supreme sachem, a medicine man, and clan mothers. More than 600 residents are descended from the original Wampanoags, and some continue to observe their ancient traditions. Today, several residential-resort communities have developed in the Mashpee area; the largest, the Country Club of New Seabury, has one of the best golf courses on the Cape. There are no hotels or inns in Mashpee, although New Seabury does have some home and condo rentals. Mashpee, with its villagelike Mashpee Commons outdoor mall, has also become a popular shopping and dining destination. Yet away from the stores, the town retains a more rural character, with wooded roads, inland ponds, and reminders of the area's original settlers.

CLOSE UP

Powwow, Wampanoag Style

DANCERS AND DRUMMERS re-creating ancient rhythms, and vivid deer skin costumes decorated with colorful beads and bold plumage are a far cry from the fried clams, shingled saltboxes, and antiques shops that typify Cape Cod, yet they represent the very essence of a culture that has made this area home for thousands of years. It was the Wampanoag tribe who peacefully greeted, assisted, and befriended the Pilgrims who came ashore in 1620. And while their presence is often overlooked amid the luxury resorts and golf courses that dominate the town of Mashpee, the tribe continues to embrace and celebrate their ancestors' way of life.

The Mashpee Wampanoag Powwow, held every year since 1924, is a lively showcase of the tribe's traditions.

Open to the public, the early July Powwow is a large gathering of local Wampanoags and numerous tribes from throughout the northeast; some even travel here from the western states. Tents and tables fill the tribal grounds, selling everything from native foods to jewelry and T-shirts. A series of intricately costumed dancing and drumming contests takes place during the three-day festival, along with one of the most dramatic events— the fireball ceremony. This ancient healing ritual involves Wampanoag males in what looks a little bit like soccer—except the ball is on fire.

The Mashpee Wampanoag tribal grounds are in Mashpee, off Great Neck Road. For more info, call the **Tribal Council** (☎ 508/477-0208).

The **Old Indian Burial Ground,** near the meetinghouse on Meeting House Road, is an 18th-century cemetery with headstones typical of the period, intricately carved with scenes and symbols and inscribed with witty sayings.

In a cavernous former church building, the **Cape Cod Children's Museum** welcomes kids with interactive play, science exhibits, a 30-foot pirate play ship, a portable planetarium, and other playtime activities. The museum is best suited for preschoolers and children in the early elementary grades. ⊠ *577 Great Neck Rd. S* ☎ *508/539-8788* ⊕ *www. capecodchildrensmuseum.org* 🖃 *$6* ☉ *Mon.–Sat. 10–5, Sun. noon–5. Reduced hrs in winter; call before visiting.*

Perfect for bird-watching, fishing, or canoeing, the **Mashpee River Woodlands** occupy 391 acres along the Mashpee River. More than 8 mi of trails meander through the marshlands and pine forests. Park on Quinaquisset Avenue, River Road, or Mashpee Neck Road (where there's a public landing for canoe access). Trail maps are available at the Mashpee Chamber of Commerce. The trails are open daily from dawn to dusk.

Where to Eat

$$–$$$ ✕ **Bleu.** Chef Frederic Feufeu, a native of the Loire Valley, brings the fla-
FodorśChoice vors of France to this urbane restaurant in the pseudo-quaint Mashpee
★   Commons retail and entertainment village. From bistro classics to haute

2

cuisine and sophisticated lunch sandwiches to decadent desserts, the flavors are astounding. Seasonal specialties include roasted filet mignon with poached foie gras, fingerling potatoes, candied shallots, and bordelaise sauce. Shrimp tempura with miso mustard sauce and Asian slaw is one of the tempting lighter and less expensive dishes served in the natty bar. There's also a jazz brunch on Sunday. ⊠ *7 Market St., Mashpee Commons* ☎ *508/539–7907* ▭ *AE, D, MC, V.*

★ $–$$$ ✕ **Siena.** A boisterous, high-ceilinged space at Mashpee Commons, this modern Italian restaurant warms the hearts of patrons with its genuinely friendly service and well-crafted Tuscan cuisine. You might start with the exceptional buffalo mozzarella salad before moving on to a wood-grilled veal chop with marsala sauce, or linguine with sautéed littleneck clams, white wine, garlic, and parsley. Several fine brick-oven pizzas are offered, too. Grand Marnier flourless chocolate cake makes for a magnificent ending. In warm weather, you can dine on the ample patio. ⊠ *11A Steeple St., Mashpee Commons* ☎ *508/477–5929 or 877/477–5929* ▭ *AE, D, MC, V.*

¢–$$ ✕ **Popponesset Inn.** The surroundings, more so than the lobster rolls, burgers, grilled swordfish, steaks, and other straightforward offerings, are exceptional here. The site is a gem, with old Cape Cod saltbox houses nearby, lovely Nantucket Sound in the background, and perfect light in the evening. The restaurant has a lounge called Poppy's and comprises several small dining rooms, some with skylights and others looking over the water through glass walls. Sit outside, either under the tent or at one of the umbrella tables. You can dance to a band on some weekends. ⊠ *95 Shore Dr., The Country Club of New Seabury* ☎ *508/477–1100* ▭ *AE, DC, MC, V* ☉ *Closed mid-Oct.–late Apr. Closed Mon.–Thurs. Sept. and Oct. No lunch Sept. and Oct.*

¢–$$ ✕ **The Raw Bar.** At this funky little seafood joint, you can pull up a bar stool and chow down on giant lobster rolls, littlenecks, cherrystones, oysters, steamers, and peel-your-own shrimp, all easily washed down with a local brew or a rum punch. Despite a few picnic tables out back, the scene here is more "bar" than "seafood shack." There's live music some nights, too. ⊠ *Popponesset Market Pl.* ☎ *508/539–4858* ▭ *AE, MC, V* ☉ *Closed late Oct.–early Apr.*

Nightlife & the Arts

Bobby Byrne's Pub (⊠ Mashpee Commons, Rtes. 28 and 151 ☎ 508/477–0600) is a comfortable pub with an outdoor café, a jukebox, and reliable pub fare.

The **Cape Cod Performing Arts Center** (☎ 508/477–2580 ⊕ www.capecodpac.org) (formerly the Boch Center for the Performing Arts) presents such top-name performers as Kathy Mattea, the Count Basie Orchestra, the Vienna Choir Boys, and the Joffrey School Dancers, as well as the Annual New England Jazz Festival in late August. Plans are under way to construct a complex of buildings, including an amphitheater to accommodate 2,000 people, on an idyllic 10-acre tract of countryside in Mashpee. Until the complex is completed, performances will be held at Mashpee Commons, in the Mashpee High School auditorium, or at other local venues.

The 90-member **Cape Symphony Orchestra** (☎ 508/362–1111 ⊕ www.capesymphony.org) comes to Mashpee in July for its annual Sounds of Summer Pops Concert (it also performs an August concert in Orleans). The performance takes place at the Mashpee Commons.

Sports & the Outdoors

BEACHES   **Attaquin Park Beach** (✉ End of Lake Ave. off Rte. 130, near Great Neck Rd. N) is a pretty, sandy place, with a spectacular view of the interconnecting Mashpee and Wakeby ponds, the Cape's largest freshwater expanse. It's popular for swimming, fishing, and boating, but resident parking stickers are required in season.

South Cape Beach is a 2½-mi-long state and town beach on warm Nantucket and Vineyard sounds, accessible via Great Neck Road south from the Mashpee rotary. You can walk to get a bit of privacy on this beach, which is wide, sandy, and pebbly in parts, with low dunes and marshland. The only services are portable toilets, although lifeguards are on duty in season. A hiking trail loops through marsh areas and ponds, linking it to the Waquoit Bay National Estuarine Research Reserve. Resident parking stickers are required for the town beach parking section, but anybody may park at the state beach section for $7 per day late May through early September (it's free off-season).

GOLF   **The Country Club at New Seabury** (✉ Shore Dr., New Seabury ☎ 508/477–9111) has a superior 18-hole, par-72 championship layout on the water as well as an 18-hole, par-70 course. Both are open to the public October through May, depending on availability; reservations two days in advance are recommended, and proper attire is required.

HIKING &   The 4 mi of walking trails at 135-acre **Lowell Holly Reservation** (✉ S. Sand-
WALKING   wich Rd. off Rte. 130 ☎ 508/679–2115 ⊕ www.thetrustees.org), administered by the Trustees of Reservations, wind through American beeches, hollies, white pines, and rhododendrons on a peninsula between Mashpee and Wakeby ponds. The reservation has picnic tables and a little swimming beach. A small free parking area is open year-round, and an additional parking lot opens from late May to early September ($6).

In summer, the **Mashpee Conservation Commission** (☎ 508/539–1400 Ext. 540 for schedules) has information about free naturalist-led guided walks of Mashpee's woods and conservation areas. Family nature walks, animal scavenger hunts, and "pond scoops" to explore aquatic life are a few of the activities offered for kids and their parents; sunrise walks on South Cape Beach and natural history tours of the Lowell Holly Reservation are also on the program.

Shopping

Mashpee Commons (✉ Junction of Rtes. 28 and 151 ☎ 508/477–5400 ⊕ www.mashpeecommons.com) has about 80 mostly upscale stores, including restaurants, art galleries, and a mix of local boutiques and national chains, in an attractive village square. There's also a multiscreen movie theater and free outdoor entertainment in summer. Some of the more unique shops include **M. Brann & Co.** (☎ 508/477–0299), a creative home-and-gift shop that carries everything from funky refrigerator magnets and unusual candlesticks to handcrafted glassware, one-of-a-kind lamps, mirrors, and furniture, with many works by New England artists; **Soft As A Grape** (☎ 508/477–5331), an elegant but sporty men's and women's clothier with several branches around the Cape; and **Cape Cod Toys** (☎ 508/477–2221), crammed full of anything the children might possibly need, including beach toys, board games, and science projects.

Popponesset Marketplace (⊠ Off Great Neck Rd. S, New Seabury, 2½ mi south of Rte. 28 from Mashpee rotary ☎ 508/477–9111 ⊕ www.popponessetmarketplace.com), open from late spring to early fall, has 20 shops (boutique clothing, home furnishings), eating places (a raw bar, pizza, ribs, Ben & Jerry's), miniature golf, and weekend entertainment (bands, fashion or puppet shows, sing-alongs).

THE UPPER CAPE ESSENTIALS

To research prices, get advice from other travelers, and book travel arrangements, visit ⊕ www.fodors.com.

Transportation

BY BOAT & FERRY
Year-round ferries to Martha's Vineyard leave from Woods Hole. Seasonal Vineyard ferries leave from Falmouth. For details ⇨ Boat and Ferry Travel *in* Smart Travel Tips A to Z in the back of this book.

BY BUS
Peter Pan Bonanza offers direct bus service to Bourne, Falmouth, and the Woods Hole steamship terminal from Boston's Logan Airport, downtown Boston, Providence (Rhode Island), Fall River, and New Bedford, as well as connecting service from New York, Connecticut, and Providence's T. F. Green Airport. Some of the buses from Boston also make stops in Wareham. Bonanza runs a service between Bourne, Falmouth, and Woods Hole year-round. Plymouth & Brockton Street Railway provides bus service to Provincetown from downtown Boston and Logan Airport, with stops en route. The Logan Direct airport express service bypasses downtown Boston and stops in Plymouth, Sagamore, Barnstable, and Hyannis.

The Cape Cod Regional Transit Authority's SeaLine, H2O Line, Barnstable Villager, and Hyannis Villager buses travel between the Upper and Lower Cape. Service is not frequent—buses depart once every hour or two, depending on the time of day—so check the schedule before you set out. To travel between Falmouth and Woods Hole, the WHOOSH trolley, also run by the Cape Cod Regional Transit Authority, is convenient. For more information, *see* Bus Travel *in* Smart Travel Tips A to Z in the back of this book.

🚌 Bus Depots **Bonanza Bus Terminals** ⊠ South Station Bus Terminal, 700 Atlantic Ave., Boston ☎ 617/720–4110 ⊠ Depot Ave., Falmouth ☎ 508/548–7588 ⊠ Steamship Authority Piers, Woods Hole ☎ 508/548–5011. **Hyannis Transportation Center** ⊠ 215

Iyannough Rd., Hyannis ☎ 508/775-8504. **Plymouth & Brockton Street Railway Terminals** ✉ South Station Bus Terminal, 700 Atlantic Ave., Boston ☎ 508/746-0378. 🚌 Bus Lines **Bonanza Bus Lines** ☎ 888/751-8800 ⊕ www.bonanzabus.com. **Cape Cod Regional Transit Authority** ☎ 800/352-7155 ⊕ www.capecodtransit.org. **Plymouth & Brockton Street Railway** ☎ 508/746-0378 ⊕ www.p-b.com.

BY TAXI
🚖 Taxi Company **All Village Taxi** ✉ Falmouth ☎ 508/540-7200.

Contacts & Resources

CONDO & HOUSE RENTALS

Donahue Real Estate lists both apartments and houses for rent in the Falmouth area. Real Estate Associates lists properties (some pricey) ranging from beach cottages to waterfront estates, with a focus on more expensive houses. It covers Falmouth, Bourne, and Mashpee, on the Upper Cape.

🏠 Local Agents **Donahue Real Estate** ✉ Falmouth ☎ 508/548-5412 ⊕ www.falmouthhomes.com. **Real Estate Associates** ✉ Falmouth, Mashpee, Sandwich ☎ 508/540-1500 📠 508/563-6943 ⊕ www.realestateassc.com.

VISITOR INFORMATION

The year-round visitor information center on Route 25, in a rest area about 3 mi west of the Bourne Bridge, is open daily 9–5 (with extended hours 8 AM–10 PM from late May to mid-October). The Cape Cod Canal Region, which includes Sandwich, Bourne, and Wareham, has information centers at the Sagamore rotary, at a train depot in Buzzards Bay, and on Route 130 in Sandwich (near the intersection with U.S. 6). 🏛 Tourist Information **Cape Cod Canal Region Chamber of Commerce** ✉ 70 Main St., Buzzards Bay 02532 ☎ 508/759-6000 ⊕ www.capecodcanalchamber.org. **Falmouth Chamber of Commerce** ✉ 20 Academy La., Falmouth 02541 ☎ 508/548-8500 or 800/526-8532 ⊕ www.falmouthchamber.com. **Mashpee Chamber of Commerce** ✉ N. Market St., Mashpee Commons [Rte. 151], 02649 ☎ 508/477-0792, 800/423-6274 outside Massachusetts ⊕ www.mashpeechamber.com.

The Mid Cape

WORD OF MOUTH

"By staying in the Mid-Cape area, you can get any-where in an hour or less."

—sherry

"My husband and I rode the Cape Cod Trail from the start in Dennis to the National Seashore non-stop—lots of fun, and I believe you could stop for ice cream and snacks every two miles if you wanted!"

—JoyInVirginia

"My personal favorite beach is Chapin in Dennis. It's on the Bay side, so the water is cooler, but re-freshing on a hot day. The sandbars are gorgeous, especially during a sunset . . .."

—klw25

Updated by
Laura V. Scheel

MORE A COLLOQUIALISM than a proper name, the designation "Mid Cape" refers to central Cape Cod, the most heavily populated—and touristed—part of the peninsula. To the north lies tranquil Cape Cod Bay, laced with wide beaches, inlets, creeks, and marshes. The tides on the bay are dramatic—at dead low some beaches double in size as tidal flats stretch out for hundreds to thousands of feet. The calmer waters on the bay side make these beaches particularly suitable for kids, and when the tide is out, they can explore and play in the tidal pools left behind.

The main thoroughfare through the north side of the Mid Cape is Route 6A, a scenic section that dates from 1684, making it one of the first major roads constructed on Cape Cod. Alternately called Old King's Highway, Main Street, and Hallet Street, the road winds through the villages of West Barnstable, Barnstable, Cummaquid, Yarmouth Port, and Dennis, with north-side harbors and beaches just a short drive from village centers. A residential and commercial mix, Route 6A is lined with antique captains' mansions and farmhouses that are now private homes, bed-and-breakfasts, art galleries, restaurants, and antiques shops. Protected by a historical society, colors and architecture along the road are kept to the standards set by early settlers.

On the south side of the Mid Cape, sunbathers flock to the expansive beaches along Nantucket Sound. The main thoroughfare here is the busy and overdeveloped Route 28, which passes through Centerville, Osterville, Hyannis, West and South Yarmouth, and Dennisport. This stretch is particularly unpleasant and tawdry between West Yarmouth and Dennisport, where it's lined with strip motels, clam shacks, miniature-golf courses, ice-cream parlors, and tacky T-shirt outlets. A draw for families in its 1960s heyday, the area hasn't seen much renovation since. However, if you stray from the congestion of Route 28, the serenity of soft sand and quiet back roads awaits. It's hard to get too lost on the Cape—you can't go far off the main roads without hitting water—so poking around is worth the risk.

Between Routes 6A and 28 is the "mid" of the Mid Cape, a mostly residential area with some historic sections, a few quiet freshwater ponds, and the commercial sections of Hyannis. Nearby are tony Osterville and Hyannis Port, a well-groomed enclave and site of the Kennedy compound.

Exploring the Mid Cape

The Mid Cape includes the towns of Barnstable, Yarmouth, and Dennis, each divided into smaller townships and villages. The town of Barnstable, for example, consists of Barnstable Village, West Barnstable, Cotuit, Marstons Mills, Osterville, Centerville, and Hyannis, with the smaller quasi villages (distinguished by their separate postal codes) of Craigville, Cummaquid, Hyannis Port, West Hyannis Port, and Wianno. Yarmouth contains Yarmouth Port, along the north shore, and the mid- and south villages of West Yarmouth and South Yarmouth. The town of Dennis's villages are easy to remember: Dennis, West Dennis, South Dennis, East Dennis, and Dennisport. Route 6A winds along the north shore through tree-shaded scenic towns and village centers, and Route 28 dips south through some of the more overdeveloped parts of the Cape. Generally speaking, if you want to avoid malls, heavy traffic, and cheesy motels, stay away from Route 28 from Falmouth to Chatham.

About the Restaurants

The Mid Cape is chock-full of eateries, ranging from sedate, high-end haute cuisine houses such as Hyannis's Paddock, the Regatta of Cotuit, and Dennis's Red Pheasant to such family-friendly places as the Red Cottage in Dennis. Expect good fun and great eats at the area's dozens of clam shacks and other super-casual restaurants along Route 28 in Yarmouth and Dennis. If you simply want lots of choices, head to Barnstable and its villages, particularly Hyannis, where a stroll down Main Street will bring you to a dozen fine restaurants ranging from lunch joints to Thai, Italian, Cajun, and upscale American dining establishments.

About the Hotels

On the northern (bay) side, Route 6A from Barnstable to Dennis has dozens of B&Bs, many in the elegant former homes of sea captains. In contrast, Route 28 on the south side has row after row of lodgings, from tacky roadside motels to medium-range family hotels, with larger seaside resorts along the side roads on Nantucket Sound. Main Street, Hyannis, is lined with motels, and several inns and B&Bs perch on side streets leading to Hyannis Harbor and Lewis Bay.

WHAT IT COSTS					
	$$$$	$$$	$$	$	¢
RESTAURANTS	over $30	$22–$30	$16–$22	$10–$16	under $10
HOTELS	over $260	$200–$260	$140–$200	$90–$140	under $90

Restaurant prices are per person for a main course at dinner. Hotel prices are for a standard double room, excluding 6% sales tax (more in some counties) and 1%–4% tourist tax.

Timing

In summer the Mid Cape bustles with tourists. But from Columbus Day weekend through April, the area is a peaceful collection of towns and villages, with beaches (no fees) for strolling, trails for walking and biking, and a wealth of shopping and entertainment. Although the year-round population has ballooned in the last decade, the off-season is still a laid-back and welcome time to catch the best of the Cape minus the crowds. Fall sees bursts of color in the easily accessed forests and marshes; winter brings a slower pace of life and a holiday spirit that locals love to celebrate with Christmas strolls featuring tours of shops, B&Bs, and old homes. Spring is also quiet, as the Mid Cape awakens to blooming trees, warmer days, reopened B&Bs, newly landscaped golf courses, and flower festivals. Boats come out of hibernation—Hyannis Whale Watcher Cruises, for instance, starts its program in May.

Barnstable

Barnstable Village is 11 mi east of Sandwich, Hyannis is 11 mi east of Mashpee.

With nearly 50,000 year-round residents, Barnstable is the largest town on the Cape, extending from the bay to the sea and comprising several prominent villages, including Centerville, Cotuit, and Osterville. The community of Hyannis feels like its own distinct municipality, but is actually a village within Barnstable.

❶ Barnstable is also the second-oldest town on the Cape—it was founded in 1639, two years after Sandwich. You can sense its history in **Barnstable Village,** on and near Main Street (Route 6A), a lovely area of large old homes dominated by the Barnstable County Superior Courthouse. In the Village Hall is the Barnstable Comedy Club, one of the oldest community theater groups in the country. Just north of the village are the marshes and beaches of Cape Cod Bay, including beautiful Sandy Neck Beach, as well as busy Barnstable Harbor. The Cape Cod Conservatory of Music and Arts and Cape Cod Community College are also in the vicinity.

The **Olde Colonial Courthouse,** built in 1772 as the colony's second courthouse, is the home of **Tales of Cape Cod** (✉ 3018 Rte. 6A, Barnstable ☎ 508/362–8927). The historical society holds a weekly slide-illustrated lecture on Tuesday in July and August, plus special events in the shoulder seasons: in May there's a lecture during Maritime Week, and in June there's one during Heritage Week. In September, a "mystery" bus trip takes visitors to areas of historic interest. While you're here, take a peek across the street at the old-fashioned English gardens at **St. Mary's Episcopal Church.**

The **Sturgis Library,** established in 1863, is in a 1644 building listed on the National Register of Historic Places. Its holdings date from the 17th century and include hundreds of maps and land charts, the definitive collection of Cape Cod genealogical material, and an extensive maritime history collection. ✉ *3090 Rte. 6A, Barnstable* ☎ *508/362–6636* ⊕ *www.sturgislibrary.org* ⊗ *Mon., Wed., Thurs., and Fri. 10–5, Tues. 1–8, Sat. 10–4.*

Opened in 2005 and continually evolving and expanding is the **Coast Guard Heritage Museum,** housed in the old Trayser building. The structure itself is on the National Register of Historic Places, and the museum is filled with all things related to this seafaring branch of the U.S. military. Artifacts and displays also highlight early lifesaving and lighthouse histories, and a small shop sells related books and items. Elsewhere on the grounds is the circa 1690 jail, with two cells bearing former inmates' graffiti; the building is undergoing extensive renovations and may not be open for the 2007 season. Call for the ongoing schedule of lectures and events. ✉ *3353 Rte. 6A, Barnstable* ☎ *508/ 362–8521* 🎟 *$3* ⊗ *Mid-May–Nov., Tues.–Sat. 10–3.*

If you're interested in Cape history, the **Nickerson Memorial Room** at Cape Cod Community College has the largest collection of Cape Cod infor-

PLEASURES & PASTIMES

BEACHES

Beach lovers will find numerous Shangri-Las throughout the Mid Cape. Sandy Neck, a peninsular strip of land that stretches across the north side of Barnstable Harbor, is one of the Top 10 beaches on Cape Cod, perfect for those who like gentle surf and long shoreline walks. Also on the north side of the Mid Cape, Dennis's Corporation Beach and Mayflower Beach are great places for kids, with wide tidal flats, snack huts, and restrooms. South-side beaches, on Nantucket Sound, include busy Craigville Beach in Centerville, popular with college students on break, and Kalmus Park Beach in Hyannis, with conditions that attract world-class windsurfers. Yarmouth's best beaches lie along its Nantucket Sound side and include Seagull Beach and Parker's River Beach.

In and among Mid Cape towns are a number of freshwater kettle ponds, created by receding glaciers eons ago. Pond beaches are usually not as crowded as ocean beaches and have plenty of appeal for those who like cooling off in gentle water without the salt and sand. In Yarmouth Port, Dennis Pond attracts families to its shallow swimming area. Dennis's Scargo Lake has two public beaches, and Hathaway's Pond in Barnstable has a nice beach and restrooms.

BICYCLING

Bike enthusiasts are well served on the Mid Cape: the scenic 25-mi Cape Cod Rail Trail begins in South Dennis, follows the paved right-of-way of the old Penn Central Railroad, and ends in South Wellfleet. For more information on the Cape Cod Rail Trail ⇨ Sports & the Outdoors *and* Riding the Rail Trail.

NIGHTLIFE & THE ARTS

Since you can pass an art gallery almost every minute on the drive along Route 6A between Barnstable and Dennis, you should stop in at some of these places, such as Cummaquid Fine Arts, which carries original contemporary art that's a decided improvement over the ubiquitous paintings of rowboats on beaches. Other gallery centers are on Main Street in both Hyannis and Osterville.

The Mid Cape is a hub for summertime entertainment. The Cape Cod Melody Tent, in Hyannis, has attracted internationally well-known performers, such as comedians Bill Cosby and George Carlin and singers Jimmy Cliff and Lyle Lovett. The Melody Tent—which really *is* a tent, albeit a large and comfortable one with a revolving stage—also produces children's matinee theater, with regular summer shows like *Sleeping Beauty* and *The Frog Prince*. Your theater needs can also be sated at the Cape Playhouse in Dennis, the country's oldest summer repertory theaters. Big stars who have cut their acting teeth here include Henry Fonda, Gregory Peck, and Bette Davis. The Cape Playhouse also offers children's theater during the season. The Barnstable Comedy Club on Route 6A in Barnstable Village presents drama, sketches, and—of course—comedic works throughout the summer.

Nightlife is abundant in the Mid Cape, from bistros and bars that

PLEASURES & PASTIMES

have regular entertainment—think Hyannis's Roadhouse Café for jazz—to hip dance clubs such as Harry's Blues Bar in Hyannis for heart-and-soul beats. Special events such as the Boston Pops Esplanade Orchestra's Pops by the Sea concert, held on the Hyannis Village Green in August, are listed in local newspapers weekly. Check out listings in the *Register,* the *Barnstable Patriot,* and the Tuesday and Friday editions of the *Cape Codder,* as well as the pullout section "Cape Week" in the Friday edition of the *Cape Cod Times.* You can pick up any of these publications at local supermarkets and convenience stores.

SPORTS & THE OUTDOORS
Numerous fishing and tour boats depart Hyannis Harbor, Barnstable Harbor, and Dennis's Sesuit Harbor for trips ranging from deep-sea fishing excursions to harbor fishing, a favorite with the kids. Barnstable Harbor is also the launch point for Hyannis Whale Watcher Cruises, which operates from spring through early fall. Canoeing and sea kayaking are excellent around the bay's marshy inlets, and windsurfing is popular at Hyannis's Kalmus Park Beach. Dennis's Swan River is great for kayaking and canoeing, and the Bass River, a border separating Yarmouth and Dennis, has river sightseeing excursions on a small boat, as well as fishing and, if you've got the permit, clamming.

Yarmouth and Dennis have conservation-land walking trails, including a Dennis trail set up for hikers with vision impairments.

SHOPPING
Throughout the villages and towns of the Mid Cape—particularly along Route 6A and the main streets of Hyannis, Centerville, Osterville, and Dennisport—are numerous boutiques, crafts shops, bookstores, antiques centers, candy shops (saltwater taffy, yes, but also exquisite chocolates and homemade fudge), and galleries. In general, look to the smaller towns and villages for specialty crafts items such as Nantucket baskets, wicker furniture, and bird-watching esoterica. The huge Cape Cod Mall, between routes 132 and 28 in Hyannis, has clothing boutiques such as Ann Taylor Loft, Gap, and Abercrombie & Fitch; jewelry stores; specialty shops; and anchor stores Macy's and Sears. Everyone is wild about Christmas Tree Shops, a local chain with stores in Yarmouth Port, West Yarmouth, West Dennis, and Hyannis that sells all sorts of amusing things at discount prices, including lava lamps, lanai furniture, candles, and cookies.

mation, including books, records, ships' logs, oral-history tapes, photographs, and films. It also has materials on the neighboring islands of Martha's Vineyard and Nantucket. ✉ *2240 Iyanough Rd., off Rte. 132, West Barnstable* ☎ *508/362–2131 Ext. 4445* ⊕ *www.capecod.mass. edu* ⊙ *Mon., Wed., and Fri. 8:30–4:30.*

❷ About 7 mi southwest of Barnstable Village, **Centerville** was once a busy seafaring village, its history evident in the 50 or so shipbuilders' and sea captains' houses along its quiet, tree-shaded streets. Offering the pleasures of sheltered ocean beaches on Nantucket Sound, such as **Craigville Beach,** and of freshwater swimming in Lake Wequaquet, it has been a popular vacation area since the mid-19th century. Shoot Flying Hill Road, named by Native Americans, is the highest point of land on the Cape, with panoramic views of Plymouth and Provincetown to the north and Falmouth and Hyannis to the south.

In a 19th-century house, the **Centerville Historical Society Museum** has furnished period rooms, Sandwich glass, miniature carvings of birds by Anthony Elmer Crowell, models of ships, marine artifacts, military uniforms and artifacts, antique tools, perfume bottles (dating from 1760 to 1920), historic costumes and quilts, and a research library. Each summer there are special costume exhibits or other shows. ✉ *513 Main St., Centerville* ☎ *508/775–0331* ⊕ *www.centervillehistoricalmuseum.org* 🎫 *$4* ⊙ *June–Oct., Wed.–Sat. noon–5.*

The **1856 Country Store** (✉ 555 Main St., Centerville ☎ 508/775–1856 or 888/750–1856 ⊕ www.1856countrystore.com) still sells penny candy, except that these days each candy costs at least 25 pennies. The store also carries newspapers, coffee, crafts, jams, and all kinds of gadgets and toys. You can sip your coffee—and take a political stance—by choosing a wooden bench out front, one is marked DEMOCRAT, and the other REPUBLICAN.

NEED A BREAK? Sample a variety of creamy homemade flavors at **Four Seas Ice Cream** (✉ 360 S. Main St., Centerville ☎ 508/775–1394 ⊕ www.fourseasicecream.com), a tradition for generations of summer visitors. The kitchen also turns out short-order lunch and dinner fare. It's open from late May to mid-September until 10:30 PM.

The **Centerville Library** (✉ 585 Main St., Centerville ☎ 508/790–6220 ⊕ www.centervillelibrary.org) has a 42-volume noncirculating set of transcripts of the Nuremberg Trials. The library is open Monday and Wednesday 10–5; Tuesday and Thursday 10–7; Friday 10–3; and Saturday 10–2; it's closed on Sunday.

❸ From Centerville, head west about 7 mi to reach **Cotuit,** a charming little community formed around seven homesteads belonging to the family of 18th-century trader Winslow Crocker. Much of the town lies along and just south of Route 28, west of Osterville and east of Mashpee, and its center is not much more than a crossroads with a post office, an old-time coffee shop, a pizza parlor, and a general store, which all seem unchanged since the 1940s. Large waterfront estates line sections of Main Street and Ocean View Drive, where small coves hide the

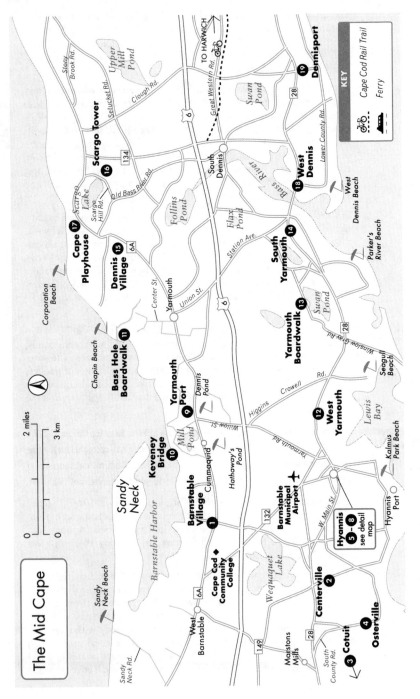

uncrowded Loop Beach and Ropes Beach. It's best to get to the beaches by bike, since traffic is light and beach parking is for residents only.

The **Cahoon Museum of American Art** is in one of the old Crocker family buildings, a 1775 Georgian colonial farmhouse that was once a tavern and an overnight way station for travelers on the Hyannis–Sandwich stagecoach line. Displays include selections from the permanent collection of American primitive paintings by Ralph and Martha Cahoon, along with other 19th- and early-20th-century artists. Special exhibitions, classes, talks, and demonstrations are held throughout the summer. ⊠ *4676 Rte. 28, Cotuit* ☎ *508/428–7581* ⊕ *www.cahoonmuseum. org* ⊡ *$4* ⊗ *Feb.–Dec., Tues.–Sat. 10–4.*

The first motor-driven fire-fighting apparatus on Cape Cod, a 1916 Model T chemical fire engine, is in the **Santuit-Cotuit Historical Society Museum,** behind the **Samuel Dottridge Homestead,** which itself dates from the early 1800s. ⊠ *1148 Main St., Cotuit* ☎ *508/428–0461* ⊡ *Free* ⊗ *Mid-June–mid-Oct., Thurs.–Sun. 2:30–5.*

Cotuit Library (⊠ 871 Main St., Cotuit ☎ 508/428–8141 ⊕ www.library. cotuit.ma.us) has a noncirculating set of luxurious leather-bound classics. Library hours are 1:30–5:30 and 7–8:30 Monday; 9:30–5:30 Tuesday and Friday; 1:30–5:30 Wednesday; 9:30–5:30 and 7–8:30 Thursday; and 10–4 Saturday. The library is closed Sunday.

❹ A wealthy Barnstable enclave 5 mi east of Cotuit, **Osterville** is lined with elegant waterfront houses, some of which are large "cottages" built in the 19th century when the area became popular with the monied set. You'll find that most beaches in the village, including the impressive **Dowses Beach,** are restricted to residents-only parking. Despite its haute homes, the village of Osterville retains the small-town charm that permeates the Cape; its Main Street and Wianno Avenue area has a collection of trendy boutiques and jewelry shops mixed with a library, a post office, and country stores. The village's festivals of Daff O'ville Day (late April) and Christmas Stroll (mid-December) are heavily attended.

The **Osterville Historical Society Museum,** in an 1824 sea captain's house, has antiques, dolls, and exhibits on Osterville's history. Two wooden-boat museums—each showcasing various sailing vessels—and the late 18th century Cammett House are also on the property. ⊠ *155 W. Bay Rd., Osterville* ☎ *508/428–5861* ⊡ *$3* ⊗ *June–Sept., Thurs.–Sun. 1:30–4:30.*

NEED A BREAK?

Gone Chocolate (⊠ 858 Main St. ☎ 508/420–0202) will tempt you with old-fashioned chocolate-pecan turtles, saltwater taffy, ice cream, and other confections.

❺–❽ **Hyannis** was named for the Native American Sachem Iyanno, who sold the area for £20 and two pairs of pants. Perhaps he would have sold it for far more had there been any indication that Hyannis would become known as the "home port of Cape Cod" or that the Kennedys would pitch so many tents here. Hyannis is effectively the transportation center of the Cape: it's near the airport, and ferries depart here for Nantucket and (in season) Martha's Vineyard. The busy roads feeding into the town are lined with the same big-box stores you'd find anywhere.

A bustling year-round hub of activity, Hyannis has the Cape's largest concentration of businesses, shops, malls, hotels and motels, restaurants, and entertainment venues. Main Street is lined with used-book and gift shops, jewelers, clothing stores, summer-wear and T-shirt shops, and ice-cream and candy stores. The street can have a somewhat forlorn, down-at-the-heels feeling, as the malls outside downtown have taken their toll on business, but there are plenty of good fun and fancy eateries here.

Perhaps best known for its association with the Kennedy clan, the Hyannis area was also a vacation site for President Ulysses S. Grant in 1874 and later for President Grover Cleveland. Today Hyannis is making an effort to preserve its historical connection with the sea. By 1840 more than 200 shipmasters had established homes in the Hyannis–Hyannis Port area. Aselton Park (at the intersection of South and Ocean streets) and the Village Green on Main Street are the sites of events celebrating this history, and Aselton Park marks the starting point of the scenic Walkway to the Sea, which extends to the dock area.

Three parallel streets run through the heart of town. Busy, shop-filled Main Street runs one-way from east to west; South Street runs from west to east; and North Street is open to two-way traffic. The airport rotary connects with heavily trafficked Routes 132 and 28 and with U.S. 6. Off Ocean Street and Sea Street lie several excellent beaches, including Kalmus Park Beach, renowned for its stiff winds and hordes of windsurfers, and the smaller Veterans Park Beach, next to the Kennedy Memorial.

⑤ In Main Street's Old Town Hall, the **John F. Kennedy Hyannis Museum** explores JFK's Cape years (1934–63) through enlarged and annotated photographs culled from the archives of the JFK Library near Boston, as well as a seven-minute video narrated by Walter Cronkite. The gift shop sells mugs, T-shirts, and presidential memorabilia. ⊠ *397 Main St., Downtown Hyannis* ☎ *508/790–3077* ⊕ *www.jfkhyannismuseum.org* ⊡ *$5* ⊙ *Mid-Apr.–Oct., Mon.–Sat. 9–5, Sun. noon–5; Nov.–early Dec. and mid-Feb.–mid-Apr., Thurs.–Sat. 10–4, Sun. noon–4. Closed Jan.*

⑥ The **St. Francis Xavier Church** (⊠ 347 South St., Downtown Hyannis ☎ 508/771–7200 ⊕ www.sfxp.org) is where Rose Kennedy and her family worshipped during their summers on the Cape; the pew that John F. Kennedy used regularly is marked with a plaque.

NEED A BREAK?

In an unlikely spot amid several industrial buildings near the airport, **Pain D'Avignon** (⊠ 192 Airport Rd. ☎ 508/778–8588 ⊕ www.french-bread.com) is nevertheless worth seeking out, especially if you're planning a picnic (although you can dine here at one of the few stainless-steel tables and chairs on a small patio). This quirky old-world-style bakery produces fine artisan breads that end up at some of the finest restaurants and gourmet shops in Boston. Drop in for delectable raisin-pecan or calamata-olive breads, cranberry bagels, chocolate-chip cookies, panini sandwiches, and fine gourmet supplies, such as cheeses, oils, and sauces.

John F.
Kennedy
Hyannis
Museum **5**

John F.
Kennedy
Memorial **7**

Kennedy
Compound **8**

St. Francis Xavier
Church **6**

Beyond the bustling docks where waterfront restaurants draw crowds and ferries, harbor-tour boats, and deep-sea fishing vessels come and go, the quiet esplanade by the **John F. Kennedy Memorial** (⊠ Off Ocean St. south of Channel Point, Hyannis Harbor) overlooks boat-filled Lewis Bay. JFK loved to sail these waters, and in 1966 the people of Barnstable erected a plaque and fountain pool here in his memory. Adjacent to the memorial is **Veterans Park,** with a beach, a tree-shaded picnic and barbecue area, and a playground.

Bismore Park (⊠ Off Ocean St., Hyannis Harbor) is part of a continuing and avid effort to revitalize downtown Hyannis and encourage folks to linger here and explore. In 2005 town planners populated the green with modest wood sheds—"shanties"—which artisans and artists rent and use as small workshops and stores. The project has proved so popular with both shoppers and sellers that an expansion is in the works.

Hyannis Port became a hot spot for Americans during the Kennedy presidency, when the **Kennedy Compound** became the summer White House. The days of hordes of Secret Service agents and swarms of tourists trampling down the bushes are gone, and the area is once again a community of quietly posh estates—though the Kennedy mystique is such that tourists still seek it out. The best way to get a glimpse of the compound is from the water on one of the many harbor tours or cruises.

Joseph P. and Rose Kennedy bought their house here—the largest one, closest to the water—in 1929 as a healthful place to summer with their soon-to-be-nine kids. (Son Ted bought the house before his mother's death in 1995.) Sons Jack and Bobby bought neighboring houses in the 1950s. Jack's is the one at the corner of Scudder and Irving, with the 6-foot-high stockade fence on two sides. Bobby's is next to it, with a white fieldstone chimney. Ted bought a home on Squaw Island, a private island connected to the area by a causeway at the end of Scudder Avenue. It now belongs to his ex-wife, Joan. Eunice (Kennedy) and Sargent Shriver have a house near Squaw Island, on Atlantic Avenue.

The compound is relatively self-sufficient in terms of entertainment: Rose Kennedy's former abode (with 14 rooms and nine baths) has a movie theater, a private beach, a boat dock, a swimming pool, a tennis court, and a sports field that was the scene of the famous Kennedy touch-football matches. Maria Shriver, Caroline Kennedy Schlossberg, and other family members have had their wedding receptions here. In the summer of 1999 family members waited at the compound, with local and international media lining the streets, for confirmation of John F. Kennedy Jr.'s death in a plane crash off Martha's Vineyard. He and his wife, Carolyn Bessette Kennedy, were flying her sister, Lauren Bessette, to the Vineyard before continuing on to a cousin's wedding in Hyannis; all three were killed.

OFF THE BEATEN PATH

CAPE COD POTATO CHIPS FACTORY – There's a standing invitation on the back of the bag: come for a free tour of the factory and get free samples of the crunchy all-natural chips hand-cooked in kettles in small batches. ⊠ *Independence Dr. (opposite Cape Cod Mall) to Breed's Hill Rd., off Rte. 132* ☎ *508/775–3358* ⊕ *www.capecodchips.com* ☉ *Weekdays 9–5.*

Hyannis Public Library (⊠ 401 Main St., Downtown Hyannis ☎ 508/775–2280) has a case full of books on JFK. Summer library hours are 11–5 Monday, Thursday, and Friday, and 11–8 Tuesday and Wednesday. The library is closed weekends in summer (Sunday and Monday in winter).

☾ Perfect for a rainy day, **Smith Family Amusement** is replete with bowling lanes, video-game rooms, and that old seaside favorite, Skee-ball. ⊠ *441 Main St., Downtown Hyannis* ☎ *508/775–3411* ☉ *Daily; hrs vary.*

Where to Stay & Eat

BARNSTABLE
$$–$$$

✗ **Dolphin Restaurant.** For the scoop on local politics, eavesdrop at the Dolphin. A popular spot among local political figures, for decades this has been the place in town where opinions clash and deals are cut. The dark, inviting interior has a colonial feel. Lunch favorites include the shrimp-and-crab melt, rib-eye steak, and fish-and-chips. Dinner consists of a straightforward, well-prepared roster of traditional steaks, chops, and seafood grills and sautés. The small but welcoming bar is a good spot to chow down if you're dining solo. ⊠ *3250 Rte. 6A* ☎ *508/362–6610* ⊕ *www.thedolphinrestaurant.com* ▤ AE, MC, V ☉ *No lunch Sun.*

The New Face of Hyannis

MORE THAN ONE MILLION PEOPLE travel to Hyannis each year—but many are merely passing *through* the town on their way to its ferry docks and boats to the outlying islands. For decades, townsfolk wished that these travelers would spend a little bit of time—and money—in Hyannis, but there wasn't much to entice them to stay.

But today, changes are afoot. In a move to become more family-friendly, sophisticated, and appealing, Hyannis has been revitalizing its downtown and waterfront areas. One pleasant improvement is the "Walkway to the Sea," completed in 2006. This wave-patterned brick path winds from Main Street at the Village Green all the way down to Bismore Park at Hyannis Harbor. Along the way are colorful art installations of lobster buoys, complete with educational

information about the fishing industry. The Village Green itself is now host to a weekly Farmers' Market, free movie showings, and band concerts in the summer.

As part of the "Harbor Your Arts" initiative, a series of wood "shanties" now populate Aselton Park along the Walkway to the Sea. Juried artists and artisans rent the sheds as both work space and selling arenas for their products. A seasonal stage, where free musical and theatrical performances will be held in summer, opened in 2006.

The entire downtown corridor is abuzz with building restorations, improvements, expansions, creative landscaping, new sidewalks, and spruced-up storefronts. You may just want to linger before catching your ferry.

$–$$$ ✕ **Barnstable Tavern & Grille.** This handsome old building right in the village center, across from the courthouse and Barnstable Comedy Club, holds both a formal restaurant and a more relaxed tavern. Fresh seafood dishes and the Tavern Keeper's Special (a medley of seafood in a casserole) are local favorites. Lighter lunch fare includes burgers, salads, and sandwiches. Look for live music on the patio Friday night. ⊠ *3176 Rte. 6A* ☎ *508/362–2355* ▭ *AE, MC, V.*

★ **¢–$** ✕ **Osterville Fish Too.** This combination seafood market and lunch place sits right on Barnstable Harbor at Millway Marina, giving it access to the freshest seafood around. It's tiny, with a fistful of outside picnic tables on a wooden deck and limited parking, but the fried clams and fish sandwiches are worth the inevitable wait. Arrive hungry and try the fat onion rings or the prodigious seafood platters (piled high with sole, shrimp, scallops, and clams). ⊠ *275 Mill Way* ☎ *508/362–2295* ▭ *MC, V* ☉ *Closed Oct.–Mar.*

¢ ✕ **Whistleberries.** Most people settle for takeout from this tiny sandwich shop, but the lucky few who manage to grab one of the three counter spots or two tables are in for an olfactory treat. Breakfast options include fresh muffins; "scrambled" eggs (they're actually steamed by the cappuccino machine); bagels; or burrito sandwiches stuffed with cheese, bacon, veggies, rice, beans, and sour cream. For lunch, try a wrap—there are many tempting choices, from barbecued chicken to Mediterranean—red pepper, hummus, tabbouleh, tomato, onion, and feta cheese folded up in a spinach tortilla. ⊠ *3261 Rte. 6A* ☎ *508/362–6717* 🖃 *No credit cards* ◎ *Closed Sun. No dinner.*

★ **$$–$$$** 🏨 **Acworth Inn.** This 1860 house 1 mi east of Barnstable Village has four large rooms and a spacious two-room suite. Rooms are decorated with soft pastels, lacy designer linens, and tasteful hand-painted furniture. The suite, with modern furnishings, also has a fireplace, whirlpool tub, TV–VCR, and refrigerator. Breakfast is family-style and includes granola, fresh muffins or homemade coffee cake, fruit, yogurt, and an entrée that might use herbs from the inn's gardens. Although the inn is not designed for small children, you can inquire about bringing older kids. ⊠ *4352 Rte. 6A* ✑ *Box 256, Cummaquid 02637* ☎ *508/362–3330 or 800/362–6363* 🖷 *508/375–0304* ⊕ *www.acworthinn.com* ☜ *4 rooms, 1 suite* ♿ *Some in-room hot tubs, some refrigerators, cable TV, some in-room VCRs; no room phones, no TV in some rooms, no kids under 12, no smoking* 🖃 *AE, D, MC, V* ⦿ *BP.*

$$–$$$ 🏨 **Ashley Manor.** Set behind hedges and a wide lawn, this B&B is a short walk from the village center. The 1699 inn has preserved its antique wide-board floors and has open-hearth fireplaces (one with a beehive oven) in the living room, the dining room, and the keeping room. The rooms are toasty, too—all but one have working fireplaces, and the suites have whirlpool tubs. Antique and country furnishings, Oriental rugs, and glimmers of brass and crystal create an elegant feel. Breakfast is served on the backyard terrace or in the formal dining room. Room TVs and phones are available on request. ⊠ *3660 Rte. 6A, Box 856, 02630* ☎ *508/362–8044 or 888/535–2246* 🖷 *508/362–9927* ⊕ *www.ashleymanor.net* ☜ *2 rooms, 4 suites* ♿ *Some in-room hot tubs, in-room data ports, tennis court, bicycles; no kids under 14, no smoking* 🖃 *D, MC, V* ⦿ *BP.*

★ **$$** 🏨 **Beechwood Inn.** Debbie and Ken Traugot's yellow-and-pale-green 1853 Queen Anne house has gingerbread trim and is wrapped by a wide porch with wicker furniture and a glider swing. Although the parlor is pure mahogany-and-red-velvet Victorian, guest rooms (all with queen- or king-size beds) have antiques in lighter Victorian styles; several have fireplaces, and one has a bay view. Bathrooms have pedestal sinks and antique lighting fixtures. Breakfast is served in the dining room, which has a pressed-tin ceiling, a fireplace, and lace-covered tables. Afternoon tea and homemade snacks are also available. ⊠ *2839 Rte. 6A, 02630* ☎ *508/362–6618 or 800/609–6618* 🖷 *508/362–0298* ⊕ *www. beechwoodinn.com* ☜ *6 rooms* ♿ *Refrigerators, cable TV, bicycles; no room phones, no TV in some rooms, no kids under 12, no smoking* 🖃 *AE, D, MC, V* ⦿ *BP.*

★ **$$** 🏨 **The Highpointe Inn.** Debbie and Rich Howard's intimate haven is nestled high on a hill overlooking dunes, the Great Salt Marsh, and the Bay at Sandy Neck. Although it's just minutes from historic Route 6A, the light and airy B&B transports you to a dreamlike getaway, offering casual luxury at its best. Each of the inn's three rooms inspire serenity with comforting colors, decor, and magical views. Breakfast includes Rich's famed French toast and Debbie's homemade goodies. ⊠ *70 High St.*

⏻ *Box 346, West Barnstable 02668* ☎ *508/362–4441 or 888/362–4441* 🖷 *508/362–4401* ⊕ *www.thehighpointeinn.com* ⇗ *3 rooms* ♿ *Wi-Fi, gym; no room phones, no room TVs, no kids under 12, no smoking* ▤ *AE, D, MC, V* �‖ *BP.*

$$ ▦ **Honeysuckle Hill.** Innkeepers Freddy and Ruth Riley provide plenty of little touches here: a guest fridge stocked with beverages, beach chairs with umbrellas (perfect for nearby Sandy Neck Beach), and an always-full cookie jar. The airy, country-style guest rooms in this 1810 Queen Anne–style cottage have lots of white wicker, featherbeds, checked curtains, and pastel-painted floors. The spacious second-floor Wisteria Room overlooking the lush yard is a particularly comfortable retreat, and the screened-in porch is a peaceful place to sip early-morning coffee. ✉ *591 Rte. 6A, West Barnstable 02668* ☎ *508/362–8418 or 866/444–5522* 🖷 *508/362–8386* ⊕ *www.honeysucklehill.com* ⇗ *4 rooms, 1 suite* ♿ *Cable TV, some in-room VCRs; no room phones, no TV in some rooms, no kids under 12, no smoking* ▤ *AE, D, MC, V* �‖ *BP.*

$$ ▦ **Lamb and Lion Inn.** Lamb and Lion occupies a 1740 farmhouse and barn, as well as several additions, with rooms and suites gathered around a courtyard and large swimming pool. Inside, some rooms are summery, with blue-and-white-stripe wallpaper and wicker chairs, while others are more staid, furnished with antiques and dark woods. The Innkeeper's Pride Suite has a fireplace and sunken tub that opens to a private deck; the rustic Barn-Stable, in the original barn, has three sleeping lofts that can accommodate six. Amenities include pickups and drop-offs from local ferries and the Barnstable Municipal Airport. A branch of Great Marsh Kayak Tours, which offers a range of boating excursions, is on the premises. ✉ *2504 Rte. 6A, Box 511, Barnstable 02630* ☎ *508/362–6823 or 800/909–6923* 🖷 *508/362–0227* ⊕ *www.lambandlion.com* ⇗ *4 rooms, 6 suites* ♿ *Some kitchens, cable TV, pool, hot tub, shop, airport shuttle, some pets allowed (fee)* ▤ *MC, V* �‖ *CP.*

CENTERVILLE, COTUIT & OSTERVILLE
$$$–$$$$ ✕ **Five Bays Bistro.** With its stylish feel and creative menu, this contemporary bistro wouldn't be out of place in Boston or Manhattan. Dishes such as Asian spring rolls or tuna with wasabi sauce draw inspiration from the East, whereas others—perhaps a linguine, duck, and artichoke appetizer or an entrée of seared halibut with shallot risotto—have a more Mediterranean flavor. If you wear black, you won't clash with the eclectic artwork on the bright yellow walls. ✉ *825 Main St., Osterville* ☎ *508/420–5559* ▤ *AE, D, MC, V* ⊗ *No lunch.*

$$$–$$$$
Fodor'sChoice ✕ **Regatta of Cotuit.** It's worth driving out of your way to this refined ★ restaurant in a handsomely restored cinnamon-hued stagecoach inn filled with wood, brass, and Oriental rugs. Chef Heather Allen turns out wonderfully inventive versions of classic regional American fare, such as foie gras and scallops with a port wine reduction and tropical-fruit chutney. The signature premium fillet of buffalo tenderloin is prepared differently each night, with seasonal starches and vegetables. The cozy taproom has its own bar menu, including globally influenced tapas (Cambodian spring rolls, Spanish-style duck empanadas) and colorful cocktails (prickly pear margaritas, apple martinis). ✉ *4631 Rte. 28, Cotuit* ☎ *508/428–5715* ⊕ *www.regattaofcotuit.com* ⇗ *Reservations essential* ▤ *AE, MC, V.*

$–$$ ✕ **Wimpy's.** No, this is not a fast-food hamburger joint—it's a Cape standby with an extensive menu that favors Italian food and fried fish, from chicken piccata to a seafood platter. Wimpy's loyal clientele fills a big family dining room, a sunny atrium, and a dark traditional tavern that has cozy booths and a fine old bar. Opt for the more inventive specials, such as tortilla-crusted salmon topped in a caper sauce, or try a simple prime rib (when available). You can get takeout here, too. ⊠ *752 Main St., Osterville* ☎ *508/428–6300, 508/428–3474 takeout* ⊟ *AE, DC, MC, V.*

★ ¢–$ ✕ **Sweet Tomatoes.** Don't be put off by the prosaic setting of this small pizza place (it's in a shopping center behind Wimpy's). Sweet Tomatoes serves absolutely tantalizing pizza made with whole wheat dough, plus a slew of calzones, panini sandwiches, grinders, and wraps, all with fresh, creative ingredients. Top picks among the pies include the Dirty Bomb, with shaved steak, portobello mushrooms, onions, peppers, mozzarella, and red sauce; and the tangy white three-cheese with mozzarella, ricotta, asiago, and garlic (try ordering it with anchovies for a little extra kick). The Mediterranean salad makes for a delicious starter. ⊠ *770 Main St., Osterville* ☎ *508/420–1717* ⊟ *MC, V.*

$–$$$ 🏨 **Tradewinds Inn.** This 6-acre property, overlooking the Atlantic Ocean and Lake Elizabeth, has large, family-friendly ocean-view rooms. There are also three efficiencies with fully equipped kitchenettes (refrigerator, stove, microwave, and cooking utensils), but skip the less attractive non-water-view rooms in the detached buildings. The furnishings are simple but well maintained, including whitewashed furniture and floral quilts. The wicker-festooned, knotty-pine-paneled lobby has a fireplace and a cocktail bar. A small sandy beach is down the path from the main lodge. ⊠ *780 Craigville Beach Rd., Centerville* ⊕ *Box 477, 02632* ☎ *508/775–0365 or 877/444–7966* ⊕ *www.twicapecod.com* 🛏 *28 rooms, 4 suites, 3 efficiencies* ⚴ *Some kitchenettes, cable TV, putting green, beach, lobby lounge; no smoking* ⊟ *AE, MC, V* ⊗ *Closed Nov.–Apr.* ¶⦿¶ *CP.*

$$ 🏨 **Josiah Sampson House.** Guest rooms in this stunning 1793 Federal-style home in Cotuit's tranquil village center have canopy beds, needlepoint rugs, antiques, and air-conditioning. Hannah's Room, the most spacious, has a queen-size four-poster bed, built-in window seats, and a massive working fireplace. Upstairs, the Sampson Room has an extra-large bathroom and a view of the backyard and handsome grounds. Tennis privileges ($8 for 1½ hours) are available at the Kings Grant Racquet Club next door. ⊠ *40 Old Kings Rd., off Main St., Cotuit* ⊕ *Box 226, 02635* ☎ *508/428–8383 or 877/574–6873* 🖷 *508/428–0116* ⊕ *www.josiahsampson.com* 🛏 *6 rooms* ⚴ *Outdoor hot tub, bicycles; no room phones, no room TVs, no kids under 10, no smoking* ⊟ *AE, MC, V* ¶⦿¶ *BP.*

$–$$ 🏨 **Centerville Corners Motor Lodge.** One of the few mid-Cape motels that's not on a traffic-choked, crassly developed road, this attractive redbrick and clapboard motor lodge is in the heart of peaceful Centerville Village, facing the wonderful Four Seas Ice Cream parlor. Although the rooms are dull and the furnishings are dated, you can't beat the location. Golf packages are available. ⊠ *1338 Craigville Beach Rd., Centerville* ⊕ *Box 507, 02632* ☎ *508/775–7223 or 800/242–1137* 🖷 *508/775–4147* ⊕ *www.centervillecorners.com* 🛏 *48 rooms* ⚴ *Some kitchenettes,*

Where to Stay & Eat in Hyannis

Restaurants ▼

Baxter's Fish N' Chips ...**1**

Brazilian Grill ...**9**

Fazio's Trattoria **2**

Grille 16 ......**4**

Harry's **10**

Misaki **12**

Naked Oyster ...**5**

The Paddock ..**11**

Roadhouse Café **8**

RööBar **7**

Sam Diego's **6**

Ying's **3**

Hotels ▼

Anchor-In **1**

Breakwaters **5**

Cape Cod Inn ...**2**

Cape Codder Resort **8**

Capt. Gosnold Village **4**

Comfort Inn Cape Cod **9**

Four Points by Sheraton Hyannis Resort **6**

Hyannis Inn Motel **3**

Simmons Homestead Inn ..**7**

KEY

❶ Restaurants

① Hotels

cable TV, Wi-Fi, indoor pool, sauna, some pets allowed (fee); no smok-ing ⊟ AE, MC, V ⊗ Closed Nov.–Apr. ⦿ BP.

HYANNIS ✕**Grille 16.** This lavish, clubby space—inside the dignified Asa Bearse
$$$–$$$$ House along the downtown shopping strip—caters to the see-and-be-seen crowd with live jazz, trendy cocktails, and big portions of creatively prepared American fare. You might kick things off with a sublime starter of Kobe beef carpaccio with roasted garlic aioli before moving on to pan-roasted wild Alaskan salmon with marinated tomatoes, Yukon potatoes, and aged balsamic vinegar and olive oil. Or test your capac-ity for huge portions with the 24-ounce prime porterhouse steak. Grille 16 is run by the same owners as the Naked Oyster, along with former NHL star Derek Sanderson. ✉ 415 Main St., Downtown Hyannis ☎ 508/778–0006 ⦿ www.grille16.com ⊟ AE, DC, MC, V ⊗ Closed Mon. No lunch.

★ $$–$$$$ ✕**The Paddock.** The Paddock is synonymous with tried-and-true formal dining on the Cape. Sumptuous upholstery in the main dining room and old-style wicker on the breezy summer porch create authentic Victorian ambience. The menu is traditional yet subtly innovative, and fresh in-gredients are combined in novel ways: baked thyme-and-cranberry en-crusted sole with a citrus beurre blanc, for example. The steak au poivre, with several varieties of crushed peppercorns, is masterful; the fire-roasted salmon comes with black-bean chili and mango salsa. ⊠ *W. Main St. rotary, next to Melody Tent, West End* ☎ *508/775–7677* ⊕ *www. paddockcapecod.com* ⊟ *AE, DC, MC, V* ⊗ *Closed mid-Nov.–Mar.*

★ **$$–$$$$** ✕ **Roadhouse Café.** Candlelight flickers off the white-linen tablecloths and dark-wood wainscoting at the Roadhouse Café, a smart choice for a night out. Popular dishes include the roasted pepper-and-goat cheese appetizer and shrimp and basil pesto over linguine. In the more casual bistro and the mahogany bar, you can order from a separate menu, which includes thin-crust pizza as well as burgers and lighter fare. Listen to excellent straight-ahead jazz on Monday night year-round in the bistro. There's a piano bar the rest of the week from early July to early September and on Friday and Saturday in the off-season. ⊠ *488 South St., Downtown Hyannis* ☎ *508/775–2386* ⊕ *www.roadhousecafe.com* ⌒ *Reservations essential* ⊟ *AE, D, MC, V* ⊗ *No lunch.*

$$–$$$ ✕ **Naked Oyster.** The big draw at this dapper restaurant with dark-wood-
Fodor'sChoice paneled walls and soft lighting is the extensive list of weekly changing
★ specials, which truly show off the kitchen's estimable talents. You'll always find several raw and "dressed" oyster dishes (such as barbecue oysters on the half shell with blue cheese, caramelized onions, and bacon) plus a nice range of salads and appetizers. Among the main dishes, consider the superb sliced duck breast with a port-wine and Rainier cherry sauce, or the sautéed shrimp in a piquant Thai peanut-cashew sauce over noodles. The oyster stew is also out of this world. ⊠ *20 Independence Dr., off Rte. 132* ☎ *508/778–6500* ⊟ *AE, D, DC, MC, V* ⊗ *No lunch weekends.*

$–$$$ ✕ **Misaki.** Tucked away on quiet West Main Street, frantically popular Misaki serves authentic Japanese food in an intimate space with tables arranged closely together. The menu has a diverse array of traditional Japanese dishes, such as vegetable tempura, yaki soba, and chicken or beef teriyaki, but the sushi and sashimi—prepared by an experienced master sushi chef—are the real stars here. Try the tuna rolls, which are delectably soft and silky. Two traditional Japanese "sitting booths" are available by reservation. ⊠ *379 W. Main St.* ☎ *508/771–3771* ⊟ *AE, MC, V.*

$–$$$ ✕ **RoöBar.** A bit of Manhattan on Main Street, RoöBar has a dark, sophisticated feel, with good music, low light, and a hip bar scene. A wood-fired oven produces "hand-spun to order" pizzas, such as Thai chicken with coconut-curry sauce. Other world-beat choices include shrimp and scallops with sweet-and-spicy Meyer lemon and crème fraîche sauce and cinnamon raisin croutons. The owner is a member of the late actor Christopher Reeve's family, and a portion of all profits goes to the Christopher Reeve Foundation for Spinal Cord Research. ⊠ *586 Main St., Downtown Hyannis* ☎ *508/778–6515* ⊕ *www.theroobar.com* ⊟ *AE, MC, V* ⊗ *Closed Mon. in off-season. No lunch.*

¢–$$$ ✕ **Baxter's Fish N' Chips.** Since fried seafood is a Cape staple, you may want to pay homage to one of the best Fry-o-lators around. Right on Hyannis Harbor, it's been a favorite of boaters and bathers alike since 1955. Generous portions of fried clams are delicious and cooked hot to order. The picnic tables outside, some set up on an old floating ferry, allow you to catch some rays while enjoying lobster, fish-and-chips, or something from the raw bar. If the weather's not on your side, there's indoor seating overlooking the harbor. A passageway off the dining room leads to Baxter's Boat House Club, a slightly more upscale space that has the same menu. ⊠ *Pleasant St., Hyannis Harbor* ☎ *508/775–4490* ⊕ *www.baxterscapecod.com* ⌲ *Reservations not accepted* ☰ *AE, DC, MC, V* ☙ *Closed mid-Oct.–Apr. and weekdays early Sept.–mid-Oct.*

¢–$$$ ✕ **Harry's.** This lovably divey-looking place serves up sizable portions of Cajun and creole dishes with great spices. The menu includes a number of meal-size sandwiches and burgers as well as blackened local fish that's done to perfection. The jambalaya will make you wonder if there's a bayou nearby. It's also a prime location for music: you can hear blues, zydeco, and folk music nightly year-round. ⊠ *700 Main St., West End* ☎ *508/778–4188* ⊕ *www.harrysbluesbar.com* ⌲ *Reservations not accepted* ☰ *AE, DC, MC, V.*

★ $–$$ ✕ **Fazio's Trattoria.** Set in an old Italian bakery building, swank but affordable Fazio's looks like the trattoria it is, with wood floors, high ceilings, and a deli case full of fresh pasta, breads, and cheeses. There's also an espresso and cappuccino bar. Chef Tom Fazio's menu leans on fresh ingredients and herbed pastas, such as basil fettuccine with shrimp, lemon, and plum tomatoes. All ravioli, pastas, and breads are homemade, and the brick-oven pizzas are delicious. Take home some fresh cannoli for dessert. ⊠ *294 Main St., Downtown Hyannis* ☎ *508/775–9400* ⊕ *www.fazio.net* ☰ *AE, MC, V* ☙ *No lunch.*

$–$$ ✕ **Sam Diego's.** The bar has a busy social scene, and the menu has satisfying—if predictable—Tex-Mex burritos, enchiladas, and fajitas. Crispy deep-fried ice cream served in a giant goblet is a house favorite; the margaritas, which come in several flavors, are another crowd-pleaser. The prop-shop furnishings may be a little cheesy—sombreros, Aztec birds, and the like—but the place is fun, friendly, and popular with families. Weekday lunch options include an all-you-can-eat chili and taco bar, and dinner is served nightly until midnight. ⊠ *950 Iyanough Rd. (Rte. 132)* ☎ *508/771–8816* ⊕ *www.samdiegos.com* ☰ *AE, D, MC, V.*

¢–$$ ✕ **Brazilian Grill.** The Cape has a large Brazilian population, and you FodorśChoice can find many of these residents, plus plenty of satisfied visitors, at this ★ all-you-can-eat *churrascaria* (Brazilian barbecue). Waiters circulate through the dining room offering more than a dozen grilled meats—beef, pork, chicken, sausage, even quail—on long swordlike skewers. You can help yourself to a buffet of salads and side dishes, including *farofa* (a couscous-like dish made of manioc [also known as cassava or yuca]), plantains, rice, and beans. The atmosphere is often loud and jovial. For dessert, the homemade flan is the best anywhere. Dine on the redbrick patio in warm weather. ⊠ *680 Main St., West End* ☎ *508/771–0109* ☰ *AE, D, DC, MC, V.*

¢–$$ ✕ **Ying's.** The huge menu at this little pan-Asian place presents Thai, Korean, and Japanese cuisines. Ying's sushi and sashimi combos are artful, and its many curried Thai seafood, noodle, and fried rice dishes range from spicy to, well, really spicy. For something different, try the Korean *bibimbap* (vegetables, beef, and egg on rice with hot sauce). Tables are set up by the windows, and there's a sushi bar and a small lounge area with a selection of Asian beers. Try the sweet and thick

Thai iced tea—you won't need dessert (but if you do, the fried ice cream is a treat). For more American-style food (as well as some Asian specialties) and nightly entertainment, check out Ying's other restaurant, the **Blue Anchor Cafe**, at 453 Main Street. ⊠ *59 Center St., East End* ☎ *508/790–2432* ⊟ *AE, MC, V.*

$$–$$$$ ⊡ **Anchor-In.** Most rooms at this pale-green motel on the north end of Hyannis Harbor have harbor views and small balconies overlooking the water. Its simple street-side appearance belies its spacious accommodations and extensive grounds. Some rooms have refrigerators, and the larger deluxe and executive rooms have wraparound porches. Lisa and Skip Simpson deliver the warm, personal service of a small B&B. Ferries to Nantucket and Martha's Vineyard are just around the corner. ⊠ *1 South St., 02601* ☎ *508/775–0357* 🖷 *508/775–1313* ⊕ *www. anchorin.com* ⥅ *43 rooms* ☖ *Some refrigerators, cable TV, Wi-Fi, pool* ⊟ *AE, D, MC, V* ⦿*⦿ CP.*

$$–$$$$ ⊡ **Four Points by Sheraton Hyannis Resort.** As chains go, it's hard to beat this low-slung compound, with its beautiful grounds, extensive services, and superior resort facilities, including a popular golf course open to the public and a top-notch spa. The lobby is elegant; the rooms, if unremarkable in decor, feature private balconies or patios and particularly comfortable mattresses. Far from traffic and close to downtown and the water, Four Points has the best locale of any Hyannis chain property. ⊠ *Scudder La., West End rotary, 02601* ☎ *508/775–7775 or 800/325–3535* 🖷 *508/778–6039* ⊕ *www.sheraton.com* ⥅ *224 rooms* ☖ *Restaurant, room service, cable TV, in-room VCRs, in-room data ports, 18-hole golf course, putting green, 2 tennis courts, 2 pools (1 indoor), health club, spa, pub, business services, meeting rooms* ⊟ *AE, D, DC, MC, V.*

$$–$$$ ⊡ **Cape Codder Resort.** Don't let the kids spy the indoor wave pool here— a fantasy of waves, waterfalls, and waterslides—or you'll never get out to see anything else on the Cape. Although it's set on an unattractive stretch of Route 132, this sprawling, family-friendly compound has quite a few amenities, including an excellent spa. Rooms range from basic to more elaborate—the Cape Codder rooms are more upscale than the standard "deluxe" ones. The best rooms face the inner courtyard, overlooking the lawn or the "beach" (a stretch of sand that's used for seasonal clambakes). The suites are huge; several have spiral staircases that lead up to a sleeping loft. Note that the hotel is sometimes packed with conventioneers and that there's no conventional pool for swimming, apart from the kid-oriented wave pool. ⊠ *1225 Rte. 132, 02601* ☎ *508/771– 3000 or 888/297–2200* 🖷 *508/771–6564* ⊕ *www.capecodderresort.com* ⥅ *252 rooms, 8 suites* ☖ *2 restaurants, room service, some in-room hot tubs, cable TV with movies and video games, in-room broadband, tennis court, exercise equipment, spa, volleyball, wine bar, playground, meeting rooms* ⊟ *AE, D, DC, MC, V.*

★ $$–$$$ ⊡ **Simmons Homestead Inn.** At this 1820 former sea captain's estate, each room in the main house or the detached barn is named for an animal. This offbeat but sophisticated inn has rooms with antique, wicker, or canopied four-poster beds topped with brightly colored quilts; some have fireplaces, and some, such as the large, cheery Bird Room, have private decks. You can borrow 10-speed mountain bikes, and Simmons Pond is a short jaunt on the property's trail. Gregarious innkeeper Bill Putman encourages you to return each evening for a wine-and-socializing hour. He'll also be happy to show you his collection of nearly 60 vintage cars or his roughly 500 vintages of single-malt Scotch. About two dozen friendly cats roam about the property. ⊠ *288 Scudder Ave., Box 578, Hyannis Port 02647* ☎ *508/778–4999 or 800/637–1649* 🖷 *508/790–1342* ⊕ *www.simmonshomesteadinn.com* 🛏 *12 rooms, 2 suites* ♨ *Hot tub, bicycles, billiards, some pets allowed (fee), no-smoking rooms; no a/c, no room phones, no room TVs* ▭ *AE, D, MC, V* ❘⊙❘ *BP.*

3

$$ 🏨 **Breakwaters.** These privately owned, weathered gray-shingle cottages rent by the week (or by the day if vacancies occur). It's a relaxed place, set on a quiet dead-end lane. Cottages are divided into one-, two-, and three-bedroom units and offer all the comforts of home. Each unit has one or two full baths; a kitchen with microwave, coffeemaker, refrigerator, toaster, and stove; TV and phone (local calls are free); and a deck or patio with a grill and picnic table. Most units have water views. An in-ground heated pool is less than 200 feet from the lifeguarded town beach on Nantucket Sound. Excluding Sunday, there is daily maid service. ⊠ *432 Sea St., Box 118, 02601* ☎🖷 *508/775–6831* ⊕ *www.capecod.com/breakwaters* 🛏 *19 cottages* ♨ *Kitchens, cable TV, pool, beach, babysitting; no a/c, no smoking* ▭ *No credit cards* ☽ *Closed mid-Oct.–Apr.*

$$ 🏨 **Comfort Inn Cape Cod.** All the rooms at this mid-range chain motel have white-oak-veneer furnishings and include one king-size or two double beds, a table and chairs or a desk and chair, and a wardrobe. Some king rooms have sofa beds. The quietest rooms are on the top floor, facing the pond and woods; all have free HBO and Nintendo, and pets are allowed. Although the location is fairly convenient to U.S. 6, the Comfort Inn is a few miles north of downtown Hyannis up traffic-choked Route 132—it is quiet and set well back from the road, though. ⊠ *1470 Rte. 132, 02601* ☎ *508/771–4804, 800/228–5150 reservations* 🖷 *508/790–2336* ⊕ *www.comfortinn-hyannis.com* 🛏 *103 rooms, 1 suite* ♨ *Cable TV with movies and video games, in-room broadband, indoor pool, gym, hot tub, sauna, meeting room, some pets allowed, no-smoking rooms* ▭ *AE, D, DC, MC, V* ❘⊙❘ *CP.*

★ $–$$ 🏨 **Capt. Gosnold Village.** An easy walk from Kalmus Beach and town, this peaceful, low-key colony of motel rooms and pink-shutter cottages is ideal for families. Kids can ride their bikes around the quiet street, and the pool is fenced in and watched over by a lifeguard. In some rooms, walls are attractively paneled with painted pine; floors are carpeted, and simple furnishings are colonial or modern. All cottages have decks and gas grills and receive maid service. Choose from efficiency units or one- to three-bedroom cottages. The cottages aren't air-conditioned, but you can rent an air-conditioning unit. ⊠ *230 Gosnold St., 02601* ☎ *508/775–9111* ⊕ *www.captaingosnold.com* 🛏 *18 units* ♨ *Picnic area, some kitchens, cable TV, pool, basketball; no a/c* ▭ *MC, V* ☽ *Closed Nov.–mid-Apr.*

¢–$$ 🏨 **Hyannis Inn Motel.** The main building of this second-oldest motel in Hyannis, a modest two-story spread, served as press headquarters during JFK's presidential campaign. Today, it's right in the heart of the downtown shopping and retail action. The main building's immaculate rooms have double, queen-size, or king-size beds; some have whirlpool tubs. Newer deluxe rooms—built in 1981 in a separate wing out back—are larger, sunnier, and quieter (they don't face Main Street) and have queen- or king-size beds, sleeper sofas, walk-in closets, and refrigerators. The restaurant serves breakfast only. ✉ *473 Main St., 02601* ☎ *508/775–0255 or 800/922-8993* 🖶 *508/771–0456* ⊕ *www.hyannisinn.com* ➯ *77 rooms* ⚒ *Restaurant, some in-room hot tubs, some refrigerators, cable TV, in-room data ports, indoor pool, sauna, lounge* 🖃 *AE, D, MC, V* ⊗ *Closed early Nov.–Feb.*

$ 🏨 **Cape Cod Inn.** This centrally located inn on downtown Main Street is within walking distance of all of Hyannis's major sights. The no-frills rooms have large double beds; most, unfortunately, have views of a drab parking lot. The inn is attached to the Duck Inn Pub, a popular local hangout where breakfast is served. ✉ *447 Main St., 02601* ☎ *508/775–3000* 🖶 *508/771–1457* ⊕ *www.capecodin.com* ➯ *37 rooms, 3 suites* ⚒ *Restaurant, cable TV, indoor pool, bar* 🖃 *AE, D, MC, V* ⑩ *CP.*

Nightlife & The Arts

THE ARTS The **Boston Pops Esplanade Orchestra** (☎ 508/362–0066 ⊕ www.artsfoundationcapecod.org) wows the crowd with its annual Pops by the Sea concert, held in August at the Hyannis Village Green. Each year a celebrity guest conductor strikes up the band for a few selected numbers; past baton bouncers have included Olympia Dukakis, Joan Kennedy, Mike Wallace, Art Buchwald, Maya Angelou, and Sebastian Junger.

In 1950 actress Gertrude Lawrence and her husband, producer-manager Richard Aldrich, opened the **Cape Cod Melody Tent** (✉ 21 W. Main St., at West End rotary, Hyannis ☎ 508/775–5630, 800/347–0808 for tickets ⊕ www.melodytent.com) to showcase Broadway musicals and concerts. Today it's the Cape's top venue for pop concerts and comedy shows; performers who have played here, in the round, include the Indigo Girls, Lyle Lovett, Tony Bennett, Bill Cosby, and Crosby, Stills & Nash. The Tent also holds an 11 AM Wednesday children's theater series in July and August.

The 90-member **Cape Symphony Orchestra,** under former D'Oyly Carte Opera conductor Royston Nash, gives regular classical and children's concerts with guest artists September through May. Performances are held at the Barnstable Performing Arts Center at **Barnstable High School** (✉ 744 W. Main St., Hyannis ☎ 508/362–1111 ⊕ www.capesymphony.org).

Opera New England of Cape Cod (☎ 508/398–1068 ⊕ www.capecodopera. org) hosts two or three performances a year, in spring and fall, by the National Lyric Opera Company.

In July and August **town-band concerts** (☎ 508/362–5230 or 877/492–6647) are held on Wednesday evening at 7:30 on the Town Green on Main Street, Hyannis.

NIGHTLIFE Hyannis is Barnstable's nightlife hub, with more than a dozen popular bars and taverns, most of them along Main Street in the heart of downtown. Elsewhere in this otherwise lightly developed town, bars and clubs are few and far between.

The **Barnstable Comedy Club** (⌧ Village Hall, Rte. 6A, Barnstable ☎ 508/362–6333 ⊕ www.barnstablecomedyclub.com), the Cape's oldest amateur theater group (it was founded in the 1920s), gives much-praised musical and dramatic performances throughout the year. Folks who appeared here before they made it big include Geena Davis, Frances McDormand, and Kurt Vonnegut, a past president of the BCC.

The British Beer Company (⌧ 412 Main St., Hyannis ☎ 508/771–1776 ⊕ www.britishbeer.com) has a hearty selection of beers, from stouts to pilsners; most nights there's also live entertainment—usually local rock bands. The BBC also has branches on the Cape in Sandwich and Falmouth.

Bud's Country Lounge (⌧ 3 Bearses Way, at Rte. 132, Hyannis ☎ 508/771–2505) has pool tables and live music, dancing, and karaoke year-round.

Club 477/Mallory Dock (⌧ 477 Yarmouth Rd., Hyannis ☎ 508/771–7511), in the old Hyannis train station, is the Cape's only gay club outside Provincetown. There's a piano bar on the lower level and a dance bar on the upper floor with music almost as hot as the crowd.

The Comedy Lounge (⌧ Radisson Hotel Hyannis, Rte. 28, Hyannis ☎ 508/771–1700), despite its location in a ubiquitous chain hotel, pulls in top comedy acts from throughout the Northeast. Shows are held Friday and Saturday.

★ **Harry's Blues Bar** (⌧ 700 Main St., Hyannis ☎ 508/778–4188 ⊕ www.harrysbluesbar.com) is hopping nearly every night year-round, drawing blues lovers of all ages. Expect to see 21-year-olds and 70-year-olds dancing up a sweat side by side. Owner Laddie Durham fills the creole joint with crowd-pleasing bands and top-notch hospitality. In summer, crowds spill over from inside onto the two decks.

The **Island Merchant** (⌧ 10 Ocean St., Hyannis ☎ 508/771–1337) showcases a fine range of acoustic, blues, jazz, and rock—even spoken-word performers. The high-octane java keeps the joint jumpin'.

Pufferbellies (⌧ 183 Rte. 28, Hyannis ☎ 508/790–4300 or 800/233–4301), in an old railroad roundhouse by the Hyannis tracks, is the Mid Cape's largest dance club, with several dance floors of swing, country line dancing, and DJ tunes, as well as eats, Internet terminals, and even volleyball courts.

★ After dinner, **RoöBar** (⌧ 586 Main St., Hyannis ☎ 508/778–6515 ⊕ www.theroobar.com) turns up the music and morphs into *the* place to see and be seen on Cape Cod. The Manhattan-esque haunt draws large crowds of attractive twenty- and thirtysomethings; expect to see lines of people out the door in summer. Personable bartenders and staff boost the already lively atmosphere.

Sports & the Outdoors

BASEBALL The **Cotuit Kettleers** of the collegiate Cape Cod Baseball League play home games at **Lowell Park** (⌧ Lowell St., 2 mi south of Rte. 28, Cotuit ☎ 508/428–3358 ⊕ www.kettleers.org) from mid-June to mid-August.

The **Hyannis Mets** (☎ 508/420–0962 ⊕ www.hyannismets.org) of the collegiate Cape Cod Baseball League play home games at **McKeon Field** (✉ High School Rd., Downtown Hyannis) from mid-June to mid-August.

BEACHES ⚠ **Daily parking fees at Barnstable beaches are $15 in season.**

Hovering above Barnstable Harbor and the 4,000-acre **Great Salt Marsh, Sandy Neck Beach** stretches some 6 mi across a peninsula that ends at **Sandy Neck Light.** The beach is one of the Cape's most beautiful—dunes, sand, and sea spread endlessly east, west, and north. The marsh used to be harvested for salt hay; now it's a haven for birds, which are out and about in the greatest numbers in morning and evening, during low tide, and during spring and fall migrations. The lighthouse, standing a few feet from the eroding shoreline at the tip of the neck, has been out of commission since 1952. It was built in 1857 to replace an 1827 light, and it used to run on acetylene gas. It's now privately owned and no longer accessible from the beach. If you like to hike, ask at the ranger station for a trail brochure. The main beach at Sandy Neck has lifeguards, a snack bar, restrooms, and showers. As you travel east along Route 6A from Sandwich, Sandy Neck Road is just *before* the Barnstable line, although the beach itself is in West Barnstable. ✉ *Sandy Neck Rd., West Barnstable* ⊘ *Daily 8 AM–9 PM, but staffed only until 5 PM.*

Hathaway's Pond (✉ Off Phinney's La., Barnstable) is a freshwater pond with a beach, restrooms, and a lifeguard (in season).

Craigville Beach, on Craigville Beach Road in Centerville, is a long, wide strand that is extremely popular with the collegiate crowd. The beach has lifeguards, showers, and restrooms, and there's food nearby.

Kalmus Park Beach, at the south end of Ocean Street in Hyannis, is a fine, wide sandy beach with an area set aside for windsurfers and a sheltered area that's good for kids. It has a snack bar, restrooms, showers, and lifeguards.

Also in Hyannis, **Veterans Park,** next to the John F. Kennedy Memorial on Ocean Street, has a small beach that's especially good for kids; it's sheltered from waves and fairly shallow. There are picnic tables, barbecue facilities, showers, and restrooms.

BICYCLING **Cascade Motor Lodge** (✉ 201 Main St., Downtown Hyannis ☎ 508/775–9717), near the bus and train station, rents three-speed and mountain bikes by the half day, full day, and week.

BOATING **Eastern Mountain Sports** (✉ 1513 Rte. 132, Hyannis ☎ 508/362–8690) rents kayaks, a variety of bicycles, and camping gear.

The catboat *Eventide* (✉ Ocean St. Dock, Hyannis ☎ 508/775–0222 or 800/308–1837 ⊕ www.catboat.com) sails in Hyannis Harbor and out into Nantucket Sound on several one- and two-hour cruises; options include a nature tour and a sunset cruise.

Hy-Line (✉ Ocean St. Dock, Hyannis ☎ 508/790–0696 ⊕ www.hy-linecruises.com) offers cruises on reproductions of old-time Maine coastal steamers. The one-hour tours of Hyannis Harbor and Lewis Bay include a view of the Kennedy compound and other points of interest.

3

FISHING **Aquarius Charters Inc.** (✉ Barnstable Harbor ☎ 508/362–9617 ⊕ www. aquariussportfishing.com) supplies all gear on its 35-foot boat and offers four-, six-, and eight-hour trips for up to six people to catch bass, blues, tuna, and shark. Reservations are recommended.

Hy-Line (✉ Ocean St. Dock, Hyannis ☎ 508/790–0696 ⊕ www.hy-linecruises.com) leads fishing trips on a walk-on basis in spring and fall, but reservations are mandatory in summer.

GOLF **Four Points by Sheraton Hyannis Resort** (✉ Scudder La., West End rotary, Hyannis ☎ 508/775–7775) has a beautifully landscaped, challenging 18-hole par-3 course called Twin Brooks; it's open to nonguests. You may bump into some famous faces; many performers from the Cape Cod Melody Tent tee off here while they're in town.

HEALTH & **Barnstable Fitness Center** (✉ 55 Attucks La., Independence Park, off Rte.
FITNESS CLUBS 132, Hyannis ☎ 508/771–7734) has an indoor pool, two aerobics rooms, cardiovascular and free-weight equipment, and a full schedule of fitness, yoga, and pilates classes. Day passes and short-term memberships are available.

Hyannis Athletic Club (✉ Sheraton Hyannis Hotel, Scudder La., West End rotary, Hyannis ☎ 508/862–2535) has two outdoor tennis courts, a fitness club, and indoor- and outdoor pools. Day- and short-term memberships are available.

HORSEBACK **Holly Hill Farm** (✉ 240 Flint St., Marstons Mills ☎ 508/428–2621
RIDING ⊕ www.hollyhillstable.com) offers horseback-riding instruction and a day camp but no trail rides.

ICE-SKATING The **Joseph P. Kennedy Jr. Memorial Skating Rink** (✉ 141 Bassett La., Hyannis ☎ 508/790–6345), named for the late Kennedy scion and war hero, offers skating October through March, with special times reserved for teenagers, youngsters, and families; skate rentals are available.

WHALE- On **Hyannis Whale Watcher Cruises** out of Barnstable Harbor, a natural-
WATCHING ist narrator comments on whale sightings and the natural history of Cape Cod Bay. Trips last about four hours, and there are concessions on board. In July and August you can cruise at sunset, too. Reservations are recommended. ✉ *Millway Marina, off Phinney's La., Barnstable ☎ 508/ 362–6088 or 888/942–5392 ⊕ www.whales.net ⚓ $35 ☉ May–Oct.*

Shopping

Main Street in downtown Hyannis has gradually been gentrified in recent years and has become one of the top shopping destinations on the Cape, buzzing with several art galleries and antiques shops, numerous clothiers, and a slew of other, mostly independent, boutiques and gift emporia. You'll also find quite a few restaurants along this walkable stretch, including several cafés that are nice for a cup of coffee or a light snack.

Black's Handweaving Shop (✉ 597 Rte. 6A, near Rte. 149, West Barn-

WORD OF MOUTH

"Hyannis is now quite a busy city, good for shopping—the mother of all Christmas Tree Shops is there, for one." —Reeder stable ☎ 508/362–3955), in a barnlike structure with working looms, makes beautiful handwoven goods in traditional and jacquard weaves. If you don't see what you want on display, you can commission it.

Cape Cod Mall (✉ Between Rtes. 132 and 28, Hyannis ☎ 508/771–0200 ⊕ www.capecodmall.com), the Cape's largest, has 120 mid- to upper-end mostly chain shops, including department stores such as Macy's and Sears; smaller anchor stores such as Marshalls, Barnes & Noble, and Best Buy; and a 12-screen movie complex.

Christmas Tree Shops (✉ 655 Rte. 132, Hyannis ☎ 508/778–5521 ⊕ www.christmastreeshops.com), a Cape mainstay, are a bargain shoppers' haven. Take home Cape souvenirs at a great discount along with just about anything you might need—or not need—to decorate your home. The Hyannis store is the largest on the Cape.

Maps of Antiquity (✉ 1022 Rte. 6A, West Barnstable ☎ 508/362–7169) sells original and reproduction maps of Cape Cod, New England, and other parts of the world. Some date to the 1700s.

★ **Oak & Ivory** (✉ 1112 Main St., Osterville ☎ 508/428–9425 ⊕ www. oakandivory.com) specializes in Nantucket lightship baskets made on the premises, as well as gold miniature baskets and scrimshaw. China, gold jewelry, and other gifts round out the selection.

The handsome flagship **Puritan of Cape Cod** (✉ 408 Main St., Hyannis ☎ 508/775–2400) store carries upscale clothing brands, from North Face to Eileen Fisher and Ralph Lauren; they also sell outdoor gear. Service is great here, and they also have four other stores around the Cape.

The **Sow's Ear Antique Company** (✉4698 Rte. 28, Cotuit ☎508/428–4931), in a late 1600s house next to the Cahoon Museum, specializes in folk art—dolls, ship models, wood carvings, antique quilts, and paintings.

West Barnstable Tables (✉ 2454 Rte. 149, West Barnstable ☎ 508/362–2676) has exquisite handcrafted tables, chairs, chests, and other furniture made from the finest woods.

The decor changes seasonally at **Whippletree** (✉ 660 Rte. 6A, West Barnstable ☎ 508/362–3320 ⊕ www.thewhippletree.com), a 1779 barn where Christmas decorations and country gift items hang from the rafters year-round. Goods include German nutcrackers, from Prussian soldiers to Casanovas.

For stunning arts and crafts imported from Africa, check out **Zizini** (✉ 382 Main St., Hyannis ☎ 508/790–2109), which carries colorful ceramic and bead necklaces, handwoven pocketbooks, carved wooden masks, and abstract soapstone carvings. The store operates on a fair trade policy, helping to support artisans who create the goods.

Yarmouth

Yarmouth Port is 3 mi east of Barnstable Village, West Yarmouth is 2 mi east of Hyannis.

Once known as Mattacheese, or "the planting lands," Yarmouth was settled in 1639 by farmers from the Plymouth Bay Colony. The town's northernmost village of **Yarmouth Port** wasn't established as a distinct village until 1829. By then the Cape had begun a thriving maritime industry, and men turned to the sea to make their fortunes. Many impressive sea captains' houses—some now B&Bs and museums—still line enchanting Route 6A and nearby side streets, and Yarmouth Port has some real old-time stores in town. A mile's drive north of Route 6A is the small but lovely Gray's Beach, where a boardwalk at Bass Hole stretches hundreds of feet over the wide marsh and the Callery-Darling conservation land trails loop through forest and marshland.

Visit the **Edward Gorey House Museum** to explore the eccentric illustrations and offbeat humor of the late acclaimed artist. The regularly changing exhibitions, arranged in the downstairs rooms of Gorey's former home, include drawings of his oddball characters and reveal the mysterious psyche of the sometimes dark but always playful illustrator. Kids enjoy the section of the house with interactive exhibits that promote Gorey's lifelong dedication to animal welfare. ✉ *8 Strawberry La., Yarmouth Port* ☎ *508/362–3909* ⊕ *www. edwardgoreyhouse.org* 🖃 *$5* 🕑 *Mid-Apr. to mid-Dec., Thurs.–Sat. 11–4, Sun. noon–4; July–Aug., Wed. 11–4; call to confirm off-season hours; closed mid-Dec.–mid-Apr.*

★ For a peek into the past, make a stop at **Hallet's,** a country drugstore preserved as it was in 1889 when it was opened by Thacher Hallet, the present owner's grandfather. Hallet served not only as druggist but also as postmaster and justice of the peace. Sit at a swivel stool at the all-marble soda fountain and order their secret-recipe ice-cream soda and, in season, an inexpensive breakfast or lunch. ✉ *139 Rte. 6A, Yarmouth Port* ☎ *508/362–3362* 🕑 *Apr.–mid-Nov.; call for hrs.*

Above Hallet's Store, the **Thacher Taylor Hallet Museum** displays photographs and memorabilia of Yarmouth Port and the Hallet family. ✉ *139 Rte. 6A, Yarmouth Port* ☎ *508/362–3362* 🖃 *Donations accepted for museum* 🕑 *Apr.–mid-Nov.; call for hrs.*

The 1886 **Village Pump** (✉ 220 Rte. 6A, Yarmouth Port), a black wrought-iron mechanism long used for drawing household water, is topped by a lantern and surrounded by ironwork with cutouts of birds and animals. In front is a stone trough that was used for watering horses. It's across from the Parnassus Book Service. The 1696 **Old Yarmouth Inn** (✉ Rte. 6A, near Summer St., Yarmouth Port ☎ 508/ 362–9962), near the village pump, is the Cape's oldest inn and a one-time stagecoach stop.

The **Botanical Trails of the Historical Society of Old Yarmouth,** behind the post office (✉ 231 Main St., Yarmouth Port), consists of 50 acres of oak and pine woods and a pond, accented by blueberries, lady's slippers, Indian pipes, rhododendrons, and hollies. Stone markers and arrows point out the 2 mi of trails; you'll find trail maps in the gatehouse mailbox. Just beyond the historical society's trails, you can find **Kelley Chapel,** built in 1873 by a father for his daughter, who was grieving over the death of her child. An iron woodstove and a pump organ dominate the simple interior. ✉ *Off Rte. 6A* 🖃 *$1 suggested donation* ☺ *Gatehouse July and Aug., daily 1–4. Trails during daylight hrs yr-round.*

The 1780 **Winslow Crocker House** is an elegantly symmetrical two-story Georgian with 12-over-12 small-pane windows and rich paneling in every room. Crocker was a well-to-do trader and land speculator; after his death, his two sons built a wall dividing the house in half. The structure was moved here from West Barnstable in 1936 by Mary Thacher, who donated it—along with her collection of 17th- to 19th-century furniture, pewter, hooked rugs, and ceramics—to Historic New England (formerly the Society for the Preservation of New England Antiquities), which operates it as a museum. ✉ *250 Rte. 6A, Yarmouth Port* ☎ *617/227-3956* ⊕ *www.historicnewengland.org* 🖃 *$5* ☺ *June–mid-Oct., 1st Sat. of month, tours at 11, noon, 1, 2, 3, and 4.*

Built in 1840 onto an existing 1740 house for a sea captain in the China trade, the **Captain Bangs Hallet House** is a white Greek Revival building with a hitching post out front and a weeping beech in back. The house and its contents typify a 19th-century sea captain's home, with pieces of pewter, china, nautical equipment, antique toys, and clothing on display. The kitchen has the original 1740 brick beehive oven and butter churns. ✉ *11 Strawberry La., off Rte. 6A, Yarmouth Port* ☎ *508/362-3021* 🖃 *$3* ☺ *June–mid-Oct., Thurs.–Sun. 1–4, tours at 1, 2, and 3.*

Purchased in 1640 and established as a prosperous farm in the late 1700s, the **Taylor-Bray Farm** (✉ Bray Farm Rd., Yarmouth Port ☎ 508/385-9407 ⊕ www.taylorbrayfarm.org) is listed on the National Register of Historic Places. Now a working farm for educational purposes, it hosts special events, such as an annual sheep shearing and a craft fair. The public is welcome to take advantage of the farm's picnic tables, walking trails, and great views of the tidal marsh year-round from dawn to dusk. Call for more information.

For a scenic loop with little traffic, turn north off Route 6A in Yarmouth Port onto Church Street or Thacher Street, then left onto Thacher Shore Road. In fall this route is especially beautiful, with impressive stands of blazing-red burning bush. Wooded segments alternate with open views of the marsh. Keep bearing right, and at the WATER STREET sign, the dirt road on the right will bring you to a wide-open view of marshland as it meets the bay. Don't drive in too far, or you may get stuck. As you ❿ come out, a right turn will take you to **Keveney Bridge,** a one-lane wooden bridge over marshy Mill Pond, and back to Route 6A.

★ ☾ ⓫ One of Yarmouth Port's most beautiful areas is Bass Hole, which stretches from Homer's Dock Road to the salt marsh. **Bass Hole Boardwalk** (⊠ Trail entrance on Center St. near Gray's Beach parking lot) extends over a marshy creek; amid the salt marshes, vegetated wetlands, and upland woods meander the 2½-mi **Callery-Darling nature trails.** Gray's Beach is a little crescent of sand with still water good for kids—but don't go beyond the roped-in swimming area, the only section where the current isn't strong. At the end of the boardwalk, benches provide a place to relax and look out over abundant marsh life and, across the creek, the beautiful, sandy shores of Dennis's Chapin Beach. At low tide you can walk out on the flats for almost a mile. It's a far cry from the 18th-century, when a harbor here was the site of a schooner shipyard.

⓬ About 4 mi south of Yarmouth Port and directly east of Hyannis, you'll find **West Yarmouth.** The commercial hub (and the major road through the community) is, for better or worse, Route 28—the part of the Cape people love to hate. As you pass through the area—probably very slowly in summer traffic—it's one motel, strip mall, nightclub, and miniature-golf course after another. In 1989, as *Cape Cod Life* magazine put it, "the town [began] to plant 350 trees in hopes that eventually the trees' leaves, like the fig leaf of Biblical lore, [would] cover the shame of unkempt overdevelopment." Regardless of the glut of tacky tourist traps, there are some interesting sights in the little villages along the way. So take Route 28 if you want to intersperse amusements with your sightseeing, because you really can amuse yourself to no end here. If you want to avoid this road entirely, a sensible option is to take speedy U.S. 6 to the exit nearest what you want to visit and then cut south across the interior. If you must travel the Route 28 area, take Buck Island Road, which runs north of and parallel to much of the busy route in West and South Yarmouth.

Yelverton Crowe settled the village of West Yarmouth in 1643 after acquiring the land from a Native American sachem. The deal they struck was that Crowe could have as much land as he could traverse in an hour in exchange for an "ox-chain, a copper kettle . . . and a few trinkets." The first settlers were farmers; when Central Wharf near Mill Creek was built in the 1830s, the town turned to more commercial ventures as it became headquarters for the growing packet service that ferried passengers from the Cape to Boston.

Listed on the National Register of Historic Places, the 1710 **Baxter Grist Mill,** by the shore of Mill Pond, is the only mill on Cape Cod powered by an inside water turbine; the others use either wind or paddle wheels. The mill was converted to the indoor metal turbine in 1860 due to the pond's low water level and the damage done to the wooden paddle wheel by winter freezes. The original metal turbine is displayed on the grounds, and a reproduction powers the restored mill. A videotape tells the mill's history. There are no scheduled hours or tours, but feel free to walk around the grounds. ⊠ *Rte. 28, across from Baxter Ave., West Yarmouth* ☎ *508/362–3021* ⊕ *www.hsoy.org/historic/baxtermill.htm.*

⓭ A unique and lovely walking trail, the **Yarmouth Boardwalk** (⊠ Off Meadowbrook La., West Yarmouth), stretches through swamp and marsh and leads to the edge of pretty Swan Pond, which is ringed with woods. To get here, take Winslow Gray Road northeast from Route 28, turn right on Meadowbrook Lane, and take it to the end.

An entertaining, educational, and occasionally hokey stop for kids, **ZooQuarium** has sea-lion shows, a petting zoo with native wildlife, a touch-friendly tidal pool, wandering peacocks, aquariums, and educational programs, plus pony rides in summer. The Children's Discovery Center presents changing exhibits such as *What's the Buzz on Bees* and *What's For Lunch* (for which kids can prepare meals for animals). ⊠ *674 Rte. 28, West Yarmouth* ☎ *508/775–8883* ⊕ *www.zooquariumcapecod. net* ⊠ *$10* ⊙ *Mid-Feb.–June and Sept.–late Nov., daily 9:30–5; July and Aug., daily 9:30–6.*

NEED A BREAK?

Jerry's Seafood and Dairy Freeze (⊠ 654 Rte. 28, West Yarmouth ☎ 508/775–9752), open year-round, serves fried clams and onion rings, along with thick frappes (milk shakes), frozen yogurt, and soft-serve ice cream at good prices.

A few miles east of West Yarmouth, you'll reach its similarly exuberant sister village, **South Yarmouth.** Here you can find charter boats, a river cruise, and boat and kayak rentals, plus seafood restaurants and markets. Like West Yarmouth, South Yarmouth has a stretch of blight and overdevelopment on Route 28, but it also has some nice beaches that are good for families. For a good indication of what the town looked like in the late 19th century, take a drive down Pleasant Street and the Main Street section south of Route 28 to view old homes in the Federal and Greek Revival styles. This section along Bass River was once home to the village's elite businessmen, bankers, and sea mer-

> **LAY OF THE LAND**
>
> Locals sometimes refer to South Yarmouth as Bass River, after the river that separates the village from West Dennis.

chants. Adding to the pastoral aura of the area is the **Judah Baker Windmill;** the grounds here are pretty and peaceful. For a closer look, the windmill is open Tuesday and Thursday during summer.

South Yarmouth was once known as Quaker Village for the large numbers of Quakers who settled the area in the 1770s after a smallpox epidemic wiped out the local Native American population. The 1809 **Quaker Meeting House** is still open for services. Two separate entrance doors and the partition down the center were meant to divide the sexes. The adjacent cemetery has simple markers with no epitaphs, an expression of the Friends' belief that all are equal in God's eyes. Behind the cemetery is a circa-1830 one-room Quaker schoolhouse. ⊠ *58 N. Main St., South Yarmouth* ☎ *508/398–3773* ⊙ *Services Sun. at 10.*

★ ☺ **Pirate's Cove** is the most elaborate of the Cape's many miniature-golf setups, with a hill, a waterfall, a stream, and the 18-hole Blackbeard's Challenge course. ⊠ *728 Rte. 28, South Yarmouth* ☎ *508/394–6200* ⊙ *July and Aug., daily 9 AM–11 PM; late Apr.–June, Sept., and Oct., most days 10–8, but call.*

🌤 For rainy-day fun, **Ryan Family Amusements** offers video-game rooms, Skee-Ball, and bowling. There's a snack bar that serves pizza, sandwiches, and beer and wine. ⊠ *1067 Rte. 28, South Yarmouth* ☎ *508/394–5644* ⊘ *Daily; hrs vary.*

Where to Stay & Eat

SOUTH
YARMOUTH
★ $$–$$$$

✕ **902 Main.** This unassuming spot sits on a prosaic stretch of Route 28, but you won't find any of the main drag's hustle and trendy commercialism in here. Acclaimed chef Gilbert Pepin and his wife, Kolleen, want you to slow down and savor the rituals and flavors of good food and good wine. The menu changes every six weeks or so but might feature wild Orleans mussels in a broth of fennel, saffron, and tomatoes, and roast rack of lamb with truffle-mashed potatoes, asparagus, spinach, and a port-wine reduction. The refined, elegant space is staffed by highly professional servers. ⊠ *902 Rte. 28* ☎ *508/398–9902* ⊕ *www.902main.com* ⊟ *AE, D, MC, V* ⊘ *Closed Mon. No lunch.*

$$–$$$

✕ **The Skipper.** This classic Cape restaurant has been around since 1936. Sit downstairs in the nautical-theme main room or upstairs on the outside deck, which has terrific views of nearby Nantucket Sound. The kitchen turns out an appealing mix of fish and shellfish dishes, plus a handful of Italian specialties and landlubber options (such as Yankee pot roast and prime rib au jus). Try the seared chili-garlic scallops or the Thai coconut shrimp-and-chicken over rice. ⊠ *152 S. Shore Dr.* ☎ *508/394–7406* ⬥ *Reservations not accepted* ⊟ *AE, D, MC, V* ⊘ *Closed Nov.–mid-Apr.*

¢–$

✕ **Ardeo.** Despite its unpromising location in a shopping plaza, this smart-casual Mediterranean bistro has built a local following for its pizzas, pastas, salads, panini sandwiches, and Middle Eastern fare. Some may find the food more Americanized than authentic, but it's tasty nonetheless. There's something for everyone here—you could bring the kids, or your grandparents, or a group of pals, and it's a good choice for vegetarians, too. ⊠ *23 V Whites Path, Union Station Plaza, South Yarmouth* ☎ *508/760–1500* ⊕ *www.ardeocapecod.com* ⊟ *AE, D, MC, V.*

$$–$$$$

🏨 **Ocean Mist.** This three-story, motel-style resort sits on its own private (if tiny) beach on Nantucket Sound. The rooms have generic modern furnishings, cable TV, and either wet bars (with sink and refrigerator) or fully stocked kitchenettes. The duplex loft suites are a step above, with cathedral ceilings, sitting areas with pullout sofas, skylights, and one or two private balconies. Continental breakfast is included late May through early September. ⊠ *97 S. Shore Dr., 02664* ☎ *508/398–2633 or 800/248–6478* ⊟ *508/760–3151* ⊕ *www.capecodtravel.com/oceanmist* ⬥ *32 rooms, 31 suites* ⬥ *Coffee shop, some kitchenettes, some minibars, some refrigerators, cable TV, indoor pool, hot tub, beach, laundry facilities, no-smoking rooms* ⊟ *AE, D, MC, V* ⊘ *Closed Dec.–mid-Feb.*

$$

FodorśChoice
★

🏨 **Capt. Farris House.** Steps from the Bass River Bridge and a short spin away from congested Route 28 sits this imposing 1845 Greek Revival home. Owners Steve and Patty Bronstein are carefully attuned to the needs of their guests while maintaining a casual our-house-is-your-house attitude. The large rooms and suites have either antique or canopied beds, plush comforters, fancy drapes, and deep tile baths (all but one with a whirlpool tub). Some have fireplaces and sundecks. Breakfast is served in the formal dining room or the greenhouse-style interior courtyard and might include quiche with pumpkin-pecan scones or thick French toast. Baked goods and coffee are available after hours. ⊠ *308 Old Main St., 02664* ☎ *508/760–2818 or 800/350–9477* ☎ *508/398–1262* ⊕ *www. captainfarris.com* ➥ *6 rooms, 4 suites* ♿ *Some in-room hot tubs, cable TV, in-room VCRs, in-room data ports; no kids under 9, no smoking* ☰ *AE, D, MC, V* �101 *BP* ⊙ *Closed Jan.*

$–$$ 🏨 **All Seasons Motor Inn.** This well-cared-for motor lodge in downtown South Yarmouth ranks above the others in town because of its great staff, a lovely outdoor pool with attractive grounds and patio furniture, and large guest rooms with clean and updated fixtures and furnishings—many have balconies or patios overlooking the pool and courtyard. Plus, it's right by the Cape Cod Creamery ice-cream shop. The dining room serves a full breakfast as well as lunch during the summer season. ⊠ *1199 Rte. 28, South Yarmouth 02664* ☎ *508/394–7600 or 800/527–0359* ☎ *508/398–7160* ⊕ *www.allseasons.com* ➥ *114 rooms* ♿ *Dining room, refrigerators, cable TV, in-room VCRs, 2 pools (1 indoors), gym, hot tub, sauna; no smoking* ☰ *AE, D, MC, V* 101 *CP.*

$–$$ 🏨 **Seaside Cottages.** Right on Nantucket Sound, this 5-acre village of Cape-style cottages (studios and one- or two-bedroom units) has a view of scalloped beaches in both directions. Seaside was built in the 1940s, and the furnishings vary from cottage to cottage, since each is individually owned. All have kitchens or kitchenettes, and many have wood-burning fireplaces. The oceanfront cottages, right off a strip of grass set with lounge- and Adirondack chairs, have the best views. Cottages in the adjacent pine grove are generally very pleasant, too. Rentals are by the week in summer; cottages can be rented by the night in late spring and fall. ⊠ *135 S. Shore Dr., 02664* ☎ *508/398–2533* ☎ *508/398–2523* ⊕ *www.seasidecapecod.com* ➥ *42 cottages* ♿ *Picnic area, some kitchens, some kitchenettes, cable TV, beach; no a/c, no room phones* ☰ *D, MC, V* ⊙ *Closed mid-Oct.–Apr.*

WEST YARMOUTH ✕ **Yarmouth House Restaurant.** This festive, family-owned green-shingle
$–$$$$ restaurant has built a devoted local following over the years. The menu has classic Italian dishes such as chicken Parmesan and veal Marsala, as well as traditional grilled steaks and plenty of fresh seafood dishes. Try the filet mignon à la Neptune (topped with lobster meat and hollandaise sauce), and accompany your meal with a selection from their long list of beers, wines, and specialty cocktails. Early-bird specials, Sunday specials, and a kids' menu are available. ⊠ *335 Rte. 28* ☎ *508/771–5454* ⊕ *www.yarmouthhouse.com* ☰ *AE, D, MC, V.*

★ ¢ ✕ **Keltic Kitchen.** If you like to start your day with a substantial meal, stop in at this friendly café for a traditional Irish breakfast—eggs, sausage, rashers (bacon), black-and-white pudding, home fries or beans, tomato, and brown bread or scones. The potato pancakes with sour cream and scallions are also tasty, as are the more "American" options, including French toast and omelets. At midday, you can still get breakfast, or choose from an assortment of sandwiches that might include corned beef or burgers. Just don't come by too late—the kitchen closes around 2 PM. ⊠ *415 Rte. 28* ☎ *508/771–4835* ☰ *No credit cards* ⊙ *No dinner.*

★ **$–$$$** 🏨 **Bayside Resort.** A bit more upscale than most of the properties along Route 28, but still with extremely reasonable rates, the Bayside overlooks pristine salt marshes and, beyond them, Lewis Bay. Although it's not right on the water, there is a small beach and a large outdoor pool with a café (there's also an indoor pool). Rooms have contemporary light-wood furnishings, and several have cathedral ceilings, whirlpool tubs, and views toward the bay. Many members of the staff have worked here for years, which helps to explain the resort's family-friendly vibe. The Bayside Resort also offers a number of package deals related to everything from golf to day trips to Martha's Vineyard and Nantucket. ✉ *225 Rte. 28, 02673* ☎ *508/775–5669 or 800/243–1114* 🖷 *508/775–8862* ⊕ *www. baysideresort.com* ⇲ *128 rooms ⚷ Restaurant, dining room, some in-room hot tubs, cable TV, 2 pools (1 indoor), gym, hot tub, sauna, beach, volleyball, pub, video game room ⊟ AE, D, MC, V* ⦿| *CP.*

$–$$$ 🏨 **Cape Point Hotel.** Families flock to this sensibly priced miniresort, taking advantage of the many amenities, large rooms, patient and friendly staff, and the fact that kids are nearly always certain to find plenty of other playmates here, especially in summer. Rooms contain simple but updated modern furniture. The poolside Cabana Grill serves lunch in July and August (it's open until 4:30). Once you've stayed here once, you're eligible to receive the Cape Point's unbelievably low-priced off-season specials. The hotel puts together some great golf packages with a number of local clubs, and the same owners run the Mariner Motor Lodge (⇨ *below*) and the even more affordable Town 'N Country Motor Lodge. ✉ *476 Rte. 28, West Yarmouth 02673* ☎ *508/778–1500 or 800/323–9595* 🖷 *508/778–5516* ⊕ *www.capepointhotel.com* ⇲ *116 rooms ⚷ Restaurant, dining room, cable TV, in-room DVDs, 2 pools (1 indoor), gym, hot tub, sauna, pub, meeting rooms, video game room ⊟ AE, D, MC, V.*

$ 🏨 **Americana Holiday Motel.** Alas, none of the motels in South Yarmouth with rates under $100 nightly in summer is especially appealing, but this dated property—with worn furnishings and drab rooms—ranks ahead of the rest, thanks to a friendly staff and clean conditions. Rooms in the rear Pine Grove section overlook serene sea pines and one of the motel's three pools, rather than traffic snarls. The two-room suites have a bedroom plus a separate living room with a sleeper sofa and VCR. Consider it only if you're on the tightest budget. ✉ *99 Rte. 28, 02673* ☎ *508/775–5511 or 800/445–4497* 🖷 *508/790–0597* ⊕ *www. americanaholiday.com* ⇲ *117 rooms, 19 suites ⚷ Coffee shop, refrigerators, cable TV, some in-room VCRs, putting green, 3 pools (1 indoor), hot tub, sauna, shuffleboard, playground ⊟ AE, D, DC, MC, V* ⦿| *CP* ⊘ *Closed Nov.–mid-Apr.*

★ **$** 🏨 **Inn at Lewis Bay.** Affordable and beautiful, this 1920s Dutch Colonial overlooks Lewis Bay, a short walk from the beach. Janet Vaughn, who owns the inn with her husband, David, is an avid quilter; her works top the antique or canopy beds and adorn the walls in the country-style rooms. Each room has a name and a theme; Whale Watch, with its distinctive navys and maroons, is one of two rooms with water views. Bountiful breakfasts are served in the dining room or on the spacious front porch, which is also a pleasant place for afternoon tea and home-baked cookies. It's in a quiet residential neighborhood south of the Route 28 fray. ⊠ *57 Maine Ave., 02673* ☎ *508/771–3433 or 800/ 962–6679* 📠 *508/790–1186* ⊕ *www.innatlewisbay.com* 🛏 *6 rooms* ⚿ *Cable TV, Wi-Fi; no room phones, no TV in some rooms, no kids under 12, no smoking* ☰ *AE, MC, V* ⏍ *BP.*

$ ⌂ **Mariner Motor Lodge.** Although crowded Route 28 is more commercial than serene, it's also home to several value-packed hotels. The Mariner, near the Hyannis–West Yarmouth line, is a good family lodging and a bargain. Although the rooms are standard-issue motel—think basic furnishings such as floral bedcovers and carpets that can take a direct hit from a spilled soft drink—the outdoor pool is heated and large, and a heated indoor pool, with an oversize whirlpool hot tub, is great for rainy days. Also on-site are a miniature-golf course and vending machines for snacks. Kids stay free, and weekday rates are reduced. ⊠ *573 Rte. 28, 02673* ☎ *508/771–7887 or 800/445–4050* 📠 *508/771–2811* ⊕ *www.mariner-capecod.com* 🛏 *100 rooms* ⚿ *Coffee shop, in-room safes, refrigerators, cable TV, miniature golf, 2 pools (1 indoor), hot tub, no-smoking rooms* ☰ *AE, D, MC, V.*

YARMOUTH PORT ✕ **Abbicci.** Set inside a dapper yellow 1755 house nestled beneath tow-
★ $$–$$$$ ering shade trees, Abbicci is an airy, smartly decorated space with a handsome black-slate bar. One of the first to bring northern Italian cooking to Cape Cod, chef-owner Marietta Hickey has remained true to tradition, offering fish and elegant pastas during summer and heartier dishes in the winter months. She prepares rich and full-tasting fare; one of the most pleasing is roast rack and grilled leg of lamb with a Cabernet mint demi-glace. Abbicci added a creative tapas menu in 2005, making this a great choice for grazing and sipping wine, too. ⊠ *43 Rte. 6A* ☎ *508/ 362–3501* ⊕ *www.abbicci.com* ☰ *AE, D, DC, MC, V.*

$$–$$$$ ✕ **Old Yarmouth Inn Restaurant & Tavern.** Established in 1696, this inn— the oldest on Cape Cod—now primarily functions as a restaurant (rooms are available in season). It comprises a main dining room, which is bright and airy, and two smaller and more intimate ones, plus the wood-paneled Tavern, which has a full bar and serves more casual fare. Fresh ingredients are a priority, so the menu changes seasonally; the wide range of meat, poultry, seafood, and pasta dishes infused with clever combinations of familiar flavors offers something for just about everyone. The Sunday brunch is popular. ⊠ *223 Rte. 6A* ☎ *508/362–9962* ⊕ *www. oldyarmouthinn.com* ☰ *AE, D, MC, V* ⊘ *Closed Mon., Jan.–May.*

$–$$$ ✕ **Inaho.** Yuji Watanabe, chef-owner of the Cape's best Japanese restau-
Fodor'sChoice rant, makes early-morning journeys to Boston's fish markets to shop
★ for the freshest local catch. His selection of sushi and sashimi is vast and artful, and vegetable and seafood tempura come out of the kitchen fluffy and light. If you're a teriyaki lover, you can't do any better than the chicken's beautiful blend of sweet and sour. One remarkable element of the restaurant is its artful lighting: small pinpoint lights on the food accentuate the presentation in a dramatic way. The serene and simple Japanese garden out back has a traditional koi pond. ⊠ *157 Rte. 6A* ☎ *508/362–5522* ☰ *MC, V* ⊘ *Closed Mon. No lunch.*

$–$$$ ⌂ **The Inn at Cape Cod.** A stately Greek Revival building with imposing columns, the inn has one of the most dramatic facades of any house on the Cape; it sits near the Botanical Trails and has its own fine gardens, patios, and tree-shaded lawns. On the first floor, the Joshua Sears Room, with a mahogany king-size four-poster bed and antique furnishings, is a traditional Victorian chamber. Upstairs, the romantic Village Suite, with an Italian armoire and cherrywood writing desk, opens to the front porch; the frilly Victorian Room has its own fireplace. Some smaller rooms, particularly the basic Guest Room, are pint-size. ⊠ *4 Summer St., 02675* ☎ *508/375–0590 or 800/850–7301* 🖷 *508/362–9520* ⊕ *www. innatcapecod.com* ⤴ *7 rooms, 2 suites* ⚘ *Cable TV, in-room VCRs, Wi-Fi; no smoking* ▭ *AE, D, DC, MC, V* ⦿ *BP.*

$–$$$ 🏨 **Liberty Hill Inn.** Smartly but traditionally furnished common areas— including the high-ceiling parlor, the formal dining room, and the wrap-around porch—are a major draw to this dignified 1825 Greek Revival house. Guest rooms in both the main building and the carriage house are filled with a mix of old-world romantic charm and modern amenities; each is uniquely decorated, and some have whirlpool tubs. Breakfast might include blueberry French toast or a frittata, and afternoon tea is also available. ⊠ *77 Rte. 6A, 02675* ☎ *508/362–3976 or 800/ 821–3977* 🖷 *508/362–6485* ⊕ *www.libertyhillinn.com* ⤴ *8 rooms, 1 suite* ⚘ *Some in-room hot tubs, cable TV, Wi-Fi; no smoking* ▭ *AE, D, MC, V* ⦿ *BP.*

★ $–$$ 🏨 **Blueberry Manor.** The living room of this 19th-century Greek Revival pairs Victorian furnishings with modern amenities, including a TV–VCR, a stereo, and a stash of puzzles, games, and books. Guest-room furnishings are traditional, but there are no fussy lace treatments or curio shelves. The Lavender Room has a queen-size four-poster bed with a handmade quilt, an antique armoire, and a modern bath under the eaves. The Rose Room has an exquisitely painted queen-size bed and cheery pink walls. The Willow Garden Suite has beam ceilings, an elegant sleigh bed, and a fireplace; it accommodates up to four and is suitable for a family. The fruit from the blueberry bushes in the lush yard turns up in homemade coffee cakes and other baked goods. Gray's Beach is within walking distance. ⊠ *438 Rte. 6A, 02675* ☎ *508/362–7620* 🖷 *508/362– 0053* ⊕ *www.blueberrymanor.com* ⤴ *3 rooms, 1 suite* ⚘ *Wi-Fi; no room phones, no room TVs, no smoking* ▭ *AE, MC, V* ⦿ *BP.*

¢–$ 🏨 **Village Inn.** Guest rooms, with wide pine floorboards, are snug in this old-fashioned 1795 sea captain's house. The Provincetown Room once served as the house's schoolroom; the original (but no longer used) light fixtures are still in place. The Wellfleet Room is tiny, but it's a great bargain for solo travelers. Families should note that the Brewster, Truro, and Hyannis rooms connect and that the first-floor Yarmouth Room is the most spacious, with its own library, bathroom with fireplace, and private entrance. The common rooms have as many books as some public libraries. Kids are welcome. It's not fancy, but it's well priced. ⊠ *92 Rte. 6A, Box 1, 02675* ☎ *508/362–3182* ⊕ *www.thevillageinncapecod. com* ⤴ *10 rooms, 8 with bath* ⚘ *No room phones, no TV in some rooms, no smoking* ▭ *MC, V* ⦿ *BP* ⊘ *Closed Nov.–Apr.*

Nightlife & the Arts

Feel as if it's been too long since you last fox-trotted? **Betsy's Ballroom** (⊠ 528 Forest Rd., South Yarmouth ☎ 508/362–9538) has Saturday-night ballroom dancing year-round on the Cape's largest dance floor. Live bands deliver swing, waltzes, and fox-trot 8 PM–11 PM. It's BYO for drinks and snacks; Betsy will provide the ice and cups. Admission is $8.50.

Cape Cod Irish Village (⊠ 512 Rte. 28, West Yarmouth ☎ 508/771–0100) has dancing to two- or three-piece bands performing traditional and popular Irish music year-round. The crowd is mostly couples and people over 35.

Oliver's (⊠ 6 Bray Farm Rd., off Rte. 6A, Yarmouth Port ☎ 508/362–6062) has live music in a variety of genres in its tavern on weekends year-round.

West Yarmouth's summertime **town-band concerts** are held on Monday in July and August at 7 PM at **Mattacheese Middle School** (⊠ Off Higgins Crowell Rd., West Yarmouth ☎ 508/778–1008).

Sports & the Outdoors

BASEBALL The **Yarmouth-Dennis Red Sox** of the collegiate Cape Cod Baseball League play home games at **Red Wilson Field** (⊠ Station Ave., South Yarmouth ☎ 508/394–9387 ⊕ www.ydredsox.org) from mid-June to mid-August.

BEACHES Parking at Yarmouth beaches for nonresidents is $12 on weekdays and $15 on weekends Memorial Day through Labor Day.

Dennis Pond (⊠ Off Summer St., Yarmouth Port) is a freshwater pond with a sandy beach, restrooms, and a seasonal snack bar. In season, a resident parking sticker is required.

The **Flax Pond** (⊠ N. Main St. between High Bank and Great Western Rds., South Yarmouth) recreation area has freshwater swimming, a lifeguard, and ducks, but no sand beach, just pine needle–covered ground. There's a pine-shaded picnic area with grills, as well as tennis and basketball courts and plenty of parking.

Parker's River Beach (⊠ South Shore Dr., South Yarmouth), a flat stretch of sand on warm Nantucket Sound, is perfect for families. It has a lifeguard, a concession stand, a gazebo and picnic area, a playground, outdoor showers, and restrooms.

Seagull Beach (⊠ Seagull Rd. off South Sea Ave., West Yarmouth), a long, wide beach along Nantucket Sound, has restrooms and a seasonal concession stand.

BIKE RENTAL **Bike Zone Inc.** (⊠ 1124 Rte. 28, South Yarmouth ☎ 508/398–5550) rents and sells bicycles; it's also a good local resource for all things related to cycling on the Cape.

BOATING **Great Marsh Kayak Tours** (⊠ Rte. 28, West Yarmouth, next to ZooQuarium ☎ 508/775–6447 or 866/395–2925 ⊠ At the Lamb and Lion Inn, 2504 Rte. 6, Barnstable ☎ 508/375–9000 or 866/675–2925) offers a range of great excursions along the water, from fly-fishing trips to sunset jaunts—you can also customize your own itinerary.

FISHING **Truman's** (⊠ 608 Rte. 28, West Yarmouth ☎ 508/771–3470) can supply you with a required freshwater license and rental gear.

GOLF **Blue Rock Golf Course** (✉ Off Great Western Rd., South Yarmouth ☎ 508/398–9295) is a highly regarded, easy-to-walk 18-hole, par-3, 3,000-yard public course crossed by a pond. The pro shop rents clubs; reservations are mandatory in season.

HEALTH & **Mid Cape Racquet Club** (✉ 193 White's Path, South Yarmouth ☎ 508/
FITNESS CLUBS 394–3511 ⊕ www.midcaperacquet.com) has one racquetball, one squash, and nine indoor tennis courts; indoor basketball; a sauna, steam room, and whirlpools; massage services; and a free-weight and cardiovascular room—plus day care. It also offers spinning, kickboxing, and body pump classes. Daily rates are available.

SOCCER The **Cape Cod Crusaders,** of the D-3 League, play action-packed home matches at the Alan Carlsen Field at **Dennis-Yarmouth Regional High School** (✉ Station Ave., South Yarmouth ☎ 508/394–1171 ⊕ www.capecodcrusaders.com) from May to mid-August.

Shopping

Cummaquid Fine Arts (✉ 4275 Rte. 6A, Cummaquid ☎ 508/362–2593) has works by contemporary resident Cape Cod artists, all beautifully displayed in an old home.

Parnassus Book Service (✉ 220 Rte. 6A, Yarmouth Port ☎ 508/362–6420), occupying a three-story 1840 former general store, has a huge selection of old and new books—Cape Cod, maritime, Americana, antiquarian, and others—and is a great place to browse. Its bookstall, outside on the building's side, is open 24 hours a day and works on the honor system—tally up your purchases and leave the money in the mail slot. Parnassus also carries Robert Bateman's nature prints.

Peach Tree Designs (✉ 173 Rte. 6A, Yarmouth Port ☎ 508/362–8317) carries home furnishings and decorative accessories; some are from local craftspeople, all are beautifully made.

Dennis

Dennis Village is 4 mi east of Yarmouth Port, West Dennis is 1 mi east of South Yarmouth.

Like Yarmouth, Dennis has a split personality. The town's southern villages, such as Dennis Port and West Dennis, tend to be heavily developed and commercialized and are more popular with families, whereas the northern section, anchored by historic **Dennis Village,** is peaceful and dignified, with countless old homes and inns lining Route 6A.

The backstreets of Dennis Village still retain the colonial charm of its seafaring days. The town, which was incorporated in 1793, was named for the Reverend Josiah Dennis. There were 379 sea captains living here when fishing, salt making, and shipbuilding were the main industries, and the elegant houses they constructed—now museums and B&Bs—still line the streets. In 1816, resident Henry Hall discovered that adding sand to his cranberry fields' soil improved the size of his harvest and the quality of the fruit. The following decades saw cranberry farming and tourism become the Cape's main commercial enterprises. Dennis has a number of conservation areas and nature trails and numerous freshwater ponds for swimming. The village center has antiques shops, general stores, a post office, and ice-cream shops. There's also a village green with a bandstand, the site of occasional summer concerts.

The **Josiah Dennis Manse,** a saltbox house with add-ons, was built in 1736 for the Reverend Josiah Dennis. Inside, the home reflects life in the Reverend Dennis's day. A child's room includes antique furniture and toys, the keeping room has a fireplace and cooking utensils, and the attic exhibits spinning and weaving equipment. Throughout you'll see china, pewter, and portraits of sea captains. The Maritime Wing has ship models, paintings, and nautical artifacts. On the grounds is a 1770 one-room schoolhouse, furnished with wood-and-wrought-iron desks and chairs. ⊠ *77 Nobscussett Rd., at Whig St., Dennis Village* ☎ *508/385–2232* ✉ *Donations accepted* ⊙ *Late June–Sept., Tues. 10–noon, Thurs. 2–4.*

> **WORD OF MOUTH**
>
> "Don't forget to play minigolf. Its illegal to leave the Cape without having played at least one round."
> –bennnie

On a clear day, you'll have unbeatable views of Scargo Lake, Dennis Village's scattered houses below, Cape Cod Bay, and distant Provincetown from the top of **Scargo Tower.** A wooden tower built on this site in 1874 was one of the Cape's first tourist attractions; visitors would pay 5¢ to climb to the top for the views. That tower burned down, and the present all-stone 30-foot tower was built in 1901 to replace it. Winding stairs bring you to the top; don't forget to read the unsightly, but amusing, graffiti on the way up. Expect crowds at sunrise and sunset. ⊠ *Scargo Hill Rd., off Rte. 6A or Old Bass River Rd., Dennis Village* ✉ *Free* ⊙ *Daily sunrise–sunset.*

NEED A BREAK?

Dip into homemade ice cream and frozen yogurt at the Ice Cream Smuggler (⊠ **716 Rte. 6A, Dennis Village** ☎ **508/385–5307), across the street from the town green and cemetery. The ginger ice cream is a specialty, but order the triple hot fudge sundae for the ultimate decadence.**

For Broadway-style dramas, comedies, and musicals, as well as kids' plays, you can attend a production at the **Cape Playhouse,** the oldest professional summer theater in the country. In 1927 Raymond Moore, who had been working with a theatrical troupe in Provincetown, bought an 1838 former Unitarian meetinghouse and converted it into a theater. The original pews still serve as seats. The opening performance was *The Guardsman,* starring Basil Rathbone; other stars who performed here in the early days—some in their professional stage debuts—include Bette Davis (who first worked here as an usher), Gregory Peck, Lana Turner, Ginger Rogers, Humphrey Bogart, Tallulah Bankhead, and Henry Fonda, who appeared with his then-unknown 20-year-old daughter, Jane. Cape resident Shirley Booth was such an admirer of the playhouse that she donated her Oscar (for *Come Back*

Little Sheba) and her Emmy (for *Hazel*) to the theater; both are on display in the lobby during the season. Behind-the-scene tours are also given in season; call for a schedule. The playhouse offers children's theater on Friday morning during July and August. Also on the 26-acre property, now known as the Cape Playhouse Center for the Arts, are a restaurant, the **Cape Cod Museum of Art,** and the **Cape Cinema,** whose exterior was designed in the style of the Congregational church in Centerville. Inside, a 6,400-square-foot mural of heavenly skies—designed by Massachusetts artist Rockwell Kent, who also designed the gold-sunburst curtain—covers the ceiling. ⌧ *820 Rte. 6A, Dennis Village* ☎ *508/385–3911 or 877/385–3911* ⊕ *www.capeplayhouse.com* ⊗ *Call for tour schedule.*

NEED A BREAK? Indulge in sumptuous baked goods at **Buckie's Biscotti** (⌧ 780 Rte. 6A, Dennis Village ☎ 508/385-4700 ⊕ www.buckiesbiscotti.com), just behind the Dennis Post Office near the Cape Playhouse. Have a slice of pie—try the Italian home-style ricotta or the key lime, arguably the Cape's best—or another tasty treat, then wash it all down with a cappuccino or latte.

The **Cape Cod Museum of Art** has a permanent collection of more than 850 works by Cape-associated artists. Important pieces include a portrait of a fisherman's wife by Charles Hawthorne, the father of the Provincetown art colony; a 1924 portrait of a Portuguese fisherman's daughter by William Paxton, one of the first artists to summer in Provincetown; a collection of wood-block prints by Varujan Boghosian, a member of Provincetown's Long Point Gallery cooperative; an oil sketch by Karl Knaths, who painted in Provincetown from 1919 until his death in 1971; and works by abstract expressionist Hans Hoffman and many of his students. The museum also plays host to interesting temporary exhibitions, film festivals, lectures, art classes, and trips. The outdoor sculpture garden has an eclectic collection on display; it's a pleasant place to take a short stroll. On Wednesday from 10 AM to 1 PM, admission is free. ⌧ *60 Hope La., on grounds of Cape Playhouse, off Rte. 6A, Dennis Village* ☎ *508/385-4477* ⊕ *www.ccmoa.org* ⌦ *$7* ⊗ *Mon.–Sat. 10–5, Sun. noon–5.*

18 In another one of those tricks of Cape geography, the village of **West Dennis** is actually south of South Dennis, on the east side of the Bass River. Dennisport is farther east, near the Harwich town line. If you're driving between West Dennis and Harwich, Lower County Road, with occasional glimpses of the sea between the cottages and beachfront hotels, is a more scenic alternative to overdeveloped Route 28.

19 The Mid Cape's last southern village is **Dennisport,** a prime summer-resort area, with gray-shingle cottages, summer houses and condominiums, and lots of white picket fences covered with rambling roses. The Union Wharf Packing Company operated here in the 1850s, and sail makers and ship chandlers lined the shore. Sunbathers now pack the sands where sea clams once laid primary claim.

| NEED A
| BREAK? | Set in a rustic mid-19th-century barn decorated with a working nickelodeon, the **Sundae School Ice Cream Parlor** (✉ 387 Lower County Rd., Dennisport ☎ 508/394–9122), open mid-April–mid-October, serves great homemade ice cream, frozen yogurt, real whipped cream, and old-fashioned sarsaparilla and cream soda from an antique marble soda fountain.

Where to Stay & Eat

DENNISPORT
$$–$$$$
Fodor'sChoice
★

✕ **Ocean House.** Overlooking Nantucket Sound, this noisy but superb restaurant has views to match the spectacular food and service. Sunday brunches (reservations strongly recommended) are decadent, with various carving stations, omelets, pancakes, and waffles made to order, and oysters and shrimp on ice, to name just a few of the selections. For dinner, try apple mustard–glazed Atlantic salmon with creamy cheddar grits, followed by caramelized sugar–encrusted vanilla-bean crème brûlée. Chef Anthony Silvestri changes the menu seasonally. ✉ *End of Depot St., Dennisport* ☎ *508/394–0700* ▭ *AE, D, MC, V.*

$–$$$

✕ **Clancy's.** A local landmark on the bucolic Swan River, Clancy's is popular—the parking lot is often jammed by 5 PM, so expect a substantial wait during peak hours in season. This is an enormous operation, with long family tables, round tables, booths, a deck overlooking the river, and two bars. On the seemingly endless menu are several variations of nachos, salads, and chili. Clancy's likes to be creative with the names of its dishes, so you can find items such as steak Lucifer (sirloin topped with lobster, asparagus, and béarnaise sauce) and a Sunday-brunch menu with the likes of crab, steak, or eggs Benny. ✉ *8 Upper County Rd.* ☎ *508/394–6661* ⊕ *www.clancysrestaurant.com* ⌔ *Reservations not accepted* ▭ *AE, DC, MC, V.*

$–$$$

✕ **Swan River Seafood Restaurant.** From the right table you can have a beautiful view of the Swan River marsh and Nantucket Sound beyond at this informal little eatery, which turns out great fresh fish in both traditional and creative preparations. Besides the usual fried and broiled choices, try mako shark au poivre or scrod San Sebastian, simmered in garlic broth with littleneck clams. There's also a take-out window. ✉ *5 Lower County Rd.* ☎ *508/394–4466* ▭ *AE, MC, V* ☉ *Closed mid-Sept.–late May. No lunch weekdays late May–mid-June.*

$$–$$$$

▥ **The Corsair and Cross Rip.** These motels, built side by side, offer clean and crisp rooms, many with captivating beach views. Rooms in the main motel buildings range from smaller "value" units with one queen bed to pricier deluxe accommodations with kitchenettes and sitting areas, plus a few spacious condo-style suites. Three large three- and four-bedroom vacation houses are also available for rent; they can sleep up to 12 and are fully equipped with luxurious amenities. Decor in the motel buildings is more basic, but between the oceanfront location (there are three private beaches) and the extensive facilities, you probably won't be spending much time in your room. There are also laundry facilities on-site. Suites and houses require a one-week minimum stay in season. ✉ *33 and 41 Chase Ave., 02639* ☎ *508/398–2279 or 800/889–8037* ⊕ *www.corsaircrossrip.com* ⇋ *37 rooms, 4 suites* ♢ *Picnic area, some kitchens, some kitchenettes, refrigerators, cable TV, 2 pools (1 indoor),* *hot tub, video game room, laundry facilities; no smoking* $\equiv$ *AE, D, MC, V* $\odot$ *Closed late Oct.–Mar.*

$$ 🏠 **English Garden Bed & Breakfast.** Anita and Joe Sangiolo—she's a former actress and he's a retired engineer—have turned their comfortable 1922 home into an equally comfortable B&B. The eight rooms are done in a cheerful country style, with quilts, four-poster or iron beds, and pine armoires; four rooms have ocean views. The adjacent carriage house has two modern suites, each with a bedroom, separate living area with gas fireplace, and kitchenette—these are available on a weekly basis. Beach chairs and towels are provided (the house is a block from the sand), and Joe has put together a meticulously detailed notebook of things to do. Film buffs take note: one of the two guest parlors has a TV–VCR and a collection of classic movies. ⊠ *32 Inman Rd., 02639* ☎ *508/398–2915 or 888/788–1908* 🖨 *508/398–2852* ⊕ *www.anenglishgardenbb.com* ♊ *8 rooms, 3 suites* ♿ *Some kitchenettes, cable TV, Internet room; no kids under 10 (except in suites), no smoking* $\equiv$ *AE, D, MC, V* $\odot$ *Closed Nov.–mid-Apr.* ⦿ *BP.*

$–$$ 🏠 **The Garlands.** Old Wharf Road in Dennisport is lined with strip motels and cottage colonies, but few places provide comfort and views to match this bi-level motel-style complex. There are 20 units in all; 18 are two-bedroom suites. Each unit has a fully equipped kitchen, private sundeck or patio, and daily maid service. The oceanfront VIP suites, simply named A and B (two bedrooms) and C and D (one bedroom), are the best picks here—the nearly floor-to-ceiling windows offer unobstructed water views; at high tide you're almost in the surf. ⊠ *117 Old Wharf Rd., Box 506, 02639* ☎ *508/398–6987* ♊ *20 suites* ♿ *Fans, kitchens, cable TV, beach; no a/c* $\equiv$ *No credit cards* $\odot$ *Closed mid-Oct.–mid-Apr.*

DENNIS VILLAGE
$$–$$$$
Fodor'sChoice
★
✕ **Red Pheasant.** This is one of the Cape's best cozy country restaurants, with a consistently good kitchen where creative American food is prepared with elaborate sauces and herb combinations. For instance, organic chicken is served with an intense preserved-lemon and fresh thyme sauce, and exquisitely grilled veal chops come with a dense red wine-and-portobello mushroom sauce. In fall, look for the specialty game dishes, including venison and quail. Try to reserve a table in the more intimate Garden Room. The expansive wine list is excellent. ⊠ *905 Rte. 6A* ☎ *508/385–2133* ⊕ *www.redpheasantinn.com* ♊ *Reservations essential* $\equiv$ *AE, D, MC, V* $\odot$ *No lunch.*

$$–$$$$ ✕ **Scargo Café.** With the Cape Playhouse right across the street, this upscale contemporary American restaurant is a favorite before- and after-show haunt. There's plenty of seafood on the eclectic menu, such as the "Seafood Romance" with clams, scallops, and shrimp, but carnivores will also take delight, with such dishes as ginger duckling, rack of lamb, and twin filet mignons. Lighter meals include scallops harpooned on a skewer and tucked in bacon, and an Asian-style fish sandwich served with seaweed salad. An added plus: the kitchen stays open until 11 PM in summer. ⊠ *799 Rte. 6A* ☎ *508/385–8200* ⊕ *www.scargocafe.com* $\equiv$ *AE, D, MC, V.*

$$–$$$ ✕ **Gina's by the Sea.** Some places are less than the sum of their parts; Gina's is more. This funky old building is tucked into a sand dune, so that the aroma of fine northern Italian cooking blends with a fresh breeze off the bay. The dining room is tasteful, cozy, and especially wonderful in fall when the fireplace is blazing. Blackboard specials could include angel-hair pasta or linguine with clams. If you don't want a long wait, come early or late. An enthusiastic staff rounds out the experience. ⊠ *134 Taunton Ave.* ☎ *508/385–3213* ⚏ *Reservations not accepted* ⊟ *AE, MC, V* ⊗ *Closed Dec.–Mar. and Mon.–Wed. Oct.–Nov.*

$–$$ ✕ **Cap'n Frosty's.** A great stop after the beach, this is where locals go to
Fodor'sChoice   get their fried seafood. This modest joint has a regular menu that in-
★   cludes ice cream, a small specials board, and a counter where you order and take a number written on a french fries box. The staff is young and hard working, pumping out fresh fried clams and fish-and-chips on paper plates. All frying is done in 100% canola oil, and rice pilaf is offered as a substitute for fries. There's seating inside as well as outside on a shady brick patio. ⊠ *219 Rte. 6A* ☎ *508/385–8548* ⚏ *Reservations not accepted* ⊟ *No credit cards* ⊗ *Closed early Sept.–Mar.*

¢   ✕ **Grumpy's Restaurant.** This airy diner consistently packs its tables and counter space year-round, and for good reason. From baked goods to waffles and eggs done any way you like them, Grumpy's jump-starts your day with generous portions for breakfast and lunch. Get here early to avoid a line that often curls out the door. ⊠ *1408 Rte. 6A* ☎ *508/385–2911* ⚏ *Reservations not accepted* ⊟ *No credit cards* ⊗ *No dinner.*

¢   ✕ **Red Cottage Restaurant.** Up Old Bass River Road ½ mi north of the town
Fodor'sChoice   hall, the Red Cottage is indeed a red cottage and serves breakfast and lunch
★   year-round. Locals pack this place even in the off-season, and you can expect a wait in the summer. The cottage is a no-frills, friendly place with food that runs the gamut from decadent stuffed French toast specials to a list of health-conscious offerings with egg whites, "lite" cheese, and turkey bacon. The grill is in plain view; if you want to watch your meal being cooked, the swivel stools at the counter have the best angle. Bottomless cups of coffee are served in an interesting collection of mismatched mugs. The breakfasts are better than the lunches, but both are no-nonsense and just plain reliably good. ⊠ *36 Old Bass River Rd.* ☎ *508/394–2923* ⚏ *Reservations not accepted* ⊟ *No credit cards* ⊗ *No dinner.*

$–$$ ⌂ **Isaiah Hall B&B Inn.** Lilacs and pink roses trail along the white picket
Fodor'sChoice   fence outside this 1857 Greek Revival farmhouse on a quiet residential
★   road near the bay. Innkeepers Jerry and Judy Neal set the scene for a romantic getaway with guest rooms that have country antiques, floral-print wallpapers, and homey touches, such as quilts and Priscilla curtains. In the attached carriage house, rooms have three walls stenciled white and one paneled with knotty pine, and some have small balconies overlooking a wooded lawn with gardens, grape arbors, and berry bushes. The carriage-house suite has a king-size bed, a separate sitting area with a pullout couch, and a refrigerator. Common areas such as the dining room are elegant. Make-it-yourself popcorn, tea, coffee, and soft drinks are always available. ⊠ *152 Whig St., Box 1007, 02638* ☎ *508/385–9928 or 800/736–0160* ⊟ *508/385–5879* ⊕ *www.isaiahhallinn.com* ⇨ *10 rooms, 2 suites* ⚏ *Picnic area, cable TV, in-room VCRs, Wi-Fi, badminton, croquet; no kids under 7, no smoking* ⊟ *AE, D, MC, V* ❏ *BP.*

3

$–$$ ☐ **Scargo Manor.** This 1895 sea captain's home has a prime location on Scargo Lake, with a private beach and dock. Inside, innkeepers Larry and Debbie Bain display a collection of art and antiques amid the Victorian furnishings. There's plenty of room to spread out on the big screened porch, in the sitting room or more formal living room, or in the cozy third-floor reading room. If you want a lake view, choose the cozy all-blue Hydrangea Room, with a pineapple-top four-poster bed and a skylight overhead. For more space, the Captain Howe's Suite has a king-size canopy bed, plus a separate sitting room with a working fireplace that's bigger than the guest rooms at many other B&Bs. Kids 5 and up are welcome. ⊠ *909 Rte. 6A, 02638* ☎ *508/385–5534 or 800/595–0034* 🖷 *508/385–9791* ⊕ *www.scargomanor.com* ⇆ *4 rooms, 2 suites* ♨ *Cable TV, beach, boating, bicycles, Internet room; no room phones, no smoking* ⊟ *AE, D, DC, MC, V* ⍾ *BP.*

WEST DENNIS ✗ **Kream 'N Kone.** The Kream 'N Kone has been going strong since 1953:
¢–$$ order up some fried clams and a shake or a soda, get a number, wait five minutes, and sit down to some of the best fast food anywhere. Fried food will overflow your paper plate onto a plastic tray, but it's so good that what you thought you'd never be able to finish somehow vanishes. The onion rings in particular are a knockout. At times the prices seem surprisingly high, but the quality and quantity of what you get are well worth the splurge. ⊠ *Corner of Rtes. 134 and 28* ☎ *508/394–0808* ⊟ *MC, V* ⍾ *Closed Nov.–Jan.*

$$$–$$$$ ☐ **Lighthouse Inn.** On a small private beach adjacent to West Dennis Beach, this venerable Cape resort has been in family hands since 1938. The main inn was built around a still-operational 1855 lighthouse. Along a landscaped lawn are 23 individual one- to three-bedroom cottages made entirely of shingles and five larger buildings with multiple guest rooms. Cottages have decks, fireplaces, two double (or one double and one king-size) beds, and sitting areas (but no kitchens). In the main inn are five guest rooms, a living room, a library, and a waterfront restaurant serving New England fare. In summer, supervised kids' activities give parents some private time. ⊠ *1 Lighthouse Rd., Box 128, 02670* ☎ *508/398–2244* 🖷 *508/398–5658* ⊕ *www.lighthouseinn.com* ⇆ *40 rooms, 23 cottages* ♨ *Restaurant, room service, refrigerators, cable TV, in-room data ports, miniature golf, tennis court, pool, beach, fishing, billiards, shuffleboard, bar, library, nightclub, recreation room, children's programs (ages 3–12), playground* ⊟ *MC, V* ⍾ *Closed mid-Oct.–mid-May* ⍾ *BP, MAP.*

$–$$ ☐ **Shady Hollow Inn.** Dedicated vegetarians, owners Ann Hart and David Dennis found B&B travel a challenge, so they opened their own veggie-friendly inn in tranquil South Dennis, well off the beaten path. Their breakfasts, which might include omelets, dairy-free baked goods, or a tofu quiche, are designed to appeal to anyone, from foodies to strict vegans. By prior arrangement, they can also prepare vegetarian dinners. Furnishings in their comfortable home are Mission-style; the guest rooms have quilt-topped beds, and the largest—the airy first-floor Westwind—has a striking painted mantel. ⊠ *370 Main St., South Dennis 02660* ☎ *508/394–7474* ⊕ *www.shadyhollowinn.com* ⇆ *4 rooms, 2 with bath* ♨ *In-room VCRs, bicycles; no room phones, no kids under 10, no smoking* ⊟ *MC, V* ⍾ *BP.*

Nightlife & the Arts

The **Cape Playhouse** (⊠ 820 Rte. 6A, Dennis Village ☎ 508/385–3911 or 877/385–3911 ⊕ www.capeplayhouse.com), an 1838 former Unitarian meetinghouse, is the oldest professional summer theater in the country. Top stars appear here each summer, and the playhouse also mounts kids' shows on Friday morning in July and August. On the grounds of the Cape Playhouse is the artsy **Cape Cinema** (☎ 508/385–2503 ⊕ www.capecinema.com), which shows foreign and first-run films throughout the summer.

Improper Bostonian (⊠ Rte. 28, Dennisport ☎ 508/394–7416), open only in summer, has a mix of live music and DJ-spun dance tunes several nights a week and attracts a young crowd.

Karl's Landmark Cafe (⊠ 645 Rte. 28, Dennisport ☎ 508/398–5551), open only in summer, shares patrons with **Improper Bostonian** across the street. Live music and DJs entertain a dancing crowd.

Lost Dog Pub (⊠ 1374 Rte. 134, Dennis Village ☎ 508/385–6177) offers basic pub eats and a relaxed social atmosphere; it's a popular place for locals and visitors to grab a beer after a long day.

Reel Art (⊠ 60 Hope La., Dennis Village ☎ 508/385–4477), at the Cape Museum of Fine Arts, shows avant-garde, classic, art, and independent films on weekends September through April. Call for a schedule.

The **Sand Bar** (⊠ Lighthouse Rd., West Dennis ☎ 508/398–7586) presents the boogie-woogie piano playing of local legend Rock King, who's been tickling the ivories—and people's funny bones—since the 1960s. The club is closed from mid-October to mid-May.

In season, you can dance to a DJ and live bands at **Sundancer's** (⊠ 116 Rte. 28, West Dennis ☎ 508/394–1600). It's closed December and January.

Sports & the Outdoors

BEACHES Parking at all Dennis beaches is $15 a day in season for nonresidents.

Chapin Beach (⊠ Chapin Beach Rd., Dennis Village) is a lovely dune-backed bay beach with long tidal flats—you can walk really far out at low tide. It has no lifeguards or services.

Corporation Beach (⊠ Corporation Rd., Dennis Village) has lifeguards, showers, restrooms, and a food stand. Once a packet landing owned by a corporation of the townsfolk, the beautiful crescent of white sand backed by low dunes now serves a decidedly noncorporate purpose as a public beach.

Mayflower Beach (⊠ Dunes Rd. off Bayview Rd., Dennis Village) reveals hundreds of feet of tidal flats at low tide. The beach has restrooms, showers, lifeguards, and a food stand.

For freshwater swimming, **Scargo Lake** (⊠ Access off Rte. 6A or Scargo Hill Rd., Dennis Village) has two beaches with restrooms, playgrounds, and a picnic area. The sandy-bottom lake is shallow along the shore, which is good for kids. It's surrounded by woods and is stocked for fishing.

The **West Dennis Beach** (⊠ Lighthouse Rd. off Lower County Rd., West Dennis) is one of the best on the south shore. A breakwater was started here in 1837 in an effort to protect the mouth of Bass River, but was abandoned when a sandbar formed on the shore side. It's a long, wide, and popular sandy beach, stretching for 1½ mi, with marshland and the Bass River across from it. Popular with windsurfers, the beach also has bathhouses, lifeguards, a playground, concessions, and parking for 1,000 cars.

BICYCLING You can pick up the 25-mi Cape Cod Rail Trail at several points along its path. In fact, riding the entire trail in one day doesn't do justice to its sights and side trips (though it certainly can be done). Many cyclists, especially those with small kids, prefer the piecemeal method because they can relax and enjoy the sights—and not turn their legs into jelly.

The ride in Dennis starts as a flat, straight spin through a small pine forest—a good warm-up exercise. Your first road crossing is at busy Great Western Road, one of the town's major thoroughfares, after which you'll pass Sand Pond and Flax Pond in Harwich. The Dennis part of the trail is short, but it's worth starting here for the ample parking at the trail's entrance and for the several bike-rental places that set up shop on Route 134.

A guidebook published by the Dennis Chamber of Commerce includes bike tours and maps. You can rent bikes from a number of places along the Cape Cod Rail Trail. **Barbara's Bike Shop** (⊠ 430 Rte. 134, Dennis Village ☎ 508/760–4723) is at the Rail Trail entrance.

BOATING **Cape Cod Waterways** (⊠ 16 Rte. 28, Dennisport ☎ 508/398–0080) rents canoes, kayaks, and electric paddleboats for leisurely travel on the Swan River.

FISHING Sesuit Harbor, on the bay side of Dennis off Route 6A, is busy with fishing and pleasure boats; several are available for fishing charters. The **Bluefish** (⊠ Sesuit Harbor ⌂ Box 113, Dennis Village 02638 ☎ 508/385–7265 ⊕ www.sunsol.com/bluefish) makes four-, six-, and eight-hour fishing excursions. The **LAD-NAV** (⊠ Sesuit Harbor ⌂ Box 2002, East Dennis 02641 ☎ 508/385–8150 ⊕ www.lad-nav.com) takes as many as six anglers per trip on a 36-foot fishing vessel.

ICE-SKATING You can ice-skate at the **Tony Kent Arena** (⊠ 8 Gages Way, South Dennis ☎ 508/760–2400) fall though spring and on Saturday in summer. Keep your eyes peeled: this is where Nancy Kerrigan and Paul Wylie train. Rental skates are available.

JOGGING **Lifecourse** (⊠ Bob Crowell Rd. and Old Bass River Rd., South Dennis) is a 1½-mi jogging trail through the woods, with 20 exercise stations along the way. It's part of a recreation area that includes basketball and handball courts, ball fields, a playground, and a picnic area.

Shopping

Antiques Center of Cape Cod (⊠ 243 Rte. 6A, Dennis Village ☎ 508/385–6400) is a large and busy market populated by more than 160 dealers offering furniture, artwork, jewelry, china, clocks, books, antique dolls, and other collectibles.

CLOSE UP

Riding the Rail Trail

IN THE LATE 1800s visitors to Cape Cod could take the train from Boston all the way to Provincetown. But with the construction of the Sagamore and Bourne bridges in the mid-1930s, the age of the automobile truly arrived on the Cape. Today, although passenger trains no longer serve Cape Cod, the former train paths provide another more leisurely way to explore the Cape—by bicycle.

The Cape's premier bike path, the Cape Cod Rail Trail, was constructed in 1978 and extended in the mid-1990s—it now offers a scenic ride from South Dennis to South Wellfleet. Following the paved right-of-way of the old Penn Central Railroad, it's 25 mi long, passing salt marshes, cranberry bogs, ponds, and Nickerson State Park, which has its own path.

Some serious bikers whiz along at top speed, but that's not the only way to travel. Along the way there are plenty of tempting places to veer off to spend an hour or two on the beach, to stop for lunch or ice cream, or just to smell the pine trees and imagine what the Cape looked like years ago. The terrain is easy to moderate in difficulty and is generally quite flat, so it's great for youngsters.

The trail starts at a parking lot off busy Route 134 south of U.S. 6, near Theophilus Smith Road in South Dennis; it ends at the post office in South Wellfleet. The Dennis Chamber of Commerce will give you a free rail trail map with distance markings to various points along the trail. The map also notes the location of parking lots en route if you want to cover only a segment: in Harwich (across from Pleasant Lake Store on Pleasant Lake Avenue), Brewster (at Nickerson State Park), and Eastham (at the Salt Pond Visitor Center). Several bike shops near the trail in Dennis, Brewster, and Eastham can also provide information as well rentals.

Experienced rail-trailers suggest breaking the trail in segments, perhaps starting in the middle near Nickerson State Park and looping to one end and back. If you want to return to your starting point by public transportation, the easiest way is to start in Dennis, ride to Orleans, and catch the bike-rack-equipped H20 Line bus back to Dennis; contact the Cape Cod Regional Transit Authority for a schedule and route information.

Remember that wheels yield to heels, so cyclists should give walkers the right-of-way. Pass slower traffic on the left, and call out a warning before you pass. Kids under 13 must wear helmets. The trail can get crowded at times; if you prefer solitude (or cooler temperatures), set out earlier in the morning or later in the afternoon.

Busy bike trails share the same fate as roads: maintenance projects and expansion. A 3-mi spur leads from the rail trail through Harwich to the Chatham line, and a new extension continues on into Chatham center. Plans to extend the trail westward into Yarmouth are also in the works. **Nickerson State Park** (☎ 508/896-3491 ⊕ www.state.ma.us/mhd/paths/webrt.htm) maintains the rail trail; to view a map of the route before you leave home, go to their Web site.

–By Carolyn Heller

Armchair Bookstore (✉ 619 Rte. 6A, Dennis Village ☎ 508/385–0900) carries a large selection of new releases, plus numerous books about Cape lore, history, and sights. Also on hand are cards and knickknacks and a kids' section with books, games, and toys.

Cape Cod Shoe Mart (✉ 271 Rte. 28, Dennisport ☎ 508/398–6000) has such brand names as Capezio, Dexter, Clark, Esprit, Nike, Reebok, L. A. Gear, and Rockport.

Emily's Beach Barn (✉ 708 Rte. 6A, Dennis Village ☎ 508/385–8328) has fashionable women's beachwear, from bathing suits and wraps to sun hats and summer dresses and tops.

★ **Robert C. Eldred Co.** (✉ 1483 Rte. 6A, East Dennis ☎ 508/385–3116 ⊕ www.eldreds.com) holds more than two-dozen auctions per year, dealing in Americana; estate jewelry; top-quality antiques; marine, Asian, American, and European art; tools; and dolls. Its "general antiques and accessories" auctions put less-expensive wares on the block.

Ross Coppelman, Goldsmith (✉ 1439 Rte. 6A, East Dennis ☎ 508/385–7900 ⊕ www.rosscoppelman.com) sells original jewelry in high-karat gold, semiprecious gemstones, and other materials (customized wedding bands are a specialty). The pieces are designed by Coppelman, a self-taught goldsmith who has been honing his craft for over 30 years. Be sure to take a peek into the tiny workshop as you enter the showroom.

Fodor'sChoice ★ **Scargo Pottery** (✉ 30 Dr. Lord's Rd. S, off Rte. 6A, Dennis Village ☎ 508/385–3894 ⊕ www.scargopottery.com) is in a pine forest, where potter Harry Holl's unusual wares—such as his signature castle birdhouses—sit on tree stumps and hang from branches. Inside are the workshop and kiln, plus work by Holl's four daughters. With luck you can catch a potter at the wheel; viewing is, in fact, encouraged.

THE MID CAPE ESSENTIALS

To research prices, get advice from other travelers, and book travel arrangements, visit www.fodors.com.

Transportation

BY BOAT & FERRY
Ferries to Nantucket and Martha's Vineyard leave from Hyannis year-round. For details, ⇨ Boat & Ferry Travel *in* Smart Travel Tips A to Z in the back of this book.

BY BUS
Hyannis is the Cape's transit hub, and is served by a number of bus routes, including the local Hyannis Villager and the Barnstable Villager lines. Buses also link Hyannis with Orleans, Woods Hole, Provincetown, Plymouth, downtown Boston, and Logan airport, as well as various towns on each route. For more information, ⇨ Bus Travel *in* Smart Travel Tips A to Z in the back of this book.

🚍 Bus Depots **Hyannis Transportation Center** ✉ 215 Iyanough Rd., Hyannis ☎ 508/775-8504 ⊕ www.capecodtransit.org. **Plymouth & Brockton Street Railway Terminals** ✉ South Station Bus Terminal, 700 Atlantic Ave., Boston ☎ 508/746-0378.

BY TAXI

There are taxi stands at the Hyannis airport, the Hyannis bus station, and the Capetown Mall, across the street from the Cape Cod Mall. In Hyannis, call Checker Taxi for pickups. Dick's Taxi will pick you up and has a stand at the airport. John's Taxi & Limousine picks up in Dennis and Harwich only but will take passengers all over the Cape. Town Taxi is found at several locations around Hyannis, including Capetown Mall, the bus station, and on W. Main Street.

🚕 Taxi Companies **Checker Taxi** ☎ 508/771-8294. **Dick's Taxi** ☎ 508/428-4918. **John's Taxi & Limousine** ☎ 508/394-3209. **Town Taxi** ☎ 508/771-5555 or 888/771-8696.

Contacts & Resources

CONDO & HOUSE RENTALS

Century 21, Sam Ingram Real Estate handles rentals throughout the Mid Cape region. Great Vacations Inc. specializes in locating vacation rentals in Brewster, Dennis, and Orleans. Peter McDowell Associates offers a wide selection of properties for rent by the week, month, or season; the company also rents larger homes for family reunions and other gatherings. Most places are in Dennis. Waterfront Rentals covers Bourne to Truro, listing everything from condos to estates.

🏠 Local Agents **Century 21, Sam Ingram Real Estate** ✉ 938 Rte. 6A, Yarmouth Port 02675 ☎ 508/362-1191 or 800/676-3340 🖶 508/362-7889 ⊕ www.century21samingram.com. **Great Vacations Inc.** ✉ 2660 Rte. 6A, Brewster 02631 ☎ 508/896-2090. **Peter McDowell Associates** ✉ 585 Main St. [Rte. 6A], Dennis 02638 ☎ 508/385-9114 or 888/385-9114 ✉ 11 Main St. [Rte. 28], Dennisport 02639 ☎ 508/394-5400 or 800/870-5401 ⊕ www.capecodproperties.com. **Waterfront Rentals** ✉ 20 Pilgrim Rd., West Yarmouth 02673 ☎ 508/778-1818 🖶 508/771-3563 ⊕ www.waterfrontrentalsinc.com.

TOURS

Cape Cod Soaring Adventures offers glider flights and lessons out of Marstons Mills.

✈ **Cape Cod Soaring Adventures** ☎ 508/420-4201 ⊕ www.capecodsoaring.com.

VISITOR INFORMATION

The Cape Cod Chamber of Commerce is open year-round, Monday–Saturday 9–5 and Sunday 10–4.

ℹ Tourist Information **Cape Cod Chamber of Commerce** ✉ Junction of U.S. 6 and 132 🖃 Box 790, Hyannis 02601 ☎ 508/862-0700 or 888/332-2732 ⊕ www.capecodchamber.org. **Dennis Chamber of Commerce** ✉ 242 Swan River Rd., West Dennis 🖃 Box 275, South Dennis 02660 ☎ 508/398-3568 or 800/243-9920 ⊕ www.dennischamber.com. **Hyannis Chamber of Commerce** ✉ 1481 Rte. 132 🖃 Box 100, Hyannis 02601 ☎ 508/362-5230 or 877/492-6647 ⊕ www.hyannis.com. **Yarmouth Chamber of Commerce** ✉ 424 Rte. 28, West Yarmouth 02673 🖃 Box 479, South Yarmouth 02664 ☎ 508/778-1008 or 800/732-1008 ⊕ www.yarmouthcapecod.com ✉ Information center ✉ U.S. 6 heading east between Exits 6 and 7 ☎ 508/362-9796.

The Lower Cape

4

WORD OF MOUTH

"As I drove back to my condo, starving, I spotted the Brewster Inn and Chowder House from the road . . .I had some of the best mahi mahi I ever ate that night! I literally had to drag myself out of there before I slipped into a culinary coma."

–T.M.

"Be sure to check out a Bay beach at low tide. If you've never seen Cape Cod Bay at low tide, you're in for a surprising treat . . . you'll be able to walk out for a mile of so!"

–ccrosner

Updated by
Laura V. Scheel

SPECKLED WITH STILL-ACTIVE CRANBERRY BOGS, sturdy trees, and pastures, the Lower Cape exudes a peaceful residential aura. You won't find roadways cluttered with minigolf complexes, trampolines, or bumper boats here. And although an influx of year-round residents has transformed much of the Upper Cape into a commuter's haven, the Lower Cape still has a quiet sense of history and simple purpose.

Rich in history and Cape flavor, Brewster and Harwich stand opposite each other in the area just shy of the Cape's elbow. Harwich, farther inland, has antique homes, rambling old burial grounds, and a modest town center with shops, restaurants, museums, churches, and public parks. Brewster is similarly historical; examples of Victorian, Greek Revival, and colonial architecture abound, most meticulously preserved. Many homes have been converted to welcoming guesthouses and bed-and-breakfasts, whereas others are privately owned.

The traditional, elegant town of Chatham perches dramatically at the end of the peninsular elbow. It's here that the Atlantic begins to wet the shores of the Cape, sometimes with frightening strength. Chatham has shown its vulnerability to the forces of nature over the years, as little by little the town's shores have succumbed to the insatiable sea.

North of Chatham is Orleans, supply center of the Lower and Outer Capes, replete with large grocery chains and shopping plazas. The famed Nauset Beach is here, its dune-backed shores crammed with sun-seeking revelers in summer. Orleans also has a rich history—you just have to leave the maze of industry to find it. Continuing north, you can reach Eastham, a town often overlooked because of its position on busy U.S. 6. It too is perfectly charming, if you know where to look.

The Lower Cape is blessed with large tracts of open space, set aside for conservation. South of Chatham, the Monomoy National Wildlife Refuge is a twin-island bird sanctuary. Here dozens of species of birds are free to feed, nest, and expand their numbers without human meddling. Recreation seekers should head straight to Nickerson State Park in Brewster to frolic in freshwater ponds or enjoy a serene bike ride under the shade of stately white pine, oak, and maple trees. In Eastham, where the Cape Cod National Seashore officially begins, the Salt Pond Visitor Center has a wealth of area information, educational programs, and guided tours.

Exploring the Lower Cape

The towns of Harwich, Chatham, Brewster, Orleans, and Eastham make up the Lower Cape. Of these, only Brewster and Orleans touch Route 6A. Harwich, Chatham, and Orleans span Route 28—but don't fear. Although it's known for traffic, Route 28's congestion eases as the road winds toward the Lower Cape. Eastham sits along U.S. 6, which is the fastest way to get to all the towns—but if you're concerned about the journey as well as the destination, it's worthwhile to amble along Route 28 or 6A. Along the way, picturesque harbors, scenic side roads, and the towns' Main Streets, antiques stores, romantic inns, and colonial homes dot the landscape. Follow Route 28 into Chatham and make your way to the Chatham Lighthouse for breathtaking views of Nantucket Sound.

About the Restaurants

Each town has its own batch of treasured and traditional restaurants, and all will be crowded in summer. A significant number of restaurants close their doors once the crowds thin in October—including the beloved fried-seafood shacks—but plenty remain open throughout the year. Fresh seafood is a major staple.

If you are celebrating a milestone or hoping to delight someone special, Brewster's Chillingsworth impresses with French-country elegance. The Chatham Bars Inn recalls an era of gentle tranquility. If you're undecided, a stroll down Chatham's Main Street will tempt your palate. The restaurants in Orleans, Brewster, Harwich, and Eastham are spread out through the towns, but top restaurants such as the Brewster Fish House are worth finding.

Most Cape towns—including Chatham, Orleans, Eastham, Brewster, and Harwich—have banished smoking from restaurants and bars; smokers can retreat for a break outdoors.

About the Hotels

Money made in early maritime fortunes helped build exquisite homes, many of which are now unique and lovely inns. Chatham is blessed with dozens of these aged beauties, most with all the modern conveniences. B&Bs and intimate guesthouses are the primary lodging choices, but even larger hotels such as Chatham Bars Inn and the Chatham Wayside Inn capture the charm of Old Cape Cod. Expect fewer hotel and motel options on this part of the Cape. However, there are a few roadside or waterfront hotels outside the town centers. These complexes, which usually welcome families with small children, can be a bit softer on the wallet.

Brewster is essentially a B&B kind of town, offering lodging in former sea captains' homes. Harwich and Orleans have a mixture of both family-friendly hotel complexes and lovingly restored inns. Eastham has quite a few large-scale hotels along U.S. 6, including a Sheraton. Don't expect to find bargains here during the high season.

Other options include camping or weekly cottage rentals—all towns have the Cape's trademark cottage colonies. Note that in summer these must be secured well in advance, usually through a local real estate agent.

WHAT IT COSTS				
$$$$	**$$$**	**$$**	**$**	**¢**
RESTAURANTS over $30	$22–$30	$16–$22	$10–$16	under $10
HOTELS over $260	$200–$260	$140–$200	$90–$140	under $90

Restaurant prices are per person for a main course at dinner. Hotel prices are for a standard double room in high season, excluding 6% state tax, local taxes, and gratuities. Some inns add a 15% service charge.

Timing

Although the crowds of summer are testament to the appeal of the Lower Cape and its spectacular beaches, outdoor pursuits, crafts and art shows, concerts, and special events, the region is becoming a popular year-round destination. Because of its ocean-side climate, spring and fall are simply lesser shades of full-blown summer. Seasonal businesses reopen in late May and early June, but lodging rates remain less pricey than during the high season, and the agonies of summertime traffic, long waits at restaurants, and parking restrictions at area beaches can be avoided. September, October, and even November are the same. The waters usually remain warm enough to swim well into October, and many shops attempt to rid their stocks of merchandise by having generous sales.

You won't get the expected splendors of New England foliage on the Lower Cape, because the landscape changes are subtle. Swaying saltmarsh grasses turn golden, cranberry bogs explode into ruby-red quilts, and the ocean relaxes into a deep, deep blue. The light becomes softer and its patterns more dramatic on both land and sea. In the towns of Harwich, Brewster, and Orleans, where the soil is substantial enough to support mighty oaks and maples, the colors of autumn do peer through. A drive along Route 6A under the canopy of changing leaves is just as breathtaking as a summer jaunt past blooming gardens.

Brewster

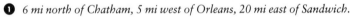 **①** *6 mi north of Chatham, 5 mi west of Orleans, 20 mi east of Sandwich.*

Brewster calls itself the Sea Captains' Town, honoring its rich heritage as a seafaring community. Historic Route 6A, the Old King's Highway, winds through its center. This road, the old stagecoach route, was once nearly the only one at this end of the Cape, and residents and legislators alike are determined to keep it well preserved. Homes and businesses must adhere to historic detail: there are no neon signs, no strip malls—only the gentle facades of a graceful era.

Named for Plymouth leader William Brewster, the area was settled in 1659 but was not incorporated as a separate town until 1803. In the early 1800s, Brewster was the terminus of a packet cargo service from Boston. In 1849 Henry David Thoreau wrote that "this town has more mates and masters of vessels than any other town in the country." Many mansions built for sea captains remain, and quite a few have been turned into handsome B&Bs (though in recent years, more than a few of these have reverted to private homes). In the 18th and 19th centuries, the bay side of Brewster was the site of a major salt-making industry. Of the 450 saltworks operating on the Cape in the 1830s, more than 60 were here.

Brewster's location on Cape Cod Bay makes it a perfect place to learn about the region's ecology. The Cape Cod Museum of Natural History is here, and the area is rich in conservation lands, state parks, forests, freshwater ponds, and brackish marshes. When the tide is low in Cape Cod Bay, you can stroll the beaches and explore tidal pools up to 2 mi

IF YOU LIKE

BEACHES

The Lower Cape is straddled by the bracing and grand Atlantic Ocean and three more mild-mannered bays—Nantucket Sound, Pleasant Bay, and Cape Cod Bay.

On the south side, Harwich Port, Harwich, and Chatham dip into the shallower and warmer Nantucket Sound. The beaches here are popular with families, ice-cream trucks, jet skiers, and windsurfers. Harwich and Chatham swimmers can also head to Pleasant Bay's shallow waters, which are also ideal for kayaking and canoeing.

Brewster's glory is Cape Cod Bay, and dozens of beaches (public and private) expand by acres at low tide. Treasure hunters can stroll the sands, keeping an eye out for shells and creatures left behind by the retreating waters.

The Lower Cape's ocean beaches are unbroken by dictates of ownership or man-made barriers from Chatham onward, so you're free to roam. Note that Chatham's ocean beaches are easily accessible by bike or foot, but there's no parking for cars. Orleans has Nauset Beach, a Cape favorite. In Eastham the National Seashore and the town maintain several beaches with exhilarating ocean swimming.

BICYCLING

The Cape's top bike route, the 25-mi Cape Cod Rail Trail, follows the paved right-of-way of the old Penn Central Railroad from South Dennis to South Wellfleet. You can also pick up the trail in Harwich, Brewster, Orleans, or Eastham. Nickerson State Park, in Brewster, has 8 mi of its own forested trails, some with access to the rail trail. From the Salt Pond Visitor Center in Eastham, take a jaunt off the rail trail and follow meandering paths leading to Nauset Beach, Coast Guard Beach, and beautiful Nauset Marsh. Or take a spin on the newly completed Old Colony Rail Trail, a nearly 15-mi paved path linking Harwich center to downtown Chatham. Cyclists in Chatham can follow the little green signs that denote the Chatham Bike Route, which runs beside the ocean, past all the stunningly majestic homes that dominate the waterfront. Use caution, though, as the roadway is shared with cars.

NIGHTLIFE & THE ARTS

Chatham's Main Street is lined with galleries and studios showcasing local and national artists. In Orleans, weekly outdoor art shows sell the works of local painters and craftspeople and have free demonstrations. Eastham and Harwich also hold outdoor arts-and-crafts forays; Harwich's biggie is the Professional Arts and Crafts Festival, held in July and August.

The Lower Cape has a strong theater tradition. The Harwich Junior Theatre stages performances year-round and offers children's classes in the summer. Community theater dominates the scene in Orleans and Chatham. Off-season, Eastham shines with the First Encounter Coffee House, a teetotaler's haven for local music and poetry readings. In Brewster, the professional Cape Cod Repertory Theatre stages productions both indoors and out under the stars.

from the shore on the Brewster flats. When it's high tide, the water is relatively warm and very calm for swimming. Both Nickerson State Park and the Punkhorn Parklands have thousands of acres through which to wander.

> **LAY OF THE LAND**
>
> In Brewster, Route 6A is also known as Main Street.

Windmills used to be prominent in Cape Cod towns; the Brewster area once had four. The 1795 **Higgins Farm Windmill** (⊠ Off Rte. 6A, just west of the Cape Cod Museum of Natural History, West Brewster ☉ Mid-June to mid-Oct., Thurs.–Sat. 1–4)—an octagonal-type mill shingled in weathered pine with a roof like an upturned boat—was moved here in 1974 and has been restored. The millstones are original. At night the mill is often spotlighted, which makes for quite a sight.

On the grounds of the Higgins Farm Windmill, the one-room **Harris-Black House** dates to 1795. Today, the restored building is partially furnished and is dominated by a brick hearth and original woodwork. ⊠ *Off Rte. 6A, just west of Cape Cod Museum of Natural History, West Brewster* ☎ 508/896–9521 ✆ *Free* ☉ *Mid-June to mid-Oct., Thurs.–Sat. 1–4.*

2 A short drive from Route 6A is the **Stony Brook Grist Mill,** a restored, operating 19th-century fulling mill (a mill that shrinks and thickens cloth), now also a museum. The old mill's waterwheel slowly turns in a small, tree-lined brook. Inside, exhibits include old mill equipment and looms; you can watch cornmeal being stone-ground and get a lesson in weaving on a 100-year-old loom. Out back, across wooden bridges, a bench has a view of the pond and of the sluices leading into the mill area.

Early each spring, in April and early May, Stony Brook's **Herring Run** boils with alewives (herring) making their way to spawning waters; it's an amazing sight. The fish swim in from Cape Cod Bay up Paine's Creek to Stony Brook and the ponds beyond it. The herring run, a rushing stream across the street from the mill, consists of ladders that help the fish climb the rocky waters. Seagulls swarm in and pluck herring from the run into midair. Sadly, disturbingly low numbers of returning herring have prompted the state to issue a three-year moratorium on fish harvests at the run. Starting with the spring of 2006, no herring can be taken from the stream, ending a long-standing tradition in hopes of increasing fish stocks. Farther down the path to the stream, there's an ivy-covered stone wishing well and a wooden bridge with a bench. ⊠ *Stony Brook Rd., West Brewster, off Rte. 6A* ☎ *No phone* ✆ *Donations accepted* ☉ *May–Aug., Thurs.–Sat. 2–5.*

3 For nature enthusiasts, a visit to the **Cape Cod Museum of Natural History** is a must; it's just a short drive west from the heart of Brewster along Route 6A. The spacious museum and pristine grounds include guided field walks, a shop, a natural-history library, lectures, classes, nature and marine exhibits such as a working beehive, and a pond- and sea-life room with live specimens. Walking trails wind through 80 acres of forest, marshland, and ponds, all rich in birds and other wildlife. The exhibit hall upstairs has a wall display of aerial photographs documenting the

FodorsChoice ★

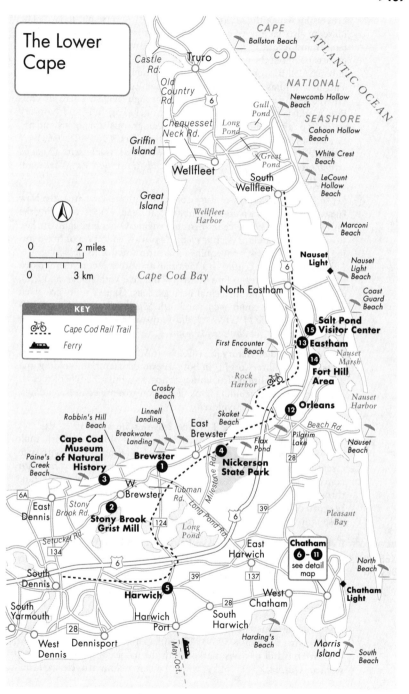

The Lower Cape

CAPE

Ballston Beach

COD

NATIONAL

Castle Rd.

Truro

Old Country Rd.

Newcomb Hollow Beach

SEASHORE

Gull Pond

Cahoon Hollow Beach

Chequesset Neck Rd.

Long Pond

Griffin Island

Great Pond

White Crest Beach

Wellfleet

South Wellfleet

LeCount Hollow Beach

Great Island

Wellfleet Harbor

Marconi Beach

Cape Cod Bay

Nauset Light

Nauset Light Beach

North Eastham

Coast Guard Beach

KEY

Cape Cod Rail Trail

Ferry

First Encounter Beach

Rock Harbor

15 Salt Pond Visitor Center

13 Eastham

Nauset Marsh

14 Fort Hill Area

Crosby Beach

Skaket Beach

Nauset Harbor

Linnell Landing

12 Orleans

Robbin's Hill Beach

Breakwater Landing

East Brewster

Beach Rd.

Pilgrim Lake

Flax Pond

Nauset Beach

Cape Cod Museum of Natural History

Brewster 1

4 Nickerson State Park

Paine's Creek Beach

3

W. Brewster

East Dennis

Stony Brook Rd.

Tubman Rd.

Long Pond Rd.

Milestone Rd.

Pleasant Bay

2 Stony Brook Grist Mill

Long Pond

East Harwich

Chatham 6–11 see detail map

North Beach

Setucket Rd.

South Dennis

South Yarmouth

5 Harwich

West Chatham

Chatham Light

Harwich Port

South Harwich

Harding's Beach

West Dennis

Dennisport

May.-Oct.

Morris Island

South Beach

0 ___ 2 miles
0 ___ 3 km

process by which the famous Chatham sandbar was split in two. The museum also has guided canoe and kayak trips from May through September and several cruises that explore Cape waterways. Onboard naturalists point out the wildlife and relay historical information about each habitat. Call for tour times and fees, and sign up as early as you can. The museum has wildlife movies and slide lectures in the auditorium on Wednesday at 7:30, from early July through August. There are children's and family activities in summer, including full- and half-day workshops and one- and two-week day camps consisting of art and nature classes for preschoolers through ninth graders. ⊠ *869 Rte. 6A, West Brewster* ☎ *508/896–3867, 800/479–3867 in Massachusetts* ⊕ *www. ccmnh.org* ⊒*$8* ⊙ *Oct.–Apr., Wed.–Sun. 11–3; Apr. and May, Wed.–Sun. 10–4; June–Sept., daily 10–4.*

☺ Set on a re-created 19th-century common with a picnic area, the **New England Fire & History Museum** exhibits 35 antique vehicles, including the only surviving 1929 Mercedes-Benz fire engine. Other highlights are late Boston Pops conductor Arthur Fiedler's private collection of fire-fighting memorabilia, 14 mannequins in historical uniforms depicting firefighters through the centuries, a Victorian apothecary shop, an animated diorama of the Chicago Fire of 1871 (complete with smoke and fire), a working forge, and medicinal herb gardens. Guided tours are given (with the last tour commencing at 3:30). ⊠ *1439 Rte. 6A, West Brewster* ☎ *508/896–5711* ⊒ *$7* ⊙ *Mid-May–early Sept., weekdays 10–4; early Sept.–mid-Oct., weekends noon–4.*

The **Brewster Ladies' Library** (⊠ 1822 Rte. 6A ☎ 508/896–3913 ⊕ www. brewsterladieslibrary.org) is in both a restored Victorian building and a more recent addition. The library is host to a full schedule of regular events for all ages, including book discussion groups, lectures, readings, and craft programs for children.

At the junction of Route 124, the **Brewster Store** (⊠ 1935 Rte. 6A ☎ 508/896–3744 ⊕ www.brewsterstore.com) is a local landmark. Built in 1852 as a church, it's a typical New England general store with such essentials as the daily papers, penny candy, and benches out front for conversation. Out back, the Brewster Scoop serves ice cream mid-June through early September. Upstairs, the old front of the store has been re-created, and memorabilia from antique toys to World War II bond posters are displayed. Downstairs there's a working antique nickelodeon.

NEED A BREAK? If you need a quick break, **Hopkins House Gift and Bakery** (⊠ 2727 Rte. 6A, East Brewster ☎ 508/896–9337) is the perfect pit stop. Wash down a chewy hermit cookie, baked with molasses and raisins, with some strong, hot coffee. A home-furnishings shop attached to the bakery might tempt you to stretch your legs a while longer.

Known as the Church of the Sea Captains, the handsome **First Parish Church** (⊠ 1969 Rte. 6A ☎ 508/896–5577), with Gothic windows and a capped bell tower, is full of pews marked with the names of famous Brewster seamen. Out back is an old graveyard where militiamen, clergy, farmers, and sea captains rest side by side. The church is the site of a summer musical program, which includes the ever-popular Tanglewood marionette show, Tuesday–Thursday mornings at 9:30.

The **Brewster Historical Society Museum,** in an 1830s house, has a sea captain's room with paintings and artifacts, an 1890 barbershop, a child's room with antique toys and clothing, a room of women's period gowns and accessories, and other exhibits on local history and architecture. Out back, a ¼-mi nature trail over dunes leads to the bay. ⊠ *3371 Rte. 6A, East Brewster* ☎ *508/896–9521* ⚏ *Free* ☉ *June and Sept., weekends 1–4; July and Aug., Tues.–Fri. 1–4.*

For a lovely hike or run through the local wilds, try the **Punkhorn Parklands,** with freshwater kettle-hole ponds and 45 mi of scenic trails meandering through 800 acres of meadows, marshes, and pine forests. ⊠ *End of Run Hill Rd., off Stony Brook Rd., West Brewster.*

4 Nickerson State Park's 1,961 acres were once part of a vast estate belonging to Roland C. Nickerson, son of Samuel Nickerson, a Chatham native who became a multimillionaire and founded of the First National Bank of Chicago. Today the land is open to the public for recreation. Roland and his wife, Addie, lavishly entertained such visitors as President Grover Cleveland at their private beach and hunting lodge in English country-house style, with coachmen dressed in tails and top hats and a bugler announcing carriages entering the front gates. Like a village unto itself, the estate gardens provided much of the household's food, supplemented by game from its woods and fish from its ponds. It also had its own electric plant and a 9-hole golf course by the water. The enormous mansion Samuel built for his son in 1886 burned to the ground 20 years later, and Roland died two weeks after the event. The grand stone mansion built to replace it in 1908 is now part of the Ocean Edge resort. In 1934 Addie donated the land for the state park in memory of Roland and their son, who died during the 1918 flu epidemic.

The park consists of acres of oak, pitch pine, hemlock, and spruce forest speckled with seven freshwater kettle ponds formed by glacial action. Some ponds are stocked with trout for fishing. You can swim in the ponds, canoe, sail, motorboat, bike along 8 mi of paved trails that have access to the Cape Cod Rail Trail, picnic, and cross-country ski in winter. Bird-watchers seek out the thrushes, wrens, warblers, woodpeckers, finches, larks, Canada geese, cormorants, great blue herons, hawks, owls, ospreys, and other species that frequent the park. Occasionally, red foxes and white-tailed deer are spotted in the woods. Both tent and RV camping are extremely popular here, and nature programs are offered in season. A map of the park is available on-site. ⊠ *3488 Rte. 6A, East Brewster* ☎ *508/896–3491* ⊕ *www.mass.gov/dcr* ⚏ *Free* ☉ *Daily dawn–dusk.*

NEED A BREAK?

Box Lunch (⊠ 302 Underpass Rd. near Cape Cod Rail Trail crossing South Brewster ☎ 508/896–1234), famous for its "rollwiches," has a few branches on the Cape. This location has the same tasty selection of breakfast and lunch roll-ups, perfect for grabbing a bite while you're on the Cape Cod Rail Trail or just touring around. In summer Box Lunch stays open until 9 PM; it closes at 4 PM when the weather turns cooler.

Where to Stay & Eat

★ **$$$$** ✕ **Bramble Inn.** Inside an inviting 1860s white house in Brewster's historical village center, this romantic property presents well-crafted, globally inspired contemporary fare in five dining rooms with floral wallpaper or wood-paneled walls, hung with gilt-framed mirrors and watercolor and oil paintings (much of the artwork is for sale). During the warmer months, dine on a patio amid fragrant flower beds. The four-course prix-fixe menu changes often and has included such memorable treats as black-bean blini topped with smoked salmon and salmon caviar, and grilled lamb stacked over pinto bean puree and a Guadalajaran-inspired rose-petal mole sauce. Sunday through Thursday you can also order à la carte from a lighter bistro menu, which is served in the bar as well as on one of the garden patios. There are also a few attractive overnight rooms. ⊠ 2019 Rte. 6A, East Brewster ☎ 508/896–7644 ▭ AE, D, MC, V ⊗ Closed Jan.–Mar. No lunch.

$$$$ ✕ **Chillingsworth.** One of the crown jewels of Cape restaurants, Chillingsworth combines formal presentation with an excellent French menu and a diverse wine cellar to create a memorable dining experience. Super-rich risotto, roast lobster, and grilled Angus sirloin are favorites. Dinner in the main dining rooms is prix fixe and includes seven courses—appetizer, soup, salad, sorbet, entrée, "amusements," and dessert, plus coffee or tea. Less expensive à la carte options for lunch, dinner, and Sunday brunch are served in the more casual, patio-style Bistro. There are also a few guest rooms here for overnighting. ⊠ 2449 Rte. 6A, East Brewster ☎ 508/896–3640 ⊕ www.chillingsworth.com ▭ AE, DC, MC, V ⊗ Closed certain days mid-Sept.–late May, call for hrs. No lunch.

FodorsChoice ★

$$–$$$ ✕ **Spark Fish.** "Spark" refers to a wood-fire grill, which the kitchen uses often. Owner Steven Parrott's menu emphasizes simple ingredients—fresh herbs, garlic, and fruit salsas—and lets the flavors of local seafood, high-quality meats, and good vegetables shine through without complicated sauces. The inside is as unfussy as the menu and, like the food, is more about elegant understatement than elaborate decoration. A full wine list is available. The canopy-covered outdoor deck is the place to be in warm weather; in the off-season, there's comfortable fireside dining. ⊠ 2671 Rte. 6A, East Brewster ☎ 508/896–1067 ▭ MC, V ⊗ No lunch.

$–$$$ ✕ **Brewster Fish House.** Long overshadowed by its pricier and snazzier neighbors, the Fish House has carved a niche for itself: Cape Cod standards such as classic scrod and New England boiled dinner share billing with both traditional and more inspired preparations of duck, rack of lamb, Cornish hen, and tenderloin of beef. Locals are known to drive from all points of the Cape to this lovably rickety restaurant for the super-fresh fish. The wine list includes a flavorful selection of by-the-glass of-

FodorsChoice ★

ferings. ✉ *2208 Rte. 6A, South Brewster* ☎ *508/896–7867* 🍽 *Reservations not accepted* ▭ *MC, V* ⊗ *Closed Jan.–Mar.*

¢–$$ ✕ **JT's Seafood.** Fresh and ample portions of fried seafood take center stage at this casual joint, which is very popular with families. Pick from several seafood platters, or gnaw on baby back ribs or burgers if you need a break from the fruits of the sea. Several items, including corn dogs, grilled cheese (lunch only), and peanut butter and jelly, are good kid-friendly choices. Place your order at the counter and sit inside or out. Leave your mark by sticking a pin in your town's name on the big map by the order counter. Takeout is also available. ✉ *2689 Main St. (Rte. 6A)* ☎ *508/896–3355* 🍽 *Reservations not accepted* ▭ *MC, V* ⊗ *Closed mid-Oct.–mid-Apr.*

$ ✕ **Brewster Inn and Chowder House.** The consistently excellent food at this long-standing Cape institution continues to live up to its great reputation among locals. Home cooking in the traditional New England style is the rule; you'll find no fancy or fussy fusion recipes here—just comfort food. Look for simple but tasty meat and seafood standards, and don't miss the rich and full-bodied New England clam chowder. The service is friendly, the prices are kind, and you won't leave hungry. The restaurant serves lunch and dinner daily year-round. ✉ *1993 Rte. 6A* ☎ *508/896–7771* ▭ *MC, V.*

¢–$ ✕ **Laurino's Tavern.** There's something timeless about this noisy pizza joint and American eatery with warm wood paneling, generous booth-style seating, and red-and-white-checkered tablecloths, plus a big patio and a playground for kids. Meatball grinders, steak-and-cheese sandwiches, and specialty pizzas are mainstays. Try a buffalo chicken pizza, topped with wing sauce and cheddar cheese, with a blue cheese dipping sauce. Lasagna, shrimp scampi, and mussels marinara are popular choices. The long, friendly bar is a great place to sit with a buddy over a beer and a big plate of Macho Nachos. In summer live music serenades the late-night crowd. ✉ *3668 Rte. 6A, East Brewster* ☎ *508/896–6135* 🍽 *Reservations not accepted* ▭ *AE, MC, V.*

★ $$$–$$$$ 🏨 **Ocean Edge.** One of the Cape's few full-service resorts, Ocean Edge is a luxury beachfront community where accommodations range from hotel rooms in the conference center to one- to three-bedroom condominiums in the woods and two- to three-bedroom beachfront villas. Condominiums have full kitchens and washer-dryers; some units have fireplaces, and many have ocean views. All rooms and condos have balconies or patios. There's also a championship 18-hole golf course and tennis courts. Clambakes, concerts, and tournaments take place throughout the summer. ✉ *2907 Rte. 6A, 02631* ☎ *508/896–9000 or 800/343–6074* 📠 *508/896–9123* ⊕ *www.oceanedge.com* 🛏 *292 condominium units, 90 rooms* 🍽 *4 restaurants, room service, driving range, golf privileges, putting greens, 9 tennis courts, 6 pools (2 indoor), ponds, gym, saunas, beach, bicycles, basketball, pub, children's programs (ages 4–17), laundry facilities, concierge, meeting rooms* ▭ *AE, D, DC, MC, V.*

$$–$$$ 🏨 **Brewster By The Sea.** Weather permitting, a three-course breakfast is served on the patio overlooking a swimming pool and 2 acres of landscaped gardens at this restored, beautifully decorated 1846 farmhouse on historic Route 6A. A fireplace is the focal point in one guest room,

and another has a king-size canopy bed and sliders that open onto a private deck. Three more guest rooms, furnished with authentic and reproduction antiques, fireplaces, and hot tubs, are in an adjacent carriage house. Afternoon tea is included. For added decadence, ask about the special in-house spa packages. ⊠ *716 Rte. 6A, 02631* ☎ *508/896–3910 or 800/892–3910* 🖨 *508/896–4232* ⊕ *www.brewsterbythesea.com* ⇱ *7 rooms, 2 suites* ⚒ *Some in-room hot tubs, cable TV, Wi-Fi, pool, hot tub, spa, bicycles; no kids under 16, no smoking* ⊟ *AE, D, MC, V* ⦿ *BP.*

$–$$ 🏠 **Candleberry Inn.** This 1790s Georgian mansion sits along a peaceful stretch of scenic Main Street and was once the home of writer Horatio Alger. The sun-filled rooms are unfussy but elegant, with Oriental rugs, wide-plank floors, original woodwork, and tall windows with the original wavy glass. Several have working fireplaces, and two particularly cozy units—the Seabreeze and Treetops rooms—have pitched ceilings and access to a deck overlooking the leafy grounds and fragrant gardens. The Seacroft Suite has French doors leading to a large sitting area. Gracious innkeepers Stuart and Charlotte Fyfe serve a delicious full breakfast out by the garden in summer and in a cozy dining room during the cooler months. ⊠ *1882 Rte. 6A, 02631* ☎ *508/896–3300 or 800/573–4769* 🖨 *508/896–4016* ⊕ *www.candleberryinn.com* ⇱ *7 rooms, 1 suite* ⚒ *Cable TV; no kids under 10, no smoking* ⊟ *AE, D, DC, MC, V* ⦿ *BP.*

$–$$ 🏠 **Isaiah Clark House.** This former 18th-century sea captain's residence, just west of the town proper, retains its wide-plank flooring and low, sloping ceilings and has a varied selection of antiques. The original inhabitants have left their mark all over the house, from the scrawled signature of 13-year-old son Jeremiah in a closet to the framed historic documents and photographs on the walls to the namesake of each of the rooms (all Clark family women). Most rooms have queen-size four-poster or canopy beds, braided rugs, and fireplaces. The extensive gardens yield some of the fruit used in the homemade pies, muffins, and breads that are served at breakfast. ⊠ *1187 Rte. 6A, 02631* ☎ *508/ 896–2223 or 800/822–4001* ⊕ *www.isaiahclark.com* ⇱ *7 rooms* ⚒ *Cable TV, Internet room; no room phones, no kids under 10, no smoking* ⊟ *D, MC, V* ⦿ *BP.*

¢–$$ 🏠 **Old Sea Pines Inn.** With its white-column portico and wraparound
Fodor'sChoice veranda overlooking a broad lawn, Old Sea Pines, which housed a
★ young ladies' boarding school in the early 1900s, resembles a vintage summer estate. Climb the sweeping staircase to guest rooms decorated with reproduction wallpaper, antiques, and framed old photographs. Some are quite large; others have fireplaces. One of the more popular rooms has a sitting area in an enclosed sunporch. Rooms in a newer building are simple, with bright white modern baths and cast-iron queen-size beds. Some rooms have shared bathrooms. The inn also holds a Sunday night Broadway musical dinner revue from mid-June through mid-September. ⊠ *2553 Rte. 6A, Box 1070, 02631* ☎ *508/896–6114* 🖨 *508/632– 0084* ⊕ *www.oldseapinesinn.com* ⇱ *24 rooms, 19 with bath, 3 suites* ⚒ *Restaurant, cable TV, Internet room, meeting rooms; no a/c, no room phones, no TV in some rooms, no kids under 8, no smoking* ⊟ *AE, D, DC, MC, V* ⊘ *Closed Jan.–Mar.* ⦿ *BP.*

¢ 🏕 **Nickerson State Park.** Shaded by a canopy of white pine, hemlock, and spruce, Nickerson State Park is a nature lover's haven. Encompassing close to 2,000 acres of wooded landscape teeming with wildlife, the park is the Cape's largest and most popular camping site. While away a summer afternoon trout fishing, walking, biking on 8 mi of paved trails (which connect to the Cape Cod Rail Trail), canoeing, sailing, motorboating, or bird-watching; there are four ponds for swimming, plus ocean beaches nearby. RVs must be self-contained. Maps and schedules of park programs are available at the park entrance. Campground reservations are accepted six months in advance, mid-April through mid-October, and sites are available on a walk-in basis only the rest of the year. There's a $9.50 fee per reservation; note that camping fees are slightly lower for in-state residents. ⚲ *Grills, flush toilets, dump station, drinking water, showers, fire grates, picnic tables, public telephone, general store, ranger station, play area, swimming (ponds)* ⇆ *420 sites, some yurts* ⊠ *3488 Rte. 6A, 02631* ☎ *508/896–3491, 877/422–6762 reservations* 🖷 *508/896–3103* ⊕ *www.mass.gov/dcr* ⊟ *$14 tent sites, $30 small yurt, $40 large yurt* ⊟ *No credit cards.*

Nightlife & the Arts

The **Cape Cod Repertory Theatre Co.** (⊠ 3379 Rte. 6A, West Brewster ☎ 508/896–1888 ⊕ www.caperep.org) performs several impressive productions, from original works to classics, in its indoor Arts and Crafts–style theater way back in the woods. The season runs from May to November. Mesmerizing entertainment for children, in the form of lively outdoor (and often interactive) theater, is provided here, too. Performances of fairy tales, music, and folk tales are given on Tuesday and Friday mornings at 10 in June, July, and August. The theater is just west of Nickerson State Park.

Sunday evenings by the bay are filled with the sounds of the **town-band concerts** (⊠ Rte. 6A, West Brewster), held in the gazebo on the grounds of Drummer Boy Park. The park is about ½ mi west of the Cape Cod Museum of Natural History, on the western side of Brewster. Families with little ones will delight in the park's playground with its ornate wood facilities.

The **Woodshed** (⊠ 1993 Rte. 6A ☎ 508/896–7771), the rustic bar at the Brewster Inn, is a good place to soak up local color and listen to pop duos or bands that perform nightly. It's open from May through October.

Sports & the Outdoors

BASEBALL The **Brewster Whitecaps** (☎ 508/385–5073 ⊕ www.brewsterwhitecaps. com) of the collegiate Cape Cod Baseball League play home games at **Cape Cod Regional Tech High School** (⊠ Rte. 124, Harwich) from mid-June to mid-August.

BEACHES **Flax Pond** (⊠ 3488 Rte. 6A, East Brewster ☎ 508/896–3491) in Nickerson State Park, surrounded by pines, has picnic areas, a bathhouse, and water-sports rentals.

Brewster's bay beaches all have access to the flats that at low tide make for very interesting tidal pool exploration. Eponymous roads to each beach branch off Route 6A; there's limited parking. All of the bay beaches require a daily, weekly, or seasonal parking pass (which for nonresidents cost $15, $40, and $125, respectively); these can be purchased at the town hall (☎ 508/896–4511). **Breakwater Landing** is one of the most popular beaches in town and has an ample parking area. **Linnell Landing** has a smaller lot and tends to fill up quickly. A favorite among the toddler crowd and the sunset seekers, **Paine's Creek** also lacks a large lot, but if you get there early enough, you can find a spot. Harder to find down a dead-end street but worth it, **Robbin's Hill** is known for its intriguing tidal pools. Farther east off Route 6A is **Crosby Beach,** ideal for beach walkers—you can trek straightway to Orleans if you so desire.

BICYCLING The **Cape Cod Rail Trail** has many access points in Brewster, among them Long Pond Road, Underpass Road, and Nickerson State Park.

Brewster Bike (⊠ 442 Underpass Rd. ☎ 508/896–8149) carries a large selection of bikes for rent.

The **Rail Trail Bike and Kayak** (⊠ 302 Underpass Rd. ☎ 508/896–8200) rents bikes, including children's bikes, and in-line skates. Parking is free, and there's a picnic area with easy access to the Rail Trail.

FISHING Many of Brewster's freshwater ponds are good for catching perch, pickerel, and other fish; five ponds are well stocked with trout. Especially good for fishing is Cliff Pond in Nickerson State Park. You'll need a **fishing license,** available from the town hall. ⊠ *2198 Main St. (Rte. 6A), East Brewster* ☎ *508/896–4506.*

GOLF The **Captain's Golf Course** (⊠ 1000 Freeman's Way, east of Rte. 6 ☎ 508/896–1716 or 877/843–9081) is an excellent public facility with two fine 18-hole courses—*Golf Digest* has named it one of the leading public courses in the nation.

Ocean Edge Golf Course (⊠ Villages Dr., off Rte. 6A, East Brewster ☎ 508/896–5911), an 18-hole, par-72 course winding around five ponds, has Scottish-style pot bunkers and challenging terrain. Three-day residential and commuter golf schools are offered in spring and early summer.

HORSEBACK RIDING **Woodsong Farm** (⊠ 121 Lund Farm Way, South Brewster ☎ 508/896–5800 ⊕ www.woodsongfarm.com) has instruction and day programs, but no rentals or trail rides; it also has a horsemanship day-camp program for kids 5–18.

TENNIS The **Ocean Edge** (⊠ 2907 Main St. [Rte. 6A], East Brewster ☎ 508/896–9000) resort has five clay and six Plexipave courts. It offers lessons and round-robins and hosts a tennis school, with weekend packages and video analysis.

Run by the town and open to the public at no charge are four **public tennis courts,** all just behind the fire and police stations on 1673 Route 6A. Two basketball courts are also available for public use.

WATER SPORTS **Cape Cod Sea Camps** (✆ Box 1880, Brewster 02631 ☎ 508/896–3451) teaches team sports, archery, art, drama, sailing, and water sports to kids ages 4–17.

Jack's Boat Rentals (✉ Flax Pond, Nickerson State Park, Rte. 6A, East Brewster ☎ 508/896–8556) rents canoes, kayaks, Seacycles, Sunfish, pedal boats, and sailboards; guide-led kayak tours are also offered.

Shopping

B. D. Hutchinson (✉ 1274 Long Pond Rd., South Brewster ☎ 508/896–6395), a watch and clock maker, sells antique and collectible watches, clocks, and music boxes.

★ **Brewster Book Store** (✉ 2648 Rte. 6A, East Brewster ☎ 508/896–6543 or 800/823–6543) prides itself on being a special Cape bookstore. It's filled to the rafters with all manner of books by local and international authors and has an extensive fiction selection and kids section. A full schedule of author signings and children's story times continues year-round.

Countryside Antiques (✉ 2052 Rte. 6A, Brewster ☎ 508/240–0525) specializes in European and Asian antique furniture, home-accent pieces, china, and silver.

HandCraft House (✉ 3996 Rte. 6A, East Brewster ☎ 508/240–1412 or 888/826–4393) has "handmade in the USA" art for the home and garden, wood sculptures, handblown glass, stoneware, watercolors, and jewelry.

Kemp Pottery (✉ 258 Rte. 6A, West Brewster ☎ 508/385–5782) has functional and decorative stoneware and porcelain, fountains, garden sculpture, pottery sinks, and stained glass.

Kings Way Books and Antiques (✉ 774 Rte. 6A, West Brewster ☎ 508/896–3639) sells out-of-print and rare books—they have a large medieval section—plus small antiques, china, glass, silver, coins, and linens.

Lemon Tree Village (✉ 1069 Rte. 6A) is a cheery complex filled with many unusual stores. You can find garden statuary, top-of-the-line cooking implements, locally made arts and crafts, pottery, birding supplies, clothing, gifts, jewelry, and toys. There's even a café next door if all that shopping makes you hungry.

Open from April through October, the **Satucket Farm Stand** (✉ 76 Harwich Rd. [Rte. 124], off Rte. 6A ☎ 508/896–5540) is a real old-fashioned farm stand and bakery. Most produce is grown on the premises, and you can fill your basket with home-baked scones and breads, fruit pies, produce, herbs, and flowers.

The **Spectrum** (✉ 369 Rte. 6A, West Brewster ☎ 508/385–3322) carries a great selection of imaginative American arts and crafts, including pottery, stained glass, and art glass.

★ **Sydenstricker Galleries** (✉ 490 Rte. 6A, West Brewster ☎ 508/385–3272) stocks glassware handcrafted by a unique process, which you can watch while you're in the shop.

Harwich

❺ *6 mi south of Brewster, 5 mi east of Dennis.*

Originally known as Setucket, Harwich separated from Brewster in 1694 and was renamed for the famous English seaport. Like other townships on the Cape, Harwich is actually a cluster of several small villages, including Harwich Port. Historically, the villages of Harwich were marked by their generous number of churches and the styles of worship they practiced—small villages often sprang up around these centers of faith.

Harwich and Harwich Port are the commercial centers, and although the two have very different natures, both have graceful old architecture and rich histories. Harwich Port is the more bustling of the two: brimming with shops, calm-water beaches, restaurants, and hotel complexes, it packs all manner of entertainment and frivolity along its roadways. Harwich is more relaxed; its commerce is more centered, and its outlying areas are graced with greenery, large shade trees, and historic homesteads. The Harwich Historical Society has a strong presence here, maintaining exhibits and artifacts significant to the town's past.

The Cape's famous cranberry industry took off in Harwich in 1844, when Alvin Cahoon was its principal grower. Today you'll still find cranberry bogs throughout Harwich, and each September the town holds a **Cranberry Festival** to celebrate the importance of this indigenous berry; the festival is usually scheduled during the week after Labor Day.

Three naturally sheltered harbors on Nantucket Sound make the town, like its English namesake, popular with boaters. You'll find dozens of elegant sailboats and elaborate yachts in Harwich's harbors, plus plenty of charter-fishing boats. Each year in August the town pays celebratory homage to its large boating population with a grand regatta, Sails Around the Cape.

Beaches are plentiful in Harwich, and nearly all rest on the warm and mild waters of Nantucket Sound. Freshwater ponds, ideal for swimming as well as small-scale canoeing and kayaking, also speckle the area. Several conservation areas have miles of secluded walking trails, many alongside vivid cranberry bogs.

Once the home of a private school offering the first high school-level curriculum in Harwich, the pillared 1844 Greek Revival building of the **Brooks Academy Museum** now houses the museum of the **Harwich Historical Society**. In addition to a large photo-history collection and exhibits on artist Charles Cahoon (grandson of cranberry grower Alvin), the sociotechnological history of cranberry culture, and shoe making, the museum has antique clothing and textiles, china and glass, fans, and toys. There's also an extensive genealogical collection for researchers. On the grounds is a powder house used to store gunpowder during the Revolutionary War, as well as a restored 1872 outhouse that could spur your appreciation for indoor plumbing. ✉ *80 Parallel St.* ☎ *508/432–8089* 💲 *Donations accepted* 🕙 *Late June–Sept., Wed.–Sat. 1–4; Oct., Thurs. and Fri. 1–4.*

☺ **Brooks Park** on Main Street (Route 28) is a good place to stretch your legs; it has a playground, picnic tables, a ball field, tennis courts, and a bandstand where summer concerts are held.

☺ For children who have spent too much time in the car watching you drive, a spin behind the wheel of one of 20 top-of-the-line go-karts at **Bud's Go-Karts** may be just the thing. ⊠ *9 Sisson Rd., off Rte. 28, Harwich Port* ☎ *508/432–4964* ⊙ *June–early Sept., Mon.–Sat. 9 AM–11 PM, Sun. 10 AM–11 PM.*

☺ **Grand Slam Entertainment** has softball and baseball batting cages and pitching machines, including one with fastballs up to 80 mph and a Wiffle-ball machine for younger kids, plus a bumper-boat pool and a video-arcade room. ⊠ *322 Rte. 28, Harwich Port* ☎ *508/430–1155* ⊕ *www.grandslamentertainment.com* ⊙ *Apr. and May and Sept.–mid-Oct., Mon.–Sat. 11–7, Sun. 11–9; June–Aug., daily 9 AM–10 PM.*

☺ The **Trampoline Center** has 12 trampolines set up at ground level over pits for safety. ⊠ *296 Rte. 28, West Harwich* ☎ *508/432–8717* ⊙ *Apr.–mid-June, weekends, hrs vary widely, call ahead; mid-June–early Sept., daily 9 AM–11 PM.*

Where to Stay & Eat

★ **$$–$$$$** ✕**Cape Sea Grille.** Sitting primly inside a dashing Gothic Victorian house on a side street off hectic Route 28, this gem with distant sea views cultivates a refined ambience with fresh flowers, white linens, and vibrant wall murals. Specialties from the ever-changing menu include crispy duck confit with Swiss chard, roasted beets, and a red-wine glaze; and grilled Atlantic salmon wrapped in prosciutto with melon, cucumbers, toasted Israeli couscous, and a wild blackberry vinaigrette. Chef-owner Douglas Ramler (formerly of Boston's noted Hamersley's Bistro) relies on the freshest ingredients. ⊠ *31 Sea St., Harwich Port* ☎ *508/432–4745* ⊟ *AE, D, MC, V* ⊙ *Closed Dec.–early Apr. No lunch.*

$$–$$$$ ✕**L'Alouette.** Owners Alan and Gretchen Champney serve authentic French food in this unassuming gray-shingle house with a loyal following among foodies in the know. Look for traditional and contemporary selections such as butter-poached lobster with a saffron-vanilla sauce, Moroccan braised lamb with preserved lemon and mint, and sun-dried-tomato-crusted halibut with a lemon, roasted garlic, and sage sauce and wilted spinach. Desserts here are a particular delight, especially the light and not-too-sweet tarte tatin. There's also a superb wine list. ⊠ *787 Rte. 28, Harwich Port* ☎ *508/430–0405* ⊟ *AE, DC, MC, V* ⊙ *No lunch.*

★ **$$–$$$** ✕**Buca's Tuscan Roadhouse.** This romantic roadhouse near the Chatham border, with a vintage Ford station wagon parked out front, has crisp red-and-white-checked tablecloths and a vibe that might just transport you to Italy—and if it doesn't, the food will. From *zuppe* to aged pecorino, Gorgonzola, and ricotta salad with figs to veal with red wine, balsamic butter, sun-dried cherries, and roasted tomatoes, this is mouthwatering Italian fare taken far beyond traditional home cooking. ⊠ *4 Depot Rd., Harwich* ☎ *508/432–6900* ⊕ *www.bucasroadhouse.com* ⊟ *MC, V* ⊙ *No lunch.*

$$–$$$ ✕ **The Port.** An urbane and homey storefront café in downtown Harwich Port, The Port was opened in 2004 by the sons of Brax Landing's former owner. The kitchen focuses on fairly traditional American fare, especially seafood, but with some inventive interpretations. You might, for instance, sample pan-seared shrimp with baby spinach and red and yellow tomatoes with a white wine–truffle sauce and angel hair pasta, or grilled pork with Jamaican jerk spices alongside lemongrass-steamed rice and veggies. The Thai-style lobster-crab cake with wasabi sour cream makes for a nice starter. The menu is long and ambitious, and there's also an extensive, well-chosen wine list. ✉ *541 Rte. 28* ☎ *508/ 430–5410* ▭ *AE, MC, V* ☾ *Closed Dec.–Apr. No lunch.*

$–$$ ✕ **Brax Landing.** In this local stalwart perched alongside busy Saquatucket Harbor, you can get a menu tip-off as you pass by tanks full of steamers and lobsters in the corridor leading to the dining room. The restaurant sprawls around a big bar that serves specialty drinks such as the Banzai (frozen piña colada with a float of dark rum). The swordfish with pineapple-mango salsa and the herb-crusted Chatham scrod are favorites, both served simply and well. And if you've been after the ultimate lobster roll—and never thought you could get full on one—sample the one at Brax Landing, bursting with the meat of a 1¼-pound lobster. There's also a notable children's menu, and Sunday brunch is an institution. ✉ *Rte. 28 at Saquatucket Harbor, Harwich Port* ☎ *508/432– 5515* ⌦ *Reservations not accepted* ▭ *AE, DC, MC, V* ☾ *Restaurant closed Jan. and Feb.; bar open yr-round.*

¢–$$ ✕ **400 East.** This big, dark restaurant buzzing with conversation is in a nondescript shopping plaza. The menu includes teriyaki chicken, prime rib, lobster ravioli, burgers, and baked scrod, but also has excellent pizza, with toppings such as wild mushrooms, blue cheese, and chicken sausage. Eating at the busy, U-shape bar is a good alternative to waiting for a table. The 400 has a cousin restaurant (also called the 400) downtown on Main Street. ✉ *1421 Rte. 39* ☎ *508/432–1800* ▭ *AE, D, MC, V.*

★ **¢–$**   ✕ **Ay! Caramba Café.** This unassuming, no-frills café in downtown Harwich is a great place to fill up on authentic Mexican fare—not easy to find in these parts—without cleaning out your wallet. Choose from tasty quesadillas, burritos, tostadas, and tacos, or go for one of the large combination plates, complete with rice and either refried beans or vegetables. More ambitious offerings include a nicely seasoned chicken mole, and Yucatán-style tuna steak with roasted pepper and pineapple salsa. The drinking crowd is young and boisterous here, and there's an extensive tequila menu—enthusiasts can even join the restaurant's Tequila Club. In warm weather, grab a seat on the outdoor patio. ✉ *703 Main St., Harwich* ☎ *508/432–9800* ⊕ *www.aycarambacafe.com* ▭ *MC, V* ☾ *Closed Sun. Nov.–Mar.*

★ **$$$$**   ▥ **Alyce's Dunscroft by-the-Sea.** This charming, luxurious beach house sits a half block from Nantucket Sound and within walking distance of several restaurants, yet it's on a peaceful street away from the crowds. The rooms, named after a diverse selection of famous couples (Scarlet and Rhett, Sonny and Cher), have many romantic amenities, including king- and queen-size lace-canopy and four-poster beds, two-person whirlpool tubs, cotton robes, and some working fireplaces. The cottage suite has a living room with a fireplace, kitchenette, and a huge Jacuzzi. In the common gathering room, you'll find a baby grand piano and extensive library. Alyce's full breakfasts are fantastic (she makes killer French toast). ⊠ *24 Pilgrim Rd., Harwich Port 02646* ☎ *508/432–0810 or 800/ 432–4345* ⊕ *www.dunscroftbythesea.com* ↪ *8 rooms, 1 cottage* ⚿ *In-room hot tubs, some kitchenettes, cable TV, beach; no kids under 16* ⊟ *AE, MC, V* ⦿ *BP.*

★ **$$$–$$$$** ⊞ **Winstead Inn and Beach Resort.** Comprising two distinct properties, the Winstead Inn and Beach Resort offer a two-for-one Cape Cod experience. Harking back to an earlier era, the airy, attractive Beach Resort sits on a private beach overlooking Nantucket Sound. You can gaze at the sweep of coast and surrounding grasslands while enjoying a generous continental breakfast from rockers and umbrella tables on the deck and wraparound porches. At the other end of the spectrum, the Winstead Inn sits along a quiet street on the edge of downtown. Greenery surrounds this Gothic Victorian house, and many of the rooms have a view of the outdoor pool. Guests at either property can use the amenities and facilities at both locations. ⊠ *114 Parallel St., 02645* ⊠ *4 Braddock La., Harwich Port 02646* ☎ *508/432–4444 or 800/870–4405* ⊕ *www.winsteadinn.com* ↪ *17 rooms, 4 suites* ⚿ *Some in-room hot tubs, some microwaves, cable TV, pool, Internet room, Wi-Fi, meeting rooms; no smoking* ⊟ *AE, MC, V* ⦿ *CP.*

$–$$$ ⊞ **Lion's Head Inn.** Actually a bit closer to Dennisport than to Harwich and Harwich Port, this well-maintained early-19th-century sea captain's home sits along a quiet street in a peaceful neighborhood a little less than a mile north of the sea. Innkeepers Marilyn and Tom Hull run this low-key, reasonably priced B&B and also rent out a pair of one-bedroom cottages with full kitchens and living rooms with double futons (so each can sleep a total of four); the cottages are available weekly in summer and for shorter stays the rest of the year. Rooms are modestly but tastefully appointed, with country quilts and a smattering of antiques. A big plus here is the large outdoor pool and attractive patio. ⊠ *186 Belmont Rd., West Harwich 02671* ☎ *508/432–7766 or 800/321–3155* ⊕ *www. capecodinns.com* ↪ *5 rooms, 1 suite, 2 cottages* ⚿ *Some kitchens, cable TV, pool; no TV in some rooms* ⊟ *D, MC, V* ⦿ *CP.*

Nightlife & the Arts

THE ARTS The **First Congregational Church** (⊠ Main St. at corner of Rtes. 39 and 124, Harwich ☎ 508/432–1053) closes its day of worship with Sunday-evening Candlelight Concerts at 7:30 from July through September.

Harwich Junior Theatre (⊠ 105 Division St., West Harwich ☎ 508/432–2002 ⊕ www.hjtcapecod.org) gives theater classes for kids year-round and presents 12 family-oriented productions.

Town-band concerts (☎ 508/432–1600) in Harwich take place in summer on Tuesday evening at 7:30 in Brooks Park.

NIGHTLIFE The **Hot Stove Saloon** (⊠ 551 Rte. 28, Harwich Port ☎ 508/432–9911) is a convivial spot for tasty pub fare and a wide selection of beers and cocktails. The baseball-themed tavern also airs sporting events on TV.

Irish Pub (✉ 126 Rte. 28, West Harwich ☎ 508/432–8808) has dancing to bands—playing Irish, American, and dance music—as well as sing-alongs, pool, darts, sports TV, and pub food in the bar.

Jake Rooney's Pub (✉ 119 Brooks Rd., off Rte. 28, Harwich Port ☎ 508/430–1100) is a comfortable watering hole. Keno and live entertainment five nights a week make it a fun place to hang out with friends.

Sports & the Outdoors

BASEBALL The **Harwich Mariners** (✉ Harwich High School, Oak St. ☎ 508/432–2000 ⊕ www.harwichmariners.org) of the collegiate Cape Cod Baseball League play home games at Whitehouse Field from mid-June through mid-August.

BEACHES Harwich has 21 beaches, more than any other Cape town. Most of the ocean beaches are on Nantucket Sound, where the water is a bit calmer and warmer. Freshwater pond beaches are also abundant. Nonresident beach parking stickers, sold at the **Harwich Community Center** (✉ 100 Oak St. ☎ 508/430–7638), cost $40 for one week, $55 for two weeks, and $75 for the season, which runs from June through Labor Day. Ask for the free map of the town's beaches when you get your sticker.

BICYCLING The **Bike Depot** (✉ 500 Depot St. ☎ 508/430–4375) has rentals, including some antique bikes. It's in North Harwich, right off the bike trail.

BOATING Whether you're in the mood to sail under the moonlight, hire a private charter, or learn to navigate yourself, **Cape Sail** (✉ 337 Squatucket Harbor, off Rte. 28, Harwich Port ☎ 508/896–2730) can accommodate any whim.

Cape Water Sports (✉ Rte. 28, Harwich Port ☎ 508/432–5996) rents Sunfish and other small sailboats by the week only.

FISHING Fishing trips are operated on a walk-on basis from spring through fall on the **Golden Eagle** (✉ Wychmere Harbor, Harwich Port ☎ 508/432–5611).

The **Yankee** (✉ Squatucket Harbor, Harwich Port ☎ 508/432–2520) invites passengers in search of fluke, scup, sea bass, and tautog aboard its 65-foot party boat. Two trips depart daily Monday through Saturday in season; there's also one on Sunday. Reservations are recommended.

GOLF **Cranberry Valley Golf Course** (✉ 183 Oak St. ☎ 508/430–5234 ⊕ www.cranberrygolfcourse.com) has a championship layout of 18 well-groomed holes surrounded by cranberry bogs.

Harwich Port Golf Club (✉ South and Forest Sts., Harwich Port ☎ 508/432–0250) has a 9-hole course that's great for beginners.

Shopping

Cape Cod Braided Rug Co. (✉ 537 Rte. 28, Harwich Port ☎ 508/432–3133) makes braided rugs in all colors, styles, and sizes.

★ **Cape Cod Lavender Farm** (✉ Corner of Rte. 124 and Weston Woods Rd., off U.S. 6, Exit 10, Harwich ☎ 508/432–8397) consists of some 14,000 lavender plants, making it one of the largest such farms on the East Coast. Apart from the plants themselves, the farm makes and sells soaps and bath salts, candles, potpourri, marmalade, lemonade, and many other lavender-infused goods and gifts. Keep your eyes peeled for their sign (on the right) as you're driving south on Route 124—it's easy to miss.

Cedar Spring Herb Farm (⊠ 159 Long Pond Dr., Harwich ☎ 508/430–4372 ⊕ www.cedarspringherbfarm.com) spreads out over 7 acres of walking trails, picnic areas, and fragrant, lush herb gardens. The emphasis here is health, both of the spiritual and physical sort; all herb products for sale are made from organic plants, and there is a full schedule of lectures, classes, and ceremonial healings and events. The farm is open from May to November.

820 Main Gallery (⊠ 820 Rte. 28, Harwich Port ☎ 508/430–7622) sells original works in oil, acrylics, watercolors, and photography, as well as limited-edition prints by established local artists. The gallery specializes in regional land- and seascapes.

The **Potted Geranium** (⊠ 188 Rte. 28, West Harwich ☎ 508/432–1114) stocks country-inspired home-related gifts, including colorful wind flags, handcrafted items, and wind chimes.

Pottery Plus (⊠ 551 Rte. 28, Harwich Port ☎ 508/430–5240) sells the pottery of artist Scott Sullivan, as well as works by other local artists.

Wychmere Book & Coffee (⊠ 521 Rte. 28, Harwich Port ☎ 508/432–7868) is a place to savor the comforts of browsing, reading, and sipping good coffee. Special events with authors and a children's summer reading hour further enhance the scene.

Chatham

6–11 *5 mi east of Harwich, 8 mi south of Orleans.*

Low-key, well-heeled Chatham feels like a sliver of Nantucket that's floated over to the Cape. It's neatly groomed and blue-blooded yet artsy, prim but eccentric, straight-arrow but with loads of personality. Originally populated by Native Americans, Chatham came into the hands of white settlers from Plymouth in 1656, when William Nickerson traded a boat for the 17 square mi of land that make up the town. In 1712 the area separated from Eastham and was incorporated as a town; the surnames of the Pilgrims who first settled here still dominate the census list. Although Chatham was originally a farming community, the sea finally lured townspeople to turn to fishing for their livelihood, and the industry has held strong to this day.

At the bent elbow of the Cape, with water nearly surrounding it, Chatham has all the charm of a quietly posh seaside resort, with plenty of shops but none of the

> **WORD OF MOUTH**
>
> "Chatham is a great little town on The Cape. The Main Street area is so cute, lots of shops and restaurants. Really good food at The Impudent Oyster. Also stop into The Chatham Squire—you can't miss these places. Check out the Lighthouse, Chatham Bars Inn, and Fish Pier." —Patty B

Atwood House
Museum **7**

Chatham
Light **9**

Fish Pier **11**

Monomoy
National
Wildlife Refuge
headquarters . .**10**

Old Grist Mill . . .**8**

Railroad
Museum **6**

crass commercialism that plagues some other towns on the Cape. And it's charming: the town has gray-shingle houses with tidy awnings and cheerful flower gardens, an attractive Main Street with crafts and antiques stores alongside dapper cafés, and a five-and-dime. It's a traditional town (said to have more registered Republican voters than any other town on Cape Cod), where elegant summer cottages share the view with stately homes rich in Yankee architectural detail. In fact, this tiny town by the sea is where you'll find some of the finest examples of bow-roof houses in the country. Chatham's nowhere near as kitschy as Provincetown, but it's not overly quaint, either—it's casual and fun, in a refined New England way.

Because of its location at the elbow, Chatham is not a town you just pass through—it's a destination in itself. During summer months, the town bursts into bloom as hydrangeas blossom in shades of cobalt blue, indigo, and deep violet. And although it can get crowded in high season—and even on weekends during shoulder seasons—Chatham remains a true New England village.

🌿 ❻ Authentic all the way, the **Railroad Museum** is in a restored 1887 depot. Exhibits include a walk-through 1910 New York Central caboose, old photographs, equipment, thousands of train models, and a diorama of the 1915 Chatham rail yards. ⊠ *153 Depot Rd., West Chatham* ☎ *No phone* ⊕ *www.chathamrailroadmuseum.com* ✉ *Free* ⊙ *Mid-June–mid-Sept., Tues.–Sat. 10–4.*

> ## ROUGH NEIGHBORHOOD
>
> Chatham's position on the confluence of Nantucket Sound and the Atlantic Ocean makes the town especially vulnerable to the destructive wrath of stormy seas. Many a home and beachfront have been lost to the tumultuous waters. But like any stalwart New England character, Chatham will continue to hold on to its fortunes, its past, and its future.

🌿 The **Play-a-round,** a multilevel wooden playground of turrets, twisting tubular slides, and jungle gyms, was designed with the input of local children and built by volunteers. There's a section for people with disabilities and a fenced-in area for small children. ⊠ *Depot Rd., across from Railroad Museum, West Chatham.*

On **Queen Anne Road** around Oyster Pond, half-Cape houses, open fields, and rolling pastures reveal the area's colonial and agricultural history.

Built by sea captain Joseph C. Atwood in 1752 and occupied by his descendants until it was sold to the Chatham Historical Society in 1926, ❼ the **Atwood House Museum** has a gambrel roof, variable-width floor planks, fireplaces, an old kitchen with a wide hearth and a beehive oven, and some antique dolls and toys. The New Gallery displays portraits of local sea captains. The Joseph C. Lincoln Room has the manuscripts, first editions, and mementos of the Chatham writer, and there is an antique tool room in the basement. The 1974 Durand Wing has collections of seashells from around the world and threaded Sandwich glass, as well as Parian-ware figures, unglazed porcelain vases, figurines, and busts. In a remodeled freight shed are murals (1932–45) by Alice Stall-knecht Wight portraying religious scenes in Chatham settings. On the grounds are an herb garden, the old turret and lens from the Chatham Light, and a simple camp house rescued from eroding North Beach. ⊠ *347 Stage Harbor Rd., West Chatham* ☎ *508/945-2493* ⊕ *www. chathamhistoricalsociety.org* ⊠ *$5* ⊙ *Mid-June–Sept., Tues.–Sat. 1–4 (opens at 10 AM on rainy days).*

❽ The **Old Grist Mill,** one of a number of windmills still on the Cape, was built in 1797 by Colonel Benjamin Godfrey for the purpose of grinding corn. How practical the mill actually was is a matter of debate: for it to work properly, a wind speed of at least 20 mph was necessary, but winds more than 25 mph required the miller to reef the sails or to quit grinding altogether. The mill was moved to its present location from Miller Hill in 1956 and extensively renovated. ⊠ *Old Mill Dr. near Mill Pond* ⊠ *Free* ⊙ *July and Aug., weekdays 10–3.*

Mill Pond is a lovely place to stop for a picnic. There's fishing from the bridge, and you'll often see bullrakers at work, plying the pond's muddy bottom with 20-foot rakes in search of shellfish.

Stage Harbor, sheltered by Morris Island, is where Samuel de Champlain anchored in 1606. The street on its north side is, not surprisingly, called Champlain Road. A skirmish here between Europeans and Native Americans marked the first bloodshed in New England between Native people and colonial settlers.

★ ❾ The famous view from **Chatham Light** (⊠ Main St. near Bridge St., West Chatham)—of the harbor, the offshore sandbars, and the ocean beyond—justifies the crowds that gather to share it. The lighthouse is especially dramatic on a foggy night, as the beacon's light pierces the mist. Coin-operated telescopes allow a close look at the famous "Chatham Break," the result of a fierce 1987 nor'easter that blasted a channel through a barrier beach just off the coast; it's now known as North and South beaches. The Cape Cod Museum of Natural History in Brewster has a display of photos documenting the process of erosion leading up to and following the break. The U.S. Coast Guard auxiliary, which supervises the lighthouse, offers tours April through September on the first and third Wednesday of the month. The lighthouse is also open by appointment and on three special occasions during the year: Seafest, an annual tribute to the maritime industry held in mid-October; mid-May's Cape Cod Maritime Week; and June's Cape Heritage Week.

Fodor'sChoice **Monomoy National Wildlife Refuge** is a 2,500-acre preserve including the ★ Monomoy Islands, a fragile 9-mi-long barrier-beach area south of Chatham. Monomoy's North and South islands were created when a storm divided the former Monomoy Island in 1978. Monomoy was itself separated from the mainland in a 1958 storm. A haven for bird-watchers, the island is an important stop along the North Atlantic Flyway for migratory waterfowl and shorebirds—peak migration times are May and late July. It also provides nesting and resting grounds for 285 species, including gulls—great black-backed, herring, and laughing—and several tern species. White-tailed deer also live on the islands, and harbor and gray seals frequent the shores in winter. The only structure on the islands is the **South Monomoy Lighthouse**, built in 1849.

Monomoy is a quiet, peaceful place of sand and beach grass, tidal flats, dunes, marshes, freshwater ponds, thickets of bayberry and beach plum, and a few pines. Because the refuge harbors several endangered species, activities are limited. Certain areas are fenced off to protect nesting areas of terns and the threatened piping plover. Several groups conduct tours of the islands, including the Massachusetts Audubon Society in South Wellfleet and the Cape Cod Museum of Natural History in Brewster, many with a focus on bird-watching. Most of these tours cost about $20 to $35 per person, depending on the length of the tour and the itinerary. In season, the *Rip Ryder* (☎ 508/945–5450 ⊕ www.monomoyislandferry.com) will take you over from Chatham for bird- or seal-watching tours; private charters are also available.

Another excellent option is **Monomoy Island Excursions** (☎ 508/430–7772), which offers seal and seabird tours and boat trips out around Monomoy Island, leaving from Saquatucket Harbor on a 43-foot high-speed catamaran.

Outermost Adventures (☎ 508/945–5858 www.outermostharbor.com) also provides water taxi services out to Monomoy Island and offers fishing, birding, and seal-watching cruises.

🔟 The **Monomoy National Wildlife Refuge headquarters** (✉ Off Morris Island Rd., Morris Island ☎ 508/945–0594 ⊕ http://monomoy.fws.gov), on the misleadingly named Morris Island (it's connected to the mainland), has a visitor center and bookstore, open daily 8–4, where you can pick up pamphlets on Monomoy and the birds, wildlife, and flora and fauna found there. A ¾-mi interpretive walking trail around Morris Island, closed at high tide, gives a good view of the refuge and the surrounding waters. The area itself is open daily for exploring from dawn to dusk.

⓫ The **Fish Pier** (✉ Shore Rd. and Barcliff Ave., North Chatham) bustles with activity when Chatham's fishing fleet returns, sometime between noon and 2 PM daily, depending on the tide. The unloading of the boats is a big local event, drawing crowds who watch it all from an observation deck. From their fishing grounds 3–100 mi offshore, fishermen bring in haddock, cod, flounder, lobster, halibut, and pollack, which are packed in ice and shipped to New York and Boston or sold at the fish market here. You might also see sand sharks being unloaded. Typically they are sent, either fresh or frozen, to French and German markets. Also here is *The Provider,* a monument to the town's fishing industry, showing a hand pulling a fish-filled net from the sea.

The **Eldredge Public Library** (✉ 564 Main St. ☎ 508/945–5170) has a special genealogy department as well as storytimes for kids, book discussion groups, and special programs and lectures.

Known for their artful contemporary treatment of blown glass, Jim Holmes and Deborah Doane of the **Chatham Glass Company** create everything from candleholders to unique vases in a vast spectrum of colors. You can watch them perform the fascinating process of glassblowing here.

⊠ *758 Main St.* ☎ *508/945–5547* ⊕ *www.chathamglass.com* ⊗ *Late May–early Sept., Mon.–Sat. 10–5; early Sept.–late May, daily 10–5.*

NEED A BREAK?
If you're looking for a fat and fancy sandwich, a morning bagel, or an afternoon cappuccino pick-me-up, stop in at the **Chatham Village Cafe** (⊠ 400 Main St. ☎ 508/945-2525). Eat inside at one of the few tables for some good streetside people-watching, or head over to the Village Green for an impromptu picnic. Head to **Buffy's** (⊠ 456 Main St. ☎ 508/945-5990) for Chatham's finest (and only homemade) ice cream. You can nosh on your cone at one of the tables set along the lawn outside, beneath a prodigious apple tree. Don't overlook the fresh-squeezed lime rickies and tangy smoothies. **Carmine's** (⊠ 595 Main St. ☎ 508/945-5300) serves some of the best New York–style pizza (by the slice or the pie) outside New York. There are just a handful of tables inside this storefront eatery in the heart of downtown, which is also an excellent source for grinders and mouthwatering gelato.

Where to Stay & Eat

$$–$$$ ✕ **Christian's.** French and New England influences are found at this landmark restaurant, although local opinions vary on the quality of the food. The menu includes grilled prime meats and fresh Cape Cod seafood, such as pepper-grilled swordfish over lobster-whipped potatoes. The mahogany-panel bar and upstairs sunroom serve a lighter menu that remains strong on seafood. As attractive as the formal downstairs may be, the upstairs is more of a happening scene, with live piano music most evenings. ⊠ *443 Main St.* ☎ *508/945-3362* ▭ *DC, MC, V* ⊗ *Closed weekdays Jan.–Mar. No lunch.*

$$–$$$
Fodor'sChoice
★ ✕ **Pisces.** An intimate dining room inside a simple yellow house not far from the Harwich border, Pisces, as its name suggests, serves coastal-inspired fare—if it swims in local waters, you can probably sample it here. A rich chowder of lobster, butternut squash, and corn is a terrific way to start your meal. Move on to Mediterranean-style fisherman's stew in saffron-lobster broth, or roasted cod with a simple but flavorful dressing of tomatoes, capers, lemon, and olive oil. Complement your dinner with a selection from the extensive wine list, which offers more than 20 vintages by the glass. ⊠ *2653 Main St., West Chatham* ☎ *508/432-4600* ▭ *MC, V* ⊗ *Closed Dec.–Mar. No lunch.*

★ **$$–$$$** ✕ **Vining's Bistro.** An exceptionally inventive menu and a determination not to rest on its laurels make this restaurant a standout. The wood grill infuses many dishes with a distinctive flavor heightened further by the chef's use of zesty rubs and spices from all over the globe. The Thai-style crab cakes come with a sharp chili-cucumber vinaigrette, and pan-roasted sea scallops are served with smoked bacon, mixed mushrooms, and caramelized red onion confit. The restaurant is upstairs at the Gallery Building, and many windows look out on the art below. Though the atmosphere is casual, this is not a family place; there is a deliberate lack of high chairs, booster seats, and kiddie meal options. ⊠ *595 Main St.* ☎ *508/945-5033* ⊕ *www.viningsbistro.com* ⊘ *Reservations not accepted* ▭ *AE, D, MC, V* ⊗ *Closed Jan.–mid-Apr.*

$-$$$ ✕ **Campari's Bistro.** It's just a short drive north of downtown, toward Pleasant Bay, to reach this reliable spot known for good regional Italian fare. The softly lighted dining room has large and comfy booths and wood paneling, and you can also dine in the casual tavern, which is more appropriate for families. Nice starters include lemon-poached shrimp wrapped in prosciutto, and crab cakes with creole mustard aioli. Seafood Florentine and veal-and-spinach-stuffed cannelloni rank among the better entrées, but the wood-fired thin-crust pizzas steal the show here. ✉ *323 Rte. 28, North Chatham* ☎ *508/945–9123* ⊕ *www.camparis.com* 🗐 *AE, D, DC, MC, V* ⊘ *No lunch.*

★ **$-$$$** ✕ **Impudent Oyster.** A cozy, festive locals' tavern with an unfailingly cheerful staff and superb but reasonably priced seafood, this always-packed restaurant sits inside a dapper house just off Main Street. It's a great place for a romantic meal or dinner with friends or kids, and the menu offers light burgers and sandwiches as well as more substantial fare. Mussels with white-wine sauce is a consistent favorite. The dining room is split-level, with a bar in back on the lower level. There's not a ton of seating, so reserve early on weekends. ✉ *15 Chatham Bars Ave.* ☎ *508/945–3545* 🗐 *AE, MC, V.*

$-$$$ ✕ **Marley's.** You'll find traditional New England fare—often served with a decidedly international flair—at Marley's, one of the best family restaurants in the area. Scallops prepared with pineapple, rum, and brown sugar and topped with a coconut-macaroon crust are a favorite. Crab cakes and Cajun blackened salmon served with poached shrimp and crabmeat are house specialties. Steak, prime rib, chicken potpie, lobster, and steamers round out the menu, which also includes several vegetarian dishes. ✉ *1077 Main St., West Chatham* ☎ *508/945–1700* 🗐 *AE, MC, V* ⊘ *No lunch.*

$$ ✕ **Chatham Squire.** If you order anything local here from the long list of tried-and-true American standbys, you won't go wrong. The fish is as fresh and good as you get on Cape Cod, and the kitchen continues to innovate while still remaining true to its Cape roots. The calamari is always tender, the New England smoked fish plate delicious, and the clam chowder is a must. Expect a long wait in season, in which case you can visit the bar and pick up on the local gossip. ✉ *487 Main St.* ☎ *508/945–0945* ⊕ *www.thesquire.com* ⌫ *Reservations not accepted* 🗐 *AE, D, MC, V.*

$$$$ ✕🏨 **Wequassett Inn Resort & Golf Club.** Twenty Cape-style cottages and
Fodor'sChoice an attractive hotel make up this traditionally elegant resort by the sea.
★ Set on 22 acres of shaded landscape partially surrounded by Pleasant Bay, the Wequassett is an informally upscale resort. An attentive staff, evening entertainment, fun in the sun, and golf at the exclusive Cape Cod National Golf Club are just a few of the benefits you can count on at Wequassett. Chef Bill Brodsky's creative globally inspired cuisine graces the menus of the three restaurants—the star being the sophisticated 28 Atlantic ($$$–$$$$), which is one of the top destination restaurants on the Cape, serving such stellar creations as yellowfin and salmon tartare, and caramelized skate wing with beet-daikon-horseradish salad and watercress jus. The Pool Bar & Grill serves cocktails, beverages, snacks, and light lunch fare poolside. After a day at the beach or on the links,

Restaurants ▼

Campari's
Bistro **5**

Chatham
Squire **3**

Christian's **1**

Impudent
Oyster **2**

Marley's **6**

Pisces **7**

Vining's
Bistro **4**

Hotels ▼

Captain's
House Inn **5**

Carriage
House Inn **6**

Chatham
Bars Inn **3**

Chatham
Wayside Inn **4**

Cranberry Inn . . . **1**

Hawthorne
Motel **2**

Nantucket
House **10**

Old Harbor
Inn **8**

Queen Anne
Inn **9**

Wequassett Inn
Resort &
Golf Club **7**

retire to your spacious room and relax amid fresh pine furniture, floral bedcovers or handmade quilts, and overflowing window boxes. Or, sip a cocktail on the lawn outside your private cottage-style room overlooking Pleasant Bay. ⌧ *173 Orleans Rd. (Rte. 28), 02633* ☎ *508/432–5400 or 800/225–7125* 🖷 *508/432–5032* ⊕ *www.wequassett.com* ⇥ *102 rooms, 2 suites* ⟁ *3 restaurants, snack bar, room service, 4 tennis courts, pool, gym, windsurfing, boating, piano bar* ▭ *AE, D, DC, MC, V* ◎ *Closed Nov.–Mar.* ⦿⧲ *FAP.*

★ **$$$–$$$$**   ✕⊞ **Queen Anne Inn.** Built in 1840 as a wedding present for the daughter of a famous clipper-ship captain, the Queen Anne first opened as an inn in 1874. Some of the large guest rooms have working fireplaces, balconies, and hot tubs. The lavish studio rooms in the Victorian cottage are particularly dashing and convey more of a colonial Caribbean flair. Lingering and lounging are encouraged—around the large heated outdoor pool, at the tables on the veranda, in front of the fireplace in the sitting room, or in the plush parlor. The place has a wonderful, cozy feel in winter, making it a great year-round option, though the restaurant is closed in winter. Opened in 2005 by locally renowned chef Toby Hill, the Eldredge Room ($$$–$$$$; closed Jan.–Apr., no lunch) turns out sublime regional American fare, including an updated fish-and-chips consisting of truffle-crusted flounder, frites, truffle tartar sauce, and malt vinaigrette, and crispy honey-Dijon venison "lollipops" with a chocolate-zinfandel dipping sauce. There's also an extensive American caviar menu. ⌧ *70 Queen Anne Rd., 02633* ☎ *508/945–0394 or 800/545–4667* 🖷 *508/945–4884* ⊕ *www.queenanneinn.com* ⇥ *33 rooms* ⟁ *Restaurant, some in-room hot tubs, cable TV, 3 tennis courts, pool, bar, Wi-Fi, meeting rooms; no smoking* ▭ *AE, D, MC, V* ◎ *Closed Jan. and Mar. (open Feb.).*

$$$$ ⊞ **Chatham Bars Inn.** Overlooking Pleasant Bay from atop a windswept bluff, Chatham Bars Inn is a grande dame hotel that has long been one of the Cape's most coveted retreats. The ground-floor lobby gives way to the formal restaurant on one side and a porch-fronted lounge on the other. Elegant guest rooms in the resort's main inn and cottages are filled with hand-painted furnishings by local artists and colorful fabrics depicting sunny seaside scenes. Adding to the well-heeled flavor of the inn is a new massive spa complex (opened in summer 2006), complete with a 4,000 square foot hydrotherapy pool. If you'd like to be as close as possible to this pampering palace, you can stay in one of the lavishly appointed suites within the new space. ⌧ *Shore Rd., 02633* ☎ *508/945–0096 or 800/527–4884* 🖷 *508/945–5491* ⊕ *www.chathambarsinn. com* ⇥ *149 rooms, 68 suites* ⟁ *4 restaurants, putting green, 3 tennis courts, pool, indoor pool, gym, spa, beach, croquet, volleyball, bar, lobby lounge, babysitting, children's programs (ages 4–14)* ▭ *AE, D, MC, V.*

★ **$$$–$$$$**   ⊞ **Captain's House Inn.** A Victorian tile ceiling, wide-board floors, and elaborate moldings and wainscoting are just part of what makes Jan and Dave McMaster's inn one of the Cape's most popular. Each room has its own personality; some are quite large, and all have fireplaces. The Hiram Harding Room, in the bow-roof Captain's Cottage, has 200-year-old hand-hewn ceiling beams, a wall of raised walnut paneling, and a large, central working fireplace. Suites in the former stables are spacious and have hot tubs, fireplaces, TV–VCRs, mini-refrigerators, and private patios or balconies. A young staff of British hospitality students serves an over-the-top full breakfast each morning and high tea in the afternoon. The herb and flower gardens and neatly trimmed lawns are stunning. ⊠ *369 Old Harbor Rd., 02633* ☎ *508/945–0127 or 800/315–0728* 🖷 *508/945–0866* ⊕ *www.captainshouseinn.com* ⇘ *12 rooms, 4 suites* ♿ *Some in-room hot tubs, some refrigerators, cable TV, in-room VCRs, pool, gym, bicycles, croquet, Wi-Fi; no kids under 12, no smoking* ▤ *AE, D, MC, V* ⦿ *BP.*

$$$–$$$$ 🏨 **Cranberry Inn.** This grand 1830s inn is a short walk east of the commercial span of Main Street, near the heart of downtown—but it has a protected marsh in its backyard. Billed as the oldest continuously operating lodging establishment in Chatham, the inn is filled with antique and reproduction furniture, plus handmade quilts, braided rugs, and other homey touches. The 18 rooms and suites come in a wide variety of shapes and sizes, some of them accommodating as many as six guests. Several rooms have fireplaces, wet bars, and private balconies. Breakfast, which is also available to the public by reservation, is served in a lovely dining room that also provides the setting for an informal afternoon tea with delicious sweets and treats. An intimate pub with a wood-burning fireplace has a full liquor license and is open to the public. On hot days you can cool off on the great big north-facing veranda overlooking Main Street. ⊠ *359 Main St., 02633* ☎ *508/945–9232 or 800/332–4667* 🖷 *508/945–3769* ⊕ *www.cranberryinn.com* ⇘ *15 rooms, 3 suites* ♿ *Dining room, cable TV, Wi-Fi, bar; no kids under 12, no smoking* ▤ *AE, D, MC, V* ⦿ *BP.*

$$–$$$$ 🏨 **Chatham Wayside Inn.** Once a stop on a turn-of-the-20th-century stagecoach route, this venerable inn is still an oasis for weary travelers. Everything is crisp and colorful here, from the floral comforters and wallpapers to freshly painted walls and bright carpeting. Some rooms have balconies, fireplaces, and hot tubs. With a great location smack-dab in the center of town, you may not have to leave your room to hear the sounds of the weekly town-band concerts. The restaurant serves reliable contemporary American fare and a very good Sunday brunch. ⊠ *512 Main St., 02633* ☎ *508/945–5550 or 800/242–8426* 🖷 *508/945–3407* ⊕ *www.waysideinn.com* ⇘ *56 rooms* ♿ *Restaurant, some in-room hot tubs, cable TV, in-room VCRs, Wi-Fi, pool, meeting rooms* ▤ *AE, D, MC, V.*

$$–$$$$ 🏨 **Hawthorne Motel.** Beyond the Hawthorne Motel's modest roadside appearance extends a private beach overlooking Pleasant Bay, the Atlantic, and Chatham Harbor. Nearly all the rooms have stunning water views. Choose from spotless, no-nonsense, simply decorated motel rooms or kitchenette efficiency units with small refrigerators, two heating plates, and a countertop-sink work area. There's also a two-bedroom cottage (rented by the week in season) with full kitchen and a separate living–dining room, plus amenities such as a VCR and an outdoor grill. The center of town is just a short walk away. Long-distance calls within the Lower 48 states are free, and the lobby has a computer with high-speed Internet access, fresh-brewed coffee, and complimentary morning newspapers. ✉ *196 Shore Rd., 02633* ☎ *508/945–0372* ⊕ *www.thehawthorne.com* ⤲ *16 rooms, 10 efficiencies, 1 cottage* ⟁ *Some kitchenettes, refrigerators, cable TV, Internet room; no smoking* ▭ *AE, D, MC, V* ☉ *Closed mid-Oct.–mid-May.*

\$\$–\$\$\$\$ ⊡ **Old Harbor Inn.** Congenial, thoughtful hosts Ray and Judith Braz run this cheery B&B set inside a handsome 1930s Colonial Revival house a few steps from Main Street and downtown shopping. You'll receive plenty of extras and treats, from in-room snack baskets and extensive complimentary bath products to hair dryers and fluffy robes. Most rooms feel distinctly Victorian in flavor—the cozy yet spacious Port Fortune room has exposed beams, pitched ceilings, white wicker furniture, and Laura Ashley linens. If it's luxury you're after, book the Stage Harbor Suite, which has a two-person Jacuzzi and separate shower. Relax out back on the deck or in the verdant, shaded garden. ✉ *22 Old Harbor Rd., 02633* ☎ *508/945–4434 or 800/942–4434* ⊕ *www. chathamoldharborinn.com* ⤲ *7 rooms, 1 suite* ⟁ *Some in-room hot tubs, refrigerators, cable TV, in-room VCRs, Wi-Fi; no room phones, no smoking* ▭ *MC, V* ◉| *BP.*

\$\$–\$\$\$ ⊡ **Carriage House Inn.** Innkeepers Jill and James Meyer have created an elegant but uncluttered B&B that offers three distinct styles for three different budgets. In the main 1890s white-clapboard house, you'll find three moderately priced rooms on the second floor, and an inviting common living room with a computer work station, DVD library, fireplace, and board games. Next door, the former stables contain three larger and more secluded rooms with high-pitched ceilings, fireplaces, and French or sliding-glass doors leading to private outdoor areas. Finally, a spacious suite affords even more space and can sleep four. The decor throughout tends toward the classic and contemporary. Each morning James prepares a delicious full breakfast, which might include gingerbread waffles or upside-down apple French toast. The beach is a mile away. ✉ *407 Old Harbor Rd., 02633* ☎ *508/945–4688 or 800/ 355–8868* ⊕ *www.thecarriagehouseinn.com* ⤲ *6 rooms, 1 suite* ⟁ *Cable TV, in-room DVDs, Wi-Fi; no kids under 12, no smoking* ▭ *AE, D, MC, V* ◉| *BP.*

\$\$ ⊡ **Nantucket House.** This handsome 1840s Greek Revival house with Doric columns and a steep roof punctuated by dormer windows originally provided shelter to a sea captain in Nantucket. In the 1860s, new owners floated the house over to the mainland, where today—close to the Harwich town line—it serves as a delightful B&B, one of Chatham's best values. Features of this airy house include wide-plank pumpkin-pine floors, ornate ceiling medallions, Laura Ashley linens, and informal but tasteful country furnishings. Guest rooms are compact without feeling cramped. Hosts Carol and Jerry Gordon are friendly but easygoing, and Carol prepares a memorable breakfast using recipes from her own cookbook, *Sleep on It.* ✉ *2647 Main St., 02659* ☎ *508/432– 5641 or 866/220–2547* ⊕ *www.chathamnantuckethouse.com* ⤲ *4 rooms, 1 suite* ⟁ *No room phones, no room TVs, no kids under 8, no smoking* ▭ *AE, MC, V* ◉| *BP.*

Nightlife & the Arts

THE ARTS **Chatham Drama Guild** (✉ 134 Crowell Rd. ☎ 508/945–0510 ⊕ www. chathamdramaguild.com) stages productions year-round, including musicals, comedies, and dramas.

The **Creative Arts Center** (✉ 154 Crowell Rd. ☎ 508/945–3583 ⊕ www. capecodcreativearts.org) thrives year-round with classes, changing gallery exhibitions, demonstrations, lectures, and other activities.

In July and August the **Guild of Chatham Painters** presents an outdoor art gallery on Thursday and Friday from 9:30 to 5 on the Main Street School's lawn. ✉ *Main St.*

The **Monomoy Theatre** (✉ 776 Main St. ☎ 508/945–1589 ⊕ www. monomoytheatre.org) stages summer productions—thrillers, musicals, classics, and modern drama—by the Ohio University Players.

Chatham's summer **town-band concerts** (✉ Kate Gould Park, Main St. ☎ 508/945–5199) begin at 8 on Friday and draw up to 6,000 people. As many as 500 fox-trot on the roped-off dance floor, and there are special dances for children and sing-alongs for all.

NIGHTLIFE **Chatham Squire** (✉ 487 Main St. ☎ 508/945–0945), with four bars—including a raw bar—is a rollicking year-round local hangout, drawing a young crowd to the bar side and a mixed crowd of locals to the restaurant.

After great success in Hyannis and Falmouth, the owners of the **RoöBar** (✉ 907 Main St. ☎ 508/945–9988 ⊕ www.theroobar.com) opened a third location in Chatham, transforming what was once a Friendly's into an elegant bar and bistro. Patrons enjoy an extensive wine list, great mixed drinks, and varied entertainment—usually rock music—on the weekends.

Wequassett Inn Resort & Golf Club (✉ 173 Orleans Rd. [Rte. 28], Pleasant Bay ☎ 508/432–5400) has a jazz duo or piano music nightly in its lounge in July and August (jacket requested).

Sports & the Outdoors

BASEBALL The **Cape Cod Baseball League,** begun in 1885, is an invitational league of college players that counts Carlton Fisk, Ron Darling, Mo Vaughn, Nomar Garciaparra, and the late Thurman Munson as alumni. Considered the country's best summer league, it's scouted by every major-league team. The 10 teams of the Cape Cod Baseball League play a 44-game season from mid-June to mid-August; games held at all 10 fields are free. The **Chatham A's** (✉ Veterans' Field, Main and Depot Sts. by rotary ☎ 508/996–5004 ⊕ www.chathamas.com) games are great entertainment.

Baseball clinics (✉ Veterans' Field, Main and Depot Sts. by rotary ☎ 508/432–6909)—for kids 6 through 8, 9 through 12, and 13 through 17—are offered in one-week sessions by the Chatham A's in summer. The other nine town teams in the Cape league also conduct clinics (☎ 508/996–5004 information).

BEACHES **Outermost Harbor Marine** (✉ Morris Island Rd., Morris Island ☎ 508/945–2030) runs shuttles to South Beach; rides cost $15 round-trip for adults (including parking).

The Cape Cod Baseball League

AT THE BASEBALL HALL OF FAME in Cooperstown, New York, you can find a poster announcing a showdown between archrivals Sandwich and Barnstable. The date? July 4, 1885. In the 120-plus years since that day, the Cape's ball-playing tradition has continued unabated. To see a game on the Cape today is to come into contact with baseball's roots—you'll remember why you love the sport.

As they have since the 1950s, top-ranked college baseball players from around the country descend on the Cape when school lets out, just in time to begin the season in mid-June. Each player joins one of the league's 10 teams, each based in a different town: the Bourne Braves, Wareham Gatemen, Falmouth Commodores, Cotuit Kettleers, Hyannis Mets, Dennis-Yarmouth Red Sox, Harwich Mariners, Brewster Whitecaps, Chatham Athletics (A's), and the Orleans Cardinals.

Players lodge with local families and work day jobs cutting lawns, painting houses, or giving baseball clinics in town parks. In the evening, though, their lives are given over to baseball.

The Cape League's motto is "Where the Stars of Tomorrow Shine Tonight." By latest count, one of every eight active major-league ballplayers spent a summer in the Cape League on the way up. You could build an all-star roster with names such as Nomar Garciaparra, Frank Thomas, Jeff Bagwell, Todd Helton, and Barry Zito.

To enshrine these heroes past, the Cape League inducted the first members into its Hall of Fame at the Heritage Museums & Gardens in Sandwich in January 2001. Among the 12 players honored were Thurman Munson, Mike Flanagan, Jeff Reardon, Mo Vaughn, and Frank Thomas.

Yet as good as the baseball is—you'll often see major-league scouts at a game—another great reason to come out to the ballpark is . . . the ballpark. Chatham's Veterans Field is the Cape's Monster Park at Candlestick Point: much like the San Francisco park, fog tends to engulf the games here. Orleans's Eldredge Park is a local favorite—immaculate, cozy, and comfortable. Some parks have bleachers; in others, it's up to you to bring your own chair or blanket and stretch out behind a dugout or baseline. Children are free to roam and can even try for foul balls—which they are, however, asked to return because, after all, balls don't grow on trees. When hunger hits, the ice-cream truck and hot-dog stand are never far away.

Games start at either 5 or 7, depending on whether the field has lights; occasionally there are afternoon games. Each team plays 44 games in a season, so finding one is rarely a problem (⊕ www. capecodbaseball.org has information). And, best of all, they're always free. The Cape's baseball scene is so American, the ambience so relaxed and refreshing, it's tempting to invoke the old *Field of Dreams* analogy. But the league needs no Hollywood comparison. This is the real thing.

—Seth Rolbein

Harding's Beach (✉ Harding's Beach Rd., off Barn Hill Rd., West Chatham), west of Chatham center, is open to the public and charges daily parking fees to nonresidents in season. Lifeguards are stationed here in summer. This beach can get crowded, so plan to arrive early or late. Nonresident parking fees at Chatham beaches are $15 daily, $60 weekly, and $125 seasonally.

BICYCLING All manner of bikes are available for rent at **Chatham Cycle** (✉ 193 Depot Rd. ☎ 508/945–8981).

Monomoy Sail & Cycle (✉ 275 Orleans Rd., North Chatham ☎ 508/945–0811) rents bicycles as well as sailboards.

BOATING **Monomoy Sail & Cycle** (✉ 275 Orleans Rd., North Chatham ☎ 508/945–0811) rents sailboards and Sunfish.

Nauti Jane's (✉ Off Rte. 28 at Wequassett Inn, Ridgevale Rd., Chatham ☎ 508/430–6893 or 508/432–4339) has Day Sailers, power boats, or peaceful kayaks for rent. The seasonal shop has two locations: one on the grounds of the Wequassett Inn and the other at Ridgevale Beach.

Rip Ryder (☎ 508/945–5450) boat tours offers naturalist-led trips that leave from the Monomoy National Wildlife Refuge area to view birds and seals and explore the rich and ever-changing habitat of the North and South Monomoy Island areas.

GOLF **Chatham Seaside Links** (✉ Seaview St., West Chatham ☎ 508/945–4774), a 9-hole course, is good for beginners.

SURFING The Lower and Outer Cape beaches, including North Beach in Chatham, are the best on the peninsula for surfing, which is tops when there's a storm offshore. Chatham does not have any surf shops, but you'll find them in nearby Orleans.

TENNIS **Chatham Bars Inn** (✉ Shore Rd. ☎ 508/945–0096 Ext. 1155) offers three waterfront all-weather tennis courts, which are open to the public by reservation for $15 an hour. You can also take lessons and visit the pro shop.

The town maintains two public tennis parks, one on Depot Road next to the Railroad Museum at No. 153 and the other at the middle school on Crowell Road.

Shopping

Main Street is a busy shopping area with a diverse range of merchandise, from the pocketbook friendly to the pricier and more upscale. Here you'll find galleries, crafts, clothing stores, bookstores, and a few good antiques shops.

Cabbages and Kings Bookstore (✉ 595 Main St. ☎ 508/945–1603) is a good independent bookstore. In addition to a full stock of literary and regional books, look for a host of unusual games, cards, and toys and a regular schedule of author appearances.

Cape Cod Cooperage (✉ 1150 Queen Anne Rd., at Rte. 137, West Chatham ☎ 508/432–0788), in an old barn, sells woodenware made in a (more than) century-old tradition by an on-site cooper (barrel maker), as well as hand-decorated furniture and crafts supplies. Daily classes are available in everything from stenciling and decorative painting to basket making and birdhouse building.

★ **Chatham Jam and Jelly Shop** (✉ 10 Vineyard Ave., at Rte. 28, West Chatham ☎ 508/945–3052 or 877/526–7467) sells delicious concoctions like rose petal jelly, apple-lavender chutney, and beach plum jam, as well as all the old standbys. All preserves are made on-site in small batches, and about 75 of the 120-plus varieties are available for sampling (which is encouraged).

Clambake Celebrations (✉ 1223C Main St. ☎ 508/945–7771 or 877/792–7771) prepares full clambakes, including lobsters, clams, mussels, corn, potatoes, onions, and sausage, for you to take out; it'll even lend you a charcoal grill. The company also delivers via air year-round if necessary. The food is layered in seaweed in a pot and ready to steam.

The **Crooked Fence** (✉ 593 Main St. ☎ 508/945–4622), tucked inconspicuously behind Dunkin' Donuts, stocks eclectic, well-chosen home furnishings and gifts, such as cast-iron planters, Nantucket baskets, wind chimes, imported Tuscan tableware, and models of vintage planes and boats.

The **East Wind Silver Co.** (✉ 878 Main St. ☎ 508/945–8935) specializes in artful silver jewelry but also sells watercolor paintings, pottery, fountains, and Tiffany-style lighting.

Marion's Pie Shop (✉ 2022 Main St. [Rte. 28], West Chatham ☎ 508/432–9439) sells homemade and home-style fruit breads, pastries, prepared foods such as lasagna, Boston baked beans, chowder base, and, of course, pies, both savory and sweet.

S. Wilder & Co. (✉ 304 Rte. 28, North Chatham ☎ 877/794–5337) displays old-style colonial crafts. Handcrafted brass and copper lanterns are made here.

Yankee Ingenuity (✉ 525 Main St. ☎ 508/945–1288) stocks a varied selection of unique jewelry and lamps and a wide assortment of unusual, beautiful trinkets at reasonable (especially for Chatham) prices.

Yellow Umbrella Books (✉ 501 Main St. ☎ 508/945–0144) has an excellent selection of new books, many about Cape Cod, as well as used books.

EN
ROUTE
North of Chatham and on the way to Orleans, you'll encounter perhaps the most beautiful stretch of Route 28, the road that's so blighted by overdevelopment in Harwich, Dennis, and Yarmouth. Along here, the narrow road twists and turns alongside the western shoreline of rippling **Pleasant Bay.** Turn east onto any number of peaceful country roads, and you'll end up near the water and within view of Nauset Spit and Pleasant Bay's several islands. This is excellent biking and jogging territory—but keep in mind that Route 28 is fairly narrow along this span, with a tiny shoulder, so keep your eye out for oncoming traffic.

Orleans

🕐 *8 mi north of Chatham, 35 mi east of Sagamore Bridge.*

Named for Louis-Philippe de Bourbon, *duc d'Orléans* (duke of Orléans), who reputedly visited the area during his exile from France in the 1790s, Orleans was incorporated as a town in 1797. Historically, it has the distinction of being the only place in the continental United States to have received enemy fire during either world war. In July 1918 a German submarine fired on commercial barges off the coast. Four were sunk, and one shell is reported to have fallen on American soil.

Today Orleans is part quiet seaside village and part bustling center with strip malls. The commercial hub of the region, Orleans is one of the more steadily populated areas, year-round, of the Lower Cape. Yet the town retains a fervent commitment to preserving its past, and residents, in support of local mom-and-pop shops, maintain an active refusal policy of many big-time corporations.

Orleans has a long heritage in fishing and seafaring, and many beautifully preserved homes remain from the colonial era. Many are found in the small village of East Orleans, home of the town's Historical Society and Museum. In other areas of town, such as down by Rock Harbor, more modestly grand homes stand near the water's edge.

As you head north, this is the first Cape town to touch both Cape Cod Bay and the Atlantic Ocean. Nauset Beach, on the Atlantic, is enormously popular. Backed by towering dunes dotted with sea grass and colorful *rosa Rugosa*, this beach could be the starting point for a long but beautiful trek clear to the very tip of the Cape. Skaket Beach, just south of Rock Harbor, is the main bay-side beach and affords both scenic views and calm, warm waters for swimming.

A walk along Rock Harbor Road, a winding street lined with gray-shingle Cape houses, white picket fences, and neat gardens, leads to the bay-side **Rock Harbor,** site of a War of 1812 skirmish in which the Orleans militia kept a British warship from docking. In the 19th century Orleans had an active saltworks, and a flourishing packet service between Rock Harbor and Boston developed. Today the former packet landing is the base of charter-fishing and party boats in season, as well as of a small commercial fishing fleet whose catch hits the counters at the fish market and small restaurant here. Sunsets over the harbor are spectacular.

The Community of Jesus, a religious community whose members come from a variety of Christian traditions, owns a large chunk of the Rock Harbor area. Their dramatic cathedral, the **Church of the Transfiguration,** showcases the work of local and international artisans, and reflects the community's dedication to the arts. Inside there's an organ with thousands of pipes, authentic frescoes depicting Biblical scenes, colorful stained-glass windows, and gorgeous, intricate mosaic work mixing religious themes with images of local flora and fauna. ⊠ *Rock Harbor Rd. across from Rock Harbor* ☎ *508/255–1054, 508/255–6204 (tours)* ⊕ *www.communityofjesus.org* ✉ *Free, donations accepted* ☉ *Tours Tues., Fri., and Sat. at 3, Thurs.–Tues. at sunset; services are open to public.*

NEED A BREAK?

The **Cottage St. Bakery** (⊠ 5 Cottage St. ☎ 508/255–2821) prepares delicious artisanal breads, pastries, cakes, and sweets, as well as healthful breakfast and lunch fare, from homemade granola to hefty sandwiches.

The 1890 **French Cable Station Museum** was the stateside landing point for the 3,000-mi-long transatlantic cable that originated in Brittany. Another cable laid between Orleans and New York City completed the France–New York link, and many important messages were communicated through the station. During World War I, when it was an essential connection between army headquarters in Washington and the American Expeditionary Force in France, the station was under guard by the marines. By 1959 telephone service had rendered the station obsolete, and it closed—but the equipment is still in place. ⊠ *41 S. Orleans Rd., East Orleans* ☎ *508/240–1735* ✉ *Donations accepted* ☉ *June, Fri.–Sun. 1–4; July–early Sept., Mon.–Sat. 1–4.*

The **Jonathan Young Windmill**, a pretty if somewhat incongruous sight on the busy highway, is a landmark from the days of salt making in Orleans, when it would pump saltwater into shallow vaults for evaporation. A program explaining the history and operation of the mill demonstrates the old millstone and grinding process. ⊠ *Rte. 6A and Town Cove, East Orleans* ☉ *July and Aug., daily 11–4; June and Sept., weekends 11–4.*

NEED A BREAK?

Grab a baked treat, chocolates of all varieties, and any number of coffee concoctions at **The Chocolate Sparrow** (⊠ 5 Old Colony Way ☎ 508/240–2230), located right by the Cape Cod Rail Trail. The adjacent Ice Cream at the Sparrow serves tasty hard and soft ice cream.

The **Academy of Performing Arts** (⊠ 5 Giddiah Hill Rd. ☎ 508/255–5510 or 508/255–1963 ⊕ www.apacape.org) offers two-week sessions of theater, music, and dance classes to kids ages 8–12, with a show at the end of each session. It also schedules year-round classes for ages four to adult in dance, music, and drama. The academy's theater is at 120 Main Street.

Snow Library (⊠ Main St. and Rte. 28 ☎ 508/240–3760) has been in operation since around 1876; today there are kids' story hours and numerous lecture programs.

Where to Stay & Eat

★ **$$–$$$$** ✕ **Abba.** Abba serves inspired pan-Mediterranean cuisine in an elegant and intimate setting. Chef and co-owner Erez Pinhas skillfully combines Middle Eastern, Asian, and Southern European flavors in such dishes as scallops with fettuccine and asparagus in a curry cream sauce, and

CLOSE UP

Rotary 101

THE ENGLISH CHEERFULLY CALL THEM "roundabouts," and while that lighthearted moniker might sound like it describes a fun (albeit slightly nauseating) carnival ride, rotaries are serious business. Uninitiated drivers are often so confused upon entering one that they either ignore all rules of the road or freeze up completely. Both reactions will likely cause horns to blare and the fists and fingers of your fellow motorists to come out in full force. But it doesn't have to be this way. Follow a few simple rules, and you'll be swinging around traffic circles like a local. The most important thing to remember is that drivers who are already in the rotary have the right of way: those entering must YIELD to the traffic in the rotary. This means that if you're approaching the rotary, you must WAIT until there is enough space for you to enter—you can't just hit the gas and hope for the best. Because if you do, you probably just caused a fellow motorist to commit another cardinal sin: stopping while in the rotary. Either that, or he just hit you. Using a rotary is actually a very simple concept. Now that you know the rules, you may even grow to appreciate their exquisite logic (at the very least, you'll see fewer unfriendly hand gestures).

–Laura V. Scheel

grilled filet mignon with Jerusalem artichokes, asparagus, pearl onions, and a morel mushroom sauce. Cushy pillows on the banquettes and soft candlelight flickering from Moroccan glass votives add a touch of opulence. ⊠ *Old Colony Way and West Rd.* ☎ *508/255–8144* ⌂ *Reservations suggested* ⊕ *www.abbarestaurant.com* ▭ *AE, D, MC, V* ⊘ *Closed Mon. No lunch.*

$$–$$$ ✕ **Academy Ocean Grill.** Owner and chef Christian Schultz, who originally opened Christian's in Chatham, has earned plenty of kudos on the Lower Cape for his artful and inventive globally influenced cooking, and his present establishment lives up to his sterling reputation. Academy Ocean Grill occupies a stately shingle house surrounded by profusive gardens—in warm weather, you can dine on the patio amid the flowers and greenery. Top dishes include chunky crab cakes, monkfish pan-seared with Thai curry, and traditional veal saltimbocca. An exceptional wine list rounds out the offerings. ⊠ *2 Academy Pl., off Rte. 28* ☎ *508/240–1585* ▭ *AE, D, MC, V* ⊘ *Closed mid-Jan.–mid-Apr.*

★ $$–$$$ ✕ **Captain Linnell House.** Sea captain Eben Linnell built this stunning mansion in the 1850s, basing its design on a neoclassical villa he'd once visited in the South of France. Linnell's masterpiece now contains one of the Cape's most esteemed formal restaurants, a longtime favorite for celebrating special occasions. A competent and polite staff serves Continental cuisine, which is consistently superb. The kitchen tends to stick with tried-and-true classics, such as herb-and-mustard-crusted rack of lamb with a pinot noir reduction, and grilled Black Angus steak au poivre with a zinfandel-peppercorn sauce. Considering the fine ingredients and opulent surroundings, it's an excellent value. ⊠ *137 Skaket Beach Rd.* ☎ *508/255–3400* ▭ *AE, MC, V* ⊘ *No lunch.*

★ **$$–$$$** ✕ **Mahoney's Atlantic Bar and Grill.** Chef Ted Mahoney cooked for years at one of Provincetown's busiest restaurants before opening this always-hopping downtown spot that serves commendable dinner fare and draws big crowds for cocktails and appetizers. The menu emphasizes grilled vegetables and polenta, drunken shellfish steamed in ale, and tuna sashimi. The bar is long and comfortable, and on many evenings you can sip your martini or California wine to live music. ⊠ *28 Main St.* ☎ *508/255–5505* 🖃 *AE, MC, V.*

★ **$$–$$$** ✕ **Nauset Beach Club.** Locals have long favored this upscale but casual trattoria on the road leading out to Nauset Beach. The kitchen produces seasonally inspired regional Italian food with an emphasis on locally harvested seafood and produce. Choose from a fixed-price option (offered daily at two early seatings; the earliest one is a bargain, starting at just $19 for three courses Sunday through Thursday) or the à la carte menu for such favorites as grilled lemon-and-cracked pepper sirloin with truffle oil and baby arugula, and pistachio-crusted rack of lamb with caramelized fennel. The off-season warms up with wood oven–fired dishes; in fall and winter, truffles appear artfully in various presentations. ⊠ *222 Main St., East Orleans* ☎ *508/255–8547* 🖃 *AE, D, DC, MC, V* ☉ *No lunch.*

$–$$$ ✕ **The Beacon Room.** Adorned with crisp linens, frilly curtains, and wood furnishings, this homey cottage bistro serves up a nice mix of seafood and meats enhanced with sophisticated and inventive flavors. Start with the Gorgonzola, sun-dried cranberry, and walnut salad, then move on to sesame-crusted salmon with cilantro oil or pecan-crusted venison with a sauce of red zinfandel and pan drippings. In warmer months, dinner on the garden patio is particularly urbane. An ambitious wine list complements the fine selection. ⊠ *23 West Rd.* ☎ *508/255–2211* ⚐ *Reservations not accepted* 🖃 *D, MC, V.*

¢–$$$ ✕ **Saltwater Grille and Binnacle Tavern.** Like siblings, these two restaurants may share the same house (an aged sea captain's dwelling) and the same parents, but that's where the similarities end. New in 2006, the Saltwater Grille portion breathed new life into the once somber upstairs dining area. Gone are the dark fabrics and heavy furniture—now it's like eating in your favorite bright beach house. You'll find grilled meats and seafood aplenty here, as well as specialty sandwiches and fat burgers. In back, the Binnacle Tavern serves delicious pizzas with some inventive toppings (apples, linguica sausage, pine nuts, Brie). There's an extensive menu of designer martinis at the Binnacle, which is also a diverting option for drinks and rounds of billiards. ⊠ *20 Rte. 28* ☎ *508/255–5149 Saltwater Grille* 🖃 *AE, D, MC, V* ⚐ *Reservations not accepted* ☉ *Saltwater Grille: closed Sun., Mon. No lunch. Binnacle: No lunch.*

★ **¢–$$** ✕ **Land Ho!** Tried-and-true tavern fare is the rule at Orleans' flagship local restaurant. The scene is usually fun and boisterous; dozens of homemade wooden signs hang from the rafters above the red-checked tablecloths. The burgers and the sea-clam pie are both excellent, and the blackboard specials change daily. This is a good place for a rainy-day lunch. On weekend nights, it livens up even more with the music of local bands. ⊠ *Rte. 6A and Cove Rd.* ☎ *508/255–5165* ⚐ *Reservations not accepted* 🖃 *AE, MC, V.*

★ ¢–$ ✗ **Sir Cricket's Fish and Chips.** For a beautifully turned-out fish sandwich, pull into this tiny local favorite, a hole-in-the-wall attached to Nauset Fish & Lobster Pool. Built mainly for takeout, this no-frills fish joint does have three or four tiny tables and a soda machine. Try the fresh oyster roll or go for a full fisherman's platter. As you eat, check out the chair seats—each is an exquisitely rendered mini-mural of Orleans history or a personality painted by legendary local artist Dan Joy. ⊠ *Rte. 6A, near Stop & Shop* ☎ *508/255–4453* ⌲ *Reservations not accepted* ▭ *No credit cards.*

$$–$$$$ ✗▣ **Orleans Inn.** This 1875 sea captain's mansion nearly met with the
Fodor'sChoice wrecking ball before Ed Maas and his family took over the place in the
★ late '90s; today the Maas clan continues to run this bustling inn and restaurant with warmth and enthusiasm. The imposing, turreted structure has two distinct faces: one turned toward a busy intersection and a large shopping plaza while the other looks longingly over tranquil Town Cove. Rooms here are simply but charmingly appointed with classic wood furniture and floral quilts on the beds; the larger waterfront suites have sitting areas and great views of the harbor. Common areas include a kitchenette with a microwave and toaster oven and a sitting room in the basement with a large TV and videos. The restaurant (¢–$$), which uses some creative ingredients in its traditional standbys, serves up large portions of fish-and-chips, grilled sirloin, and grilled salmon with orange-honey glaze. There's also an excellent Sunday brunch. Remarkably, the inn has no cancellation fee: you must pay in full for your stay at the time of booking, but even if you cancel the day of arrival, you'll receive a full refund. Local and long-distance phone calls are complimentary, too. ⊠ *21 Rte. 6A, 02653* ☎ *508/255–2222* ⊟ *508/255–6722* ⊕ *www.orleansinn. com* ⇖ *8 rooms, 3 suites* ⌂ *Restaurant, refrigerators, cable TV, Wi-Fi, pub; no smoking* ▭ *AE, MC, V* ▢◐ *CP.*

★ $$$–$$$$ ▣ **A Little Inn on Pleasant Bay.** Run by sisters Sandra Zeller and Pamela Adam and Sandra's husband, Bernd Zeller—all of whom have extensive corporate and hospitality backgrounds—this gorgeously decorated inn occupies a 1798 building set on a bluff beside a cranberry bog, across Route 28 from the bay for which it's named. The main house has four rooms, and two adjoining nearby buildings contain another five rooms. Many of the accommodations look clear out to the bay, and others face the lush gardens. The Mercury room has French doors leading out to a private garden patio, and the spacious Wianno room is warmed by a fireplace and has a lovely sitting area. The roomy, modern bathrooms are among the nicest of any hotel on the Cape. The breakfast buffet includes a dazzling variety of fresh fruits, baked goods, smoked fish, cold cuts, fine cheeses, yogurts, cereals, and other treats. It's more substantial than many full breakfasts, and you can enjoy it while sitting on the pretty patio, admiring Pleasant Bay in the distance. ⊠ *654 S. Orleans Rd., Box 190, South Orleans 02662* ☎ *508/255–0780 or 888/332–3351* ⊕ *www. alittleinnonpleasantbay.com* ⇖ *9 rooms* ⌂ *Wi-Fi, dock; no room phones, no room TVs, no kids under 10, no smoking* ▭ *AE, MC, V* ▢◐ *CP.*

★ $–$$$ ▣ **Cove Motel.** Consisting of two main buildings overlooking Orleans Town Cove, this tidy but prosaic year-round motel has large rooms, most with decks or patios overlooking the water. Furnishings are undistinguished but updated and pleasant, and rooms have tasteful, neutral color schemes. Some units have fireplaces and kitchens, and two-room suites can comfortably accommodate four guests. An attractive picnic area overlooks the heated pool. You can't beat the location, and in summer you'll receive a complimentary boat tour around Town Cove. ✉ *13 Rte. 28, Box 279, 02653* ☎ *508/255–1203 or 800/343–2233* ⊕ *www.thecoveorleans.com* ⇨ *37 rooms, 10 suites* ♿ *Some kitchens, some microwaves, refrigerators, cable TV, in-room DVDs, pool, meeting rooms* ▭ *MC, V.*

$–$$ 🏨 **Skaket Beach Motel.** Rooms in this convenient-to-everything inland motel overlooking a busy intersection are well sized; a handful of suites have kitchens and two or three bedrooms. Outdoor facilities include horseshoes, a heated pool, and grills. ✉ *203 Rte. 6A, 02643* ☎ *508/255–1020 or 800/835–0298* 🖷 *508/255–6487* ⊕ *www.skaketbeachmotel.com* ⇨ *40 rooms, 6 suites* ♿ *Some kitchens, refrigerators, cable TV, pool, croquet, horseshoes* ▭ *MC, V* ⊘ *Closed late Nov.–Mar.* ⦿ *CP.*

¢–$$ 🏨 **Nauset House Inn.** You could easily spend a day trying out all the places to relax here. There's a parlor with comfortable chairs and a large fireplace, an orchard set with picnic tables, and a lush conservatory with a weeping cherry tree in its center. Rooms in both the main building and the adjacent Carriage House have stenciled walls, quilts, and unusual antique pieces, as well as hand-painted furniture, stained glass, and prints done by one of the owners. The beach is ½ mi away (they'll set you up with beach chairs and towels), and the attractions of town are close—but not too close. Those rooms with a shared bath all cost $85 or less. ✉ *143 Beach Rd., Box 774, East Orleans 02643* ☎ *508/255–2195* ⊕ *www.nausethouseinn.com* ⇨ *14 rooms, 8 with bath* ▭ *D, MC, V* ⊘ *Closed Nov.–Mar.* ⦿ *BP.*

Nightlife & the Arts

The **Academy Playhouse** (✉ 120 Main St. ☎ 508/255–1963), one of the oldest community theaters on the Cape, stages 12 or 13 productions year-round, including original works.

The **Cape & Islands Chamber Music Festival** (☎ 508/945–8060 ⊕ www.capecodchambermusic.org) presents three weeks of top-caliber performances, including a jazz night, at various locations in August.

The **Stages Theatre Company** (☎ 508/255–3999 ⊕ www.gdaf.org) puts on music and theater events several times a year. The group is affiliated with the Community of Jesus; performances are held on the Community's grounds at Rock Harbor.

Land Ho! (✉ Rte. 6A and Cove Rd. ☎ 508/255–5165) has live local bands frequently and throughout the year.

Mahoney's Atlantic Bar and Grill (✉ 28 Main St. ☎ 508/255–5505) regularly has live jazz and blues in the bar area; call for times.

Free ocean-side concerts are held in the gazebo at **Nauset Beach** each Monday evening from 7 to 9 in July and August. The resident fried-clam shack stays open until 10.

Sports & the Outdoors

BASEBALL The **Orleans Cardinals** (☎ 508/255–0793 ⊕ www.orleanscardinals.com)
of the collegiate Cape Cod Baseball League play home games at **Eldredge
Park** (✉ Rte. 28) from mid-June to mid-August.

BEACHES The town-managed **Nauset Beach** (✉ Beach Rd., Nauset Heights ☎ 508/
240–3780)—not to be confused with Nauset Light Beach on the National
Seashore—is a 10-mi sweep of sandy ocean beach with low dunes and
large waves good for bodysurfing or board surfing. The beach has lifeguards, restrooms, showers, and a food concession. Despite its size, the
massive parking lot often fills up when the sun is strong; arrive quite early
or in the late afternoon if you want to claim a spot. The beach is open
to off-road vehicles with a special permit. Daily parking fees are $15; a
one-week pass costs $50, and a season pass is $110. Entrance is free with
a resident sticker. For more information, call the parks department.

Freshwater seekers can access **Pilgrim Lake** (✉ Pilgrim Lake Rd. off
Monument Rd. and Rte. 28, South Orleans), which has the same parking and sticker fees as Nauset Beach.

NEED A
BREAK?
Eldia Market & Coffeehouse (✉ 210 Main St., East Orleans ☎ 508/255–
7469) has become a favorite local hangout; it's a great spot to pick up a nice
bottle of wine, sip a steaming espresso, or check your e-mail. The sandwich
and soup menu has some great offerings, but the biggest surprise is the wine
selection, which includes hard-to-find boutique wines at decent prices.
There's also free Wi-Fi.

Skaket Beach (✉ Skaket Beach Rd., Namskaket ☎ 508/240–3775) on
Cape Cod Bay is a sandy stretch with calm, warm water good for children. It's a good place to watch motorboats, fishing charters, and sailboats as they leave the channel at Rock Harbor or take in the spectacular
evening sunsets. There are restrooms, lifeguards, and a snack bar. Daily
parking fees are the same as at Nauset Beach.

BOATING **Arey's Pond Boat Yard** (✉ 43 Arey's La., off Rte. 28, South Orleans ☎ 508/
255–0994) has a sailing school with individual and group lessons.

What kid doesn't want to put on an eye-patch and sail the seven seas?
Make your little buccaneer's fantasy a reality on a trip with **Pirate Adventures** on the *Sea Gypsy* (✉ Behind Goose Hummock, off Rte. 6A,
Orleans ☎ 508/255–8811). You'll fire cannons, get your face painted,
hear tall tales, and, of course, find buried treasure. Six trips depart daily
and ply the waters of Town Cove from mid-June through Labor Day.

FISHING Many of Orleans's freshwater ponds offer good fishing for perch, pickerel, trout, and more. The required fishing license, along with rental gear,
is available at the **Goose Hummock Shop** (✉ 15 Rte. 6A ☎ 508/255–0455),
which also rents kayaks and gives kayaking lessons and tours.

Rock Harbor Charter Boat Service (✉ Rock Harbor ☎ 508/255–9757, 800/
287–1771 in Massachusetts) goes for bass and blues in the bay from
spring through fall. Walk-ons and charters are both available.

HEALTH &
FITNESS CLUBS **Willy's Gym** (⊠ 21 Old Colony Way ☎ 508/255–6826 ⊕ www.willysgym. com) is one of the Cape's top fitness facilities, with state-of-the-art cardio and weight-training equipment and studios for yoga, pilates, martial arts, aerobics, and dance classes. Daily, weekly, and monthly passes are available, and there's also a full range of classes for kids. The onsite Kembali Spa offers a wide range of massage and treatment options. This 27,000 square foot location is the original Willy's; the one in Eastham is even larger.

SPAS **Heaven Scent You** (⊠ 13 Cove Rd. ☎ 508/240–2508) offers massage, spa services, and beauty treatments—everything you need for some relaxation and rejuvenation.

After an extensive renovation of an aged Victorian in 2006, the formerly hidden day spa **Welstar** (⊠ 42 S. Orleans Rd. ☎ 508/240–1422 or 800/893–6008 ⊕ www.dayspacapecod.com) now has a prominent location on busy Route 28 in the center of Orleans. Decadent specialty treatments include crystal balancing (for refocusing the body's energy), seaweed contouring masks, warm stone massages, facials, manicures, pedicures, and many more esoteric treats.

SPORTING
GOODS–RENTALS **Nauset Sports** (⊠ Jeremiah Sq., Rte. 6A at rotary ☎ 508/255–4742) rents surf-, body, skim, and wake boards; kayaks; wet suits; in-line skates; and tennis rackets.

For bike rentals just across the way from the Cape Cod Rail Trail, head to **Orleans Cycle** (⊠ 26 Main St. ☎ 508/255–9115).

SURFING The Lower and Outer Cape beaches, including Nauset Beach in Orleans, are the best spots for surfing, especially when there's a storm offshore. For a surf report—water temperature, weather, surf, tanning factor— call ☎ 508/240–2229.

Pump House Surf Co. (⊠ 9 Rte. 6A ☎ 508/240–2226) rents wet suits and surfboards, and sells boards and gear.

Shopping

Baseball Shop (⊠ 26 Main St. ☎ 508/240–1063) sells licensed products relating to baseball and other sports—new and collectible cards (and nonsports cards) as well as hats, clothing, and videos.

Bird Watcher's General Store (⊠ 36 Rte. 6A ☎ 508/255–6974 or 800/562–1512) stocks nearly everything avian but the birds themselves: feeders, paintings, houses, books, binoculars, calls, bird-theme apparel, and more.

Karol Richardson (⊠ 47 Main St. ☎ 508/255–3944) sells fine contemporary clothing, plus silk wraps and scarves, hats, shoes, handbags, and handcrafted jewelry. You'll usually pay more for the quality goods here, but bargains can be found at the shop's off-season warehouse sales.

Kemp Pottery (⊠ 9 Rte. 6A ☎ 508/255–5853) displays functional and decorative stoneware and porcelain, fountains, garden sculpture, sinks, and stained glass.

Oceana (⊠ 1 Main St. Sq. ☎ 508/240–1414) has a beautiful selection of nautical-theme home accents, gifts, and jewelry, as well as colorful hooked rugs made by Cape artist Claire Murray.

The **Orleans Farmers' Market** (⊠ Old Colony Way across from Capt'n Elmers ☎ 508/255–0951) is the place to go for local delicacies such as fresh produce, flowers, and homemade goodies. It's open 8–noon Saturday mornings throughout the summer. Be forewarned—early birds get the best selection, and things tend to disappear quickly.

Village Market Farm Stand (⊠ 199 Main St., East Orleans ☎ 508/255–1949) sells local produce, fresh sandwiches and roll-ups, salads (salad bar or prepared varieties), homemade soup, ice cream, fresh-baked breads, and other supplies for a great picnic. A wide assortment of flowers, both dried and fresh, are sold, adding great color to the beautiful, beamed old-style barn.

ART & CRAFTS The **Addison Art Gallery** (⊠ 43 Rte. 28 ☎ 508/255–6200), in four rooms
GALLERIES   of a brick-red Cape house, represents more than two dozen regional artists. Peruse the collection of contemporary works, many of which were inspired by life on Cape Cod. The sculpture garden in the side yard is a perfect complement to the tasteful gallery. Receptions, where you can often meet the week's featured artist, are held year-round from 5 to 7 on Saturday night.

The **Hogan Art Gallery** (⊠ 39 Main St. ☎ 508/240–3655) showcases colorful white-line woodblocks, paintings, and pastels by artist Ruth Hogan, as well as 20th-century American regional paintings by her husband, Frank. There's also a nice selection of painted furniture.

Left Bank Gallery (⊠ 8 Cove Rd. ☎ 508/247–9172) carries an eclectic mix of handcrafted jewelry, fine art by both local and national artists, hand-painted furniture, pottery, and handmade clothing.

On Tuesday and Sunday in July and August, **Nauset Painters** (Tuesday ⊠ Depot Sq. at Old Colony Way ⊠ Sunday ⊠ Sandwich Cooperative Bank, 51 Main St.) presents outdoor juried art shows.

The **Orleans Art Association** holds outdoor art shows from 10 to 5 each Thursday and Friday in July and August on the grounds of the American Legion Hall ⊠ *137 Main St.*

At various times in June, July, and August, the **Orleans Professional Arts and Crafts Association** (⊠ Rte. 28) sponsors a giant outdoor show on the grounds of the Nauset Middle School featuring the works of more than 100 artists and craftspeople. For specific dates and times check the free town guide published by the Chamber of Commerce.

The **Star Gallery** (⊠ 76 Rte. 6A ☎ 508/240–7827) specializes in contemporary and less traditional art; watch for Saturday-evening artist receptions in July and August.

★ **Tree's Place** (⊠ Rte. 6A at Rte. 28 ☎ 508/255–1330 or 888/255–1330), one of the Cape's best and most original shops, has a collection of handcrafted kaleidoscopes, as well as art glass, hand-painted porcelain and pottery, handblown stemware, jewelry, imported ceramic tiles, and fine art. Tree's displays the work of New England artists, including Robert Vickery, Don Stone, and Elizabeth Mumford (whose popular folk art is bordered in mottos and poetic phrases). Champagne openings are held on Saturday night in summer.

Eastham

13 *3 mi north of Orleans, 6 mi south of Wellfleet.*

Often overlooked on the speedy drive up toward Provincetown on U.S. 6, Eastham is a town full of hidden treasures. Unlike other towns on the Cape, it has no official town center or Main Street; the highway bisects Eastham, and the town is spread out on both Cape Cod Bay and the Atlantic. Amid the gas stations, convenience stores, restaurants, and large motel complexes, Eastham's wealth of natural beauty takes a little exploring to find.

One such gem is the National Seashore, which officially begins here and comprises thousands of acres of wooded areas, salt marshes, and wild, open ocean beaches. The Salt Pond Visitor Center just off U.S. 6 is one of Cape Cod National Seashore's main centers, host to numerous nature and history programs and lectures; it also maintains a paved bike path. Nearby is the much-beloved Nauset Light, the red-and-white-stripe lighthouse saved from imminent destruction when it was moved from its perilous perch atop eroding cliffs. The Fort Hill area is another pretty spot, with lots of walking trails and a stately old mansion called the Penniman House.

It was here in 1620 that an exploring band of *Mayflower* passengers met the Nauset tribe on a bay-side beach, which they then named First Encounter Beach. The meeting was peaceful, but the Pilgrims moved on to Plymouth anyway. Nearly a quarter century later, they returned to settle the area, which they originally called by its Native American name, Nawsett. Eastham was incorporated as a town on June 7, 1651.

Like many other Cape towns, Eastham started as a farming community and later turned to the sea and to salt making for its livelihood; at one time there were more than 50 saltworks in town. A less typical industry that once flourished here was asparagus growing; from the late 1800s through the 1920s, Eastham was known as the asparagus capital of the United States. The runner-up crop, Eastham turnips, are still the pride of many a harvest table.

★ **14** The road to the Cape Cod National Seashore's **Fort Hill Area** (⊠ Fort Hill Rd., off U.S. 6) winds past the **Captain Edward Penniman House,** ending at a parking area with a lovely view of old farmland traced with stone fences that rolls gently down to **Nauset Marsh** and a red-maple swamp. Appreciated by bird-

WORD OF MOUTH

"The most beautiful, although not long, hike is Fort Hill in Eastham. A definite MUST. Beautiful views of the ocean and also a marsh walk."   –ccrosner watchers and nature photographers, the 1-mi **Red Maple Swamp Trail** begins outside the Penniman House and winds through the area, branching into two separate paths, one of which eventually turns into a boardwalk that meanders through wetlands. The other path leads directly to Skiff Hill, an overlook with benches and informative plaques that quote Samuel de Champlain's account of the area from when he moored off Nauset Marsh in 1605. Also on Skiff Hill is Indian Rock, a large boulder moved to the hill from the marsh below. Once used by the local Nauset tribe as a sharpening stone, the rock is cut with deep grooves and smoothed in circles where ax heads were whetted.

The French Second Empire–style **Captain Edward Penniman House** was built in 1868 for a whaling captain. The impressive exterior is notable for its mansard roof; its cupola, which once commanded a dramatic view of bay and sea; and its whale-jawbone entrance gate. The interior is open for guided tours or for browsing through changing exhibits. Call ahead to find out when tours are available. ⊠ *Fort Hill Rd., Fort Hill Area* ☎ *508/255–3421* ⬚ *Free* ☉ *Weekdays 1–4.*

The park at Samoset Road has as its centerpiece the **Eastham Windmill**, the oldest windmill on Cape Cod. A smock mill built in Plymouth in the early 1680s, it was moved to this site in 1793 and is the only Cape windmill still on the site where it was used commercially. The mill was restored by local shipwreck historian William Quinn and friends. The park often comes alive with town festivals and concerts, and occasionally demonstrations are given on the inner workings of the mill. Each September, just after Labor Day, Eastham celebrates its history and the change of the season with the annual Windmill Weekend, an event with a full roster of activities for all ages. ⊠ *U.S. 6 at Samoset Rd.* ⬚ *Free* ☉ *Late June–early Sept., Mon.–Sat. 10–5, Sun. 1–5.*

Frozen in time, the 1741 **Swift-Daley House** was once the home of Gustavus Swift, founder of the Swift meatpacking company. Inside the full Cape with bow roof you can find beautiful pumpkin-pine woodwork and wide-board floors, a ship's-cabin staircase that, like the bow roof, was built by ships' carpenters, and fireplaces in every downstairs room. The colonial-era furnishings include an old cannonball rope bed, tools, a melodeon (similar to an accordion), and a ceremonial quilt decorated with beads and coins. Among the antique clothing is a stunning 1850 wedding dress. Out back is a tool museum. ⊠ *U.S. 6, next to Eastham post office* ☎ *No phone* ⊕ *www.easthamhistorical.org* ⬚ *Free* ☉ *July and Aug., weekdays 10–1; Sept., Sat. 10–1.*

A great spot for watching sunsets over the bay, **First Encounter Beach** (⊠ End of Samoset Rd. off U.S. 6) is rich in history. Near the parking lot, a bronze marker commemorates the first encounter between local Native Americans and passengers from the *Mayflower*, led by Captain Myles Standish, who explored the entire area for five weeks in November and December 1620 before moving on to Plymouth. The remains of a navy target ship retired after 25 years of battering now rest on a sandbar about 1 mi out.

The Cape's most expansive national treasure, the **Cape Cod National**
Seashore was established in 1961 under the administration of President
John F. Kennedy, for whom Cape Cod was home and haven. The 27,000-
acre seashore, extending from Chatham to Provincetown, encompasses
and protects 30 mi of superb ocean beaches; great rolling dunes; swamps,
marshes, and wetlands; pitch pine and scrub oak forest; all kinds of
wildlife; and a number of historic structures. Self-guided nature trails,
as well as biking and horse trails, lace through these landscapes. Hiking trails lead to a red-maple swamp, **Nauset Marsh,** and to **Salt Pond,**
in which breeding shellfish are suspended from floating "nurseries"; their
offspring will later be used to seed the flats. Also in the seashore is the
Buttonbush Trail, a nature path for people with vision impairments. A
hike or bike ride to Coast Guard Beach leads to a turnout looking out
over marsh and sea. A section of the cliff here was washed away in 1990,
revealing the remains of a prehistoric dwelling.

15 **Salt Pond Visitor Center** is the first visitor center of the Cape Cod National Seashore that you encounter as you travel down-Cape toward the
tip (the other, the **Province Lands Visitor Center,** is in Provincetown).
The Salt Pond Visitor Center offers guided walks, tours, boat trips, demonstrations, and lectures from mid-April through Thanksgiving, as well
as evening beach walks, campfire talks, and other programs in summer.
The center includes a museum with displays on whaling and the old saltworks, as well as early Cape Cod artifacts including scrimshaw, the journal that Mrs. Penniman kept while on a whaling voyage with her
husband, and some of the Pennimans' possessions, such as their tea service and the captain's top hat. A good bookstore and an air-conditioned
auditorium showing films on geology, sea rescues, whaling, Henry
David Thoreau, and Guglielmo Marconi are also here. Something's
going on most summer evenings at the outdoor amphitheater, from
slide-show talks to military-band concerts. ⊠ *Doane Rd. off U.S. 6* ☏ *508/*
255–3421 ⊕ *www.nps.gov/caco* ⊠ *Free* ☉ *Daily 9–4:30 (hrs extended*
slightly in summer).

Roads and bicycle trails lead to **Coast Guard and Nauset Light beaches**
(⊠ Off Ocean View Dr.), which begin an unbroken 30-mi stretch of barrier beach extending to Provincetown—the "Cape Cod Beach" of
Thoreau's 1865 classic, *Cape Cod.* You can still walk its length, as Thoreau
did, though the Atlantic continues to claim more of the Cape's eastern
shore every year. The site of the famous beach cottage of Henry Beston's
1928 book, *The Outermost House,* is to the south, near the end of Nauset spit. Designated as a literary landmark in 1964, the cottage was, alas,
destroyed in the Great Blizzard of February 1978.

Moved 350 feet back from its perch at cliff's edge in 1996, the much-
photographed red-and-white **Nauset Light** (⊠ Ocean View Dr. and Cable
Rd. ☏ 508/240–2612 ⊕ www.nausetlight.org) still tops the bluff where
the Three Sisters Lighthouses once stood; the Sisters themselves can be
seen in a little landlocked park surrounded by trees, reached by paved
walkways off Nauset Light Beach's parking lot. How the lighthouses
got there is a long story. In 1838 three brick lighthouses were built 150

feet apart on the bluffs in Eastham overlooking a particularly danger-ous area of shoals (shifting underwater sandbars). In 1892, after the erod-ing cliff dropped the towers into the ocean, they were replaced with three wooden towers. In 1918 two were moved away, as was the third in 1923. Eventually the National Park Service acquired the Three Sisters and brought them together in the inland park, where they would be safe, rather than returning them to the eroding coast. The Fresnel lens from the last working lighthouse is on display at the **Salt Pond Visitor Cen-ter.** Lectures on and guided walks to the lighthouses are conducted throughout the season.

Where to Stay & Eat

$-$$ ✕ **Fairway Restaurant and Pizzeria.** The friendly family-run Fairway spe-cializes in Italian comfort food and pizzas. Attached to the Hole in One Donut Shop (very popular among locals), the Fairway puts a jar of crayons on every paper-covered table and sells its own brand of root beer. Entrées come with salad and homemade rolls. Try the eggplant Parmesan, fettuccine and meatballs, or a well-stuffed calzone. You can order from the extensive breakfast menu from 6:30 to 11:30 AM. ⊠ *4295 U.S. 6* ☎ *508/255–3893* ⚓ *Reservations not accepted* ⊗ *No lunch* ⊟ *AE, D, DC, MC, V.*

¢-$$ ✕ **The Friendly Fisherman.** Not just another roadside lobster shack with buoys and nets for decoration, this place is serious about its fresh seafood. It's both a great place to pick up ingredients to cook at home—there's a fish and produce market on-site—and a good bet for dining out on such favorites as fish-and-chips, fried scallops, and lobster. The market also sells homemade pies, breads, soups, stews, and pasta. ⊠ *U.S. 6, North Eastham* ☎ *508/255–6770 or 508/255–3009* ⊟ *AE, MC, V* ⊗ *Closed Nov.–Apr.*

$$$-$$$$ 🏠 **Fort Hill Bed and Breakfast.** Gordon and Jean Avery run this enchant-
Fodor's Choice ing bed-and-breakfast in an 1864 Greek Revival farmhouse nestled in
★ the tranquil Fort Hill area. The location is perfect—minutes off busy Route 6, but steps away from quiet, secluded trails that wind through cedar forests, fields crisscrossed by old stone fences, and a red maple swamp. Two cozy suites in the main house, tastefully decorated with period pieces and an-tiques, share a living room with fireplace. The crown jewel, however, is the light and airy Nantucket Cottage, modeled after a Truro barn. It's so homey—with stone floors, a gas fireplace, a classic white-and-blue Cape Cod bedroom loft, and a private garden—that you'll want to move in. Breakfasts are superb, with offerings like oven-poached pears in sweet cream, and buttermilk-currant scones; the cheesy-chive egg soufflé is a masterpiece. ⊠ *75 Fort Hill Rd., 02642* ☎ *508/240–2870* ⊕ *www. forthillbedandbreakfast.com* 🛏 *2 rooms, 1 cottage* ♿ *Some kitchenettes, some microwaves, refrigerators, cable TV, some in-room VCRs, some in-room DVDs, Wi-Fi* ⊟ *No credit cards* ⊙I *BP.*

$$$-$$$$ 🏠 **Whalewalk Inn & Spa.** This 1830 whaling master's home is on three
Fodor's Choice landscaped acres. Wide-board pine floors, fireplaces, and 19th-century
★ country antiques provide historical appeal. Rooms in the main inn have four-poster twin, double, or queen-size beds; floral fabrics; and antique or reproduction furniture. Suites with fully equipped kitchens are in the converted barn and guesthouse. A secluded saltbox cottage has a fire-

place, kitchen, and private patio. Deluxe rooms in the carriage house have fireplaces, hot tubs, and air-conditioning. The property also has an opulent state-of-the-art spa, complete with a small resistance pool and fitness center. Above the spa is the inn's most sumptuous suite, with vaulted ceilings, fireplace, entertainment center, and two-person hot tub. Breakfast is served in the cheerful sunroom or on the garden patio. ⊠ *220 Bridge Rd., 02642* ☎ *508/255–0617 or 800/440–1281* ⊕ *www. whalewalkinn.com* ⤴ *11 rooms, 6 suites* ⚒ *Some in-room hot tubs, some kitchens, some refrigerators, cable TV, in-room VCRs, indoor pool, gym, hot tub, sauna, spa, bicycles; no smoking* ⊟ *MC, V* ⊺◯⊺ *BP.*

★ **$$–$$$$** 🏨 **Penny House Inn.** Tucked behind a wave of privet hedge, this rambling gray-shingle inn's spacious rooms are furnished with antiques, collectibles, and wicker. The luxurious accommodations are cozy rather than stuffy; many are romantic, with whirlpool tubs, fireplaces, or both. Some rooms are larger, with sitting areas; suites have separate bedrooms and sitting rooms and can sleep up to five. Take a dip in the saltwater pool, or indulge in a massage, facial, or mud wrap in the on-site spa room. Common areas include a Great Room with lots of windows and a selection of videos, a combination sunroom-library, and a garden patio with umbrella tables. A full homemade breakfast starts the day, and afternoon tea is available. ⊠ *4885 County Rd. (U.S. 6), 02642* ☎ *508/ 255–6632 or 800/554–1751* 🖷 *508/255–4893* ⊕ *www.pennyhouseinn. com* ⤴ *9 rooms, 3 suites* ⚒ *Some in-room hot tubs, some refrigerators, cable TV, in-room VCRs, in-room data ports, saltwater pool, spa, library; no smoking* ⊟ *AE, D, MC, V* ⊺◯⊺ *BP.*

$–$$$$ 🏨 **Four Points Sheraton.** This reliable if ordinary midrange chain hotel is at the entrance to the National Seashore. Rooms have views of the tropical indoor pool (with lush plants, pirate-theme bar, and resident live parrot), the parking lot, or the woods. Outside rooms are a little bigger and brighter and have mini-refrigerators. ⊠ *3800 U.S. 6, 02642* ☎ *508/255–5000 or 800/533–3986* 🖷 *508/240–1870* ⊕ *www. capecodfourpoints.com* ⤴ *107 rooms, 2 suites* ⚒ *Restaurant, room service, refrigerators, cable TV, Wi-Fi, 2 tennis courts, 2 pools, gym, hot tub, saunas, lobby lounge, meeting rooms* ⊟ *AE, D, DC, MC, V.*

$–$$$$ 🏨 **Inn at the Oaks.** If it weren't for this three-story inn's vivid-yellow paint job, it would be lost among the trees, even though it's right along U.S. 6. Both the Cape Cod Rail Trail and the Salt Pond Visitor Center are just across the road. Victorian touches at this 19th-century refuge include graceful high ceilings and intricate interior wood molding. Each room has antiques, brass beds, and soft down comforters, plus a few modern amenities such as DVD players; some have claw-foot tubs, which are great to slide into after a day at the beach. ⊠ *3085 U.S. 6, 02642* ☎ *508/255–1886* 🖷 *508/240–0345* ⊕ *www.innattheoaks.com* ⤴ *10 rooms, 4 suites* ⚒ *Cable TV, in-room DVDs, Wi-Fi, hot tub, massage, recreation room, some pets with fee* ⊟ *AE, D, MC, V* ⊺◯⊺ *BP.*

¢–$$ 🏨 **Ocean Park Inn.** Rooms at this property, run by the same owners as the adjacent Four Points Sheraton, are clean, simple, and straightforward. There are larger family units available—one with a fireplace—but most rooms are for double occupancy, with full- or queen-size beds. You are welcome to use the amenities, including the pools and tennis courts, of the Four Points Sheraton. ⊠ *3900 U.S. 6, 02642* ☏ *508/255–1132 or 800/862–5550* 🖶 *508/255–5250* ⊕ *www.capecodopi.com* 🛏 *54 rooms, 1 suite* ♿ *Picnic area, microwaves, refrigerators, cable TV, laundry facilities* ⊟ *AE, D, DC, MC, V* ⊗ *Closed Nov.–Mar.*

¢–$ 🏨 **Cove Bluffs Motel.** This old-fashioned haven for nature lovers and families is nestled among the trees and within walking distance of Orleans Town Cove and several nature trails. Settle into a standard motel room or choose a more self-sufficient getaway in studio or two-bedroom housekeeping units with stoves, refrigerators, and microwaves. Grounds include basketball courts, shuffleboard, swing sets, a playhouse, a sandbox, grills, and swinging hammocks in the shade. ⊠ *U.S. 6 and Shore Rd., Box 297, 02642* ☏ *508/240–1616* ⊕ *www.capecod-orleans.com/covebluffs* 🛏 *5 rooms, 8 housekeeping units* ♿ *Cable TV, pool, basketball, shuffleboard, laundry facilities, no-smoking rooms* ⊟ *MC, V* ⊗ *Closed Nov.–Mar.*

¢ 🏨 **Hostelling International–Mid Cape.** On three wooded acres near the Cape Cod Rail Trail and a 15-minute walk from the bay, this hostel has cabins that sleep six to eight each; two can be used as family cabins. It has a common area and a kitchen, and there are a number of guest programs. ⊠ *75 Goody Hallet Dr., 02642* ☏ *508/255–2785* ⊕ *www.usahostels.org* 🛏 *8 cabins* ♿ *Kitchen, Ping-Pong, volleyball; no a/c, no room TVs* ⊟ *MC, V* ⊗ *Closed mid-Sept.–mid-May.*

⚠ **Atlantic Oaks Campground.** This campground in a pine and oak forest is less than a mile north of the Salt Pond Visitor Center and minutes from Cape Cod National Seashore. Primarily an RV camp (year-round hookups are available), it offers limited tenting as well. You can rent bikes, and there's direct access to the Cape Cod Rail Trail. Reservations are essential during peak season. ♿ *Grills, flush toilets, full hookups, drinking water, guest laundry, showers, fire grates, picnic tables, electricity, public telephone, general store, play area, swimming (pond and ocean)* 🛏 *99 RV sites, 12 tent sites* ⊠ *3700 U.S. 6, 02642* ☏ *508/255–1437 or 800/332–2267* 🖶 *508/247–8216* ⊕ *www.atlanticoaks.com* 💲 *$36 no hookups, $50 full hookups* ⊟ *D, MC, V* ⊗ *Closed Nov.–Apr.*

Nightlife & the Arts

The **Cape Cod National Seashore** (☏ 508/255–3421 information) sponsors summer-evening programs, such as slide shows, sunset beach walks, concerts by local groups or military bands, and campfire sing-alongs.

The **Eastham Painters Guild** holds outdoor art shows every Thursday, Friday, and holiday weekend from 9 to 5, July through October, at the Schoolhouse Museum. ⊠ *Next to Salt Pond Visitor Center, off U.S. 6.*

First Encounter Coffee House (⊠ Chapel in the Pines, Samoset Rd. ☏ 508/255–5438) presents a mixture of professional and local folk and blues in a smoke-and-alcohol-free environment, with refreshments available during intermission. National acts are booked for the second and fourth Saturday. It's closed May and December.

Sea Dog Restaurant & Saloon (⊠ 4100 U.S. 6 ☏ 508/255–2650) serves pub food and drinks in a lively atmosphere. Live acoustic music is played year-round on varying nights; call for a schedule. It's closed Tuesday.

Sports & the Outdoors

BEACHES On the bay side of the Outer Cape, **First Encounter Beach** (⊠ End of Samoset Rd. off U.S. 6) is open to the public and charges daily parking fees of $15 to nonresidents in season (weekly and season passes are also available; call the town hall at ☎ 508/240–5972). Parking fees or passes also apply to several other bay beaches and ponds, both saltwater and freshwater.

★ **Coast Guard Beach** (⊠ Off Ocean View Dr.), part of the National Seashore, is a long beach backed by low grass and heathland. A handsome former Coast Guard station is also here, though it's not open to the public. The beach has no parking lot of its own, so park at the Salt Pond Visitor Center or at the lot up Doane Road from the center and take the free shuttle to the beach. At high tide the size of the beach shrinks considerably, so watch your blanket. There are showers here, and lifeguards are posted between June and August. A daily charge of $15 for cars or a season pass (by far the best bargain) for $45 grants admission to all six National Seashore swimming beaches.

Fodor'sChoice **Nauset Light Beach** (⊠ Off Ocean View Dr.), adjacent to Coast Guard
★ Beach, continues the National Seashore landscape of long, sandy beach backed by tall dunes, grass, and heathland. It has showers and lifeguards in summer, but as with other National Seashore beaches, there's no food concession. Nauset charges $15 daily per car; a $45 season pass admits you here and to the other five National Seashore swimming beaches.

BICYCLING The **Idle Times Bike Shop** (⊠ 4550 U.S. 6 and Brackett Rd. ☎ 508/255–8281) provides bikes of all sizes and types and is right near the Cape Cod Rail Trail.

The **Little Capistrano Bike Shop** (⊠ Salt Pond Rd. across from Salt Pond Visitor Center ☎ 508/255–6515) has plenty of bikes and trailers available for rent and is between the Cape Cod Rail Trail and the National Seashore Bike Trail.

Nauset Trail, maintained by the Cape Cod National Seashore, stretches 1½ mi from Salt Pond Visitor Center through groves of apple and locust trees to Coast Guard Beach.

HEALTH & **Willy's Gym** (⊠ 4730 U.S. 6, North Eastham ☎ 508/255–6370 ☎ 508/
FITNESS CLUBS 255–6826) is the astounding 100,000 square foot branch of the original Willy's in Orleans. Kids will love Play World, a massive indoor playground. Other facilities include an Olympic-size, SaltSystem indoor pool, a rock-climbing wall, an indoor NBA basketball court, and indoor and outdoor tennis courts, along with a vast selection of exercise machines and studio classes. After your workout, relax in the hot tub, steam room, or sauna—or book a massage or skincare treatment at Kembali Spa. You can also peruse the pro shop, or perhaps grab a bite at the Tiger restaurant . . . and if you run out of things to do, there's even free Wi-Fi access on-site. Willy's also hosts free movie nights and other arts and community programs, which are open to the public. You can buy a day, week, or month pass.

CLOSE UP

Year-Round on the Cape

THE BEAUTY AND ABUNDANCE of our beaches, striking sunsets and blooming flora, ice-cream and lobster shacks, the lush landscapes and temperate climate perfectly suited for countless outdoor activities, from biking to sailing to golf to slow strolls through town or along the harbor—the appeal of summers on Cape Cod is obvious. More than 4 million visitors flock to the Cape during the high season, from day-trippers to temporary residents, and many have made a Cape trip a summer tradition, returning year after year. What might seem less obvious—at least, to those who don't live here—is what the Cape has to offer during the rest of the year.

Cape Codders and visitors agree that it takes a special kind of person to live on the Cape year-round: one who can endure the brutal weather and stark isolation of the winter months. In fact, among locals, there is a pecking order for those who call Cape Cod home. Those who live here full-time are called residents or year-rounders; this is not to be confused with being a native Cape Codder. Having been born on the Cape holds a special distinction; if you were not, you are a "washashore," and there is no exception to this rule. The truest salt-of-the-earth natives boast generations of family born on the peninsula, and being a native who has chosen to stay and raise a family here is a point of pride; it takes a hardy person with a true love for all that nature cooks up to ride out a lifetime on these windswept shores.

It isn't always easy to live in Cape Cod. In addition to the rough winters, being here year-round is a financial challenge for a large portion of the Cape's 220,000 permanent residents. Many take on several jobs or work off-Cape and commute home each night to make ends meet. But to a Cape resident, life here is more than worth these difficulties. All of us, native and washashore alike, are bound by our common affection and respect for the ocean and the Cape's environment, and this sentiment runs deep, even on the darkest days of winter. Full-year residents see the beauty in every season on the Cape. Although we love summers here—for many of the same reasons that draw the tourists—we live for the off-season. Come Labor Day, the crowds disappear and traffic congestion subsides, and Cape residents eagerly reclaim our beaches and resume our quiet everyday lives. For the next nine months, until Memorial Day comes around again, we return to our seaside walks on crisp mornings, the familiar smell of low tide and the marshes on the way to work, and kayaking, fishing, and sunset strolls to end the day. To us, this is the Cape's true personality—one most visitors don't see.

Tourism in the shoulder season has increased in recent years, as more people discover that the simple beauty of the Cape's natural surroundings is more serene and easily appreciated without the summer crowds. The Cape no longer rolls up its sidewalks and packs away the fun after Labor Day, and many businesses now open for the season as early as March or April. Those who come here in the few weeks before or after the high season are treated to a taste of what Cape residents love so much about their home. Before the summer crush hits, Cape Cod awakens with beauty in spring. Cheery daffodils line the streets, birds dart through the air in hypnotizing formations, bunnies hop through yards, and fishing for schoolie (baby striped bass) begins. And after Labor Day, temperatures stay mild through early to mid-October. This is, for many, the ideal time to enjoy the shores—the waters have had time to warm from months of summer sun, parking restrictions are lifted, and beachgoers have all the space they need to spread out. Autumn leaves and cranberry harvests paint the area with brilliant swaths of color, creating stunning views.

But visitors still tend to shy away from the peninsula once the first hints of cold air blow in. Some are surprised to learn that average winter temperatures on the Cape are actually milder than on the mainland. Despite this, the colder months are known to bring some difficult weather conditions, but Cape locals know how to make the best of it. Fall and winter nor'easters—powerful storms that carry in cold air from Canada—leave us in awe of the ocean's power. Most of us are content to observe these captivating scenes from indoors, but some local surfers will brave the action off the Lower Cape. These infamous storms also strengthen the sense of community here, as we check on our neighbors and help each other board up buildings and tie down our belongings. Some residents view the harsh weather as character building, a challenge to overcome. I share my life with a Cape native who says, "I have a certain sense of satisfaction knowing that I beat the weather. When I come home from work on those days when it is 10 degrees out with 40 mph winds and I just put a cap on a roof, I feel a real sense of accomplishment."

The Atlantic surrounds us and we are at the whim of Mother Nature's brew. Yet, even living just steps from the shore, we are always trying to get closer to nature. Peek into the home of a Cape resident and you're likely to see windowsills lined with seashells, sea glass, driftwood, fish bones, and pieces of mystery items that landed on our shores. You might see mantels made of driftwood or driveways of crushed shell. We use clamshells as ashtrays, soap dishes, and coin holders. The longer you live here, the more you bring the outdoors in as close as possible. The connection to the ocean grows stronger and freeing as material needs lessen. Life simplifies, and crossing the bridge to leave for good becomes inconceivable.

–Lori A. Nolin

SURFING　Eastham's ocean beaches are great for surfing and trying out a new sport that's gaining in popularity: kiteboarding. Basically a combination of surfing and windboarding, kiteboarding is a speedy sport that will definitely get your blood pumping.

Little Overhead Surf & Kiteboard (✉ 4900 U.S. 6 ☎ 508/240–1455 ⊕ www. littleoverhead.com) has a full stock of surfboards and kiteboards, as well as all the necessary accoutrements; they even provide instruction.

THE LOWER CAPE ESSENTIALS

To research prices, get advice from other travelers, and book travel arrangements, visit www.fodors.com.

Transportation

BY BOAT & FERRY

In season, the ferry from Harwich to Nantucket is a less hectic alternative to the Hyannis crowd. For details ⇨ Boat & Ferry Travel *in* Smart Travel Tips A to Z in the back of this book.

BY BUS

A bus connecting Hyannis and Orleans serves the Lower Cape region. For details ⇨ Bus Travel *in* Smart Travel Tips A to Z in the back of this book.

BY TAXI

John's Taxi & Limousine picks up only in Dennis and Harwich but will take you anywhere on the Cape.

🚖 Taxi Companies **Eldredge Taxi** ✉ Chatham ☎ 508/945-0068. **John's Taxi & Limousine** ☎ 508/394-3209.

Contacts & Resources

CONDO & HOUSE RENTALS

Commonwealth Associates can assist in finding vacation rentals in the Harwiches, including waterfront properties. Great Locations Inc. specializes in vacation rentals in Brewster, Dennis, and Orleans.

🏠 Local Agents **Commonwealth Associates** ✉ Harwich Port ☎ 508/432-2618 ⊕ www. commonwealthrealestate.com. **Great Locations Inc.** ✉ Brewster ☎ 508/896-2090 or 800/626-9984 ⊕ www.greatlocationsre.com.

TOURS

The Cape Cod Museum of Natural History offers a two-hour cruise from Orleans through Nauset Marsh. Early morning cruises include breakfast in a nearby restaurant. During evening tours enjoy cocktails and appetizers on board. Tours run daily, Tuesday through Friday until Labor Day, and then weekends until Columbus Day. Guided natural history tours of Chatham's Monomoy Islands are also available through the museum.

To sightsee from the air, contact Chatham Municipal Airport.

Fees & Schedules **Cape Cod Museum of Natural History** ☎ 508/896-3867 ⊕ www. ccmnh.org. **Chatham Municipal Airport** ⊠ George Ryder Rd., West Chatham ☎ 508/ 945-9000.

VISITOR INFORMATION

Some local chambers of commerce are open only in season. The Brewster Chamber of Commerce is in the Brewster town offices building. The office includes a visitor center and the offices of the Brewster Chamber of Commerce and Board of Trade United.

Tourist Information **Brewster Chamber of Commerce** ⊠ 2198 Main St. [Rte. 6A], Box 1241, 02631 ☎ 508/896-3500 ⊕ www.brewstercapecod.org. **Chatham Chamber of Commerce** ⓘ Box 793, 02633 ☎ 508/945-5199 or 800/715-5567 ⊕ www. chathamcapecod.org ⊠ Seasonal visitor center ⊠ Rtes. 28 and 137, South Chatham ⊠ Information booth ⊠ 533 Main St., Chatham. **Eastham Chamber of Commerce** ⊠ U.S. 6 at Fort Hill Rd., Box 1329, 02642 ☎ 508/240-7211 ⊕ www.easthamchamber.com. **Harwich Chamber of Commerce** ☎ 508/432-1600 or 800/442-7942 ⊕ www.harwichcc. com ⊠ Seasonal visitor center ⊠ One Schoolhouse Rd. and Rte. 28, Harwich Port. **Orleans Chamber of Commerce** ⓘ Box 153, 02653 ⊠ Information booth ⊠ 44 Main St. ☎ 508/255-1386 or 800/856-1386 ⊕ www.capecod-orleans.com.

The Outer Cape

WORD OF MOUTH

"You can't go wrong with any of the beaches on the Cape Cod National Seashore."

—Boss Ton

"I like Provincetown because the ocean is as much a part of the downtown as are the smells of garlic and wood fires."

—outofblue

By Andrew
Collins

TECHNICALLY PART OF THE LOWER CAPE, the Outer Cape is nonetheless its own entity, forming the wrist and fist of Cape Cod. There's a sense of abandon here, in the hedonistic summertime frenzy of Provincetown and out on the windswept landscape of dunes and marshes. As you drive down here, the land flattens out, vegetation gets sparser and more coniferous, and the sea feels closer as the land narrows. Much of the region is undeveloped, protected by the Cape Cod National Seashore. Long, straight, dune-backed beaches appear to go on forever; inland, trails wind through wind-stunted forests of scrub pine, beech, and oak. Wellfleet is a quiet town, with art galleries, upscale shops, and a calm—but active—harbor. With an expanse of high dunes, estuaries, salt marshes, pine forests, rivers, and winding back roads, Truro is the least-populated, least-developed town on the entire Cape.

The promise of solitude has long drawn artists and writers out here. Provincetown has two faces—a quiet little fishing village in winter and a magnet for throngs of pleasure seekers (including a substantial gay and lesbian community) in summer, who come for the rugged beaches, photogenic streets lined with historic homes, zany nightlife, shops selling everything from antiques to zoot suits, and the galleries, readings, and art classes that carry on Provincetown's rich history as an art colony.

5

Exploring the Outer Cape

Making your way around narrow Outer Cape, you really have one key option for getting around: driving along U.S. 6. There are some less congested but slower and indirect roads between the area's two least-developed communities, Wellfleet and Truro. In Wellfleet, many businesses and attractions are strung along U.S. 6, but there's also a compact downtown with art galleries, cafés, and boutiques that's ideal for strolling. Truro has just the tiniest commercial district and its few attractions are best reached by car, as they're somewhat far apart. In Provincetown, on the other hand, a car—especially in summer—can actually be a hindrance. This is a walkable town with two main thoroughfares, Commercial and Bradford streets. You could easily spend a full day or two just walking around downtown and checking out the dozens and dozens of shops, galleries, and restaurants. Provincetown also has some excellent beaches, which are a short drive or bike ride from downtown.

Numbers in the margin correspond to the Outer Cape and Provincetown maps.

About the Restaurants

Dining on the Outer Cape means everything from humble fried-clam shacks to candlelit elegance. Many restaurants have withstood the tests of time and fashion and have developed loyal followings that keep their doors open year after year. Menus frequently highlight local seafood. Wellfleet's restaurants, while not inexpensive, cater as much to families as to adult sophisticates and typically have menus offering a wide range of items, from less expensive burgers and fried-seafood platters to creatively prepared steaks and fish grills. Truro has just a handful of restau-

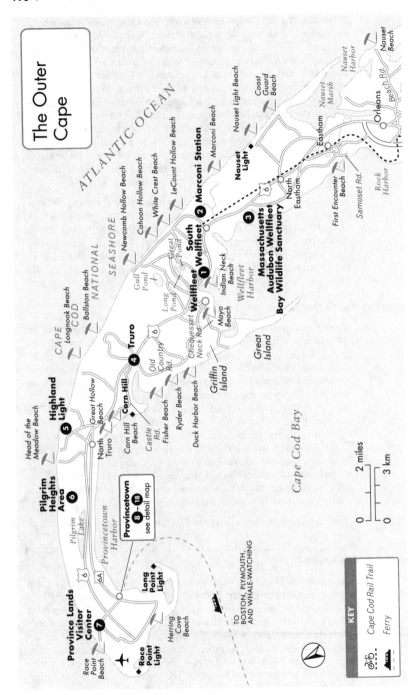

The Outer Cape

ATLANTIC OCEAN

CAPE COD NATIONAL SEASHORE

Head of the Meadow Beach

Longnook Beach

Newcomb Hollow Beach

Cahoon Hollow Beach

White Crest Beach

LeCount Hollow Beach

Marconi Beach

Nauset Light Beach

Coast Guard Beach

Nauset Beach

Nauset Harbor

Nauset Marsh

Orleans

Beach Rd.

Rock Harbor

Samoset Rd.

First Encounter Beach

North Eastham

Eastham

6

Nauset Light ◆

② **Marconi Station**

① **South Wellfleet**

Wellfleet

Great Pond

Gull Pond

Long Pond

Ballston Beach

Indian Neck Beach

Wellfleet Harbor

③ **Massachusetts Audubon Wellfleet Bay Wildlife Sanctuary**

Chequesset Neck Rd.

Mayo Beach

Great Island

Griffin Island

Duck Harbor Beach

Ryder Beach

Fisher Beach

Castle Rd.

Corn Hill Beach ◆

Corn Hill

④ **Truro**

Old Country Rd.

6

Great Hollow Beach

North Truro

⑤ **Highland Light**

⑥ **Pilgrim Heights Area**

Pilgrim Lake

6

6A

Provincetown Harbor

Provincetown
⑧–⑱ see detail map

⑦ **Province Lands Visitor Center**

Long Point Light ◆

Herring Cove Beach

Race Point Light ◆

Race Point Beach

Cape Cod Bay

TO BOSTON, PLYMOUTH, AND WHALE-WATCHING

0   2 miles
0   3 km

KEY

◦╍◦ *Cape Cod Rail Trail*

▬ ▬ ▬ *Ferry*

rants spread out along the byways. Provincetown opens a world of great variation to the eager diner. There are a number of snazzy, hip restaurants in town, all aglow with candles, crystal, and fine linens, but you'll find an equal number of lively and boisterous cafés. Many have outdoor seating, providing good views of the town's constant action. Smoking is banned inside all of the town's bars and restaurants.

In the height of the summer season, you may have to wait awhile for a table—even if you have a reservation. To make matters worse, in the past few years Cape Cod has been experiencing a labor shortage; good help is at a premium, and this has caused some restaurants to shorten their season or reduce their hours.

About the Hotels

Lodging options on the Outer Cape are diverse. Wellfleet has several cozy inns and bed-and-breakfasts in the center of town, with a few larger motels on busy U.S. 6. Despite the strict building codes, there are a surprising number of large (though not imposing) hotel complexes and cottage colonies spread out along Cape Cod Bay in North Truro. These places may be crowded, but they're also right on the sand, with commanding views of sunsets and the Provincetown skyline.

Provincetown's lodging scene has changed dramatically in recent years, as a number of old guest houses and inns have been sold and converted to private homes. Those that remain have mostly transformed themselves from modest, affordable lodgings to sophisticated—and quite pricey—fine inns. With the shrinkage in available rooms, it's become even harder to find a room during the summer months. Minimum stays of at least three nights are often the norm during the peak season and holiday times, and sometimes there's a week minimum in July and August. That being said, more and more Provincetown properties have begun staying open for most or even all of the year—if you don't feel a need to visit during the busiest time of year, consider the quieter, yet still wonderfully atmospheric, off months. May, June, September, and October are especially nice, as most of the town's restaurants and shops are still open then, but hotel rates are lower and rooms easier to find.

WHAT IT COSTS					
	$$$$	$$$	$$	$	¢
RESTAURANTS	over $30	$22–$30	$16–$22	$10–$16	under $10
HOTELS	over $260	$200–$260	$140–$200	$90–$140	under $90

Restaurant prices are per person for a main course at dinner. Hotel prices are for a standard double room, excluding 6% sales tax (more in some counties) and 1%–4% tourist tax.

Timing

Prime time on the Outer Cape—when everything is open—is from Memorial Day to around Columbus Day; July and August are by far

GREAT ITINERARIES

Numbers in the text correspond to numbers in the margin and on the Outer Cape map.

As you first enter **Wellfleet** ❶, make a point of stopping at historic **Marconi Station** ❷, which was the landing point for the transatlantic telegraph early in the 20th century. It's also worth walking the short but stunning White Cedar Swamp Trail. In Wellfleet, you can lose yourself among the many art galleries and distinctive shops, or plan a more outdoorsy adventure. Stroll along the sand or go for a swim in the water—Wellfleet has several beaches on both the bay and the ocean. You might also rent a canoe or kayak and tour the marshes. Bird-watchers should make a point of visiting the **Massachusetts Audubon Wellfleet Bay Wildlife Sanctuary** ❸.

Truro ❹ solidly represents the quietude of this end of the Cape, at

least until you reach seasonally bustling 🏛 **Provincetown** ❼-❽, out at the tip. Catch a whale-watch boat from P-town (as Provincetown is almost universally known)—the Cape ranks fourth in the world for sighting whales. Take a trolley tour in town or bike through the National Seashore on its miles of trails. Climb the Pilgrim Monument for a spectacular view of the area—on an exceptionally clear day you can see the Boston skyline. Visit the museums and shops and art galleries, or spend the afternoon swimming and sunning on one of the beaches. To escape the crowds, walk across the breakwater to Long Point. Rent a sailboat or relax in the sand, taking in the splendid views of the bay. Then choose from an abundance of restaurants and the Cape's wildest nightlife.

the most crowded times. The shoulder seasons of late May and June, and after Labor Day, have become more and more popular with child-less travelers who aren't locked into a school schedule. Rates are lower during these times, and restaurants and shops are still open. If the weather has been generous, swimming is still a pleasant possibility.

Wellfleet pretty much seals itself up after Columbus Day; most galleries and restaurants close, leaving just a handful of year-round businesses. But you'll have the entire outside world to explore, now free of thousands of others trying to do the same thing. Ocean climates keep winters milder than on the mainland. It's quiet—beautifully so—and distractions and pleasures take on a more basic flavor.

Provincetown clears out as well, but not as fully as Wellfleet. Various theme weekends throughout the year have boosted tourism in the off-season, and there are always readings, films, and places to eat. The off-season is truly a time to discover the essence of the place, see its changing natural beauty, and experience a more restful and relaxed pace.

Wellfleet & South Wellfleet

❶ *6 mi north of Eastham, 13 mi southeast of Provincetown.*

Still famous for its world-renowned and succulent namesake oysters and, with Truro, for having been a colonial whaling and cod-fishing port, Wellfleet is today a tranquil community; many artists and writers call it home. Less than 2 mi wide, it's one of the most attractively developed Cape resort towns, with a number of fine restaurants, historic houses, art galleries, and a good old Main Street in the village proper. The South Wellfleet section of town extends to the North Eastham border and has a wonderful Audubon sanctuary and a drive-in theater that doubles on weekends as a flea market. There's no village center here, just a handful of motels, restaurants, and businesses along busy U.S. 6.

The downtown center of Wellfleet is quite compact, so it's actually best to leave your car in one of the public parking areas and take off on foot. Historic buildings that once housed oyster and fish-drying shacks or stately residences now contain upscale art galleries, designer-clothing stores, and restaurants. Wellfleet's small-town nature still somehow accommodates the demands of a major tourist industry; the year-round population of around 2,800 residents explodes to more than 18,000 people in July and August.

Tourism isn't the only industry, though. Fishing boats still head out from the harbor daily in search of scallops, cod, and other fish. Shellfishing accounts for a major portion of the town's economy. Whaling played a role in the 18th and 19th centuries; a raucous whaling tavern once thrived out on the now-sunken Billingsgate Island. Dozens of world-traveling sea captains found their way to Wellfleet as well, the effect evident in many of the grand old houses that line the narrow streets of town. The Wellfleet Historical Society is a fine stop for those who wish to see the town as it was in its early days. Natural splendor, as well as history and sophisticated artistic culture, accounts for Wellfleet's popularity. The beaches are spectacular, with their towering sand dunes, bracing surf, and miles of unfettered expanse. Seemingly endless wooded paths in the domain of the National Seashore make for terrific walking and hiking trails, and the sheltered waters of the tidal Herring River and Wellfleet Harbor are a favorite destination for canoeists, kayakers, windsurfers, and sailors.

★ ❷ **Marconi Station,** on the Atlantic side of the Cape's forearm, is the site of the first transatlantic wireless station erected on the U.S. mainland. Italian radio and wireless-telegraphy pioneer Guglielmo Marconi sent the first American wireless message from here to Europe—"most cordial greetings and good wishes" from President Theodore Roosevelt to King Edward VII of England—on January 18, 1903. The station broadcasted news for 15 years. An outdoor shelter contains a model of the original station, of which only fragments remain as a result of cliff erosion; parts of the tower bases are sometimes visible on the beach below, where they fell. The Cape Cod National Seashore's administrative headquarters is here, and though it is not an official visitor center, it can provide information at times when the centers are closed. Inside there's a

PLEASURES & PASTIMES

BEACHES

Ocean beaches on the Cape Cod National Seashore have cold water and serious surf and are backed by dunes. They're also contiguous: you can walk from Eastham to Provincetown if you've got the stamina. On the Cape Cod Bay side, you'll find warmer and more gentle waters. The tides are pivotal here: at low tide the flats expose vast, sandy expanses, and to get thoroughly wet, you'll have to trek out a ways. Bay-side beachgoers also get more time in the sun—the majestic dunes on the ocean side block the descending late-afternoon sun—and sunsets on the bay are spectacular.

NIGHTLIFE & THE ARTS

Many credit the unusual light and extraordinary beauty of the Outer Cape with creating its strong, vibrant artistic tradition. Wellfleet's town center has nearly two dozen art galleries, all representing local and national artists. Works aren't limited to sea and landscapes, either—you can also find abstract works and fine crafts.

Truro has fewer galleries, but its artistic history is rich. Painter Edward Hopper spent many years here in his modest home overlooking Cape Cod Bay; numerous recognizable scenes of Truro exist among his work. The Center for the Arts at Castle Hill has held summer classes in art, writing, and crafts for more than 30 years.

Provincetown is well known for its history as an artists' community. Many world-famous artists made their homes here—some started art schools that are still in operation.

Today, Provincetown may have more galleries per block than any other New England town. Friday night is gallery night; stroll the streets and pop in on one of the many champagne artist receptions.

P-town also has an active, gay-popular nightlife, from pulsating dance clubs to pool halls, with lots of live entertainment. Drag shows, theater, comedy routines, and music concerts are held regularly throughout the summer. Wellfleet has a few more peaceful options, such as restaurant taverns that occasionally stay open late with live music performances.

SHOPPING

Shoppers on the Outer Cape never have to worry about the uniqueness of their purchases—all stores are individually owned, one-of-a-kind establishments. Wellfleet shoppers will find a wealth of fine arts and crafts to choose from, as well as a couple of small, chic designer-clothing stores. On the same street, you could walk away with a funky Indonesian sarong for the beach and a handcrafted, gold and gem-studded ring costing thousands of dollars. The Wellfleet Flea Market—great for bargain hunting—is held four days a week in summer. In Provincetown, there's a little bit of everything—from the most civilized and expensive art galleries to the sunglasses hut. Aptly named Commercial Street is a tightly packed thoroughfare dominated by pedestrians ambling in and out of boutiques. During fall months, when shops are eager to clean out their inventories before winter sets in, you can find some great sales.

mock-up of the spark-gap transmitter Marconi used. Off the parking lot, a 1½-mi trail and boardwalk lead through the **Atlantic White Cedar Swamp,** one of the most beautiful trails on the seashore; free maps and guides are available at the trailhead. **Marconi Beach,** south of the station on Marconi Beach Road, is another of the National Seashore's ocean beaches. ⊠ *Marconi Site Rd., South Wellfleet* ☎ *508/349–3785* ⊕ *www. nps.gov/caco* 🖙 *Free* ☉ *Daily 8–4:30.*

For a **scenic loop** through a classic Cape landscape near Wellfleet's Atlantic beaches—with scrub and pines on the left, heathland meeting cliffs and ocean below on the right—take LeCount Hollow Road just north of the Marconi Station turnoff. All the beaches on this strip rest at the bottom of a tall grass-covered dune, which lends dramatic character to this outermost shore. The first of the four, **LeCount Hollow,** is restricted to residents or

WORD OF MOUTH

"If you're here on a weekend, drive along Ocean View Drive in Wellfleet, and at White Crest Beach, on the Atlantic, you will see kite surfers riding the waves, as well as the wind riders catching the thermal winds off the dunes." –capecodshanty

temporary residents in season, as is the last, **Newcomb Hollow,** with a scalloped shoreline of golden sand. In between, **White Crest** and **Cahoon Hollow** are town-managed public beaches. Cahoon has a hot restaurant and dancing spot, the Beachcomber. Backtrack to Cahoon Hollow Road and turn west for the southernmost entrance to the town of Wellfleet proper, across U.S. 6.

NEED A BREAK?

The **Blue Willow** (⊠ South Wellfleet Post Office Sq., 1426 U.S. 6 ☎ 508/349–0900) is tiny, but the food is grand, transcending what you'd find in other take-out places. Treats like crab cakes, crispy duck, tarragon chicken salad, and pasta dishes are made on the premises. For breakfast, there are daily frittata and quiche specials, as well as muffins, scones, and pastries. Outside is a mini–farmers' market with fresh vegetables and flowers. Right at the Cape Cod Rail Trail, it's a good spot to grab a snack or pick up the complete makings of a beach picnic or fine dinner. It's across from the chamber of commerce information booth and open daily year-round.

Wellfleet's **First Congregational Church** (⊠ 200 Main St., Downtown Wellfleet ☎ 508/349–6877), a courtly 1850 Greek Revival building, is said to have the only town clock in the world that strikes on ship's bells. The church's interior is lovely, with pale blue walls, a brass chandelier hanging from an enormous gilt ceiling rosette, subtly colored stained-glass windows, and pews curved to form an amphitheater facing the altar and the 738-pipe Hook and Hastings tracker-action organ, dating from 1873. To the right is a Tiffany-style window depicting a clipper ship. Concerts are given in July and August on Sunday at 8 PM.

For a glimpse into Wellfleet's past, the diminutive **Wellfleet Historical Society Museum** exhibits furniture, paintings, shipwreck salvage, needle-

Rainy Day Fun

YOU CAN COUNT ON plenty of wonderful things on Cape Cod: stunning beaches, fresh lobster, distinguished art galleries. Great weather, however, isn't always a sure thing. The Cape averages 3 to 4 inches of rain per month, and extended periods of inclement weather are not unheard of, no matter the season. Rain does not, however, have to put a damper on your vacation fun. If you look around a bit, you can find plenty to keep you busy in these parts, from a day at the spa to an umbrella-covered stroll along the beach.

Here are 15 engaging activities for rainy days on the Cape:

1. **Have a bowl of chowder.** Nothing takes the nip off a rainy day better than a steaming hot bowl of clam chowder, and the Cape has more than a few outstanding restaurants specializing in this longtime favorite. Top picks include the Lobster Pot (Provincetown), the Chatham Squire (Chatham), and Mill Way Fish and Lobster (Barnstable).

2. **Go storm-watching.** If it's a windy, exciting storm, grab lunch at a waterfront restaurant and enjoy watching the dramatically crashing surf outside your window. Some excellent choices for this activity include Fanizzi's by the Sea in Provincetown, Brax Landing in Harwich, and Fishmonger's Café in Woods Hole.

3. **Visit the Cape Cod Children's Museum.** Filled with interactive exhibits and games, plus a 30-foot play pirate ship, this Mashpee wonderland is geared mostly to kids around eight and younger.

4. **Curl up with a book in front of the fire.** You may think it odd to book a room with a fireplace on Cape Cod, since you'll be out beachcombing and strolling all day long. But on rainy days—even in summer—a fireplace can be a real treasure, and quite a few inns and vacation rentals have in-room fireplaces.

5. **Sample some fine wines.** In East Falmouth, Cape Cod Winery produces six well-respected wines, some of which have won medals in prestigious competitions.

6. **See a performance at the Cape Playhouse.** This famous 26-acre compound comprises the main theater, the Cape Museum of Fine Arts, and the Cape Cinema; there's children's theater on Friday mornings in July and August.

7. **Visit the Sandwich Glass Museum.** On artsy Cape Cod, you can always pass time on a rainy day by visiting local art galleries, but for a truly memorable art encounter, drop by this museum that traces the history of the prestigious glassmaking company. Glassblowing demonstrations are held throughout the summer.

8. **Take a whale-watching trip.** You're every bit as likely to see whales when it rains as when it's sunny, and two well-known Provincetown whale-watching tour operators—Dolphin Fleet and Portuguese Princess—offer these trips rain or shine, as does Hyannis's Whale Watcher Cruises. If you're prone to seasickness, however, beware of the stormy seas.

9. **Work up a sweat at the gym.** Willy's Gym in North Eastham and Orleans, the Mid Cape Racquet Club in

South Yarmouth, and Falmouth Sports Center in Woods Hole all have indoor racquetball, squash, tennis, and basketball courts, plus indoor heated pools and all the usual workout amenities.

10. **Head to a Christmas Tree Shops**—you'll find them in Sagamore, Yarmouthport, Orleans, Falmouth, West Yarmouth, West Dennis, and Hyannis (the largest of the bunch). These massive, rambling shops are loaded with bargain-priced goods, from kitschy treasures to discontinued bulk items. If you're a bargain hunter, you could lose yourself here for hours.

11. **Book a spa treatment.** Several Cape hotels have opened full-service spas (open to guests and nonguests) in recent years: the Crowne Pointe Inn in Provincetown, the Cape Codder Resort in Hyannis, and Dan'l Webster Inn in Sandwich. There's also a full-service spa, Kembali, at both Willy's Gym locations, in Eastham and Orleans. You don't have to travel far for a relaxing deep-tissue massage or algae wrap.

12. **Go for a walk on the beach.** Don't assume that the beach is worth a visit only when it's sunny outside—a rainy stroll can also be highly enjoyable. You won't encounter big crowds, and you may see some interesting wildlife. Plus, once you've gotten a little wet, you may forget about the showers and enjoy the brooding ocean and bay views more.

13. **Take some pictures.** As long as you have an umbrella and proper attire in which to stow your camera and protect it from the elements, consider a day of photo touring. Cape Cod offers plenty of intriguing photo-ops in the rain, from windswept sand dunes at Cape Cod National Seashore to dramatic street scenes in Provincetown and Dennis.

14. **Head to the library.** Each town on the Cape has a public library, and many sponsor children's programs, lectures, storytelling, art installations, and author readings.

15. **Attend a matinee at the movies.** Movie theaters large and small can be found throughout the Cape, and although they get crowded when it rains, most offer lower-priced tickets early in the day. The famed Wellfleet Drive-In presents movies rain or shine.

–by Andrew Collins

work, navigation equipment, early photographs, Native American artifacts, and clothing. Short guided walks around the center of town are given Tuesday and Friday mornings at 10:15 in July and August for $3. ⊠ *266 Main St., Downtown Wellfleet* ☎ *508/349–9157* ⊕ *www. wellfleethistoricalsociety.com* 🖮 *$1* ☉ *Late June–mid-Sept., Wed., Thurs., and Sat. 1–4, Tues. and Fri. 10–4.*

The **Wellfleet Public Library** (⊠ 55 W. Main St., Downtown Wellfleet ☎ 508/349–0310 ⊕ www.wellfleetlibrary.org) reflects the literary life of Wellfleet with readings, lectures, and exhibits by noted writers and artists in the community, and the collection of books for adults and children is impressive. Also available are videos, books on tape, and Internet access. Among the writers who have spent time here are Mary McCarthy, Edmund Wilson, Annie Dillard, and Marge Piercy.

Main Street is a good place to start if you're in the mood for shopping. **Commercial Street** has all the flavor of the fishing town that Wellfleet remains; galleries and shops occupy small weathered-shingle houses. A good stroll around town would take in Commercial and Main streets, ending perhaps at **Uncle Tim's Bridge** (⊠ Off E. Commercial St., Downtown Wellfleet). The short walk across this arching landmark—with its beautiful, much-photographed view over marshland and a tidal creek—leads to a small wooded island.

NEED A BREAK?

Box Lunch (⊠ 50 Briar La. ☎ 508/349–2178) is a popular Cape franchise that you may have seen elsewhere, but this is the original location. It serves up hot and cold roll-up sandwiches, a style it claims to have invented and perfected. A wide variety of fillings are available for breakfast, lunch, or early dinner. This tiny place gets ferociously busy in the summer season—call your order in ahead of time if you can. Pop inside dainty **On the Creek Cafe** (⊠ 55 Commercial St. ☎ 508/349–9841) for bracing java elixirs, hearty breakfasts, and creative lunch fare. It overlooks Duck Creek and has dining on the patio. Several galleries and B&Bs are within walking distance. It's closed November–April.

Commercial Street leads to the **Wellfleet Pier** (☎ 508/349–9818 for a fishing permit), busy with fishing boats, sailboats, yachts, charters, and party boats. At the twice-daily low tides, you can dig on the tidal flats for oysters, clams, and quahogs.

Chequessett Neck Road makes for a pretty 2½-mi drive from the harbor to the bay past Sunset Hill—a great place to catch one. At the end, on the left, is a parking lot and wooded picnic area from which nature trails lead off to **Great Island** (⊠ Off Chequessett Neck Rd., west of Downtown Wellfleet), perfect for beachcombers and solitude seekers. The "island" is actually a peninsula connected by a sand spit built by tidal action. More than 7 mi of trails wind along the inner marshes and the water—these are the most difficult paths on the seashore because they're mostly in soft sand. In the 17th century, a tavern and shore whaling lookout towers stood here; residents pastured animals and engaged in oystering and cranberry harvesting. By 1800 the hardwood forest that had covered the island had been cut down for use in the building of ships and homes. The pitch pines and other growth you see here (and all over the Cape) today were introduced in the 1830s to keep the soil from washing into the sea. Cape Cod National Seashore offers occasional guided hikes on Great Island and, from February through April, seal walks. To the right of the Great Island lot, a road leads to **Griffin Island,** which has its own walking trail.

Fodor'sChoice

A trip to the Outer Cape isn't complete without a visit to the **Massachusetts Audubon Wellfleet Bay Wildlife Sanctuary,** an 1,100-acre haven for more than 250 species of birds attracted by the varied habitats found here. The jewel of the Massachusetts Audubon Society, the sanctuary is a superb place for walking, birding, and watching the sun set over the salt marsh and bay. The **Esther Underwood Johnson Nature Center** contains two 700-gallon aquariums that offer an up-close look at marine life common to the Cape's tidal flats and marshlands. Other rotating exhibits illustrate different facets of the area's ecology and natural history. From the center you can hike five short nature trails, including a fascinating Boardwalk Trail that leads over a salt marsh to a small beach—or you can wander through the Butterfly Garden. Note that as of this writing the center was closed for repairs and reconstruction, and there's no timetable in place as to when it will reopen—check first before going. The center's interpretive programs are still in place, however, and the sanctuary remains open for hiking.

The Audubon Society is host to naturalist-led wildlife tours around the Cape, including trips to the Monomoy Islands, year-round. There are bay cruises; bird, wildlife, and insect walks; hikes; snorkeling; winter seal cruises; and birding, canoe, and kayak trips. The sanctuary also has camps for children in July and August and weeklong field schools for adults. Phone reservations are required for some programs. ⊠ *291 U.S. 6* ☎ *508/349–2615* ⊕ *www.wellfleetbay.org* 🖃 *$5* ☉ *Trails daily 8 AM–dusk; nature center late May–mid-Oct., daily 8:30–5; mid-Oct.–late May, Tues.–Sun. 8:30–5.*

Where to Stay & Eat

$–$$$ ✕ **Bookstore and Restaurant.** This quirky place, with great views of Wellfleet Harbor and Great Island, serves consistently tasty—if predictable—fare. It's attached to a funky vintage bookstore close to the town docks, and there's ample outdoor seating. The kitchen serves American classics, from grilled filet mignon and vegetable penne primavera to fresh seafood (the shellfish comes right from Wellfleet Harbor), including a first-rate oyster stew. There's live music on weekends in summer, and the adjoining Bombshelter sports bar is a diverting spot to watch a game on TV. ⊠ *50 Kendrick Ave., across from Mayo Beach* ☎ *508/349–3154* ⊕ *www.wellfleetoyster.com* 🖃 *AE, D, MC, V* ☉ *Closed Jan.–mid-Feb.*

$–$$$ ✕ **Lighthouse Restaurant.** A line snakes out the door of this simple wood-frame house on summer mornings for classic bacon-and-egg breakfasts and tasty blueberry pancakes. Try a plate of steamers and a beer for lunch and perhaps chowder, cod fritters, lemon-butter scallops, and another beer for dinner—but keep in mind that it's as much about the value and the people-watching here as the food itself. Mexican fare, margaritas, and Dos Equis beer are served on Thursday. There's a large deck, and downstairs you can order coffees, gelato, and lighter fare from the Lighthouse To-Go-Shoppe. ✉ *Main St., Downtown Wellfleet* ☎ *508/349–3681* ⊕ *www.mainstreetlighthouse.com* ⌖ *Reservations not accepted* ▭ *D, MC, V.*

$–$$$ ✕ **PJ's Family Restaurant.** There's always a good-size but fast-moving line here, waiting for a heap of steamers or a creamy soft-serve cone. At PJ's you place your order and take a number. Food is served in utilitarian style: Styrofoam soup bowls, paper plates, plastic forks. The lobster-and-corn chowder doesn't have much lobster in it, so stick to the traditional clam chowder. Fried calamari and clam or oyster plates are generous and fresh. Try the dense, spicy stuffed clams and a pile of crispy onion rings. ✉ *U.S. 6 near Downtown Wellfleet exit* ☎ *508/349–2126* ⌖ *Reservations not accepted* ▭ *MC, V* ⊗ *Closed Nov.–mid-Apr.*

$–$$$ ✕ **Van Rensselaer's.** This cavernous, casual family seafood restaurant across from Marconi Station—not too far from the Eastham town line—stands out for its nice mix of traditional standbys (baked-stuffed lobster, prime rib) and more creative offerings. You might start with lobster cakes in a lemon beurre blanc or steamed littleneck clams with lemongrass-ginger-soy butter. Favorite main dishes include potato-crusted salmon with lobster-butter, and cranberry-orange duck with sweet-potato puree. The restaurant also serves breakfast as well as an excellent Sunday brunch, where you might try smoked salmon Benedict or, if you're looking to fuel up for the day, the all-you-can-eat breakfast buffet. The same family has run the place since 1968. ✉ *U.S. 6* ☎ *508/349–2127* ⊕ *www.vanrensselaers.com* ▭ *AE, D, DC, MC, V* ⊗ *Closed Nov.–mid-Apr. No lunch.*

$–$$$ ✕ **Wicked Oyster.** In a rambling, gray clapboard house just off U.S. 6 on Fodor'sChoice the main road into Wellfleet village, the Wicked Oyster serves up the ★ most innovative fare in Wellfleet. Try the rosemary-and-scallion-crusted half rack of lamb over roasted-shallot-and-garlic potato salad, or the local mussels in tomato broth with smoky bacon, cilantro, jalapeño, and lime. Oyster stew and the Harry's Bar open-face burger (with caramelized onions, fresh mozzarella, and Worcestershire mayonnaise) are among the top lunch dishes. Breakfast is a favorite here—try the smoked salmon Benedict. There's also an outstanding wine list. Live music is offered many nights, and in the dining room hang changing exhibits of paintings and photography. ✉ *50 Main St., Wellfleet* ☎ *508/349–3455* ▭ *AE, D, MC, V* ⊗ *No dinner Wed.*

★ **$–$$$** ✕ **Winslow's Tavern.** Known as Aesop's Table until new owners took over in 2005 and completely renovated the interior, this 1805 Federal-style captain's house contains five dining rooms; try for a table on the porch overlooking the center of town. The kitchen specializes in bistro-inspired seafood, mostly with American and Italian preparations. Bacon-wrapped scallops with mango chutney, garlic-and-butter-grilled lobster with sweet-corn relish, and roasted pork loin chop with oven-roasted tomatoes and cilantro-walnut relish rank among the better dishes. Head to the cozy lounge upstairs (it's open until 1 AM) for a drink—it's filled with plush sofas. The same owners run the popular Moby Dick's seafood restaurant. ✉ *316 Main St., Downtown Wellfleet* ☎ *508/349–6450*

⊕ *www.winslowstavern.com* ▭ *AE, DC, MC, V* ⊗ *Closed mid-Oct.–mid-May.*

¢–$$$ ✗ **Marconi Beach Restaurant.** The nondescript interior of this cavernous restaurant in South Wellfeet may not inspire you, but once you pull up and smell the enticing aroma of barbecue from the smoker in back, it's hard to resist the temptation to step inside for a meal. Drop in for a lighter dish, such as a pulled pork sandwich or a few littlenecks and oysters from the raw bar, or savor a more substantial meal, perhaps a platter of smoked barbecue ribs, a grilled Porterhouse steak, or fish-and-chips. It's all pretty tasty, but the barbecue stands out—you could order most of the other items on the menu at any nearby steak and seafood joint. ⊠ *545 U.S. 6* ☎ *508/349–6025* ⊕ *www.marconibeachrestaurant.net* ▭ *AE, D, MC, V* ⊗ *Closed mid-Oct.–early Apr.*

¢–$$$ ✗ **Moby Dick's.** A meal at this good-natured, rough-hewn fish shack with a hyper-nautical theme is an absolute Cape Cod tradition for some people. There's a giant blackboard menu (order up front, and food is brought to you); a big, breezy screened-in porch in which to eat; and red-checkered tablecloths. Go for the Nantucket Bucket—a pound of whole-belly Monomoy steamers, a pound of native mussels, and corn on the cob served in a bucket. Also consider the rich and creamy lobster bisque or the complete lobster-in-the-rough dinner. Bring your own libations, and if you need to kill time, stop inside Moby's Cargo, the bustling gift shop next door. ⊠ *U.S. 6 near Truro border* ☎ *508/349–9795* ⊕ *www.mobydicksrestaurant.com* ⌳ *Reservations not accepted* ▭ *MC, V* ⊗ *Closed mid-Oct.–Apr.* ⌸ *BYOB.*

$–$$ ✗ **Finely JP's.** Chef John Pontius consistently turns out wonderful, affordable food full of the best Mediterranean and local influences and ingredients at his beloved restaurant along U.S. 6. The unassuming roadhouse restaurant was redesigned and enlarged in 2006—it's now a handsome, Arts and Crafts–inspired structure. Appetizers are especially good, among them oysters *Bienville* (baked in a white wine–cream sauce topped with Parmesan cheese and bread crumbs), and jerk-spiced duck salad with a raspberry vinaigrette. The Wellfleet paella draws rave reviews and a steady handful of locals, but the chef is not afraid to cook down-home barbecue pork ribs, either. Off-season hours vary, so call ahead—and be sure not to confuse this place with PJ's. ⊠ *554 U.S. 6, South Wellfleet* ☎ *508/349–7500* ⌳ *Reservations not accepted* ▭ *D, MC, V* ⊗ *Closed some nights during off-season. No lunch.*

Fodor'sChoice
★

★ **¢–$$** ✗ **Mac's Seafood.** Right at Wellfleet Harbor, this ambitious little spot has some of the freshest seafood around. There's not a whole lot of seating here—some inside and some outside on picnic tables—but when you've got a succulent mouthful of raw oyster or fried scallop, who cares? You can always sit along the pier and soak up the great water views while you chow down. This place serves a vast variety of seafood, plus sushi, Mexican fare (grilled-scallop burritos), linguica sausage sandwiches, and raw-bar items. There's also a selection of smoked fish, pâtés, lobster, and fish you can take home to grill yourself. Mac's also has two take-out seafood markets (open year-round) in downtown Wellfleet and Truro, and in spring 2006, they added **Mac's Shack** (91 Commercial St., 508/349–6333), a funky sit-down BYOB restaurant in a rambling mid-19th-century barn overlooking Duck Creek, with a lobster boat on the roof. ✉ *Wellfleet Town Pier, Wellfleet Harbor* ☎ *508/349–0404* ⊕ *www.macsseafood.com* ▭ *MC, V* ⊘ *Closed mid-Oct.–late May.*

¢–$ ✕ **Flying Fish.** Set inside a handsome little Cape-style house with wood floors and a simple dining room, this downtown café serves a wide range of foods—spinach-feta pizzas, Greek salads, curried chicken salad sandwiches, hummus platters, Häagen-Dazs ice cream, smoothies, and a full range of coffees and pastries. It's perfect for a full sit-down meal or a quick bite on the go. Don't forget to check out the selection of fresh-baked pastries. ✉ *28 Briar La.* ☎ *508/349–7292* ▭ *MC, V* ⊘ *Closed Oct.–Apr.*

$$–$$$$ 🏠 **Surf Side Colony Cottages.** Scattered on either side of Ocean View Drive,
Fodor\$Choice accommodations here range from units in a piney grove to well-equipped
★ ocean-side cottages; all accommodate two or more guests (six can stay in the largest units). The cottages are a one-minute walk from the Maguire's Landing town beach (LeCount Hollow), a beautiful wide strand of sand, dunes, and surf. Though most of the exteriors are retro-cool Floridian, with pastel shingles and flat roofs, cottage interiors are Cape-style, including knotty-pine paneling. All units have phones, wood-burning fireplaces, screened porches, kitchens, and grills. Some have roof decks with an ocean view and outdoor showers. Ocean-side cottages have dishwashers. ✉ *Ocean View Dr.* 🖃 *Box 937, South Wellfleet 02663* ☎ *508/349–3959* 🖷 *508/349–3959* ⊕ *www.surfsidevacation. com* ⇆ *20 cottages* ♨ *BBQs, kitchens, some pets (fee)* ⟳ *1- to 2-wk minimum in summer* ▭ *MC, V* ⊘ *Closed Nov.–Mar.*

$$–$$$ 🏠 **Aunt Sukie's Bayside Bed & Breakfast.** Hosts Sue and Dan Hamar treat you like you're actual guests in their home, a part-contemporary, part-antique inn with three rooms and multiple decks. It's set on the marsh grass fronting Wellfleet Harbor and Cape Cod Bay, along a quiet residential stretch of road near Power's Landing. The birds, the water, and the stunning bay views will probably be enough to keep you content in the shade of trees with a pair of binoculars. Rooms are welcoming, with flowered quilts and private decks, and the two upstairs beds grant vistas of the water without a lift of the head. The room in the antique portion of the home has a gas fireplace, a brick patio, and a grand claw-foot tub. The owners also have a full house for rent about a mile away; it comfortably accommodates two couples or a family of four and is rented weekly from May through October. ✉ *525 Chequessett Neck Rd., 02667* ☎ *508/349–2804 or 800/420–9999* ⊕ *www.auntsukies.com* ⇆ *2 rooms, 1 suite* ♨ *Refrigerators, Wi-Fi, beach; no room TVs, no kids under 10, no smoking* ▭ *MC, V* ⊘ *Closed Nov.–mid-June* ⵔ *CP.*

$$ 🏠 **Blue Gateways.** This inn—a home built in 1712—combines the simple comforts of colonial times with a modern sense of leisure. The original three-sided fireplace still reigns on the ground floor, which has wide-plank pine floors and generous beams. Upstairs are three ample guest rooms with quilts, antiques, hooked rugs, and private bathrooms. Gardens, fish-filled ponds, and private sitting areas are just outside. Common areas include a chess table, plenty of reading materials, a sunporch with cable TV and a VCR, and a small kitchen area with a microwave and refrigerator. It's a short walk from downtown Wellfleet's galleries

and restaurants. ✉ *252 Main St., 02667* ☎ *508/349–7530* ⊕ *www. bluegateways.com* 🛏 *3 rooms* ♨ *No room phones, no room TVs, no kids under 12, no smoking* ▭ *AE, D, MC, V* ⊘ *Closed early Sept.–late May* ◉ *CP.*

★ **\$\$** 🏠 **Stone Lion Inn.** B&Bs are meant to feel a bit like homes away from home—places to feel welcome, at ease, and taken care of. All of these requirements are met at the Stone Lion Inn, a gracious mansard roof Victorian just outside the town center and a short walk away from both the harbor and the village. Rooms have queen beds, ceiling fans to encourage the breezes, hardwood floors, and antiques to reflect the 19th-century era in which the house was built. Relax amid the gardens, in the outdoor shower, or in the pretty common room. New Yorkers may recognize the subtle Brooklyn theme—nostalgic, yet happily devoid of frenzy. ✉ *130 Commercial St., 02667* ☎ *508/349–9565* 🖷 *508/349– 9697* ⊕ *www.stonelioncapecod.com* 🛏 *3 rooms, 1 apartment, 1 cottage* ♨ *Internet room; no room phones, no room TVs, no kids under 10, no smoking* ▭ *MC, V* ◉ *BP.*

★ **\$\$** 🏠 **Wellfleet Motel & Lodge.** A mile from Marconi Beach, opposite the Audubon sanctuary, this immaculate and tasteful (although somewhat pricey) highway-side complex sits on 12 beautifully groomed, wooded acres. Rooms in the single-story motel are renovated each winter; those in the two-story lodge are bright and spacious, with king- or queen-size beds and balconies or patios. The property offers direct access to the Cape Cod Rail Trail. ✉ *146 U.S. 6* 🔖 *Box 606, South Wellfleet 02663* ☎ *508/349–3535 or 800/852–2900* 🖷 *508/349–1192* ⊕ *www. wellfleetmotel.com* 🛏 *57 rooms, 8 suites* ♨ *Restaurant, cable TV, in-room broadband, 2 pools (1 indoor), hot tub, basketball, bar, meeting room* ▭ *AE, DC, MC, V* ⊘ *Closed Dec.–Mar.*

\$–\$\$ 🏠 **Southfleet Motor Inn.** Geared toward active families, this carefully maintained motor inn is directly across from the entrance to the National Seashore at Marconi Station for easy access to ocean beaches. Bring your bikes to cruise the 25-mi Cape Cod Rail Trail. Rooms, which have utilitarian furnishings and an assortment of beds, can sleep up to five people. The pools and game room (with a Ping-Pong table) keep the kids busy and happy. ✉ *U.S. 6, across from Marconi Station, 02667* ☎ *508/ 349–3580 or 800/334–3715* ⊕ *www.southfleetmotorinn.com* 🛏 *30 rooms* ♨ *2 restaurants, BBQs, refrigerators, cable TV, 2 pools (1 indoor), hot tub, sauna, lounge, basketball, bikes, video game room, laundry facilities; no smoking* ▭ *AE, MC, V* ⊘ *Closed mid-Oct.–late-Apr.*

¢**–\$\$** 🏠 **Even'tide.** Long a summer favorite, this motel is set back off the main road, surrounded by 5 acres of trees and lawns; it's close to the Cape Cod Rail Trail. A central attraction is the 60-foot indoor pool (although Wellfleet's beaches are also close by). Rooms have simple modern furnishings; choose from doubles, two-room family suites, and efficiencies with kitchens. Cottages speckled about the property are available for stays of a week or longer. The staff is friendly and enthusiastic. ✉ *650 U.S. 6, South Wellfleet 02663* ☎ *508/349–3410 or 800/368–0007* 🖷 *508/349–7804* ⊕ *www.eventidemotel.com* 🛏 *31 units, 10 cottages* ♨ *BBQs, some kitchens, refrigerators, cable TV, miniature golf, indoor pool, basketball, Ping-Pong, shuffleboard, playground, some Wi-Fi,*

5

laundry facilities; no smoking ⏎ *1- or 2-wk minimum for cottages in summer* ⊟ *MC, V* ☉ *Closed Nov. and Dec.*

¢–$ ⊞ **Holden Inn.** If you're watching your budget and can deal with modest basics, try this old-timey place on a tree-shaded street just outside the town center but within walking distance of several galleries and restaurants. Rooms are simply decorated with Grandma's house–type wallpapers, ruffled sheer or country-style curtains, and antiques such as brass-and-white-iron or spindle beds or marble-top tables. Private baths with old porcelain sinks are available in the adjacent 1840 and 1890 buildings. The lodge has shared baths, an outdoor shower, and a large screened-in porch with a lovely view of the bay and Great Island, far below. The main house has a common room and a screened front porch with rockers and a bay view through the trees. ⊠ *140 Commercial St., Box 816, Wellfleet 02667* ☎ *508/349–3450* ⊕ *www.theholdeninn.com* ⏎ *26 rooms, 10 with bath* ⟡ *No room phones, no room TVs, no smoking* ⊟ *No credit cards* ☉ *Closed Nov.–Apr.*

¢–$ ⊞ **Inn at Duck Creeke.** Set on 5 wooded acres by a duck pond, a creek, and a salt marsh, this old inn consists of a circa-1815 main building and three other houses from the same era. Rooms in the main inn (except rustic third-floor rooms) and in the Saltworks house have a simple charm. Typical furnishings include claw-foot tubs, country antiques, lace curtains, chenille spreads, and rag rugs on hardwood floors. The two-room Carriage House is cabinlike, with rough barn-board and plaster walls. There's full-service dining at Sweet Seasons or pub dining with entertainment at the Tavern Room. ⊠ *70 Main St., Box 364, Wellfleet 02667* ☎ *508/349–9333* ⊕ *www.innatduckcreeke.com* ⏎ *26 rooms, 17 with bath* ⟡ *2 restaurants; no room phones, no room TVs* ⊟ *AE, MC, V* ☉ *Closed Nov.–late Apr.* ⦿ *CP.*

Nightlife & the Arts

THE ARTS During July and August the **First Congregational Church** (⊠ 200 Main St., Downtown Wellfleet ☎ 508/349–6877) trades the serenity of worship for Sunday evening concerts. The music begins at 8 PM and could include opera, blues, jazz, or chamber music.

The drive-in movie is alive and well on Cape Cod at the **Wellfleet Drive-In Theater** (⊠ 51 U.S. 6, South Wellfleet ☎ 508/349–7176), which is right by the Eastham town line. Films start at dusk nightly in season, and there's a miniature-golf course on the premises.

Art galleries are open for cocktail receptions to celebrate show openings on Saturday evening in July and August during the **Wellfleet Gallery Crawl.** You can walk from gallery to gallery, meeting the featured artists and checking out their works.

★ The well-regarded **Wellfleet Harbor Actors Theater** (⊠ Kendrick St. past E. Commercial St., near Wellfleet Harbor ☎ 508/349–6835 or 866/252–9428 ⊕ www.what.org) presents world premieres of American plays, satires, farces, and black comedies in its mid-May–mid-October season. This is the place for provocative experimental theater.

NIGHTLIFE **Beachcomber** (⊠ 1120 Calloon Hollow Rd., off Ocean View Dr. ☎ 508/
★ 349–6055) is big with the college crowd. It's right on the beach, with

national touring acts most nights, weekend happy hours with live reggae, and dancing nightly in summer. You can order appetizers, salads, burgers, seafood, and barbecue indoors or at tables by the beachfront bar. There's also a raw bar. Beachcomber is closed October–April.

A number of organizations sponsor outdoor activities at night, including the **Massachusetts Audubon Wellfleet Bay Wildlife Sanctuary**'s night hikes and lecture series.

In the venerable Inn at Duck Creeke, the **Tavern Room** (⌧ 70 Main St., U.S. 6 exit to Downtown Wellfleet ☎ 508/349–7369), set in an 1800s building with a beam ceiling, a fireplace, and a bar covered in nautical charts, has live entertainment—anything from jazz and pop to country and Latin ensembles. Munchies are served alongside a menu of traditional and Latin/Caribbean-inspired dishes.

Kick up your heels and grab a twirling partner for a long-standing Wellfleet tradition, the **Wednesday Night Square Dance.** Down at the town pier in July and August, the music and live calling by master caller Irvin "Toots" Tousignant begins at 7 and lasts as long as *you* can.

Sports & the Outdoors

The state-of-the-art Skateboard Park down at **Baker's Field** (⌧ Kendrick Ave. just past Wellfleet Town Pier, near Wellfleet Harbor) was professionally designed for tricks and safety; it's manned by local teens.

BEACHES **Public Beaches.** Extensive storm-induced erosion has made the cliffs to most of Wellfleet's ocean beaches quite steep—so be prepared for a taxing trek up and down the dune slope.

Cahoon Hollow Beach (⌧ Ocean View Dr.) has lifeguards, restrooms, and a restaurant and music club on the sand. This beach tends to attract younger and slightly rowdier crowds; it's a big Sunday-afternoon party place. There are daily parking fees of $15 for nonresidents in season only; parking is free for those with beach stickers.

Fodor'sChoice **Marconi Beach** (⌧ Off U.S. 6), part of the Cape Cod National Seashore, ★ charges $15 for daily parking or $45 for a season pass that provides access to all six National Seashore swimming beaches. There are lifeguards, restrooms, and outdoor showers.

Mayo Beach (⌧ Commercial St., adjacent to Wellfleet Pier) is free, but swimming here is pleasant only around high tide—once the water recedes, it's all mud and sharp shells. You can park for free at the small lot by Great Island on the bay.

White Crest Beach (⌧ Ocean View Dr.) is a prime surfer hangout where the dudes often spend more time waiting for waves than actually riding them. Lifeguards are on duty daily 9–5 from July through Labor Day weekend. If you're up to the challenge, join one of the spontaneous volleyball games that frequently pop up. There are daily parking fees of $15 for nonresidents in season only; parking is free for those with beach stickers.

Restricted Beaches. Resident or temporary resident parking stickers are required for access to Wellfleet beaches in season only, from the last week of June through Labor Day. To get a three-day ($30), weekly ($60), or season ($200) pass, visit the Beach Sticker Booth on the town pier with your car registration in hand and a proof-of-stay form, available from rental agencies and hotels. For the rest of the year anyone can visit the beaches for free. Note that people arriving on foot or by bicycle can visit the beaches at any time; the sticker is for parking only. These parking restrictions apply to all beaches listed below.

For information about restricted beaches, call the **Wellfleet Chamber of Commerce** (☎ 508/349–2510).

☾ **Duck Harbor Beach** (✉ End of Chequessett Neck Rd.) seems like it's nearly at the end of the world. Its shores are on the warm waters of Cape Cod Bay, and there's plenty of room to wander and find your own private space. You can look out to Provincetown across the bay, but the finest view by far is the nightly sunset.

Indian Neck Beach (✉ Pilgrim Spring Rd. off U.S. 6) is on the bay side, fronting Wellfleet Harbor, and is thus affected by the tides. Low tide reveals plenty of beach but less water—you'll have to walk way out before your hips get wet. It's a good spot to watch the comings and goings of fishing boats from Wellfleet Pier. With it's shallow and calm waters, warmer temperatures, and ample opportunity for treasure hunting at low tide, it's also a great beach for families.

★ **LeCount Hollow Beach** (✉ Ocean View Dr.) is the beach closest to U.S. 6 in South Wellfleet, along the meandering Ocean View Drive. The dunes are steep here, so be prepared to carry all beach belongings down (and up) the sandy slope.

Newcomb Hollow Beach (✉ Ocean View Dr.) is the northernmost beach on the Wellfleet strip, closest to Truro. If you keep your eyes on the horizon, it's not at all uncommon to see the distant spout of a passing whale. This beach is also a popular nighttime fishing spot.

The **Wellfleet Ponds,** nestled in the woods between U.S. 6 and the ocean, were formed by glaciers and are fed by underground springs. Mild temperatures and clear, clean waters make swimming here pleasant for the whole family, a refreshing change from the bracing salty surf of the Atlantic. The ponds are also perfect for canoeing, sailing, or kayaking (boats are available from Jack's Boat Rentals). A Wellfleet beach sticker is required to visit these fragile ecosystems in season (the sticker is only for cars, though—anyone can walk or ride a bike over to the ponds). Motorized boats are not allowed.

BICYCLING   The Cape Cod Rail Trail ends at the South Wellfleet post office. Other scenic routes for bicyclists include winding, tree-lined Old County Road, just outside Wellfleet center at the end of West Main Street. Ambitious riders can bike all the way to Truro on this often bumpy road, but be sure to watch for vehicular traffic around the tight curves. Ocean View Drive, on the ocean side, winds through miles of wooded areas; there are several ponds along the route that are perfect for taking a quick dip. The Wellfleet Chamber of Commerce publishes a pamphlet, "Bicycling in Wellfleet," with an annotated map.

Idle Times Bike Shop, Inc. (⊠ U.S. 6, just west of Cahoon Hollow Rd. ☎ 508/349–9161) opens Memorial Day and rents bikes, trailer bikes (a tandem bike with a backseat for children who are big enough to pedal), and trailer attachments for the littler passengers. The shop also handles repairs and sells parts and assorted accessories. Depending on the crowds and weather, it usually remains open until Columbus Day.

BOATING **Jack's Boat Rental** (⊠ Gull Pond, south of U.S. 6 ☎ 508/349–7553 ⊠ U.S. 6, west of Downtown Wellfleet exit ☎ 508/349–9808 long-term rentals) has canoes, kayaks, Sunfish, pedal boats, surfboards, Boogie boards, and sailboards. Guided kayak tours are also available.

Wellfleet Marine Corp. (⊠ Wellfleet Town Pier, Wellfleet Harbor ☎ 508/349–2233) rents sailboats and motorboats in various sizes by the hour or the day.

FISHING You can climb aboard the charter boat *Jac's Mate* (⊠ Wellfleet Town Pier, Wellfleet Harbor ☎ 508/255–2978 ⊕ http://users.rcn.com/jacsmate) for fishing expeditions in search of bass and blues.

The *Naviator* (⊠ Wellfleet Town Pier, Wellfleet Harbor ☎ 508/349–6003 ⊕ www.naviator.com) operates fishing trips on a walk-on basis from spring through fall. Rods, reels, and bait are included.

GOLF & TENNIS Wellfleet maintains several tennis courts at **Baker's Field** near the town pier. Call the **Recreation Department** (☎ 508/349–0330) for fees and reservations.

Chequessett Yacht Country Club (⊠ 680 Chequessett Neck Rd., west of Downtown Wellfleet ☎ 508/349–3704) is a semiprivate club (public use on space-available basis) with a 9-hole golf course and five hard-surface tennis courts by the bay. Lessons are available.

Oliver's (⊠ U.S. 6, west of Downtown Wellfleet exit ☎ 508/349–3330), which has one Truflex and seven clay courts, offers tennis lessons and arranges matches.

SURFING Atlantic-coast **Marconi** and **White Crest** beaches are the best for surfing. Surfboard rentals can be arranged at Jack's Boat Rental.

Shopping

ART GALLERIES **Andre Pottery** (⊠ 5 Commercial St., Downtown Wellfleet ☎ 508/349–2299 ⊕ www.andrepottery.com) specializes in handmade bowls, vases, and pitchers, mostly in greens, blues, and grays, the shades of the sea and shore.

Blue Heron Gallery (⊠ 20 Bank St., Downtown Wellfleet ☎ 508/349–6724 ⊕ www.blueheronfineart.com) is one of the Cape's best galleries, with contemporary works—including Cape scenes, jewelry, sculpture, and pottery—by regional and nationally recognized artists, among them Steve Allrich and Del Filardi.

★ **Brophy's Fine Art** (⊠ 313 Main St., Downtown Wellfleet ☎ 508/349–6479 ⊕ www.brophysfineart.com), one of the few year-round shops in Wellfleet, carries a nice selection of pottery, jewelry, and landscape paintings by several prominent New England artists as well as the beautiful stained-glass works of owner Thomas Brophy.

Cove Gallery (✉ 15 Commercial St., Downtown Wellfleet ☎ 508/349–2530 ⊕ www.covegallery.com) displays the works of John Grillo, Tomie dePaola, and Leonard Baskin, among others. The gallery hosts Saturday-night artist receptions in July and August.

Davis Gallery (✉ 2766 U.S. 6, east of Downtown Wellfleet exit ☎ 508/349–0549 ⊕ www.thedavisgallery.com) makes its home in what was once an ugly building on the highway. The owners have turned the place into a very respectable and attractive gallery showcasing contemporary art and fine crafts. There's also a pleasant outdoor sculpture gallery.

Jacob Fanning Gallery (✉ 25 Bank St., Downtown Wellfleet ☎ 508/349–9546 ⊕ www.jacobfanningcapecod.com) showcases the art, furniture, and decorative pieces of several established local artists, including Joyce Zavorskas, Jane Lincoln, and Lynn Shaler.

★ **Kendall Art Gallery** (✉ 40 Main St., Downtown Wellfleet ☎ 508/349–2482 ⊕ www.kendallartgallery.com) carries eclectic modern works, including Harry Marinsky's bronzes in the sculpture garden, photography by Walter Baron and Alan Hoelzle, watercolors by Walter Dorrell, and contemporary art by several prominent Chinese artists. Receptions are held on Saturday evenings.

Left-Bank Gallery (✉ 25 Commercial St. ☎ 508/349–9451 ✉ 3 W. Main St., Downtown Wellfleet ☎ 508/349–7939 ⊕ www.leftbankgallery.com) has two branches. The larger one, on Commercial Street, displays the larger works of local and national artists and sells fine crafts in the back room facing Duck Creek. The other gallery has fine handcrafted jewelry, silk and chenille scarves, hats, and small works of original art and photography.

Nicholas Harrison Gallery (✉ 275 Main St., Downtown Wellfleet ☎ 508/349–7799 ⊕ thenicholasharrisongallery.com) has made a name for itself in the area of lovely and unusual American crafts, including beautiful lamps, resin-and-silver jewelry, and hand-painted cabinets. Owners Mark and Laura Evangelista are also accomplished potters, and you'll see their vibrant ceramic works here as well.

Sandpiper Gallery (✉ 95 Commercial St., Downtown Wellfleet ☎ 508/349–9500 ⊕ www.sandpipergallery.us), an impressive space, carries a wide range of oils, watercolors, photography, etchings, and jewelry by both regional and national talents.

Fodor'sChoice ★ **Wellfleet Glass Works** (✉ 15½ Bank St., Downtown Wellfleet ☎ 508/349–0200 ⊕ www.wellfleetglassworks.com) carries a wide assortment of contemporary glassware, sculpture, and jewelry created by owners Jason and Erin Robicheau; you can come in to watch glassblowing demonstrations throughout the day.

SPECIALTY STORES **Abiyoyo** (✉ 286 Main St., Downtown Wellfleet ☎ 508/349–3422) has a full line of Wellfleet T-shirts and sweatshirts, along with shoes, children's clothing, and bath and beauty products.

Chocolate Sparrow (✉ 326 Main St., Downtown Wellfleet ☎ 508/349–1333) makes nine types of fudge, luscious hand-dipped chocolates, and a wide array of decadent baked goods and sweets. This is a seasonal branch of the well-known shop that began in Eastham and also has a location in Orleans; it's open May through early September.

Eccentricity (✉ 361 Main St., Downtown Wellfleet ☎ 508/349–3634) keeps the corner of Main and Briar offbeat. One of the most interesting stores on the Cape, it sells gorgeous kimonos, ethnic-inspired cotton clothing, African carved-wood sculptures, barbershop paintings, odd Mexican items, and trinkets. The owners also run Off Center, a similarly lively shop across the street.

Frances Francis (✉ 326 Main St., Downtown Wellfleet ☎ 508/314–6464) is a fine source of stylish, contemporary women's wear and snappy accessories.

★ **Herridge Books** (✉ 11 E. Main St., between U.S. 6 and town center, Downtown Wellfleet ☎ 508/349–1323) is the perfect store for a town that has been host to so many writers. Its dignified literary fiction, art and architecture, literary biography and letters, mystery, Americana, sports, and other sections are full of used books in very nice condition. Herridge also carries new editions on the Cape and its history.

Jules Besch Stationers (✉ 15 Bank St., Downtown Wellfleet ☎ 508/349–1231) has extraordinary cards, fine stationery, journals, papers, and pens. Proprietor Michael Tuck's warm and welcoming nature is as beautiful as his products are; he also offers full calligraphy services.

Karol Richardson (✉ 11 W. Main St., Downtown Wellfleet ☎ 508/349–6378) fashions women's wear in luxurious fabrics and sells interesting shoes, hats, and jewelry.

Kite Gallery (✉ 75 Commercial St., Downtown Wellfleet ☎ 508/349–7387) overlooks a salt marsh and stocks kites and all kinds of colorful beach toys, windsocks, flags, and garden goodies.

Pickle and Puppy (✉ 355 Main St., Downtown Wellfleet ☎ 508/349–0606) has a bit of everything: housewares, T-shirts, fanciful foodstuffs, ceramics, and luxury bath and beauty-parlor items, plus a selection of unusual children's toys, games, and puzzles.

Secret Garden (✉ Main St., Downtown Wellfleet ☎ 508/349–1444) doesn't waste any precious space—the walls are covered from floor to ceiling with whimsical folk art pieces, handbags, clothing, and decorative accessories. They also have good buys on sterling silver jewelry.

Wellfleet Marketplace (✉ 295 Main St., Downtown Wellfleet ☎ 508/349–3156), which opened in 2005, is *the* place to pick up gourmet foods in town. Besides a branch of Mac's Seafood, you'll also find great deli treats, organic produce, and other tasty foods.

FLEA MARKET   The giant **Wellfleet Flea Market** (✉ 51 U.S. 6, South Wellfleet ☎ 508/
Fodor'sChoice   349–0541) sets up shop in the parking lot of the Wellfleet Drive-In The-
★   ater mid-April–June and September and October, weekends and Monday holidays 8–4; July and August, Monday holidays, Wednesday and Thursday, and weekends 8–4. You'll find antiques, sweat socks, old advertising posters, books, Beanie Babies, Guatemalan sweaters, plants, trinkets, and plenty more. On Monday and Tuesday in July and August

the vendors make way for large arts-and-crafts shows. A snack bar and playground keep fatigue at bay.

EN ROUTE If you're in the mood for a quiet, lovely ride winding through what the Cape might have looked like before Europeans arrived, follow **Old County Road** from Wellfleet to Truro on the bay side. It's bumpy and beautiful, with a stream or two along the way. So cycle on it, or drive slowly, or just stop and walk to take in the nature around you.

Truro

❹ *2 mi north of Wellfleet, 7 mi southeast of Provincetown.*

Settled in 1697, Truro has had several names. It was originally called Pamet after the local Native Americans, but in 1705 the name was changed to Dangerfield in response to all the sailing mishaps off its shores. "Truroe" was the final choice, named for a Cornish town that homesick settlers thought it resembled; the final 'e' was eventually dropped. The town relied on the sea for its income—whaling, shipbuilding, and cod fishing were the main industries.

Today Truro is a town of high dunes, estuaries, and rivers fringed by grasses, rolling moors, and houses sheltered in tiny valleys. It's a popular retreat for artists, writers, politicos, and numerous vacationing psychoanalysts. Edward Hopper summered here from 1930 to 1967, finding the Cape light ideal for his austere brand of realism. One of the largest towns on the Cape in terms of land area—almost 43 square mi—it's also the smallest in population, with about 1,400 year-round residents. Truro is also the Cape's narrowest town, and from a high perch you can see the Atlantic Ocean on one side and Cape Cod Bay on the other.

If you thought neighboring Wellfleet's downtown was small, wait until you see—or don't see—Truro's. It consists of a post office, a town hall, and a shop or two—you'll know it by the sign that says DOWNTOWN TRURO at a little plaza entrance. Truro also has a library, a firehouse, and a police station, but that's about all. The North Truro section contains most of the town's restaurants and accommodations, most either along U.S. 6 or fronting the bay along Route 6A (Shore Road), just south of the Provincetown border. Many who live or vacation in Truro choose it for its easygoing, quiet personality and lack of development—and it's close proximity to the excitement and commerce of Provincetown.

For a few hours of exploring, take the children to **Pamet Harbor** (✉ Depot Rd.). At low tide you can walk out on the flats and discover the creatures of the salt marsh. A nearby plaque identifies plants and animals and describes the area's ecological importance.

On **Corn Hill** (✉ Off Corn Hill Rd.), near the beach area of the same name, a tablet commemorates the finding of a buried cache of corn by Myles Standish and the *Mayflower* crew. They took it to Plymouth and used it as seed, returning later to pay the Native Americans for what they'd taken. The **Truro Center for the Arts at Castle Hill,** in a converted 19th-century barn, has summer arts-and-crafts workshops for children, as well as courses and single classes in art, crafts, photography, and writ-

Truro's Edward Hopper

THE OUTER CAPE has inspired thousands of acclaimed artists, but perhaps none is more closely associated with its serene yet romantic landscape than Edward Hopper, the esteemed realist painter who lived in Truro for most of the last four decades of his life. Quiet Truro, with its peaceful, sandy lanes, suited the introspective Hopper perfectly.

Hopper, born in Nyack, New York, in 1882, enjoyed little commercial or critical success before middle age. Early in his career, he worked as a commercial illustrator to support himself while living in New York City's Greenwich Village. At age 43 he married Josephine Nivison. It was during the 1920s, after his marriage, that Hopper achieved marked success as both an oil painter and watercolorist and became known for his starkly realistic scenes, often depicting public places filled with people, such as his most iconic work, *Nighthawks*.

Edward and Josephine first summered in Truro in 1930, and a few years later they designed their own Truro home. Much of Hopper's work conveyed the emptiness and alienation of big-city life, and although his Cape paintings were similar in their simplicity, they nevertheless offered a slightly more hopeful vision, if for no other reason than their tendency to focus more on the region's sensuous luminosity than strictly on lonely or bored people.

Most famously, his Truro work captured the undulating auburn hills along Pamet Road in *Corn Hill Truro Cape Cod*. Other notable paintings that portray the Outer Cape include *Cape Cod Evening* (1939), *Route 6 Eastham* (1941), *Martha McKeen of Wellfleet* (1944), and *Cape Cod Morning* (1950).

–by Andrew Collins

ing for adults. Teachers have included notable New York- and Province-town-based artists. ⊠ *10 Meetinghouse Rd.* ☎ *508/349–7511* ⊕ *www.castlehill.org.*

NEED A BREAK? **Jams** (⊠ 14 Truro Center Rd., off U.S. 6 in Truro Center ☎ 508/349-1616) has fixings for a great picnic lunch: sandwiches, fresh produce, a bottle of wine or Evian, or a sweet treat. Unless you like getting your knees knocked, don't bother sitting at the bench outside—besides, the best part of the Cape awaits just outside the door.

Built at the turn of the 20th century as a summer hotel, the **Highland House Museum,** operated by the Truro Historical Society, has 17th-century firearms, mementos of shipwrecks, early fishing and whaling gear, ship models, a pirate's chest, and scrimshaw. One room exhibits wood carvings, paintings, blown glass, and ship models by Courtney Allen, artist and founder of Truro's historical society. The museum also holds local art and artifact shows each year. ⊠ *6 Lighthouse Rd., off S. Highland Rd., North Truro* ☎ *508/487–3397* ⊕ *www.trurohistorical.org* ⌦ *$4; $6 for combo admission with Highland Light* ⊙ *Late May–Sept., Mon.–Sat. 10–4:30, Sun. 1–4:30.*

❺ Truly a breathtaking sight, **Highland Light**, also called Cape Cod Light, is the Cape's oldest lighthouse. It was the last to become automated, in 1986. The first light on this site, powered by 24 whale-oil lamps, began warning ships of Truro's treacherous sandbars in 1798—the dreaded Peaked Hills Bars alone, to the north, claimed hundreds of ships. The current light, a white-painted 66-foot tower built in 1857, is powered by two 1,000-watt bulbs reflected by a huge Fresnel lens; its beacon is visible for 20 mi.

One of four active lighthouses on the Outer Cape, Highland Light has the distinction of being listed in the National Register of Historic Places. Henry David Thoreau used it as a stopover in his travels across the Cape's backside (as the Atlantic side of the Outer Cape is called). Erosion threatened to cut this lighthouse from the 117-foot cliff on which it stood and drop it into the sea; thanks to a concerted effort by local residents and lighthouse lovers, the necessary funds were raised, and the lighthouse was moved back 450 feet to safety (while remaining surrounded by the Highland Links golf course). Twenty-five-minute tours of the lighthouse are given daily in summer. Children must be at least 51 inches tall to climb the tower. ⊠ *Off S. Highland Rd.* ☎ *508/487–3397* ⊕ *www.trurohistorical.org* ⌦ *$4; $6 for combo admission with Highland House Museum* ⊙ *Mid-May–mid-Oct., daily 10–5:30.*

The gardens of **A Touch of Heaven** are beautiful—and, unlike most gardens, are meant to be picked. The lawns are set with benches and birdbaths, and the flowers are so abundant that you won't feel guilty about gathering a bunch to take home. ⊠ *Pond Village Heights, North Truro* ☎ *No phone* ⌦ *Free* ⊙ *Daily dawn–dusk.*

Worth a stop as much for its verdant grounds and tranquil setting inside a rambling 1830s farmhouse as for its enjoyable (and increasingly respectable) wines, **Truro Vineyards of Cape Cod Winery** produces a Cabernet Franc, a blush, and a Chardonnay. They also make a red table wine that's flavored with cranberries and known for its unusual bottle, shaped like a lighthouse—it's a fun souvenir. ⊠ *Rte. 6A, North Truro* ☎ *508/487–6200* ⊕ *www.trurovineyardsofcapecod.com* ⊙ *Apr., Fri.–Sun. noon–5; May–Nov., Mon.–Sat. 11–5, Sun. noon–5; Dec., Fri. and Sat. 11–4, Sun. noon–4* ⌦ *Free.*

❻ At the **Pilgrim Heights Area** (⊠ Off U.S. 6) of the Cape Cod National Seashore, a short trail leads to the spring where members of a Pilgrim exploring party stopped to refill their casks, tasting their first New England water in the process. Walking through this still-wild area of oak, pitch pine, bayberry, blueberry, beach plum, and azalea gives you a taste of what it was like for these voyagers in search of a new home. "Being thus passed the vast ocean . . ." William Bradford wrote in *Of Plimoth Plantation,* "they had no friends to welcome them, no inns to entertain them or refresh their weather-beaten bodies; no houses, or much less towns to repair to, to seek for succour."

From an overlook you can see the bluffs of High Head, where glaciers pushed a mass of earth before melting and receding. Another path leads to a swamp, and a bike trail leads to Head of the Meadow Beach, often a less crowded alternative to others in the area.

Where to Stay & Eat

$–$$$$ ✕**Whitman House.** What began as a modest pancake house has been transformed by the Rice family into a vast—if touristy—restaurant, but pewter plates, candlelight, and rustic wood accents make the place feel comfortably tavernlike. Seafood, steaks, and surf-and-turf combos (consider the crabmeat casserole with petite filet mignon) keep the menu uncomplicated, and the portions ample. Lunch and lighter dinner fare are served daily in the Bass Tavern. If you have to wait for a table, browse in the adjacent Amish quilt shop. ⊠ *Off U.S. 6* ☎ *508/487–1740* ⊕ *www.whitmanhouse.com* ☐ *AE, D, DC, MC, V* ☉ *Closed Jan.–Mar.*

$–$$$ ✕**Adrian's.** Adrian Cyr's restaurant crowns a high bluff overlooking Pilgrim Lake and all of Provincetown; his cooking also hits great heights. Cayenne-crusted salmon with maple-mustard sauce is just one of the well-prepared dishes here. Tuscan salad is also a hit, with tomatoes, olives, fresh basil, plenty of garlic, and balsamic vinegar. Pizzas, too, are standouts, especially one made with cornmeal dough and topped with shrimp and artichokes. The outdoor deck overflows at the popular breakfasts and brunches, served every day in season and weekends in spring and fall—try the cranberry pancakes with orange butter. ⊠ *Outer Reach Hotel, 535 U.S. 6, North Truro* ☎ *508/487–4360* ⊕ *www.adriansrestaurant. com* ☐ *AE, MC, V* ☉ *Closed mid-Oct.–late May. No lunch.*

$–$$$ ✕**Blacksmith Shop.** Here's where Truro locals like to linger at the bar, gossiping about what's going on in town while choosing from an eclectic menu with everything from seafood to Italian and Asian dishes. The cozy, wood-beamed restaurant looks like it might once have been a place to bring your horse for shoeing, but these days it's a nice out-of-the-way spot for company. There are excellent steaks as well as an oven-baked pistachio-crusted salmon with pistachio oil, Thai shrimp and scallops with coconut curry, and a pan-roasted rack of lamb with a cranberry-port reduction. It's also a good bet for a burger or lighter dinner fare. Local shellfishermen deliver excellent quahogs and oysters, then hang around to gossip. ⊠ *17 Truro Center Rd., off Rte. 6A, Truro Center* ☎ *508/349–6554* ☐ *AE, MC, V* ☉ *Closed Mon.–Wed. Nov.–May.*

★ **$–$$$** ✕**Terra Luna.** An insider's favorite for wonderfully fresh and inventive bistro fare, Terra Luna has an intimate art-filled dining room with lace curtains and simple wooden tables. The food is stylish, with sophisticated sauces for both fish and meat dishes. The littleneck clams with sausage, fennel, garlic, and tomatoes is a house favorite, and spicy stuffed lamb chops are an excel-

---

WORD OF MOUTH

"Terra Luna in Truro has never let me down."   –lizag

---

lent alternative to the usual fish. For dessert, don't miss the unusual black-berry polenta custard. ⊠ *104 Shore Rd. (Rte. 6A), North Truro* ☎ *508/487–1019* ▤ *AE, MC, V* ⊘ *Closed late Oct.–May. No lunch.*

$$ ▦ **Crow's Nest Resort.** Amid the mostly run-of-the-mill motels and cot-
Fodor'sChoice tage compounds along Route 6A in North Truro, this beautifully refur-
★ bished all-suites beachfront property stands head and shoulders above the rest. It's been around since the mid-1960s, but the rooms are refresh-ingly contemporary with tile and oak floors, modern kitchen appliances, light-wood furniture, and country quilts. Ground-floor units front an attractive wooden deck overlooking the bay, and upstairs units have pri-vate balconies with similar views. You can choose from studio, two-bed-room, and three-bedroom units, and all have full kitchens, fireplaces, Jacuzzi tubs, and washers and dryers, making them perfect for longer stays. The resort also rents three attractive beachfront bungalows, called Crown's Nest Cottages, about a half-mile away. Given the prime loca-tion, friendly service, and top-notch facilities and furnishings, this is one of the Outer Cape's best bargains for families and friends traveling to-gether. ⊠ *496 Rte. 6A, Box 177, 02652* ☎ *508/487–9031 or 800/499–9799* ⊕ *www.caperesort.com* ⇄ *21 suites* ⌂ *Kitchens, in-room hot tubs, cable TV, in-room DVDs, in-room broadband* ▤ *AE, MC, V* ⊘ *Closed late Nov.–early Apr.*

$$ ▦ **Moorlands Inn.** The creative works of innkeepers Bill and Skipper Evaul—artists and musicians—fill the walls and rooms of this tower-ing Queen Anne Victorian beauty. Antiques adorn the bright rooms in the main house; the spacious penthouse has a full kitchen, two bedrooms, and a deck. Those staying in the Carriage House have their own out-door whirlpool, and all guests can use the communal hot tub out back. The apartments and cottages operate on the European plan. ⊠ *11 Hughes Rd., Box 384, North Truro 02652* ☎ *508/487–0663* ⊕ *www.themoorlands.com* ⇄ *1 room, 2 suites, 1 apartment, 3 cottages* ⌂ *Some kitchens, cable TV, some in-room VCRs, outdoor hot tubs, croquet; no a/c in some rooms* ▤ *MC, V* ⏐◉⏐ *BP.*

$$ ▦ **Top Mast Resort.** This North Truro beach motel complex, which sits on 52 acres across U.S. 6 from Cape Cod National Seashore, had seen better days before its owners purchased two adjacent buildings and began an extensive refurbishment and expansion during the spring of 2006 (they expect work to be complete in spring 2007). Improvements include new kitchen appliances and cabinets, tile flooring and new carpeting, and attractive furnishings. As of this writing, the Top Mast was also build-ing a new office, restaurant, pool, tennis courts, and a playground. Most rooms are along the beach, but there are also some significantly less expensive units in a building across the road, facing the swimming pool and landscaped gardens. Two cottages are available on a weekly basis. ⊠ *209 Rte. 6A* ⌂ *Box 44, North Truro 02652* ☎ *508/487–1189 or 800/917–0024* ⊕ *www.topmastresort.com* ⇄ *67 rooms, 2 cottages* ⌂ *Restaurant, BBQs, some kitchens, refrigerators, microwaves, cable TV, in-room broadband, pool* ▤ *MC, V* ⊘ *Closed late Oct.–early May.*

¢–$$ ▦ **Cape View Motel.** The true appeal of this tan-clapboard roadside motel is its noble perch on a westward bluff, looking out over Cape Cod Bay sunsets and the distant lights of Provincetown. Deluxe rooms have private balconies, as well as fully equipped kitchenettes and a king bed or two doubles. The style inside can't compete with the vistas outside, but the rooms are clean, simple, reasonably priced, and a 10-minute drive to Provincetown. Free coffee and doughnuts are provided in the morning. ✉ *Junction of U.S. 6 and Rte. 6A, Box 114, 02652* ☎ *508/487–0363 or 800/224–3232* ⊕ *www.capeviewmotel.com* ➫ *32 rooms* ♿ *Some kitchenettes, refrigerators, cable TV, pool* ☰ *AE, MC, V* ☯ *Closed mid-Oct.–mid-Apr.*

$ ☶ **Sea Gull Motel.** This motel's location, right on the beach and close to the Provincetown border, is its real draw. It's been family run for decades, so you may feel like you're spending time in someone's summerhouse. Most rooms have splendid water views; lodging is in standard motel rooms, motel studios, and beach apartments—the latter two are rented weekly, but you can rent rooms by the night. ✉ *Rte. 6A* ☍ *Box 126, North Truro 02652* ☎ *508/487–9070* ⊕ *www.capecodtravel.com/ seagullmotel* ➫ *26 rooms* ♿ *Refrigerators, cable TV* ☰ *AE, D, MC, V* ☯ *Closed mid-Oct.–mid-May.*

★ ¢ ☶ **Hostelling International–Truro.** In a former Coast Guard station right on the dunes, this handsome, well-placed, and nicely maintained hostel has kitchen facilities, a common area, and naturalist-led programs—not to mention panoramic views of the ocean and dunes. It's also right by the ½-mi-long Cranberry Bog Trail, which takes you by a refurbished cranberry bog and an old bog house. The dorm rooms are single-sex, and there are no curfews or lockouts—just come and go as you like. Guided kayak tours are available. ✉*N. Pamet Rd., Box 402, Truro 02666* ☎ *508/349–3889 or 888/901–2086* ⊕ *www.capecodhostels.org* ➫ *42 beds, 2 private rooms* ☰ *MC, V* ☯ *Closed early Sept.–late-June.*

Sports & the Outdoors

BEACHES Parking at a number of Truro's **town beaches** is reserved for residents and renters in season, although anyone can walk or bicycle in. Ask at the **town hall** (☎ 508/349–3635) about a obtaining seasonal sticker.

Corn Hill Beach (✉ Corn Hill Rd.), on the bay, has beautiful views of Provincetown. The waters are generally calm and warm, typical of bay beaches. There are restrooms on-site. Parking requires a Truro beach sticker or a $15 daily fee.

Truro has several other accessible beaches stretched along Cape Cod Bay. All are beautiful and ideal for long, lazy days of watching boats go by and taking in views of Provincetown in the distance.

Cold Storage Beach (✉ Pond Rd. off Rte. 6A [Shore Rd.]) is just as popular with anglers looking for passing blues and stripers as it is with sunseekers and swimmers. A Truro beach sticker is required for parking.

Just off one of Truro's backcountry roads, **Fisher Road Beach** (✉ Fisher Rd.) has a smaller parking area, so it's usually quiet. A Truro beach sticker is required for parking.

To get to **Great Hollow Beach** (✉ Great Hollow Rd. off U.S. 6) you must be ready to scale some moderate stairs from the parking lot to the sands below. A Truro beach sticker is required for parking.

5

Ryder Beach (✉ Ryder Beach Rd. off Old County Rd.) rests just below a rise in the small dunes. A Truro beach sticker is required for parking.

On the ocean side, three spectacular beaches are marked by massive dunes and bracing surf.

★ **Ballston Beach** (✉ Pamet Rd.) lies at the end of the winding, residential Pamet Road, backed by the golden hills that artist Edward Hopper made famous in his Truro paintings. Parking is reserved for residents and renters in season, although anyone can walk or bicycle in.

FodorśChoice **Coast Guard Beach** (✉ Coast Guard Rd.) sits just down the road from
★ Highland Light. Parking is for residents and renters with stickers only, although anyone can walk or bicycle in to enjoy this pristine swath of golden sand that stretches for miles in either direction and sees relatively few crowds—even in the heart of summer. Keep in mind that the parking area is small and tends to fill quickly.

Head of the Meadow Beach (✉ Head of the Meadow Rd. off U.S. 6) in North Truro, part of the Cape Cod National Seashore, is often less crowded than other beaches in the area. The bathhouse burned down, so it has only temporary restroom facilities available in summer and no showers. The daily parking fee is $15 in season; you can also purchase a season pass ($45) that is good for all National Seashore locations.

A not-so-secret favorite of nude sunbathers, **Longnook Beach** (✉ Long Nook Rd.) shares the senses of wildness and isolation synonymous with Truro's outer reaches. Truro beach stickers are required for parking.

BICYCLING The **Head of the Meadow Trail** provides 2 mi of easy cycling between dunes and salt marshes from High Head Road, off Route 6A in North Truro, to the Head of the Meadow Beach parking lot.

★ **Cape Outback Adventures** (☎ 508/349–1617 or 800/864–0070 ⊕ www. capeoutback.com) has friendly instruction and guided tours for kayakers, mountain bikers, and beginning surfers. Times and location are arranged by phone, and owner Richard Miller and his staff provide equipment. Kayak trips explore areas in both Wellfleet and Truro, and off-road mountain-biking excursions take place in the vast wooded areas within the National Seashore. Surfing instruction is available by the hour. These trips are designed for all ages and skill levels.

GOLF The **Highland Golf Links** (✉ Lighthouse Rd., North Truro ☎ 508/487–
★ 9201), a 9-hole, par-36 course on a cliff overlooking the Atlantic and Highland Light, is unique for its resemblance to Scottish links.

SURFING **Longnook Beach** (✉ End of Long Nook Rd., off U.S. 6) is good for surfing.

Shopping
Atlantic Spice Co. (✉ U.S. 6 at Rte. 6A, North Truro ☎ 508/487–6100 ⊕ www.atlanticspice.com) has spices, teas, and potpourris, as well as herbs, dried flowers, soaps, sauces, and kitchenware items.

Whitman House Quilt Shop (⊠ County Rd. just off U.S. 6, North Truro ☎ 508/487–3204 ⊕ www.whitmanhouse.com) sells Amish quilts and other country items.

Provincetown

 7 mi northwest of Truro, 27 mi north of Orleans, 62 mi from Sagamore Bridge.

The Cape's smallest town in area and its second smallest in year-round population, Provincetown is a place of liberating creativity, startling originality, and substantial diversity. Like so much of Cape Cod, it's also a town that's become progressively—and rather dramatically—more upscale and sophisticated in recent years. A number of the casual—if cheesy—T-shirt and souvenir shops that once lined the town's main drag, Commercial Street, have given way to first-rate art galleries and upscale boutiques. Many of the town's funky B&Bs and inns, which once felt more like glorified boarding houses than proper accommodations, have been sold as private homes or transformed into fabulous, upscale hideaways with fine antiques, flat-screen TVs and DVD players, and cushy amenities.

With the change has come at least a mild concern that Provincetown may become too upscale and cosmopolitan for its own good—but so far there's little evidence that this lovably eccentric, individualistic place will ever become any less freespirited. A strong sense of community spirit and civic pride remains. In the busy downtown, Portuguese-American fishermen mix with painters, poets, writers, whale-watching families, cruise-ship passengers on brief stopovers, and gay and lesbian residents and visitors. In summer Commercial Street is packed with sightseers and shoppers hunting for treasures in the overwhelming number of galleries and crafts shops. At night raucous music and people spill out of bars, drag shows, and sing-along lounges galore. It's a fun, crazy place, with the extra dimension of the fishing fleet unloading their catch at MacMillan Wharf, in the center of the action.

The town's 8 square miles are also rich in history. The fist at the very tip of the Cape, Provincetown has shores that curve protectively around a natural harbor, perfect for sailors from any epoch to anchor. Historical records suggest that Thorvald, brother of Viking Leif Erikson, came ashore here in AD 1004 to repair the keel of his boat and consequently named the area Kjalarness, or Cape of the Keel. Bartholomew Gosnold came to Provincetown in 1602 and named the area Cape Cod after the abundant codfish he found in the local waters.

The Pilgrims remain Provincetown's most famous visitors. On Monday, November 21, 1620, the *Mayflower* dropped anchor in Provincetown Harbor after a difficult 63-day voyage from England. While in the harbor the passengers signed the Mayflower Compact, the first document to declare a democratic form of government in America. One of the first things the ever-practical Pilgrims did was come ashore to wash their clothes, thus beginning the ages-old New England tradition of Monday wash day.

Provincetown

EAST END

TO
ROUTE 6A

Provincetown Harbor

750 yards

750 meters

MacMillan Wharf

Duck Pond

Shank Painter Pond

WEST END

TO
RACE POINT
LIGHT

TO
LONG POINT
LIGHT

Province Lands Rd.

Fine Arts Work Center ...**12**
MacMillan Wharf **9**
Mayflower Compact
Plaque **14**
Octagonal house **15**
Pilgrim Monument **8**
Pilgrim Plaque **17**

Provincetown
Art Association and
Museum **10**
Provincetown Inn **18**
Provincetown
Public Library **11**
Seth Nickerson House ...**16**
Town hall **13**

They lingered for five weeks before moving on to Plymouth. Plaques and parks throughout town commemorate the landing.

Incorporated as a town in 1727, Provincetown was for many decades a bustling seaport, with fishing and whaling as its major industries. In the late 19th century, groups of Portuguese fishermen and whalers began to settle here, lending their expertise and culture to an already cosmopolitan town. Fishing is still an important source of income for many Provincetown locals, but now the town ranks among the world's leading whale-watching—rather than whale-hunting—outposts.

GHOST SHIP

During the American Revolution, Provincetown Harbor was controlled by the British, who used it as a port from which to sail to Boston and launch attacks on colonial and French vessels. In November 1778, the 64-gun British frigate *Somerset* ran aground and was wrecked off Provincetown's Race Point. Every 60 years or so, the shifting sands uncover its remains.

Artists began coming here in the late 1890s to take advantage of the unusual Cape Cod light—in fact, Provincetown is the nation's oldest continuous art colony. Poets, writers, and actors have also been part of the art scene. Eugene O'Neill's first plays were written and produced here, and the Fine Arts Work Center continues to have in its ranks some of the most important writers working today.

During the early 1900s, Provincetown became known as Greenwich Village North. Artists from New York and Europe discovered the town's unspoiled beauty, special light, lively community, and colorful Portuguese flavor. By 1916, with five art schools flourishing here, painters' easels were nearly as common as shells on the beach. This bohemian community, along with the availability of inexpensive summer lodgings, attracted young rebels and writers as well, including John Reed (*Ten Days That Shook the World*) and Mary Heaton Vorse (*Footnote to Folly*), who in 1915 began the Cape's first significant theater group, the Provincetown Players. The young, then unknown Eugene O'Neill joined them in 1916, when his *Bound East for Cardiff* premiered in a tiny wharfside East End fish house. After 1916 the Players moved on to New York. Their theater, at present-day 571 Commercial Street, is long gone, but a model of it and the old Lewis Wharf on which it stood is on display at the Pilgrim Monument museum.

Near the Provincetown border, **massive dunes** actually meet the road in places, turning U.S. 6 into a sand-swept highway. Scattered among the dunes are primitive cottages called dune shacks, built from flotsam and other found materials, that have provided atmospheric as well as cheap lodgings to a number of famous artists and writers over the years—among them poet Harry Kemp, Eugene O'Neill, e. e. cummings, Jack Kerouac, and Norman Mailer. The few surviving shacks are privately leased from the Cape Cod National Seashore, whose proposal to demolish the shacks was halted by their inclusion on the National Register of Historic Places in 1988. The dunes are fragile and should not be walked on, but paths lead through them to the ocean. You can see some of the shacks by van on Art's Dune Tours.

The **Province Lands** begin at High Head in Truro and stretch to the tip of Provincetown. The area is scattered with ponds, cranberry bogs, and scrub; unfortunately, this terrain provides optimal conditions for the deer tick, which can cause Lyme disease, so use extra caution. More than 7 mi of bike and walking trails lace through forests of stunted pines, beech, and oak and across desertlike expanses of rolling dunes. Protected against development, the Province Lands are the "wilds" of the Cape.

A beautiful spot to stop for lunch before biking to the beach, the **Beech Forest picnic area** (⊠ Race Point Rd., east of U.S. 6) in the National Seashore borders a small pond covered with water lilies. The adjacent bike trails lead to Herring Cove and Race Point beaches, which are both part of the National Seashore.

❼ Inside the **Province Lands Visitor Center** in the Cape Cod National Seashore, you'll find literature and nature-related gifts, frequent short films on local geology, and exhibits on the life of the dunes and the shore. You can also pick up information on guided walks, birding trips, lectures, bonfires, and other current programs throughout the seashore, as well as on the Province Lands' own beaches, Race Point and Herring Cove, and walking, biking, and horse trails. Don't miss the wonderful 360-degree view of the dunes and the surrounding ocean from the observation deck. ⊠ *Race Point Rd., east of U.S. 6* ☎ *508/487–1256* ⊕ *www.nps. gov/caco* ☜ *Free* ☉ *May–Oct., daily 9–5.*

Not far from the present Coast Guard station is the **Old Harbor Station,** a U.S. Life Saving Service building rescued from an eroding beach and towed here by barge from Chatham in 1977. It's reached by a boardwalk across the sand, and plaques along the way tell about the lifesaving service and the whales seen offshore. Inside are displays of such equipment as Lyle guns, which shot rescue lines out to ships in distress when seas were too violent to launch a surfboat, and breeches buoys, in which passengers were hauled across those lines to safety. There are reenactments of this old-fashioned lifesaving procedure at 6:30 on Thursday night in summer. ⊠ *Race Point Beach, end of Race Point Rd.* ☎ *No phone* ☜ *Donations accepted; Thurs. night $3* ☉ *July and Aug., daily 3–5 (also 6–8 on Thurs.).*

★ Provincetown's main downtown thoroughfare, **Commercial Street,** is 3 mi from end to end. In season, driving from one end to the other could take forever, so wear comfortable shoes and get ready to walk (although going on foot will take awhile, too, due to the crowds). You'll see signs for parking lots as you head into town. Take a casual stroll and check out the many architectural styles (Greek Revival, Victorian, Second Empire, and Gothic, to name a few) used in the design of the impressive houses for wealthy sea captains and merchants. Be on the lookout for blue plaques fastened to housefronts explaining their historical significance—practically the entire town has been designated part of the

Provincetown Historic District. The Historical Society puts out a series of walking-tour pamphlets—available for about $1 each at many shops in town as well as at the chamber of commerce visitor center—with maps and information on the history of many buildings and the (more or less) famous folk who have occupied them. You may also want to pick up a free Provincetown gallery guide.

The center of town is where the crowds and most of the touristy shops are. The quiet East End is mostly residential, with an increasing number of nationally renowned galleries; the similarly quiet West End has a number of small inns with neat lawns and elaborate gardens.

NEED A BREAK?

The **Aquarium Shops Food Court** (⊠ 205–209 Commercial St.) contains a handful of excellent little fast-food spots. Grab outstanding Mexican fare at **Big Daddy's Burritos**; Asian snacks at **Fortune Cookie**; silky smooth Italian ice cream, hot cocoa, and smoothies at **I Dream of Gelato**; and casual American fare at **Jaqui's Juke Joint**. The **Provincetown Fudge Factory** (⊠ 210 Commercial St., Downtown Center ☎ 508/487-2850 ⊕ www.ptownfudge.com), across from the post office, makes silky peanut-butter cups, chocolates, saltwater taffy, yard-long licorice whips, custom-flavor frozen yogurt, and the creamiest fudge on the Cape—and will ship sweet goodies to you, too.

★ ❽ The first thing you'll see in Provincetown is the **Pilgrim Monument**. This grandiose edifice, which seems somewhat out of proportion to the rest of the low-rise town, commemorates the Pilgrims' first landing in the New World and their signing of the Mayflower Compact (the first colonial-American rules of self-governance) before they set off from Provincetown Harbor to explore the mainland. Climb the 116 steps and 60 short ramps of the 252-foot-high tower for a panoramic view—dunes on one side, harbor on the other, and the entire bay side of Cape Cod beyond. On an exceptionally clear day you can see the Boston skyline. At the tower's base is a museum of Lower Cape and Provincetown history, with exhibits on whaling, shipwrecks, and scrimshaw; a diorama of the *Mayflower;* and another of a glass factory.

The tower was erected of granite shipped from Maine, according to a design modeled on a tower in Siena, Italy. President Theodore Roosevelt laid the cornerstone in 1907, and President Howard Taft attended the 1910 dedication. On Thanksgiving Eve, in a ceremony that includes a museum tour and open house, 5,000 white and gold lights that drape the tower are illuminated—a display that can be seen from as far away as the Cape Cod Canal. They are lighted nightly into the New Year. ⊠ *High Pole Hill Rd.* ☎ *508/487–1310* ⊕ *www.pilgrim-monument. org* ⊠ *$7* ⊙ *Apr.–June, Sept., and Oct., daily 9–4:15; July and Aug., daily 9–6:15; Nov., Fri.–Sun. 9–4:15.*

❾ **MacMillan Wharf**, with its large municipal parking facility, is a sensible place to start a tour of town. It's one of five remaining wharves of the original 54 that once jutted into the bay. The wharf serves as the base for P-town whale-watch boats, fishing charters, and party boats. The **Chamber of Commerce** is also here, with all kinds of information and events schedules. Kiosks at the wharf have restroom and parking-lot locations, bus schedules, and other information for visitors.

The former Provincetown Marina building, on MacMillan Wharf, holds the **Expedition *Whydah* Sea Lab and Learning Center,** a home for artifacts recovered from the pirate ship *Whydah*, which sank off the coast of Wellfleet in 1717. The *Whydah* is the only pirate shipwreck ever authenticated anywhere in the world, and the museum, though tiny, is entertaining and educational, with one display on the restoration and conservation processes and another on the untold story of the 18th-century pirating life. The curators hope to eventually collect all the recovered pieces; some are on loan to other museums across the country. ⊠ *16 MacMillan Wharf, Downtown Center* ☎ *508/487–8899 or 800/949–3241* ⊕ *www.whydah. com* ✉ *$8* ⊙ *June–early Sept., daily 9–8; Apr., May, and early Sept.–Oct., weekdays 10–4, weekends 10–5; Nov. and Dec., weekends 10–4.*

⑩
Fodor'sChoice
★

Founded in 1914 to collect and show the works of artists with Provincetown connections, the **Provincetown Art Association and Museum** (PAAM) has a 1,650-piece permanent collection, displayed in changing exhibits that mix up-and-comers with established 20th-century figures, including Milton Avery, Philip Evergood, William Gropper, Charles Hawthorne, Robert Motherwell, Claes Oldenburg, Man Ray, John Singer Sargent, Andy Warhol, and Agnes Weinrich. Some of the work hung in the four bright galleries is for sale. The museum store carries books of local interest, including works by or about area artists and authors, as well as posters, crafts, cards, and gift items. PAAM-sponsored year-round courses (one day and longer) offer the opportunity to study under such talents as Hilda Neily, Franny Golden, and Doug Ritter. A stunning, contemporary wing was added in 2005, greatly expanding the exhibit space. ⊠ *460 Commercial St., East End* ☎ *508/487–1750* ⊕ *www.paam. org* ✉ *$3 donation suggested* ⊙ *Late May–early July and Sept., daily noon–5, also Fri. and Sat. 8 PM–10 PM; early July and Aug., daily noon–5 and 8 PM–10 PM; Oct.–May, Thurs.–Sun. noon–5.*

★ ⑪ In 2005, the **Provincetown Public Library** moved into the beautifully restored and redesigned Center Methodist Church, a towering 1860 beauty in the East End whose steeple you can see from the harbor and much of town. On rainy days, this is a wonderful place to read, work, or check your e-mail on one of the several public computers. You can also check out *The Rose Dorothea*, a half-scale replica of an early 1900s fishing schooner that was built by some 15 Provincetown fishermen and woodworkers as a tribute to the town's rich nautical heritage. The 62-foot-long boat has ingeniously been built into the the library's second floor. Architecturally, this is one of the town's most striking and distinctive buildings, but it's also a great cultural resource, hosting children's storytelling on Wednesday and Saturday mornings, educational workshops, and other community events. There's also a children's room with computers, books, and educational resources. As of this writing, the building's lower level was still under construction—it will eventually house a gallery space showing rotating local exhibits. ⊠ *356 Commercial St., East End* ☎ *508/487–7094* ⊕ *www.ptownlib.com* ✉ *Free*

⊙ Mon. and Fri. 10–5, Tues. and Thurs. noon–8, Wed. 10–8, Sat. 10–2, Sun. 1–5.

NEED A
BREAK?
Wired Puppy (⊠ 379 Commercial St., East End ☎ 508/487–0017) is a slick but comfy Internet café with hardwood floors and mod seating. They serve outstanding organic coffees and teas—the knowledgeable staff can help you choose just the right beverage—plus a nice variety of cookies, brownies, and treats. There's free Wi-Fi if you bring your own laptop, or you can borrow a laptop here.

⑫ To see or hear the work of up-and-coming artists, visit the gallery or attend a reading at the **Fine Arts Work Center** (FAWC). A nonprofit organization founded in 1968, the FAWC sponsors 10 writers and 10 artists from October through May each year, providing them with a place to live and work, a stipend, and access to artists and teachers. A summer program has open-enrollment workshops in both writing and the visual arts. The buildings in the complex around the center, which it owns, were formerly part of Day's Lumber Yard Studios, built above a lumberyard by a patron of the arts to provide poor artists with cheap accommodations. Robert Motherwell, Hans Hoffmann, and Helen Frankenthaler have been among the studios' roster of residents over the years. ⊠ *24 Pearl St., East End* ☎ *508/487–9960* ⊕ *www.fawc.org* ⊠ *Free, $5 for events and readings* ⊙ *Weekdays 9–5, events are usually held in evening.*

⑬ The **town hall** was used by the Provincetown Art Association as its first exhibit space. Paintings donated to the town over the years—including Provincetown scenes by Charles Hawthorne and WPA-era murals by Ross Moffett—are still displayed here. ⊠ *260 Commercial St., Downtown Center* ☎ *508/487–7000* ⊙ *Weekdays 8–5.*

⑭ In a little park behind the town hall is the **Mayflower Compact Plaque** (⊠ Bradford St., Downtown Center), carved in bas-relief by sculptor Cyrus Dalin and depicting the historic signing.

⑮ An **octagonal house** (⊠ 74 Commercial St., West End) built in 1850 is an interesting piece of Provincetown architecture in the West End. The house is not open to the public.

⑯ The oldest building in town, dating from 1746, is the small Cape-style **Seth Nickerson House** (⊠ 72 Commercial St., West End), which is still a private home. It was built by a ship's carpenter, with massive pegged, hand-hewn oak beams and wide-board floors. Modern renovations have somewhat obscured the glimpse into centuries past that it once possessed, but it's still impressive.

⑰ The bronze **Pilgrim Plaque** (⊠ West end of Commercial St., Downtown Center), set into a boulder at the center of a little park, commemorates the first footfall of the Pilgrims onto Cape soil—Provincetown's humble equivalent to Plymouth Rock.

⑱ In the **Provincetown Inn** (⊠ 1 Commercial St., West End ☎ 508/487–9500) you can see a series of 19 murals, painted in the 1930s from old postcards, depicting life in the 19th-century town. The inn still operates as a hotel; the murals are in the lobby and hallways.

Where to Stay & Eat

$$-$$$$ ✕ **Cafe Edwige.** A longtime East End restaurant set rather discreetly up a flight of stairs, Cafe Edwige consists of an intimate dining room with varnished-wood floors and dim lighting, and a casual side patio with tile tables and billowing drapes. Start things off at the bar with one of their signature white-ginger cosmos, and perhaps the tuna-avocado tartare appetizer with sweet-chili vinaigrette and wasabi cream, which has long been a staple here. Popular entrées from the contemporary menu include the Provincetown paella, with lobster, shrimp, squid, clams, chicken, chorizo, and saffron-arborio rice; or the grilled New Zealand rack of lamb with a feta-risotto-spinach cake, haricot vert, and a lamb demi-glace. For breakfast, consider the omelet with Portobello mushrooms and Brie. ✉ *333 Commercial St.* ☎ *508/487-4020* ▭ *MC, V* ⊙ *Closed Oct.–Apr., Mon.–Thurs. May–mid-June, and Wed.*

$$-$$$$
Fodor'sChoice
★ ✕ **Devon's.** This unassuming, tiny white cottage—with a dining room that seats just 37 lucky patrons—serves up some of the best food in town. Specialties from the oft-changing menu include pan-seared halibut with caramelized orange glaze, black rice, and sautéed beet greens; and free-range seared duck with a Syrah reduction, red onion marmalade, and couscous primavera. Another plus is their great little wine list. Be sure to save some room for knockout dessert selections like blackberry mousse over ginger-lemon polenta cake with wildberry coulis. Devon's also serves up a terrific breakfast each day, where you might sample truffle cheese-and-baby spinach omelets with rosemary homefries. Hours are limited in May and October; it's best to phone ahead. ✉ *401½ Commercial St.* ☎ *508/487-4773* ⊕ *www.devons.org* ⩜ *Reservations essential* ▭ *MC, V* ⊙ *Closed Wed. and Nov.–Apr.*

★ **$$-$$$$** ✕ **Front Street.** Front Street is very good and quite romantic, if not as revered by locals as it used to be (in part because several noteworthy competitors have opened in recent years). Here classic Italian cooking is linked to offerings from Greece, southern France, and even North Africa. There's a nightly char-grilled fish special: match salmon, swordfish, or tuna with a Latin, Berber, or Cajun spice rub; lemon-caper butter; or a ginger-soy-wasabi glaze. Other stellar dishes include Carolina crab–stuffed filet mignon and a truffled veal-and-lobster napoleon. The wine list is also a winner. Finish things off with raspberry-chocolate tiramisu. ✉ *230 Commercial St.* ☎ *508/487-9715* ⊕ *www.frontstreetrestaurant. com* ⩜ *Reservations essential* ▭ *AE, D, MC, V* ⊙ *Closed Jan.–mid-May and Tues. No lunch.*

$$-$$$$
Fodor'sChoice
★ ✕ **The Mews.** This perennial favorite with magnificent harbor views focuses on seafood with a cross-cultural flair. Some popular entrées include roasted vegetable and polenta lasagna with a tomato-olive sauce; and an 8-ounce flatiron steak and scallops with chili butter and a savory bread pudding of applewood-smoked bacon and mushrooms. A piano bar upstairs serves lunch (weekdays in summer) and dinner from a light, less-expensive café menu (burgers, tarragon chicken potpie). The view of the bay from the bar is nearly perfect, and the gentle lighting makes this a romantic spot to have a drink. Brunch is also served daily in season. The restaurant claims its vodka bar is New England's largest. ✉ *429 Commercial St.* ☎ *508/487-1500* ⊕ *www.mews.com* ▭ *AE,*

Where to Eat in Provincetown

Bayside Betsy's **17**
Bubala's by the Bay **16**
Cafe Edwige **7**
Chach **19**
Ciro & Sal's **2**
Clem & Ursie's **20**
Devon's **4**

Fanizzi's by the Sea **1**
Front Street **13**
Lobster Pot **8**
Lorraine's **18**
L'Uva **11**
The Mews **3**
Napi's **6**

Post Office Café **9**
Provincetown
  Portuguese Bakery **10**
Ross' Grill **12**
Spiritus **15**
Thai Aroi **14**
Tofu A Go-Go **5**

D, DC, MC, V ⊗ *Closed Jan. No lunch weekdays off-season or Sat. mid-Oct.–late May.*

★ **$$–$$$$** ✕ **Ross' Grill.** Likening itself to a French bistro with American tastes, the kitchen here is modest but busy, preparing everything from scratch, including its signature hand-cut, double-dipped french fries. Local fish and shellfish dominate the menu; a favorite is the sautéed local sea scallops with leeks, garlic, and pear tomatoes over linguine. Portions are generous—you'll get eight meaty racks of baby New Zealand lamb—and prices are reasonable. Choose from 75 wines by the glass. The location is grand: up on the second floor of the Whaler's Wharf complex, views of Province-town Harbor are unlimited. It's a popular place, so expect a wait. ⊠ *237 Commercial St.* ☎ *508/487–8878* ⌂ *Reservations not accepted* ☐ *AE, MC, V* ⊗ *Closed Tues. and Wed. Jan.–Apr.*

$–$$$$ ✕ **Ciro & Sal's.** Tucked inside a cozy house down an alley behind Commercial Street, this longtime local favorite offers a low-key, romantic alternative to some of the town's busier restaurants. The most memorable tables are inside a cozy brick wine cellar; the rest fill a pair of art-filled dining rooms; one is warmed by a huge fireplace. You can also relax with a cocktail on the garden patio. The restaurant is justly known for its fresh pastas and bountiful antipasto selections. Favorite entrées include calamari sautéed with anchovies, lemon, garlic, and cream; and chicken livers sautéed with prosciutto, Marsala wine, and sage. Hours vary during the off-season—call ahead. ⊠ *4 Kiley Ct.* ☎ *508/487–6444* ⊕ *www.ciroandsals.com* ☐ *AE, D, MC, V* ⊗ *Closed Jan. No lunch.*

★ **$$–$$$** ✕ **L'Uva.** L'Uva—which occupies an 1840s cottage—ranks among Provincetown's most sophisticated and memorable small restaurants. The menu works off a novel premise: it's divided into four distinct culinary categories—Italian, French, Spanish, and American—and everything is prepared with artful, innovative flair. For instance, the filet mignon comes with a star-anise demi-glace, the cod is wrapped in flaky phyllo dough and paired with a feathery spinach-cream sauce, and the filet mignon comes with a tamarind-and-chipotle demi-glace. For dessert, dive into the lavender or ginger crème brûlée. ⊠ *133 Bradford St.* ☎ *508/487–2010* ⊕ *www.luvarestaurant.com* ☐ *AE, MC, V* ⊗ *Closed Dec.–Apr. No lunch.*

$$–$$$ ✕ **Napi's.** A steady favorite for its lively ambience and dependable Mediterranean fare, Napi's presents a long and varied menu. The food and the interior share a penchant for unusual, striking juxtapositions—a classical sculpture in front of an abstract canvas, for instance. On the gustatory front, look for sharp combinations such as shrimp Santa Fe, sautéed with tequila, fresh lime juice, cilantro, garlic, roasted chipotle peppers, and black beans with a zippy gazpacho garnish. A cashew vegetable stir-fry is just one of several very nice vegetarian dishes. ⊠ *7 Freeman St.* ☎ *508/487–1145 or 800/571–6274* ⊕ *www.napis-restaurant.com* ☐ *AE, D, DC, MC, V* ⊗ *No lunch May–Sept.*

$–$$$ ✕ **Bayside Betsy's.** Named for the feisty chef and co-owner, this campy, infectiously fun bar-and-grill serves a mix of homespun American favorites and slightly more contemporary dishes, such as lobster tortellini, seafood wontons with orange-horseradish sauce, and classic steamed mussels in white wine with garlic, shallots, and tomatoes. Nightly specials

Where to Stay in Provincetown

EAST END

TO ROUTE 6A

Provincetown Harbor

MacMillan Wharf

750 yards
750 meters

TO RACE POINT BEACH

Duck Pond

Shank Painter Pond

TO RACE POINT LIGHT

TO LONG POINT LIGHT

WEST END

Province Lands Rd.

Streets: Howland, Harry Kemp Way, Bradford St., Priscilla Alden, Brewster, Pearl, Conwell, Law, Arch, Center, Johnson, Standish, Cemetery, Alden, Ryder, Winslow, Gosnold, Masonic, Prince, Carver, Court, Winthrop, Central St., Commercial St., Pleasant, Franklin, Nickerson, Tremont St., Soper, W. Vine, Blueberry, Creek Rd., Shank Painter Rd., Jerome Rd.

Ampersand Guesthouse **17**
Anchor Inn **14**
Benchmark Inn & Central **4**
Best Western Chateau Motor Inn **9**
Brass Key **13**
Christopher's by the Bay .. **8**
The Commons **5**
Crown & Anchor **11**
Crowne Pointe Historic Inn and Spa ...**12**
1807 House **18**
Fairbanks Inn **10**
Inn at Cook Street **2**
Officer's Quarters **15**
Oxford House **16**
Race Point Lighthouse .. **20**
Red Inn **19**
Seasons **7**
Snug Cottage **3**
Somerset House Inn **6**
Watermark Inn **1**

often reflect the luck of local fishermen. You might try pan-seared scallops with chorizo tossed with fettuccine. You can expect reliable food for breakfast (try the banana-walnut pancakes), lunch, and dinner year-round, but the real draws are the colorful people-watching, good-natured attitude, and nice views of Provincetown Harbor. ⊠ *177 Commercial St.* ☎ *508/487–6566* ⊕ *www.baysidebetsys.com* ⊟ *AE, D, MC, V* ☺ *Closed Mon.–Wed. Nov.–May.*

$–$$$ ✕ **Bubala's by the Bay.** Look for the bright yellow building adorned on top with campy carved birds. The kitchen rarely stops, serving breakfast, lunch, and dinner; it's strong on seafood bought directly off local boats. Lobster salad, seafood cassoulet with white beans and chorizo, and grilled venison rack with currant, sage, and shiitake demi-glace are wonderfully fresh and tasty. The wine list is priced practically at retail, and the U-shaped bar picks up into the evening. Outdoor seating is a social focal point, whereas quieter indoor seating reaches right down to the bay. It's one of the few Commercial Street restaurants with off-street parking. ⊠ *183 Commercial St.* ☎ *508/487–0773* ⊕ *www. bubalas.com* ⊟ *AE, D, MC, V* ☺ *Closed late Oct.–late Apr.*

★ **$–$$$** ✕ **Fanizzi's by the Sea.** A dependable, year-round East Ender that sits directly over the bay and offers fine water views, Fanizzi's presents a varied menu heavy on comfort food (including a memorable chicken potpie), but often with a few creative twists. The baked cod is served with a tangy coating of almonds and mustard, and the hearty roasted half chicken is glazed with fresh garlic, lemon juice, rosemary, and thyme. You can order burgers and substantive dinner salads, including a fine salmon Caesar. The dining room, lined with large windows, is softly lighted and casual. ⊠ *539 Commercial St.* ☎ *508/487–1964* ⊟ *AE, D, DC, MC, V.*

$–$$$ ✕ **Lobster Pot.** Provincetown's Lobster Pot is fit to do battle with all the lobster shanties anywhere (and everywhere) else on the Cape—it's often jammed with tourists, but that's truly a reflection of the consistently high quality. The hardworking kitchen turns out classic New England cooking: lobsters, generous and filling seafood platters (try the seafood Pico with a half lobster, shrimp, littlenecks, mussels, calamari, and fish over pasta with tomatoes, rose wine, onions, and garlic), and some of the best chowder around. The Asian bouillabaisse is another favorite. The upstairs deck overlooks the comings and goings of the harbor and is a great spot for lunch. There's also a take-out lobster market and bakery on the premises. You'll have to wait in line, but you'll be in the center of town—an ideal place for people-watching. ⊠ *321 Commercial St.* ☎ *508/487–0842* ⊕ *www.ptownlobsterpot.com* ⌲ *Reservations not accepted* ⊟ *AE, D, DC, MC, V* ☺ *Closed Jan.*

★ **$–$$$** ✕ **Lorraine's.** In a cozy cottage toward the West End, Lorraine's has an intimate feel, but the nouvelle Latin American–inspired menu is as good as ever. An appetizer of blackened seafood tostadas with black bean-and-corn relish packs a punch, and the tender, slow-cooked pork carnitas are a revelation. Also wonderful is a mesquite-grilled rack of lamb with roasted-garlic chipotle demi-glace. The bar draws a loyal, lively crowd and is famous for its long list of premium tequilas. A tantalizing brunch is served in summer—consider the chorizo with scrambled eggs, tortillas, and beans. ✉ *133 Commercial St.* ☎ *508/487–6074* ⊕ *www.lorrainesrestaurant.com* ▤ *MC, V* ⊘ *Closed Mon.–Wed. Nov.–Mar. No lunch.*

¢–$$$ ✕ **Clem & Ursie's.** It's worth the short drive or long walk from downtown
Fodor'sChoice to sample the tantalizing seafood prepared at this colorful café,
★ grocery market, cocktail bar, and bakery. The mammoth menu touches on just about every kind of food from the ocean: tuna steaks, crab claws, squid stew, Japanese baby octopus salad, hot lobster rolls, lobster scampi—even sushi. The Buffalo shrimp are addictive, and be sure to try the Portuguese clam pie. A nice range of nonfishy items is offered, too, from pulled pork barbecue to bacon cheeseburgers—plus great desserts like pistachio cake and stuffed ice-cream sandwiches dipped in chocolate. You order and pay at the counter and grab a seat inside the decidedly casual dining room; they bring your chow out to you. The market has the best selection of cheeses in town plus countless seafood items, oils and vinegars, and gourmet goods. ✉ *85 Shank Painter Rd.* ☎ *508/487–2333* ⊕ *www.clemandursies.com* ▤ *MC, V* ⊘ *Closed mid-Nov.–mid-Apr.*

¢–$$ ✕ **Post Office Cafe.** A dapper yet casual bistro beneath Provincetown's favorite cabaret bar, the Post Office serves food most nights until 1 AM, making it one of the area's best options for late-night snacking. The kitchen turns out a mix of substantial but straightforward American entrées, such as scallops Alfredo, along with lighter pub favorites. Sandwiches are a specialty; consider the grilled yellowfin tuna and greens on focaccia, or the grilled portobello mushroom with artichokes, sundried tomatoes, roasted red peppers, feta cheese, and mixed greens on a pita. The place becomes increasingly festive—even a little raucous—the later it gets. ✉*303 Commercial St.* ☎ *508/487–3892* ▤ *AE, D, MC, V.*

¢–$$ ✕ **Thai Aroi.** Bringing a much-needed dose of Asian deliciousness to the Outer Cape, this cozy eatery inside the shaggy Gifford House Inn serves reasonably authentic, well-seasoned fare. You might start with a salad of spicy minced chicken with fresh ginger, lime, and roasted peanuts, or the fried crab rolls. Excellent main dishes include sweet-and-sour squid with stir-fried pineapple and veggies, basil fried rice with tofu and vegetables, salmon pad thai, and boneless duck with tamarind sauce. ✉ *9 Carver St.* ☎ *508/487–0889* ▤ *MC, V.*

¢–$ ✕ **Chach.** A cute, airy, and contemporary clapboard restaurant out on Shank Painter Road toward the beach, Chach is a big hit with locals. It's a sweet little place serving creative omelets (try one with green chili, cheddar, and sour cream), vanilla custard French toast with Vermont maple syrup, fried chicken salad with buttermilk dressing, and falafel sandwiches with cucumber-mint sauce. Fresh ingredients and artful presentation make this a winner. Closing time is 3 PM. ✉ *73 Shank Painter Rd.* ☎ *508/487–1530* ▤ *MC, V* ⊘ *No dinner.*

¢–$ ✕ **Provincetown Portuguese Bakery.** This town standby makes fresh Portuguese breads and pastries and serves breakfast and lunch all day from March to October. Although it may be difficult to choose among the sweet splendor, favorite pastries include *malassadas,* a sweet fried dough; lemon custard; sponge cake with Bavarian creme; and the more unusual *trutas,* with rich, sweet potato filling. It's open until 11 PM in summer.

✉ *299 Commercial St.* ☎ *508/487–1803* ▭ *No credit cards* ⊘ *Closed Nov.–Feb. No dinner.*

¢–$ ✕ **Spiritus.** The local bars close at 1 AM, at which point this pizza joint–coffee stand becomes the town's epicenter. It's the ultimate place to see and be seen, pizza slice in hand and witty banter at the ready. In the morning, the same counter serves restorative coffee and croissants as well as Häagen-Dazs ice cream. ✉ *190 Commercial St.* ☎ *508/487–2808* ▭ *No credit cards* ⊘ *Closed Nov.–Apr.*

¢–$ ✕ **Tofu A Go-Go.** This popular spot for light snacks and quick meals serves
Fodor'sChoice consistently fresh vegetarian and vegan fare to a wildly devoted cadre
★ of regulars. It's open for three meals daily. Try tofu breakfast burritos in the morning or gazpacho and the hummus-and-tabouli platter at lunch. Enticing dinner specialties include brown rice with tamari-ginger sauce, grilled tofu, black and pinto beans, greens, and seaweed; tempeh Reuben sandwiches; and Thai veggie burritos. There's a casual dining area upstairs and more seating out on a front deck with great views of passersby along Commercial Street. ✉ *336 Commercial St.* ☎ *508/487–6237* ⊕ *www.tofuagogo.com* ▭ *No credit cards* ⊘ *Closed Wed. No dinner early Sept.–May.*

$$$–$$$$ ⊞ **Benchmark Inn & Central.** Made up of two separate buildings on a quiet, narrow street just a block from downtown, this is an inn of simple, refined luxury. Rooms are painted in soothing neutral tones, floors are bare wood, and fresh flowers are placed atop every stainless-steel wet bar; the bathrooms have marble tile and hair dryers. Most rooms have private entrances and fireplaces; some have skylights and private balconies with rooftop and water views. When you're ready to turn in, indulge in the nightly turndown service. There are also three very large and cushy penthouse suites. ✉ *6 and 8 Dyer St., 02657* ☎ *508/487–7440 or 888/487–7440* 🖷 *508/487–3446* ⊕ *www.benchmarkinn.com* 🛏 *11 rooms, 3 suites* ♻ *Minibars, refrigerators, cable TV, in-room VCRs, Wi-Fi, pool, 2 hot tubs, sauna, laundry service, concierge, airport shuttle; no smoking* ▭ *AE, MC, V* ⊘ *Closed Jan.–late Feb.*

★ $$–$$$$ ⊞ **Anchor Inn.** Run by the same talented team that operates the West End's Red Inn, this regal, turreted beach house in the heart of Provincetown enjoys a wonderful location just steps from bars, shops, and restaurants as well as unobstructed water views from most rooms (rooms without water views cost a fraction of the price). White-picket porches and balconies envelope the inn's dapper shingle exterior. You won't find frill and excess here—the airy rooms are done in a palette of whites and tans, with tasteful wicker furniture and, in many cases, four-poster beds and fireplaces. Four cottage units have private entrances, and the three most romantic accommodations occupy the turret. With a spacious lobby and professional staff, the Anchor feels more like a small luxury hotel than a typical Provincetown guesthouse, but an air of informality keeps the vibe relaxed and fun. There's a substantial Continental breakfast buffet in the morning. ✉ *175 Commercial St., west of Downtown Center, 02657* ☎ *508/487–0432 or 800/858–2657* ⊕ *www.anchorinnbeachhouse.com* 🛏 *25 rooms* ♻ *Some in-room hot tubs, refrigerators, cable TV, in-room VCRs* ▭ *MC, V* ◉⬚ *CP.*

$$–$$$$ ⊡ **Brass Key.** One of the Cape's most luxurious small resorts, this metic-
Fodor'sChoice ulously-kept year-round getaway comprises a beautifully restored main
★ house—originally an 1828 sea captain's home—and several other care-
fully groomed buildings and cottages. Rooms mix antiques with such
modern amenities as Bose stereos and TV–VCRs (loaner laptops and
iPod docks are also available). Deluxe rooms come with gas fireplaces
and whirlpool baths or French doors opening onto wrought-iron bal-
conies. A widow's-walk sundeck has a panoramic view of Cape Cod
Bay. Complimentary cocktails are served in the courtyard; in winter, wine
is served before a roaring fire in the common room. As is true of many
of Provincetown's smaller hotels, the Brass Key draws a largely gay clien-
tele, especially in summer, but the owners and staff make everyone feel
welcome and pampered. ⊠ *67 Bradford St., 02657* ☎ *508/487–9005
or 800/842–9858* 🖷 *508/487–9020* ⊕ *www.brasskey.com* ⇆ *42 rooms
⌂ In-room safes, some in-room hot tubs, cable TV, in-room VCRs, Wi-
Fi, pool, hot tubs; no kids under 16, no smoking* ⊟ *AE, D, MC, V* ⭗ *CP.*

$$–$$$$ ✕⊡ **Crown & Anchor.** If you're looking to eat, sleep, and live amid the
pulsing entertainment center of Provincetown, this is the place. Upstairs
from the daily clamor of drag shows and discos are 18 rooms handsomely
adorned with Oriental rugs and deep cranberry hues. Deluxe rooms have
two-person whirlpool tubs, fireplaces, and private balconies facing
Provincetown Harbor; all rooms have the choice of a king or two full-
size beds. In addition, two rooms are fully ADA compliant. One draw-
back, however, is that you can hear the din and vibration of music and
conversation downstairs in the bars and discos until about midnight or
1 AM on many evenings. Complimentary continental breakfast is served,
but why not take advantage of the choice room service and simply stay
in bed? Later in the day, stop by the open-air Central House Bar & Grill
($–$$$, closed Wed. and Thurs.) for commendable contemporary Amer-
ican fare, such as pomegranate-honey-glazed chicken with grilled pineap-
ple relish; and scallops baked in parchment with baby spinach, citrus
butter, and orange zest. A highly professional staff with a great attitude
holds everything together. ⊠ *247 Commercial St., 02657* ☎ *508/487–
1430* 🖷 *508/487–3237* ⊕ *www.onlyatthecrown.com* ⇆ *18 rooms* ⌂ *2
restaurants, some in-room hot tubs, microwaves, minibars, refrigera-
tors, cable TV, Wi-Fi, pool, beach, 5 bars, lounge, cabaret, dance club,
business services* ⊟ *AE, D, MC, V* ⭗ *CP.*

$$–$$$$ ✕⊡ **Crowne Pointe Historic Inn and Spa.** Created meticulously from six
Fodor'sChoice different buildings, this inn has not left a single detail unattended. Own-
★ ers Tom Walter and David Sanford skillfully mix luxury and comfort.
Period furniture and antiques fill the common areas and rooms; a queen-
size bed is the smallest you'll find, dressed in 250-thread-count linens,
with treats on the pillow for nightly turndown service. Many rooms have
fireplaces: in one room, you can view the flames from your bed or the
whirlpool tub. Penthouse suites have two floors of living space with a
full kitchen, and many rooms have private balconies with water or
town views. The grounds are accented with brick pathways, flowers,
and trees. Start the day with a full, hot breakfast, then graze on freshly
baked treats and wine and cheese in the afternoon. Opened in 2005,
The Bistro at Crowne Pointe ($–$$$) serves finely crafted, healthful, mod-

ern American food, such as duck wontons with a tamarind-citrus dipping sauce, and Moroccan-spiced rack of lamb with red couscous, apricot-pistachio tapenade, and green beans. In the handsome, full-service Shui Spa (open to guests and the public by reservation), you might opt for such soothing treatments as Shiatsu massage, craniosacral therapy, or the honey-almond body polish. ✉ *82 Bradford St., 02657* ☎ *508/ 487–6767 or 877/276–9631* 🖷 *508/487–5554* ⊕ *www.crownepointe. com* ☞ *37 rooms, 3 suites* ☼ *Some in-room hot tubs, some kitchens, some microwaves, refrigerators, cable TV, in-room VCRs, Wi-Fi, pool, 2 outdoor hot tubs, spa, laundry service, concierge, business services, airport shuttle; no smoking* ▤ *AE, D, MC, V* ⦿ *BP.*

\$\$–\$\$\$\$ 🏠 **Officer's Quarters.** Built in 1887 for a sea captain, this stately mansard-roof Victorian is only a short walk from the center of town and is across the street from Provincetown Bay. The owners have done a wonderful job adding their own touches while maintaining this B&B's outstanding reputation. Room 3, done in vibrant reds, has a four-poster bed, a gas fireplace, and private access to the garden. Most rooms have water views; some have private decks. ✉ *164 Commercial St., 02657* ☎ *508/487–1850 or 800/400–2278* ⊕ *www.officersquarters.org* ☞ *6 rooms* ☼ *Refrigerators, cable TV, in-room VCRs, Wi-Fi, hot tub, some pets allowed (fee); no smoking* ▤ *D, MC, V* ⦿ *CP.*

\$\$–\$\$\$\$ ✕🏠 **Red Inn.** A rambling red 1915 house that once was host to Franklin and Eleanor Roosevelt, this small, luxurious inn has been completely refurbished after several years of neglect. Most of the airy rooms afford bay views, and all are fitted with big plush beds with high-thread-count linens, goosedown comforters, and pillow-top mattresses. Other luxe amenities include radio–CD players, phones with voice mail, and high-speed Internet. The Cape Light Room contains a decorative fireplace with an ornate hand-painted fresco, and the secluded Chauffer's Cottage has a living room with a soaring vaulted ceiling and a sundeck with far-reaching water views. The intimate, low-key restaurant (\$\$–\$\$\$\$) serves inventive contemporary fare but can be hit-or-miss in terms of both food and service. You might start off with the sweet and chunky lobster-corn chowder before moving on to pepper-crusted filet mignon with truffle-mashed potatoes and onion-garlic-butter sauce. Brunch is served Thursday through Sunday. ✉ *15 Commercial St., 02657* ☎ *508/ 487–7334 or 866/473–3466* 🖷 *508/487–5115* ⊕ *www.theredinn.com* ☞ *4 rooms, 2 suites, 2 cottages* ☼ *Restaurant, room service, in-room hot tubs, refrigerators, cable TV, in-room VCRs, in-room broadband, massage, free parking; no kids under 18, no smoking* ▤ *AE, MC, V* ⦿ *CP.*

★ \$\$–\$\$\$\$ 🏠 **Somerset House Inn.** In 2005 new owners took over this cheerful property known for its hip, whimsical decor and superb personal service—and they've done an excellent job with it. From the outside, the inn looks like a classic 1830s Provincetown house, but inside it's a cozy den of mod sofas and cool colors. A communal computer is equipped with high-speed wireless, and you'll find reams of magazines throughout the common areas. The sleekly furnished rooms are compact but charming. Some have eclectic themes—safari, Asia, modern—and all have updated amenities, such as flat-screen TVs, DVD players, and L'Occitaine toiletries. The third-floor units, with pitched ceilings, are especially romantic; some have fireplaces. Somerset House serves one of the better breakfasts in town and also has an extensive afternoon wine-and-cheese social. ⊠ *378 Commercial St., east of Downtown Center, 02657* ☎ *508/487–0383 or 800/575–1850* 🖷 *508/487–4237* ⊕ *www.somersethouseinn.com* 🛏 *12 rooms* ♨ *Some in-room hot tubs, refrigerators, cable TV, in-room DVDs, Wi-Fi* ═ *AE, MC, V* ¶◎¶ *BP.*

$$–$$$$ 🖼 **Watermark Inn.** A modern all-suites inn facing the bay at the very east end of Commercial Street, the Watermark has enormous accommodations with separate living–dining rooms, making it a favorite for longer stays (weekly or daily rates are available in summer; rates are daily the rest of the year). Although these airy suites with tall windows feel more like rental condos than hotel rooms, they do come with fine linens and daily maid service. It's a very private setup, and guests enjoy plenty of independence. Four suites on the top level have private sundecks and panoramic water views; two less-expensive ground-floor units overlook a courtyard. ⊠ *603 Commercial St., 02657* ☎ *508/487–0165* 🖷 *508/487–2383* ⊕ *www.watermark-inn.com* 🛏 *10 suites* ♨ *Some kitchens, some kitchenettes, cable TV; no smoking* ═ *MC, V.*

$$–$$$ 🖼 **Best Western Chateau Motor Inn.** This inn may be part of a chain, but the personal attention of owners Charlotte and Bill Gordon, whose family has run the place for decades, shows in the landscaped grounds and in the well-maintained modern rooms with wall-to-wall carpeting and tile baths. Atop a hill with expansive views of marsh, dunes, and sea, the motel is a longish walk to the center of town but relatively close to beaches. There's talk of the hotel eventually going condo, but it's expected to remain open through at least 2007. ⊠ *105 Bradford St. Ext., Box 558, 02657* ☎ *508/487–1286 or 800/528–1234* 🖷 *508/487–3557* ⊕ *www.bestwestern.com/chateaumotorinn* 🛏 *54 rooms* ♨ *Refrigerators, cable TV, in-room broadband, pool; no smoking* ═ *AE, D, DC, MC, V* ⊘ *Closed Nov.–Apr.* ¶◎¶ *CP.*

★ $$–$$$ 🖼 **Inn at Cook Street.** In winter 2006, this attractive East End inn just off Bradford Street sold to a developer who planned to convert it into condos, but Connecticut transplants Lisa Feistel and Doreen Birdsell quickly stepped in, snapped it up, and turned it back into a terrific place to stay. The enthusiastic new innkeepers have done an admirable job decorating the 1836 Greek Revival where author Michael Cunningham penned *Home at the End of the World* one winter. The sophisticated rooms have high-thread-count linens, flat-screen TVs, and well-placed reading lights; two have decks, three have fireplaces, and three have private entrances. Continental breakfast includes organic cappuccino, herbal teas, fruit and breads, and a hot entrée such as pancakes or an omelet. Guests can relax in a hammock out back amid the fragrant gardens or walk a block to the galleries along Commercial Street. ⊠ *7 Cook St., 02657* ☎ *508/487–3894 or 888/266–5655* ⊕ *www.innatcookstreet.com* 🛏 *4 rooms, 1 suite, 2 cottages* ♨ *BBQ, some kitchenettes, refrigerators, cable TV, in-room DVDs, Wi-Fi; no children under 16* ═ *MC, V* ¶◎¶ *BP.*

★ $$–$$$ 🖼 **Oxford House.** Run by the former owners of the outstanding Beaconlight Guesthouse, the Oxford sits in the heart of the West End along a quiet lane and is decorated in the spirit of a British country house. Rooms come with linen robes, CD player/radios, phones with voice mail, and beds that have 480-thread-count linens and fluffy duvets. You can save a bundle by booking either the Merton or Hertford rooms, which share a bath; the Worcester Room has its own private entrance. The evening wine hour is a great time to mingle with fellow guests. All phone calls within the continental United States are free. ⊠ *8 Cottage St., 02657* ☏ *508/487–9103 or 888/456–9103* ⊕ *www.oxfordguesthouse. com* ⟿ *5 rooms, 3 with bath, 1 suite* ⚫ *Refrigerators, cable TV, in-room VCRs, Wi-Fi, business services* ⊟ *AE, D, MC, V* ⦿ *CP.*

$–$$$ ⊡ **Fairbanks Inn.** This meticulously restored colonial inn a block from Commercial Street includes the 1776 main house and auxiliary buildings. Guest rooms have four-poster or canopy beds, Oriental rugs on wide-board floors, and antique furnishings; some have fireplaces or kitchens. Many original touches remain here, from the 18th-century wallpaper to artifacts from the inn's first residents. The baths are on the small side, but they help preserve the colonial integrity of the home. The garden and the wicker-filled sunporch are good places for afternoon cocktails or breakfast—which you can also enjoy inside before the warm glow of the fireplace on cold days. ⊠ *90 Bradford St., 02657* ☏ *508/487–0386 or 800/324–7265* ⊕ *www.fairbanksinn.com* ⟿ *13 rooms, 1 efficiency* ⚫ *Some kitchens, cable TV, some in-room VCRs, Wi-Fi, free parking* ⊟ *AE, MC, V* ⦿ *CP.*

$$ ✕⊡ **The Commons.** Built as an inn in the 1860s, this property was purchased by a new owner in 2006; as of this writing, a complete refurbishment was in the works (it's expected to be completed by spring 2007). The already tasteful rooms are being given hip makeovers, but the original wide-board floors and marble-tile baths will still figure prominently in the design. Most rooms claim a view of the bay; some have balconies, and appealing common areas include a sundeck and tranquil garden. The swanky new Level Bistro ($$–$$$) serves food all day and presents such innovative mod-American fare as truffle crab salad, steak tartare, and cinnamon-lobster bisque. Brunch is outstanding. You can relax in the garden or at the deck bar that overlooks the bay. There's also a casual sandwich shop and coffee bar on premises called Buttery. ⊠ *386 Commercial St., 02657* ☏ *508/487–7800 or 800/487–0784* 🖷 *508/487–0358* ⊕ *www.commonsghb.com* ⟿ *12 rooms, 2 suites* ⚫ *Restaurant, café, cable TV, Wi-Fi, bar, airport shuttle* ⊟ *AE, MC, V* ⊘ *Restaurant closed Jan. and Feb., inn closed Dec.–Apr.* ⦿ *CP.*

$$ ⊡ **Race Point Lighthouse.** One of the most unusual lodging opportunities on the Cape, the restored 1840 keeper's house at the stunning Race Point Lighthouse has three sparsley furnished guest rooms with lace curtains, braided rugs, and simple wooden chests and tables—pillows and blankets are provided, but you'll need to bring your own linens, towels, drinking water, and food. The house does have solar-powered electricity and central heating. You don't stay here because it's cushy, but rather to enjoy the seclusion and romance of staying at an authentic, working lighthouse with a pristine beach just outside the window. Opportunities to see whales, dolphins, and migratory birds abound, both from the grounds and from the house itself. A gift shop on premises sells shrimshaw, sweatshirts, ballcaps, and other keepsakes. The maximum stay is four nights. If you're not able to spend the night, keep in mind that the lighthouse itself is open for tours a few Saturdays per month from mid-May through mid-October. ⊠ *Off Race Point Rd. at Cape Cod National Seashore* 🕭 *Box 570, North Truro 02652* ☎ *508/487–9930* ⊕ *www. racepointlighthouse.net* 🛏 *3 rooms* ⚲ *BBQs, refrigerators; no room phones, no room TVs* 🖃 *No credit cards* ☉ *Closed mid-Oct.–Apr.*

$$ 🏨 **Seasons.** This petite 1860s cream-color Victorian with a Dutch-style gambrel roof is an outstanding value. Owners John Mirthes and Rick Reynolds run a relaxed ship, freely offering guests advice on local restaurants and lending out chairs, towels, and cooler bags for the beach. Rick is a professional chef and prepares exceptional breakfasts replete with filling hot entrées, such as pumpkin pancakes with maple-poached pears, that can render lunch unnecessary. Rooms contain mostly classic Victorian pieces, wallpapers, and fabrics—it's a little old-fashioned, especially compared with all the flashier and more social guesthouses in town, and that's a big reason many guests here come back year after year. Save a hello for sweet old Buster, the house cat. ⊠ *160 Bradford St., east of Downtown Center, 02657* ☎ *508/487–2283 or 800/563– 0113* ⊕ *www.provincetownseasons.com* 🛏 *5 rooms* ⚲ *Some refrigerators, cable TV, in-room VCRs; no room phones* 🖃 *MC, V* ⊺◎⊺ *BP.*

$$ 🏨 **Snug Cottage.** Noted for its extensive floral gardens and enviable perch atop one of the larger bluffs in town, this convivial Arts and Crafts–style inn dates to 1825 and is decked in smashing English country antiques and fabrics. The oversize accommodations have distinctly British names (Victoria Suite, Royal Scott); most are full suites with sitting areas, and many have wood-burning fireplaces and private outdoor entrances. The Churchill Suite has 10 big windows overlooking the flowers and bushes outside, and the York Suite has a partial view of Cape Cod Bay. All rooms have phones with voice mail and high-speed Internet, plus clock radios with CD players. Nightly turndown service and plush robes in each room lend a touch of elegance. ⊠ *178 Bradford St., east of Downtown Center, 02657* ☎ *508/487–1616 or 800/432–2334* 🖷 *508/487–5123* ⊕ *www.snugcottage.com* 🛏 *3 rooms, 5 suites* ⚲ *Some kitchenettes, cable TV, in-room DVDs, Wi-Fi; no smoking* 🖃 *AE, D, MC, V* ⊺◎⊺ *BP.*

$–$$ 🏨 **Ampersand Guesthouse.** Helpful, low-key owners Robert Vetrick and Ken Janson (the latter an architect) run this peaceful West End inn that feels far from the din of Commercial Street but is actually just a short walk away. This natty mid-19th-century Greek Revival guesthouse contains nine eclectically furnished rooms, many with high-pitched ceilings, fireplaces, and tall windows—furnishings tend toward simple, understated, and elegant. For more seclusion, book the studio apartment in the neighboring carriage house, which also has a kitchen. Guests relax in the leafy yard with pretty gardens, or out on the sundeck on the second floor, with views of the harbor a couple of blocks away. Robert bakes fresh muffins each morning as part of the continental breakfast, which is served before a fireplace on cooler days. ⊠ *6 Cottage St., West End, 02657* ☎ *508/487–0959* ⊕ *www.ampersandguesthouse.com* 🛏 *9 rooms, 1 apartment* ⚲ *Some kitchens, some refrigerators, in-room VCRs* 🖃 *AE, MC, V* ⊺◎⊺ *CP.*

$–$$ FodorśChoice ★ 🏨 **Christopher's by the Bay.** The rooms in this elegant but reasonably priced art-inspired inn are named after the greats—Rembrandt, Picasso, Monet, van Gogh—and are elegantly appointed with brass beds and rich fabrics. Many of these tall-windowed rooms have great views of the bay, and all receive plenty of light. The building is a graceful old Victorian surrounded by carefully maintained gardens and brick patios. Rooms on the upper floors share bathrooms. Set back from the bustle, it's just a quick walk from the center of town. ⊠ *8 Johnson St., east of Downtown Center, 02657* 🏠 *508/487–9263* 🖼 *877/487–9263* ⊕ *www.christophersbythebay.com* ⟿ *10 rooms, 5 with bath* ⌂ *Refrigerators, cable TV, in-room VCRs, Wi-Fi* ⊟ *AE, MC, V* ⍑⊙⍑ *BP.*

★ **$–$$** 🖭 **1807 House.** This weathered, craggy old house that dates to 1783 (it was moved to this spot in 1807, hence the name) doesn't look like much more than a cottage from the quiet stretch of Commercial Street it faces, but behind the facade you'll find a beautifully kept inn with cozy, low-ceilinged rooms. Several tastefully furnished and very private apartments and studios are in back. The dramatic Red Room, overlooking Provincetown Bay, contains a hulking four-poster mahogany bed, and the Artist's Studio, perhaps the most romantic unit, occupies a second-floor perch with a balcony affording water views; French doors lead into this light-flooded room with a high cathedral ceiling. This is one of the West End's little treasures—and a good value to boot. ⊠ *54 Commercial St., West End, 02657* 🖼 *508/487–2173 or 888/522–1807* ⊕ *www.1807house.com* ⟿ *3 rooms, 1 suite, 4 apartments* ⌂ *Some kitchens, refrigerators, cable TV, in-room VCRs* ⊟ *AE, MC, V* ⍑⊙⍑ *CP.*

Nightlife & the Arts

THE ARTS   **Provincetown Inn** (⊠ 1 Commercial St., West End 🖼 508/487–9500) hosts several unusual theater productions in summer; look for shows performed by C.A.P.E. Inc. Theatre and those offered during the Provincetown Fringe Festival in August. The inn also hosts nights of live music.

The annual **Provincetown International Film Festival** (🖼 508/487–3456 ⊕ www.ptownfilmfest.com) has become so popular that most of the screenings sell out. Aside from a full schedule of independent films, there are guest appearances by such notables as director John Waters, Lily Tomlin, and Christine Vachon. The festival hits town in mid-June.

Established in 2004 as the new home base for both the **Provincetown Repertory Theatre** and the **Provincetown Theatre Company** (🖼 508/487–8673 ⊕ www.ptowntheatrecompany.org), the **Provincetown Theater** (⊠ 238 Bradford St., Downtown Center 🖼 508/487–7487, box office 508/487–9793 ⊕ www.ptowntheater.org, box office www.ptowntix.com) is host to a wide variety of performances throughout the year, especially during the summer high season. The Provincetown Repertory Theatre has a summer lineup of classic and modern drama, with Equity actors and local talent. The Provincetown Theatre Company presents classics, modern drama, and works by local authors, as well as staged readings and playwriting workshops.

NIGHTLIFE   **Atlantic House** (⊠ 4 Masonic Pl., Downtown Center 🖼 508/487–3821),
★ the grandfather of the gay nightlife scene, is the only gay bar open year-round. It has several lounge areas and an outdoor patio.

Boatslip Beach Club (⊠ 161 Commercial St., Downtown Center, toward West End 🖼 508/487–1669) holds a gay and lesbian late-afternoon tea

Provincetown: America's Gay Summer Playground

AMERICA'S ORIGINAL GAY RESORT, Provincetown developed as an artists' colony at the turn of the 20th century. In 1899, a young artist and entrepreneur named Charles Hawthorne founded the Cape Cod School of Art. Within 20 years, a half dozen art schools opened, the Provincetown Art Association staged its first exhibitions, and the Provincetown Players, a small band of modernist theater folk, began to produce plays on a small wharf in the town's East End.

After a year in Provincetown the players moved to New York City's Greenwich Village, where gay culture was already thriving. This kinship helped spur Provincetown's early flourishing as a gay community. Tourism became a significant revenue source, and local homes began letting rooms to the hundreds of writers, painters, and other creative spirits drawn to the town's thriving arts community.

Over the next few decades, many innovative writers and artists spent time in Provincetown, including several openly gay luminaries such as Truman Capote and Tennessee Williams. The town became identified increasingly for its willingness to flout convention, and it was by the 1960s a haven for anyone whose artistic leaning, political platform, or sexual persuasion was subject to persecution elsewhere in America. This hotbed of counterculture naturally nurtured one of the country's most significant gay communities.

Today Provincetown is as appealing to artists as it is to gay and lesbian—as well as straight— tourists. The awareness brought by the AIDS crisis and, most recently, Massachusetts's becoming the first state to legalize same-sex marriage has turned the town into the most visibly gay vacation community in America.

–by Andrew Collins

dance daily in summer and on weekends in spring and fall on the outdoor pool deck. The club has indoor and outdoor dance floors. There's ballroom dancing here, in addition to two-stepping Thursday through Sunday nights. There was talk of converting the Boatslip into condos in 2006, but as of this writing an agreement was tentatively in place to keep it operating as is.

The **Cape Cod National Seashore** schedules summer evening programs, such as slide shows, sunset beach walks, concerts (local groups, military bands), and sing-alongs, at its **Province Lands Visitor Center** (⊠ Race Point Rd., east of U.S. 6 ☎ 508/487–1256); sunset campfire talks are also held on the beaches in Provincetown.

Club Euro (⊠ 258 Commercial St., Downtown Center ☎ 508/487– 2505) has weekend concerts by big names in world music, including African music, Jamaican reggae, Chicago blues, and Louisiana zydeco.

The venue, an 1843 Congregational church that later housed a movie theater, is an eerie ocean dreamscape with sea-green walls with a half-submerged, three-dimensional mermaid spouting fish, and a black ceiling high above. Pool tables and a late-night menu are available.

★ The gay-oriented **Crown & Anchor Complex** (✉ 247 Commercial St., Downtown Center ☎ 508/487–1430) has plenty of action—perhaps the most in town—with a video bar, several stages, and a giant disco called Paramount. Seven nightly shows in summer range from cabaret to comedy.

Governor Bradford Restaurant (✉ 312 Commercial St., Downtown Center ☎ 508/487–9618) is perhaps better known as a sometimes-rowdy pool and dance hall. In the afternoon you can play chess or backgammon at the tables by the window. After 8 PM, the place revs up with live music or a DJ spinning everything from hip-hop to disco.

Pied Piper (✉ 193A Commercial St., Downtown Center, toward West End ☎ 508/487–1527) draws hordes of gay men to its post–tea dance gathering at 6:30 every evening in July and August and weekends during the shoulder seasons. Later in the evening, the crowd is mostly (though not exclusively) women. The club has a deck overlooking the harbor, a small dance floor with a good sound system, and two bars.

The **Post Office Cabaret** (✉ 303 Commercial St., Downtown Center ☎ 508/487–3892) has long been a dishy and lively spot for piano cabaret. The upstairs lounge draws some of the top talents in the region, and downstairs an excellent restaurant serves dependable American bistro fare until 1 AM most nights.

The **Squealing Pig** (✉ 335 Commercial St., Downtown Center, toward East End ☎ 508/487–5804) has DJs presenting rock, hip-hop, reggae, and house; they also show late-night movies on Monday. There's never a cover charge.

Vixen (✉ 336 Commercial St., Downtown Center ☎ 508/487–6424), a lively women's club, gets packed with dancers. On most nights, before the dance crowd sets in, there are both national and local women entertainers. Look for live music and comedy. There are also a couple of pool tables in the front room.

Whalers' Wharf (✉ 237–241 Commercial St., Downtown Center) resembles an old European marketplace, with a brick pathway that leads straight to the beach and a rotunda theater alive with street performers and entertainment. The first floor of the building holds shops; upstairs are artists' studios and a museum dedicated to the town's history. At the **New Art Cinema** (☎ 508/487–9355, 508/487–4269 box office) moviegoers can view the latest in independent films, classics, and movies you won't find in the usual megaplex. As of this writing, New Art was building a brand-new cinema, Internet café, creperie, and live-theater stage across the street (it was slated to have opened by the end of summer 2006), but movies will also continue to be shown at Whalers' Wharf.

Sports & the Outdoors

BEACHES The entire stretch of Commercial Street is backed by the waters of Provincetown Harbor, and most hotels have private beaches. Farther into town there are plenty of places to settle on the sand and take a refreshing dip—just be mindful of the busy boat traffic.

Herring Cove Beach is relatively calm and warm for a National Seashore beach, but it's not as pretty as some because its parking lot isn't hidden behind dunes. However, the lot to the right of the bathhouse is a great place to watch the sunset. There's a hot-dog stand, as well as showers and restrooms. Lifeguards are on duty in season. From mid-June through Labor Day, parking costs $15 per day, or $45 for a yearly pass to all National Seashore beaches.

For a day of fairly private beachcombing and great views, you can walk across the stone jetty at low tide to **Long Point,** a sand spit south of town with two lighthouses and two Civil War bunkers—called Fort Useless and Fort Ridiculous because they were hardly needed. It's a 2-mi walk across soft sand—beware of poison ivy and deer ticks if you stray from the path—or hire a boat at **Flyer's** (☎ 508/487–0898) to drop you off and pick you up; the cost is $8 one-way, $12 round-trip.

Fodor'sChoice **Race Point Beach** (✉ Race Point Rd., east of U.S. 6), one of the Cape Cod
★ National Seashore beaches in Provincetown, has a wide swath of sand stretching far off into the distance around the point and Coast Guard station. Behind the beach is pure duneland, and bike trails lead off the parking lot. Because of its position on a point facing north, the beach gets sun all day long (east coast beaches get fullest sun early in the day). Parking is available, there are showers and restrooms, and lifeguards are stationed in season. From mid-June through Labor Day, parking costs $15 per day, or $45 for a yearly pass good at all National Seashore beaches.

BICYCLING **Arnold's** (✉ 329 Commercial St., Downtown Center ☎ 508/487–0844) rents all types of bikes, including children's.

The **Beech Forest bike trail** (✉ Off Race Point Rd., east of Rte. 6) in the National Seashore offers an especially nice ride through a shady forest to Bennett Pond.

Gale Force Bikes (✉ 144 Bradford St. Ext. ☎ 508/487–4849 ⊕ www.galeforcebikes.com) stocks a wide variety of bikes for sale and for rent; it's also a good source for parts and repairs.

The **Province Lands Trail** is a 5¼-mi loop off the Beech Forest parking lot on Race Point Road, with spurs to Herring Cove and Race Point beaches and to Bennett Pond. The paths wind up and down hills amid dunes, marshes, woods, and ponds, affording spectacular views. More than 7 mi of bike trails lace through the dunes, cranberry bogs, and scrub pine of the National Seashore, with many access points, including Herring Cove and Race Point.

P'town Bikes (✉ 42 Bradford St., east of Downtown Center ☎ 508/487–8735 ⊕ www.ptownbikes.com) has Trek and Mongoose mountain bikes at good rates, and you can reserve online. The shop also provides free locks and maps.

BOATING & **Bay Lady II Excursion Schooner** (✉ MacMillan Wharf, Downtown Cen-
KAYAKING ter ☎ 508/487–9308 ⊕ www.sailcapecod.com), a beautiful 73-foot sailing vessel, heads out for two-hour cruises three times daily. You're welcome to bring your own spirits and snacks for this scenic and peaceful sail.

Flyer's Boat Rental (✉ 131A Commercial St., West End ☎ 508/487–0898 ⊕ www.flyersboats.com) has kayaks, surfbikes, Sunfish, Hobies, Force 5s, Lightnings, powerboats, and rowboats. Flyer's will also shuttle you to Long Point.

Venture Athletics Kayak Shop (✉ 237 Commercial St., Unit 13A, Downtown Center ☎ 508/487–9442 ⊕ www.ventureathletics.com) rents kayaks and equipment and offers guided kayak tours. The company also operates the nearby **Venture Athletics Outdoor Shop** (✉ 220 Commercial St., Downtown Center ☎ 508/487–2395), which sells all kinds of sporting gear and clothing.

FISHING You can go after fluke, bluefish, and striped bass on a walk-on basis from spring through fall with **Cee Jay Fishing Parties** (✉ MacMillan Wharf, Downtown Center ☎ 508/487–4330).

TENNIS **Bissell's Tennis Courts** (✉ 21 Bradford St. Ext., east of Downtown Center ☎ 508/487–9512) has five clay courts and offers lessons. It's open from late May through September.

Provincetown Tennis Club (✉ 288 Bradford St. Ext., east of Downtown Center ☎ 508/487–9574) has five clay and two hard courts open to non-members; you can also take lessons with the resident tennis pro.

TOURS **Art's Dune Tours** (✉ Commercial and Standish Sts., Downtown Center
Fodor'sChoice ☎ 508/487–1950 ⊕ www.artsdunetours.com) has been taking eager pas-
★ sengers into the dunes of Province Lands since 1946. Bumpy but controlled rides transport you through sometimes surreal sandy vistas peppered with beach grass and along shoreline patrolled by seagulls and sandpipers. Tours are filled with lively tales, including the fascinating history of the exclusive (and reclusive) dune shacks (18 still stand today). These 1- to 1½-hour tours are offered several times daily; especially intriguing are the sunset and moonlight tours. Rides coupled with clambakes or barbecues are popular; call for availability and pricing.

Harbor Tours on the **Viking Princess** (✉ MacMillan Wharf, Downtown Center ☎ 508/487–7323 ⊕ www.capecodecotours.com) are given in mornings throughout the summer. These narrated excursions tell stories of shipwrecks and pirate raids and pass by Civil War forts and the Long Point Lighthouse. There are also sunset cruises, "critter cruises" with onboard naturalists, and kids-oriented "pirate fun cruises."

★ **P-town Pedicab** (☎ 508/487–0660 ⊕ www.ptownpedicabs.com) provides highly enjoyable town tours in vehicles you won't find in too many places around the country. A guide pedals you and up to two more guests around town in an open-air three-wheel chariot-like cab, pointing out

Dune Shacks

CLOSE UP

PROVINCETOWN'S rich artistic legacy continues to manifest itself in the dozens of galleries along Commercial Street and through countless resident writers and painters. But out along the seashore, along a 3-mi stretch of sand extending from about Race Point to High Head (in Truro), you can see a more unusual remnant of the town's artistic past—the dune shacks.

These small, austere structures were built by the Life Saving Service in the 19th century to house seamen. Sometime around the 1920s, long after the dune shacks ceased housing life-saving personnel, many of the community's creative or eccentric spirits began using them as retreats and hideaways. Probably the most famous of these was playwright Eugene O'Neill, who purchased one and spent many summers there with his wife, Agnes Boulton. O'Neill penned *Anna Christie* (1920) and *The Hairy Ape* (1921) while living in his shack, and in doing so gave the whole collection of dune shacks something of an arty cachet.

Other Provincetown artists soon followed O'Neill, including the self-proclaimed "poet of the dunes," Harry Kemp, who wrote many a verse about the seashore's stark, desolate splendor. Author Hazel Hawthorne-Werner wrote *The Salt House*, a memoir tracing her time amid the dunes, in 1929. It's said that this book helped get the shacks, along with the entire dunes district, onto the National Register of Historic Places, helping to preserve them for years to come. In later years, Jack Kerouac, e. e. cummings, Norman Mailer, and Jackson Pollack also lived in these primitive structures.

The dune shacks haven't been modernized much—none has electricity, running water, or toilets. You stay in them for a chance to be with nature and perhaps commune with the spirits of artists who have gone before you. The dune shacks are now all set along the part of the Cape Cod National Seashore that is known as the Province Lands. The park owns most of the Provincetown dune shacks, though a few are managed by nonprofit groups aimed at preserving them and their legacy. Some of these organizations, such as the Peaked Hills Bars Trust and the Provincetown Community Compact, allow visitors to stay in the dune shacks through a variety of arrangements. Both groups run an artist-in-residence program—artists can apply for short stays in some of the shacks during the summer season. Only a handful of applicants are admitted each year.

If you're not an artist, you can enter a lottery for the opportunity to lease one of the shacks for a week in spring or fall. If you're interested in applying to spend time in a dune shack or you'd like to join one of the nonprofit organizations that sponsors them, contact **Dune Shacks** (Box 1705, Provincetown 02657, 508/487-3635).

If you're simply interested in exploring the terrain and seeing the shacks, you can either book a tour with **Art's Dune Tours** (508/487-1950 or 800/894-1951, www.artsdunetours.com), or park behind the Cape Inn, on Snail Road just off U.S. 6, where a 3-mi trail winds through the dunes and past many of the dune shacks.

—by Andrew Collins

local sights and offering an unusual perspective on this already unusual town. The company also offers customized gallery-hopping, ghost–graveyard, shopping, and history tours. It's a memorable way to see the area.

Provincetown Trolley (☎ 508/487–9483 ⊕ www.provincetowntrolley. com) offers 40-minute narrated tours of Provincetown, which leave from outside town hall every 30 minutes daily 10–4, and every hour daily 5–7 PM. The ride takes you through downtown, out to the Provincetown Monument, and by the beaches; the fare is $8.

WHALE-
WATCHING
One of the joys of Cape Cod is spotting whales swimming in and around the feeding grounds at Stellwagen Bank, about 6 mi off the tip of Provincetown. On a sunny day the boat ride out into open ocean is part of the pleasure, but the thrill, of course, is in seeing these great creatures. You might spot minke whales; humpbacks (who put on the best show when they breach); finbacks; or perhaps the most endangered great whale species, the right whale. Dolphins are a welcome sight as well; they play in the boat's bow waves. Many people also come aboard for birding, especially during spring and fall migration. You can see gannets, shearwaters, and storm petrels, among many others. Several boats take you out to sea (and bring you back) with morning, afternoon, or sunset trips lasting from three to four hours. All boats have food service, but remember to take sunscreen and a sweater or jacket—the breeze makes it chilly. Some boats stock seasickness pills, but if you're susceptible, come prepared.

The municipal parking area by the harbor in Provincetown fills up by noon in summer; consider taking a morning boat to avoid crowds and the hottest sun. Although April may be cold, it's one of the better months for spotting whales, who at that time have just migrated north after mating and are very hungry. Good food is, after all, what brings the whales to this part of the Atlantic.

Dolphin Fleet tours are accompanied by scientists from the Center for Coastal Studies in Provincetown, who provide commentary while collecting data on the whale population they've been monitoring for years. They know many of the whales by name and will tell you about their habits and histories. Reservations are required. ⊠ *Ticket office: Chamber of Commerce building at MacMillan Wharf, Downtown Center* ☎ *508/240–3636 or 800/826–9300* ⊕ *www.whalewatch.com* ⚏ *$30* ☉ *Tours mid-Apr.–Oct.*

The *Portuguese Princess* sails with a naturalist on board to narrate. The snack bar sells Portuguese specialties. *Tickets* ⊠ *70 Shank Painter Rd., ticket office, east of Downtown Center* ⊠ *Whale Watchers General Store, 309 Commercial St., Downtown Center* ☎ *508/487–2651 or 800/442–3188* ⊕ *www.princesswhalewatch.com* ⚏ *$30* ☉ *Tours mid-May–Oct.*

Shopping

ART GALLERIES
★
Albert Merola Gallery (⊠ 424 Commercial St., Downtown Center, toward East End ☎ 508/487–4424 ⊕ www.albertmerolagallery.com) focuses on 20th-century and contemporary master prints and Picasso ceramics. The gallery showcases artists from in and around Province-

town, Boston, and New York, including James Balla, Richard Baker, and iconic gay filmmaker and arbiter of bad taste, John Waters.

Berta Walker Gallery (✉ 208 Bradford St., east of Downtown Center, toward East End ☎ 508/487–6411 ⊕ www.bertawalker.com) specializes in Provincetown-affiliated artists, including Selina Trieff and Nancy Whorf, and such Provincetown legends as Ross Moffett, Charles Hawthorne, Hans Hofmann, and Karl Knaths.

Charles-Baltivik Gallery (✉ 432 Commercial St., east of Downtown Center, toward East End ☎ 508/487–3611 ⊕ www.cbgallery.net) features several leading contemporary artists and has a small sculpture garden.

The **DNA Gallery** (✉ 288 Bradford St., east of Downtown Center, toward East End ☎ 508/487–7700 ⊕ www.dnagallery.com) represents artists working in various media, including many emerging talents.

★ **Gallery Voyeur** (✉ 444 Commercial St., east of Downtown Center, toward East End ☎ 508/487–3678 ⊕ www.voy-art.com) shows artist-owner Johniene Papandreas' provocative, larger-than-life portraits, which are inspired by Classical and Romantic artists of the past.

Hilda Neily Art Gallery (✉ 432 Commercial St., Downtown Center, toward East End ☎ 508/487–6300 ⊕ www.hildaneilygallery.com) is named for its featured artist, who was once a student of impressionist painter Henry Hensche.

★ **Julie Heller Gallery** (✉ 2 Gosnold St., Downtown Center ☎ 508/487–2169 ⊕ www.juliehellergallery.com) has contemporary artists as well as some Provincetown icons. The gallery has works from the Sol Wilson and Milton Avery estates, as well as from such greats as Robert Motherwell, Agnes Weinrich, and Blanche Lazzell.

Rice/Polak Gallery (✉ 430 Commercial St., Downtown Center, toward East End ☎ 508/487–1052 ⊕ www.ricepolakgallery.com) stocks a remarkably comprehensive and eclectic variety of contemporary works, from paintings and pastels to photography and sculpture.

★ The **Schoolhouse Galleries** (✉ 494 Commercial St., Downtown Center, toward East End ☎ 508/487–4800 ⊕ www.theschoolhousegalleries.com), in an 1844 former school, shows the works of more than 25 local and national artists and photographers.

Simie Maryles Gallery (✉ 435 Commercial St., Downtown Center, toward East End ☎ 508/487–7878 ⊕ www.simiemaryles.com) represents about 15 contemporary artists, most of whom work in traditional styles. Oil paintings, glasswork, ceramics, and metal sculpture are among the strong suits here.

The **William-Scott Gallery** (✉ 439 Commercial St., Downtown Center, toward East End ☎ 508/487–4040 ⊕ www.williamscottgallery.com) primarily shows contemporary works such as John Dowd's reflective, realistic Cape 'scapes.

Farland Provisions (⊠ 150 Bradford St., Downtown Center ☎ 508/487–0045) proffers all kinds of fine foods and snacks, including excellent deli sandwiches.

Forbidden Fruit (⊠ 173 Commercial St., Downtown Center, toward West End ☎ 508/487–9800) is a one-stop shop for all irreverent and offbeat gifts, from strange costumes to erotic trinkets to Gothic tchotchkes.

Impulse (⊠ 188 Commercial St., Downtown Center, toward West End ☎ 508/487–1154) has contemporary American crafts, including jewelry and an extraordinary kaleidoscope collection. The Autograph Gallery exhibits framed photographs, letters, and documents signed by celebrities.

ID (⊠ 220A Commercial St., Downtown Center, toward West End ☎ 508/487–1154) stocks a wonderful array of Mexican pottery, cool clocks, offbeat jewelry, and retro-hip greeting cards and stationery.

Kidstuff (⊠ 371 Commercial St., Downtown Center, toward East End ☎ 508/487–0714) carries unusual, colorful children's wear.

Lady'Z Vintage Clothing (⊠ 389 Commercial St., Downtown Center, toward East End ☎ 508/487–2251) offers racks of sexy, campy, bold, and offbeat secondhand fashions. It's a favorite of drag queens, who especially favor the costume jewelry and boas, but there are all kinds of cool threads here.

★ **Marine Specialties, Inc.** (⊠ 235 Commercial St., Downtown Center ☎ 508/487–1730) is full of treasures, knickknacks, and clothing. Here you can purchase some very reasonably priced casual- and military-style clothing, as well as seashells, marine supplies, stained-glass lamps, candles, rubber sharks (you get the idea), and prints of old advertisements.

Moda Fina (⊠ 349 Commercial St., Downtown Center ☎ 508/487–6632) displays an eclectic selection of women's fashions, shoes, and jewelry—everything from flowing linen or silk eveningwear to funky and casual pieces. Unique Mexican crafts are also for sale.

Now Voyager Bookstore (⊠ 357 Commercial St., Downtown Center ☎ 508/487–0848) is a first-rate independent bookstore with an emphasis on lesbian and gay titles; the store hosts prominent authors throughout the year (especially in summer) and has a small art gallery.

Peter's Royal Navy (⊠ 120 Commercial St., Downtown Center, toward West End ☎ 508/487–7141), with its whimsical window displays, appeals to fans of all things British with a great selection of linens, authentic Royal Navy flatware, Bay Rhum toiletries, antique model ships, and fine nautical memorabilia.

Provincetown Antique Market (⊠ 131 Commercial St., Downtown Center, toward West End ☎ 508/487–1115) has one of the town's better selections of vintage lighting, jewelry, Bakelite, costumes, toys, textiles, and furnishings.

Remembrances of Things Past (⊠ 376 Commercial St., Downtown Center, toward East End ☎ 508/487–9443) deals with articles from the 1920s to the 1960s, including Bakelite and other jewelry, telephones, neon items, ephemera, and autographed celebrity photographs.

Silk & Feathers (✉ 377 Commercial St., Downtown Center, toward East End ☎ 508/487–2057) carries an assortment of fine lingerie, women's clothing, and jewelry.

Tim's Used Books (✉ 242 Commercial St., Downtown Center ☎ 508/487–0005) is packed with volumes of volumes—rooms of used-but-in-good-shape books, including some rare and out-of-print texts.

★ **Utilities** (✉ 393 Commercial St., Downtown Center, toward East End ☎ 508/487–6800) supplies customers with some of the coolest kitchen and bathroom gadgetry and decorative pieces around.

Wa (✉ 184 Commercial St., Downtown Center, toward West End ☎ 508/487–6355) is an oasis of peace and Zen-like tranquillity. Unusual- and Japanese-inspired items include fountains, home accent pieces, and framed (and sometimes frightening) tropical insects.

West End Antiques (✉ 146 Commercial St., Downtown Center, toward West End ☎ 508/487–6723) sells everything from $4 postcards to a $3,000 model ship. Handmade dolls and high-quality glassware—Steuben, Orrefors, and Hawkes—are also available.

THE OUTER CAPE ESSENTIALS

To research prices, get advice from other travelers, and book travel arrangements, visit www.fodors.com.

Transportation

BY BOAT & FERRY

In season, ferries run from Provincetown to Boston and Plymouth. For more information, ⇨ Boat & Ferry Travel *in* Smart Travel Tips A to Z in the back of this book.

BY BUS

Plymouth & Brockton Street Railway provides bus service to Provincetown from downtown Boston or Logan Airport, with stops en route. For more information, ⇨ Bus Travel *in* Smart Travel Tips A to Z in the back of this book.

The Shuttle, run by the Cape Cod Regional Transit Authority, provides a much-needed transportation boost. The route begins at Horton's Camping Resort in Truro and continues to Provincetown along Route 6A; it stops wherever a passenger or roadside flagger dictates. Once in Provincetown, the shuttle continues up Bradford Street, with alternating trips to Herring Cove Beach and Pilgrim Park as well as summertime service up to Provincetown Airport and Race Point Beach. It runs every 20 minutes and is outfitted to carry bicycles. The service is popular and reasonably priced ($1 for a single fare, $3 for a day pass), and the only trouble seems to be finding parking on the Truro end (plans are in the works to find alternative parking areas). The shuttle runs from late May until mid-October, with more limited service during the spring and fall.

There are no bus stations or depots, per se, in the Outer Cape, though there are designated stops within each town: in Provincetown, in front of the Chamber of Commerce office on Commercial Street; in Truro, at Dutra's Market–Route 6A (Shore Road); in North Truro, at Depot Road, near the Truro Post Office and Jams store; in Wellfleet, at D&D market on U.S. 6 and in Wellfleet Village; and in South Wellfleet on Main Street in front of Town Hall.

⛟ Bus Lines **Plymouth & Brockton Street Railway** ☎ 508/746-0378 ⊕ www.p-b.com. **Shuttle** ☎ 800/352-7155 ⊕ www.capecodtransit.org.

BY TAXI
The companies below provide cab service throughout the Outer Cape. Mercedes Cab Co. offers local and long-distance service in vintage Mercedes sedans.

⛟ Taxi Companies **Cape Cab** ✉ Provincetown ☎ 508/487-2222. **Queen Cab** ✉ Provincetown ☎ 508/487-5500.

Contacts & Resources

CONDO & HOUSE RENTALS
Cape Cod Realty lists rentals for Wellfleet; Atlantic Bay Real Estate specializes in Provincetown rentals but covers all of the Outer Cape. Ruth Gilbert Real Estate also lists Provincetown vacation rentals. Kinlin Grover Vacation Rentals lists available apartments and houses on the Outer Cape.

⛟ Local Agents **Atlantic Bay Real Estate** ✉ Provincetown ☎ 508/487-2430 ⊕ www.atlanticbayre.com. **Cape Cod Realty** ✉ Wellfleet ☎ 508/349-2245 ⊕ www.capecodrealty.net. **Ruth Gilbert Real Estate** ✉ Provincetown ☎ 508/487-2004 ⊕ www.ruthgilbertrealestate.com. **Kinlin Grover Vacation Rentals** ✉ Wellfleet ☎ 508/349-9000 or 800/444-6756 ⊕ www.vacationcapecod.com.

TOURS
For other tours, including whale-watching trips ⇨ Outdoor Activities and Sports *in* Provincetown, *above.*

VISITOR INFORMATION
The Provincetown Chamber of Commerce is open from March until New Year's Day and has the only staffed visitor center in town, just off Commercial Street near MacMillan Wharf. The Provincetown Business Guild specializes in gay tourism and is open year-round to offer answers over the phone or send out its directory—but it has no visitor center. The Truro Chamber of Commerce and Wellfleet Chamber are open from mid-May through mid-October.

⛟ Tourist Information **Provincetown** ✉ 307 Commercial St., Box 1017, 02657 ☎ 508/487-3424 ⊕ www.ptownchamber.com. **Provincetown Business Guild (gay and lesbian)** ✉ 3 Freman St., No. 2, Box 421-94, 02657 ☎ 508/487-2313 or 800/637-8696 ⊕ www.ptown.org. **Truro** ✉ U.S. 6 at Head of the Meadow Rd. ⛟ Box 26, North Truro 02652 ☎ 508/487-1288 ⊕ www.trurochamberofcommerce.com. **Wellfleet** ⛟ Box 571, 02667 ☎ 508/349-2510 ✉ Information center off U.S. 6 in South Wellfleet ⊕ www.wellfleetchamber.com.

Martha's Vineyard

WORD OF MOUTH

"In Aquinnah, we took numerous photographs of the beautiful cliffs and striking brick lighthouse. The cliffs had colorful strata in the afternoon light. What a gorgeous place!"

—volcam

"I prefer Martha's Vineyard for its more varied terrain and views, beautiful beaches, rolling hills, and indescribable Aquinnah clay cliffs. You can see it all from a tour bus on a day trip"

—Kingajh

By Andrew
Collins

FAR LESS DEVELOPED THAN CAPE COD—thanks to a few local conservation organizations—yet more cosmopolitan than neighboring Nantucket, Martha's Vineyard is an island with a double life. From Memorial Day through Labor Day the quieter, some might say real, Vineyard quickens into a vibrant, star-studded place. Edgartown floods with people who come to wander narrow streets flanked with elegant boutiques, stately whaling captains' homes, and charming inns. The busy main port, Vineyard Haven, welcomes day-trippers fresh off ferries and private yachts to browse in its own array of shops. Oak Bluffs, where pizza and ice-cream emporiums reign supreme, attracts diverse crowds with its boardwalk-town air and nightspots that cater to high-spirited, carefree youth.

Summer regulars include a host of celebrities, among them William Styron, Art Buchwald, Walter Cronkite, Beverly Sills, Patricia Neal, Spike Lee, and Diane Sawyer. Former president Clinton and his wife, Senator Hillary Clinton, are frequent visitors. Concerts, theater, dance performances, and lecture series draw top talent to the island; a county agricultural fair, weekly farmers' markets, and miles of walking trails provide earthier pleasures.

Most people know the Vineyard's summer persona, but in many ways its other self has even more appeal, for the off-season island is a place of peace and simple beauty. Drivers traversing country lanes through the agricultural center of the island find time to linger over pastoral and ocean vistas, without being pushed along by a throng of other cars, bicycles, and mopeds. In nature reserves, the voices of summer are gone, leaving only the sounds of birdsong and the crackle of leaves underfoot. Private beaches open to the public, and the water sparkles under crisp, blue skies.

Locals are at their convivial best off-season. After the craziness of their short moneymaking months, they reestablish contact with friends and take up pastimes temporarily crowded out by work. The result for visitors—besides the extra dose of friendliness—is that cultural, educational, and recreational events continue year-round.

About the Restaurants

From fried fish at roadside stands to boiled lobster and foie gras at fancy French restaurants and a growing array of international influences—Thai, Brazilian, Japanese, Mexican, to name just a few—the Vineyard serves an amazing variety of culinary choices.

The majority of eating establishments, both take-out and sit-down, are concentrated in the three Down-Island towns of Vineyard Haven, Oak Bluffs, and Edgartown. As you travel Up-Island—to West Tisbury, Chilmark, and Aquinnah—choices dwindle, especially when it comes to sit-down dinners. Sadly, Vineyard diners—all-American institutions where you can get an honest, no-frills meal at reasonable prices—are a dying breed. Luckily, you can pick up sandwiches, pastries, and other to-go specialties at a number of places around the island, and with good planning you can eat well on a modest budget and splurge for an elegant dinner.

Most restaurants are open on weekends starting in late spring, and by Memorial Day weekend most are serving daily. Although the season seems to stretch longer each year, most restaurants remain open full time through Columbus Day weekend, then only weekends through Thanksgiving (a small handful of die-hard restaurants remain open year-round). Dress, even for the up-scale spots, is casual; a man in a sport jacket is a rare sight. Reservations are highly recommended in the summer months.

About the Hotels

The variety of lodging options on Martha's Vineyard ranges from historic whaling captains' mansions filled with antiques to sprawling modern oceanfront hotels to cozy cottages in the woods. When choosing your accommodations, keep in mind that each town has a different personality: Oak Bluffs tends to cater to a younger, active, nightlife-oriented crowd; Edgartown is more subdued and dignified. Chilmark has beautiful beaches and miles of conservation lands, but not much of a downtown shopping area. Vineyard Haven provides a nice balance of downtown bustle and rustic charm. Bear in mind that many of the island's B&Bs, set in vintage homes filled with art and antiques, have age restrictions—call ahead if you're traveling with a family. And remember that in July and August, the height of the summer season, minimum stays of as many as four nights may be required. If you're planning to visit for a week or more, consider renting a house. For more lodging information, including rental properties and B&Bs ⇨ Lodging *in* Smart Travel Tips at the back of this book.

You should make reservations for summer stays as far in advance as possible; late winter is not too early. Rates in season are very high but can fall by as much as 50% in the off-season. The Martha's Vineyard Chamber of Commerce (⇨ Visitor Information in Martha's Vineyard Essentials at the end of this chapter) maintains a listing of availability in the peak tourist season, from mid-June to mid-September.

BYOB

Part of how the Vineyard maintains its charm—and part of what makes it somewhat frustrating as well—is that alcoholic beverages are sold in retail stores and in restaurants in only two towns: Edgartown and Oak Bluffs. At restaurants in the so-called "dry" towns of Vineyard Haven, West Tisbury, Chilmark, and Aquinnah you can BYOB, but only if you've had the foresight to visit a "wet" town for provisions first. Once you're at the restaurant, expect to be charged up to $6 for corkage fees (this includes the opening of the bottle and the provision of glasses).

WHAT IT COSTS					
	$$$$	$$$	$$	$	¢
RESTAURANTS	over $30	$22–$30	$16–$22	$10–$16	under $10
HOTELS	over $260	$200–$260	$140–$200	$90–$140	under $90

Restaurant prices are per person for a main course at dinner. Hotel prices are for a standard double room, excluding 6% sales tax (more in some counties) and 1%–4% tourist tax.

Martha's Vineyard

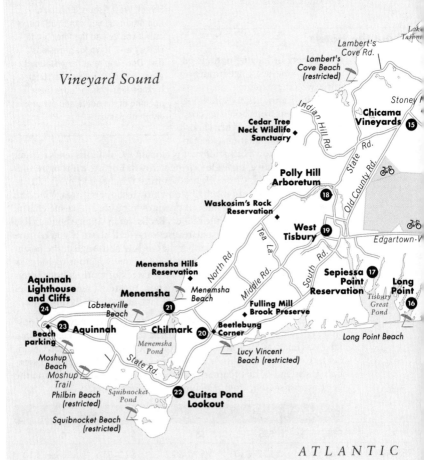

Vineyard Sound

Lambert's Cove Rd.

Lambert's Cove Beach (restricted)

Stoney

Lake Tashm

Chicama Vineyards ⑮

Cedar Tree Neck Wildlife Sanctuary ♦

Indian Hill Rd.

State Rd.

Old County Rd.

Polly Hill Arboretum ⑱

Waskosim's Rock Reservation ♦

West Tisbury ⑲

Edgartown-V

Tea La.

North Rd.

Menemsha Hills Reservation ♦

Middle Rd.

South Rd.

Sepiessa Point Reservation ⑰

Long Point ⑯

Aquinnah Lighthouse and Cliffs ㉔

Menemsha ㉑

Menemsha Beach ♦

Fulling Mill Brook Preserve ♦

Lobsterville Beach

Beach parking ♦ ㉓ Aquinnah

Chilmark ⑳

Beetlebung Corner ♦

Tisbury Great Pond

Long Point Beach

Moshup Beach ♦

Moshup Trail

Menemsha Pond

Lucy Vincent Beach (restricted)

State Rd.

Philbin Beach (restricted)

Squibnocket Pond

㉒ Quitsa Pond Lookout

Squibnocket Beach (restricted)

ATLANTIC

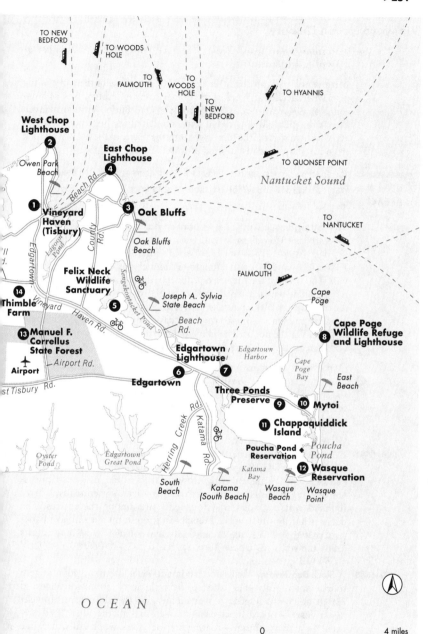

TO NEW
BEDFORD

TO WOODS
HOLE

TO
FALMOUTH

TO
WOODS
HOLE

TO
NEW
BEDFORD

TO HYANNIS

**West Chop
Lighthouse**
2

Owen Park
Beach

**East Chop
Lighthouse**
4

Nantucket Sound

TO QUONSET POINT

TO
NANTUCKET

**1 Vineyard
Haven
(Tisbury)**

Beach Rd.

County Rd.

Lagoon Pond

3 Oak Bluffs

Oak Bluffs
Beach

TO
FALMOUTH

Cape
Poge

**Felix Neck
Wildlife
Sanctuary**

Sengekontacket Pond

Joseph A. Sylvia
State Beach

**Cape Poge
Wildlife Refuge
and Lighthouse**
8

**14
Thimble
Farm**

Vineyard Haven Rd.

5

Beach
Rd.

**Edgartown
Lighthouse**

Edgartown
Harbor

Cape
Poge
Bay

East
Beach

**13 Manuel F.
Correllus
State Forest**

✈
Airport

Airport Rd.

Edgartown
6

7

Three Ponds
Preserve
9

10 Mytoi

st Tisbury Rd.

Herring Creek Rd.

Katama Rd.

**11 Chappaquiddick
Island**

*Poucha
Pond*

Oyster
Pond

Edgartown
Great Pond

**Poucha Pond
Reservation** ♦

Katama
Bay

**12 Wasque
Reservation**

South
Beach

Katama
(South Beach)

Wasque
Beach

Wasque
Point

OCEAN

0   4 miles

0   6 km

Vineyard Haven (Tisbury)

❶ *7 mi southeast of Woods Hole, 3½ mi west of Oak Bluffs, 8 mi northwest of Edgartown.*

Most people call this town Vineyard Haven because of the name of the port where ferries arrive, but its official name is Tisbury. Not as high-toned as Edgartown or as honky-tonk as Oak Bluffs, Vineyard Haven blends the past and the present with a touch of the bohemian. Visitors arriving here step off the ferry right into the bustle of the harbor, a block from the shops and restaurants of Main Street.

▌NEED A
BREAK?

The delicious breads, pastries, and quick-lunch items at **Black Dog Bakery** (✉ 11 Water St. ☎ 508/693-4786) are simply not to be missed—it's a popular stop for good reason.

The stately, neoclassic 1844 **Association Hall** houses the town hall and the Katharine Cornell Memorial Theatre, created in part with funds that Cornell (1898-1974)—one of America's foremost stage actresses in the 1920s, '30s, and '40s and a longtime summer resident—donated in her will. The walls of the theater on the second floor are painted with murals depicting whaling expeditions and a Native American gathering, and the ceiling resembles a blue sky with seagulls overhead. Island artist Stan Murphy painted the murals on the occasion of the town's tercentenary in 1971. The theater occasionally holds performances of plays, concerts, and dances. ✉ *51 Spring St.* ☎ *508/696-4200.*

One of two lighthouses that mark the opening to the harbor, the 52-
❷ foot white-and-black **West Chop Lighthouse** was built of brick in 1838 to replace an 1817 wood building. It's been moved back from the edge of the eroding bluff twice. ✉ *W. Chop Rd. (Main St.)* ⊕ *www.marthasvineyardhistory.com.*

Where to Stay & Eat

$$$-$$$$ ✕ **Le Grenier.** Owner-chef Jean Dupon has been serving classic French food since the late 1970s above the M. V. Bagel Authority at the upper end of Vineyard Haven's downtown. All this time, he's been consistently loyal to the French standards: frogs' legs, sweetbreads, lobster flambéd with calvados, and tournedos are among the entrées. The decor is hardly stuffy in the French tradition; rather, it's almost backyard casual, with a string of lightbulbs and souvenir wine-bottle corks lining the walls. ✉ *Upper Main St.* ☎ *508/693-4906* ▤ *AE, MC, V* ⛛ *BYOB* ☉ *No lunch.*

$$-$$$$ ✕ **Black Dog Tavern.** This island landmark—which is more popular with tourists than locals—lies just steps from the ferry terminal in Vineyard Haven. In July and August, the wait for breakfast (with an expansive omelet assortment) can be as much as an hour from 8 AM on. Why? Partly because the ambience inside—roaring fireplace, dark-wood walls, maritime memorabilia, and a grand view of the water—makes everyone feel so at home. The menu is heavy on local fish, chowders, and chops. Lighter fare is available until 7 PM in the Black Dog Bakery Cafe. ✉ *Beach St.* ☎ *508/ 693-9223* ⛝ *Reservations not accepted* ▤ *AE, D, MC, V* ⛛ *BYOB.*

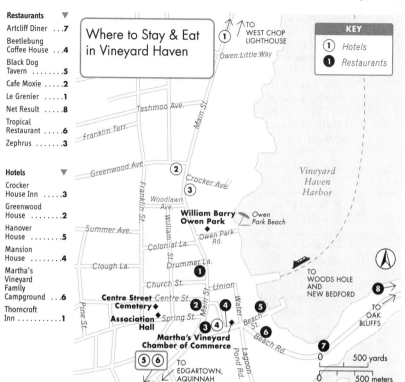

Restaurants ▼

Artcliff Diner ...**7**

Beetlebung
Coffee House ...**4**

Black Dog
Tavern **5**

Cafe Moxie **2**

Le Grenier **1**

Net Result **8**

Tropical
Restaurant **6**

Zephrus **3**

Hotels ▼

Crocker
House Inn **3**

Greenwood
House **2**

Hanover
House **5**

Mansion
House **4**

Martha's
Vineyard
Family
Campground ...**6**

Thorncroft
Inn **1**

Where to Stay & Eat in Vineyard Haven

KEY
① Hotels
❶ Restaurants

$$–$$$$ ✕ **Cafe Moxie.** Open year-round, this classy restaurant has a handsome wooden bar (though it's a dry town) and local artists' work on the walls. Chef Austin Racine's mussels, steamed in garlic and ginger and served over noodles, are a favorite. For something fancier, try a duck breast wrapped in Swiss chard over a white-bean-and-duck ragout, or herbed gnocchi with garlic, leeks, roasted tomato, and chèvre. Hours tend to vary at a whim, so call first. ⊠ *Main St. at Centre St.* ☎ *508/693–1484* ▭ *D, MC, V* Ⓨ *BYOB* ⊘ *Closed Mon. No dinner Tues. and Oct.–Apr.*

$$–$$$$ ✕ **Zephrus.** Mansion House owners Sherman and Susan Goldstein run this ambitious restaurant next to their hotel. The menu favors inventive takes on American classics, such as grilled rack of spring lamb with sweet onion–jalapeño chutney with whipped Yukon potatoes and wilted baby spinach, and baked cod crusted with Cape Cod potato chips. There's also a Chocaholic's Platter of assorted cakes, chocolate mousse, and fresh strawberries to dip into warm caramel and roll in shaved chocolate. ⊠ *9 Main St.* ☎ *508/693–3416* ⊕ *www.mvmansionhouse.com* ▭ *AE, MC, V* Ⓨ *BYOB.*

$$–$$$ ✕ **Tropical Restaurant.** The house specialty at this roadside restaurant is *rodizio*, a Brazilian style of barbecue where slow-roasted meats—in this case beef, chicken, sausage, pork, and lamb—are carved table-side

and served continuously throughout your meal. Along with rice and beans, side dishes include collard greens and yucca. ⊠ *Five Corners* ☎ *508/ 696–0715* ▤ *MC, V* ⓘ *BYOB.*

¢–$$$ ✕ **Net Result.** It may not have quite the ambience of the fish markets in Menemsha, but this simple take-out market and restaurant in a shopping center just outside downtown Vineyard Haven serves some of the best food around, including superb clam chowder, hefty scallop and oyster platters, steamed lobsters, grilled swordfish sandwiches, and crab salad. There are always additional daily specials that reflect what's been caught that day, and Net Result also has a sushi counter: the Martha's Vineyard roll is a favorite, packed with tuna, salmon, yellowtail, and avocado and wrapped in seaweed. You can dine at picnic tables outside and view Vineyard Haven's harbor across the busy road. ⊠ *Tisbury Marketplace 79 Beach Rd.* ☎ *508/693–6071* ⊕ *www.mvseafood.com* ▤ *MC, V.*

¢–$ ✕ **Artcliff Diner.** This vintage diner has been a year-round breakfast and lunch meeting place for locals since 1943. Owner–chef Gina Stanley, who was on call to make desserts for Blair House when she lived in Washington, D.C., serves anything but ordinary diner fare. She whips up pecan pancakes with real rum raisins for breakfast, and crepes with chèvre, arugula, or almost anything you ask for at lunch. ⊠ *39 Beach Rd.* ☎ *508/ 693–1224* ▤ *No credit cards* ☉ *Closed Wed. No dinner.*

¢ ✕ **Beetlebung Coffee House.** This cozy coffeehouse is within easy walking distance of the ferry terminal and downtown shops and restaurants. A hip crowd convenes here for the great sandwiches (try the Taos panini, with flame-roasted New Mexico green chilies, turkey, and cheddar), designer-coffee drinks, and delicious desserts. The breakfast "eggwich," with Black Forest ham, poached egg, and Vermont cheddar, is a treat. There's an attractive side patio that's perfect on a warm afternoon. ⊠ *32 Beach St.* ☎ *508/696–7122* ▤ *MC, V.*

★ $$$$ ▥ **Crocker House Inn.** This 1924 farmhouse-style inn is tucked into a quiet lane off Main Street, minutes from the ferries and Owen Park Beach. The rooms are decorated casually with understated flair—pastel-painted walls, softly upholstered wing-back chairs, and white-wicker nightstands. Each contains a small, wall-mounted "honor bar," with a disposable camera, suntan lotion, and other useful sundries. Three rooms have soothing whirlpool tubs, and two have fireplaces. No. 6, with a small porch and a private entrance, has the best view of the harbor. Breakfast is served at a large farmer's table inside the small common room and kitchen area. Jeff and Jynell Kristal are the young, friendly owners, and Jynell also creates whimsically painted glassware, which is available for sale. ⊠ *12 Crocker Ave., Box 1658, 02568* ☎ *508/693–1151 or 800/772–0206* ⊕ *www.crockerhouseinn.com* ⇆ *8 rooms* ♨ *Some in-room hot tubs; no kids under 12, no smoking* ▤ *MC, V* ⦿ *CP.*

$$$$ ▥ **Mansion House.** There has been a hostelry on this Main Street site just above Vineyard Haven Harbor since 1794; today's Mansion House opened in 2003. Apart from the cheerful, summery rooms—some with balconies, some with gas fireplaces, some with soaking tubs—the cupola deck provides a pleasant spot for a respite. It affords sweeping views of the harbor, the town, and the lagoon that stretches between Vineyard Haven and Oak Bluffs. Afternoon cookies and lemonade are served there

or you can BYOB. The hotel's Zephrus Restaurant serves commendable contemporary American fare and is also a nice spot for cocktails. ✉ *9 Main St., Box 428, 02568* ☎ *509/693–2200 or 800/332–4112* ⊕ *www. mvmansionhouse.com* ⇆ *32 rooms, 11 suites* ⌂ *Restaurant, room service, refrigerators, cable TV, pool, health club, spa, Internet* ▤ *AE, D, MC, V* ⑂ *CP.*

$$$$ ⊞ **Thorncroft Inn.** On 3½ wooded acres about 1 mi from the ferry, this inn's main building, a 1918 Craftsman bungalow, combines fine colonial and richly carved Renaissance Revival antiques with tasteful reproductions to create a somewhat formal environment. Ten of the rooms have working fireplaces. Most rooms have canopy beds; three rooms have two-person whirlpool baths, and two have private hot-tub spas. Rooms in the carriage house, set apart from the main house via a breezeway, are more secluded. ✉ *460 Main St., Box 1022, 02568* ☎ *508/693– 3333 or 800/332–1236* 🖶 *508/693–5419* ⊕ *www.thorncroft.com* ⇆ *14 rooms, 1 cottage* ⌂ *Dining room, some in-room hot tubs, some refrigerators, in-room VCRs, library; no kids under 13, no smoking* ▤ *AE, D, DC, MC, V* ⑂ *BP.*

$$–$$$ ⊞ **Greenwood House.** A low-key bed-and-breakfast on a quiet lane around the corner from Vineyard Haven's public library, the Greenwood House is one of the better values in town. Affable innkeepers Kathy Stinson and Larry Gomez own this homey, three-story Arts and Crafts–style cottage with classic shingle siding and a shaded yard. The rooms are decorated with a mix of antiques and contemporary pieces, including brass and four-poster beds, island artwork, and functional but attractive nightstands and bureaus. It's a 10- to 15-minute walk from the ferry and even closer to many shops and restaurants. ✉ *40 Greenwood Ave., Box 2734, 02568* ☎ *508/693–6150 or 866/693–6150* 🖶 *508/696– 8113* ⊕ *www.greenwoodhouse.com* ⇆ *4 rooms* ⌂ *Refrigerators, library; no smoking* ▤ *AE, D, MC, V* ⑂ *BP.*

$$–$$$ ⊞ **Hanover House.** Set on ½ acre of landscaped lawn on a busy road— but within walking distance of the ferry—this three-property inn consists of a classic, home-style B&B, a country inn, and a carriage house. Rooms are decorated with a combination of antiques and reproduction furniture, and each has individual flair: in one, an antique sewing machine serves as the TV stand. The three carriage house suites have private decks or patios, and two have kitchenettes. ✉ *28 Edgartown Rd., Box 2108, 02568* ☎ *508/693–1066 or 800/339–1066* ⊕ *www. hanoverhouseinn.com* ⇆ *12 rooms, 3 suites* ⌂ *Some kitchenettes, Internet room* ▤ *AE, D, MC, V* ☉ *Closed Dec.–Mar.* ⑂ *CP.*

★ **¢–$** ⛺ **Martha's Vineyard Family Campground.** Wooded sites, a ball field, a camp store, bicycle rentals, and electrical and water hookups are among the facilities at this 20-acre campsite a few miles from Vineyard Haven. A step up from tents are 21 rustic one- or two-room cabins, which come with electricity, refrigerators, gas grills, and combinations of double and bunk beds (but bring your own bedding). The campground also has hookups for trailers. This is the only campsite on the island, so book early; discounts are available for extended stays. No dogs or motorcycles are allowed. ✉ *569 Edgartown Rd., Box 1557, 02568* ☎ *508/693– 3772* 🖶 *508/693–5767* ⊕ *www.campmvfc.com* 🖀 *$36–$100* ⇆ *130*

6

tent sites, 50 RV sites, 21 cabins ♿ *Picnic area, some refrigerators, bi-cycles, recreation room, shop, playground, laundry facilities* ▭ *D, MC, V* ⊘ *Closed mid-Oct.–mid-May.*

Nightlife & the Arts

The **Vineyard Playhouse** (✉ 24 Church St. ☎ 508/693–6450 or 508/696–6300) has a year-round schedule of professional productions. From mid-June through early September, a troupe performs drama, classics, and comedies on the air-conditioned main stage; summer Shakespeare and other productions take place at the natural amphitheater at Tashmoo Overlook on State Road in Vineyard Haven—bring insect repellent and a blanket or lawn chair. Children's programs and a summer camp are also scheduled, and local art exhibitions are held throughout the year. The theater is wheelchair-accessible and provides hearing devices.

Sports & the Outdoors

Lake Tashmoo Town Beach (✉ End of Herring Creek Rd.) provides swimmers with access to the warm, relatively shallow, brackish lake—or cooler, gentler Vineyard Sound. **Owen Park Beach** (✉ Off Main St.), a small, sandy harbor beach, is just steps away from the ferry terminal in Vineyard Haven, making it a great spot to catch some last rays before heading home. **Tisbury Town Beach** (✉ End of Owen Little Way off Main St.) is a public beach next to the Vineyard Haven Yacht Club.

Shopping

All Things Oriental (✉ 123 Beach Rd. ☎ 508/693–8375) sells new and antique jewelry, porcelains, paintings, furniture, and more, all with an Asian theme.

★ **Belushi Pisano Gallery** (✉ 18 State Rd. ☎ 508/696–8988), operated by Victor Pisano and Judith Belushi Pisano, is an extension of the Second Chance Foundation, a nonprofit organization that aims to assist artists on Martha's Vineyard during times of financial duress; proceeds from the gallery's sales fund the foundation. It's a handsome space carrying works in all types of media by more than 20 of the island's top artists. There's also a small coffeehouse.

Bowl & Board (✉ 35 Main St. ☎ 508/693–9441) is summer-home central. It carries everything you need to cozy up in a summer rental.

Bramhall & Dunn (✉ 19 Main St. ☎ 508/693–6437) carries crafts, linens, hand-knit sweaters, and fine antique country-pine furniture.

Bunch of Grapes Bookstore (✉ 44 Main St. ☎ 508/693–2291) sells new books and sponsors book signings.

Midnight Farm (✉ 18 Water-Cromwell La. ☎ 508/693–1997), co-owned by Carly Simon and Tamara Weiss, stocks furniture, clothes, shoes, jewelry, linens, dinnerware, books, soaps, candles, garden supplies, snack foods, and, of course, Carly's books and CDs.

Rainy Day (✉ 66 Main St. ☎ 508/693–1830), as the name suggests, carries gifts and amusements that are perfect for one of the island's gloomy rainy days, when you just need a warm, dry diversion. You'll find toys, crafts, cards, soaps, and more.

Tisbury Antiques & Interiors (✉ 339 State Rd. ☎ 508/693–8333) carries a vast selection of 18th- and 19th-century English, French, and Italian antiques, plus fine lighting fixtures, Cornishware, estate jewelry, and vintage books and postcards.

Wind's Up! (✉ 199 Beach Rd. ☎ 508/693–4340) sells swimwear, windsurfing and sailing equipment, Boogie boards, and other outdoor gear.

Oak Bluffs

❸ *3½ mi east of Vineyard Haven.*

Circuit Avenue is the bustling center of the Oak Bluffs action, with most of the town's shops, bars, and restaurants. Colorful gingerbread-trimmed guesthouses and food and souvenir joints enliven Oak Bluffs Harbor, once the setting for several grand hotels (the 1879 Wesley Hotel on Lake Avenue is the last remaining one). This small town is more high spirited than haute, more fun than refined.

❹ The **East Chop Lighthouse** was built out of cast iron in 1876 to replace an 1828 tower (used as part of a semaphore system of visual signaling between the island and Boston) that burned down. The 40-foot structure stands high atop a 79-foot bluff with spectacular views of Nantucket Sound. ✉ *E. Chop Dr.* ☎ *508/627–4441* 💲 *$3* ⊙ *Late June–mid-Sept., Sun. 1 hr before sunset–1 hr after sunset.*

6

NEED A BREAK?

The **Coop de Ville** (✉ Dockside Marketplace, Oak Bluffs Harbor ☎ 508/693–3420) teems with people eager to sample simple fried seafood and raw bar delectables (the oysters are fantastic). Eat out on the patio deck overlooking the water to enjoy the view. It's open May to mid-October.

🐿 A National Historic Landmark, the **Flying Horses Carousel** is the nation's oldest continuously operating carousel. Handcrafted in 1876 (the horses have real horse hair and glass eyes), the ride gives children a taste of entertainment from a TV-free era. ✉ *Oak Bluffs Ave.* ☎ *508/693–9481* 💲 *Rides $1.50, book of 8 tickets $10* ⊙ *Late May–early Sept., daily 10–10; Easter–late May, weekends 10–5; early Sept.–mid-Oct., weekdays 11–4:30, weekends 10–5.*

★ Don't miss **Oak Bluffs Campground,** a 34-acre warren of streets tightly packed with more than 300 Carpenter Gothic Victorian cottages with wedding-cake trim, gaily painted in pastels. As you wander through this fairy-tale setting, imagine it on a balmy summer evening, lighted by the warm glow of hundreds of Japanese paper lanterns hung from every cottage porch. This describes the scene on Illumination Night at the end of the Camp Meeting season—which is attended these days by some fourth- and fifth-generation cottagers. Attendees mark the occasion as they have for more than a century, with lights, song, and open houses for families and friends. Note that because of overwhelming crowds of onlookers in seasons past, the date is not announced until the week before. One-hour tours are conducted Tuesday and Thursday, July and August, at 10 AM. ✉ *Off Circuit Ave.* ☎ *508/693–0525* 💲 *Tour $10.*

Restaurants ▼

Jimmy Seas 5

Linda Jean's 6

Lola's 7

Lookout Tavern . .2

Offshore Ale
Company 4

Sharky's
Cantina 3

Smoke 'n
Bones 9

Sweet Life
Café 8

Tsunami 1

Hotels ▼

Attleboro
House 1

Dockside Inn . . .4

MV Surfside
Motel 5

Oak Bluffs
Inn 2

Oak House 6

Pequot Hotel . . .3

Where to Stay & Eat
in Oak Bluffs

Where to Stay & Eat

$$$–$$$$
Fodor'sChoice
★
✕ **Sweet Life Café.** Housed in a charming Victorian house, this island fa-
vorite's warm tones, low lighting, and handsome antique furniture will
make you feel like you've entered someone's home—but the cooking is
more sophisticated than home-style. Dishes on the menu are prepared
in inventive ways; duck breast is roasted with a lavender-rosemary-honey
glaze, and the chèvre ravioli comes with a savory curry sauce. The
desserts are superb; try the warm chocolate fondant (a sort of soufflé)
with toasted-almond ice cream. There's outdoor dining by candlelight
in a shrub-enclosed garden, with heaters for cold nights. The same own-
ers run **Slice of Life** (⊠ 50 Circuit Ave. ☎ 508/693–3838), a more ca-
sual, less expensive bakery and café nearby. ⊠ *Upper Circuit Ave. at
far end of town* ☎ *508/696–0200* ⌫ *Reservations essential* ⊟ *AE, D,
MC, V* ✆ *Closed Jan.–Mar.*

$$–$$$$
✕ **Jimmy Seas.** The irresistible fragrance of sautéed garlic wafting out
these doors beckons lovers of the "stinking rose." Most dishes come in
the pan they're cooked in and are among the biggest portions you'll find
on the island. Classic red-sauce Italian dishes include *vongole* (whole
littleneck clams) marinara and linguine puttanesca. A brightly colored
porch and painted ceilings add to the place's charm. ⊠ *32 Kennebec
Ave.* ☎ *508/696–8550* ⌫ *Reservations not accepted* ⊟ *MC, V.*

$$–$$$$ ✕ **Lola's.** This festive spot draws a party crowd. On one side, a spirited bar hosts live music; an enclosed patio for dining and a large separate dining room are on another side. Ribs as well as Southern and Louisiana standards such as crawfish étoufée and grilled swordfish with Key lime dill sauce fill the long menu; Sunday mornings are reserved for an all-you-can-eat buffet brunch, often with live gospel or jazz. This is more of a scene than a relaxing dining spot. However, the bar is big and welcoming, and the wall mural is full of familiar local faces. Lighter, less expensive fare, such as chicken jambalaya and fried catfish, is available from the pub menu. ⊠ *Beach Rd., about 1 mi from Oak Bluffs* ☎ *508/693–5007* ▭ *DC, MC, V.*

$$–$$$$ ✕ **Tsunami.** In this quaint converted gingerbread house overlooking the harbor, chef Ricardo Reno focuses on Thai flavors but also samples from the cuisines of Japan, China, Burma, and France. You might start with tempura calamari with coconut-sambal sauce before moving on to pad thai with shrimp, or pan-roasted sole with a citrus-mint reduction and jasmine rice. The small upstairs dining room is decorated with a minimalist touch; downstairs is a handsome mahogany bar with several small tables. The dinner menu, which includes sushi and sake, is served on both levels. ⊠ *6 Circuit Ave. Ext.* ☎ *508/696–8900* ▭ *AE, MC, V* ☉ *Closed mid-Oct.–mid-May.*

$–$$$$ ✕ **Offshore Ale Company.** The island's first and only microbrewery restaurant has become quite popular. There are private wooden booths, dark wood throughout, a dartboard in the corner, and live music throughout the year (Wednesday-night Irish music jams are a hoot). Take your own peanuts from a barrel by the door and drop the shells on the floor; then order from a menu that includes steaks and burgers, chicken, gumbo, and fish. However, to truly appreciate the beer, try it with one of the wood-fired brick-oven pizzas. ⊠ *30 Kennebec Ave.* ☎ *508/693–2626* ⌲ *Reservations not accepted* ☉ *No lunch Mon. and Tues. Oct.–May* ▭ *AE, MC, V.*

$–$$$ ✕ **Smoke 'n Bones.** This is the island's only rib joint, with its own smoker out back and a cord of hickory, apple, oak, and mesquite wood stacked up around the lot. Treats from the smoker include Asian-style dry-rubbed ribs and North Carolina–style pulled pork. The place has a cookie-cutter, prefab feeling, with all the appropriate touches—neon flames around the kitchen and marble bones for doorknobs. If you're a true rib aficionado, this may not satisfy you, but on the Vineyard it's an offbeat treat. ⊠ *Siloam Rd., about 7 blocks from Oak Bluffs* ☎ *508/696–7427* ⌲ *Reservations not accepted* ▭ *MC, V.*

¢–$$ ✕ **Lookout Tavern.** There are two things about this easygoing Oak Bluffs seafood joint that make it stand out. First, its rustic dining room affords direct views of the sea and incoming ferry boats—it's truly the perfect "lookout" if you love watching boats ply the island's waters. Second, it serves the usual seafood platters plus first-rate sushi, from the salmon and tuna rolls to more unusual treats, like the Inkwell Roll, with barbecued eel, cucumber, avocado, crabmeat, and seaweed salad. Highlights from the traditional menu include the grilled Cuban sandwich, the snow-crab dinner, fish-and-chips, or the fried scallop plate. ⊠ *8 Seaview Ave. Ext.* ☎ *508/696–9844* ▭ *AE, D, DC, MC, V.*

★ ¢–$$ ✕ **Sharky's Cantina.** This small storefront restaurant opened in 2006 to rave reviews. Sharky's serves tasty–somewhat creative–Mexican and Southwestern fare and great drinks, and you may wait awhile to get a table. But once you're in, savor spicy tortilla soup, lobster quesadillas, steak burritos, chicken mole, and Gaucho-style skirt steak. There's an extensive margarita list (they're strong here), and for dessert try apple-pie empanadas drizzled with caramel sauce. Limited items from the menu are served until around midnight during the summer season. ☒ *31 Circuit Ave.* ☎ *508/ 693–7501* ⌂ *Reservations not accepted* ▤ *AE, MC, V.*

★ ¢–$ ✕ **Linda Jean's.** This is a classic local hangout, a diner that serves food the way a diner should: with hearty helpings and inexpensive prices. Want breakfast at 6 AM? No problem. Want breakfast at 11:30 AM? No problem. Tired of the gourmet world and want comfortable booths, friendly waitresses, and few frills? No problem. The only problem: you may have to wait—even at 6 AM. ☒ *34 Circuit Ave.* ☎ *508/693–4093* ⌂ *Reservations not accepted* ▤ *No credit cards.*

$$$–$$$$ ▦ **Oak Bluffs Inn.** A tan octagonal viewing tower dominates this rosy-hue Victorian B&B with a veranda on Oak Bluffs' main street, a short stroll from the beach. Victorian and country pieces fill the high-ceilinged rooms, all of which have private baths and gauzy white curtains; one has a four-poster bed. ☒ *64 Circuit Ave., at Pequot Ave., Box 2546, 02557* ☎ *508/693–7171 or 800/955–6235* 🖷 *508/693–8787* ⊕ *www. oakbluffsinn.com* ⬎ *9 rooms* ⌂ *No smoking* ▤ *AE, MC, V* ⊘ *Closed Nov.–early Apr.* ⍐ *CP.*

$$–$$$ ▦ **Dockside Inn.** This gingerbread Victorian-style inn built in 1989, decked with broad porches, sits right by the dock, steps from the ferry landing and downtown shops, restaurants, and bars. Kids are welcome, and they'll have plenty to do in town and at nearby beaches. Some rooms open onto building-length balconies. ☒ *9 Circuit Ave. Exit, Box 1206, 02557* ☎ *508/693–2966 or 800/245–5979* 🖷 *508/696–7293* ⊕ *www. vineyardinns.com* ⬎ *17 rooms, 5 suites, 2 apartments* ⌂ *Some kitchens, some kitchenettes, some in-room hot tubs, cable TV, hot tub* ▤ *AE, MC, V* ⊘ *Closed late Oct.–mid-May* ⍐ *CP.*

$$–$$$ ▦ **Martha's Vineyard Surfside Motel.** These two buildings stand right in the thick of things, steps from restaurants and nightlife, so it tends to get noisy in summer. Rooms are spacious and bright (especially corner units), smartly decorated with carpets, stylish wallpaper, tile floors, and fairly standard but attractive chain-style furnishings that include a table and chairs. Deluxe rooms have water views. Four suites have whirlpool baths, and two are wheelchair-accessible. The staff is helpful and courteous. ☒ *70 Oak Bluffs Ave., Box 2507, 02557* ☎ *508/693–2500 or 800/537–3007* 🖷 *508/693–7343* ⊕ *www.mvsurfside.com* ⬎ *34 rooms, 4 suites* ⌂ *Restaurant, in-room hot tubs, refrigerators, in-room broadband, some pets allowed (fee)* ▤ *AE, D, MC, V.*

★ $$–$$$ ▦ **Oak House.** The wraparound veranda of this courtly pastel-painted 1872 Victorian looks across a busy street to the beach and out across Nantucket Sound. Several rooms have private terraces or balconies; if you're bothered by noise, ask for a room in back. Ceilings, wall paneling, wainscoting, and furnishings are all in richly painted or polished oak, and all this well-preserved wood creates an appropriate setting for the choice antique furniture and nautical-theme accessories. An elegant afternoon tea with cakes and cookies is served in a glassed-in sunporch. ✉ *75 Sea View Ave., Box 299, 02557* 🕾 *508/693–4187 or 800/245–5979* 🖷 *508/696–7385* ⊕ *www.vineyardinns.com* 🛏 *10 rooms, 2 suites* ☖ *No kids under 10, no smoking* 🚬 *AE, D, MC, V* ⊙ *Closed mid-Oct.–mid-May* ❧ *CP.*

$–$$$ 🏨 **Pequot Hotel.** The bustle of downtown Oak Bluffs is a pleasant five-minute walk past Carpenter Gothic houses from this casual cedar-shingle inn on a tree-lined street. The furniture is quirky but comfortable; the old wing has the most atmosphere. In the main section of the building, the first floor has a wide porch with rocking chairs—perfect for enjoying coffee or tea with the cookies that are set out in the afternoon—and a small breakfast room where you help yourself to bagels, muffins, and cereal in the morning. The hotel is one block from the beaches that line Oak Bluffs–Edgartown Road. ✉ *19 Pequot Ave., 02557* 🕾 *508/693–5087 or 800/947–8704* 🖷 *508/696–9413* ⊕ *www.pequothotel.com* 🛏 *29 rooms, 1 3-bedroom apartment* ☖ *Dining room, cable TV, Wi-Fi; no room phones* 🚬 *AE, MC, V* ⊙ *Closed mid-Oct.–Apr.* ❧ *CP.*

$ 🏨 **Attleboro House.** This guesthouse, part of the Methodist Association Camp Grounds, is across the street from busy Oak Bluffs Harbor. The big 1874 gingerbread Victorian, an inn since its construction, has wraparound verandas on two floors and small, simple rooms with powder-blue walls, lacy white curtains, and a few antiques. Some rooms have sinks. Singles have three-quarter beds, and every room is provided linen exchange (but no chambermaid service) during a stay. The five shared baths are rustic and old but clean. ✉ *42 Lake Ave., Box 1564, 02557* 🕾 *508/693–4346* 🛏 *11 rooms with shared bath* ☖ *No room TVs* 🚬 *AE, D, MC, V* ⊙ *Closed Oct.–May* ❧ *CP.*

Nightlife & the Arts

Dark and crowded, the **Island House** (✉ 11 Circuit Ave. 🕾 508/693–4516) hosts a mixture of rock, blues, and reggae for younger crowds whose ears crave volume.

The **Lampost** (✉ 6 Circuit Ave. 🕾 508/696–9352) is a good, old-fashioned neighborhood bar with a DJ and dancing. In addition to events such as an '80s night, a Brazilian night, and a Hawaiian night, there are also swing nights. The bar attracts a young crowd.

Lola's (✉ Beach Rd. 🕾 508/693–5007), a popular restaurant, has a lively bar that hosts local musicians. There's a great pub menu year-round, and you can also get regular restaurant cuisine at the bar.

The island's only family brewpub, **Offshore Ale** (✉ Kennebec Ave. 🕾 508/693–2626) hosts live Latin, folk, and blues year-round and serves its own beer and ales and a terrific pub menu. Cozy up to the fireplace with a pint on cool nights.

The **Ritz Café** (✉ 4 Circuit Ave. 🕾 508/693–9851) is a popular year-round bar with a pool table that's removed in the summer to make way for dancing. There's an eclectic mix of live performances, including rock, blues, and reggae, from Monday through Saturday in summer and on weekends in the off-season.

Sports & the Outdoors

BEACH **Joseph A. Sylvia State Beach** (⊠ Between Oak Bluffs and Edgartown, off Beach Rd.) is a 6-mi-long sandy beach with a view of Cape Cod across Nantucket Sound. Food vendors and calm, warm waters make this a popular spot for families.

FISHING **Dick's Bait & Tackle** (⊠ New York Ave. ☎ 508/693–7669) rents gear, sells accessories and bait, and keeps a current copy of the fishing regulations.

GOLF **Farm Neck Golf Club** (⊠ County Rd. ☎ 508/693–3057), a semiprivate club on marsh-rimmed Sengekontacket Pond, has a driving range and 18 holes in a championship layout. Reservations are required 48 hours in advance.

Shopping

Book Den East (⊠ 71 New York Ave. ☎ 508/693–3946) stocks 20,000 out-of-print, antiquarian, and paperback books.

B*tru (⊠ 40 Circuit Ave. ☎ 508/693–5222) sells wonderfully stylish, off-beat, funky clothing and accessories.

If you're looking for out-of-the-ordinary, **Craftworks** (⊠ 42 Circuit Ave. ☎ 508/693–7463) carries outrageous painted furniture, ceramic figures, folk art, and home accessories—all handmade by American artists.

Laughing Bear (⊠ 33 Circuit Ave. ☎ 508/693–9342) carries women's clothing made of Balinese or Indian batiks plus jewelry and accessories from around the world.

The **Secret Garden** (⊠ 41 Circuit Ave. ☎ 508/693–4759), set in a yellow gingerbread cottage, has a complete line of Shelia collectibles—miniature wooden versions of Camp Ground houses and other island landmarks.

ART GALLERIES **Cousen Rose Gallery** (⊠ 71 Circuit Ave. ☎ 508/693–6656) displays works by many island artists, including Myrna Morris, John Breckenridge, Marietta Cleasby, Deborah Colter, Lynn Hoefs, Ray Prosser, and Renee Balter. During the summer months, be sure to inquire about children's art classes.

Dragonfly Gallery (⊠ Dukes County and Vineyard Aves. ☎ 508/693–8877) changes shows weekly and holds artist receptions—featuring jazz pianist John Alaimo—every other Saturday during the summer from 4 to 7 PM. Check the local papers for a schedule of artists.

The **Firehouse Gallery** (⊠ 635 Dukes County Ave., at Vineyard Ave. ☎ 508/693–9025) is home to the Martha's Vineyard Center for the Visual Arts. It holds weekly shows throughout the summer, featuring island and off-island artists; check the local paper for details.

Edgartown

❻ *6 mi southeast of Oak Bluffs.*

★ Stop at a complex of buildings and lawn exhibits that constitutes the **Martha's Vineyard Historical Society** to orient yourself historically before making your way around town. The opening hours and admission listed below apply to all the buildings and exhibits—including the Thomas Cooke House, the Francis Foster Museum, the Capt. Francis Pease House, and the Carriage Shed—and the Huntington Reference Library of Vineyard History, which contains archives of oral history, letters, and law documents. The museum sells an excellent Edgartown walking-tour booklet full of anecdotes and the history of the people who have lived in the town's houses over the past three centuries; you can purchase the booklet at the entrance gatehouse in summer or at the library in winter. ⊠ *Cooke and School Sts.* ☎ *508/627–4441* ⊕ *www.marthasvineyardhistory.org* 🖃 *$7* ⊗ *Mid-Mar.–mid-June and early Oct.–late Dec., Wed.–Fri. 1–4, Sat. 10–4; mid-June–early Oct., Tues.–Sat. 10–5; early Jan.–mid-Mar., Sat. 10–4.*

Once a well-to-do whaling center, Edgartown remains the Vineyard's toniest town and has preserved parts of its elegant past. Sea captains' houses from the 18th and 19th centuries, ensconced in well-manicured gardens and lawns, line the streets. The island's oldest dwelling is the 1672 **Vincent House Museum.** A tour of this weathered-shingle farmhouse takes you along a time line that starts with the sparse furnishings of the 1600s and ends in a Federal-style parlor of the 1800s. ⊠ *Main St.* ☎ *508/627–4440* ⊕ *www.mvpreservation.org/tours.html* 🖃 *Museum $5* ⊗ *May–mid-Oct., Mon.–Sat. 10:30–3.*

❼ The **Edgartown Lighthouse,** surrounded by a public beach, provides a great view (but seaweedy bathing). The white cast-iron tower was floated by barge from Ipswich, Massachusetts, in 1938. ⊠ *Off N. Water St.*

NEED A BREAK?

If you need a pick-me-up, pop into **Espresso Love** (⊠ 3 S. Water St. ☎ 508/627–9211) for a cappuccino and a homemade raspberry scone or blueberry muffin. If you prefer something cold, the staff also makes fruit smoothies. Light lunch fare is served: bagel sandwiches, soups, and delicious pastries and cookies—all homemade, of course.

★ ♻ ❺ The 350-acre **Felix Neck Wildlife Sanctuary,** a Massachusetts Audubon Society preserve 3 mi outside Edgartown toward Oak Bluffs and Vineyard Haven, has 2 mi of hiking trails traversing marshland, fields, woods, seashore, and waterfowl and reptile ponds. Naturalist-led events include sunset hikes, stargazing, snake or bird walks, and canoeing. ⊠ *Off Edgartown–Vineyard Haven Rd.* ☎ *508/627–4850* 🖃 *$4* ⊗ *Center June–Aug., Mon.–Sat. 8–4, Sun. 10–3; Sept.–May, Tues.–Sat. 8–4, Sun. noon–4. Trails daily sunrise–7 PM.*

Where to Stay & Eat

$$$–$$$$ ✕ **Alchemy Bistro and Bar.** According to the menu, the dictionary meaning of *alchemy* is "a magic power having as its asserted aim the discovery of a panacea and the preparation of the elixir of longevity"—lofty goals for a French-style bistro. This high-class version has elegant gray wainscoting, classic paper-covered white tablecloths, old wooden floors, and an opening cut into the ceiling to reveal the second-floor tables. The only things missing are the patina of age, experience, cigarette smoke—and French working folk's prices—but you can expect quality and imag-

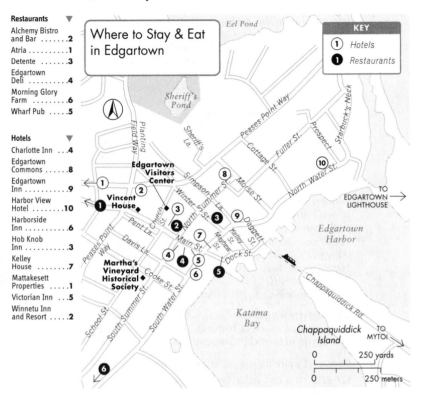

Restaurants ▼

Alchemy Bistro
and Bar 2

Atria 1

Detente 3

Edgartown
Deli 4

Morning Glory
Farm 6

Wharf Pub 5

Hotels ▼

Charlotte Inn . . .4

Edgartown
Commons 8

Edgartown
Inn 9

Harbor View
Hotel 10

Harborside
Inn 6

Hob Knob
Inn 3

Kelley
House 7

Mattakesett
Properties 1

Victorian Inn . . .5

Winnetu Inn
and Resort 2

ination. One example is the fried cornmeal-dusted soft-shell crab with lemon risotto, sweet peas, and artichokes. The alcohol list, long and complete, includes cognacs, grappas, and beers. ⊠ *71 Main St.* ☎ *508/627–9999* ▤ *AE, MC, V.*

$$$–$$$$
Fodor'sChoice
★
✕ **Atria.** One of the island's more urbane venues, Atria feels like a big-city bistro and cocktail lounge, with a swank dining room, glam crowd, and artful food presentations. Chef Christian Thornton uses eclectic, globally influenced ingredients to come up with such entrées as pan-seared duck breast with duck-confit spring rolls, baby bok choy, and fresh plum sauce; and wok-fired cracked lobster with whipped potatoes. Top starters include steak tartar with crisp shallots, capers, truffle oil, and aged balsamic vinegar; and braised-veal-cheek ravioli with stuffed squash blossoms, shaved Parmesan, and truffle oil. The chocolate-molten cake with cappuccino ice cream is a great finish. ⊠ *137 Main St.* ☎ *508/627–5850* ▤ *AE, MC, V.*

$$$–$$$$
✕ **Detente.** A dark, intimate wine bar and restaurant with hardwood floors and rich banquette seating, Detente serves more than a dozen wines by the glass as well as numerous half-bottles. Even if you're not much of an oenophile, it's worth a trip just for the innovative food. Try the unusual starter of truffled peaches with warm taleggio cheese and mizuna, followed by such choice entrées as roasted wild boar chop over caponata

with fennel-potato tortellini in a pine-nut emulsion with caper berries; or lemon-honey–basted halibut with potato au gratin, truffled leek purée, roasted artichokes, and oven-dried tomatoes. ⊠ *Nevin Sq., off Water St.* ☎ *508/627–8810* ▭ *AE, MC, V* ☉ *Closed Tues. and Feb. and Mar. No lunch.*

$–$$$ ✕ **Wharf Pub.** The name may sound generic, and the menu tends toward the predictable—shrimp scampi, prime rib, burgers, and steaks—but this lively bar and grill in the heart of Edgartown earns kudos for its well-prepared food, inviting dining room and pair of bars, and easygoing vibe. Standouts include the grilled flank steak with fries and a horseradish cream sauce, and the Cobb salad with ham and chicken. You can tune in to a game on the TV or mingle with locals. It's nothing fancy, but this year-round mainstay is consistently reliable and a great bet for singles, groups of friends, and—especially during the day—families. ⊠ *Lower Main St.* ☎ *508/627–9966* ▭ *AE, D, MC, V.*

★ **¢–$** ✕ **Morning Glory Farm.** Fresh farm greens in the salads and vegetables in the soups; homemade pies, cookies, and cakes; and a picnic table and grass to enjoy them on make this an ideal place for a simple country lunch. ⊠ *West Tisbury Rd.* ☎ *508/627–9003* ▭ *No credit cards.*

¢ ✕ **Edgartown Deli.** A no-frills place with a down-home, happy feeling, this deli has walls and a glass counter plastered with specials written on multicolored paper. Brightly lighted booths fill one side of the room, and customers line up at the counter for orders to go. Breakfast specials, served from 8 until 10:45, include egg, cheese, and *linguiça* (garlicky Portuguese sausage) on a roll. Lunch sandwiches include corned beef and Swiss, roast beef, turkey, pastrami, or steak and cheese. ⊠ *52 Main St.* ☎ *508/627–4789* ⌦ *Reservations not accepted* ▭ *No credit cards* ☉ *Closed Nov.–Apr. No dinner.*

$$$$ 🏠 **Charlotte Inn.** From the moment you walk up to the dark-wood Scottish barrister's check-in desk at this regal 1864 inn, you'll be surrounded by the trappings and customs of a bygone era. Guests' names are handwritten into the register by the dignified and attentive staff. Beautiful antique furnishings, objets d'art, and paintings fill the property—the book you pick up in your room might be an 18th-century edition of Voltaire, and your bed could be a hand-carved four-poster. All rooms have hair dryers and robes; rooms in the carriage house have fireplaces and French doors that open into the brick courtyard as well as private patios. The elegant atmosphere that pervades the property extends to the inn's swank restaurant, the Terrace. ⊠ *27 S. Summer St., 02539* ☎ *508/627–4751* ⎙ *508/627–4652* ⊕ *www.relaischateaux.com* ⇆ *21 rooms, 2 suites* ⌂ *Restaurant, in-room broadband, library; no kids under 14* ▭ *AE, MC, V* ⦿ *CP.*

FodorsChoice

★

★ **$$$$** 🏠 **Harbor View Hotel.** The centerpiece of this historic hotel is a gray-shingle, 1891 Victorian building with wraparound veranda and a gazebo. Accommodations are also in a complex of nearby buildings in a residential neighborhood. The contemporary town houses have cathedral ceilings, decks, kitchens, and large living areas with sofa beds. Rooms in other buildings, however, resemble upscale motel rooms, so ask for a main-building or town-house room. A beach, good for walking, stretches ¾ mi from the hotel's dock, and the sheltered bay is a great place for kids to swim. Packages and theme weekends are available. The hotel is also home to the Coach House restaurant. ⊠ *131 N. Water St., Box 7, 02539* ☎ *508/627–7000 or 800/225–6005* 🖷 *508/742–1042* ⊕ *www.harborview.com* ↹ *102 rooms, 22 suites* ⚐ *2 restaurants, room service, some kitchenettes, cable TV, refrigerators, 2 tennis courts, pool, dock, laundry service, concierge, business services* ☰ *AE, DC, MC, V.*

$$$$ 🏨 **Harborside Inn.** Right on the harbor, with boat docks at the end of its nicely landscaped lawn, this large inn provides a central town location, harbor-view decks, and plenty of amenities. Seven two- and three-story buildings sprawl around formal rose beds, brick walkways, a brick patio, and a heated pool. Rooms have colonial-style but modern furnishings, brass beds and lamps, and textured wallpapers. ⊠ *3 S. Water St., Box 67, 02539* ☎ *508/627–4321 or 800/627–4009* 🖷 *508/627–7566* ⊕ *www. theharborsideinn.com* ↹ *89 rooms, 3 suites* ⚐ *Refrigerators, cable TV, pool, hot tub, sauna, dock* ☰ *AE, MC, V* ☉ *Closed mid-Nov.–mid-Apr.*

$$$$ 🏨 **Hob Knob Inn.** This 19th-century Gothic Revival inn blends the amenities and service of a luxury hotel with the ambience and charm of a small B&B. A short walk from the harbor, it's on the main road into town—but far enough out to avoid crowds. Rooms are gracious and quite large by island standards; the upper floors have dormer windows. Art and antiques help capture the island's rural, seaside charm, and many rooms overlook the spectacular gardens. The inn also runs fishing trips and charters on its 27-foot Boston Whaler. Full breakfast and lavish afternoon tea are included. ⊠ *128 Main St., 02539* ☎ *508/627–9510 or 800/ 696–2723* 🖷 *508/627–4560* ⊕ *www.hobknob.com* ↹ *17 rooms, 1 suite* ⚐ *Cable TV, Wi-Fi, gym, massage, sauna, bicycles, meeting rooms; no kids under 10* ☰ *AE, MC, V* ⦿ *BP.*

$$$$ 🏨 **Kelley House.** In the center of town, this sister property of the Harbor View combines services and amenities with a country-inn feel. The 1742 white clapboard main house and the adjacent Garden House are surrounded by pink roses. Large suites in the Chappaquiddick House and the two spacious town houses in the Wheel House have porches (most with harbor views) and living rooms. The Newes from America, with original hand-hewn timbers and ballast-brick walls, serves light fare and microbrewed beers on tap. ⊠ *23 Kelley St., Box 37, 02539* ☎ *508/ 627–7900 or 800/225–6005* 🖷 *508/627–8142* ⊕ *www.kelley-house.com* ↹ *42 rooms, 9 suites, 2 town-house units* ⚐ *Restaurant, some kitchens, cable TV, 2 tennis courts, pool, pub, babysitting, laundry service, business services* ☰ *AE, DC, MC, V* ☉ *Closed mid-Oct.–Apr.* ⦿ *CP.*

$$$$ 🏨 **Mattakesett Properties.** This attractive resort complex, which lies just down the road from its sister resort, the Winnetu, sits close to South Beach. Mattakesett differs from the Winnetu in that all of its units are owner-furnished town houses and condominiums with three to four bedrooms; guests at either property can use the amenities at both. All homes have fireplaces and decks. The children's programs are extensive, and the pool and barbecue grills make this a favorite for families. Bookings at Mattakesett are taken on a per-week basis only. A vintage fire truck and livery are used to shuttle you around the area. ⊠ *Katama Rd., RFD 270, 02539* ☎ *508/627–4747 or 978/443–1733* ⊕ *www.winnetu.com/ mattakesett.htm* ↹ *92 units* ⚐ *Kitchens, cable TV, some in-room broad-*

band, some Wi-Fi, 10 tennis courts, pool, theater, children's programs (ages 3–12), laundry facilities ▭ *AE, MC, V* ⊘ *Mattakesett closed Nov.–Apr.*

$$$$
Fodor's Choice
★

▣ **Winnetu Inn and Resort.** A departure from most properties on the island, the contemporary Winnetu—styled after the grand multistory resorts of the gilded age—both encourages families and provides a contemporary seaside-resort experience for couples. This all-suites property has units that can sleep up to 11 guests. All have kitchens and decks or patios with views. Room decor is stylish and modern but casual enough so that kids feel right at home. The resort arranges bicycling and kayaking trips, lighthouse tours, and other island activities. The General Store carries snacks, and Lure, the only restaurant on the island with a south-facing water view, prepares tasty box lunches for the beach. (It's open to the public and specializes in gourmet fish fare.) The staff will stock your kitchen in advance of your arrival on request. Clambakes are held on the grounds on Wednesday evening. In summer, all stays must be a minimum of three nights. ⊠ *Katama Rd., RFD 270, 02539* ☎ *508/627–4747 or 978/443–1733* ⊕ *www.winnetu.com* ⇆ *22 suites* ⚒ *Restaurant, snack bar, kitchens, cable TV, in-room VCRs, in-room broadband, putting green, 10 tennis courts, pool, gym, croquet, Ping-Pong, library, children's programs (ages 3–12), laundry facilities, concierge, business services, Internet room, meeting rooms* ▭ *MC, V* ⊘ *Closed Dec.–mid-Apr.*

6

★ **$$$–$$$$**
▣ **Victorian Inn.** White with the classic black shutters of the town's historic homes and fronted by ornate columns, this appropriately named inn sits a block from the downtown harbor; it was built as the home of 19th-century whaling captain Lafayette Rowley. Today the inn's three floors are done in dark woods and bold floral wallpapers, with rugs over wood floors. Several rooms hold handmade reproduction four-poster beds. Breakfast, served in season in the brick-patio garden, includes creative muffins and breads. ⊠ *24 S. Water St., 02539* ☎ *508/627–4784* ⊕ *www.thevic.com* ⇆ *14 rooms* ⚒ *No kids under 8* ▭ *MC, V* ⦿▮ *BP.*

$–$$$$
▣ **Edgartown Inn.** The inside of the former home of whaling captain Thomas Worth still evokes its late 18th century origins. In fact, its cozy parlor and antique-filled rooms look as if the captain still lives here. The inn was also the spot where Nathaniel Hawthorne wrote much of his "Twice Told Tales" during a stay. Many an Edgartonian joins inn guests in the paneled dining room or back garden for breakfast in summertime. ⊠ *56 N. Water St., 02539* ☎ *508/627–4794* 🖷 *508/627–9420* ⊕ *www.edgartowninn.com* ⇆ *20 rooms, 4 with shared bath* ▭ *No credit cards.*

$$–$$$
▣ **Edgartown Commons.** This condominium complex of seven buildings, which includes an old house and motel rooms set around a busy pool, is just a couple of blocks from town. Studios and one- or two-bedroom condos all have full kitchens, and some are very spacious. Each has been decorated by its individual owner, so the decor varies—some have an older look, others are new and bright. Definitely family-oriented, the place is abuzz with kids; rooms away from the pool are quieter. ⊠ *20 Pease's Point Way, Box 1293, 02539* ☎ *508/627–4671, 800/439–4671 in eastern Massachusetts* 🖷 *508/627–4271* ⊕ *www.edgartowncommons.com* ⇆ *35 units* ⚒ *Picnic area, some kitchens, cable TV, pool, playground, laundry facilities; no room phones* ▭ *AE, MC, V* ⊘ *Closed mid-Oct.–Apr.*

Nightlife & the Arts

The **Atria Bar** (⊠ 137 Main St. ☎ 508/627–5850) is off the beaten path, but it's a quiet, comfortable place to escape the summer crowds. Enjoy one of the clever drinks, including the Aunt Katherine Manhattan (Maker's Mark and sweet vermouth, served neat), and the Espresso Martini (Stoli vanilla vodka, Kahlúa, Tia Maria, and a shot of fresh espresso).

Outerlands (⊠ Martha's Vineyard Airport, Edgartown–West Tisbury Rd. ☎ 508/693–1137), formerly Hot Tin Roof, is a venue where big-name acts such as Medeski, Martin and Wood, Ben Lee, Kate Taylor, and the Derek Trucks Band play.

The Wharf (⊠ Lower Main St. ☎ 508/627–9966) is a great spot for tasty food and a terrific place for cocktails, people-watching, and listening to live rock and pop music.

Sports & the Outdoors

Bend-in-the-Road Beach (⊠ Beach Rd.), the town's public beach, is backed by low, grassy dunes and wild roses. **Little Beach** (⊠ End of Fuller St.) is a lesser-known beach that looks like a crooked pinkie pointing into Eel Pond; it's a great place for bird-watching (be careful of the fenced-off piping plover breeding grounds in the dunes).

Big Eye Charters (☎ 508/627–3649) leads fishing charters from Edgartown Harbor. **Coop's Bait and Tackle** (⊠ 147 W. Tisbury Rd. ☎ 508/627–3909) sells accessories and bait, rents fishing gear, and books fishing charters.

Shopping

Claudia (⊠ 35 Winter St. ☎ 508/627–8306) brings you back to another era with its clever windows, antique display cases, and fabulous French fragrances. You'll find designer, vintage-looking, and fine gold and silver jewelry in a variety of price ranges.

David Le Breton, the owner of **Edgartown Books** (⊠ 44 Main St. ☎ 508/627–8463), is a true bibliophile. He carries a large selection of current and island-related titles and will be happy to make a summer reading recommendation.

The **Edgartown Scrimshaw Gallery** (⊠43 Main St. ☎508/627–9439) showcases a large collection of scrimshaw, including some antique pieces.

Lamplighter Corner (⊠ 89 Pease's Point Way S ☎ 508/627–4656) has artisans making brass and copper lanterns; it also sells 18th- and 19th-century American furniture.

The **Old Sculpin Gallery** (⊠ 58 Dock St. ☎ 508/627–4881) is the Martha's Vineyard Art Association's headquarters.

Chappaquiddick Island

⓫ *1 mi southeast of Edgartown.*

A sparsely populated area with many nature preserves, Chappaquiddick Island makes for a pleasant day trip or bike ride on a sunny day. The "island" is actually connected to the Vineyard by a long sand spit that begins in South Beach in Katama. It's a spectacular 2¾-mi walk, or you can take the ferry, which departs about every five minutes from 7 AM to midnight daily, June to mid-October.

⑨ The Land Bank's 226-acre **Three Ponds Preserve** (✉ Off Chappaquiddick Rd.) is a popular, scenic picnicking spot. Mown grasses surround a serpentine pond with an island in its center and a woodland backdrop behind—a truly lovely setting. Across the road are fields, woods, and another pond.

★ ⑩ The Trustees of Reservations' 14-acre **Mytoi** preserve is a quiet, Japanese-inspired garden with a creek-fed pool spanned by a bridge and rimmed with Japanese maples, azaleas, bamboo, and irises. The garden was created in 1958 by a private citizen. Restroom facilities are available. ✉ *Dike Rd., ⅕ mi from intersection with Chappaquiddick Rd.* ☎ *508/627–7689* 🖾 *Free* ☉ *Daily sunrise–sunset.*

⑧ A conglomeration of habitats where you can swim, walk, fish, or just sit and enjoy the surroundings, the **Cape Poge Wildlife Refuge** (✉ East end of Dike Rd., 3 mi from Chappaquiddick ferry landing), on the easternmost shore of Chappaquiddick Island, is more than 6 square mi of wilderness. Its dunes, woods, cedar thickets, moors, salt marshes, ponds, tidal flats, and barrier beach serve as an important migration stopover and nesting area for numerous sea- and shorebirds. The best way to get to the refuge is as part of a naturalist-led **jeep drive** (☎ 508/627–3599).

★ ⑫ The 200-acre **Wasque Reservation** (pronounced *wayce*-kwee) is mostly a vast beach. Closing off the south end of Katama Bay, this is where Chappaquiddick connects to the mainland Vineyard. You can fish, sunbathe, take the trail by Swan Pond, walk to the island's southeasternmost tip at Wasque Point, or dip into the surf—use caution, as the currents are strong. Wasque Beach is accessed by a flat boardwalk with benches overlooking the west end of Swan Pond. It's a pretty walk skirting the pond, with ocean views on one side and poles for osprey nests on the other. Atop a bluff is a pine-shaded picnic grove with a spectacular, practically 180-degree panorama. ✉ *At east end of Wasque Rd., 5 mi from Chappaquiddick ferry landing* ☎ *508/627–7260* 🖾 *Cars $3, plus $3 per adult late May–mid-Sept.; free rest of yr* ☉ *Property 24 hrs. Gatehouse late May–mid-Oct., daily 9–5.*

Sports & the Outdoors

BEACHES **East Beach,** one of the area's best beaches, is accessible by car from Dike Road. There is a $3 fee to enter the beach. **Wasque Beach,** at the Wasque Reservation, is an uncrowded ½-mi sandy beach with a parking lot and restrooms. The surf and currents are sometimes strong.

West Tisbury

⑲ *8 mi west of Edgartown, 6½ mi south of Vineyard Haven.*

West Tisbury retains its rural appeal and maintains its agricultural tradition at several active horse and produce farms. The town center looks very much like a small New England village, complete with a white steepled church.

★ ⑱ A rich and expansive collection of flora and serene walking trails are the attractions of the **Polly Hill Arboretum.** Horticulturist and part-time Vineyard resident Polly Hill, now in her nineties, has over the years tended some 2,000 species of plants and developed nearly 100 species herself on her old sheep farm in West Tisbury. On site are azaleas, tree peonies, dogwoods, hollies, lilacs, magnolias, and more. Hill raised them from seeds without the use of a greenhouse, and her patience is the inspiration of the arboretum. Now run as a nonprofit center, the arboretum also runs guided tours, a lecture series, and a visitor center and gift shop. ⊠ *809 State Rd.* ☎ *508/693–9426* ⊕ *www.pollyhillarboretum.org* ▨ *$5* ☉ *Grounds daily sunrise–sunset. Visitor center late May–mid-Oct., daily 9:30–4; guided tours by appointment.*

NEED A BREAK?
Step back in time with a visit to **Alley's General Store** (⊠ State Rd. ☎ 508/693-0088), the heart of town since 1858. Alley's sells a truly general variety of goods: everything from hammers to housewares and dill pickles to sweet muffins as well as great things you find only in a country store. There's even a post office inside. Behind the parking lot, Back Alley's serves tasty sandwiches and pastries to go year-round.

⑯ **Long Point,** a 633-acre Trustees of Reservations preserve with an open area of grassland and heath, provides a lovely walk with the promise of a refreshing swim at its end. The area is bounded on the east by freshwater Homer's Pond, on the west by saltwater Tisbury Great Pond, and on the south by fantastic, mile-long South Beach on the Atlantic Ocean. Long Cove Pond, a sandy freshwater swimming pond, is an ideal spot for bird-watchers. ⊠ *Mid-June–mid-Sept., turn left onto unmarked dirt road (Waldron's Bottom Rd., look for mailboxes) ³⁄₁₀ mi west of airport on Edgartown–West Tisbury Rd.; at end, follow signs to Long Point parking lot. Mid-Sept.–mid-June, follow unpaved Deep Bottom Rd. (1 mi west of airport) 2 mi to lot* ☎ *508/693–7392* ▨ *Mid-June–mid-Sept., $7 per vehicle, $3 per adult; free rest of yr* ☉ *Daily 9–6.*

⑮ A rather unique island undertaking, the **Chicama Vineyards** is the fruit of the Mathiesen family's labors. From 3 acres of trees and rocks, George—a broadcaster from San Francisco—his wife, Cathy, and their six children have built a fine vineyard. They started in 1971 with 18,000 vinifera vines, and today the winery produces nearly 100,000 bottles a year from Chardonnay, Cabernet, and other European grapes. Chenin blanc, Merlot, and a cranberry dessert wine are among their 10 or more tasty varieties. A shop selling their wine, along with herbed vinegars, mustards, jellies, and other foods prepared on the premises, is open year-round. ⊠ *Stoney Hill Rd.* ☎ *508/693–0309* ⊕ *www.chicamavineyards.com* ▨ *Free tours and tastings* ☉ *Late May–mid-Oct., Mon.–Sat. 11–5, Sun. 1–5; call for off-season hrs and tastings.*

⑭ In season you can pick your own strawberries, raspberries, and flowers at **Thimble Farm,** where you can also buy preboxed fruit if you're not feeling quite so agrarian. The farm also sells cut flowers, melons, pumpkins, hydroponic tomatoes, and other produce. ⊠ *Stoney Hill Rd.* ☎ *508/693–6396* ☉ *June–early Oct., Tues.–Sun. 10–5.*

Restaurants ▼

The Aquinnah
Restaurant **4**

At the
Cornerway **6**

The Bite **2**

Bittersweet **7**

Home Port **5**

Lambert's Cove
Country Inn **1**

Larsen's **3**

Hotels ▼

Beach Plum
Inn **5**

Duck Inn **6**

Inn at Blueberry
Hill **3**

Lambert's Cove
Country Inn **1**

Martha's
Vineyard
International
Hostel **2**

Menemsha
Inn and
Cottages **4**

Outermost
Inn **7**

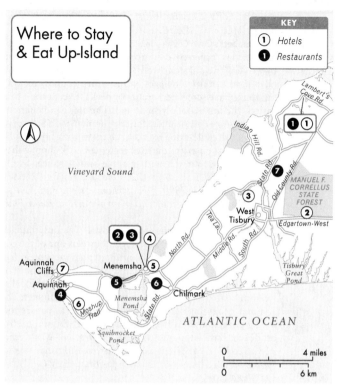

Where to Stay & Eat Up-Island

KEY

① *Hotels*

❶ *Restaurants*

Vineyard Sound

MANUEL F. CORRELLUS STATE FOREST

West Tisbury

Edgartown-West

Aquinnah Cliffs

Menemsha

Chilmark

Aquinnah

Menemsha Pond

Moshup Trail

Squibnocket Pond

ATLANTIC OCEAN

Tisbury Great Pond

0   4 miles
0   6 km

6

★ ⑬ At the center of the island, the **Manuel F. Correllus State Forest** is a 5,000-acre pine and scrub-oak forest crisscrossed with hiking trails and circled by a paved but rough bike trail (mopeds are prohibited). You'll also find a 2-mi nature trail, a 2-mi par fitness course, and horse trails. The West Tisbury side of the state forest joins with an equally large Edgartown parcel to virtually surround the airport. ⊠ *Headquarters on Barnes Rd. by airport* ☎ *508/693–2540* ⊠ *Free* ⊙ *Daily sunrise–sunset.*

⑰ A paradise for bird-watchers, **Sepiessa Point Reservation** consists of 164 acres on splendid Tisbury Great Pond, with expansive pond and ocean views, walking trails around coves and saltwater marshes, bird-watching, horse trails, swimming, and a boat launch. ⊠ *New La., which becomes Tiah's Cove Rd., off W. Tisbury Rd.* ☎ *508/627–7141* ⊠ *Free* ⊙ *Daily sunrise–sunset.*

Where to Stay & Eat

$$$–$$$$ ✕ **Bittersweet.** A pronounced Mediterranean flavor enhances the progressive American cuisine that chef Job Yacubian creates here. Rosemary, olives, and celery hearts are part of the braised lamb shank, and the pan-roasted skate wing is flavored with kumquats and almonds, cauliflower, and capers. The menu is exciting, but keep in mind that this place can get a bit noisy. ⊠ *State Rd.* ☎ *508/696–3966* ⚓ *Reservations essen-tial* ▤ *MC, V* 🍷 *BYOB.*

$$–$$$$
Fodor'sChoice
★

✕⊞ **Lambert's Cove Country Inn.** A narrow road winds through pine woods and beside creeper-covered stone walls to this secluded inn surrounded by gardens and old stone walls. Rooms in the rambling 1790 farmhouse have light floral wallpapers and a sunny, country feel. Those in out-buildings have screened porches or decks. Except for a brief winter va-cation, the inn is open year-round. The soft candlelight and excellent contemporary cuisine make the restaurant ($$–$$$; reservations essen-tial) a worthwhile stop. Try the crab cakes with caper aioli and shaved-fennel salad, or a main course of center-cut pork chop with roasted sweet potatoes, broccoli rabe, and an apple brandy sauce. ⊠ *Off Lambert's Cove Rd.* ✍ *R.R. 1, Box 422, Vineyard Haven 02568* ☎ *508/693–2298* 🖷 *508/693–7890* ⊕ *www.lambertscoveinn.com* ⇗ *15 rooms* ⚐ *Restaurant, tennis court; no room phones, no room TVs* ▤ *AE, MC, V* 🍽 *BP.*

¢

⊞ **Martha's Vineyard International Hostel.** The only budget, roof-over-your-head alternative in season, this hostel is one of the country's best. The large, common kitchen is outfitted with multiple refrigerators and stoves (barbecue grills are available, too), the common room has a fire-place and plenty of books, and you'll catch wind of local events on the bulletin board. Morning chores are required in summer. The hostel runs summer programs on island history, as well as nature tours. It's near a bike path, and 2 mi from the airport and about 3 mi from the near-est beach. Buses stop out front. ⊠ *Edgartown–West Tisbury Rd., Box 158, 02575* ☎ *508/693–2665* ⊕ *www.usahostels.org* ⇗ *78 dorm-style beds* ⚐ *Volleyball, laundry facilities* ▤ *MC, V* ☉ *Closed mid-Oct.–mid-Apr.*

Nightlife & the Arts

WIMP (⊠ Grange Hall, State Rd. ☎ 508/939–9368), the island's pre-mier comedy improvisation troupe, performs Wednesday at 8 PM from mid-June to mid-October.

Sports & the Outdoors

Lambert's Cove Beach (⊠ Lambert's Cove Rd.), one of the island's pret-tiest, has fine sand and clear water. The Vineyard Sound Beach has calm waters; it's good for children.

Shopping

The **Granary Gallery at the Red Barn** (⊠ Old County Rd. ☎ 508/693–0455) displays early-American furniture and exhibits artworks by island and international artists.

Chilmark

20 *5½ mi southwest of West Tisbury.*

Chilmark is a rural village where ocean-view roads, rustic woodlands, and lack of crowds have drawn chic summer visitors and resulted in stratospheric real estate prices. Laced with rough roads and winding stone fences that once separated fields and pastures, Chilmark reminds people of what the Vineyard was like in an earlier time, before the developers came.

NEED A BREAK? The **Chilmark Store** (⊠ 7 State Rd. ☎ 508/645–3655) serves up pizza, burgers, salads, and deli sandwiches—it's a solid take-out lunch spot. If you've bicycled into town, the wooden rockers on the porch may be just the place to take a break—or find a picnic spot of your own nearby to enjoy a fish burger or a slice of the pizza of the day. It's open from May to mid-October.

Where to Stay & Eat

$$$–$$$$ ✕ **At the Cornerway.** Jamaican chef Deon Thomas brings cuisine rich in his home island's flavors to this American-style bistro. Adventurous diners can try braised goat shoulder with prunes and pearl onions; those with less exotic tastes can choose from offerings like duck, lamb, venison, or garlic-crusted snapper. Whichever pleases your palate, make sure to finish with either the coconut bread pudding or chocolate rum cake. If you want to hear what your dinner companions have to say, ask for a corner seat away from the atrium. The acoustics are terrible in this barnlike structure that once hosted square dances. ⊠ *Beetlebung Corner* ☎ *508/645–9300* ▬ *AE, MC, V* ⛟ *BYOB.*

$$$–$$$$ ✕▢ **Inn at Blueberry Hill.** Exclusive and secluded, this cedar-shingle retreat on 56 acres of former farmland puts you in the heart of the rural Vineyard. The restaurant, Theo's ($$–$$$$), is relaxed and elegant, with fresh, health-conscious food that is thoughtfully prepared. You might dine on maple-spiced duck breast with sweet-potato gnocchi, or seared sea scallops with a basil-grapefruit-tarragon beurre blanc. A cold breakfast is included in the room rate, and a box lunch is available for a picnic on the beach (the inn runs a guest shuttle to Lucy Vincent and Squibnocket beaches). Rooms are sparsely but tastefully decorated with simple island-made furniture; most have glass doors that open onto terraces or private decks. There is a large parlor-library with a fireplace. ⊠ *74 North Rd., 02535* ☎ *508/645–3322 or 800/ 356–3322* 🖶 *508/645–3799* ⊕ *www.blueberryinn.com* 🛏 *25 rooms* ⛵ *Restaurant, tennis court, pool, gym, hot tub, massage, meeting room, airport shuttle; no kids under 12, no smoking* ▬ *AE, MC, V* ⊙ *Closed Nov.–Apr.* ⛆ *CP.*

Sports & the Outdoors

★ A dirt road leads off South Road to beautiful **Lucy Vincent Beach,** which in summer is open only to Chilmark residents and those staying in town.

Squibnocket Beach (⊠ off South Rd.), on the south shore, is a narrow stretch of boulder-strewn coastline that is part smooth rocks and pebbles, part fine sand. The area has good waves, and it's popular with surfers. During the season, this beach is restricted to residents and visitors with passes.

Shopping

★ **Chilmark Chocolates** (⊠ State Rd. ☎ 508/645–3013) sells superior chocolates and what might just be the world's finest butter crunch, which you can sometimes watch being made in the back room.

CLOSE UP

Martha's Vineyard Trivia

The year-round population of the island is about 15,000. On any given day in summer, the population increases fivefold, to an estimated 75,000.

Some four decades after the island was charted in 1602, Bay Colony businessman Thomas Mayhew struck a deal with the Crown and purchased Martha's Vineyard, as well as Nantucket and the Elizabeth Islands, for £40.

Jeanne and Hugh Taylor, the latter the brother of recording star James Taylor, operate the Outermost Inn, by the lighthouse in Aquinnah.

Total shoreline: 126 mi. Total land area: 100 square mi.

Martha's Vineyard was formed more than 20,000 years ago as great sheets of ice, as thick as 2 mi, descended from the frigid northern climes into what is now New England, pushing great chunks of earth and rock before them. When the glaciers melted and receded, the island, as well as Nantucket and Cape Cod, remained in their wake.

When residents say they are going "Up-Island," they mean they're heading to the western areas of Aquinnah, Chilmark, Menemsha, and West Tisbury. The designation is based on nautical terminology, where heading west means going "up" in longitude. "Down-Island" refers to Vineyard Haven, Oak Bluffs, and Edgartown.

During the height of the 19th-century whaling era, it was considered good luck to have an Aquinnah Wampanoag on board. The Wampanoags were renowned as sailors and harpooners. Town residents voted to change the name of Gay Head to Aquinnah in 1997, and the official change was signed into law on May 7, 1998.

The North American continent's last heath hen, an eastern prairie chicken, died in a forest fire on Martha's Vineyard in 1932. A monument to it stands in the State Forest just off the West Tisbury-Edgartown Road.

West Tisbury resident, farmer, and sailor Joshua Slocum became the first man to sail solo around the world. He set out in 1895 in his 36-foot sloop and returned three years later. Ten years later he was lost at sea.

Despite the fact that Great Harbour was renamed Edgartown after the young son of the Duke of York, the unfortunate three-year-old died one month before the name became official.

Menemsha

★ *1½ mi northwest of Chilmark.*

Unspoiled by the "progress" of the past few decades, the working port of Menemsha is a jumble of weathered fishing shacks, fishing and pleasure boats, drying nets, and lobster pots. Several scenes from the movie *Jaws* were filmed here. The village is popular with cyclists who like to stop for ice cream or chowder.

Where to Stay & Eat

$$$–$$$$ ✕ **Home Port.** A classic seafood-in-the-rough experience since the 1930s, this breezy seasonal island institution serves absolutely the freshest lobster around, plus steamers, scallops, and local fish. The fishing nets and other nautical paraphernalia hanging on the knotty-pine walls bring you back to a bygone era. Sailors from all around southern New England savor the chance to pull into Menemsha for a meal at this stalwart, where commoners often rub shoulders with celebs. You can also get your meal to go and enjoy it on the lawn or by the dock overlooking the harbor. ✉ *At end of North Rd.* ☎ *508/645–2679* ⚓ *Reservations essential* ➦ *MC, V* ⛄ *BYOB* ⊗ *Closed mid-Oct.–mid-Apr. No lunch.*

¢–$$ ✕ **Larsen's.** Basically a retail fish store, Larsen's has a raw take-out
Fodor'sChoice counter and will also boil lobsters for you. A plate of fresh littlenecks
★ or cherrystones goes for $9 a dozen. Oysters—at $15 a dozen—are not a bad alternative. There's also seafood chowder and a variety of smoked fish and dips. Bring your own bottle of wine or beer, buy your dinner here, and then set up on the rocks, the docks, or the beach: there's no finer alfresco rustic dining on the island. Larsen's closes at 6 PM weekdays, 7 PM weekends. ✉ *Dutcher's Dock* ☎ *508/645–2680* ➦ *MC, V* ⛄ *BYOB* ⊗ *Closed mid-Oct.–mid-May.*

¢–$ ✕ **The Bite.** Fried everything—clams, fish-and-chips, you name it—is on the menu at this simple, roadside shack, where two outdoor picnic tables are the only seating options. Small, medium, and large are the three options: all of them are perfect if you're craving that classic seaside fried lunch. But don't come on a rainy day, unless you want to get wet—the lines here can be long. To beat the crowds, try arriving between traditional mealtimes. The best advice, however, is to be patient and don't arrive too hungry. The Bite is open 11 AM–3 PM in spring and fall and until 8:45 PM in summer. ✉ *Basin Rd.* ☎ *509/645–9239* ➦ *No credit cards* ⊗ *Closed Oct.–late May.*

★ **$$$–$$$$** ▦ **Beach Plum Inn.** This mansard-roof inn, bought by the nearby Menemsha Inn in 2005, is surrounded by 7 acres of lavish formal gardens and lush woodland; it sits on a bluff over Menemsha Harbor. The floral-theme rooms—five in the main house and four in cottages—have gorgeous furnishings; in the Daffodil room, bathed in shades of yellow and blue, you'll find a hand-painted queen bed and a romantic balcony. A vaulted, beamed ceiling rises over the bedroom of the secluded Morning Glory Cottage. ✉ *North Rd., 02552* ☎ *508/645–9454 or 877/ 645–7398* ⊕ *www.beachpluminn.com* ➥ *9 rooms* ⚷ *Some in-room hot tubs, refrigerators, cable TV, tennis court, concierge; no smoking* ➦ *AE, D, MC, V* ⊗ *Closed Dec.–Apr.* ⦿⏐ *BP.*

$$$–$$$$ ▦ **Menemsha Inn and Cottages.** For 40 years the late *Life* photographer Alfred Eisenstaedt returned to his cottage on the hill here for the panoramic view of Vineyard Sound and Cuttyhunk beyond the trees below. These cottages, all with screened porches, fireplaces, and kitchens, tumble down a hillside behind the main house and vary in privacy and views. You can also stay in the 1989 inn building or the pleasant Carriage House. All rooms have private decks, most with sunset views. Suites include sitting areas, desks, and big tiled baths. A continental breakfast is served in a solarium-style breakfast room with a deck facing the ocean. Passes and shuttle transportation to both Squibnocket and Lucy Vincent Beaches are provided. ✉ *North Rd., Box 38, 02552* 🕾 *508/645–2521* ⊕ *www.menemshainn.com* ⌂ *15 rooms, 11 cottages, 1 2-bedroom house* ♿ *Some kitchens, some refrigerators, cable TV, in-room VCRs, in-room data ports, tennis court, gym, Ping-Pong* ▭ *MC, V* ⊗ *Closed Dec.–mid-Apr.* ⦿| *CP.*

Sports & the Outdoors

Menemsha Hills Reservation (✉ North Rd. just north of Menemsha) has 4 mi of some of the most challenging, steep, and breathtaking hiking trails on the island, including a stroll up to Martha's Vineyard's second-highest point and another ramble that descends down through the windswept valley to boulder-strewn Vineyard Sound Beach.

Aquinnah

❷❸ *6½ mi west of Menemsha, 10 mi southwest of West Tisbury, 17 mi southwest of Vineyard Haven.*

Aquinnah, called Gay Head until the town voted to change its name in 1997, is an official Native American township. The Wampanoag tribe is the guardian of the 420 acres that constitute the Aquinnah Native American Reservation. Aquinnah (pronounced a-*kwih*-nah) is Wampanoag for "land under the hill." The town is best known for the red-hued Aquinnah Cliffs.

❷❷ **Quitsa Pond Lookout** (✉ State Rd.) has a good view of the adjoining Menemsha and Nashaquitsa ponds, the woods, and the ocean beyond.

❷❹ A National Historic Landmark, the spectacular **Aquinnah Cliffs** are part
Fodor'sChoice of the Wampanoag reservation land. These dramatically striated walls of
★ red clay are the island's major attraction, as evidenced by the tour bus–filled parking lot. Native American crafts and food shops line the short approach to the overlook, from which you can see the Elizabeth Islands to the northeast across Vineyard Sound and Noman's Land Island—part wildlife preserve, part military bombing-practice site—3 mi off the Vineyard's southern coast. ✉ *State Rd.*

The brick **Aquinnah Lighthouse** is stationed precariously atop the rapidly eroding cliffs. It's open to the public on summer weekends at sunset, weather permitting. ✉ *Lighthouse Rd.* 🕾 *508/645–2211* 🎫 *$2.*

Where to Stay & Eat

$$–$$$$ ✕ **The Aquinnah Restaurant.** At the far end of the row of fast-food take-out spots and souvenir shops at the Gay Head Cliffs is this restaurant owned and operated by members of the Vanderhoop and Madison families, native Wampanoags. The family took back the lease in 2000 after a four-year hiatus, and the restaurant has regained its reputation as a homey place to eat. For breakfast try the Tomahawk Special, two homemade fish cakes covered with salsa on top of poached eggs with melted cheddar cheese. The lunch menu includes sandwiches, burgers, and healthy-sounding salads. Dinner entrées include sautéed shrimp, scallops, and lobster with rotini in a chardonnay sauce, and striped bass in a mussel-and-saffron sauce. The home-baked pies (banana cream, pecan,

or fruit) come wrapped in a moist and flaky crust. ⊠ *State Rd.* ☎ *508/645–3867* ⊟ *MC, V* ⊗ *Closed mid-Oct.–mid-Apr.*

★ **$$$$**   ✕⚏ **Outermost Inn.** This B&B by the Aquinnah Cliffs stands alone on acres of moorland, a 10-minute walk from the beach. The house is wrapped in windows revealing views of sea and sky in three directions, and there are great views of the Aquinnah Lighthouse from the wide porch and patio. The inn is clean and contemporary, with white walls and polished light-wood floors. Each room has a phone, and one has a whirlpool tub. The restaurant, open to the public, serves dinner nightly in summer and is all prix fixe at $72 (reservations are essential, and it's BYOB). ⊠ *Lighthouse Rd.* ⚏ *R.R. 1, Box 171, 02535* ☎ *508/645–3511* 🖷 *508/645–3514* ⊕ *www.outermostinn.com* ⇘ *7 rooms* ⚭ *Restaurant, some in-room hot tubs; no a/c, no kids under 12, no smoking* ⊟ *AE, D, MC, V* ⊗ *Closed mid-Oct.–May* ⦿ *BP.*

★ **$–$$**   ⚏ **Duck Inn.** The Duck Inn, originally an 18th-century home built by Native American seafarer George Belain, sits on a bucolic 5-acre bluff overlooking the ocean, with the Aquinnah Lighthouse standing sentinel to the north. The eclectic, fun interior blends peach stucco walls, Native American rugs and wall hangings, and ducks. Three upstairs rooms come with balconies; a suite in the stone-wall lower level (cool in summer, warm in winter) has views of the rolling fields; and a small attached cabin (closed in winter) with separate bath is the least expensive room. The first floor's common room, with a working 1928 Glenwood stove, piano, and fireplace, is the heart of the inn. Massage and facial therapies are available, and the healthful breakfast fare includes waffles with strawberries and omelets or chocolate crepes. This inn is very informal—kids and pets are welcome—and one night is free with a week's stay. ⊠ *10 Duck Pond Way, off State Rd., Box 160, 02535* ☎ *508/645–9018* 🖷 *508/645–2790* ⇘ *4 rooms, 1 suite* ⚭ *Outdoor hot tub, massage, meeting room, some pets allowed* ⊟ *MC, V* ⦿ *BP.*

MARTHA'S VINEYARD ESSENTIALS

To research prices, get advice from other travelers, and book travel arrangements, visit www.fodors.com.

Transportation

BY AIR

⇨ Air Travel *in* Smart Travel Trips in the back of this book.

BY BIKE

Martha's Vineyard offers superb terrain for biking—you can pick up a map that shows the island's many dedicated bike paths from the chamber of commerce. Several shops throughout the island rent bicycles, many of them close to the ferry terminals. Martha's Vineyard Strictly Bikes rents bike racks for your car.

🚲 Bike Rentals **DeBettencourt's** ⊠ Circuit Ave. Exit, Oak Bluffs ☎ 508/693–0011. **Edgartown Bicycles** ⊠ Upper Main St., Edgartown ☎ 508/627–9008. **Martha's Vineyard Strictly Bikes** ⊠ 24 Union St., Vineyard Haven ☎ 508/693–0782.

BY BOAT & FERRY
⇨ Boat & Ferry Travel *in* Smart Travel Trips in the back of this book.

BY BUS
The big buses of the Martha's Vineyard Transit Authority (VTA) provide regular service to all six towns on the island, with frequent stops in peak season and very limited service in winter. The fare is $1 per town, including the town of departure. One-day ($6), three-day ($15), and one-week ($25) passes are available at the Edgartown Visitors Center. The VTA also has two free in-town shuttle-bus routes, one in Edgartown and one in Vineyard Haven.

🚍 Bus Information **Martha's Vineyard Transit Authority** (VTA) 📞 508/693-9940 ⊕ www.vineyardtransit.com.

BY CAR
Traffic can be a challenge on Martha's Vineyard, especially in season, but driving can be worth the hassle if you really want to see the whole island and travel freely among towns. Bringing a car over on the ferry in summer, however, requires reservations far in advance, costs almost double what it does in the off-season, and necessitates standing in long lines—it's sometimes easier and more economical to rent a car once you're on the island, and then only for the days when you plan to explore. Where you stay and what you plan on seeing can greatly influence your transportation plans; discuss the different options for getting around Martha's Vineyard with your innkeeper or hotel staff as soon as you've booked a room.

Note that permits, fees, and certain equipment is needed for driving on Katama Beach and Wasque Reservation. Contact the chamber of commerce or park rangers for details.

You can book rentals on Martha's Vineyard through the Woods Hole ferry terminal free phone. The agencies listed below have rental desks at the airport. Cost is $80–$170 per day for a sedan; renting a four-wheel-drive vehicle costs around $150 per day (seasonal prices fluctuate widely).

🚗 Martha's Vineyard Agencies **AAA Island** 📞 508/627-6800 or 800/627-6333 ⊕ www.mvautorental.com. **Adventure Rentals** ✉ Beach Rd., Vineyard Haven 📞 508/693-1959 ⊕ www.adventurerentalsmv.com.

BY TAXI
Taxis meet all scheduled ferries and flights, and there are taxi stands by the Flying Horses Carousel in Oak Bluffs, at the foot of Main Street in Edgartown, and by the steamship office in Vineyard Haven. Fares range from $6 within a town to $35–$40 one-way from Vineyard Haven to Aquinnah.

Rates double between 1 AM and 7 AM. Note that limousine companies often provide service both on- and off-island.

🚕 Martha's Vineyard Taxi Companies **AdamCab** 📞 508/627-4462 or 800/281-4462 ⊕ www.adamcab.com. **All Island Taxi** 📞 508/693-2929. **Mario's** 📞 508/693-8399. **Martha's Vineyard Taxi** 📞 508/693-8660.

Contacts & Resources

TOURS

Liz Villard's Vineyard History Tours leads walking tours of Edgartown's "history, architecture, ghosts, and gossip," including a stop at the Vincent House. Tours are run from April through December; call for times. Liz and her guides also lead similar tours of Oak Bluffs and Vineyard Haven. Walks last a little more than an hour.

🚩 **Vineyard History Tours** ☎ 508/627-8619.

VISITOR INFORMATION

The Martha's Vineyard Chamber of Commerce is two blocks from the Vineyard Haven ferry. The chamber information booth by the Vineyard Haven steamship terminal is open late May to the last weekend in June, Friday–Sunday 8–8; July–early September, daily 8–8; and early September–mid-October, Friday–Sunday 8:30–5:30. The chamber itself is open weekdays 9–5. There are also town information kiosks on Circuit Avenue in Oak Bluffs and on Church Street in Edgartown.

🚩 Tourist Information **Martha's Vineyard Chamber of Commerce** ✉ Beach Rd. 🗐 Box 1698, Vineyard Haven 02568 ☎ 508/693-4486 or 800/505-4815 🌐 www.mvy.com.

6

Nantucket

WORD OF MOUTH

"I keep going back to Nantucket for the natural beauty of its beaches, the sense of being far away from the mainland, and the smell of Rosa rugosa everywhere outside of Town."

–MarieF

It's not for everyone. The prices are out of control: gas, houses, rents, meals, goods and services, ferry tickets for your auto, etc., etc. But for many of us, it's the BEST."

–rhkkmk

By Sandy
MacDonald

FOR THE FIRST TIME SINCE ITS GOLDEN AGE as a world-renowned whaling capital in the early 1800s, the tiny island of Nantucket is decidedly on a roll. Modest shingled cottages that might have gone begging for a buyer a few decades ago now fetch an easy million-plus. The more than 800 pre-1840 structures that compose the core of Nantucket Town—a National Landmark Historic District—only rarely change hands, and then at exalted prices. As for the trophy houses—mega-mansions built in the hinterlands for rich arrivistes—they're consistently off the charts, setting new records only to break them.

Still, Nantucket's ascending chic isn't what attracts most people to the island in the first place, or keeps them coming back. Its allure has more to do with how, at the height of summer, a cooling fog will drift in across the multihued moors; or the way rambling wild roses, the gaudy pink Rosa rugosa, perfume a hidden path to the beach.

Essentially Nantucket is *all* beach—a boomerang-shape sand spit consisting of detritus left by a glacier that receded millennia ago. Off Cape Cod, some 26 mi out to sea, the island measures 3½ by 14 mi at its widest points, while encompassing—such are the miracles of inlets and bays—about 80 mi of sandy shoreline, all of it open, as a matter of local pride, to absolutely everyone.

The small commercial area of Nantucket Town is the center of island activity, just as it has been since the early 1700s. It's only a few square blocks of mostly historical buildings, lovingly restored inns, and boutiques and galleries leading up from the pretty harbor and waterfront, where the ferries dock. Beyond it, quiet residential roads fan out to points around the island; Siasconset (known locally as 'Sconset) lies 8 mi to the east, Surfside 3 mi to the south, and Madaket 6 mi west of town. Thus far, the outlying areas appear relatively rural; however, increasing "infill" threatens the tranquillity.

Still, on a day when sun scintillates on sand and the thrumming waves hint at an eternal rhythm, it's hard to imagine that anything could ever go too terribly wrong here. As summer succeeds summer, children will continue to construct their fanciful if foredoomed sand castles and marvel over the odd treasures the tides drag in. Adults will gladly play along, if allowed, remembering their own seemingly endless days of summer and imagining more of the same for their children's children and so on and on. Perfection can be surprisingly simple, after all, and even if Nantucket's current cachet should fade, the island's timeless pleasures will endure.

About the Restaurants

For such a tiny island, Nantucket is rife with great restaurants—"world class" would not be an exaggeration. Of course, with New York–level sophistication come New York–level prices. And whereas the titans of industry who flock here for a bit of high-rent R&R might not blink at the prospect of a $40 or even $50 entrée, the rest of us must sometimes suppress a nervous gulp. Is it worth it? Again and again, in venues that vie for the title of most recherché, the answer is yes.

Reservations can be hard to come by in high season, or during popular weekends such as December's Christmas Stroll and the Daffodil Festival in April, so plan and make dinner reservations well ahead. You may still be able to squeeze into a popular establishment at the last minute if you're willing to eat unfashionably early or decadently late. In any month other than July or August, call ahead to check hours of operation.

About the Hotels

From small bed-and-breakfasts to the island's few surviving grand hotels, Nantucket knows the value of hospitality. A unique "product" plus good service—as busy as this little island gets—are the deciding factors that keep visitors coming back year after year. The majority of lodgings are in town, convenient to the shops and restaurants; the downside is that you may be subjected to street noise on summer evenings. Those seeking quiet might prefer the inns on the periphery of town, a 5- to 10-minute walk from Main Street. The most remote inns, in Sconset and Wauwinet, also tend to be among the most expensive. Families with children will probably want to consider the larger, less formal hotels, since many of the small, historic B&Bs are furnished with antiques.

Nantucket is notoriously expensive, so don't expect to find many bargains in terms of lodging, especially in summer. The best rates can be found in the off-season; however, the spring and fall shoulder seasons are also growing in popularity, and such special-event weekends as the Daffodil Festival in late April and Christmas Stroll in early December command peak-season rates. Most inns charge upward of $150 a night in summer, and many go higher. The only truly "budget" facility you'll find is the youth hostel, which is also the only option for roughing it, since camping is prohibited anywhere on-island.

WHAT IT COSTS					
	$$$$	$$$	$$	$	¢
RESTAURANTS	over $30	$22–$30	$16–$22	$10–$16	under $10
HOTELS	over $260	$200–$260	$140–$200	$90–$140	under $90

Restaurant prices are per person for a main course at dinner. Hotel prices are for a standard double room, excluding 6% sales tax (more in some counties) and 1%–4% tourist tax.

Nantucket Town

30 mi southeast of Hyannis, 107 mi southeast of Boston.

At the height of its prosperity in the early 19th century, the little town of Nantucket was the foremost whaling port in the world. Shipowners and sea captains built elegant mansions, which today remain remarkably unchanged, thanks to a very strict building code initiated in the 1950s. The entire town of Nantucket is now an official National Historic District encompassing more than 800 pre-1840 structures within 1 square mi.

Nantucket

Given its compact nature, Nantucket definitely merits consideration as a day trip—a prospect made easier by the introduction of fast ferries (the crossing now takes an hour) from Hyannis. Day-trippers usually take in the architecture and historical sites and browse the pricey boutiques. After dining at one of the many delightful restaurants, you can hop a ferry back—or, if you're not in a hurry, stay the night at one of the town's luxurious historic inns.

Nantucket Town has one of the country's finest historical districts, with beautiful 18th- and 19th-century architecture and a museum of whaling history. The **Nantucket Historical Association (NHA)** (☎ 508/228–1894 NHA ⊕ www.nha.org) maintains an assortment of venerable properties in town, including the gloriously expanded Whaling Museum. An $18 pass gets you into all of the association's sites.

FodorśChoice
★

❶ African Meeting House. When the island abolished slavery in 1773, Nantucket became a destination for free blacks and escaping slaves. The African Meeting House was built in the 1820s as a schoolhouse, and it functioned as such until 1846, when the island's schools were integrated. A complete restoration has returned the site to its authentic 1880s appearance. ⊠ 29 York St. ☎ 508/228–9833 ⊕ www.afroammuseum. org ⌨ Free ☽ July and Aug., Tues.–Sat. 11–3, Sun. 1–3.

⓮ Brant Point Light. This 26-foot-tall, white-painted beauty has views of the harbor and town. The point was once the site of the second-oldest lighthouse in the country (1746); the present, much-photographed light was built in 1902. ⊠ End of Easton St., across footbridge.

★ **⓬ First Congregational Church.** The tower of this church provides the best view of Nantucket—for those willing to climb its 92 steps. Rising 120 feet, the tower is capped by a weather vane depicting a whale catch. Peek in at the church's 1852 trompe l'oeil ceiling. ⊠ 62 Centre St. ☎ 508/228–0950 ⊕ www.nantucketfcc.org ⌨ Tower tour $2.50 ☽ Mid-June–mid-Oct., Mon.–Sat. 10–4, and Fri. and Sat. Daffodil and Memorial weekends; services Sun. 9 and 10 AM.

❻ Hadwen House. The pair of magnificent white porticoed Greek Revival mansions on upper Main Street—commonly referred to as the Two Greeks—were built in 1845 and 1846 by wealthy factory owner William Hadwen. No. 94, built as a wedding gift for his adopted niece, was modeled on the Athenian Tower of the Winds, with Corinthian capitals on the entry columns, a domed-stair hall with statuary niches, and an oculus. The Hadwens' own domicile, at No. 96, is now a museum, and its contents reflect how the wealthy of the period lived. Inside, on a guided tour, you'll see such architectural details as the grand circular staircase, fine plasterwork, and carved Italian-marble mantels. ⊠ 96 Main St. ☎ 508/228–1894 ⊕ www.nha.org ⌨ NHA Combination Pass or Historic Sites Pass only ☽ Mid-May–mid-Oct., Mon.–Sat. 10–5, Sun. noon–5.

❿ Main Street. After the Great Fire of 1846 leveled all its wooden buildings, Main Street was widened to prevent future flames from hopping across the street. The cobblestone thoroughfare has a harmonious symmetry: the Pacific Club anchors its foot, and the Pacific National Bank,

Nantucket Town

KEY

ℹ️ *Tourist information*

TO
JETTIES
BEACH

0 — 330 yards
0 — 330 meters

Nantucket Harbor

Children's Beach

TO HYANNIS

TO HYANNIS, MARTHA'S VINEYARD

Steamboat Wharf

Old North Wharf

Straight Wharf

Lily Pond Park

Murray's Toggery

Old South Wharf

Commercial Wharf

Town Pier

TO 'SCONSET

TO SURFSIDE BEACH

African Meeting House 1
Brant Point Light 14
First Congregational Church 12
Hadwen House 6
Hinchman House Natural Science Museum 3
Loines Observatory 2
Main Street 10
Maria Mitchell Aquarium 9
Maria Mitchell Association Science Library 4
Mitchell House 5
Nantucket Atheneum ..11
Oldest House 15
Pacific National Bank ...8
"Three Bricks" 7
Vestal Street Observatory 5
Whaling Museum 13

another redbrick building, squares off the head. The cobblestones were brought to the island as ballast in returning ships and laid to prevent the wheels of carts heavily laden with whale oil from sinking into the dirt. At the center of Lower Main is an old horse trough, today overflowing with flowers. From here the street gently rises; at the bank it narrows to its prefire width and leaves the commercial district for an area of mansions that escaped the blaze.

NEED A BREAK? You can breakfast or lunch inexpensively at several lunch counters, including **Congdon's Pharmacy** (⌧ 47 Main St. ☎ 508/228-0020) and the **Nantucket Pharmacy** (⌧ 45 Main St. ☎ 508/228-0180). "The Strip," a hodgepodge of fun fast-food eateries on Broad Street near Steamboat Wharf, is another good option.

★ ☺ Besides fresh-squeezed juices, the **Juice Bar** (⌧ 12 Broad St. ☎ 508/228-5799), open April–mid-October, serves homemade ice cream and frozen yogurt with waffle cones and toppings. Long lines signal that good things come to those who wait.

Maria Mitchell Association (MMA). Established in 1902 by Vassar students and astronomer Maria Mitchell's family, the association administers the ❺ **Mitchell House** (⌧ 1 Vestal St. ☎ 508/228-2896 ⊕ www.mmo.org ❹ ✉ $5 or MMA pass), the **Maria Mitchell Association Science Library** (⌧ 2 Vestal St. ☎ 508/228-9219 ⊕ www.mmo.org ✉ reserved for scholars, by appointment), the ❸ **Hinchman House Natural Science Museum** (⌧ 7 Milk St. ☎ 508/228-0898 ⊕ www.mmo.org ✉ $5 or MMA ❾ pass), the **Maria Mitchell Aquarium** (⌧ 28 Washington St., near Commercial Wharf ☎ 508/228-5387 ⊕ www.mmo.org ✉ $4 or MMA ❺ pass), the **Vestal Street Observatory** (⌧ 3 Vestal St. ☎ 508/228-9273 ❷ ⊕ www.mmo.org ✉ $5 or MMA pass), and the **Loines Observatory** (⌧ 59 Milk St. Ext. ☎ 508/228-9273 ⊕ www.mmo.org ✉ $10). The MMA Museum Pass is a combination admission ticket to the Mitchell House, the Hinchman House, the Vestal Street Observatory, and the aquarium; it's $15 for adults and $10 for senior citizens and children ages 6 to 14. In summer, the association conducts inexpensive classes for adults and children on astronomy, natural science, and Nantucket history. ⌧ *4 Vestal St.* ☎ *508/228-9198* ⊕ *www.mmo.org.*

★ ☺ ⓫ **Nantucket Atheneum.** Nantucket's town library is a great white Greek Revival building, with a windowless facade and fluted Ionic columns. Completed in 1847 to replace a structure lost to the 1846 fire, it's one of the oldest libraries in continuous service in the United States. Astronomer Maria Mitchell was its first librarian. Opening ceremonies included a dedication by Ralph Waldo Emerson, who—along with Daniel Webster, Henry David Thoreau, Frederick Douglass, Lucretia Mott, and John James Audubon—later delivered lectures in the library's second-floor Great Hall. During the 19th century the hall was the center of island culture—a role it fulfills to this day. The adjoining Atheneum Park is a great place to relax for a while, and the spacious Weezie Library for Children hosts readings and activities—a welcome respite for a rainy day. ⌧ *1 India St.* ☎ *508/228-1110* ⊕ *www.nantucketatheneum. org* ☉ *Late May–early Sept., Mon., Wed., Fri., and Sat. 9:30–5, Tues.*

and Thurs. 9:30–8; early Sept.–late May, Tues. and Thurs. 9:30–8, Wed., Fri., and Sat. 9:30–5.

⑮ Oldest House. History and architecture buffs should be sure to get a look at this hilltop house, also called the Jethro Coffin House, built in 1686 as a wedding gift for Jethro and Mary Gardner Coffin. The most striking feature of the saltbox is the massive central brick chimney with a brick horseshoe adornment said to ward away witches. Other highlights are the enormous hearths and diamond-pane leaded-glass windows. Cutaway panels show 17th-century construction techniques. An NHA interpreter will tell you about the home's history and the interior's sparse furnishings, including an antique loom. ⊠ *Sunset Hill (a 10- to 15-min walk along Centre St. from Main St.)* ☏ *508/228–1894* ⊕ *www.nha. org* ✉ *NHA Combination Pass or Historic Sites Pass* ☉ *Mid-May–mid-Oct., Mon.–Sat. 10–5, Sun. noon–5.*

❽ Pacific National Bank. Like the Pacific Club (a social club that counts whalers' descendants among its members) it faces, the bank, dating to 1818 and still in use today, is a monument to the far-flung voyages of the Nantucket whaling ships it financed. Inside, above old-style teller cages, are 1954 murals of scenes from the whaling days. Note the **Meridian Stone** on the south side of the building and to the left—it's about 3 feet high and pointed on top. Placed here in the 1830s by astronomers Maria Mitchell and her father, William, it marks the town's precise meridian—an important point to early navigators. ⊠ *61 Main St.*

★ ❼ "Three Bricks." Many of the mansions of the golden age of whaling were built on Upper Main Street. These well-known identical redbrick homes, with columned Greek Revival porches at their front entrances, were built between 1836 and 1838 by whaling merchant Joseph Starbuck for his three sons. They are not open to the public. ⊠ *93–97 Main St.*

Immersing you in Nantucket's whaling past with exhibits that include a fully rigged whaleboat and a skeleton of a 46-foot sperm whale, the **⑬ Whaling Museum**—a complex that includes a restored 1846 spermaceti candle factory—is a must-see. The museum received a $14 million expansion and refurbishment in 2005. Items on view in the handsome galleries include harpoons and other whale-hunting implements; portraits of whaling captains and their wives (a few of whom went whaling as well); the South Seas curiosities they brought home; a large collection of sailors' crafts, a full-size tryworks once used to process whale oil aboard ship; and the original 16-

Fodor'sChoice
★

GREASY LUCK

Nantucket's preeminence as the world's whaling capital (at least until the early 1800s, when New Bedford's deeper harbor took the lead) resulted from a fluke, when, in 1712, Captain Christopher Hussey's crew speared a sperm whale. The whale's waxy spermaceti, it was found, could be used for candles in place of lantern oil, produced by the messy, endless task of cooking down whale blubber. The captains made out like bandits—their grand houses still stand as proof—but the trade went into a downward spiral with the discovery of petroleum in 1836.

foot-high 1850 lens from Sankaty Head Lighthouse. The Children's Discovery Room provides interactive learning opportunities. Be sure to climb—or take the elevator—up to the observation deck for a view of the harbor. ⊠ *13–15 Broad St.* ☎ *508/228–1894* 🖃 *$15 or NHA Combination Pass* ☉ *Jan.–mid-Apr., Fri.–Sun. 11–4; mid-Apr.–mid-May and mid-Oct.–mid-Dec., Thurs.–Mon. 11–4; mid-May–mid-Oct., Mon.–Wed., Fri., and Sat. 10–5, Thurs. 10–8, Sun. noon–5.*

Where to Eat

★ **$$$$** ✕ **the pearl.** This ultracool space—a sophisticated upstairs cousin to the Boarding House—is seriously chic, with a white onyx bar lighted in a Curaçao blue and, behind an aquarium divider, cushy leather banquettes. These—plus the garden porch, where tasting dinners can be prearranged—are the power seats. However, everyone is well served by Seth Raynor's enthusiasm for the flavors of Asian cuisine. It may be tough to choose between the rice-flour pillows enrobing "Lobi-Yaki" (Japanese lobster knuckle fritters) and the wok-fried lobster with lo-mein and grilled lime—so do yourself a favor and order both. ⊠ *12 Federal St.* ☎ *508/228–9701* ⊕ *www.boardinghouse-pearl.com* 🖃 *AE, MC, V* ☉ *Closed mid-Oct.–Mar. No lunch.*

$$$$ ✕ **Water Street.** Two stylish young couples have transformed a tired old standby (formerly Vincent's) into a chic eatery with cinnamon walls and handsome leather highback chairs. The locally provisioned cuisine calls on micro-diced taste explosions—star anise-scented pineapple sparks the seared foie gras, and charred-tomato gazpacho underlies the fresh-caught striped bass. The Bartlett Farm corn chowder, which packs a bonus crab tempura, is nonpareil, and the closing "Study in Chocolate" is deeply satisfying. ⊠ *21 S. Water St.* ☎ *508/228–0189* 🖃 *D, MC, V* ☉ *Closed Jan.–Mar.*

$$$–$$$$ ✕ **American Seasons.** At once playful and tasteful, this intimate space
Fodor'sChoice arrayed with folk art—you'll be dining on a lacquered game table—is
★ commensurately romantic. It's not just the subdued lighting and smooth service. Chef Michael LaScola demonstrates his full culinary genius in festively presented dishes that roam the nation, from the Pacific Coast to New England, by way of the Wild West and Down South. From his signature foie gras crème brûlée to ancho-rubbed duck breast with Medjool date browned butter and blood orange atop almond-strewn quinoa, expect spectacular pan-regional pyrotechnics. ⊠ *80 Centre St.* ☎ *508/228–7111* 🖃 *AE, MC, V* ☉ *Closed Jan.–mid-Apr. No lunch.*

$$$–$$$$ ✕ **The Boarding House.** Beyond the throngs of twentysomethings mingling at the bar, you'll encounter a culinary oasis, a vaulted semi-subterranean space reminiscent of a private wine cellar, with leather banquettes circling antique-gold walls. Here, under the watchful eye of star chef–owner Seth Raynor, chef de cuisine Erin Zircher showcases her skill with Mediterranean market cuisine. Comfort is the universal watchword: the "rustic pasta gratin" is essentially mac 'n' cheese, Italian style (lavished with rapini and fresh ricotta), and the grilled lamb steak comes sided with light chickpea panisse (fritter). The chocolate chocolate-chip cookies (like mini-molten cakes)—served with a shot glass of chocolate malted milk—are not to be missed. Come summer, you can sample from the menu at the sidewalk café—provided you succeed in snagging a table. ✉ *12 Federal St.* ☎ *508/228–9622* ⊕ *www.boardinghouse-pearl. com* ▭ *AE, MC, V.*

★ $$$–$$$$ ✕ **Brant Point Grill.** With its beautiful broad lawn set harborside, the Brant Point Grill—in-house restaurant for the elegant White Elephant hotel—proffers a straightforward haute-steak house menu, with a few New American frills on the side: be sure to order the cinnamon-dusted sweet potato fries. You may also be tempted by the likes of grilled tuna with wasabi mascarpone, or fire-cone salmon grilled in plain sight, on cedar planks poised downwind from a blazing brazier. The desserts are fabulous (Guinness ice-cream mud pie). Brace yourself for Sunday brunch, featuring a make-your-own Bloody Mary station. ✉ *50 Easton St.* ☎ *508/325–1320 or 800/445–6574* ⊕ *www.whiteelephanthotel.com* ▭ *AE, D, DC, MC, V* ⊙ *Closed Jan.–Mar.*

★ $$$–$$$$ ✕ **DeMarco.** Northern Italian cuisine debuted on-island at this cored-out clapboard house in 1980, slightly ahead of the wave. The delights endure: "badly cut" homemade pasta, for instance, in a sauce of wild mushrooms, prosciutto, and fresh sage, or luscious lobster cannelloni enrobed in a corn zabaglione. Truffle-braised lamb shank—served with creamy, rosemary-scented polenta—gets a regional tweak from tart cranberries. Otherwise, the approach is faithfully classicist, right through the exemplary tiramisu. ✉ *9 India St.* ☎ *508/228–1836* ▭ *AE, D, MC, V* ⊙ *Closed Mid-Oct.–late May. No lunch.*

★ $$$–$$$$ ✕ **Languedoc Bistro.** The only thing not exquisitely Gallic about this auberge-style restaurant, founded in 1975, is the portioning: American appetites will be satisfied—and then some—by the supersize rib chop, not to mention the oven-roasted lobster swimming in creamy polenta and festooned with parsnip "ribbons." Dining moods are divided into two modes: you can opt for the fairly formal upstairs rooms or the bistro-style conviviality of the cellar. In season, the patio is a lovely place to toy with a salad composé of Chioggia beets and Hubbardston chèvre mousse—or to tackle a decadent, over-generous dessert. ✉ *24 Broad St.* ☎ *508/228–2552* ⊕ *www.lelanguedoc.com* ♿ *Reservations essential* ▭ *AE, MC, V* ⊙ *Closed Jan.–mid-Apr.*

$$$–$$$$ ✕ **Oran Mór.** Like his predecessor, Peter Wallace, chef-owner Christopher Freeman abandoned the cushy confines of Topper's at the Wauwinet to strike out on his own at this tasteful eatery. Copper-encased stairs lead to a wine bar and a trio of rooms now warmed to a buttery yellow. Freeman's signature dishes—for example, his lobster Navarin, in a heavenly sauce that tastes like bisque squared—have likewise made the leap, as did his sommelier (wines ascend well into four figures). Freeman's fans are sure to follow. One cautionary note: as at the Wauwinet, the culinary aesthetic can sometimes be so refined as to read a little wan. ✉ *2 S. Beach St.* ☎ *508/228–8655* ⊕ *www.oranmorbistro.com* ▭ *AE, MC, V* ⊙ *No lunch.*

$$$–$$$$ ✕ **Straight Wharf.** This loftlike restaurant with harborside deck has enjoyed legendary status since the mid-'70s, when chef Marion Morash used to get a helping hand from culinary buddy Julia Child. The young couple who took over in 2006—Gabriel Frasca and Amanda Lydon—were fast-rising stars on the Boston restaurant scene, but their approach here is more studied than flashy. Favoring local produce and catches, they con-

7

American
Seasons 5

Arno's 21

Black-Eyed
Susan's 9

The Boarding
House 12

Brant Point
Grill 1

The
Brotherhood 4

Centre Street
Bistro 8

Cioppino's 7

Company of the
Cauldron 11

DeMarco 10

Even Keel
Cafe 20

Fifty-Six
Union 24

Fog Island
Café 16

Languedoc
Bistro 6

LoLa 41 2

Oran Mór 3

the pearl 13

Ships Inn 22

Slip 14 19

Starlight
Café 17

Straight
Wharf 18

29 Fair Street ..23

21 Federal 14

Water Street ...15

Where to Eat
in Nantucket Town

coct stellar dishes like stuffed zucchini flowers with saffron tomato vinaigrette, and wild Chatham halibut with garlic-chive spaetzle. Everything from cuisine to service is just right, if a bit on the pricey side. If you'd like a preview, try the less costly café menu at the adjoining bar—if you can get in. ⊠ *6 Harbor Sq., Straight Wharf* ☎ *508/228-4499* ⊕ *www. straighwharfrestaurant.com* ☰ *AE, MC, V* ⊗ *Closed Mid-Oct.–mid-May.*

$$$–$$$$ ✕ **29 Fair Street.** When the owners of the Summer House took over the venerable Woodbox (a 1709 abode which spent the past half-century as a restaurant–rooming house), they brightened up the interior with colorful silk pillows and installed Bretagne-bred Charles Salliou as chef. His innovations, such as Mediterranean fish soup, impart a sunny touch, and his classic training shines when it comes to the beef Wellington and breakfast popovers for which the Woodbox was famed. The heaping salads—with smoked trout or duck confit—are fabulous, as is the lobster in angelhair filo. The deserts are a Francophile's dream come true. ⊠ *29 Fair St.* ☎ *508/228-0587* ⚠ *Reservations essential* ☰ *No credit cards* ⊗ *Closed Mon. and Jan.–Apr. No lunch.*

$$$–$$$$ ✕ **21 Federal.** An avatar of the New American culinary revolution since 1985, 21 Federal retains its creative edge, thanks to the ever-avant menus of chef Russell Jaehnig. Nothing is too outré, mind you, in this handsome 1847 Greek Revival house with sconce-lighted, dove-gray interiors. But the food has a spark to match the spirited clientele: try the slow-roasted portobello mushroom with Parmesan pudding or the seared foie gras with roasted peach tarte tatin. ⊠ *21 Federal St.* ☎ *508/ 228-2121* ☰ *AE, MC, V* ⊗ *Closed Jan.–Mar.*

$$–$$$$ ✕ **Cioppino's.** Tracy Root's elegant house-restaurant has been popular since day one (in 1990). Beyond the signature dish—a San Franciscan seafood stew—the menu is ambitious, marrying classic technique and contemporary taste. Piling perfectly grilled lobster tails (that's not a typo) and claws atop linguini with pesto is a luscious and memorable way to serve that coveted crustacean. Desserts—especially the tangy housemade key lime pie—have their own following. ⊠ *20 Broad St.* ☎ *508/ 228-4622* ⊕ *www.cioppinos.com* ☰ *D, DC, MC, V* ⊗ *Closed Nov.–Apr.*

$$–$$$$ ✕ **Fifty-Six Union.** You can tell there's a playful spirit at work here, just from the overdressed mannequin usually propped up at a café table out front. Venture inside, though, and you'll find a city-sophisticated space, with a civilized grown-ups bar. Inside or out (the lovely garden out back harbors a chef's table), Peter Jannelle's cuisine delivers global pizzazz. You'll want to make a habit of the truffle-asiago frites, not to mention the mussels in mild Thai curry broth, and the Javanese spicy fried rice. ⊠ *56 Union St.* ☎ *508/228-6135* ☰ *AE, MC, V* ⊗ *No lunch.*

$$–$$$$ ✕ **LoLa 41.** A hopping bar scene—LoLa 41 became *the* place to hang the minute it opened—somewhat impedes the culinary experience here, but an evolving menu means that chefs at this trendy Galley Beach off-shootcome up with compelling new dishes every few weeks. Just one bite, and you'll be hooked on the calamari doused with ultraspicy Korean claypot-aged *kochujang* (a chili bean paste). ⊠ *15 S. Beach St.* ☎ *508/ 325-4001* ☰ *MC, V.*

$$–$$$$ ✕ **Ships Inn.** Tucked into the *rez-de-chaussée* (demi-basement) of Captain Obed Starbuck's handsome 1831 mansion, this peach-tint, candlelit restaurant is a light and lovely haven where French cuisine meets a California sensibility and both cultures are the richer for it. If you want to eat healthy, you can—but why not sin a little and sup on warm cauliflower soup with Vermont cheddar, or a deft and delicate lobster with fennel beurre blanc? Compound the transgression with the soufflé du jour. ✉ *13 Fair St.* ☎ *508/228–0040* ⊕ *www.shipsinnnantucket.com* 🖃 *AE, D, MC, V* ✆ *Closed Nov.–Apr. No lunch.*

★ **$$$** ✕ **Company of the Cauldron.** This tiny dining room, a sconce-lighted haven of architectural salvage, is served by an even smaller kitchen, from whence chef-owner All Kovalencik issues only one menu per evening. Fans gladly forgo multiple choice when the chef's choice is invariably so dead-on. Rundowns of the weekly roster are available over the phone or online, and a typically tantalizing lineup might start with jumbo lump crab cakes with orange basil oil, then hardwood-grilled rack of lamb with blackberry Merlot sauce, followed by chocolate ganache with grilled fresh figs and cinnamon syrup. Given the close quarters, expect to come away not only sated but better acquainted with your near neighbors—and in love with Mary Keller's celestial harp. ✉ *7 India St.* ☎ *508/228–4016* ⊕ *www.companyofthecauldron.com* 🍴 *Reservations essential* 🖃 *MC, V* ✆ *Closed Dec.–mid-May. No lunch.*

$$–$$$ ✕ **Arno's.** Arno's, which has a prime location right on Main Street, presents lush breakfasts (some featuring lobster), hearty lunches, and fairly ambitious dinners, all with generous portions. (Warning: the salads could constitute meals in themselves.) Molly Dee's nostalgic canvases adorn the brick walls, and a bar invites adult schmoozing. Expect some envious looks—from inside and outside—if you get the prime spot in the storefront window. ✉ *41 Main St.* ☎ *508/228–7001* 🖃 *AE, D, DC, MC, V* ✆ *Closed mid-Jan.–Mar.*

★ **$$–$$$** ✕ **Black-Eyed Susan's.** From a passing glance, you'd never peg this seemingly humble storefront as one of Nantucket's chic eateries—but as the invariable lines attest, it is. The luncheonette setup is offset by improbably fancy glass chandeliers, and foodies lay claim to the stools to observe chef Jeff Worster's often pyromaniacal "open kitchen." The dinner menu, which changes every three weeks, ventures boldly around the world. The breakfasts (served until 1 PM) include such eye-openers as sourdough French toast with orange, Jack Daniels butter, and pecans. ✉ *10 India St.* ☎ *508/325–0308* 🖃 *No credit cards* 🍷 *BYOB* ✆ *Closed Nov.–Mar. No dinner Sun. No lunch.*

🕘 **$$–$$$** ✕ **The Brotherhood.** No, it's not really an 1840s whaling bar—though the atmospheric basement, which dates all the way back to 1972, presents a more convincing front than the open, family-friendly upper floors added in 2005. Upstairs or down, you can dive into the same juicy burgers and signature curly fries. ✉ *23 Broad St.* ☎ *508/228–2551* ⊕ *www.brotherhoodofthieves.com* 🖃 *MC, V.*

★ **$$–$$$** ✕ **Centre Street Bistro.** Tiny—there are 20 seats indoors, and as many out—and perfect, this gem of a bistro is a find that devoted locals almost wish they could keep to themselves. Chef–owners Tim and Ruth Pitts's sizzling cuisine is a match for the persimmon-orange color scheme of this cozy hideaway lined with cushioned banquettes and splashed with exuberant flower paintings. The "short stack" appetizer—seared tuna atop a sesame-noodle griddle cake—is a poem of bold flavorings and textural contrasts, and the massive beef tenderloin with goat cheese and white truffle oil all but demands a doggie bag. Portions are lavish—even on desserts—and prices modest. ⊠ *29 Centre St.* ☎ *508/228–8470* ⊟ *MC, V.*

☼ **$$–$$$** ✕ **Even Keel Cafe.** This former ice-cream parlor, with its tin ceilings and pretty backyard patio, is no mere restaurant—it's the very heart of town (especially off-season, when patrons are treated to two-for-one entrées). It's the first place to head for a fancy coffee, a light pastry binge, or a creative meal. The lobster risotto, studded with Bartlett Farm corn, holds its own against contenders at the fanciest restaurants in town. ⊠ *40 Main St.* ☎ *508/228–1979* ⊕ *www.evenkeelcafe.com* ⊟ *AE, MC, V.*

$$–$$$ ✕ **Slip 14.** With its picturesque setting at the end of a shell-lined lane flanked by galleries, Slip 14 is an ideal spot to while away a summer night: portions are large, prices are fair—and all is well with the world. Skip the dull lobster cake, but feast on the likes of seared dayboat scallops swimming in vanilla-scented corn fondue, and definitely succumb to any cobbler you encounter on the dessert list. ⊠ *14 Old South Wharf* ☎ *508/228–2033* ⊟ *MC, V* ۞ *Closed Nov.–Apr.*

$$–$$$ ✕ **Starlight Café.** This tiny movie-theater anteroom and enclosed patio, spiffed up with cinematic artifacts, offers a casual menu—think mac 'n' cheese with lobster. It's ideal for a pre- or post-flick feed, and yes, you're allowed to take your drinks into the theater. Also, with a dinner reservation you can get a movie reservation—a great way to leapfrog the line. ⊠ *1 N. Union St.* ☎ *508/228–4479* ⊕ *www.starlightnantucket.com* ⊟ *AE, D, MC, V* ۞ *Closed Nov.–Apr.*

☼ **$–$$** ✕ **Fog Island Café.** Cherished year-round for its exceptional breakfasts, Fog Island is just as fine a spot for lunch—or, in season, a charitably priced dinner. The storefront space is cheerily decked out in a fresh country style (echoed in the friendly service), and chef-owners Mark and Anne Dawson—both Culinary Institute of America grads—seem determined to provide the best possible value to transients and natives alike. Consider starting the day with pesto scrambled eggs and ending it with sesame-crusted tuna with Thai noodles. ⊠ *7 S. Water St.* ☎ *508/228–1818* ⊟ *MC, V* ۞ *Closed Jan.–Mar.*

NANTUCKET TOWN OUTSKIRTS ⇨ *Where to Stay & Eat Outside Nantucket Town map for these properties.*

$$$$ ✕ **Galley Beach.** A beloved institution since 1958, this modest cottage plunked right on the Cliffside Beach Club's swath of sand has managed to stay fresh and luxe thanks to three generations of restaurateurs who know how to spot and foster talent in the kitchen. These days, that's W. Scott Osif, whose resume spans Philadelphia's Le Bec Fin and New York's City Hall. The menu mostly sticks to the safe side (a peril of catering to the moneyed crowd), but Osif occasionally kicks loose with dishes like lobster poached in chipotle and lime butter. Everything—even staid options—is very, very good. The deck, with its gay blue-and-white awning ringed with red geraniums, takes in a 180-degree beach view; it's perfectly oriented to capture what photographers call "the golden moment." ⊠ *54 Jefferson Ave.* ☎ *508/228–9641* ⊕ *www.galleybeach.com* ⊟ *AE, MC, V* ۞ *Closed Oct.–mid-May.*

$$$–$$$$ ✕ **Seagrille.** Though it may lack the flashy profile of other top island restaurants, this mid-island eatery deserves its popularity. The lobster bisque alone, even without the bonus of a dilled *en croute bonnet*, warrants a following, as does the free-form seafood ravioli. Off-season, the dining room, with its murals of wharf and street scenes, is a peaceful haven. When summer arrives, so do the crowds. ⊠ *45 Sparks Ave.* ☎ *508/325–5700* ⊕ *www.theseagrille.com* ▤ *AE, MC, V.*

$$–$$$ ✕ **Cinco.** With this eclectic tapas oasis, affable owner Michael Sturgis
Fodor'sChoice has made mid-island a true dining destination. The festive mood is ir-
★ resistible, starting with the setting (candlelit rooms painted in dark, sexy colors) and culminating in a parade of thrilling "small plates" meant for sharing. Don't be surprised if you find yourself getting possessive over the grilled lamb chops sauced with lime "mojo," say, or the lobster tail with blood orange butter—just order more for the table. Chef Tim Thacher-Renshaw tinkers with the menu daily. ⊠ *5 Amelia Dr.* ☎ *508/325–5151* ⊕ *www.cinco5.com* ▤ *AE, MC, V* ⊘ *Closed Jan.–Mar. No lunch.*

$$–$$$ ✕ **Sfoglia.** Culinary Institute of America grads Ron and Colleen Suhanosky appointed their celery-tinted trattoria with mismatched tables (including some enamel-top honeys from the '40s), chairs, crockery—even silverware. You'll feast on home-style Italian dishes such as minted gnocchi, or chicken "al mattone" (cooked under a brick). Desserts—Colleen's province—include rustic seasonal tarts and seductive semifreddos. ⊠ *130 Pleasant St.* ☎ *508/325–4500* ⊕ *www.sfogliarestaurant.com* ▤ *No credit cards.*

¢–$ ✕ **The Downyflake.** Locals flock here for bountiful breakfasts—featuring much sought-after homemade doughnuts—and well-priced lunches, from codfish cakes to burgers. ⊠ *18 Sparks Ave.* ☎ *508/228–4533* ▤ No *credit cards* ⊘ *No dinner.*

Where to Stay

⏲ **$$$$** ▦ **The Beachside at Nantucket.** Nantucket has only one "motel" in the classic rooms-around-a-pool configuration, and it's a honey—not at all out of place amid its tony neighbors. Between the town and Jetties Beach (both are within a bracing 10-minute walk), the complex ascends to two stories; rooms—decor is of the cheery wicker-and-florals school—have little pool-view terraces separated by whitewashed latticework. Families naturally flock here, but business travelers are equally well served. ⊠ *30 N. Beach St., 02554* ☎ *508/228–2241 or 800/322–4433* 🖷 *508/228–8901* ⊕ *www.thebeachside.com* 🛏 *87 rooms, 3 suites* ⌂ *Refrigerators, cable TV, Wi-Fi, heated outdoor pool, meeting rooms, some pets allowed, no-smoking rooms* ▤ *AE, D, DC, MC, V* ⊘ *Closed early Dec.–late Apr.* ⫿◯⫿ *CP.*

⏲ **$$$$** ▦ **The Cottages at the Boat Basin.** These weathered-shingle cottages sit on South Wharf, amid the yachts—you could reserve a mooring and bring your own boat. Cottages range from studios to three bedrooms, and each has attractive modern decor with a nautical flavor: white walls, navy blue rugs, and light-wood floors and furniture. All have water views, though they're not always equal—some cottages have picture windows—plus a little garden terrace. ⊠ *New Whale St., Box 1139, 02554* ☎ *508/325–1499 or 866/838–9253* 🖷 *508/228–7639* ⊕ *www.*

The Beachside at
Nantucket **1**

Brant Point
Inn & Atlantic
Mainstay **2**

Carlisle House
Inn **3**

The Cottages at
Boat Basin **15**

Harbor House
Village **4**

Jared Coffin
House **13**

Nantucket
Whaler **10**

Nesbitt Inn **11**

The Periwinkle . .**9**

Pineapple
Inn **14**

Safe Harbor **5**

Seven Sea
Street **7**

Ships Inn **17**

Union Street
Inn **16**

The Veranda
House **8**

VNH/
Hotel Green . . .**12**

White
Elephant **6**

Where to Stay in Nantucket Town

thecottagesnantucket.com ⤻ *23 cottages* ⚿ *Kitchenettes, cable TV, in-room VCRs, Wi-Fi, dock, marina, some pets allowed* ☰ *AE, D, DC, MC, V* ☾ *Closed late Oct.–mid-May* ⓘ *BP.*

☼ **$$$$** ⊡ **Harbor House Village.** An 1886 grand hotel forms the core of this family-oriented complex, where nicely landscaped brick walkways lead to a half-dozen town houses and an outdoor heated pool. Rooms are decorated in a sunny pale-pine-and-wicker motif, and many come with private balconies. Babysitters are on call in season, and children's programs are offered from mid-June to Labor Day. ⊠ *S. Beach St., Box 1139, 02554* ☎ *508/228–1500 or 866/325–9300* ⎙ *508/228–7639* ⊕ *www.harborhousevillage.com* ⤻ *104 rooms* ⚿ *Restaurant, cable TV, pool, lounge, children's programs (ages 3–13), concierge, business services, meeting rooms* ☰ *AE, D, DC, MC, V* ☾ *Closed late Oct.–late Apr.* ⓘ *CP.*

★ **$$$$** ⊡ **Nantucket Whaler.** Let's not mince words: the suites carved out of this 1850 Greek Revival house are gorgeous. Neither Calliope Ligelis nor Randi Ott, the New Yorkers who rescued the place in 1999, had any design experience, but they approached the project as if preparing to welcome friends. Each suite has a private entrance and the wherewithal to whip up a meal. The spacious bedrooms are lavished with flowers, well-chosen antiques, and fine linens, including plush robes. Couples who have come to explore not so much the island as one another will scarcely have to come up for air. ⊠ *8 N. Water St., Box 1337, 02554* ☎ *508/228–6597 or 888/808–6597* ⎙ *508/228–6291* ⊕ *www.nantucketwhaler.com* ⤻ *12 suites* ⚿ *Minibars, cable TV, in-room DVD/VCR, boccie, croquet; no kids under 12, no smoking* ☰ *AE, MC, V* ☾ *Closed mid-Dec.–mid-Apr.*

$$$$ ⊡ **Seven Sea Street.** If this red-oak post-and-beam B&B looks awfully well preserved, that's because it was custom-built in 1987. Decked out in Early American style (decorative stenciling, fishnet-canopy beds, braided rugs), it offers the ambience of antiquity without all the creaky drawbacks. The Deluxe Suite, with its cathedral ceiling, full kitchen, gas fireplace, and harbor view, warrants a leisurely stay. ⊠ *7 Sea St., 02554* ☎ *508/228–3577* ⎙ *508/228–3578* ⊕ *www.sevenseastreetinn.com* ⤻ *13 rooms, 2 suites* ⚿ *Refrigerators, cable TV, in-room VCRs, hot tub, library, Wi-Fi; no kids under 5, no smoking* ☰ *AE, D, MC, V* ⓘ *CP.*

$$$$ ⊡ **Union Street Inn.** Ken Withrow worked in the hotel business, Deborah Withrow in high-end retail display, and guests get the best of both worlds. This 1770 house, a stone's throw from the bustle of Main Street, has been respectfully yet lavishly restored. Guests are treated to Frette linens, plump duvets, and lush robes (the better to lounge around in, my dear), as well as a full gourmet breakfast served on the tree-shaded garden patio. ⊠ *7 Union St., 02554* ☎ *508/228–9222 or 800/225–5116* ⎙ *508/325–0848* ⊕ *www.unioninn.com* ⤻ *12 rooms* ⚿ *Cable TV; no kids under 12, no smoking* ☰ *AE, MC, V* ⓘ *BP.*
*Fodor's*Choice
★

$$$$ ⊡ **VNH (Vanessa Noel Hotel) and Hotel Green.** Minimalist chic has waltzed in the door—in a sweet pair of kitty heels. Opened in 2002 by native New Yorker and island shoe designer Vanessa Noel, VNH is a living catalog of trendy decor: each of the eight rooms (some admittedly as small as shoeboxes) boasts Armani Casa bedside tables, Philippe Starck bathroom fixtures, Mascioni linens, and Bulgari toiletries. Though the concept might seem a bit at odds with the island aesthetic, you'd be hard pressed to name a hotel with these touches—plus flat-screen plasma TVs and direct phone lines—outside a metropolis. Organo-purists will want to check out Noel's 2006 addition a few doors down: the 10-room Hotel Green—distinguished by its grass windowboxes—has milk-painted walls, hemp shower curtains (the water is dechlorinated), and ayurvedic body products. The inns share an outdoor breakfast café. ⊠ *5 Chestnut St., at Centre St., 02554* ☎ *508/228–5300* ⊕ *www.vanno.com* ⟿ *18 rooms* ⚏ *Minibars, cable TV, bar; no kids* ▭ *AE, D, MC, V.*

$$$$ ▣ **White Elephant.** The White Elephant, a 1920s behemoth right on Nantucket Harbor, seems determined to keep raising the bar in service and style. The complex—a main building plus a cluster of cottages in a breezy country-chic decor—hugs the harbor, leaving just enough room for an emerald lawn and the veranda of its in-house restaurant, the Brant Point Grill. Prices are lofty but, for the echelon it attracts, not all that extreme. ⊠ *Easton St., Box 1139, 02554* ☎ *508/228–2500 or 800/445–6574* 🖷 *508/325–1195* ⊕ *www.whiteelephanthotel.com* ⟿ *21 rooms, 31 suites, 11 cottages* ⚏ *Restaurant, room service, refrigerators, cable TV, in-room VCRs, in-room data ports, Wi-Fi, in-room safes, exercise equipment, dock, lounge, library, laundry service, concierge, business services, meeting rooms* ▭ *AE, D, DC, MC, V* ⊗ *Closed Jan.–Mar.* ❚◯❙ *BP.*

★ **$$$–$$$$** ▣ **Jared Coffin House.** The largest house in town when it was built in 1845, this three-story brick manse is still plenty impressive. The antiques-filled parlors are a study in timeless good taste. The inn's umbrella extends to two other nearby buildings, the handsomest of which is the 1842 Greek Revival Harrison Gray House. Rooms vary greatly in terms of size and grandeur (the inn even has some very affordable singles). ⊠ *29 Broad St., Box 1580, 02554* ☎ *508/228–2405 or 800/248–2405* ⊕ *www.jaredcoffinhouse.com* ⟿ *43 rooms* ⚏ *Cable TV, Wi-Fi, bar, concierge, meeting rooms; no a/c in some rooms, no smoking* ▭ *AE, D, DC, MC, V* ⊗ *Closed early Dec.–mid-May* ❚◯❙ *BP.*

★ **$$$–$$$$** ▣ **Pineapple Inn.** No expense was spared in retrofitting this 1838 Greek Revival captain's house for its new role as pamperer. It's decorated with impeccable taste, with down quilts and marble-finished baths. Breakfast is served in a formal dining room or beside the garden fountain. Whaling captains displayed a pineapple on their stoops upon completion of a successful journey, signaling the neighbors to come celebrate; here that spirit prevails daily. ⊠ *10 Hussey St., 02554* ☎ *508/228–9992* 🖷 *508/325–6051* ⊕ *www.pineappleinn.com* ⟿ *12 rooms* ⚏ *Cable TV, Wi-Fi* ▭ *AE, MC, V* ⊗ *Closed mid-Dec.–late Apr.* ❚◯❙ *CP.*

★ **$$$–$$$$** ▣ **The Veranda House.** A fixture since the early 1880s, the former Overlook, whose tiers of balconies take in a sweeping harbor vista, has been treated to a trendy overhaul. The exterior may look unchanged, but the rooms got a makeover that introduced Frette linens, Simon Pearce lamps, Italian-tile rain showers, and the like. Breakfasts are equally lush, featuring frittatas and artisanal cheeses. ⊠ *3 Step La., Box 1112, 02554* ☎ *508/228–0695* ⊕ *www.theverandahouse.com* ⟿ *15 rooms, 1 suite* ⚏ *Concierge, Wi-Fi; no kids under 10* ▭ *AE, D, MC, V* ⊗ *Closed early Dec. to mid-May* ❚◯❙ *BP.*

$$–$$$$ ▣ **The Periwinkle.** Sara Shlosser-O'Reilly's B&B has spark—and a variety of rooms ranging from affordable singles to nice-size quarters with

CLOSE UP

Navigating the Rental Market

IF YOU'RE GOING TO BE staying for a week or more, you might want to consider renting a cottage or house—an arrangement that gives you a chance to settle in and get a real taste of island living. Many visitors, especially those with children, find renting more relaxing than staying in a hotel or an inn. With your own kitchen, you'll save money by eating in; plus you can enjoy such homey summer pleasures as barbecues. Though decor can vary from chichi to weatherworn, most cottages come equipped with all you'll need to ensure a comfortable stay. Steer clear of a house without linens; it's a sign of bad things to come. The better houses come fully accoutered: not just with basics but with luxury touches like cable or satellite TV, a CD player, gourmet kitchen implements, beach chairs, and bikes.

Finding a great cottage or house can be tough, however, especially since so many are rented a year or more in advance by returning guests. The time to start your search is a summer ahead, though you can occasionally find a property as late as spring. A good way to shop is to stop in and visit Realtors when you happen to be in town. Be prepared for a bit of sticker shock, though. Prices are generally about twice what you'd have to pay on Cape Cod or even the Vineyard. In summer, very rustic (read shabby) rentals start at about $1,200 a week and can run to many times that ($3,500 and up) for multibedroom or waterfront properties.

Congdon & Coleman Real Estate ⊠ 57 Main St. ☎ 508/325–5000 or 800/325–5232 ⊟ 508/325–5025 ⊕ www.congdonandcoleman.com has been serving buyers and renters since 1931.

Lucille Jordan Real Estate ⊠ 8 Federal St. ☎ 508/228–4449 ⊕ www.jordanre.com has a broad rental inventory; check the photos lining the storefront windows.

The **Maury People** ⊠ 35–37 Main St. ☎ 508/228–1881 ⊟ 508/228–1481 ⊕ www.maurypeople.com, associated with Sotheby's, has more than 1,000 private homes in its rental inventory, including historic and beach homes; service is not only knowledgeable but personable.

Preferred Properties ⊠ 76 Easton St. ☎ 508/228–2320 or 800/338–7715 ⊟ 508/228–8464 ⊕ www.preferredpropertiesre.com is a Christie's affiliate whose offerings range "from cottages in the sand to castles on the cliff."

canopied king-size beds and harbor views. In one especially pretty setting, the blue-ribbon pattern of the wallpaper matches the cushions and canopy: it's like living in a nicely wrapped gift. ⊠ 7–9 N. Water St., Box 1436, 02554 ☎ 508/228–9267 or 800/588–0078 ⊟ 508/325–0245 ⊕ www.theperiwinkle.com ⋈ 16 rooms, 1 cottage ⚬ Cable TV; no smoking ⊟ D, MC, V ⊙ CP.

¢–$$$$ 🏠 **Carlisle House Inn.** A sister property to Marblehead's handsome Harbor Light Inn, this 1765 beauty shares the same traditionalist taste and dedication to comfort. Many rooms have four-poster beds and charming flocked wallpaper; one, overlooking the garden, is wood-paneled.

The location couldn't be more convenient or the breakfast room cheerier. ⊠ *26 N. Water St., 02554* ☎ *508/228–0720* 🖷 *781/639–1004* ⊕ *www.carlislehouse.com* 🗩 *14 rooms* ⚕ *No a/c in one room, no room phones, no smoking* ▤ *AE, MC, V* ⊗ *Closed Jan.–Mar.* ⑩| *CP.*

♻ **$$$** ▦ **Safe Harbor.** The name is apt: children *and* pets are welcome at this homey B&B with an enviable location mere steps from Children's Beach. Some of the rooms harboring American and Oriental antiques have water views; some have private decks. Everyone's welcome to sit on the wide front porch and enjoy the ocean breezes. ⊠ *2 Harborview Way, 02554* ☎🖷 *508/228–3222 or 800/651–9262* ⊕ *www.beesknees.net/safeharbor* 🗩 *5 rooms* ⚕ *Wi-Fi, some pets allowed* ▤ *AE, MC, V* ⑩| *CP.*

★ **$$$** ▦ **Ships Inn.** This 1831 home exudes history: built for whaling captain Obed Starbuck, it was later the birthplace of abolitionist Lucretia Mott. A dozen guest rooms, named for the ships Starbuck commanded, are furnished with period antiques and pretty wall coverings. The basement has a restaurant of the same name (delighted murmurings waft up); it generates a wonderful continental breakfast and afternoon tea. ⊠ *13 Fair St., 02554* ☎ *508/228–0040 or 888/872–4052* ⊕ *www.shipsinnnantucket.com* 🗩 *13 rooms, 11 with bath* ⚕ *Restaurant, refrigerators, cable TV; no kids under 8* ▤ *AE, D, MC, V* ⊗ *Closed Nov.–Apr.* ⑩| *CP.*

$$–$$$ ▦ **Brant Point Inn & Atlantic Mainstay.** You can't beat the edge-of-town location (Jetties Beach is a mere five-minute walk), especially given the modest rates that prevail at this pair of handsome post-and-beam guest houses. Innkeeper Thea Kaizer grew up in a Nantucket inn; her husband, Peter, leads fishing charters, and should you catch something, he'll expedite it to the restaurant of your choice. ⊠ *6 N. Beach St., 02554* ☎ *508/228–5442* 🖷 *508/228–8498* ⊕ *www.brantpointinn.com* 🗩 *17 rooms, 2 suites* ⚕ *Refrigerators, cable TV* ▤ *AE, MC, V* ⑩| *CP.*

¢**–$$** ▦ **Nesbitt Inn.** The last real deal left in town, this homey Victorian has been in the same family since 1914. Fourth-generation proprietors Joanne and Steve Marcoux are so nice, and the rates so reasonable, you're willing to overlook the shared baths and gently worn furnishings. Here you'll find the authentic, pre-glitz Nantucket. ⊠ *21 Broad St., Box 1019, 02554* ☎ *508/228–0156* 🖷 *508/228–2446* 🗩 *12 rooms share 3 baths, 1 room with private bath, 2 cottages* ⚕ *No smoking* ▤ *MC, V* ⑩| *CP.*

NANTUCKET TOWN OUTSKIRTS ⇨ *Where to Stay & Eat Outside Nantucket Town map for these properties.*

★ ♻ **$$$$** ▦ **Cliffside Beach Club.** Which way to the beach? You're on it: this snazzily updated 1920s beach club stakes its claim with a flotilla of colorful umbrellas—somewhat miffing natives, who consider sand rights anathema. Local politics aside, this is one prime chunk of gentle bay beach, and the complex makes the most of its site, with a gorgeous cathedral-ceiling lobby decorated with hanging quilts and rooms of every size and shape enhanced by island-made modern furnishings. Best of all, you can traipse across the sand to Galley Beach, one of the best restaurants around. ⊠ *46 Jefferson Ave., Box 449, 02554* ☎ *508/228–0618 or 800/932–9645* ⊕ *www.cliffsidebeach.com* 🗩 *26 rooms, 3 suites, 2 apartments, 1 cottage* ⚕ *Restaurant, some kitchenettes, refrigerators, cable TV, in-*

room data ports, gym, hot tub, massage, beach, pool ⊟ *AE* ⊘ *Closed mid-Oct.–May* ¶ *CP.*

¢ ⊞ **Robert B. Johnson Memorial Hostel.** One of the country's most picturesque hostels, this 49-bed Hostelling International facility occupies a former 1873 lifesaving station—known as "The Star of the Sea"—right on Surfside Beach, a 3 mi ride from town on the bike path. Dorm rooms (the three private rooms book quickly) are divided into men's, women's, and coed; the common areas include a kitchen. There's no lockout (customary at many urban hostels) and—huzzah—no curfew. Reservations are always a good idea, and essential come summer. ⊠ *31 Western Ave., 02554* ☎ *508/228–0433* ⊕ *www.usahostels.org/cape/nantucket_index. htm* ⇄ *49 dorm-style beds* ⚲ *Picnic area, beach, volleyball* ⊟ *MC, V* ⊘ *Closed mid-Oct.–early May.*

Nightlife & the Arts

The phrase "Nantucket nightlife" verges on an oxymoron—and, during the off-season, it's virtually a nonentity. If it's glitz and nonstop action you're after, better stick to the mainland. On the other hand, if you like live music, you will never go lacking—at least in season.

For listings of events, see the *Inquirer and Mirror* (⊕ www.ack.net), the *Nantucket Independent* (⊕ www.nantucketindependent.com), and the free weekly *Yesterday's Island* (⊕ www.yesterdaysisland.com). Posters around town announce coming attractions: check the board outside the Hub, a newsstand at the corner of Federal and Main streets.

FILM   The **Nantucket Film Festival** (☎ 508/325–6274 or 212/642–6339 ⊕ www. nantucketfilmfestival.org), held each June, emphasizes the importance of strong scripts. The final playlist—about two dozen short and feature-length films—always includes a few world premieres, and many selections have gone on to considerable commercial success. Shows tend to sell out, so it's best to buy ahead. A Week Pass, though pricey ($375), gives you priority in the inevitable lines, as well as access to certain seminars. Alternately, daily passes ($50) can also be useful. Informal daily coffee-klatch events—such as close-up discussions with directors—held at a local restaurant, are always interesting.

The **Starlight Theatre** (⊠ 1 N. Union St. ☎ 508/228–4435 ⊕ www. stariglightnantucket.com) is a small screening room appended to a café of the same name. It presents two shows nightly in season, plus sporadic matinees.

MUSIC   The **Boston Pops Esplanade Orchestra** (☎ 508/825–8248) puts on a blowout concert in mid-August on Jetties Beach to benefit the Nantucket Cottage Hospital.

The **Nantucket Arts Council** (⊠ Box 554, 02554 ☎ 508/228–8588) sponsors a music series (jazz, country, classical) September to June.

The **Nantucket School of Music** (⊠ 11 Centre St. ☎ 508/228–3352) arranges year-round choral and instrumental instruction and sponsors and puts on concerts; choristers are always welcome.

Nantucket Musical Arts Society (☎ 508/228–1287) mounts concerts by internationally acclaimed musicians Tuesday evenings at 8:30 July through August. The concerts are mostly classical but sometimes venture into jazz.

The **Nantucket Park & Recreation Commission** (✉ Children's Beach bandstand, off Harbor View Way ☎ 508/228–7213) hosts free concerts (and the occasional theater production) from July 4 to Labor Day. Programs begin at 6 PM, range from jazz and classical to pop, and include such local favorites as Ecliff & the Swingdogs. Bring blankets, chairs, and bug repellent.

The **Noonday Concert Series** (✉ Unitarian Universalist Church, 11 Orange St. ☎ 508/228–5466), Thursday at noon in July and August, brings in stellar performers and also showcases outstanding local musicians. Past concerts have included organ, bluegrass, and classical music.

BARS & CLUBS   The **Chicken Box** (The Box; ✉ 14 Dave St., off Lower Orange St. ☎ 508/228–9717 ⊕ www.chickenbox.com) rocks! Live music—including some big-name bands—plays six nights a week in season, and weekends throughout the year. On the off nights, you can always play pool, foosball, or darts.

The **Muse** (✉ 44 Surfside Rd. ☎ 508/228–6873 ⊕ www.museack.com) is *the* place to catch big-name acts year-round. DJs spin between sets and on nights when there's no live act. The barnlike Muse accommodates some 370 people, who also have the option of playing pool or Ping-Pong or scarfing pies produced on-site at **Muse Pizza** (☎ 508/228–1471).

THEATER   **Theatre Workshop of Nantucket** (✉ Methodist Church, 2 Centre St. ☎ 508/228–4305 ⊕ www.theatreworkshop.com), a community theater since 1956, stages plays, musicals, and readings year-round.

Sports & the Outdoors

BEACHES   A calm area by the harbor, **Children's Beach** (off Harbor View Way) is an easy walk north from the center of town and a perfect spot for small children. The beach has a grassy park with benches, a playground, lifeguards, a café, picnic tables, showers, and restrooms. Tie-dyeing classes are offered Friday at noon mid-July through August.

Cisco (✉ Hummock Pond Rd., South Shore) has heavy surf, lifeguards, but no food or restrooms. It's not easy to get to or from Nantucket Town, though: it's 4 mi from town, and there are no bike trails to it, so you'll have to ride in the road, walk, drive, or take a taxi. Also, the dunes are severely eroded, so getting down onto the beach can be difficult. Still, the waves make it a popular spot for body- and boardsurfers.

Dionis Beach (✉ Eel Point Rd.) is, at its entrance, a narrow strip of sand that turns into a wider, more private strand with high dunes and fewer children. The beach has a rocky bottom and calm, rolling waters; there are lifeguards on duty and restrooms. Take the Madaket Bike Path to Eel Point Road, about 3 mi west of town.

★   A short bike- or shuttle-bus ride from town, **Jetties Beach** (Hulbert Ave., 1½ mi northwest of Straight Wharf) is the most popular family beach because of its calm surf, lifeguards, bathhouse, restrooms, and snack bar. It's a good place to try out water toys: kayaks, sailboards, and day-sailers are rented in summer. On shore it's a lively scene with playground and volleyball nets on the beach and adjacent tennis courts. There is a boardwalk to the beach and you can watch the ferries pass.

Known for great sunsets and surf, **Madaket Beach** (⊠ Off Madaket Rd., Madaket) is reached by shuttle bus from Nantucket Town or the Madaket Bike Path (5 mi from Upper Main Street) and has lifeguards, but no restrooms. The West End, for food, is nearby.

Fodor'sChoice ★   **Surfside Beach** (⊠ Surfside Rd., South Shore) is the island's most popular surf beach, with lifeguards, restrooms, a snack bar, and a wide strand of sand. It pulls in college students as well as families and is great for kite flying and surf casting. It's accessible via the Surfside Bike Path (3 mi) or shuttle bus.

> ### MICHELANGELO ON THE BEACH
>
> Buddhas, dragons, mermaids, and, of course, whales inhabit Jetties Beach during the annual Sandcastle & Sculpture Day in August. Creative concoctions, often with maritime themes, emerge from the sand: porpoises, submarines, spaceships, flowers, and the famous lightship baskets are carefully and creatively crafted out of sand, shells, seaweed, and even beach litter (you may even see a castle or two). Anyone can stake out a patch of sand. There are prizes in several age groups and categories, so grab a shovel, bucket, turkey baster (a secret weapon for blowing sand), rake, and sunscreen and join the fun. Registration forms are available at the chamber office, 48 Main Street.

BIKING   The best way to tour Nantucket is by bicycle. Nearly 28 mi of paved bike paths wind through all types of terrain from one end of the island to the other; it is possible to bike around the entire island in a day. Most paths start within ½ mi of town, and all are well marked. Several lead to beaches. And if you're without your wheels, it's easy enough to rent some. The paths are also perfect for runners and bladers—but not mopeds, which are forbidden. Note that Nantucket now requires all bike riders—including adults—to wear a helmet.

The easy 3-mi **Surfside Bike Path** leads to Surfside, the island's premier ocean beach. A drinking fountain and rest stop are placed at about the halfway point.

Milestone Bike Path, a straight shot linking Nantucket Town and Sconset, is probably the most monotonous of the paths but can still be quite pleasant. It's 6 mi—paired with the scenic Polpis Path, it becomes a 14-mi island loop.

At 1.2 mi, the **Cliff Road Path,** on the north shore, is one of the easiest bike paths, but it's still quite scenic, with gentle hills. It intersects with the Eel Point and Madaket paths.

The **Eel Point/Dionis Beach Path** starts at the junction of Eel Point Road and Madaket Road and links the Cliff Road and Madaket bike paths to Dionis Beach. It's less than a mile long.

The **Madaket Path** starts at the intersection of Quaker and Upper Main Street and follows Madaket Road out to Madaket Beach, on the island's west end and about 5 mi from the edge of Nantucket Town. About one-third of the way, you could turn off onto Cliff Road Path or the Eel Point/Dionis Beach Path.

Young's Bicycle Shop (✉ 6 Broad St., Steamboat Wharf ☎ 508/228–1151 ⊕ www.youngsbicycleshop.com), established in 1931, rents bicycles, including tandems and children's equipment; weekly rates are available. The knowledgeable third-generation Young family and staff will send you off with everything you need—an excellent touring map, a helmet, and a quaint little Portuguese basket for your handlebars.

BIRD-WATCHING Hundreds of species flock to the island's moors, meadows, and marshes in the course of a year. Birds that are rare in other parts of New England thrive here, because of the lack of predators and the abundance of wide-open, undeveloped space. Almost anywhere outside of town you're sure to see interesting bird life, not just in migratory season but year-round. Set up your spotting scope near the salt marsh at Eel Point any time of year and you're bound to see shorebirds feeding—low tide is the best time. Endangered piping plovers and least terns nest on the ocean side in spring. Folger's Marsh about 3 mi east of town and the Harbor Flats at the end of Washington Street on the eastern edge of town are also good shorebird-watching sites. Inland, a walk through Sanford Farm from Madaket Road to the south shore, traversing upland, forest, heath, and shore habitats, will bring you in range of Savannah sparrows, yellow warblers, osprey, and red-tailed hawks, the island's most common raptor. Be on the lookout for the protected Northern harrier. For woodland species, check out the trails through Windswept Cranberry Bog or the Masquetuck Reservation near Polpis Harbor.

Eco Guides: Strong Wings (✉ 9 Nobadeer Farm Rd. ☎ 508/228–1769 ⊕ www.strongwings.org) customizes environmentally savvy birding tours based on interest and group size and, depending on your preferred degree of difficulty, can include a hike, a bike ride, or a casual stroll.

The **Maria Mitchell Association** (MMA; ✉ 4 Vestal St. ☎ 508/228–0898 ⊕ www.mmo.org) leads marine-ecology field trips and nature and bird walks weekly in spring and early summer and three times a week from June through Labor Day.

BOATING During July and August, Nantucket is *the* place to study, close-up, some of the world's most splendid yachts—and the well-to-do people who own and sail them. Don't be surprised if you see yachts with piggyback motor launches, automobiles, and helicopters. Most of them spend a few days here, many from a tour that originated in the Mediterranean via the Caribbean. If you don't happen to own a floating palace, you can still hit the water—Nantucket has plenty of boat charters, rentals, and scenic cruises.

Nantucket Boat Rentals (✉ Slip 1, Straight Wharf ☎ 508/325–1001 ⊕ www.nantucket.net/boating/boatrentals) rents powerboats, for up to 10 passengers; security deposits are required.

Nantucket Community Sailing (✉ 4 Winter St. ☎ 508/228–6600 ⊕ www.nantucketcommunitysailing.org) rents Sunfish sailboats, sailboards, and kayaks from Jetties Beach (Memorial Day–Labor Day); it also has youth and adult instructional sailing programs, as well as adaptive watersport clinics for disabled athletes. NCS's Outrigger Canoe Club—a Polynesian tradition—meets on Jetties Monday, Wednesday, and Friday at 5:30 in season.

Sea Nantucket (⊠ Washington St., ¼ mi southeast of Commercial Wharf ☎ 508/228–7499) rents kayaks and small sailboats by the hour or half day at the vest-pocket Francis Street Beach.

Anna W. II (⊠ Slip 11, Straight Wharf ☎ 508/228–1444) is a 1961 Maine lobster boat that's been converted to accommodate tables with booth seating. Kid-friendly trips (ages 4 and up only) include a Marine Life Discovery Cruise, on which fisherman and self-taught naturalist Captain Bruce Cowan tours the jetties, trap-hauling for lobsters, fish, crabs, and eels, as well as Ice Cream cruises featuring complimentary servings of everyone's favorite food. On the Sunset Cruise, couples or families are welcome to bring a picnic supper and a bottle of wine.

★ The *Endeavor* (⊠ Slip 1015, Straight Wharf ☎ 508/228–5585 ⊕ www. endeavorsailing.com), a charter replica Friendship sloop, makes four daily 1½-hour trips out to the jetties and into the sound. Private charters and special theme trips for children—"Pirate Adventure" and "Songs and Stories of the Sea"—are available.

Shearwater Excursions (☎ 508/228–7037 ⊕ www.explorenantucket. com) mount various seaborne ecotours aboard a 50-foot power catamaran. One option is a two-hour trip to view Muskeget Island's 2,500 resident gray seals; one-hour lobster cruises to nearby Tuckernuck Island are offered on a flexible schedule out of Madaket. Sunday is for whale-watching 15–30 mi southeast of Nantucket; Captain Blair Perkins guarantees a sighting, which means that if no mammals show up, you can go again for free. The Shearwater is also available for private evening charters.

FISHING Surf fishing is very popular on Nantucket, especially in the late spring when bluefish are running (the best place to go after them is Great Point). Freshwater fishing is also an option at many area ponds.

Many of the fishing charters will gladly make detours to spot whales.

Captain Peter Kaizer likes to say "Fishing's fun, catching's better." A former commercial fisherman, he guarantees you'll bring home something to eat by taking you to the fishies' favorite clandestine hangouts aboard the *Althea K* (☎ 508/228–3471 ⊕ www.altheakcharter.com). Kaizer also runs whale-watching and charter cruises from an insider's perspective.

Captain Tom's Charters (⊠ Public Landing, Madaket ☎ 508/228–4225 ⊕ www.captaintomscharters.com) win consistent "best of" awards for Tom Mleczko's hands-on expertise. Choose among rips, bars, surf, open water, and flats (the latter for the added challenge of sight fishing with fly rods).

A permit is required for **shellfishing,** specifically foraging for littleneck and cherrystone clams, quahogs, scallops, oysters, steamers, and mussels. You can pick one up—along with tips on where and how to get the best catch—at the **Marine and Coastal Resources Department** (✉ 34 Washington St. ☎ 508/228–7261 ⊕ www.nantucket-ma.gov/departments/marine/marine.html).

GOLF **Miacomet Golf Club** (✉ 12 W. Miacomet Ave. ☎ 508/325–0333 ⊕ www.miacometgolf.com) is a public links-style course owned by the Land Bank and built over natural terrain—mostly coastal heathland. It has 18 very flat holes.

HIKING Nantucket supports approximately 1,200 species of vegetation: that's a greater variety than is found in any other area of equivalent size in the United States. It has 82 mi of beaches, and though almost 97% of the shoreline is privately owned, it's a point of pride that almost all is open for public use. There are hardwood forests, salt marshes, cranberry bogs, squam swamps, freshwater ponds, and coastal heathlands, and, with Martha's Vineyard and nearby Tuckernuck Island, the island holds more than 90% of the acreage of sandplain grassland *worldwide*. The island is home to a huge number of deer; significant colonies of harbor seals, gray seals, and harbor porpoises; turtles, frogs, rabbits, voles, and other reptiles and small field mammals. A lack of land-bound predators such as skunks and raccoons allows bird populations to thrive, and hundreds of species either live on the island or pass through on their annual migrations.

Almost all of the 9,000 acres maintained by the **Nantucket Conservation Foundation** (✉ 118 Cliff Rd. ☎ 508/228–2884 ⊕ www.nantucketconservation.com) are open to the public; though only a few trails are marked, you can feel free to wander knowing that you can't get lost—if you keep going in one direction, you're bound to hit a road or a beach eventually. The foundation, open weekdays 8–5, puts out maps and informative brochures on the most popular hiking spots. Remember that these conservation areas are set aside to preserve and protect Nantucket's fragile ecosystems—tread carefully—and also be aware that ticks are a serious problem here. Dress accordingly and carry plenty of repellent.

A 5- to 10-minute bike ride from Nantucket Town on the way to Madaket, the **Sanford Farm, Ram Pasture, and the Woods** (✉ Madaket Rd., between Milford and Cliff Rds.) comprises 300 acres that were saved from developers by the Nantucket Conservation Foundation in 1971. The southern edge of the property borders the ocean.

The **Tupancy Links** (✉ 165 Cliff Rd., 1¼ mi west of town) runs between the Cliff Road bike path and Nantucket Sound. It's a smaller property that passes mainly through grassland populated by plants like false heather, oxeye daisy, and Queen Anne's lace, and it provides wonderful views once you reach the overlook at the water's edge. The cliff is only 42 feet above sea level, but from it you can see great stretches of the island's north shore.

SURFING   The relatively mild breakers at Cisco Beach make picking up the sport easier than it might be in, say, Maui. **Nantucket Island Surf School** (☎ 508/560-1020 ⊕ www.surfack.com) owner Gary Kohner and his crew can tell you everything you need to know to get up and cruising, from surfing etiquette to ocean safety. Group and private lessons and equipment and wet-suit rental are available.

TENNIS   **The Jetties Beach Tennis Courts** (☎ 508/325–5334), six contiguous asphalt courts overseen by the Park & Recreation department, charge a nominal fee 8 AM–6 PM in season and are much in demand, so reserve early in the day. Early- and latecomers play free, and off-season, you're golden: they leave the nets up year-round.

Nantucket Tennis and Swim Club (⊠ 23 Nobadeer Farm Rd., near airport ☎ 508/228–3700 ⊕ www.nantuckettennis.com ☉ Memorial Day–Columbus Day, daily 7 AM–9:30 PM) has nine fast-dry clay courts, five lighted courts, and a pro shop. Lessons, rentals, clinics, and round-robins are available.

Shopping

The historic center of town doubles as the commercial district: shops are concentrated primarily in the grid formed by Main, Centre, Broad, and Easy streets, with a few shops trailing off along the periphery. The former boathouses of Straight Wharf and Old South Wharf, retrofitted as shops and galleries, attract well-heeled browsers as well. The necessities of island life—hardware, office supplies, etc.—tend to be clustered mid-island, where new stores offering nonessentials are gradually making inroads as well.

Most of Nantucket's shops are seasonal, opening in time for the Daffodil Festival in late April and closing soon after Christmas Stroll in early December; a hardy few stay open year-round and often offer rather astounding bargains off-season. On summer weekends, many shops stay open late (until 9 or 10). Most galleries hold their openings on Friday evenings.

ANTIQUES   **Barrington Antiques** (⊠ 0 Washington St. ☎ 508/228–4515 ⊕ www.michaelbarringtonantiques.com) is packed with treasures, some sizable and "important."

G. K. S. Bush (⊠ 13 Old South Rd. ☎ 508/325–0300) carries ultra-high-end American antique furniture, paintings, and decorative arts (winter headquarters are on New York's Upper East Side).

Lynda Willauer Antiques (⊠ 2 India St. ☎ 508/228–3631) has amassed a stellar cache of American and English furniture, plus fine collectibles, including Chinese export porcelain and majolica.

★ **Nantucket Country** (⊠ 38 Centre St. ☎ 508/228–8868 ⊕ www.nantucketcountryantiques.com) has an especially rich inventory of quilts and flags; another specialty—in addition to maritime and "Nantucketiana"—is antique children's toys.

Nina Hellman Marine Antiques & Americana (✉ 48 Centre St. ☎ 508/228–4677 ⊕ www.nauticalnantucket.com) carries scrimshaw, whaling artifacts, ship models, instruments, and other marine antiques, plus folk art and Nantucket memorabilia. Charles Manghis, a contemporary scrimshaw artist, demonstrates and exhibits his craft here.

Fodor'sChoice ★ **Rafael Osona Auctions** (✉ American Legion Hall, 21 Washington St. ☎ 508/228–3942 ⊕ www.rafaelosonaauction.com) holds auctions of fine antiques most Saturday mornings from Memorial Day weekend to early December; the items—furniture, decorative accessories, art, jewelry, and more—are previewable two days in advance.

Established in 1927, **Sylvia Antiques** (✉ 6 Ray's Ct. ☎ 508/228–0960 ⊕ www.sylviaantiques.com) retains the richest stash of island-related antiquities.

PETTICOAT ROW

During the whaling era—a time, remember, when women were generally considered better seen than heard—a circumstance developed in Nantucket Town that was perhaps unique in the country: a large portion of Centre Street shops near Main Street were almost completely run by women merchants. It eventually became known as Petticoat Row, and it still exists today. Women have always played a strong role in Nantucket's history, partly because of the Quaker philosophy of sexual equality and partly because on whaling expeditions men could be gone for years at a time—and it was up to women to keep the town going. They became leaders in every arena, from religion to business.

★ **Weeds** (✉ 14 Centre St. ☎ 508/228–5200 ⊕ www.weedsnantucket.com) marries mere age with pure style; it's a delight to peruse.

ART GALLERIES The **Artists' Association of Nantucket** (✉ 19 Washington St. ☎ 508/228–0772 ⊕ www.nantucketarts.org) is the best place to get an overview of the work being done on-island; many members have galleries of their own.

★ At **The Brigham Galleries** (✉ 54 Center St. ☎ 508/925–2525 ⊕ www.thebrighamgalleries.com) Sara Boyce has an entire Federal-style house in which to showcase her excellent, at times playful taste; portrait commissions are a specialty.

The **Gallery at Four India** (✉ 4 India St. ☎ 508/228–8509 ⊕ www.galleryatfourindia.com) is a quiet, spacious refuge, with highly sought-after American and marine paintings dating from the 1850s to 1940s, plus a small sampling of contemporary realism.

★ Tucked amid a row of shingled former boathouses, the **South Wharf Gallery** (✉ 21 Old South Wharf ☎ 508/228–0406 ⊕ www.southwharfgallery.com) has been showing top local work since 1978; an annex at 3 India Street was added in 2006.

BOOKS Check the Nantucket Room at the back of **Mitchell's Book Corner** (✉ 54 Main St. ☎ 508/228–1080 ⊕ www.mitchellsbookcorner.com) for regional titles. The front is filled with an astute sampling covering a broad range of categories. Author signings are held on summer Saturdays.

Nantucket Bookworks (⊠ 25 Broad St. ☎ 508/228–4000 ⊕ www. nantucketbookworks.com) carries an extensive inventory, with an emphasis on literary works and Nantucket-specific titles, as well as children's books and gift items.

CLOTHING **Eye of the Needle and Eye of the Needle Girls** (⊠ 14–14A Federal St. ☎ 508/ ★ 228–1923 and 508/228–4449) is a microcosm of urban fashion trends, playfully leavened.

She's back! The splashy resort wear so popular in the '60s is enshrined at the **Lilly Pulitzer Shop** (⊠ 5 S. Water St. ☎ 508/228–0569 ⊕ www. lillyshop.com).

Mallory Alfano (⊠ 32 Center St. ☎ 508/228–0569) combs the international boutique market to stock her namesake store with exquisite, of-the-moment accessories.

Murray's Toggery Shop (⊠ 62 Main St. ☎ 508/228–0437 ⊕ www. nantucketreds.com) can claim credit for introducing the signature "Nantucket reds" (⇨ Nantucket Reds box)—now available in a range of styles for men, women, and children.

Murray's Warehouse (⊠ 7 New St. ☎ 508/228–3584 ⊕ www. nantucketreds.com) offers discounts of up to 75% on surplus stock from Murray's Toggery Shop.

Something about the Nantucket lifestyle prompts hat hunger. **Peter Beaton** (⊠ 16½ Federal St. ☎ 508/228–8456 ⊕ www.peterbeaton.com) shows an international array of beauties, all customizable with special trim, along with a smattering of clothing.

Vanessa Noel (⊠ 5 Chestnut St., at Centre St. ☎ 508/228–6030 ⊕ www. vanessanoel.com) creates ultraglam shoes—they're expensive, to be sure, but fans gladly toe the line.

Island loyalties might be tested, but the **Vineyard Vines** (⊠ 2 Harbor Sq. ☎ 800/892–4982 ⊕ www.vineyardvines.com) line—from flip-flops to bathing trunks, not to mention the ties that started it all—is just so irresistibly preppy, resistance is futile.

Fodor'sChoice The inviting windows of **Vis-a-Vis** (⊠ 34 Main St. ☎ 508/228–5527 ★ ⊕ www.visavisnantucket.com) display relaxed-luxe women's fashions amid antique home furnishings, some of which, including hooked rugs, quilts, and collectibles, are also for sale.

CRAFTS **Claire Murray** (⊠ 11 S. Water St. ☎ 508/228–1913 or 800/252–4733 ⊕ www.clairemurray.com) carries the designer's Nantucket-theme and other hand-hooked rugs and rug kits, quilts, and knitting and needlework kits; this little shop is where the empire got started.

Erica Wilson Needle Works (⊠ 25 Main St. ☎ 508/228–9881) embodies the enthusiasms of the famous British-born designer, an island resident since 1958. In addition to her own embroidery and needlepoint

Nantucket Reds

BERMUDA HAS ITS SHORTS, FIJI ITS SARONGS. Nantucket's totemic clothing items are made of cotton dyed red so as to fade to a dull salmon shade. The reds were something of a secret code until they were singled out by *The Official Preppy Handbook* in 1980: "By their pink shirts ye shall know them" might be the watchwords for Nantucketers among the worldwide sailing community. Now reds are as site-specific as Martha's Vineyard's Black Dog line (attempting to compete, of late, with a satellite shop on Straight Wharf).

The principal purveyor of Nantucket reds is Murray's Toggery Shop on Main Street, which has catered to conservative dressers since the early 1900s. (Roland Macy worked here at his father's shop in the early 1800s before setting off to rewrite retailing history.) From baby togs to tote bags, you'll find everything you could want here in the way of reds. But for that weathered look that sets them off so well, you'll have to get out on the water.

kits, the store carries winning clothing and accessories for women (look for Heidi Weddendorf's Nantucket knot jewelry), baby gifts, and appealing elements of home decor.

Since 1927, the **Four Winds Craft Guild** (⌧ 6 Ray's Ct. ☎ 508/228–9623 ⊕ www.sylviaantiques.com) has showcased local folk arts, including scrimshaw and lightship baskets (old and new), ship models, and duck decoys; the guild also offers a kit for making your own lightship basket. A satellite shop within the historic Pacific Club at 1 Main Street displays outstanding new work.

★ **Nantucket Looms** (⌧ 16 Federal St. ☎ 508/228–1908 ⊕ www.nantucketlooms.com) stocks luscious woven-on-the-premises textiles and chunky Susan Lister Locke jewelry, among other adornments for self and home.

JEWELRY **Diana Kim England, Goldsmiths** (⌧ 56 Main St. ☎ 508/228–3766 or 800/343–1468 ⊕ www.dianakimengland.com) has created an elegant contemporary line featuring unusual gems such as tourmaline, chalcedony, and tanzanite.

The **Golden Basket** (⌧ 44 Main St. ☎ 508/228–4344 or 800/626–2758 ⊕ www.thegoldenbasket.com) was founded in 1977 by designer Glenaan M. Elliott, who fashioned the first miniature lightship basket. Other popular motifs include starfish and shells.

Siasconset & Wauwinet

★ *7 mi east of Nantucket Town.*

First a fishing outpost and then an artist's colony (Broadway actors favored it in the late 19th century), Siasconset—or 'Sconset, in the local vernacular—is a charming cluster of rose-covered cottages linked by driveways of crushed clamshells; at the edges of town, the former fishing shacks give way to magnificent sea-view mansions. The small town center consists of a market, post office, café, lunchroom, and liquor store–cum–lending library.

The tiny settlement of Wauwinet, a few miles north, is in a haulover–spit of land so narrow, boats can be dragged across it—leading to the immense curving sandbar of Coskata, Great Point, and Coatue.

⑥ Altar Rock. Altar Rock Road, a dirt track about 3 mi west of the Milestone Road Rotary on Polpis Road, leads to the island's highest point, Altar Rock, from which the view is spectacular. The hill overlooks open moor and bog land—technically called lowland heath—which is very rare in the United States. The entire area is laced with paths leading in every direction. Don't forget to keep track of the trails you travel to find your way back.

OFF THE BEATEN PATH **MILESTONE BOG –** The 200-plus acres of cranberry bogs, surrounded by conservation land, is always a beautiful spot to visit, particularly in the fall. The sight of bright red berries and the moors' rich autumn colors is not to be missed. ⊠ *Off Milestone Rd., west of Siasconset.*

⑦ Nantucket Life Saving Museum. Items displayed in this re-creation of the 1874 Life Saving Service station that still stands on Surfside Beach (it's a hostel now), include original rescue equipment and boats, artifacts recovered from the *Andrea Doria* wreck, and photos and accounts of daring rescues. There are several rare pieces: for instance, one of four surviving surfboats and an equally well preserved original beach cart. ⊠ *158 Polpis Rd.* ☎ *508/228–1885* ⊕ *www.nantucketlifesavingmuseum. com* ⊠ *$5* ⊙ *Mid-June–mid-Oct., daily 9:30–4.*

② Sankaty Head Lighthouse. The red-and-white-striped beacon overlooking the sea on one side and the Scottish-looking links of the private Sankaty Head Golf Club on the other is one of New England's many endangered lighthouses. It's not open to the public, but you can approach it, via a seashell gravel road. ⊠ *Baxter Rd.*

NEED A BREAK? For a great picnic in Sconset, stop at **Claudette's** (⊠ Post Office Sq. ☎ 508/ 257–6622) for a box lunch to go; or dig right in on the shady patio. It's open mid-May through mid-October.

③ Sesachacha Pond. This kettle pond (pronounced *sah*-kah-cha) off Polpis Road is a good spot for bird-watching. It's circled by a walking path that leads to an Audubon wildlife area and is separated from the ocean by a narrow strand on its east side. It provides a good view of Sankaty Head Lighthouse.

① Siasconset Casino. Despite its name, this property dating to 1899 has never been used for gambling—the meaning of "casino" was broader back when it was built—but was instead used from the beginning as a theater venue, particularly during the actors'-colony heyday, and as a gathering place. Some theater can still be seen here, but it's primarily a tennis club and informal cinema. ⊠ *New St.* ☎ *508/257–6661.*

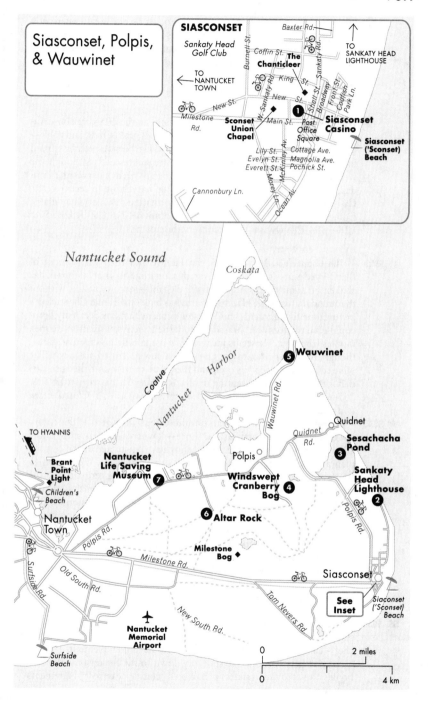

Siasconset, Polpis, & Wauwinet

SIASCONSET

Sankaty Head Golf Club

Baxter Rd.

TO SANKATY HEAD LIGHTHOUSE

Coffin St. **The Chanticleer**

TO NANTUCKET TOWN

Burnett St.

King St.

New St.

W-Sankaty Rd.

Sankaty Rd.

Shell St.

Broadway

Front St.

Codfish Park Ln.

New St.

Milestone Rd.

Main St.

Sconset Union Chapel

Post Office Square

❶ **Siasconset Casino**

Siasconset ('Sconset) Beach

Lily St.

Evelyn St.

Everett St.

Cottage Ave.

Magnolia Ave.

Pochick St.

McKinley Av.

Morey Ln.

Ocean Av.

Cannonbury Ln.

Nantucket Sound

Coskata

Harbor

Coatue

Nantucket

❺ **Wauwinet**

TO HYANNIS

Brant Point Light

Children's Beach

Nantucket Town

Surfside Rd.

Nantucket Life Saving Museum ❼

Polpis

Windswept Cranberry Bog ❹

❻ **Altar Rock**

Wauwinet Rd.

Quidnet Rd.

Quidnet

❸ **Sesachacha Pond**

Sankaty Head Lighthouse ❷

Polpis Rd.

Polpis Rd.

Old South Rd.

Milestone Rd.

Milestone Bog ◆

New South Rd.

Tom Nevers Rd.

Siasconset

See Inset

Siasconset ('Sconset) Beach

✈ **Nantucket Memorial Airport**

Surfside Beach

0 ___ 2 miles

0 ___ 4 km

⑤ Wauwinet. Now it's a hamlet of beach houses on the northeastern end of Nantucket. But early European settlers found the neck of sand above it to be the easiest way to get to the ocean for fishing. Instead of rowing around Great Point, fishermen would go to the head of the harbor and haul their dories over the narrow strip of sand and beach grass separating Nantucket Harbor from the ocean. Hence the name for that strip: the haulover.

④ Windswept Cranberry Bog. Throughout the year, the 205-acre conservation area off Polpis Road is a beautiful tapestry of greens, reds, and golds—and a popular hangout for many bird species. The bog is especially vibrant in mid-October, when the cranberries are harvested. (Although the weekend after Columbus Day has historically been a harvesting holiday, a glut in the market has cancelled the harvesting in recent years. Call the Chamber of Commerce for information.) A map is available from the **Nantucket Conservation Foundation** (⊠ 118 Cliff Rd. ☎ 508/ 228–2884 ⊕ www.nantucketconservation.com).

Where to Stay & Eat

$$$$ ╳ **The Chanticleer.** Now that Susan Handy and chef Jeff Worster of Black-Eyed Susan's have taken over, this longtime Sconset landmark has shaken off some of its starch. It's still elegant—more so, really, without the attendant fussiness. Handy's charm has blossomed amid Chanticleer's picturesque rose gardens, and Worster's cuisine remains decidedly Francophile, in the form of "brasserie moderne": vichyssoise, fruits de mer, moules frites, etc. He seems incapable of containing his creative streak, though: the new mandate just gives him a new palette to play with. The wine cellar is as "deep" as ever, and the porch overlooking the herb garden is the most coveted seating of all. ⊠ *9 New St., Siasconset* ☎ *508/ 257–6231* ⚠ *Reservations essential* ☰ *AE, MC, V* ☺ *Closed Mon. and mid-Oct.–early May.*

★ **$$$$** ╳ **Topper's.** The Wauwinet—an ultraluxuriously restored 19th-century inn on Nantucket's northeastern shore—is where islanders and visitors alike go to experience perfection. Many take advantage of the complimentary launch, the *Wauwinet Lady* out of Straight Wharf, which frames the journey with a scenic harbor tour. Having traipsed past the croquet lawn, one enters a creamy-white dining room awash with lush linens and glorious flowers. David Daniel's cuisine delivers on the fantasy with a menu of intentional "simplicity"—if that's how you would describe butter-basted lobster, for instance, paired with glazed Thumbelina carrots and tempura sea beans, or sake-poached Ahi tuna with truffled crab angliotti. Portions may be on the nouvellish (read "puny") side, and this is not what you'd call vibrant cuisine: it's delicate bordering on bland. Still the experience as a whole is soothing and special. ⊠ *120 Wauwinet Rd., Wauwinet* ☎ *508/228–8768* ⊕ *www.wauwinet.com* ⚠ *Reservations essential* ☰ *AE, D, DC, MC, V* ☺ *Closed Nov.–Apr.*

$$–$$$$ ╳ **The Summer House Beachside Bistro.** Where some hoteliers might in-
FodorsChoice stall a poolside snack bar, the Summer House imported a top French
★ chef—Charles Salliou—to create a real restaurant en plein air. The terraced potagere flanking the stairway down to the cluster of white umbrellas attests to the freshness of Salliou's "cuisine de terroir" ingredients

Where to Stay & Eat
Outside Nantucket Town

KEY
① Hotels
① Restaurants

ATLANTIC OCEAN

Nantucket Sound

TO MARTHA'S VINEYARD (SUMMER ONLY)
TO HYANNIS

See "Where to Eat in Nantucket Town" & "Where to Stay in Nantucket Town" maps

Restaurants ▶

The Chanticleer	.8
Cinco	.5
The Downyflake	.4
Galley Beach	.1
Seagrille	.2
Sfoglia	.3
The Summer House Beachside Bistro	.6
The Summer House Restaurant	.7
Topper's	.9

Hotels ▶

Cliffside Beach Club	.1
Robert B. Johnson Memorial Hostel	.2
The Summer House	.3
Wade Cottages	.4
The Wauwinet	.5

(he's a gifted gardener, too, to wrest such bounty from the sand). Prize dishes include a light, lyrical clam chowder (made with Vermont cream) and halibut with a champagne, ginger, and chive sauce. Fresh-made sorbets top off a lovely night under the stars. ⊠ *17 Ocean Ave., Siasconset* ☎ *508/257–4542* ⊕ *www.thesummerhouse.com* ▤ *AE, MC, V* ⊘ *Closed mid-Sept.–late June.*

★ **$$–$$$$**   ✕ **The Summer House Restaurant.** An integral element of the rose-canopied complex that epitomizes Sconset, the dining room is also abloom, with lavish floral displays set against a background of pastel linen and white wicker. Now that Chef Salliou, having wowed regulars at the Beachside Bistro, has reassumed the reins of the main dining room as well, everyone's the richer. Expect a skilled Gallic take on New England staples such as lobster bisque; duck meets a tart counterpart in locally harvested cranberries. ⊠ *17 Ocean Ave., Siasconset* ☎ *508/257–9976* ⊕ *www.the-summer-house.com* ⌂ *Reservations essential* ▤ *MC, V* ⊘ *Closed mid-Oct.–mid-May.*

$$$$ 🏨 **Summer House.** Perched on a bluff overlooking Sconset Beach, this cluster of rose-covered cottages—cobbled from salvage in the 1840s—epitomizes Nantucket's enduring allure. The rooms, though small, are intensely romantic, with lace coverlets and pale pine armoires; most have marble baths with whirlpool tubs, and one has a fireplace. Contemplative sorts can claim an Adirondack chair on the lawn. Others may want to race down to the beach, perhaps enjoying lunch beside the heated pool en route. ⊠ *17 Ocean Ave., 02564* ☎ *508/257–4577* ᵬ *508/257–4590* ⊕ *www.thesummerhouse.com* ⇨ *10 rooms* ⌂ *2 restaurants, some in-room hot tubs, pool, bar, piano bar* ▤ *AE, MC, V* ⊘ *Closed Nov.–late Apr.* ⓣⓞⓘ *CP.*

$$$$ 🏨 **Wauwinet.** This resplendently updated 1850 resort straddles a

FodorśChoice   "haulover" poised between ocean and bay—which means beaches on

★   both sides. Head out by complimentary van or launch to partake of utmost pampering (the staff-to-guest ratio exceeds one-on-one). Optional activities include sailing, water-taxiing to a private beach along Coatue, and touring the Great Point nature preserve by Land Rover. Of course, it's tempting just to stay put, what with the cushy country-chic rooms and a splendid restaurant, Topper's. ⊠ *120 Wauwinet Rd., Wauwinet* ᵭ *Box 2580, Nantucket 02584* ☎ *508/228–0145 or 800/426–8718* ᵬ *508/228–7135* ⊕ *www.wauwinet.com* ⇨ *25 rooms, 5 cottages* ⌂ *Restaurant, room service, 2 tennis courts, beach, boating, mountain bikes, croquet, bar, library, concierge, business services; no kids under 12, no smoking* ▤ *AE, DC, MC, V* ⊘ *Closed Nov.–Apr.* ⓣⓞⓘ *BP.*

☾ **$$–$$$$**   🏨 **Wade Cottages.** This Sconset complex of guest rooms, apartments, and cottages couldn't be better situated for beach aficionados. The buildings, in the same family since the 1920s, are arranged around a central lawn with a great ocean view, shared by most of the rooms. Furnishings tend to be of the somewhat worn beach-house school, but you'll be too busy—and happy—to waste a moment critiquing. ⊠ *Shell St., Box 211, Siasconset 02564* ☎ *508/257–6308* ᵬ *508/257–4602* ⊕ *www.wadecottages.com* ⇨ *8 rooms, 4 with bath; 6 apartments; 3 cottages* ⌂ *Badminton, Ping-Pong, laundry facilities* ▤ *AE, MC, V* ⊘ *Closed mid-Oct.–late May* ⓣⓞⓘ *CP.*

Nightlife

BARS The bar at the **Summer House Restaurant** (✉ 17 Ocean Ave. ☎ 508/257–9976) is hands down the most romantic spot for a cocktail on-island. A pianist entertains devotees, who cluster around the bar or claim comfortable armchairs.

FILM The **Siasconset Casino** (✉ New St., Siasconset ☎ 508/257–6661) shows first-run movies, auditorium-style, Tuesday, Thursday, and Sunday evenings at 8:30, June through Labor Day. Old hands know to bring pillows.

Sports & the Outdoors

BEACHES **Siasconset Beach** (✉ End of Milestone Rd.) has a lifeguard (the surf runs moderate to heavy) but no facilities; restaurants are a short walk away.

BICYCLING The 6½-mi **'Sconset Bike Path** starts at the rotary east of Nantucket Town and parallels Milestone Road, ending in 'Sconset. It is mostly level, with some gentle hills.

HIKING & CONSERVATION AREAS Probably the most interesting property, from a visitor's perspective, is **Squam Swamp** (✉ Wauwinet Rd., ¼ mi past Pocomo Rd.), a 294-acre parcel whose 19 trail markers are coordinated to points on a self-guided brochure. You'll pass through glades of ferns (including fiddlehead, edible in the spring), stands of high-bush blueberries, shadbush, and arrowwood, and portions of hardwood forest. The pamphlet also points out specific markers along the way, such as a partially uprooted tree at the edge of the trail, a boulder that recalls Nantucket's geologic past, and a vernal pool, an ecosystem crucial to the breeding of amphibians and currently threatened throughout the United States. The swamp is on the right as you drive out Wauwinet Road.

TENNIS **Siasconset Casino** (✉ 10 New St., Siasconset ☎ 508/257–6585) is a private club with 11 outdoor courts. Some nonmember court time is available; call ahead for information.

NANTUCKET ESSENTIALS

To research prices, get advice from other travelers, and book travel arrangements, visit www.fodors.com.

Transportation

BY BOAT & FERRY

⇨ Boat & Ferry Travel *in* Smart Travel Trips in the back of this book.

Nantucket has first-class marina and mooring amenities for yacht and boat owners.

🚩 **Marina Contacts Madaket Marine** ☎ 508/228-1163 ⊕ www.madaketmarine.com. **Nantucket Boat Basin** ☎ 508/325-1333 or 800/626-2628 🖳 508/228-8941 ⊕ www.nantucketboatbasin.com. **Nantucket Moorings** ☎ 508/228-4472 🖳 508/228-7441 ⊕ www.nantucketmoorings.com.

BY BUS

The Nantucket Regional Transit Authority (NRTA) runs shuttle buses in town and to Madaket, mid-island areas (including the airport and

Surfside Beach), and Sconset. Service is available May to late September. Fares are $1 to $2, depending on the route. Each of the routes has its own schedule (you can pick one up at the Chamber of Commerce, Visitor Services, the NRTA office, or at most any bus stop); service generally begins at 7 AM and ends at 11:30 PM. All shuttle buses have bike racks and lifts. Fares are $1 in town or mid-island; $2 to Madaket, Surfside, the airport, or Sconset; seniors pay half-fare and children under 7—and pets—ride free. Passes run $7 for one day, $12 for three, $20 for seven, $50 for 30, and $80 for the season, with attendant discounts available. Passes for up to a week can be bought on-board; longer-term passes can be purchased at the NRTA office.

🚌 Bus Information **Nantucket Regional Transit Authority (NRTA)** ⊠ 22 Federal St., Nantucket 02554 ☎ 508/228-7025 ⊕ www.shuttlenantucket.com.

BY CAR
The Chamber of Commerce strongly discourages bringing cars to Nantucket. They're really not needed—unless you're planning to stay a week or more, and renting far out of town, off the bus routes. The town itself is entirely walkable, and keeping a car there is not practical; the longest you're allowed to park is one-half to two hours at a time ("summer specials"—supplemental police personnel—mark tires with chalk). The entire island is easily accessible by bike, taxi, or public transportation.

If you're still determined to rent a car while on Nantucket, book early—and expect to spend at least $95 a day during high season.

🚗 Nantucket Agencies **Nantucket Island Rent A Car** ⊠ Nantucket Memorial Airport ☎ 508/228-9989 ⊕ www.nantucketislandrentacar.com. **Nantucket Windmill Auto Rental** ⊠ Nantucket Memorial Airport ☎ 508/228-1227 ⊕ www.nantucketautorental. com. **Young's Bicycle Shop** ⊠ 6 Broad St. ☎ 508/228-1151 🖶 508/228-3038 ⊕ www.youngsbicycleshop.com.

BY TAXI
Taxis usually wait outside the airport, on Steamboat Wharf, and at the foot of Main Street. Rates are flat fees, based on one person with two bags before 1 AM: $6 within town (1½-mi radius), and, from town, $9 to the airport, $18 to Sconset, and $20 to Wauwinet.

🚕 Nantucket Taxi Companies **All Point Taxi** ☎ 508/228-5779. **Breeze Taxi** ☎ 508/325-2170. **Val's Cab Service** ☎ 508/228-9410.

Contacts & Resources

EMERGENCIES
There is no 24-hour pharmacy on the island. Call the **Nantucket Cottage Hospital** (⊠ 57 Prospect St. ☎ 508/228–8100 ⊕ www.nantuckethospital.org), in case of an emergency.

For police, fire department, or emergency medical technicians dial 911.

INTERNET, MAIL & SHIPPING
The main post office is right in the center of town; if lines are daunting, try the mid-island annex at 115 Pleasant Street. There's a UPS Store off Surfside Road ☎ 508/325–8884. You'll find a FedEx box

(pickup is early: 4 PM) at the Steamship office, and another near the airport. The Atheneum offers free Internet access, including Wi-Fi, and the Even Keel doubles as an Internet café.

▸ Internet Access **Even Keel Café** ✉ 40 Main St. ☎ 508/228-1979 ⊕ www.evenkeelcafe.com. **Nantucket Atheneum** ✉ 1 India St. ☎ 508/228-1110 ⊕ www.nantucketatheneum.org.

▸ Mail & Shipping **FedEx** ☎ 800/238-5355 ⊕ www.fedex.com. **The UPS Store** ✉ 2 Windy Way ☎ 508/325-8884. **U.S. Post Office** ✉ 5 Federal St. ☎ 508/228-1067 ✉ Annex, 115 Pleasant St. ☎ 508/228-4143.

MONEY MATTERS

ATMS ATMs are ubiquitous—you'll find them at the airport, ferry terminals, and supermarkets. The following are accessible 24 hours.

▸ 24-Hour ATM Locations **Fleet Bank** ✉ Pacific National, 15 Sparks Ave. ✉ Pacific Club, Main and S. Water Sts. **Nantucket Bank** ✉ 2 Orange St. ✉ 104 Pleasant St. ✉ 1 Amelia Dr.

TOUR OPTIONS

ADVENTURE TOURS No matter what you want to do around Nantucket, be it kayaking, mountain biking, climbing, birding, hiking, snorkeling, or scuba diving, Eco Guides: Strong Wings can customize a small-group tour.

▸ Tour Operator **Eco Guides: Strong Wings** ✉ 9 Nobadeer Farm Rd. ☎ 508/228-1769 ⊕ www.strongwings.org.

NATURE TOURS Great Point Natural History Tours, led by knowledgeable naturalists, are sponsored by the Trustees of Reservations. Group tours are about three hours long, and you see the sights via Jeep. The Maria Mitchell Association leads marine-ecology field trips and nature and bird walks weekly in the spring and early summer months and three times a week from June through Labor Day.

▸ Tour Operators **Great Point Natural History Tours** ☎ 508/228-6799 ⊕ www.thetrustees.org. **Maria Mitchell Association** (MMA) ✉ 4 Vestal St. ☎ 508/228-9198 ⊕ www.mmo.org.

VAN TOURS Sixth-generation Nantucketer Gail Johnson of Gail's Tours narrates a lively 1½-hour van tour of the island's highlights: the moors, the cranberry bogs, and the lighthouses, in addition to Nantucket Town. The 13-passenger cranberry-red van heads out at 10, 1, and 3 in season; pickups at in-town inns can be arranged.

▸ **Gail's Tours** ☎ 508/257-6557 ⊕ www.nantucket.net/tours/gails.

WALKING TOURS Walking tours generally cover the major sights within the historic district. The Nantucket Historical Association's 90-minute Historic Nantucket Walking Tours (offered several times a day in season) provide an overview of the island's history and encompass such sites as Petticoat Row, upper Main Street, and the wharfs, churches, and library. Nantucket Walking Tours offer evening walks in season, covering a plethora of special interests (including nautical Nantucket, the women of Nantucket, and the popular Ghost Tour). Twelfth-generation islander Dirk Gardiner Roggeveen leads 90- to 120-minute tours in the afternoons (except Sunday); children are welcome to tag along for free.

The self-guided Black Heritage Trail tour covers nine sites in and around town, including the African Meeting House, the Whaling Museum, and the Atheneum. The trail guide is free from the Friends of the African Meeting House on Nantucket, which also leads a "Walk the Black Heritage Trail" tour by appointment in season.

🛈 Tour Operators **Friends of the African Meeting House on Nantucket** ✉ York and Pleasant Sts. ☎ 508/228-9833 ⊕ www.afroammuseum.org/afmnantucket.htm. **Historic Nantucket Walking Tours** ✉ Whaling Museum, 15 Broad St. ☎ 508/325-1894 ⊕ www. nha.org. **Nantucket Walking Tours** ☎ 508/228-4572. **Walking Tours with Dirk Gardiner Roggeveen** ☎ 508/221-0075.

VISITOR INFORMATION

You can stop by the Nantucket Visitor Services and Information Bureau, open weekdays 9–6 year-round, to get your bearings, as well as maps, brochures, island information, and advice. The bureau is also a great resource if you need a room at the last minute—they track cancellations daily and might be able to refer you to an inn with newly available rooms. It's in the center of town, within a couple of blocks of both ferry landings, each of which also has a NVS booth in season. The Chamber of Commerce is another great place to get maps and island information; it's open weekdays 9–5, year-round.

🛈 Tourist Information **Nantucket Visitor Services and Information Bureau** ✉ 25 Federal St., 02554 ☎ 508/228-0925 ⊕ www.nantucket.net/town/departments/visitor. html. **Nantucket Chamber of Commerce** ✉ 48 Main St., upstairs ☎ 508/228-1700 ⊕ www.nantucketchamber.org.

SMART TRAVEL TIPS

There are planners and there are those who, excuse the pun, fly by the seat of their pants. We happily place ourselves among the planners. Our writers and editors try to anticipate all the issues you may face before and during any journey, and then they do their research. This section is the product of their efforts. Use it to get excited about your trip to Cape Cod, Nantucket, and Martha's Vineyard; to inform your travel planning; or to guide you on the road should the seat of your pants start to feel threadbare.

AIR TRAVEL

Most long-distance travelers visiting Cape Cod head to a major gateway, such as Boston or Providence, RI, and then rent a car to explore the region. Flying time to Boston or Providence is 1 hour from New York, 2½ hours from Chicago, 6 hours from Los Angeles, and 3½ hours from Dallas.

Boston's Logan Airport is one of the nation's most important domestic and international airports, with direct flights from all over North America and Europe (as well as other continents). Providence's efficient T. F. Green Airport receives very few international flights (mostly from Canada) but offers a wide range of direct domestic flights to East Coast and Midwest destinations; it serves the western United States to a lesser extent. Discount carrier Southwest also flies out of Providence, which helps keep fares down.

Another option is connecting from a major airport to one of the two airports on the Cape, the most popular being Barnstable Municipal Airport in Hyannis, which has direct service to Boston, Providence, and New York (La Guardia), as well as to Martha's Vineyard and Nantucket. The other, Provincetown Airport, has direct flights to Boston. Flying to either of these smaller airports can be costly, especially during busy times in summer, but it can also save you plenty of time when compared with driving to the Mid, Lower, or Upper Cape from Boston or New York City. There are also numerous flights to

Air Travel
Airports
Beaches
Bike Travel
Boat & Ferry Travel
Bus Travel
Bus Travel to & from Cape Cod
Business Hours
Car Rental
Car Travel
Eating Out
Emergencies
Gay & Lesbian Travel
Health
Holidays
Insurance
For International Travelers
Lodging
Media
Money Matters
Packing
Phones
Restrooms
Sightseeing Tours
Sports & the Outdoors
Taxes
Time
Tipping
Tours & Packages
Travel Agencies
Visitor Information
Web Sites

Nantucket and Martha's Vineyard from Hyannis, Boston, New Bedford, and Providence, and you can fly between Nantucket and Martha's Vineyard as well.

CARRIERS

All of the nation's major airlines—as well as many international airlines—serve Boston's Logan Airport, and all major national carriers serve Providence. Hyannis's Barnstable Municipal Airport is serviced by US Airways Express (with service to Boston and NYC's La Guardia), Nantucket Airlines (with service to Nantucket), Island Airlines (with service to Nantucket), and Cape Air (with service to Boston, Providence, Nantucket, and Martha's Vineyard); Provincetown Airport is serviced by Cape Air (with service to Boston).

🔢 Major Airlines **American Airlines** ☎ 800/433-7300 ⊕ www.aa.com. **Continental Airlines** ☎ 800/523-3273 ⊕ www.continental.com. **Delta Airlines** ☎ 800/221-1212 ⊕ www.delta.com. **Northwest Airlines** ☎ 800/225-2525 ⊕ www.nwa.com. **Southwest Airlines** ☎ 800/435-9792 ⊕ www.southwest.com. **United Airlines** ☎ 800/864-8331 ⊕ www.united.com. **US Airways** ☎ 800/428-4322 ⊕ www.usairways.com.

🔢 Smaller Airlines **Cape Air** ☎ 508/771-6944 or 800/352-0714 ⊕ www.flycapeair.com. **Island Airlines** ☎ 508/775-6606 or 800/248-7779 ⊕ www.nantucket.net/trans/islandair. **Nantucket Airlines** ☎ 508/228-6234 or 800/635-8787 ⊕ www.nantucketairlines.com. **US Airways Express** ☎ 800/428-4322 ⊕ www.usair.com.

CHECK-IN & BOARDING

Double-check your flight times, especially if you made your reservations far in advance. Airlines change their schedules, and alerts may not reach you. Always **bring a government-issued photo I.D. to the airport** (even when it's not required, a passport is best), and **arrive when you need to and not before.** Check-in usually at least an hour before domestic flights and two to three hours for international flights. But many airlines have more stringent advance check-in requirements at some busy airports. The TSA estimates the waiting time for security at most major airports and publishes the information on its Web site.

Note that if you aren't at the gate at least 10 minutes before your flight is scheduled to take off (sometimes earlier), you won't be allowed to board.

Minimize the time spent standing line. Buy an e-ticket, check in at an electronic kiosk, or—even better—check in on your airline's Web site before you leave home. These days, most domestic airline tickets are electronic; international tickets may be either electronic or paper. Also, pack light and limit carry-on items to only the essentials.

You usually pay a surcharge (up to $50) to get a paper ticket, and its sole advantage is that it may be easier to endorse over to another airline if your flight is cancelled and the airline with which you booked can't accommodate you on another flight. With an e-ticket, the only thing you receive is an e-mailed receipt citing your itinerary and reservation and ticket numbers. Be sure to carry this with you as you'll need it to get past security. If you lose your receipt, though, you can simply print out another copy or ask the airline to do it for you at check-in.

Particularly during busy travel seasons and around holiday periods, if a flight is oversold, the gate agent will usually ask for volunteers and will offer some sort of compensation if you are willing to take a different flight. **Know your rights.** If you are bumped from a flight *involuntarily,* the airline must give you some kind of compensation if an alternate flight can't be found within one hour. If your flight is delayed because of something within the airline's control (so bad weather doesn't count), then the airline has a responsibility to get you to your destination on the same day, even if they have to book you on another airline and in an upgraded class if necessary. Read your airline's Contract of Carriage; it's usually buried somewhere on the airline's Web site.

Be prepared to quickly adjust your plans by programming a few numbers into your cell: your airline, an airport hotel or two, your destination hotel, your car service, and/or your travel agent.

CUTTING COSTS

It's always good to **comparison shop.** Web sites (aka. consolidators) and travel agents can have different arrangements with the airlines and offer different prices for exactly the same flight and day. Certain Web sites have tracking features that will e-mail you immediately when good deals are posted. Other people prefer to stick with one or two frequent-flier programs, racking up free trips and accumulating perks that can make trips easier. On some airlines, perks include a special reservations number, early boarding, access to upgrades, and more roomy economy-class seating.

Check early and often. Start looking for cheap fares up to a year in advance, and keep looking until you see something you can live with; you never know when a good deal may pop up. That said, **jump on the good deals.** Waiting even a few minutes might mean paying more. For most people, saving money is more important than flexibility, so the more affordable nonrefundable tickets work. Just remember that you'll pay dearly (often as much as $100) if you must change your travel plans. Check on prices for departures at different times of the day and to and from alternate airports, and look for departures on Tuesday, Wednesday, and Thursday, typically the cheapest days to travel. Remember to **weigh your options,** though. A cheaper flight might have a long layover rather than being nonstop, or landing at a secondary airport might substantially increase your ground transportation costs.

Note that many airline Web sites—and most ads—show prices *without* taxes and surcharges. Don't buy until you know the full price. Government taxes add up quickly. Also **watch those ticketing fees.** Surcharges are usually added when you buy your ticket anywhere but on an airline's own Web site. (By the way, that includes on the phone–even if you call the airline directly—and for paper tickets regardless of how you book).

⧉ Online Consolidators AirlineConsolidator.com ⊕ www.airlineconsolidator.com for international tickets. **Best Fares** ⊕ www.bestfares.com; $59.90 annual membership. **Cheap Tickets** ⊕ www.

cheaptickets.com. **Expedia** ⊕ www.expedia.com. **Hotwire** ⊕ www.hotwire.com is a discounter. **lastminute.com** ⊕ www.lastminute.com specializes in last-minute travel; the main site is for the UK, but it has a link to a U.S. site. **Luxury Link** ⊕ www.luxurylink.com has auctions (surprisingly good deals) as well as offers at the high-end side of travel. **Onetravel.com** ⊕ www.onetravel.com. **Orbitz** ⊕ www.orbitz.com. **Priceline.com** ⊕ www.priceline.com is a discounter that also allows bidding. **Travel.com** ⊕ www.travel.com allows you to compare its rates with those of other booking engines. **Travelocity** ⊕ www.travelocity.com charges a booking fee for airline tickets but promises good problem resolution.

ENJOYING THE FLIGHT

Get the seat you want. Avoid those on the aisle directly across from the lavatories. Most frequent fliers say those are even worse than the seats that don't recline (e. g., those in the back row and those in front of a bulkhead). For more legroom, you can request emergency-aisle seats, but only do so if you're capable of moving the 35- to 60-pound airplane exit door—a Federal Aviation Administration requirement of passengers in these seats. Seats behind a bulkhead also offer more legroom, but they don't have under-seat storage. Often, you can pick a seat when you buy your ticket on an airline's Web site. But it's not always a guarantee, particularly if the airline changes the plane after you book your ticket; check back before you leave. SeatGuru.com has more information about specific seat configurations, which vary by aircraft.

Fewer airlines are providing free food for passengers in economy class. **Don't go hungry.** If you're scheduled to fly during meal times, verify if your airline offers anything to eat; even when it does, be prepared to pay. If you have dietary concerns, request special meals. These can be vegetarian, low-cholesterol, or kosher, for example.

Ask the airline about its children's menus, activities, and fares. On some lines infants and toddlers fly for free if they sit on a parent's lap, and older children fly for half price in their own seats. Also inquire about policies involving car seats; having one may limit where you can sit. While you're at it, ask about seatbelt extenders for car seats. And note that you can't count on a flight attendant to automatically produce an extender; you may have to inquire about it again when you board.

HOW TO COMPLAIN

If your baggage goes astray or your flight goes awry, complain right away. Most carriers require that you **file a claim immediately.** The Aviation Consumer Protection Division of the Department of Transportation publishes *Fly-Rights,* which discusses airlines and consumer issues and is available online. You can also find articles and information on mytravelrights.com, the Web site of the nonprofit Consumer Travel Rights Center.

🚹 Airline Complaints **Office of Aviation Enforcement and Proceedings** (Aviation Consumer Protection Division) ☎ 202/366-2220 ⊕ airconsumer.ost. dot.gov. **Federal Aviation Administration Consumer Hotline** ☎ 866/835-5322 ⊕ www.faa.gov.

AIRPORTS

The major gateways to Cape Cod are Boston's Logan International Airport (BOS) and Providence's T. F. Green Airport (PVD). Smaller airports include the Barnstable (HYA), Martha's Vineyard (MVY), Nantucket (ACK), New Bedford (EWB), and Provincetown (PVC) municipal airports.

Long layovers don't have to be only about sitting around or shopping. These days they can be about burning off vacation calories. Check out www.airportgyms.com for lists of health clubs that are in or near many U.S. and Canadian airports.

🚹 Airlines & Airports **Airline and Airport Links. com** ⊕ www.airlineandairportlinks.com has links to many of the world's airlines and airports. Boston: **Logan International Airport** ☎ 617/561-1806 or 800/235-6426 ⊕ www.massport.com/logan. Hyannis: **Barnstable Municipal Airport** ☎ 508/775-2020 ⊕ www.town.barnstable.ma.us. Martha's Vineyard: **Martha's Vineyard Airport** ☎ 508/693-7022 ⊕ www.mvyairport.com. Nantucket: **Nantucket Memorial Airport** ☎ 508/325-5300 ⊕ www. nantucketairport.com. New Bedford: **New Bedford Regional Airport** ☎ 508/991-6161 ⊕ www.ci.new-bedford.ma.us. Providence: **T. F. Green Airport** ☎ 401/737-8222 or 888/268-7222 ⊕ www.pvd-ri.

com. Provincetown: **Provincetown Airport** ☎ 508/ 487-0241.

🚹 Airline Security Issues **Transportation Security Administration** ⊕ www.tsa.gov/public has answers for almost every question that might come up.

TRANSFERS BETWEEN AIRPORTS

Aristocrat Limousine, Escort Coach, and King's Coach provide chartered limo service from Boston and Providence to the Cape; call ahead for reservations. Rates vary greatly, depending on your Cape destination, which airport you're flying into, and what kind of car or van you book.

🚹 Limousine Agencies **Aristocrat Limousine** ☎ 508/420-5466 or 800/992-6163 ⊕ www. aaristocratlimo.com. **Escort Coach** ☎ 508/548-8116 or 800/564-8116 ⊕ www.whitetielimo.com. **King's Coach** ☎ 508/771-1000 or 800/272-9892 ⊕ www. capecodlimo.com.

BEACHES

In season, you must pay to park at public beaches. Parking at "restricted" beaches is available only to residents and to visitors with permits. If you're renting a house, you can purchase a weekly beach permit; contact the local town hall for details. Walkers and cyclists do not need permits to use restricted beaches. The official season generally begins the last weekend in June and ends on Labor Day. Note that the lots are often open to all early in the morning (before 8) and late in the afternoon (after 4 or 5), even at resident beaches in season.

BIKE TRAVEL

Biking is very popular on Cape Cod and the islands, which have an abundance of excellent bike trails, some of them as busy as the region's roads in summer. Note that Massachusetts law requires children under 13 to wear protective helmets while riding a bike, even as a passenger. For information on trails, maps, and rentals ⇨ listings for specific towns.

🚹 Bike Maps **Rubel Bike Maps** ✉ Box 401035, Cambridge, MA 02140 ⊕ www.bikemaps.com.

BIKES IN FLIGHT

Most airlines accommodate bikes as luggage, provided they are dismantled and boxed; check with individual airlines about packing requirements. Some airlines sell bike boxes, which are often free at bike shops, for about $20 (bike bags can be considerably more expensive). International travelers often can substitute a bike for a piece of checked luggage at no charge; otherwise, the cost is about $100. Most U.S. and Canadian airlines charge $40–$80 each way.

BOAT & FERRY TRAVEL

In season, ferries connect Boston and Plymouth with Provincetown.

Ferries to Martha's Vineyard leave Woods Hole year-round. In summer you can also catch Vineyard ferries in Falmouth and Hyannis. All provide parking lots where you can leave your car overnight ($10–$15 per night). A number of parking lots in Falmouth hold the overflow of cars when the Woods Hole lot is filled, and free shuttle buses take passengers to the ferry, about 15 minutes away. Signs along Route 28 heading south from the Bourne Bridge direct you to open parking lots, as does AM radio station 1610, which you can pick up within 5 mi of Falmouth.

Ferries to Nantucket leave Hyannis year-round. In season, a passenger ferry connects Nantucket with Martha's Vineyard, and a cruise from Hyannis makes a day trip with stops at both islands. From New Bedford you can take a ferry to Martha's Vineyard from mid-May to mid-October and to Cuttyhunk Island year-round (although between mid-October and mid-April, the schedule is very limited).

FERRIES TO PROVINCETOWN

Bay State Cruise Company offers both standard and high-speed ferry service between Commonwealth Pier in Boston and MacMillan Wharf in Provincetown. High-speed service runs a few times daily from late May through early October and costs $68 round-trip; the ride takes 90 minutes. Standard service runs weekends from late June through early September and costs $29 round-trip; the ride takes three hours. On either ferry, the round-trip charge for bikes is $10.

Boston Harbor Cruises also offers high-speed service several times daily from mid-

June to early September, with more limited service mid-May to mid-June and early September to mid-October. Rates are $70 round-trip and $10 for bikes.

Capt. John Boats runs a seasonal ferry between Plymouth and Provincetown, with daily service from late June through early September and weekend service from late May to mid-June. The boat departs from State Pier (near the *Mayflower II*) in Plymouth and docks at MacMillan Wharf in Provincetown. The trip takes approximately 90 minutes. A round-trip ticket costs $35, the one-way fare is $20 (no one-way in July and August), and bikes cost $5 each way.

Boat & Ferry Lines Bay State Cruise Company ☎ 617/748-1428 ⊕ www.baystatecruisecompany. com. **Boston Harbor Cruises** ☎ 617/227-4320 or 877/733-9425 ⊕ www.bostonharborcruises.com. **Capt. John Boats** ☎ 508/747-2400 or 800/242-2469 ⊕ www.provincetownferry.com.

FERRIES TO CUTTYHUNK ISLAND

The M/V *Alert II* runs ferries between New Bedford and Cuttyhunk Island, daily mid-June through mid-September, several times a week from mid-April to mid-June and from mid-September to mid-October, and once a week the rest of the year. Same-day round-trip fare is $24, one-way $17, bicycles $3.50 each way. The ride takes about an hour.

Boat & Ferry Information M/V *Alert II* ⊠ Fisherman's Wharf/Pier 3, New Bedford ☎ 508/992-1432 ⊕ www.cuttyhunk.com.

FERRIES TO MARTHA'S VINEYARD

The Steamship Authority runs the only car ferries, which make the 45-minute trip from Woods Hole to Vineyard Haven year-round and to Oak Bluffs from late May through mid-October. There are several runs per day, but fewer during the off-season. In summer and on autumn weekends, you *must* have a reservation if you want to bring your car (passenger reservations are never necessary). You should **make car reservations as far ahead as possible;** in season the reservations office is open daily 7 AM–9 PM. You can also make car reservations online at the Steamship Authority's Web site. In season, standby car reservations are not available. One-way passenger fare year-round is $6.50; bicycles are $3. The cost for a car traveling one-way in season (April–October) is $62 (not including passengers); off-season cars cost $38. Call or check the Web site for off-season rates.

The *Island Queen* makes the 35-minute trip from Falmouth Harbor to Oak Bluffs from late May through early October. Ferries run multiple times a day from mid-June through early September, with less frequent service in the spring and fall; call for schedules. Round-trip fare is $12, bikes $6. Only cash and traveler's checks are accepted for payment.

Patriot Boats runs a Falmouth Harbor to Oak Bluffs high-speed ferry year-round, with several trips Monday through Saturday; there's no service on Sunday or holidays. The company also operates a year-round 24-hour water taxi and offers boat charters. The ferry costs $8 one-way, and the ride takes 30 minutes.

Hy-Line offers both high-speed and conventional ferry service from Hyannis. The conventional ferries offer a 95-minute run from Hyannis to Oak Bluffs early May–late October. One-way fare is $16.50; bicycles cost $5. The high-speed run takes 55 minutes and costs $29 one-way from late May through late October and $15 one-way the rest of the year; it costs $5 for bikes. The parking lot fills up in summer, so **call to reserve a parking space** in high season. From June to mid-September, Hy-Line's Around the Sound cruise makes a one-day round-trip from Hyannis with stops at Nantucket and Martha's Vineyard ($70).

The New England Fast Ferry Company makes the hour-long trip by high-speed catamaran from New Bedford to Oak Bluffs and Vineyard Haven from mid-May to mid-October, several times daily. One-way is $29, bicycles $5.

🚢 **Boat & Ferry Information Hy-Line** ✉ Ocean St. dock ☎ 508/778–2600 or 800/492–8082 ⊕ www. hy-linecruises.com. *Island Queen* ✉ Falmouth Harbor ☎ 508/548–4800 ⊕ www.islandqueen.com. **New England Fast Ferry** ✉ State Pier Ferry Terminal ☎ 866/683–3779 ⊕ www.nefastferry.com.

Patriot Boats ✉ 227 Clinton Ave., Falmouth Harbor ☎ 508/548–2626 or 800/734–0088 ⊕ www. patriotpartyboats.com. **Steamship Authority** ☎ 508/477–8600 information and car reservations, 508/693–9130 on the Vineyard ⊕ www. steamshipauthority.com.

FERRIES TO NANTUCKET

The Steamship Authority runs car-and-passenger ferries from Hyannis to Nantucket year-round, a 2¼-hour trip. There's also high-speed passenger ferry service, which takes only an hour. Note that there are no standby car reservations on ferries to Nantucket. One-way passenger fare is $14, bicycles $6. Cost for a car traveling one-way April through October is $175; November through April, $115. One-way high-speed passenger ferry fare is $29.50, bicycles $6.

Hy-Line's high-end, high-speed *Grey Lady* ferries run between Hyannis and Nantucket year-round in an hour. Such speed has its downside in rough seas—lots of bucking and rolling that some find literally nauseating. Seating ranges from benches on the upper deck to airline-like seats in side rows of the cabin to café-style tables and chairs in the cabin front. Make reservations in advance, particularly during the summer months or for holiday travel. One-way fare is $36, bicycles $5.

Hy-Line's slower ferry makes the roughly two-hour trip from Hyannis between early May and late October. The M/V *Great Point* offers a first-class section ($23.50 one-way) with a private lounge, restrooms, upholstered seats, carpeting, complimentary continental breakfast or afternoon cheese and crackers, a bar, and a snack bar. Standard one-way fare is $16.50, bicycles $5.

From Harwich Port, the Freedom Cruise Line runs express high-speed 75-minute ferries to Nantucket between late May and early October, allowing you to explore the rose-covered isle without having to brave the crowds of Hyannis. Round-trip fare is $54 ($34 one-way), $12 for bikes. Sightseeing and seal cruises are also offered daily.

🚢 **Boat & Ferry Information Freedom Cruise Line** ✉ Saquatucket Harbor, Harwich Port ☎ 508/432–

8999 ⊕ www.nantucketislandferry.com. **Hy-Line**
✉ Ocean St. dock ☏ 508/778-2600 or 800/492-
8082 ⊕ www.hy-linecruises.com. **Steamship Authority** ✉ South St. dock ☏ 508/477-8600, 508/
495-3278 on Nantucket for reservations ⊕ www.
steamshipauthority.com.

BUS TRAVEL

The Cape Cod Regional Transit Authority
operates several bus services that link
Cape towns. All buses are wheelchair ac-
cessible and equipped with bike racks.
The SeaLine runs along Route 28 Monday
through Saturday between Hyannis and
Woods Hole (one-way fare $3.50, from
Hyannis to Woods Hole; shorter trips cost
less), with stops including Mashpee Com-
mons, Falmouth, and the Woods Hole
Steamship Authority docks. The SeaLine
connects in Hyannis with the Plymouth &
Brockton line as well as the Barnstable
Villager, another bus line that runs along
Route 132 between Hyannis and Barnsta-
ble Harbor, stopping at the Cape Cod
Mall. It also connects with the Hyannis
Villager, which runs through Hyannis.
The driver will stop when signaled along
the route.

The H2O Line offers daily regularly scheduled service year-round between Hyannis
and Orleans along Route 28. The Hyannis–Orleans fare is $3.50; shorter trips are
less. Buses connect in Hyannis with the
SeaLine, the Barnstable Villager, and Plymouth & Brockton lines.

The b-bus is composed of a fleet of minivans that will transport passengers door to
door between any towns on the Cape. You
must register in advance to use the b-bus
service (you pay in advance by a prepaid
account system); phone the Cape Cod Regional Transit Authority 11–5 on weekdays to sign up. You must also make
advance reservations when you want to
ride the b-bus. After you are enrolled, call
for reservations 8–5 on weekdays; reservations may be made up to a week in advance. Service runs seven days a week,
year-round. The cost is $2.50 per ride plus
10¢ per mile.

The Flex bus, a new Cape Cod Regional
Transit Authority route, runs between the

Harwichport Chamber of Commerce and
Dutra's Market in North Truro, with stops
in Brewster, Orleans, Eastham, and
Wellfleet. Riders can also schedule addi-
tional off-route stops by calling the Cape
Cod Regional Transit Authority. All one-
way fares are $1.00, and buses run
Monday-Saturday year-round.

The Cape Cod Regional Transit Authority
also runs the seasonal trolleys in Falmouth, Mashpee, Hyannis, Yarmouth, and
Dennis. Fares and times vary; call for more
information.

On the Outer Cape, Cape Cod Regional
Transit Authority's Provincetown Shuttle
serves North Truro and Provincetown
daily from late May through mid-October,
with more-limited service during the late
fall and early spring, and no service in
winter. The route begins at Dutra's Market
in Truro and continues to Provincetown
along Route 6A; it stops wherever a passenger or roadside flagger dictates. Once
in Provincetown, the shuttle continues up
Bradford Street, with alternating trips to
Herring Cove Beach and Pilgrim Park as
well as summertime service up to
Provincetown Airport and Race Point
Beach. It runs every 20 minutes and is outfitted to carry bicycles. The service is popular and reasonably priced ($1 for a single
fare, $3 for a day pass).

The big buses of the Martha's Vineyard
Transit Authority (VTA) provide regular
service to all six towns on the island, with
frequent stops in peak season and quite
limited service in winter. The fare is $1 per
town, including the town of departure.
One-day ($6), three-day ($15), and one-
week ($25) passes can be purchased on the
bus and at Steamship Authority terminals.
The VTA also has two free in-town shuttle-bus routes, one in Edgartown and one
in Vineyard Haven.

The Nantucket Regional Transit Authority
(NRTA) runs shuttle buses in town and to
Madaket, mid-island areas (including the
airport, Sconset, Surfside Beach, and Jetties Beach). Service is available late May to
early September. Fares are $1 to $2, depending on the route.

🚌 Bus Information **Bonanza** ☎ 508/548-7588 or 888/751-8800 ⊕ www.bonanzabus.com. **Cape Cod Regional Transit Authority** ☎ 508/790-2613 or 800/352-7155 ⊕ www.capecodtransit.org. **Greyhound** ☎ 800/231-2222 ⊕ www.greyhound.com. **Martha's Vineyard Transit Authority** (VTA) ☎ 508/693-9940 ⊕ www.vineyardtransit.com. **Nantucket Regional Transit Authority** (NRTA) ✉ 22 Federal St., Nantucket 02554 ☎ 508/228-7025 ⊕ www.shuttlenantucket.com. **Plymouth & Brockton Street Railway** ☎ 508/746-0378 ⊕ www.p-b.com.

BUS TRAVEL TO & FROM CAPE COD

Greyhound serves Boston and Providence from all over the United States; from there you can connect to Greyhound's affiliate, Bonanza Bus Lines, which serves Barnstable, Bourne, Eastham, Falmouth, Hyannis, North Truro, North Eastham, Orleans, Otis Air Base (in Sandwich), Provincetown, Sagamore Circle, Truro, Wellfleet, and Woods Hole on the Cape, plus nearby Fall River, New Bedford, and Plymouth. The Plymouth & Brockton Street Railway buses travel all the way to Provincetown from Boston and Logan Airport, with stops en route at a number of towns throughout the Cape.

🚌 Bus Information **Greyhound** ☎ 800/231-2222 ⊕ www.greyhound.com.

BUSINESS HOURS

Hours on the Cape and the islands can sometimes differ from those elsewhere in New England, as many businesses and attractions are open only seasonally or have limited hours during the quieter months, from mid-fall to mid-spring. Within the region, shops and other businesses in the towns near the Cape as well as on the Upper Cape and even as far out as Barnstable and Hyannis tend to be less seasonal, catering to the larger year-round populations in those areas. The farther out you go, toward the Lower Cape and Outer Cape and on the islands, the more likely you are to encounter businesses that close or keep shorter hours off-season.

MUSEUMS & SIGHTS

Museum and attraction hours vary widely from place to place and from season to season. Some places are staffed by volunteers and have limited hours (open just a few hours a day several days a week) even in summer, although major museums and attractions are generally open daily in summer. Always check the hours of a place you plan to visit ahead of time.

SHOPS

Banks are usually open weekdays from 9 to 3 and some Saturday mornings. The post office is open from 8 to 5 weekdays and often on Saturday morning. Shops in more heavily settled areas, particularly in indoor and strip malls, typically open at 9 or 10 daily and stay open until anywhere from 6 PM to 10 PM on weekdays and Saturday, and until 5 or 6 on Sunday. Hours vary greatly, so call ahead when in doubt.

On major roads and in some densely populated areas, you'll usually find at least one or two pharmacies and gas stations open 24 hours. Throughout the region, most bars and discos stay open until 1 or 2 AM.

CAR RENTAL

Request car seats and extras such as GPS when you book, and make sure that a confirmed reservation guarantees you a car. Agencies sometimes overbook, particularly for busy weekends and holiday periods. Rates are sometimes—but not always—better if you book in advance or reserve through a rental agency's Web site. There are other reasons to book ahead, though: for popular destinations, during busy times of the year, or to ensure that you get a certain type of car (vans, SUVs, exotic sports cars).

In Massachusetts you must be 21 to rent a car, and rates may be higher if you're under 25. When picking up a car, non-U.S. residents will need a reservation voucher (for prepaid reservations made in the traveler's home country), a passport, a driver's license, and a travel policy that covers each driver.

Base rates in Boston begin at $25–$40 a day and $170–$250 a week for an economy car with air-conditioning, automatic transmission, and unlimited mileage; rates tend to be slightly lower out of Providence and slightly higher out of Hyannis, but much depends on availability, which changes regularly. Keep in mind that taxes and a variety of surcharges typically add 30% to 40% to your total bill.

You can book car rentals on Martha's Vineyard through the Woods Hole ferry terminal free phone. A handful of local agencies, listed below, have rental desks at the airport. The cost is $90–$150 per day for a sedan. Renting a four-wheel-drive vehicle costs around $160 per day (seasonal prices fluctuate widely).

If you're determined to rent a car while on Nantucket, be sure to book early. Expect to spend about $85 a day during high season.

CUTTING COSTS

Really weigh your options. Find out if a credit card you carry or organization or frequent-renter program to which you belong has a discount program. And check that such discounts really are the best deal. You can often do better with special weekend or weekly rates offered by a rental agency. (And even if you only want to rent for five or six days, ask if you can get the weekly rate; it may very well be cheaper than the daily rate for that period of time.)

Price local car-rental companies as well as the majors. Also investigate wholesalers, which don't own fleets but rent in bulk from those that do and often offer better rates (note you must usually pay for such rentals before leaving home). Consider adding a car rental onto your air/hotel vacation package; the cost will often be cheaper than if you had rented the car separately on your own.

When traveling abroad, **look for guaranteed exchange rates,** which protect you against a falling dollar. With your rate locked in, you won't pay more, even if the price goes up in the local currency. (Note to self: not the best thing if the dollar is surging rather than plunging.)

Beware of hidden charges. Those great rental rates may not be so great when you add in taxes, surcharges, cancellation penalties, taxes, drop-off charges (if you're planning to pick up the car in one city and leave it in another), and surcharges (for being under or over a certain age, for addi-

tional drivers, or for driving over state or country borders or out of a specific radius from your point of rental).

Note that airport rental offices often add supplementary surcharges that you may avoid by renting from an agency whose office is just off airport property. Don't buy the tank of gas that's in the car when you rent it unless you plan to do a lot of driving. Avoid hefty refueling fees by filling the tank at a station well away from the rental agency (those nearby are often more expensive) just before you turn in the car.

⚑ Automobile Associations U.S.: **American Automobile Association (AAA)** ☎ 315/797-5000 ⊕ www.aaa.com; most contact with the organization is through state and regional members. **National Automobile Club** ☎ 650/294-7000 ⊕ www.thenac.com; membership is open to California residents only.

⚑ Cape Cod Agency Rent-A-Wreck of Hyannis ☎ 508/771-9667 or 888/486-1470 ⊕ www.rentawreck.com.

⚑ Martha's Vineyard Agencies AAA Island ☎ 508/627-6800 or 800/627-6333 ⊕ www.mvautorental.com. **Adventure Rentals** ⊠ Beach Rd., Vineyard Haven ☎ 508/693-1959 ⊕ www.adventurerentalsmv.com.

⚑ Nantucket Agencies Affordable Rentals ⊠ 6 S. Beach St. ☎ 508/228-3501 or 877/235-3500. **Nantucket Island Rent A Car** ⊠ Nantucket Memorial Airport ☎ 508/228-9989 or 800/508-9972 ⊕ www.nantucketislandrentacar.com. **Nantucket Jeep Rental** ☎ 508/228-1618. **Nantucket Windmill** ⊠ Nantucket Memorial Airport ☎ 508/228-1227 or 800/228-1227 ⊕ www.nantucketautorental.com.

⚑ Major Agencies Alamo ☎ 800/462-5266 ⊕ www.alamo.com. **Avis** ☎ 800/230-4898 ⊕ www.avis.com. **Budget** ☎ 800/527-0700 ⊕ www.budget.com. **Hertz** ☎ 800/654-3131 ⊕ www.hertz.com. **National Car Rental** ☎ 800/227-7368 ⊕ www.nationalcar.com.

INSURANCE

Everyone who rents a car wonders about whether the insurance that the rental companies offer is worth the expense. No one—not even us—has a simple answer. It all depends on how much regular insurance you have, how comfortable you are with risk, and whether or not money is an issue.

If you own a car and carry comprehensive car insurance for both collision and liability, your personal auto insurance will probably cover a rental, but read your policy's fine print to be sure. If you don't have auto insurance, then you should probably buy the collision- or loss-damage waiver (CDW or LDW) from the rental company. This eliminates your liability for damage to the car. Some credit cards offer CDW coverage, but it's usually supplemental to your own insurance and rarely covers SUVs, minivans, luxury models, and the like. If your coverage is secondary, you may still be liable for loss-of-use costs from the car-rental company (again, read the fine print). But no credit-card insurance is valid unless you use that card for *all* transactions, from reserving to paying the final bill.

You may also be offered supplemental liability coverage; the car-rental company is required to carry a minimal level of liability coverage that covers all renters, but it's rarely enough to cover claims in a really serious accident if you're at fault. Your own auto insurance policy will protect you if you own a car; if you don't, you have to decide if you are willing to take the risk.

U.S. rental companies sell CDWs and LDWs for about $15 to $25 a day; supplemental liability is usually over $10 a day. The car-rental company may offer you all sorts of other policies, but they're rarely worth the cost. Personal accident insurance, which is basic hospitalization coverage, is an especially egregious rip-off if you already have health insurance.

Note that you can decline the insurance from the rental company and purchase it through a third-party provider such as Travel Guard (www.travelguard.com)—$9 per day for $35,000 of coverage. That's sometimes just under half the price of the CDW offered by some car-rental companies. Also, Diners Club offers primary CDW coverage on all rentals reserved and paid for with the card. This means that Diners Club's company—not your own car insurance—pays in case of an accident. It *doesn't* mean your car-insurance company won't raise your rates once it discovers you had an accident.

CAR TRAVEL

To reach Cape Cod from Boston (60 mi), take Route I–93 south, then Route 3 south, and cross the Sagamore Bridge. After finding your way out of a rotary, you'll be on U.S. 6, the Cape's main artery, leading toward Hyannis and Provincetown. From western Massachusetts, northern Connecticut, and upstate New York, take I–84 east to the Massachusetts Turnpike (I–90) and take I–495 south to the Bourne Bridge. From New York City and southern Connecticut and Rhode Island, take I–95 north toward Providence, where you pick up I–195 east (toward Fall River–New Bedford) to Route 25 east to the Bourne Bridge. From the Bourne Bridge you can take Route 28 south to Falmouth and Woods Hole (about 15 mi), or follow signs to U.S. 6 if you're headed elsewhere on the Cape.

Driving times can vary widely, depending on traffic. In good driving conditions you can reach the Sagamore Bridge from Boston in about 1½ hours, the Bourne Bridge from New York City in about 5 hours.

On summer weekends, when more than 100,000 cars a day cross each bridge, **make every effort to avoid arriving in late afternoon,** especially on holidays. And be sure to give yourself extra time if you're driving to any of the ferry terminals to Nantucket and Martha's Vineyard. U.S. 6 and Route 28 are heavily congested eastbound on Friday evening, westbound on Sunday afternoon, and in both directions on Saturday (when rental homes change hands). On the north shore, the Old King's Highway—Route 6A—parallels U.S. 6 and is a scenic country road passing through occasional towns.

When you're in no hurry, use back roads—you won't get there any faster, but they're less frustrating and much more rewarding. Heading from the Bourne Bridge toward Falmouth, County Road and Route 28A are prettier alternatives to Route 28, and Sippewisset Road meanders near Buzzards Bay between

West Falmouth and Woods Hole. Just remember that some of these roads travel through residential areas, so keep your speed down.

Driving to Provincetown from other points on the Cape is mostly a scenic adventure. The wooded surrounds of Truro break into a breathtaking expanse of open water and sand dunes, with the skyline of Provincetown beyond. The busiest time is early morning—especially on days when the sun is reluctant to shine—when it seems that everyone on Cape Cod is determined to make it to Provincetown. Traffic is heaviest around Wellfleet, and because the road is just two lanes until North Truro, it can be slow going. Except during the traffic-heavy season, you'll find the drive from Wellfleet to Provincetown beautiful and only 25 minutes in duration.

Traffic delays often result from congestion at the Sagamore and Bourne bridges, but as of this writing, the state was replacing the much-despised traffic rotary on the mainland side of the Sagamore Bridge with a direct "flyover" road, which will connect Route 3 to the bridge, with exits leading to and from U.S. 6. The state predicts this will cut down the average trip onto the Cape by about 20 minutes. Construction is slated for completion in spring 2007.

Traffic can be a challenge on the islands, especially in season. Nantucket is small enough that one can easily get around on foot or by public transportation, but on Martha's Vineyard, it can be handy to have a car if you really want to see the whole island and travel freely among the different towns. Bringing a car over on the ferry in summer requires reservations far in advance, costs almost double what it does off-season, and necessitates standing in long lines—it's sometimes easier and more economical to rent a car once you're on the island, and then only for the days you plan on exploring. And consider public transportation and taxis if you're only making a few trips to different parts of the island, which has very good bus service that can get you to just about every major sight, village, and beach. Where you stay and what you plan on seeing can greatly

influence your transportation plans. As soon as you've booked a room, discuss the different options for getting around Martha's Vineyard with your innkeeper or hotel staff.

PARKING
Parking, in general, is a great challenge across much of Cape Cod and the islands from mid-June through early September, although many towns have metered lots and street parking or flat-fee or hourly pay lots. Popular and congested downtowns such as Falmouth, Provincetown, Hyannis, Oak Bluffs, Nantucket Town, and Chatham tend to prove especially tough. A number of smaller communities even have free street parking and municipal lots. In general, however, anytime you can walk, bike, or cab it somewhere, or you're able to travel in one car instead of two or more, do so. Off-season, parking is rarely a problem anywhere on the Cape or islands.

RULES OF THE ROAD
In Massachusetts, highway speed limits are 55 mph near urban areas, 60 or 65 mph elsewhere. Speed limits on U.S. 6 on the Cape vary as it changes from four lanes to two lanes. Radar detectors are legal in Massachusetts.

Massachusetts permits a right turn on a red light (*after* a full stop) unless a sign says otherwise. Also, when you approach one of the Cape's numerous rotaries (traffic circles), note that the vehicles already in the rotary have the right of way and that those vehicles entering the rotary must yield. Be careful: some drivers forget (or ignore) this principle.

Massachusetts law requires that drivers **strap children under age five (or under 40 pounds) into approved child-safety seats.** Kids ages 5 to 12 must wear seatbelts. Drivers (but not other passengers over age 12) are legally required to wear seatbels, but they can only be ticketed for not wearing them if they're pulled over for some other reason.

EATING OUT
The restaurants we list are the cream of the crop in each price category. Note that

ordering a lobster dinner, which can be far more expensive than other menu items, may push your meal into a higher price category than the restaurant's price range shows. Properties indicated by a ✕🏠 are lodging establishments whose restaurant warrants a special trip.

Unless otherwise noted, the restaurants listed in this guide are open daily for lunch and dinner.

In general, when you order a regular coffee, you get coffee with milk and sugar.

CATEGORY	COST
$$$$	over $30
$$$	$22–$30
$$	$16–$22
$	$10–$16
¢	under $10

Per person for a main course at dinner

Was the service stellar or not up to snuff? Did the food give you shivers of delight or leave you cold? Did the prices and portions make you happy or sad? Rate restaurants and write your own reviews in Travel Ratings or start a discussion about your favorite places in Travel Talk on www.fodors.com. Your comments might even appear in our books. Yes, you, too, can be a correspondent!

CUTTING COSTS

Even the best of the region's restaurants offer slightly scaled-down portions of pricier dinner menus during lunchtime. Any time of day, you can indulge in fresh local seafood and clambakes at **seat-yourself shanties** for a much lower price than their fine-dining counterparts. Often the tackier the decor (plastic fish on the walls), the better the seafood. These laid-back local haunts usually operate a fish market on the premises and are in every town on the Cape.

Bear in mind that Cape Cod waters are occasionally plagued by red tide, an insidious algae that infests shellfish; 2005 saw a particular bad strain, which led to skyrocketing prices for fried whole-belly clams, but area waters were generally back to normal in 2006. During these times, you can still usually find most shellfish on menus, as it's easily brought in from other parts of

the country, but whole-belly clams are expensive when shipped in from elsewhere, and menu prices reflect this.

RESERVATIONS & DRESS

Regardless of where you are, it's a good idea to make a reservation if you can. In some places, it's expected. We only mention specifically when reservations are essential (there's no other way you'll ever get a table) or when they are not accepted. For popular restaurants, book as far ahead as you can (often 30 days), and reconfirm as soon as you arrive. (Large parties should always call ahead to check the reservations policy.) We mention dress only when men are required to wear a jacket or a jacket and tie.

WINE, BEER & SPIRITS

Massachusetts is not a major wine-growing area, but Westport Rivers Winery in Westport and the Cape Cod Winery in East Falmouth produce respectable vintages. The family that owns Westport Rivers also runs the local Buzzards Bay Brewing Co. Wines from Truro Vineyards of Cape Cod are local favorites.

In Massachusetts, you can generally buy alcoholic beverages (wine, beer, and spirits) in liquor stores, known locally as package stores. A few exceptions allow some grocery stores to sell wine and beer. All of the towns on Martha's Vineyard except Oak Bluffs and Edgartown are "dry" and don't sell alcohol, although as of this writing, the town of Vineyard Haven was considering allowing the sale of alcohol in restaurants.

EMERGENCIES

Cape Cod Hospital has a 24-hour emergency room. For rescues at sea, call the Coast Guard. Boaters should use Channel 16 on their radios.

🚑 Emergency Services **Ambulance, fire, police** ☎ 911 or dial township station. **Coast Guard** ☎ 508/888-0335 in Sandwich and Cape Cod Canal, 508/945-0164 in Chatham ⊕ www.uscg.mil.
🏥 Hospitals **Cape Cod Hospital** ✉ 27 Park St., Hyannis ☎ 508/771-1800 or 877/227-3263 ⊕ www.capecodhealth.org. **Falmouth Hospital** ✉ 100 Ter Heun Dr., Falmouth ☎ 508/548-5300 or 877/227-3263 ⊕ www.capecodhealth.org/falmouthhospital. **Jordan Hospital** ✉ 275 Sandwich St., Plymouth

☎ 508/746-2000 ⊕ www.jordan.org. **Martha's Vineyard Hospital** ✉ Linton La., Oak Bluffs ☎ 508/693-0410 ⊕ www.marthasvineyardhospital. com. **Nantucket Cottage Hospital** ✉ 57 Prospect St., Nantucket ☎ 508/228-1200 ⊕ www. nantuckethospital.org. **St. Luke's Hospital** ✉ 101 Page St., New Bedford ☎ 508/997-1515 ⊕ www. southcoast.org/services/stlukes.html.
🚩 **24-Hour Pharmacies CVS Falmouth** ✉ 105 Rte. 28, Falmouth ☎ 508/540-4307. **CVS Hyannis** ✉ 176 North St., Hyannis ☎ 508/775-8462. **CVS Plymouth** ✉ 8 Pilgrim Hill Rd., Plymouth ☎ 508/ 747-1465.
🚩 **Late-Night Pharmacy Leslie's Drug Store** ✉ 65 Main St., Vineyard Haven ☎ 508/693-1010.

GAY & LESBIAN TRAVEL

Provincetown, at the tip of the Cape, is one of the East Coast's leading lesbian and gay seaside destinations, and it also has a large year-round lesbian and gay community. Dozens of P-town establishments, from B&Bs to bars, cater specifically to lesbian and gay visitors, and all of the town's restaurants are gay friendly; many are gay-owned and -operated. Hyannis has Cape Cod's sole gay bar outside P-town, but attitudes throughout Cape Cod tend to be extremely accepting and tolerant toward gays and lesbians. Martha's Vineyard, although lacking any gay-specific nightlife, has a number of gay-friendly businesses and accommodations and has become increasingly popular as a gay vacation spot in recent years. Nantucket is also quite tolerant but has less of a gay following than the Vineyard. In 2004, Massachusetts became the first state in the nation to legalize same-sex marriage.

For details about the gay and lesbian scene, consult *Fodor's Gay Guide to the USA* (available in bookstores everywhere).
🚩 **Gay- & Lesbian-Friendly Travel Agencies Different Roads Travel** ☎ 760/325-6964 or 800/429-8747 (Ext. 14) ✉ lgernert@tzell.com. **Kennedy Travel** ✉ 130 W. 42nd St., Suite 401, New York, NY 10036 ☎ 800/237-7433 or 212/840-8659 🖷 212/730-2269 ⊕ www.kennedytravel.com. **Now, Voyager** ✉ 4406 18th St., San Francisco, CA 94114 ☎ 415/626-1169 or 800/255-6951 🖷 415/626-8626 ⊕ www.nowvoyager.com. **Skylink Travel and Tour/ Flying Dutchmen Travel** ☎ 707/546-9888 or 800/ 225-5759; serving lesbian travelers.

HEALTH

LYME DISEASE

Lyme disease, so named for its having been first reported in the town of Lyme, Connecticut, is a potentially debilitating disease carried by deer ticks, which thrive in dry, brush-covered areas, especially on Cape Cod. Always **use insect repellent**; outbreaks of Lyme disease all over the region make it imperative that you protect yourself from ticks from early spring through summer. To prevent bites, **wear light-colored clothing and tuck pant legs into socks.** Look for black ticks about the size of a pinhead around hairlines and the warmest parts of the body. If you have been bitten, **consult a physician, especially if you see the telltale bull's-eye bite pattern.** Influenza-like symptoms often accompany a Lyme infection. Early treatment is imperative.

PESTS & OTHER HAZARDS

Cape Cod's greatest insect pest is mosquitoes, which are at their worst after snowy winters and wet springs. The best protection is **repellent containing DEET.** A particular pest of coastal areas, especially salt marshes, is the greenhead fly. Their bite is nasty, and they are best repelled by a liberal application of Avon Skin So Soft.

Poison ivy is a pervasive vinelike plant, recognizable by its leaf pattern: three shiny green leaves together. In spring new poison-ivy leaves are red; likewise, they can take on a reddish tint as fall approaches. The oil from these leaves produces an itchy skin rash that spreads with scratching. If you think you may have touched some leaves, **wash as soon as you can** with soap and cool water.

SHELLFISHING

Cape Cod attracts seafood lovers who enjoy harvesting their own clams, mussels, and even lobsters; permits are required, and casual harvesting of lobsters is strictly forbidden. Amateur clammers should be aware that New England shellfish beds are periodically visited by red tides, during which microorganisms can render shellfish (excluding lobsters, scallops, and all fin fish) poisonous. To keep abreast of the situation, inquire when you apply for a license (usually at town halls or police stations) and pay attention to red tide postings as you travel. Cape Cod had a particularly devastating red tide breakout in 2005, but 2006 saw relatively few problems.

🚩 Lyme Disease Info **Massachusetts Department of Public Health** ☎ 508/947-1231, 866/627-7968 public health hotline ⊕ www.state.ma.us/dph. **National Centers for Disease Control and Prevention** ☎ 888/232-3228 general information, 877/394-8747 travelers' health line, 800/311-3435 public inquiries 🖷 888/232-3299 ⊕ www.cdc.gov.

HOLIDAYS

Major national holidays are New Year's Day; Martin Luther King Jr. Day (3rd Mon. in Jan.); Presidents' Day (3rd Mon. in Feb.); Memorial Day (last Mon. in May); Independence Day; Labor Day (1st Mon. in Sept.); Thanksgiving Day (4th Thurs. in Nov.); Christmas Eve and Christmas Day; and New Year's Eve.

INSURANCE

What kind of coverage do you honestly need? Do you even need trip insurance at all? Take a deep breath and read on.

We believe that comprehensive trip insurance is especially valuable if you're booking a very expensive or complicated trip (particularly to an isolated region) or if you're booking far in advance. Who knows what could happen six months down the road? But whether or not you get insurance has more to do with how comfortable you are assuming all that risk yourself.

Comprehensive travel policies typically cover trip-cancellation and interruption, letting you cancel or cut your trip short because of a personal emergency, illness, or, in some cases, acts of terrorism in your destination. Such policies also cover evacuation and medical care. Some also cover you for trip delays because of bad weather or mechanical problems as well as for lost or delayed baggage. Another type of coverage to look for is financial default—that is, when your trip is disrupted because a tour operator, airline, or cruise line goes out of business. Generally you must buy this when you book your trip or shortly thereafter, and it's only available to you if your operator isn't on a list of excluded companies.

Expect comprehensive travel insurance policies to cost about 4% to 7% of the total price of your trip (it's more like 12% if you're over age 70). A medical-only policy may or may not be cheaper than a comprehensive policy. Always read the fine print of your policy to make sure that you are covered for the risks that are of the most concern to you. Compare several policies to make sure you're getting the best price and range of coverage available.

🚩 Insurance Comparison Sites **Insure My Trip. com** ⊕ www.insuremytrip.com. **Square Mouth.com** ⊕ www.quotetravelinsurance.com.

🚩 Comprehensive Travel Insurers **Access America** ☎ 866/807-3982 ⊕ www.accessamerica.com. **CSA Travel Protection** ☎ 800/873-9855 ⊕ www. csatravelprotection.com. **HTH Worldwide** ☎ 610/254-8700 or 888/243-2358 ⊕ www.hthworldwide. com. **Travelex Insurance** ☎ 888/457-4602 ⊕ www.travelex-insurance.com. **Travel Guard International** ☎ 715/345-0505 or 800/826-4919 ⊕ www.travelguard.com. **Travel Insured International** ☎ 800/243-3174 ⊕ www.travelinsured.com.

FOR INTERNATIONAL TRAVELERS

CURRENCY

The dollar is the basic unit of U.S. currency. It has 100 cents. Coins are the penny (1¢); the nickel (5¢), dime (10¢), quarter (25¢), and half-dollar (50¢); and the very rare golden $1 coin and even rarer silver $1. Bills are denominated $1, $5, $10, $20, $50, and $100, all mostly green and identical in size; designs and background tints vary. You may come across a $2 bill, but the chances are slim.

CUSTOMS

🚩 **U.S. Customs and Border Protection** ⊕ www. cbp.gov.

DRIVING

Driving in the United States is on the right. Speed limits are posted in miles per hour along roads and highways (usually between 55 mph and 70 mph). Watch for lower limits in small towns and on back roads (usually 30 mph to 40 mph). Most states require front-seat passengers to wear seat belts; many states require children to sit in the back seat and to wear seat belts. In major cities, rush hour is between 7 and

10 AM; afternoon rush hour is between 4 and 7 PM. To encourage carpooling, some freeways have special lanes for so-called high-occupancy vehicles (HOV)—cars carrying more than one passenger—ordinarily marked with a diamond.

Highways are well paved. Interstate highways—limited-access, multilane highways whose numbers are prefixed by "I–"—are the fastest routes. Interstates with three-digit numbers encircle urban areas, which may have other limited-access expressways, freeways, and parkways as well. Tolls may be levied on limited-access highways. So-called U.S. highways and state highways are not necessarily limited-access but may have several lanes.

Gas stations on the Cape are plentiful (although less so on the islands, where you should keep in mind that gas is also much more expensive than on the mainland). Most stations stay open late (24 hours along large highways and in big cities), except in rural areas, where Sunday hours are limited and where you may drive long stretches without a refueling opportunity. Along larger highways, roadside stops with restrooms, fast-food restaurants, and sundries stores are well spaced. State police and tow trucks patrol major highways and lend assistance. If your car breaks down on an interstate, pull onto the shoulder and wait for help, or have your passengers wait while you walk to an emergency phone (available in most states). If you carry a cell phone, dial *55, noting your location on the small green roadside mileage markers.

ELECTRICITY
The U.S. standard is AC, 110 volts/60 cycles. Plugs have two flat pins set parallel to each other.

EMBASSIES
🛈 **Australia** ☎ 202/797-3000 ⊕ www.austemb. org. **Canada** ☎ 202/682-1740 ⊕ www. canadianembassy.org. **United Kingdom** ☎ 202/ 588-7800 ⊕ www.britainusa.com.

EMERGENCIES
For police, fire, or ambulance dial 911 (0 in rural areas).

HOLIDAYS
Major national holidays are New Year's Day (Jan. 1); Martin Luther King Day (3rd Mon. in Jan.); Presidents' Day (3rd Mon. in Feb.); Memorial Day (last Mon. in May); Independence Day (July 4); Labor Day (1st Mon. in Sept.); Columbus Day (2nd Mon. in Oct.); Thanksgiving Day (4th Thurs. in Nov.); Christmas Eve and Christmas Day (Dec. 24 and 25); and New Year's Eve (Dec. 31).

MAIL
You can buy stamps and aerograms and send letters and parcels in post offices. Stamp-dispensing machines can occasionally be found in airports, bus and train stations, office buildings, drugstores, and the like. U.S. mail boxes are stout, dark blue, steel bins at strategic locations in major cities; pickup schedules are posted inside the bin (pull down the handle to see them). Parcels more than 1 pound must be mailed at a post office or at a private mailing center.

Within the United States, a first-class letter weighing 1 ounce or less costs 39¢, and each additional ounce costs 24¢; postcards cost 24¢. A 1-ounce airmail letter to most countries costs 84¢, an airmail postcard costs 75¢; to Canada and Mexico, a 1-ounce letter costs 63¢, a postcard 55¢. An aerogram—a single sheet of lightweight blue paper that folds into its own envelope, stamped for overseas airmail—costs 75¢ regardless of its destination.

To receive mail on the road, have it sent c/o General Delivery at your destination's main post office (use the correct five-digit ZIP code). You must pick up mail in person within 30 days and show a driver's license or passport.

🛈 **DHL** ☎ 800/225-5345 ⊕ www.dhl.com. **Federal Express** ☎ 800/463-3339 ⊕ www.fedex.com. **Mail Boxes, Etc.** (The UPS Store) ☎ 800/789-4623 ⊕ www.mbe.com. **United States Postal Service** ⊕ www.usps.com.

PASSPORTS & VISAS
Visitor visas aren't necessary for citizens of Australia, Canada, the United Kingdom, as well as for most citizens of European Union countries if you're coming for tourism and

staying for fewer than 90 days. If you require a visa, the cost is $100 and, depending on where you live, the waiting time can be substantial. Apply for a visa at the U.S. consulate in your place of residence; look at the U.S. State Department's special Visa Web site for further information.

🛃 Visa Information **Destination USA** ⊕ www. unitedstatesvisas.gov.

PHONES

All U.S. telephone numbers consist of a three-digit area code and a seven-digit local number. (The area code for Cape Cod and the islands is 508). Within many local calling areas, you dial only the seven-digit number; in others, you must dial "1" first and then the area code. To call between area-code regions, dial "1" then all 10 digits; the same goes for calls to numbers prefixed by "800," "888," "866," and "877"—all toll free. For calls to numbers preceded by "900" you must pay—usually dearly.

For international calls, dial "011" followed by the country code and the local number. For help, dial "0" and ask for an overseas operator. The country code is 61 for Australia, 64 for New Zealand, 44 for the United Kingdom. Calling Canada is the same as calling within the United States. Most phone books list country codes and U.S. area codes. The country code for the United States is 1.

For operator assistance, dial "0." To obtain someone's phone number, call directory assistance at 555–1212 or occasionally 411 (free at many public phones). You can reverse the charges on a long-distance call by calling "collect"; dial "0" instead of "1" before the 10-digit number.

At pay phones, instructions often are posted. Usually you insert coins in a slot (usually 25¢–50¢ for local calls) and wait for a steady tone before dialing. When you call long-distance, the operator tells you how much to insert; prepaid phone cards, widely available in various denominations, can be used from any phone. Follow the directions to activate the card (there is usually an access number and then an activation code for the card), then dial your number.

The United States has several GSM (Global System for Mobile Communications) networks, so multiband mobile phones from most countries (except for Japan) work here. Unfortunately, it's almost impossible to buy a pay-as-you-go mobile SIM card in the U.S.—which allows you to avoid roaming charges—without a phone. That said, cell phones with pay-as-you-go plans are available for well under $100. The cheapest ones with decent national coverage are the GoPhone from Cingular and Virgin Mobile, which only offers pay-as-you-go service.

📱 Cell Phone Contacts **Cingular** ☎ 888/333-6651 ⊕ www.cingular.com. **Virgin Mobile** 🖷 No phone ⊕ www.virginmobileusa.com.

LODGING

Accommodations on the Cape and islands range from campsites to B&Bs to luxurious self-contained resorts offering all kinds of sporting facilities, restaurants, entertainment, services (including business services and children's programs), and all the assistance you'll ever need in making vacation arrangements.

Because real-estate prices have skyrocketed throughout the region in the past few years, many motels and hotels have been developed into more lucrative condominiums, and quite a few bed-and-breakfasts have been sold and converted back to private homes. The effect is that the Cape has fewer lodging options than it has had in years, and lodging rates have risen a bit, too. That said, there are still plenty of overnight options.

Single-night lodgings for those just passing through can be found at countless tacky but cheap and conveniently located little roadside motels, as well as at others that are spotless and cheery yet still inexpensive, or at chain hotels at all price levels; these places often have a pool, TVs, or other amenities to keep children entertained in the evening. Bear in mind that many Cape accommodations, even simple motels, have two-, three-, and even four-night minimum stays on weekends in high season, generally from around Memorial Day through Labor Day. It's still worth checking with a property to see if you can stay for fewer days, especially if you're planning to come out for a last-minute visit, but be warned that finding a single-night accommodation on a June, July, or August weekend can prove extremely challenging.

Because of extremely high demand for accommodations on the islands, it's best to reserve especially well in advance when planning a stay on Nantucket or Martha's Vineyard, especially from June through early September. If you're looking to visit during the summer months or over a popular weekend, such as the Nantucket Daffodil Festival or Christmas Stroll, it's not a bad idea to book a full year in advance. Most inns on the islands require prepayment or nonrefundable deposits as well as three-night (or more) minimums in summer. And rates can be very high, averaging $250 a night or more on Nantucket and only slightly less on Martha's Vineyard.

Families may want to **consider condominiums, cottages, and efficiencies,** which offer more space; living areas; kitchens; and sometimes laundry facilities, children's play areas, or children's programs. Especially as single-night lodging options on the Cape diminish in number, this is an increasingly popular option, although many condo and cottage rentals have one-week minimum stays, especially in summer.

The lodgings we list are the cream of the crop in each price category. We always list the facilities that are available—but we don't specify whether they cost extra: when pricing accommodations, always ask what's included and what costs extra. Properties indicated by a ✕⊞ are lodging establishments whose restaurant warrants a special trip even if you are not staying at that establishment.

CATEGORY	COST
$$$$	over $260
$$$	$200–$260
$$	$140–$200
$	$90–$140
¢	under $90

All prices are for a standard double room in high season, excluding a variable state tax and gratuities. Some inns add a 15% service charge.

Most hotels and other lodgings require you to give your credit card details before they will confirm your reservation. If you don't feel comfortable e-mailing this information, ask if you can fax it (some places even prefer faxes). However you book, get confirmation in writing and have a copy of it handy when you check in. If you book through an online travel agent, discounter, or wholesaler, you might even want to confirm your reservation with the hotel before leaving home—just to be sure everything was processed correctly.

Be sure you understand the hotel's cancellation policy. Some places allow you to cancel without any kind of penalty—even if you prepaid to secure a discounted rate—if you cancel at least 24 hours in advance. Others require you to cancel a week in advance or penalize you for the cost of one night. Small inns and B&Bs are most likely to require you to cancel far in advance. Most hotels allow children under a certain age to stay in their parents' room at no extra charge, but others charge for them as extra adults; find out the cutoff age for discounts.

Assume that hotels operate on the European Plan (**EP,** no meals) unless we specify that they use the Breakfast Plan (**BP,** with full breakfast), Continental Plan (**CP,** Continental breakfast), Full American Plan (**FAP,** all meals), Modified American Plan (**MAP,** breakfast and dinner) or are **all-inclusive** (all meals and most activities).

Did the resort look as good in real life as it did in the photos? Did you sleep like a baby, or were the walls paper thin? Did you get your money's worth? Rate hotels and write your own reviews in Travel Ratings or start a discussion about your favorite places in Travel Talk on www.fodors.com. Your comments might even appear in our books. Yes, you, too, can be a correspondent!

CONDO & HOUSE RENTALS

If you want a home base that's roomy enough for a family and comes with cooking facilities, consider a furnished rental. These can save you money, especially if you're traveling with a group. Home-exchange directories sometimes list rentals as well as exchanges.

Many travelers to the Cape and the islands rent a house if they're going to stay for a week or longer rather than stay at a B&B or hotel. These can save you money; however, some rentals are luxury properties, economical only when your party is large. Many local real-estate agencies deal with rentals, and most specialize in a specific area; see the end of each chapter for information on agents in your area.

If you do decide to rent, be sure to book a property well in advance of your trip, as many properties are rented out to the same families or groups year after year. Rental choices are often even more abundant in the smaller, quieter towns, such as Yarmouth, Chatham, Wellfleet, and Truro, or Up-Island on Martha's Vineyard.

🚪 International Agent **Hideaways International** ✉ 767 Islington St., Portsmouth, NH 03801 ☎ 603/430-4433 or 800/843-4433 🖨 603/430-4444 ⊕ www.hideaways.com, annual membership $185.

BED-AND-BREAKFASTS

Bed-and-breakfast inns have long been very popular on Cape Cod and the islands. Many of them occupy stately old sea captains' homes and other 17th-, 18th-, and 19th-century buildings; others are in newer homes.

In many cases, B&Bs are not appropriate for families—noise travels easily, rooms are often small, and the furnishings are often fragile—so be sure to ask. Many B&Bs do not provide phones or TVs in guest rooms, some are not air-conditioned, and nearly all prohibit smoking indoors (some allow smoking on the grounds).

In summer you should reserve lodgings as far in advance as possible—several months for the most popular inns. Assistance with last-minute reservations is available at the Cape Cod Chamber of Commerce information booths and through the chamber of commerce's Web site (⇨ Web Sites). Off-season, rates are much reduced, and you may find that it's easier to get to know your innkeeper.

Numerous B&B reservation agencies can aid you in choosing an inn.

🚪 Reservation Services **Bed & Breakfast.com** ☎ 512/322-2710 or 800/462-2632 ⊕ www. bedandbreakfast.com also sends out an online newsletter. **Bed & Breakfast Inns Online** ☎ 615/868-1946 or 800/215-7365 ⊕ www.bbonline.com. **BnB Finder.com** ☎ 212/432-7693 or 888/547-8226 ⊕ www.bnbfinder.com.

🚪 Reservation Services on the Cape **Bed and Breakfast Cape Cod** ☎ 508/255-3824 or 800/541-6226 ⊕ www.bedandbreakfastcapecod.com. **DestINNations** ☎ 207/563-2506 or 800/333-4667 ⊕ www.destinnations.com.

🚪 Reservation Services on the Islands **Martha's Vineyard and Nantucket Reservations** ☎ 508/693-7200 ⊕ www.mvreservations.com. **Nantucket Accommodation** ☎ 508/228-9559 ⊕ www.nantucketaccommodation.com. **Nantucket Concierge** ☎ 508/228-8422 ⊕ www.nantucketconcierge.com.

CAMPING

There are many private and state-park camping areas on Cape Cod. For additional details on camping in specific areas, look for the ⚠ icon in that area's Dining and Lodging section.

HOME EXCHANGES

With a direct home exchange, you stay in someone else's home while they stay in yours. Some outfits also deal with vacation homes, so you're not actually staying in someone's full-time residence, just their vacant weekend place.

🚪 Exchange Clubs **HomeLink International** ☎ 800/638-3841 ⊕ www.homelink.org; $80 yearly for Web-only membership; $125 with Web access and two directories. **Home Exchange.com** ☎ 800/877-8723 ⊕ www.homeexchange.com; $59.95 for a 1-year online listing. **Intervac U.S.** ☎ 800/756-4663 ⊕ www.intervacus.com; $78.88 for Web-only membership; $126 includes Web access and a catalog.

HOSTELS

Hostels offer barebones lodging at low, low prices—often in shared dorm rooms with shared baths—to people of all ages, though the primary market is young travelers, especially students. Most hostels serve breakfast; dinner and/or shared cooking facilities may also be available.

In some hostels, you aren't allowed to be in your room during the day, and there may be a curfew at night. Nevertheless, hostels provide a sense of community, with public rooms where travelers often gather to share stories. Many hostels are affiliated with Hostelling International (HI), an umbrella group of hostel associations with some 4,500 member properties in more than 70 countries. Other hostels are completely independent and may be nothing more than a really cheap hotel.

Membership in any HI association, open to travelers of all ages, allows you to stay in HI-affiliated hostels at member rates. One-year membership is about $28 for adults; hostels charge about $10–$30 per night. Members have priority if the hostel is full; they're also eligible for discounts around the world, even on rail and bus travel in some countries.

Cape Cod has some excellent hostels. In season, when all other rates are jacked up beyond belief, hostels are often the only budget-accommodation option, but you must plan ahead to reserve space. The hostel in Eastham has eight cabins that each sleep six to eight; two can be used as family cabins. In the Truro hostel, accommodations are dormitory-style. You may luck out on last-minute cancellations, but it would be unwise to rely on them. *See the* lodging listings in the appropriate chapters for specifics.

🏠 **Hostelling International–USA** ☎ 301/495-1240 ⊕ www.hiusa.org.

HOTELS
Weigh all your options (we can't say this enough). Join "frequent guest" programs. You may get preferential treatment in room choice and/or upgrades in your favorite chains. Check general travel sites and hotel Web sites as not all chains are represented on all travel sites. Always research or inquire about special packages and corporate rates. If you prefer to book by phone, note you can sometimes get a better price if you call the hotel's local toll-free number (if one is available) rather than the central reservations number.

If your destination's high season is December through April and you're trying to book, say, in late April, you might save considerably by changing your dates by a week or two. Note, though, that many properties charge peak-season rates for your entire stay even if your travel dates straddle peak and nonpeak seasons. High-end chains catering to businesspeople are often busy only on weekdays and often drop rates dramatically on weekends to fill up rooms. **Ask when rates go down.**

Watch out for hidden costs, including resort fees, energy surcharges, and "convenience" fees for such things as unlimited local phone service you won't use and a free newspaper—possibly written in a language you can't read. Always verify whether local hotel taxes are or are not included in the rates you are quoted, so that you'll know the real price of your stay. In some places, taxes can add 20% or more to your bill. If you're traveling overseas **look for price guarantees,** which protect you against a falling dollar. With your rate locked in, you won't pay more, even if the price goes up in the local currency.

All hotels listed have private bath unless otherwise noted.

🏠 Discount Hotel Rooms **Accommodations Express** ☎ 800/444-7666 or 800/277-1064. **Hotels.com** ☎ 800/219-4606 or 800/364-0291 ⊕ www.hotels.com. **Quikbook** ☎ 800/789-9887 ⊕ www.quikbook.com. **Turbotrip.com** ☎ 800/473-7829 ⊕ w3.turbotrip.com.

MEDIA

NEWSPAPERS & MAGAZINES
Glossy regional magazines include *Cape Cod Life* (⊕ www.capecodlife.com) and *Cape Cod Magazine* (⊕ www.capecodmagazine.com), which both have articles about Cape people and places; and *Provincetown Arts* (⊕ www.provincetownarts.org), which focuses on Provincetown artists, performers, and writers, and also publishes essays, fiction, interviews, and poetry.

The *Cape Cod Times* (⊕ www.capecodonline.com/cctimes) is a daily newspaper with news from around the Cape and elsewhere. In Provincetown look for the *Provincetown Banner* (⊕ www.provincetownbanner.com) and *Provincetown Magazine* (⊕ www.ptownmag.com), both weeklies, for art and entertainment listings.

The *Martha's Vineyard Times* (⊕ www.mvtimes.com) and *Vineyard Gazette* (⊕ www.mvgazette.com) are the main news sources on Martha's Vineyard. On Nantucket, look for the free tabloid-format weekly *Yesterday's Island* (⊕ www.yesterdaysisland.com) and the regular island newspaper, the *Inquirer and Mirror* (⊕ www.ack.net).

MONEY MATTERS

Prices throughout this guide are given for adults. Substantially reduced fees are almost always available for children, students, and senior citizens. For information on taxes *see* Taxes.

ATMS

Cape Cod has several ATMs in each town.

CREDIT CARDS

Throughout this guide, the following abbreviations are used: **AE**, American Express; **D**, Discover; **DC**, Diners Club; **MC**, MasterCard; and **V**, Visa.

It's a good idea to inform your credit card company before you travel. Otherwise, the credit-card company might put a hold on your card owing to unusual activity—not a good thing halfway through your trip. Record all your credit card numbers—as well as the phone numbers to call if your cards are lost or stolen—in a safe place so you're prepared should something go wrong. Both MasterCard and Visa have general numbers you can call (collect if you're abroad) if your card is lost, but you're better off calling the number of your issuing bank since MasterCard and Visa usually just transfer you to your bank; your bank's number is usually printed on your card.

▪ Reporting Lost Cards American Express ☎ 800/992-3404 in the U.S. or 336/393-1111 collect from abroad ⊕ www.americanexpress.com. **Diners Club** ☎ 800/234-6377 in the U.S. or 303/799-1504 collect from abroad ⊕ www.dinersclub.com. **Discover** ☎ 800/347-2683 in the U.S. or 801/902-3100 collect from abroad ⊕ www.discovercard.com. **MasterCard** ☎ 800/622-7747 in the U.S. or 636/722-7111 collect from abroad ⊕ www.mastercard.com. **Visa** ☎ 800/847-2911 in the U.S. or 410/581-9994 collect from abroad ⊕ www.visa.com.

TRAVELER'S CHECKS & CARDS

Some consider this the currency of the cave man, and it's true that fewer establishments accept traveler's checks these days. Nevertheless, they're a cheap and secure way to carry extra money, particularly on trips to urban areas. Both Citibank (under the Visa brand) and American Express issue traveler's checks in the United States, but Amex is better known and more widely accepted; you can also avoid hefty surcharges by cashing Amex checks at Amex offices. Whatever you do, keep track of all the serial numbers in case the checks are lost or stolen.

American Express now offers a stored-value card called a Travelers Cheque Card, which you can use wherever American Express credit cards are accepted, including ATMs. The card can carry a minimum of $300 and a maximum of $2,700, and it's a very safe way to carry your funds. Although you can get replacement funds in 24 hours if your card is lost or stolen, it doesn't really strike us as a very good deal. In addition to a high initial cost ($14.95 to set up the card, plus $5 each time you "reload"), you still have to pay a 2% fee for each purchase in a foreign currency (similar to that of any credit card). Further, each time you use the card in an ATM you pay a transaction fee of $2.50 on top of the 2% transaction fee for the conversion—add it all up and it can be considerably more than you would pay for simply using your own ATM card. Regular traveler's checks are just as secure and cost less.

▪ American Express ☎ 888/412-6945 in the U.S., 801/945-9450 collect outside of the U.S. to add value or speak to customer service ⊕ www.americanexpress.com.

PACKING

Why do some people travel with a convoy of suitcases the size of large-screen TVs and yet never have a thing to wear? How do others pack a toaster-oven-size duffle with a week's worth of outfits *and* supplies for every possible contingency? We realize that packing is a matter of style—a very personal thing—but there's a lot to be said for traveling light. The tips in this section will help you win the battle of the bulging bag.

Make a list. In a recent Fodor's survey, 29% of respondents said they make lists (and often pack) at least a week before a trip. Lists can be used at least twice—once to pack and once to repack at the end of your trip. You'll also have a record of the contents of your suitcase, just in case it disappears in transit.

Think it through. What's the weather like? Is this a business trip or a cruise or resort vacation? Going abroad? In some places and/or sights, traditions of dress may be more or less conservative than you're used to. As your itinerary comes together, jot activities down and note possible outfits next to each (don't forget those shoes and accessories).

Edit your wardrobe. Plan to wear everything twice (better yet, thrice) and to do laundry along the way. Stick to one basic look—urban chic, sporty casual, etc. Build around one or two neutrals and an accent (e.g., black, white, and olive green). Women can freshen looks by changing scarves or jewelry. For a week's trip, you can look smashing with three bottoms, four or five tops, a sweater, and a jacket you can wear alone or over the sweater.

Be practical. Put comfortable shoes at the top of your list. (Did we need to tell you this?) Pack items that are lightweight, wrinkle resistant, compact, and washable. (Or this?) Stack and then roll your clothes when packing, so they'll wrinkle less. Unless you're on a guided tour or a cruise, select luggage that you can readily carry. Porters, like good butlers, are hard to find these days.

Check weight and size limitations. In the United States you may be charged extra for checked bags weighing more than 50 pounds. Abroad some airlines don't allow you to check bags weighing more

than 60 to 70 pounds, or they charge outrageous fees for every pound your luggage is over. Carry-on size limitations can be stringent, too.

Check carry-on restrictions. Research restrictions with the TSA. Rules vary abroad, so check them with your airline if you're traveling overseas on a foreign carrier. Consider packing all but essentials (travel documents, prescription meds, wallet) in checked luggage. This leads to a "pack only what you can afford to lose" approach that might help you streamline.

Lock it up. If you must pack valuables, use TSA-approved locks (about $10) that can be unlocked by all U.S. security personnel.

Tag it. Always put tags on your luggage with some kind of contact information; use your business address if you don't want people to know your home address. Put the same information (and a copy of your itinerary) inside your luggage, too.

Rethink valuables. On U.S. flights, airlines are liable for only about $2,800 per person for bags. On international flights, the liability limit is around $635 per bag. But items like computers, cameras, and jewelry aren't covered, and as gadgetry regularly goes on and off the list of carry-on no-no's, you can't count on keeping things safe by keeping them close. Although comprehensive travel policies may cover luggage, the liability limit is often a pittance. Your home-owner's policy may cover you sufficiently when you travel—or not.

Report problems immediately. If your bags—or things in them—are damaged or go astray, file a written claim with your airline *before you leave the airport.* If the airline is at fault, it may give you money for essentials until your luggage arrives. Most lost bags are found within 48 hours, so alert the airline to your whereabouts for two or three days. If your bag was opened for security reasons in the United States and something is missing, file a claim with the TSA.

🛂 Complaints **U.S. Transportation Security Administration Contact Center** ☎ 866/289-9673 ⊕ www.tsa.gov.

WHAT YOU'LL NEED IN CAPE COD & THE ISLANDS

Only a few Cape Cod and island restaurants require a jacket and tie, as do some dinner cruises; the area prides itself on informality. Do **pack a sweater or jacket, even in summer,** for nights can be cool. For suggested clothing to minimize bites from deer ticks and to prevent Lyme disease, *see* Health. Perhaps most important of all, **don't forget a swimsuit** (or two).

In your carry-on luggage, pack an extra pair of eyeglasses or contact lenses and enough of any medication you take to last a few days longer than the entire trip. You may also ask your doctor to write a spare prescription using the drug's generic name, as brand names may vary from country to country. Check *Fodor's How to Pack* (available at online retailers and bookstores everywhere) for more tips.

PHONES

Eastern Massachusetts has a 10-digit dialing system. You have to **dial the area code plus the seven-digit number for all local calls.** To call another region, as always, dial "1," then all 10 digits; the same goes for calls to numbers prefixed by 800, 888, 866, and 877.

RESTROOMS

In each Cape or island town, the tourist information office or chamber of commerce office (⇨ Visitor Information) has a restroom or can refer you to the nearest facilities. Gas stations usually have restrooms as well. If you're driving between Boston and the Cape on Route 3, there are restrooms in the Tourist Information Center at Exit 5.

The Bathroom Diaries is a Web site that's flush with unsanitized info on restrooms the world over—each one located, reviewed, and rated.

🚻 Find a Loo **The Bathroom Diaries** ⊕ www. thebathroomdiaries.com.

SIGHTSEEING TOURS

BOAT TOURS

Cape Cod Canal Cruises (two or three hours, narrated) leave from Onset, just northwest of the Bourne Bridge. A Sunday

jazz cruise, sunset cocktail cruises, and Friday and Saturday dance cruises are also available. Children 12 and under cruise free on Family Discount Cruises, Monday–Saturday at 4. Cruises cost between $11 and $17.

Patriot Boats has two-hour day and sunset cruises from Falmouth Harbor on the 74-foot schooner *Liberté II* in July and August. Another sunset cruise, which operates on Friday and Saturday evenings, passes six lighthouses in the Falmouth area. Fishing charters are also available.

Hy-Line runs one-hour narrated boat tours of Hyannis Harbor, including a view of the Kennedy compound. Sunset and evening cocktail cruises are also available; ticket prices for all tours range between $12 and $15.

The gaff-rigged schooner *Bay Lady II* makes two-hour sails, including a sunset cruise, across Provincetown Harbor into Cape Cod Bay; fares are $15 to $20. Private charters are also available.

🚢 Fees & Schedules *Bay Lady II* ✉ MacMillan Wharf, Provincetown ☎ 508/487-9308 ⊕ www. sailcapecod.com. **Cape Cod Canal Cruises** ✉ Onset Bay Town Pier, Onset ☎ 508/295-3883 ⊕ www.hy-linecruises.com. **Hy-Line** ✉ Ocean St. dock, Pier 1, Hyannis ☎ 508/778-2600 or 800/492-8082 ⊕ www.hy-linecruises.com. **Patriot Boats** ✉ 227 Clinton Ave., Falmouth ☎ 508/548-2626 or 800/734-0088 ⊕ www.patriotpartyboats.com.

TRAIN & TROLLEY TOURS

The Cape Cod Central Railroad offers two-hour, 42-mi narrated rail tours from Hyannis to the Cape Cod Canal (fare $17) from late May through October; trains generally run daily, but call for a schedule. You can have your fill of cranberry bogs, marshes, and woodlands, as well as such unusual sights as the Barnstable House of Corrections, where you'll spot inmates farming in the fields. From Hyannis, sit on the right side of the train for the best views. The second hour and its narration are a bit subdued, as you're traveling back the way you came, but the scenery and loud whistle blasts ought to keep you alert and engaged. There's also a three-hour, adults-only dinner train where you can settle back and watch the scenery as you nosh; it runs Thursday through Saturday in summer and less frequently spring and fall. The cost is $59.95 per person. Another dinner train, geared toward families, with a kids' menu and activities, runs on Tuesday evening and costs $39.95 for adults and $25.95 for kids under 12. A lunch train operates midweek from June through October and costs $36.95 per person.

The Provincetown Trolley offers 40-minute narrated tours of Provincetown, leaving from outside town hall every 30 minutes daily 10–4, and every hour daily 5–7 PM. The ride takes you through downtown, out to the Provincetown Monument, and by the beaches. The fare is $9.

🚊 Fees & Schedules **Cape Cod Central Railroad** ✉ Hyannis Train Depot, 252 Main St., Hyannis ☎ 508/771-3800 or 888/797-7245 ⊕ www. capetrain.com. **Provincetown Trolley** ☎ 508/487-9483 ⊕ www.provincetowntrolley.com.

WALKING TOURS
Colonial Lantern Tours offers guided evening walking tours April through November of the original Plymouth plantation site and historic district, as well as the nightly "Ghostly Haunts and Legends" tour highlighting Plymouth's more macabre history. The cost is $15.

Liz Villard's Vineyard History Tours leads walking tours of Edgartown's "history, architecture, ghosts, and gossip," including a stop at the Vincent House. Tours are run from April through December; call for times. Liz and her guides also lead similar tours of Oak Bluffs and Vineyard Haven. Walks last a little over an hour. Sixth-generation Nantucketer Gail Johnson of Gail's Tours narrates a lively 1½-hour van tour of the island's highlights.

🚊 Fees & Schedules **Colonial Lantern Tours** ✉ 5 North St., Plymouth ☎ 508/747-4161 or 800/698-5636 ⊕ www.plimouth.com. **Gail's Tours** ☎ 508/257-6557 ⊕ www.nantucket.net/tours/gails. **Vineyard History Tours** ☎ 508/627-8619 ⊕ www.mvpreservation.org/tours.html.

SPORTS & THE OUTDOORS
For further details on enjoying the outdoors, including water sports *see* the appropriate regional chapter.

BASEBALL
The Cape Cod Baseball League, considered the country's best summer league, is scouted by all the major-league teams. Ten teams play a 44-game season from mid-June to mid-August; admission is free to games at all 10 fields, although donations are accepted. The teams also conduct baseball clinics for children and teens.

🚊 **Cape Cod Baseball League** ☎ 508/432-6909 ⊕ www.capecodbaseball.org.

BICYCLING
In the Plymouth area, the Myles Standish State Forest (⇨ Sports & the Outdoors *in* the Approaching the Cape chapter) has 15 mi of bike trails. Fall River and New Bedford are predominantly urban areas that are not well suited for cyclists, but nearby, many local roads in Westport and South Dartmouth are pleasant biking spots. In the New Bedford suburb of Fairhaven, the Phoenix bike trail is a 3.3-mi rail trail that begins at the intersection of Ferry and Main streets. It runs east to the Mattapoisett town line.

Despite the heavy summertime traffic, the Outer Cape is quite blessed with bike trails. Off-road, the sandy, pine needle–covered trails of miles of fire roads traverse the National Seashore on the ocean side, from Wellfleet all the way on up to Truro. Bikers with thick wheels, stamina, and ambition will find hours of uninterrupted time with which to ride these trails, coming upon little other life than squirrels, birds, and the occasional deer. Provincetown is very bike friendly, as cycling is a far better way to get around than driving in summer. There are several stunning trails within the grounds of the Province Lands that will take riders through dunes and forest and alongside salt marshes.

Martha's Vineyard has superb terrain for biking—you can pick up a map that shows the island's many dedicated bike paths from the chamber of commerce. Several shops throughout the island rent bicycles, many of them close to the ferry terminals.

FISHING
Charter boats and party boats (per-head fees, rather than the charters' group rates)

fish in season for bluefish, tuna, marlin, and mako and blue sharks. Throughout the year there's bottom fishing for flounder, tautog, scup, fluke, cod, and pollack.

The Cape Cod Chamber of Commerce's *Sportsman's Guide* provides fishing regulations, surf-fishing access locations, a map of boat-launching facilities, and more. The state Division of Fisheries and Wildlife has a book with dozens of maps of Cape ponds; the maps are also available on the Division's Web site. Remember, you'll need a license for freshwater fishing, available for a nominal fee at bait-and-tackle shops. Molly Benjamin's fishing column in the Friday *Cape Cod Times* gives the latest information about fishing on the Cape—what's being caught and where.

GOLF

The Cape Cod Chamber of Commerce produces a "Golf Map of Cape Cod," locating dozens of courses on the Cape. Summer greens fees range from $25 to about $100.

TAXES

The state hotel tax varies from town to town but never exceeds 9.7%.

SALES TAX

Massachusetts state sales tax is 5%.

TIME

Cape Cod is in the eastern standard time zone. When it is noon in Cape Cod it is 9 AM in Los Angeles, 11 AM in Chicago, 5 PM in London, and 3 AM the following day in Sydney.

TIPPING

The customary tipping rate for taxi drivers is 15%–20%, with a minimum of $2; bellhops are usually given $2 per bag in luxury hotels, $1 per bag elsewhere. Hotel maids should be tipped $2 per day of your stay. A doorman who hails or helps you into a cab can be tipped $1–$2. You should also tip your hotel concierge for services rendered; the size of the tip depends on the difficulty of your request, as well as the quality of the concierge's work. For an ordinary dinner reservation or tour arrangements, $3–$5 should do; if the concierge scores seats at a popular restau-

rant or show or performs unusual services (getting your laptop repaired, finding a good pet-sitter, etc.), $10 or more is appropriate.

Waiters should be tipped 15%–20%, though at higher-end restaurants, a solid 20% is more the norm. Many restaurants add a gratuity to the bill for parties of six or more. Ask what the percentage is if the menu or bill doesn't state it. Tip $1 per drink you order at the bar, though if at an upscale establishment, those $15 martinis might warrant a $2 tip.

TOURS & PACKAGES

GUIDED TOURS

Guided tours are a good option when you don't want to do it all yourself. You travel along with a group (sometimes large, sometimes small), stay in pre-booked hotels, eat with your fellow travelers (sometimes included in the price of your tour, sometimes not), and follow a schedule. But not all guided tours are a "If This is Tuesday, It Must Be Belgium" kind of experience. A knowledgeable guide can take you places that you might never discover on your own, and you may be pushed to see more than you would have otherwise. Tours aren't for everyone, but they can be just the thing for trips to places where making travel arrangements is difficult or time-consuming (particularly when you don't speak the language). Whenever you book a guided tour, find out what's included and what isn't. A "land-only" tour includes all your travel (by bus, in most cases) in the destination, but not necessarily your flights to or even within it. Also, in most cases, prices in tour brochures don't include fees and taxes. And remember that you'll be expected to tip your guide (in cash) at the end of the tour.

VACATION PACKAGES

Packages *are not* guided tours. Packages combine airfare, accommodations, and perhaps a rental car or other extras (theater tickets, guided excursions, boat trips, reserved entry to popular museums, transit passes), but they let you do your own thing. During busy periods, packages may be your only option because flights and rooms may be otherwise sold out. Packages will definitely save you time. They can also save you money, particularly in peak seasons, but—and this is a really big "but"—you should price each part of the package separately to be sure. And be aware that prices advertised on Web sites and in newspapers rarely include service charges or taxes, which can up your costs by hundreds of dollars.

Note that local tourism boards can provide information about lesser-known and small-niche operators that sell packages to just a few destinations. And don't always assume that you can get the best deal by booking everything yourself. Some packages and cruises are sold only through travel agents.

Each year consumers are stranded or lose their money when packagers—even large ones with excellent reputations—go out of business. How can you protect yourself? First, always pay with a credit card; if you have a problem, your credit-card company may help you resolve it. Second, buy trip insurance that covers default. Third, choose a company that belongs to the United States Tour Operators Association, whose members must set aside funds ($1 million) to cover defaults. Finally choose a company that also participates in the Tour Operator Program of the American Society of Travel Agents (ASTA), which will act as mediator in any disputes. You can also check on the tour operator's reputation among travelers by posting an inquiry on one of the Fodors.com forums.

🖪 Organizations **American Society of Travel Agents** (ASTA) ☎ 703/739–2782 or 800/965–2782 24-hr hotline ⊕ www.astanet.com. **United States Tour Operators Association** (USTOA) ☎ 212/599–6599 ⊕ www.ustoa.com.

TRAVEL AGENCIES

If you use an agent—brick-and-mortar or virtual—you'll pay a fee for the service. And know that the service you get from some online agents isn't comprehensive. For example Expedia or Travelocity don't search for prices on budget airlines like JetBlue, Southwest, or small foreign carriers. That said, some agents (online or not)

do have access to fares that are difficult to find otherwise, and the savings can more than make up for any surcharge.

A knowledgeable brick-and-mortar travel agent can be a godsend if you're booking a cruise, a package trip that's not available to you directly, an air pass, or a complicated itinerary including several overseas flights. What's more, travel agents that specialize in a destination may have exclusive access to certain deals and insider information on things such as charter flights. Agents who specialize in types of travelers (senior citizens, gays and lesbians, naturists) or types of trips (cruises, luxury travel, safaris) can also be invaluable.

A top-notch agent planning your trip to Russia will make sure you get the correct visa application and complete it on time; the one booking your cruise may get you a cabin upgrade or arrange to have a bottle of champagne chilling in your cabin when you embark. And complain about the surcharges all you like, but when things don't work out the way you'd hoped, it's nice to have an agent to put things right.

🖪 Agent Resources **American Society of Travel Agents** ☎ 703/739–2782 ⊕ www.travelsense.org. 🖪 Online Agents **Expedia** ⊕ www.expedia.com. **Onetravel.com** ⊕ www.onetravel.com. **Orbitz** ⊕ www.orbitz.com. **Priceline.com** ⊕ www.priceline.com. **Travelocity** ⊕ www.travelocity.com.

VISITOR INFORMATION

Before you go, contact the state's office of tourism and the area's chambers of commerce for general information, seasonal events, and brochures. For specific information on Cape Cod's state forests and parks, the area's farmers' markets and fairs, or wildlife, contact the special-interest government offices below. You can also check Web sites on the Internet (⇨ Web Sites). When you arrive, stop by the local chamber of commerce for additional information—each chamber is stocked with local brochures and produces a comprehensive annual guidebook on each town.

The Army Corps of Engineers has a 24-hour recreation hotline for canal-area events, weather, and tidal and fishing information.

🛈 General Cape Contacts **Cape Cod Chamber of Commerce** ✉ U.S. 6 and 132, Hyannis 02601 ☎ 508/862-0700 or 888/332-2732 🖷 508/862-0727 ⊕ www.capecodchamber.org. **Cape Cod National Seashore** ☎ 508/349-3785 ⊕ www.nps.gov/caco.

🛈 General Islands Contacts **Martha's Vineyard Chamber of Commerce** ✉ Beach Rd. ⬡ Box 1698, Vineyard Haven 02568 ☎ 508/693-4486 or 800/505-4815 ⊕ www.mvy.com. **Nantucket Chamber of Commerce** ✉ 48 Main St., 2nd fl., 02554 ☎ 508/228-1700 ⊕ www.nantucketchamber.org. **Nantucket Visitor Services and Information Bureau** ✉ 25 Federal St., 02554 ☎ 508/228-0925 ⊕ www.nantucket.net/town/departments/visitor.html.

🛈 Massachusetts Contacts **Department of Agricultural Resources** ☎ 617/626-1700 ⊕ www.state.ma.us/dfa. **Department of Conservation and Recreation** ☎ 617/626-1250 ⊕ www.mass.gov/dcr. **Department of Fish and Game** ☎ 508/792-7270 ⊕ www.state.ma.us/dfwele. **Massachusetts Office of Travel & Tourism** ✉ 10 Park Plaza, Suite 4510, Boston 02116 ☎ 800/227-6277, 800/447-6277 brochures 🖷 617/973-8525 ⊕ www.massvacation.com.

WEB SITES

We're really proud of our Web site: Fodors.com is a great place to begin any journey. Scan Travel Wire for suggested itineraries, travel deals, restaurant and hotel openings, and other up-to-the-minute info. Check out Booking to research prices and book plane tickets, hotel rooms, rental cars, and vacation packages. Head to Talk for on-the-ground pointers from travelers who frequent our message boards. You can also link to loads of other travel-related resources.

After your trip, be sure to rate the places you visited and share your experiences and travel tips with us and other Fodorites in Travel Ratings and Talk on www.fodors.com.

GENERAL INFORMATION

For general information, visit the Cape Cod Chamber of Commerce online at ⊕ www.capecodchamber.org. Other resources include the Cape Cod Information

Center (⊕ www.allcapecod.com) and Cape Cod Online (⊕ www.capecodonline.com); also *see* Visitor Information.

TRANSPORTATION

Smart Traveler (⊕ www.smarttraveler.com) provides real-time updates on traffic conditions on Cape Cod (just click on the link for Boston, and you'll find a further link to Cape Cod). You can look at live Web cam pictures of the Bourne and Sagamore bridges at the Cape Cod USA site (⊕ www.capecodlivecam.com), as well as Web cam pictures of Commercial Street in Provincetown, the harbor in Hyannis, and the beach at Wellfleet.

For Cape Cod bus and trolley schedules, check with the Cape Cod Regional Transit Authority (⊕ www.capecodtransit.org). The transportation information site of the Cape Cod Commission (⊕ www.gocapecod.org) has links to transportation providers, updates on transportation-related construction projects, and information on bicycling and walking, including updates on the Cape Cod Rail Trail. The Massachusetts Bicycle Coalition (⊕ www.massbike.org) has information for bicyclists. Rails-to-Trails Conservancy (⊕ www.railtrails.org) provides general information about rail trails, such as the Cape Cod Rail Trail.

Island ferry information and schedules are available online from the Steamship Authority (⊕ www.islandferry.com) and from Hy-Line (⊕ www.hy-linecruises.com). For information on the Boston to Provincetown ferries, visit the site of Bay State Cruise Company (⊕ www.baystatecruisecompany.com) or Boston Harbor Cruises (⊕ www.bostonharborcruises.com).

DISABILITY ACCESS

The Directory of Accessible Facilities lists accessible recreational facilities in Massachusetts (⊕ www.mass.gov/dcr/universalaccess/index.htm). Cape Cod Disability Access Directory (⊕ www.capecoddisability.org) has useful information about facilities on Cape Cod.

INDEX

A

Abba ✕, 169–170
Abbicci ✕, 118
Academy of Performing Arts, 169
Acworth Inn 🖼, 98
Adventure Isle, 52
African Meeting House, 284
Air travel, 277, 319–322, 339
Airports, 322
Albert Merola Gallery, 242–243
Alley's General Store, 270
Alter Rock, 310
Alyce's Dunscroft by-the-Sea 🖼, 150–151
American Seasons ✕, 288
Anchor Inn 🖼, 230
Annual Bourne Scallop Fest, 23
Aptucxet Trading Post Museum, 50, 52
Aqua Grille ✕, 59
Aquarium Shops Food Court, 221
Aquariums
Nantucket, 286
West Yarmouth, 114
Woods Hole, 66
Aquinnah, 276–277
Aquinnah Cliffs, 276
Aquinnah Lighthouse, 276–277
Arbor Restaurant ✕, 276–277
Army Corps of Engineers, 53
Art galleries and museums, 17. ⇨ *Also* Museums
approaching the Cape, 40, 42–43
Lower Cape, 147, 153, 176
Martha's Vineyard, 256, 262, 268, 272
Mid Cape, 93, 111, 121, 123
Nantucket, 307
Outer Cape, 207–208, 210–211, 222, 223, 242–243
Upper Cape, 57–58, 62
Ashumet Holly and Wildlife Sanctuary, 67
Association Hall, 252
Atlantic House, 236
Atlantic Oaks Campground 🖼, 182
Atlantic White Cedar Swamp, 195
ATMs (automated teller machines), 317, 338

Atria ✕, 264
Attaquin Park Beach, 82
Atwood House Museum, 155–156
Ay! Caramba Cafe ✕, 150

B

Back Eddy ✕, 38
Baker's Field, 205
Ballston Beach, 216
Barnstable, 88, 91, 93–110
Barnstable Comedy Club, 107
Barnstable County Fair, 22
Barnstable Village, 88
Baseball, 52, 76, 107–108, 120, 145, 149, 152, 164, 165, 174, 341
Bass Hole Boardwalk, 113
Bates, Katharine Lee, 63–64
Battleship Cove, 36
Baxter Grist Mill, 113
Bay Lady II Excursion Schooner, 18
Bayside Resort 🖼, 117
Beach House Oceanfront B&B 🖼, 34
Beach Plum Inn 🖼, 275
Beachcomber ✕, 204–205
Beaches, 17, 322
approaching the Cape, 35, 38, 39, 42, 44
Lower Cape, 137, 145–146, 152, 164, 166, 174, 178, 179, 183
Martha's Vineyard, 256, 262, 268, 269, 272, 273
Mid Cape, 89, 93, 108, 120, 128–129
Nantucket, 301–302, 315
Outer Cape, 194, 195, 205–206, 215–216, 239
Upper Cape, 49, 53–54, 62, 77, 82
Bean & Cod (shop), 78
Bed-and-breakfasts, 41, 42, 180, 336
Beech Forest picnic area (Cape Cod National Seashore), 220
Beechwood Inn 🖼, 98
Belfry Inne & Bistro ✕🖼, 60
Belushi Pisano Gallery, 256
Bend-in-the-Road Beach, 268
Big Daddy's Burritos ✕, 221
Bismore Park, 95
Black Dog Tavern ✕, 252

Black-Eyed Susan's ✕, 292
Black's Handweaving Shop, 109–110
Blessing of the Fleet (festival), 22
Bleu ✕, 80–81
Blue Willow ✕, 195
Blueberry Manor 🖼, 119
Boat tours, 340
Boating, 18
Lower Cape, 147, 152, 166, 174
Mid Cape, 108, 120, 129
Nantucket, 303–304
Outer Cape, 207, 240
Bobby Byrne's Pubs, 61, 81
Borden, Lizzie, 36
Boston Pops Esplanade Orchestra, 106, 300
Botanical Trails of the Historical Society of Old Yarmouth, 112
Bourne, 48, 50, 52–54
Box Lunch (Brewster) ✕, 142
Box Lunch (Wellfleet) ✕, 198
Bramble Inn ✕, 142
Brant Point Grill ✕, 289
Brant Point Light, 284
Brass Key 🖼, 231
Brazilian Grill ✕, 103
Breakwater Landing (beach), 146
Brewster, 136, 138, 140–147
Brewster Book Store, 147
Brewster Fish House ✕, 142–143
Brewster Historical Society Museum, 141
Brewster in Bloom (festival), 21
Brewster Ladies' Library, 140
Brewster Store, 140
Brigham Galleries, 307
British Beer Company (pub), 61, 107
Brooks Academy Museum, 148
Brooks Park, 149
Brophy's Fine Art, 207
Brown Jug (shop), 62
Buca's Tuscan Roadhouse ✕, 149
Buckie's Biscotti ✕, 123
Bud's Country Lounge, 107
Bud's Go-Karts, 149
Buffy's (ice cream shop), 18, 158
Butler's Colonial Donut House, 38

C

Cahoon Hollow Beach, *195, 205*
Cahoon Museum of American Art, *93*
Calendar of events, *21–24*
Callery-Darling nature trails, *113*
Camping, *53, 145, 182, 255–256, 257, 336*
Cape & Islands Chamber Music Festival, *23, 173*
Cape Cinema, *123, 128*
Cape Cod. ⇨ *See* Lower Cape; Mid Cape; Outer Cape; Upper Cape
Cape Cod Antique Dealers Association Annual Antiques Show, *22*
Cape Cod Baseball League, *14, 164, 165*
Cape Cod Canal Visitor Center, *58*
Cape Cod Children's Museum, *80*
Cape Cod Community College, *88, 91*
Cape Cod Factory Outlet Mall, *54*
Cape Cod Lavender Farm, *152–153*
Cape Cod Maritime Days, *21*
Cape Cod Melody Tent, *106*
Cape Cod Museum of Art, *123*
Cape Cod Museum of Natural History, *138, 140*
Cape Cod National Seashore, *179, 182, 237*
Cape Cod Performing Arts Center, *81*
Cape Cod Potato Chips Factory, *96*
Cape Cod Rail Trail (bike path), *130, 146*
Cape Cod Repertory Theatre Co., *145*
Cape Cod Theater Project, *76*
Cape Cod Winery, *68*
Cape Outback Adventures, *216*
Cape Playhouse, *122–123, 128*
Cape Poge Wildlife Refuge, *269*
Cape Sea Grille ✕, *149*
Cape Symphony Orchestra, *82, 106*
Cap'n Frosty's ✕, *126*
Captain Bangs Hallet House, *112*

Captain Edward Penniman House, *177, 178*
Capt. Farris House 🏨, *115–116*
Capt. Gosnold Village 🏨, *105*
Captain Linnell House ✕, *170*
Captain's House Inn 🏨, *161–162*
Car rental, *326–328*
Car travel, *170, 278, 316, 328–329, 332–333*
Carmine's ✕, *158*
Carriage House Craft Center, *32*
Centerville, *91, 99–101*
Centerville Historical Society Museum, *91*
Centerville Library, *91*
Centre Street Bistro ✕, *292–293*
Chapin Beach, *128*
Chapoquoit Beach, *77*
Chapoquoit Grill ✕, *73*
Chappaquiddick Island, *268–269*
Charles D. and Margaret K. Spohr Garden, *64*
Charlotte Inn 🏨, *265*
Chatham, *153–164, 166–167*
Chatham Glass Company, *157–158*
Chatham Jam and Jelly Shop, *167*
Chatham Light, *156*
Chatham Village Cafe ✕, *158*
Chicama Vineyards, *270*
Children's Beach, *301*
Chillingsworth ✕, *142*
Chilmark, *272–273*
Chilmark Chocolates, *273*
Chilmark Store, *273*
Chocolate Sparrow ✕, *169*
Christmas by the Sea (festival), *21*
Christmas Tree Shops, *54, 110*
Christopher's by the Bay 🏨, *235–236*
Church of the Transfiguration, *168–169*
Churches, *63, 94, 112, 140–141, 151, 168–169, 195, 284*
Cinco ✕, *294*
Cisco (beach), *301*
Claudette's ✕, *310*
Clem & Ursie's ✕, *229*
Cliffside Beach Club 🏨, *299–300*
Climate, *16*

Club 477/Mallory Dock, *107*
Coast Guard Beach, *179, 183, 216*
Coast Guard Heritage Museum, *88*
Cold Storage Beach, *215*
Cole's Hill, *30, 32*
College Light Opera Company, *75*
Colonial Lantern Tours, *30*
Comedy Lounge, *107*
Commercial Street (Provincetown), *220–221*
Commercial Street (Wellfleet), *198*
Company of the Cauldron ✕, *292*
Conant House, *64*
Condos, *84, 132, 186, 246, 335–336*
Congdon's Pharmacy ✕, *286*
Congregational Church (Falmouth), *63*
Coonamessett Farm, *68*
Coop de Ville ✕, *257*
Corn Hill, *210*
Corn Hill Beach, *215*
Corporation Beach, *128*
Cottage St. Bakery ✕, *169*
Cotuit, *91, 93, 99–101*
Cotuit Library, *93*
Cove Motel 🏨, *172–173*
Craigville Beach, *108*
Credit cards, *6, 338*
Crocker House Inn 🏨, *254*
Crosby Beach, *146*
Crowne Pointe Historic Inn & Spa ✕🏨, *231–232*
Crows Nest Resort 🏨, *214*
Currency, *332*
Customs and duties, *332*
Cuttyhunk Fishing Club B&B 🏨, *41*
Cuttyhunk Island, *41*

D

DeMarco ✕, *289*
Demarest Lloyd State Park, *39*
Dennis, *121–129, 131*
Dennis Pond, *120*
Dennis Village, *121, 125–127*
Dennisport, *123, 124–125*
Devon's ✕, *224*
Dexter Gristmill, *56*
Dionis Beach, *301*
Disabilities and accessibility, *344*
Dowses Beach, *93*
Duck Harbor Beach, *206*

Duck Inn 🏨 , 277
Dunbar Tea Shop ✕ , 56
Dune shacks, 241
Dunes, 219–220, 240

E

Earl of Sandwich Motor Manor
🏨 , 61
East Beach, 269
East Chop Lighthouse, 257
East Falmouth, 67
East Sandwich Beach, 62
Eastham, 177–183, 186
Eastham Windmill, 178
Edgartown, 262–268
Edgartown Lighthouse, 263
Edward Gorey House Museum,
111
Eight Cousins Children's Books
(shop), 79
1856 Country Store, 91
1807 House 🏨 , 236
Eldia Market & Coffeehouse,
174
Eldredge Public Library, 157
Electricity, 333
Embassies and consulates, 333
Emergencies, 316, 330–331,
333
Episcopal Church of the
Messiah, 66–67
Espresso Love ✕ , 263
Esther Underwood Johnson
Nature Center, 199
Europa (shop), 79
Expedition Whydah Sea Lab
and Learning Center, 222
Eye of the Needle and Eye of
the Needle Girls (shop), 308

F

Fall foliage, 23
Fall River, 36–37
Fall River Historical Society, 36
Falmouth, 63–79
Falmouth Heights Beach, 77
Falmouth Historical Society, 64
Falmouth Museum on the
Green, 63–64
Falmouth Road Race, 23, 78
Falmouth Theater Guild, 76
Fanizzi's by the Sea ✕ , 228
Fazio's Trattoria ✕ , 103
Feast of the Blessed
Sacrament, 23
Felix Neck Wildlife Sanctuary,
263
Ferry travel. ⇨ See Boat and
ferry travel

Festivals and seasonal events,
21–24, 42, 173
Film, 236, 238, 300
Fine Arts Work Center, 223
Finely JP's ✕ , 201
First Congregational Church
(Harwich), 151
First Congregational Church
(Nantucket), 284
First Congregational Church
(Wellfleet), 195, 204
First Encounter Beach, 178,
183
First Parish Church, 140–141
Fish Pier, 157
Fisher Road Beach, 215
Flat Pond Trail, 67–68
Flax Pond, 120, 145
Flying Horse Carousel, 257
Fort Hill Area, 177–178
Fort Hill Bed & Breakfast 🏨 ,
180
Fort Phoenix State Beach
Reservation, 42
Fortune Cookie ✕ , 221
Four Seas Ice Cream, 91
Freestone's City Grill ✕ , 42
French Cable Station Museum,
169
Front Street ✕ , 224

G

Gallery Voyeur, 243
Gardens, 40, 64, 212, 269
Giving Tree Gallery (gallery),
62
Golf, 35, 62, 82, 109, 121,
146, 152, 166, 207, 216,
262, 305, 342
Gone Chocolate (shop), 93
Grand Slam Entertainment
(batting cages), 149
Great Hollow Beach, 215
Great Island, 198–199
Great Marsh Kayak Tours, 18
Great Salt Marsh, 108
Green Briar Herb Festival,
21
Green Briar Nature Center and
Jam Kitchen, 58–59
Grews Pond, 77
Griffin Island, 199

H

Hadwen House, 284
Hallet's (country drugstore),
18, 111
Handworks (shop), 79

Handy's Tavern, 43
Harbor View Hotel 🏨 ,
265–266
Harding's Beach, 166
Harlow Old Fort House, 30
Harris-Black House, 138
Harry's Blues Bar, 107
Harwich, 148–153
Harwich Cranberry Festival, 23
Harwich Historical Society, 148
Hathaway's Pond, 108
Head of the Meadow Beach,
216
Health and fitness clubs, 109,
121, 175, 183
Health concerns, 331–332
Hedge House Museum, 30
Heritage Museums and
Gardens, 57–58, 61
Herridge Books, 209
Herring Cove Beach, 239
Herring Run, 138
Herring Run Visitor Center, 54
Higgins Farm Windmill, 138
Highland Golf Links, 216
Highland House Museum,
211–212
Highland Light, 212
Highpointe Inn 🏨 , 98–99
Hiking, 54, 82, 305, 315
Hinchman House Natural
Science Museum, 286
Hobbamock's Homestead, 32
Holidays, 332, 333
Home exchanges, 336
Hopkins House Gift and
Bakery ✕ , 140
Hopper, Edward, 211
Horseback riding, 78, 109,
146
Horseneck Beach State
Reservation, 38
Hostelling International-Truro
🏨 , 215
Hostels, 182, 215, 272,
336–337. ⇨ Also Lodging
House and apartment rentals,
41, 84, 132, 186, 246,
298, 335–336
Houses, historic, 30, 57,
63–64, 93, 112, 122, 138,
155, 177, 178, 223, 284,
286, 287
Howlingbird (shop), 79
Hoxie House, 57
Hy-Line (cruises), 18
Hyannis, 93–96, 97,
101–106
Hyannis Public Library, 96

I

I Dream of Gelato, *221*
Ice-cream, *18*
Ice Cream Smuggler (ice cream parlor), *122*
Ice-skating, *54, 78, 109, 129*
Impudent Oyster ✕, *159*
Inaho ✕, *118*
Indian Neck Beach, *206*
Inn at Cook Street 🏠, *233*
Inn at Lewis Bay 🏠, *117–118*
Inn at Sandwich Center 🏠, *60–61*
Inn on the Sound 🏠, *71*
Insurance, *327–328, 332*
International travelers, tips for, *332–334*
Internet, *316–316*
Irish dancing, *120*
Isaiah Hall B&B Inn 🏠, *126*
Island Merchant (club), *107*
Itinerary recommendations, *19–20*

J

Jams ✕, *211*
Jaqui's Juke Joint ✕, *221*
Jared Coffin House 🏠, *297*
Jerry's Seafood and Dairy Freeze ✕, *18, 114*
Jettie's Beach, *301–302*
Joe's Lobster Mart, *62*
Jogging and running, *129*
John Alden House Museum, *33*
John F. Kennedy Hyannis Museum, *94*
John F. Kennedy Memorial, *95*
Jonathan Young Windmill, *169*
Joseph A. Silvia State Beach, *262*
Josiah Dennis Manse, *122*
Judah Baker Windmill, *114*
Juice Bar, *286*
Julie Heller Gallery, *243*
Julia Wood House, *63–64*

K

Kalmus Park Beach, *108*
Kayaking, *240*
Kelley Chapel, *112*
Keltic Kitchen ✕, *116*
Kendall Art Gallery, *208*
Kennedy, John F., *94, 95–96*
Kennedy Compound, *95–96*
Keveney Bridge, *112*

L

La Cucina Sul Mare ✕, *70*
Lake Tashmoo Town Beach, *256*
Lambert's Cove Beach, *272*
Lambert's Cove Country Inn ✕🏠, *272*
Land Ho! ✕, *171*
Languedoc Bistro ✕, *289*
Larsen's ✕, *275*
Leary Family Amusement Center, *64*
LeCount Hollow (beach), *195, 206*
Liam Maguire's (pub), *76*
Lighthouses, *15, 67, 108, 156, 157, 179–180, 212, 234–235, 252, 257, 263, 276, 284, 310*
Lighting of the Monument (festival), *24*
Linda Jean's ✕, *260*
Linnell Landing (beach), *146*
Little Beach, *268*
Little Inn on Pleasant Bay 🏠, *172*
Lobster Hut ✕, *34*
Loines Observatory, *286*
Long Point, *270*
Long Point (beach), *239*
Longnook Beach, *216*
Lorraine's ✕, *228–229*
Lowell Holly Reservation, *82*
Lucy Vincent Beach, *273*
L'Uva ✕, *226*

M

MacMillan Wharf, *221–222*
Mac's Seafood ✕, *201–202*
Medaket Beach, *302*
Maggie's Homemade Ice Cream ✕, *43*
Mahoney's Atlantic Bar and Grill ✕, *171*
Mail and shipping, *316–317, 333*
Main Street (Nantucket Town), *284, 286*
Main Street (Wellfleet), *198*
Manuel F. Correllus State Forest, *271*
Marconi Beach, *195, 205*
Marconi Station, *193, 195*
Maria Mitchell Aquarium, *286*
Maria Mitchell Association (MMA), *286*
Maria Mitchell Association Science Library, *286*
Marine Biological Laboratory-Woods Hole Oceanographic Institution Library, *65*
Marine Specialties (shop), *244*
Marion, *42–44*
Marion Art Center, *42–43*
Marion General Store, *43*
Martha's Vineyard Family Campground, *255–256*
Martha's Vineyard Historical Society, *262–263*
Mashpee, *79–83*
Mashpee Commons (shops), *82–83*
Mashpee Conservation Commission, *82*
Mashpee Powwow (festival), *22, 80*
Mashpee River Woodlands, *80*
Massachusetts Audubon Wellfleet Bay Wildlfe Sanctuary, *17, 199, 205*
Massachusetts Maritime Academy, *50*
Maxwell & Co. (shop), *79*
Mayflower Beach, *128*
Mayflower Compact Plaque, **223**
Mayflower II (ship replica), *30*
Mayo Beach, *205*
Meal plans, *6*
Media, *337–338*
Megansett Beach, *77*
Menauhant Beach, *77*
Menemsha, *274–276*
Menemsha Hills Reservation, *276*
Meridian Stone, *287*
Mews ✕, *224, 226*
Mile Stone Bog, *310*
Mill Pond (Chatham), *156*
Mitchell House, *286*
Money matters, *317, 338*
Monomoy Island Excursions (cruises), *157*
Monomoy National Wildlife Refuge, *18, 156–157*
Monomoy National Wildlife Refuge headquarters, *157*
Monument Beach, *53*
Morning Glory Farm ✕, *265*
Mostly Hall B&B 🏠, *72*
Museums. ⇨ *Also* Art galleries and museums
in Barnstable, 88, 91
in Bourne, 50, 52
in Brewster, 138, 140, 141
Coast Guard, 88
in Centerville, 91

in Chatham, *155–156*
children, *57, 80*
in Cotuit, *93*
in Dennis, *123*
in Edgartown, *263*
in Fall River, *29, 36*
in Falmouth, *63–64*
fire-fighting, *140*
glass, *56*
in Harwich, *148*
history, *30, 32, 33, 50, 52,
  57–58, 63–64, 66, 88, 91, 93,
  94, 111, 140, 141, 148,
  155–156, 195, 198, 211–212,
  284, 286, 310*
hours, *326*
in Hyannis, *94*
in Nantucket, *284, 286,
  287–288, 310*
natural history, *50, 52, 138,
  140, 286*
in New Bedford, *29, 40*
oceanography, *50*
in Orleans, *169*
in Plymouth, *29, 30, 32, 33*
in Provincetown, *222*
quilting, *93*
railroads, *155*
in Sandwich, *56, 57–58*
transatlantic cable, *169*
in Truro, *211–212*
in Wellfleet, *195, 198*
whaling, *40, 287–288*
in Woods Hole, *66*
in Yarmouth Port, *111*
M/V *Alert II* ferry, *41*
Myles Standish State Forest, *35*

N

Naked Oyster ✕, *102*
Nantucket Atheneum,
  286–287
Nantucket Country (shop),
  306
Nantucket Historical
  Association, *284*
Nantucket Life Saving
  Museum, *310*
Nantucket Looms (shop), *309*
Nantucket Pharmacy ✕, *286*
Nantucket Town, *282,
  284–309*
Nantucket Whaler 🏠 , *296*
National Marine Fisheries
  Service Aquarium, *66*
National Marine Life Center,
  50
National Monument to the
  Forefathers, *28*

Nauset Beach, *173, 174*
Nauset Beach Club ✕, *171*
Nauset Light, *179–180*
Nauset Light Beach, *179, 183*
Nauset Marsh, *177–178, 179*
Nauset Trail, *183*
New Bedford, *39–42*
New Bedford Art Museum, *40*
New Bedford Whaling
  Museum, *40*
New Bedford Whaling
  National Historical Park, *40*
New England Fire & History
  Museum, *140*
New England Jazz Festival, *23*
Newcomb Hollow Beach, *195,
  206*
Nickerson Memorial Room,
  88, 91
Nickerson State Park, *130,
  141, 145*
Nightlife. ⇨ See Arts and
  nightlife under specific
  areas
Nimrod Inn (club), *76*
902 Main ✕, *115*
Nobska Light, *67*
Nye Barn, *32*

O

Oak & Ivory (shop), *110*
Oak Bluffs, *257–262*
Oak Bluffs Campground, *257*
Oak House 🏠 , *260–261*
Ocean Edge 🏠 , *143*
Ocean House ✕, *124*
Octagonal house, *223*
Old Country Road, *210*
Old Grist Mill, *156*
Old Harbor Station, *220*
Old Indian Burial Ground, *80*
Old Sea Pines Inn 🏠 , *144*
Old Silver Beach, *77*
Old Town Cemetery, *57*
Olde Colonial Courthouse, *88*
Oldest House, *287*
On the Creek Café, *198*
Orleans, *168–177*
Orleans Art Association, *176*
Orleans Inn ✕🏠 , *172*
Osterville, *93, 99–101*
Osterville Fish Too ✕, *97*
Osterville Historical Society
  Museum, *93*
Outdoor activities and sports,
  341–342. ⇨ Also specific
  sports
Outermost Adventures
  (cruises), *157*

Outermost Inn ✕🏠 , *277*
Owen Park Beach, *256*
Oxford House 🏠 , *233–234*

P

Packing for the trip, *338–340*
Pacific National Bank, *287*
Paddock ✕, *101–102*
Pain D'Avignon, *94*
Paine's Creek (beach), *146*
Pairpoint Glass Company, *52*
Pamet Harbor, *210*
Parker's River Beach, *120*
Parks, *35, 40, 95, 108, 141,
  149*
Passports and visas, *333–334*
Pearl, The ✕, *288*
Penny House Inn 🏠 , *181*
Pete's Place Rentals 🏠 , *41*
Pie in the Sky ✕, *66*
Pilgrim Hall Museum, *32*
Pilgrim Heights Area (Cape
  Code National Seashore),
  212–213
Pilgrim Lake, *174*
Pilgrim Monument, *221*
Pilgrim Plaque, *223*
Pineapple Inn 🏠 , *297*
Pirate's Cove (miniature
  golf), *114*
Pisces ✕, *158*
Play-a-round (playground),
  155
Pleasant Bay, *167*
Plimoth Plantation, *32, 33*
Plymouth, *28, 30, 32–35*
Plymouth Bay Winery, *32*
Plymouth Long Beach, *35*
Plymouth Rock, *30*
Plymouth Rock Trolley, *28*
Polly Hill Arboretum, *270*
Popponesset Marketplace
  (shop), *83*
Pops by the Sea (concert), *23*
Portuguese Festival, *22*
Price categories
  approaching the Cape, *27*
  dining, *330*
  lodging, *335*
  Lower Cape, *135*
  Martha's Vineyard, *249*
  Mid Cape, *87*
  Nantucket, *282*
  Outer Cape, *191*
  Upper Cape, *48*
Province Lands, *220*
Province Lands Trail, *239*
Province Lands Visitor Center,
  179, 220, 237

Provincetown, *217–245*
Provincetown Art Association and Museum, *222*
Provincetown Fudge Factory ✕, *221*
Provincetown Inn, *223, 236*
Provincetown International Film Festival, *236*
Provincetown Public Library, *222–223*
Provincetown Trolley, *242*
P-Town Pedicab, *240, 242*
Pufferbellies (dance club), *107*
Punkhorn Parklands, *141*

Q
Quaker Meeting House, *114*
Queen Anne Inn ⛉, *161*
Queen Anne Road (Chatham), *155*
Quitsa Pond Lookout, *276*

R
Race Point Beach, *239*
Racquetball, *78*
Rafael Osona Auctions, *307*
Rail trail, *130*
Railroad Museum, *155*
Rainy day fun, *196–197*
Red Cottage Restaurant ✕, *126*
Red Maple Swamp Trail, *178*
Red Pheasant ✕, *125*
Regatta of Cotuit ✕, *99*
Restaurants, *6, 15, 329–331.*
⇨ *Also under specific areas*
price categories, 27, 48, 87, 135, 191, 249, 282, 330
Restrooms, *340*
Rip Ryder (cruises), *157*
Roadhouse Café ✕, *102*
Robbin's Hill (beach), *146*
Robert C. Eldred Co. (auctions), *131*
Rock Harbor, *168*
Roo Bar City Bistro ✕, *69*
Rose Cheeks (shop), *79*
Ross' Grill ✕, *226*
Rotary, *170*
Rotch-Jones-Duff House and Garden Museum, *40*
Route 6A, *62–63*
Running, *78*
Ryan Family Amusement Center, *115*
Ryder Beach, *216*

S
Sagamore, *52*
Sagamore flyover, *55*
St. Francis Xavier Church, *94*
Salt Pond, *179*
Salt Pond Visitor Center, *179*
Samuel Dottridge Homestead, *93*
Sandwich, *55–63*
Sandwich Auction House, *62*
Sandwich Boardwalk, *58*
Sandwich Fish Hatchery, *58*
Sandwich Glass Museum, *56*
Sandy Neck Beach, *108*
Sandy Neck Light, *108*
Sankaty Head Lighthouse, *310*
Santuit-Cotuit Historical Society Museum, *93*
SBLI Falmouth Road Race, *23, 78*
Scargo Lake, *128*
Scargo Tower, *122*
Schoolhouse Galleries, *243*
Scusset Beach State Reservation ⛉, *53–54*
Seafest, *23*
Seagull Beach, *120*
Seaman's Bethel, *40*
Sepiessa Point Reservation, *271*
Sesachacha Pond, *310*
Seth Nickerson House, *223*
Sharky's Cantina ✕, *260*
Shawme-Crowell State Forest ⛉, *61*
Shawme Pond, *56*
Shining Sea Trail, *77–78*
Shopping. ⇨ *See under specific areas*
Siasconset, *309–312, 314–315*
Siasconset Casino, *310*
Siasconset Beach, *315*
Siena ✕, *81*
Sightseeing tours, *340–341*
approaching the Cape, 30, 35
Lower Cape, 186–187
Martha's Vineyard, 279
Mid Cape, 132
Nantucket, 317–318
Outer Cape, 240, 246
Silvershell Beach, *44*
Simmons Homestead Inn ⛉, *104–105*
Sippican Harbor, *43*
Sippican Historical Society, *42*
Sir Cricket's Fish and Chips ✕, *172*
Skaket Beach, *174*
Smith Family Amusement, *96*

Snow Library, *169*
Soccer, *121*
Somerset frigate, *219*
Somerset House Inn ⛉, *232–233*
Soundfest Chamber Music Festival, *22*
Sounds of Summer Pops Concert, *22, 23*
South Cape Beach, *67, 82*
South Dartmouth, *39*
South Monomoy Lighthouse, *157*
South Wellfleet, *193, 195, 198–210*
South Wharf gallery, *307*
South Yarmouth, *114, 115–116*
Spas, *175*
Sparrow House, *30*
Spooner House, *30*
Sports and outdoor activities. ⇨ *See* Outdoor activities and sports
Squibnocket Beach, *273*
Stage Harbor, *156*
Stir Crazy ✕, *52*
Stone Lion Inn ⛉, *203*
Stony Brook Grist Mill, *138*
"Strip, The", *286*
Sturgis Library, *88*
Summer House Beachside Bistro ✕, *312, 314*
Summer House Restaurant ✕, *314*
Sundae School Ice Cream Parlor, *18, 124*
Surf Drive Beach, *77*
Surf Side Colony Cottages ⛉, *202*
Surfside Beach, *302*
Surfing, *166, 175, 186, 207, 216, 306*
Sweet Life Café ✕, *258*
Sweet Tomatoes ✕, *100*
Swift-Daley House, *178*
Sydenstricker Galleries (shop), *147*
Symbols, *6*

T
Tabor Academy, *43*
Tales of Cape Cod (historical society), *88*
Taxes, *342*
Taxis, *45, 84, 132, 186, 246, 278, 316*
Taylor-Bray Farm, *112*
Telephones, *334, 340*

Tennis, *78, 146, 166, 207, 240, 306, 315*
Terra Luna ✕, *213–214*
Thacher Taylor Hallet Museum, *111*
Theater, *42, 122–123, 151, 236, 256, 300, 301*
Thimble Farm, *270*
Thornton W. Burgess Museum, *57*
"Three Bricks", *287*
Three Ponds Preserve, *269*
Tidal Flats Recreation Area, *54*
Time, *342*
Tipping, *342*
Tisbury Town Beach, *256*
Titcomb's Bookshop, *62*
Tofu A Go-Go ✕, *230*
Tony Andrews Farm and Produce Stand, *68*
Topper's ✕, *312*
Touch of Heaven (gardens), *212*
Tours and packages, *342–343*
Town Hall (Provincetown), *223*
Town Neck Beach, *62*
Train tours, *340–341*
Trampoline Center, *149*
Transportation, *344*
Travel agencies, *331, 343*
Trolleys, *28, 242, 340–341*
Truro, *210–217*
Truro Center for the Arts at Castle Hill, *210–211*
Truro Vinyards of Cape cod Winery, *212*

U

Uncle Tim's Bridge, *198*
Union Street Inn 🏨, *296*
Utilities (shop), *245*

V

Veranda House 🏨, *297*
Vestal Street Observatory, *286*
Veterans Park, *95, 108*
Victorian Inn 🏨, *267*
Village Green (Falmouth), *63*
Village Pump, *111*

Vincent House Museum, *263*
Vineyard Haven (Tisbury), *252–257*
Vining's Bistro ✕, *158*
Vis-à-vis (shop), *308*
Visas, *333–334*
Visitor information, *45, 84, 132, 187, 249, 279, 318, 343–344*

W

Walking tours and trails, *54, 82, 113, 178, 198–199, 279, 271, 276, 305, 315, 317–318, 341*
Waquoit, *67*
Waquoit Bay National Estuarine Research Reserve, *67–68*
Washburn Island, *68*
Wasque Beach, *269*
Wasque Reservation, *269*
Water sports, *146–147*
Water Wizz Water Park, *44*
Wauwinet, *309–310, 312*
Wauwinet 🏨, *314*
Weather information, *16*
Web sites, *344*
Weeds (shop), *307*
Wellfleet, *193, 195, 198–210*
Wellfleet Chamber of Commerce, *206*
Wellfleet Drive-In Theater, *204*
Wellfleet Flea Market, *209–210*
Wellfleet Gallery Crawl, *204*
Wellfleet Glass Works, *208*
Wellfleet Harbor Actors Theater, *204*
Wellfleet Motel & Lodge 🏨, *203*
Wellfleet Pier, *198*
Wellfleet Ponds, *206*
Wellfleet Public Library, *198*
Wellfleet Scenic loop, *195*
Wequassett Inn Resort & Golf Club ✕🏨, *159, 161*
West Chop Lighthouse, *252*
West Dennis, *123, 127*
West Dennis Beach, *129*

West Tisbury, *269–272*
West Yarmouth, *113, 116–118*
Westport, *37–38*
Westport Rivers Vineyard and Winery, *37–38*
Whalewalk Inn & Spa 🏨, *180–181*
Whale-watching, *109, 242*
Whaling Museum, *40, 287–288*
White Crest Beach, *195, 205*
White Horse Beach, *35*
WHOI Exhibit Center, *66*
Wicked Oyster ✕, *200*
Windmills, *56, 113, 114, 138, 156, 169, 178*
Windswept Cranberry Bog, *312*
Wineries, *32, 37–38, 68, 212, 270*
Winnetu Inn and Resort 🏨, *267*
Winslow Crocker House, *112*
Winslow's Tavern ✕, *200–201*
Winstead Inn and Beach Resort 🏨, *151*
Wired Puppy ✕, *223*
Wood Neck Beach, *77*
Woods Hole, *64–66*
Woods Hole Folk Music Society, *76*
Woods Hole Historical Museum, *66*
Woods Hole Oceanographic Institute, *65–66*
Woods Hole Passage 🏨, *75*
Woods Hole Theater Company, *76*

Y

Yarmouth, *110–121*
Yarmouth Boardwalk, *113–114*
Yarmouth Port, *111, 118–119*

Z

ZooQuarium, *114*

PHOTO CREDITS

Cover Photo (Brand Point Lighthouse, Nantucket): *Atlantide Phototravel/Corbis*. 7, *Joe Viesti/viestiphoto. com*. 12, *Walter Bibikow/viestiphoto.com*. 13 (left), *Raymond Forbes/age fotostock*. 13 (right), *Walter Bibikow/viestiphoto.com*. 14, *Joe Viesti/viestiphoto.com*. 15, *Raymond Forbes/age fotostock*. 17, *Susan Rosenberg*. 18, *Joe Viesti/viestiphoto.com*. 21, *Raymond Forbes/age fotostock*. 22, *Jeff Greenberg/age fotostock*. 23 (left), *Strauss/Curtis/age fotostock*. 23 (right), *Craig Lovell/viestiphoto.com*. 24, *Susan Rosenberg*.

ABOUT OUR WRITERS

Former Fodor's staff editor and longtime Cape Cod contributor Andrew Collins updated the Outer Cape and Martha's Vineyard chapters for this edition, as well as the information in the front of the book. Andrew grew up in New England and has visited Cape Cod for many years, writing about it for *Fodor's Gay Guide to the USA*, several other Fodor's titles related to New England, and a number of newspapers and magazines. He has contributed to *Fodor's New Mexico, Travel & Leisure, Out Traveler, Sunset,* and *New Mexico Magazine,* and teaches a course on travel writing for New York City's Gotham Writers' Workshon

tributed to others. She has also written about the island for publications such as *Boston Magazine* and *New England Travel & Life.* For this book, she covered Nantucket's good life—including dining, lodging, nightlife, the arts, and shopping.

Laura V. Scheel updated the Approaching Cape Cod, Upper Cape, Mid Cape, and Lower Cape chapters of this edition. She has written frequently for Fodor's, contributing to titles such as *Fodor's Maine Coast* and *Fodor's The Thirteen Colonies.* When not writing about travel, history, and the arts, she raises oysters in Wellfleet on the Outer Cape.

Nantucket r
seasoned tr
several New

ill DeSousa of
tions & Com-
assistance.

DATE DUE

MAY 1 5 2007

Demco